T0325054

Big Data Analytics Techniques for Market Intelligence

Dina Darwish
Ahram Canadian University, Egypt

A volume in the Advances in Business Information
Systems and Analytics (ABISA) Book Series

Published in the United States of America by
  IGI Global
  Engineering Science Reference (an imprint of IGI Global)
  701 E. Chocolate Avenue
  Hershey PA, USA 17033
  Tel: 717-533-8845
  Fax: 717-533-8661
  E-mail: cust@igi-global.com
  Web site: http://www.igi-global.com

Library of Congress Cataloging-in-Publication Data

Names: Darwish, Dina (Dina Gamal), 1981- editor.
Title: Big data analytics techniques for market intelligence / edited by
  Dina Darwish.
Description: Hershey,PA : Engineering Science Reference, [2024] | Includes
  bibliographical references and index. | Summary: "Through a
  comprehensive exploration of various techniques and methodologies, this
  book offers a solution to the hurdles encountered in extracting
  meaningful information from Big Data. Covering the entire lifecycle of
  Big Data analytics, including preprocessing, analysis, visualization,
  and utilization of results, the book equips readers with the knowledge
  and tools necessary to unlock the power of Big Data and generate
  valuable market intelligence"-- Provided by publisher.
Identifiers: LCCN 2023033291 (print) | LCCN 2023033292 (ebook) | ISBN
  9798369304136 (hardcover) | ISBN 9798369304143 (paperback) | ISBN
  9798369304150 (ebook)
Subjects: LCSH: Marketing research--Data processing. | Big data--Industrial
  applications. | Quantitative research--Methodology. | Data mining.
Classification: LCC HF5415.2 .B475 2024 (print) | LCC HF5415.2 (ebook) |
  DDC 658.8/3--dc23/eng/20231109
LC record available at https://lccn.loc.gov/2023033291
LC ebook record available at https://lccn.loc.gov/2023033292

This book is published in the IGI Global book series Advances in Business Information Systems and Analytics (ABISA) (ISSN: 2327-3275; eISSN: 2327-3283)

British Cataloguing in Publication Data
A Cataloguing in Publication record for this book is available from the British Library.

All work contributed to this book is new, previously-unpublished material. The views expressed in this book are those of the authors, but not necessarily of the publisher.

For electronic access to this publication, please contact: eresources@igi-global.com.

Advances in Business Information Systems and Analytics (ABISA) Book Series

Madjid Tavana
La Salle University, USA

ISSN:2327-3275
EISSN:2327-3283

MISSION

The successful development and management of information systems and business analytics is crucial to the success of an organization. New technological developments and methods for data analysis have allowed organizations to not only improve their processes and allow for greater productivity, but have also provided businesses with a venue through which to cut costs, plan for the future, and maintain competitive advantage in the information age.

The **Advances in Business Information Systems and Analytics (ABISA) Book Series** aims to present diverse and timely research in the development, deployment, and management of business information systems and business analytics for continued organizational development and improved business value.

COVERAGE

- Legal information systems
- Business Information Security
- Data Strategy
- Big Data
- Business Models
- Business Process Management
- Statistics
- Data Management
- Strategic Information Systems
- Data Analytics

IGI Global is currently accepting manuscripts for publication within this series. To submit a proposal for a volume in this series, please contact our Acquisition Editors at Acquisitions@igi-global.com or visit: http://www.igi-global.com/publish/.

Titles in this Series

For a list of additional titles in this series, please visit: www.igi-global.com/book-series/advances-business-information-systems-analytics/37155

Data-Driven Decision Making for Long-Term Business Success
Sonia Singh (Toss Global Management, UAE) S. Suman Rajest (Dhaanish Ahmed College of Engineering, India) Slim Hadoussa (Brest Business School, France) Ahmed J. Obaid (University of Kufa, Iraq) and R. Regin (SRM Institute of Science and Technology, India)
Business Science Reference • copyright 2024 • 484pp • H/C (ISBN: 9798369321935) • US $285.00 (our price)

Leveraging AI and Emotional Intelligence in Contemporary Business Organizations
Dipanker Sharma (Central University of Himachal Pradesh, India) Bhawana Bhardwaj (Central University of Himachal Pradesh, India) and Mohinder Chand Dhiman (Kurukshetra University, India)
Business Science Reference • copyright 2024 • 449pp • H/C (ISBN: 9798369319024) • US $270.00 (our price)

Evolution of Cross-Sector Cyber Intelligent Markets
Eugene J. Lewis (Capitol Technology University, USA)
Business Science Reference • copyright 2024 • 300pp • H/C (ISBN: 9798369319703) • US $275.00 (our price)

Data-Driven Intelligent Business Sustainability
Sonia Singh (Toss Global Management, UAE) S. Suman Rajest (Dhaanish Ahmed College of Engineering, India) Slim Hadoussa (Brest Business School, France) Ahmed J. Obaid (University of Kufa, Iraq) and R. Regin (SRM Institute of Science and Technology, India)
Business Science Reference • copyright 2024 • 490pp • H/C (ISBN: 9798369300497) • US $265.00 (our price)

Information Logistics for Organizational Empowerment and Effective Supply Chain Management
Hamed Nozari (Department of Management, Azad University of the Emirates, Dubai, UAE)
Business Science Reference • copyright 2024 • 275pp • H/C (ISBN: 9798369301593) • US $275.00 (our price)

Leveraging ChatGPT and Artificial Intelligence for Effective Customer Engagement
Rohit Bansal (Department of Management Studies, Vaish College of Engineering, Rohtak, India) Abdul Hafaz Ngah (Faculty of Business Economics and Social DevelopmentUniversiti Malaysia Terenganu, Malaysia) Aziza Chakir (FSJES AC, Hassan II University, Casablanca, Morocco) and Nishita Pruthi (Maharshi Dayanand University, India)
Business Science Reference • copyright 2024 • 320pp • H/C (ISBN: 9798369308158) • US $265.00 (our price)

701 East Chocolate Avenue, Hershey, PA 17033, USA
Tel: 717-533-8845 x100 • Fax: 717-533-8661
E-Mail: cust@igi-global.com • www.igi-global.com

Editorial Advisory Board

Table of Contents

Detailed Table of Contents

Chapter 1
Dina Darwish, Ahram Canadian University, Egypt

Big data refers to data collections that are either too huge or too complex for traditional data-processing application software to manage. The three major concepts initially associated with big data are volume, variety, and velocity. The fourth major concept, veracity, is concerned with the accuracy or believability of the data. Big data analytics is the act of acquiring and analyzing massive volumes of data to discover market trends, insights, and patterns that may help firms in making better business decisions. Across all corporate sectors, improving efficiency results in more shrewd operations overall, more profits, and happy customers. This chapter gives an overview on how to store and manage big data, importance of big data analytics, how to apply big data analytics using different methods and tools to benefit businesses, and big data analytics applications in various fields, as well as challenges facing big data analytics.

Chapter 2
Dina Darwish, Ahram Canadian University, Egypt

Market intelligence, a field that depends on data analytics to gather corporate insights for better decision-making, has embraced big data analytics as a disruptive technology that will transform it. It is necessary to talk about the big data analytics landscape from a market perspective. The idea of big data and its use in market intelligence have drawn a lot of attention in recent years due to their immense potential to have an impact on the market. Market intelligence (MI) involves obtaining and examining data on trends, rivalry, and customer monitoring that pertains to a company's market. Big data analytics tools can examine past marketing data to learn more about what occurred and why. There is a need to focus on the data sources, techniques, and applications associated with critical marketing perspectives. This chapter focusses on how big data analytics can be gathered and analyzed to benefit market intelligence.

Chapter 3
Smrity Prasad, Christ University, India
Kashvi Prawal, Penn State University, USA

Big data analysis is the process of looking through and gleaning important insights from enormous, intricate datasets that are too diverse and massive to be processed via conventional data processing techniques. To find patterns, trends, correlations, and other important information entails gathering, storing, managing, and analyzing massive amounts of data. Datasets that exhibit the three Vs—volume, velocity, and variety—are referred to as "big data." The vast amount of data produced from numerous sources, including social media, sensors, devices, transactions, and more, is referred to as volume. The rate at which data is generated and must be processed in real-time or very close to real-time is referred to as velocity. Data that is different in its sorts and formats, such as structured, semi-structured, and unstructured data, is referred to as being varied.

    Jignesh Patil, Rajiv Gandhi Institute of Technology, India
    Sharmila Rathod, Rajiv Gandhi Institute of Technology, India

Businesses need all data to be controlled centralized, and most corporations utilize analysis to learn where their company stands in the market. Big data tools and approaches are being used by researchers and practitioners to compute performance utilizing various algorithms. It is obvious that organisations require strong understanding of their consumers, commodities, and laws; nevertheless, with the aid of big data, organisations may find new methods to compete with other organizations. This study will focus on big data techniques and algorithms to find patterns to apply on the business cases which are lagging. Technology is simply a tool used by the business elite to keep their clientele close by. It has successfully aided the organisation in achieving cost savings, making quicker, better decisions using business big data cycle and collaborative filtering.

    Ganesh B. Regulwar, Vardhaman College of Engineering, India
    Ashish Mahalle, G.H. Raisoni College of Engineering, Nagpur, India
    Raju Pawar, G.H. Raisoni College of Engineering, Nagpur, India
    Swati K. Shamkuwar, G.H. Raisoni College of Engineering, Nagpur, India
    Priti Roshan Kakde, G.H. Raisoni College of Engineering, Nagpur, India
    Swati Tiwari, G.H. Raisoni College of Engineering, Nagpur, India

Big data is a term used to describe data sets that are too large or intricate for traditional data processing systems to handle. Big data collection, filtering, and feature extraction are significant procedures in data science that enable organizations to scrutinize vast amounts of data to obtain insights and make well-informed decisions. Following filtration, feature extraction is executed to identify vital patterns and relationships in the data using techniques such as clustering, principal component analysis, and association rule mining. The primary objective of big data collection, filtering, and feature extraction is to identify valuable information that can aid in decision-making, enhance operations, and develop new products and services. These processes are essential for organizations that aspire to remain competitive and at the forefront of the constantly changing data landscape.

Chapter 6

"Unleashing the Power of Big Data: Innovative Approaches to Preprocessing for Enhanced Analytics" is a groundbreaking chapter that explores the pivotal role of preprocessing in big data analytics. It introduces diverse techniques to transform raw, unstructured data into a clean, analyzable format, addressing the challenges posed by data volume, velocity, and variety. The chapter emphasizes the significance of preprocessing for accurate outcomes, covers advanced data cleaning, integration, and transformation techniques, and discusses real-time data preprocessing, emerging technologies, and future directions. This chapter is a comprehensive resource for researchers and practitioners, enabling them to enhance data analytics and derive valuable insights from big data.

Big data analysis techniques are the methods and tools utilized for extracting insights and knowledge from vast and intricate datasets. Due to the increasing velocity, volume, and variety of data being produced, conventional data analysis methods have become inadequate. Therefore, big data analysis techniques employ advanced computational and statistical methods to extract treasured information from big data. There are several big data analysis techniques, including data mining, natural language processing, machine learning, predictive analytics, and deep learning. For example, data mining involves identifying patterns and relationships within data sets, while machine learning enables systems to learn from data without explicit programming. Additionally, natural language processing focuses on analyzing human language, and predictive analytics utilizes statistical modeling techniques to predict future outcomes. Deep learning, which uses neural networks to model complex data patterns, is also a common big data analysis technique.

Chapter 8

As data plays a role in machine learning and provides insights across various sectors, organizations are placing more emphasis on collecting, organizing, and managing information. However, traditional methods of analysing data struggle to keep up with the increasing complexity and volume of big data. To extract insights from datasets, advanced techniques like machine learning and deep learning have emerged. In the field of self-driving cars, analysing sensor data relies on methodologies developed from data analytics. These trends extend beyond cases; big data and deep learning are driving forces supported by enhanced processing capabilities and the expansion of networks. Managing the complexities involved in processing amounts of data requires scalable architectures that leverage distributed systems, parallel processing techniques and technologies such as GPUs. This development is particularly relevant for industries like banking, healthcare, and public safety, which have pressing demands, for transparency and interpretability in models.

Chapter 9

Big data refers to the large volume of data which can be processed to get the relevant, required, and meaningful data within less time. It is required to apply sophisticated methods and techniques to process big data. There are many methods and techniques available, like regression analysis, time series analysis, sentiment analysis, descriptive analysis, predictive analysis, association analysis with sampling, machine learning, visualization techniques, classification, and qualitative and quantitative analysis. In the future, there is a need to enhance the performance of these techniques due to increasing size of data. Many applications are based on any of these techniques to process the large volume of data in order to retrieve the meaningful data. It is expected, big data analysis techniques will filter and process the large volume and find the relevant one. Analysis of big data is very helpful in many areas like businesses, industries, and other sectors.

Chapter 10

New privacy rules and responsible data use are pushing companies to find clever ways to learn from data without exposing personal details. This chapter explains different techniques that protect privacy while still gaining insights. They provide strong privacy guarantees so organizations can use and share data safely. Real-world examples show how companies in marketing, healthcare, banking, and other industries apply these techniques to drive business value through secure collaboration and accelerated innovation. Recommendations help teams choose and test the right privacy tools for their needs. With the proper privacy toolbox, market intelligence can thrive in an era of ethical data analysis. Organizations that embrace privacy-first practices will gain a competitive advantage and consumer trust. This chapter equips teams to adopt modern privacy-preserving approaches to tap hidden insights in data while respecting user confidentiality.

Chapter 11

Dishant Banga, Bridgetree, USA

In today's data-driven world, organizations across industries are grappling with vast amounts of data, and the realm of market intelligence is no exception. The explosive growth of big data has created both opportunities and challenges for businesses seeking to gain valuable insights from their data assets. This chapter proposes to explore the significance of big data visualization with key performance indicator (KPI) dashboards as a powerful technique to visualize and extract actionable intelligence from complex datasets in the context of market intelligence. This chapter provides a comprehensive overview of KPI dashboards as these are essential tools for monitoring and analyzing business performance and to make data-driven decisions. The chapter explores the importance of KPIs, the design and implementation of KPI dashboards in big data. Additionally, it discusses the benefits and challenges associated with these tools, along with real-world examples of their successful implementation.

Chapter 12

Shahanawaj Ahamad, University of Hail, Saudi Arabia
S. Janani, Periyar Maniammai Institute of Science and Technology, India
Veera Talukdar, D.Y. Patil International University, India
Tripti Sharma, Rungta College of Engineering and Technology, India
Aradhana Sahu, Rungta College of Engineering and Technology, India
Sabyasachi Pramanik, Haldia Institute of Technology, India
Ankur Gupta, Vaish College of Engineering, Rohtak, India

This chapter describes how one may stock clinical data in digital forms, such as patient reports as an electronic health record, and how one may create meaningful information from these records utilizing analytics methods and tools. Apollo Hospital is the biggest hospital in West Bengal. It collects a huge quantity of heterogeneous data from various sources, including patient health records, lab test results, digital diagnostic supplies, healthcare insurance data, social media data, pharmaceutical data, gene expression records, transactions, and data from MY hospital's Mahatma Gandhi Memorial Medical College. Data analytics could be used to organise this data and make it retrievable. As a result, the term "big data" may be used. Big data is defined as exceptionally big datasets which may be analysed computationally to uncover trends, patterns, and relationships, as well as visualisation, querying, information privacy, and predictive analytics on a huge dataset.

Chapter 13

Munir Ahmad, Survey of Pakistan, Pakistan

OpenStreetMap (OSM) emerges as a dynamic asset for market intelligence, opening a plethora of possibilities for businesses and organizations to enrich their strategies and decision-making processes. By tapping into the geospatial wealth offered by OSM, enterprises can glean valuable insights into market dynamics, consumer preferences, and competitive landscapes. This information can equip them to refine supply chain logistics, make well-informed choices about expansion initiatives, and seamlessly amalgamate diverse data sources to gain a holistic market perspective. OSM's utility can be extended to analyzing market share and extracting invaluable consumer behavior insights. Its adaptability can lend itself to tailor-made data amalgamation, facilitating bespoke market intelligence solutions. Additionally, OSM can be proved instrumental in amplifying digital marketing endeavors, fine-tuning SEO tactics, and delivering accessible public datasets, catering to businesses seeking seamless geospatial data integration.

Chapter 14

    Neepa Biswas, Narula Institute of Technology, India
    Sudarsan Biswas, RCC Institute of Information Technology, India
    Kartick Chandra Mondal, Jadavpur University, India
    Suchismita Maiti, Narula Institute of Technology, India

Business organizations are trying to focus from the traditional extract-transform-load (ETL) system towards real-time implementation of the ETL process. Traditional ETL process upgrades new data to the data warehouse (DW) at predefined time intervals when the DW is in off-line mode. Modern organizations want to capture and respond to business events faster than ever. Accessing fresh data is not possible using traditional ETL. Real-time ETL can reflect fresh data on the warehouse immediately at the occurrence of an event in the operational data store. Therefore, the key tool for business trade lies in real-time enterprise DW enabled with Business Intelligence. This study provides an overview of ETL process and its evolution towards real-time ETL. This chapter will represent the real-time ETL characteristics, its technical challenges, and some popular real-time ETL implementation methods. Finally, some future directions towards real-time ETL technology are explored.

Chapter 15

    N. Abinaya, Hindusthan College of Arts and Sciences, India
    A. V. Senthil Kumar, Hindusthan College of Arts and Sciences, India
    Ankita Chaturvedi, IIS University (deemed), India
    Ismail Bin Musirin, Universiti Teknologi MARA, Malaysia
    Manjunatha Rao, National Assessment and Accreditation Council, India
    Gaganpreet Kaur, Chitkara University Institute of Engineering and Technology, Chitkara University, India
    Sarabjeet Kaur, Zakir Husain Delhi College Evening, India
    Omar S. Saleh, Studies, Planning, and Followup Directorate, Iraq
    Ravisankar Malladi, Koneru Lakshmaiah Education Foundation, India
    Nitin Arya, India Para Power Lifting, India

The proliferation of linked devices and the Internet have made it easier for hackers to infiltrate networks, which can result in cyber attacks, financial loss, healthcare information theft, and cyber war. As a result, network security analytics has drawn a lot of interest from researchers lately, especially in the field of anomaly detection in networks, which is seen to be essential for network security. Current methods are ineffective mostly because of the large amounts of data that linked devices have amassed. It is essential to provide a framework that can manage real-time massive data processing and identify network irregularities. This study makes an effort to solve the problem of real-time anomaly detection. This work has examined both the key features of related machine learning algorithms and the most recent real-time big data processing technologies for anomaly detection. The recognized research problems of massive data processing in real-time for anomaly detection are described at this point.

Shweta Dewangan, ICFAI University, India
Sanjeev Kumar, Lovely Professional University, India

This study intends to investigate the application of artificial intelligence (AI) technologies in Industry 5.0, concentrating on the joint component that promotes interaction and collaboration between humans and machines. The artificial intelligence may improve human capacities, increase productivity, and make it easier to establish new business models. In addition, the study examines the ethical concerns and societal repercussions related to the use of AI in Industry 5.0. The research outlines critical success factors, difficulties, and best practices for effectively collaboratively leveraging AI within the framework of Industry 5.0. The results of this research provide organizations and policymakers with insights and recommendations that can help them use the synergy of AI and Industry 5.0 to generate collaborative innovation and achieve sustainable growth. Human-centricity, socio-environmental sustainability, and resilience are some of the aims that Industry 5.0 has the potential to support.

Kriti Saroha, CDAC, Noida, India
Mukesh Sehrawat, IAMR Group of Institutions, India
Vishal Jain, Sharda University, India

The rapid transformation in the business domain enhances the understanding that to achieve competitive advantage, corporates need to understand customer sentiments. The abundance of customer data as customer feedback, product reviews, and posts on social media platforms provides an in-depth insight that can navigate strategic decisions and inflate customer experiences. In this context, the unification of machine learning and sentiment analysis emerges as a potent combination for extracting emotional traces from volumes of unstructured text data. This chapter searches into the sphere of analysis techniques of sentiment analysis for analyzing customer feedback, where the convergence of advanced machine learning techniques with sentiment analysis methods empowers businesses to derive valuable insights from the feedback gathered from various touch points. By decoding sentiments and opinions hidden within textual data, this approach enables organizations to capture a clear view on customer satisfaction, identify their pain points, uncover emerging trends, and tailor offerings accordingly.

Dwijendra Dwivedi, Krakow University of Economics, Poland
Saurabh Batra, Delhi University, India

Computer vision technology can be used for instant car damage recognition by analyzing images of damaged vehicles to detect and identify the location and severity of any damages. Technology can accurately classify damage into categories such as small, medium, or high severity. This can help insurance companies and other relevant stakeholders quickly process claims, reduce fraudulent claims, and improve the overall claims process efficiency. The conventional car damage assessment process is time-consuming, labor-intensive, and prone to errors. Computer vision models offer a new solution to detect car insurance fraud by identifying the damage severity and streamlining the claims process. AI can automate the process by analyzing images of damaged cars and generating a breakdown of the damage. The authors propose a unique computer vision process that can help identify small, medium, and high severity of damages and validate investigators' recommendations to detect anomalies in real-time.

Chapter 19

There is no future without big data as users, applications are continuously increasing and processed information expected to use in Healthcare, e-Commerce, Aviation, Education, etc. One can say it is just the beginning of big-data-era (BDE) computing. Everyone expects that 'ready to use' data must be available instantly and hence new techniques and algorithms must be developed to store handle and find the required 'relevant' data. However, to predict and find the relevant data many researchers suggested taking care about handling the 'context'. Many people process big datasets with missing contexts, and considering the datasets or attributes as per their convenience. In future it is also expected to focus on data quality because many applications will use this ready to process data as an input. Decision making is possible with recent machine learning applications and selection of data. It involves carefully selecting the data and removing incomplete, invalid, inaccurate data. Therefore, it is suggested to get ready for the future of big data with innovative ways, techniques, and algorithms.

Preface

Big data is a term for large amounts of data that are too difficult or large for normal data-processing tools to handle. Big data analytics is the process of collecting, studying, and analyzing huge amounts of data to find market trends, insights, and patterns that can help companies make better business choices. This information is quickly and easily accessible, which lets companies come up with smart plans to keep their competitive edge.

Big data size has been a shifting target for several years, ranging from a few dozen terabytes to many zetabytes of data. To extract insights from diverse, complex, and large data sets, Big data necessitates a combination of approaches and technologies with novel forms of integration. Big data is defined by the following characteristics: volume, variety, velocity, veracity, value, and variability.

Volume is the amount of data generated and stored. The scale of the data impacts its worth and possible insight, as well as whether it may be deemed Big data or not. Big data size is typically larger than terabytes and petabytes.

Variety is concerned with data kind, and nature. RDBMSs, one of the early technologies, were able to handle structured data well and efficiently. The existing tools and technologies were put under test by the shift from structured to semi-structured or unstructured data types and natures.

Velocity is the rate at which data is produced and processed in order to satisfy the requirements and difficulties that stand in the way of growth and development. Real-time access to Big data is frequent. Big data is created more frequently compared to small data. The frequency of creation and the frequency of handling, recording, and publication are two types of velocity that are relevant to Big data.

Veracity is the quality and value of the data as well as its trustworthiness or truthfulness. To be useful for analysis, Big data must not only be huge in size but also trustworthy. An accurate analysis can be hampered by the wide variations in the quality of the data that have been collected.

Value is concerned with the informational worth that can be obtained through the processing and analysis of massive datasets. A review of Big data's other characteristics can be used to gauge value as well. Value may also be a representation of how profitable was the data that was gleaned from the study of Big data.

Variability represents the quality of Big data that refers to its varying formats, structures, or sources. Big data can consist of both structured and unstructured data, as well as both types combined. Big data analysis could incorporate unprocessed data from several sources. Unstructured data conversions into structured data may also be a part of the processing of raw data.

Market intelligence (MI) is the gathering and analysis of market-related data, including trends, competitor, and customer (targeted, lost, and current) monitoring. It is a subset of competitive intelligence (CI), which is data and information gathered by firms to provide continuing insight into market trends including competitors' and consumers' values and preferences. MI acts as a framework for the distribution and application of resources and procedures, together with an organization's marketing expertise. It is used to give businesses ongoing strategic marketing planning so they may monitor their marketing positions and improve their ability to accomplish goals and get an advantage over competitors.

Although MI processes have been utilized in many organizations' strategic market planning, it is still unclear what are the hard and soft benefits of employing a MI process for an organization. The advantages of a good MI process can be divided into three categories: better and faster decisions, time and cost savings, and organizational learning and new ideas; however, in general, it can increase an organization's profitability and competitiveness. The competitiveness of an organization grows when more MI is collected since it allows organizations to innovate by enhancing current processes and boosting the potential to locate and produce new goods.

Depending on how organizations perceive it, MI is implemented in a variety of ways. Information Analysis, which is the intelligence obtained from the gathered information, Information Activation, which is the use of the intelligence to implement and develop marketing plans, and Information Acquisition, which is the gathering of marketing information necessary for current and future customer needs, are the three primary activities that comprise MI.

Organizations model MI based on four stages: collection, validation, processing, and communication. Although frameworks are adaptable, these four steps are the basis for modeling MI. Throughout the operations, data mining techniques are utilized to aid in the collection and analysis of retrieved data and information. Businesses must continuously monitor MI in order to enhance their strategic and tactical marketing strategies. The focus of these procedures is on the three actions that define MI. The model can be modified and adapted as needed, and it can be deployed in its entirety or in sections.

Big data analytics is a process carried out by specialized software tools that integrate numerous data mining approaches and algorithms. To understand what happened in the past and why, Big data analytics solutions can examine historical marketing data (such as clients' purchase histories from a customer relationship management (CRM) system). Focus needs to be placed on the data sources, techniques, and applications associated with the five critical marketing perspectives—people, product, place, price, and promotion—that serve as the cornerstone of marketing intelligence.

The following nine stages make up the *Big data analytics lifecycle*. Business Case Evaluation, Data Identification, Data Acquisition & Filtering, Data Extraction, Data Validation & Cleansing, Data Aggregation & Representation, Data Analysis, Data Visualization, and Use of Analysis Results.

The Big Data analytics lifecycle must begin with a well-defined business case that provides a clear understanding of the analysis's justification, goals, and objectives. Before continuing on to the actual hands-on analytical duties, the *Business Case Evaluation stage* requires the preparation, analysis, and approval of a business case. An examination of a business case for Big data analytics helps decision-makers comprehend the business resources that will be required and the business issues that will be addressed by the analysis. During this stage, further identification of Key Performance Indicators (KPIs) can aid in determining assessment criteria and direction for evaluating analytic results. If KPIs are not readily available, SMART (Specific, Measurable, Attainable, Relevant, and Timely) goals should be developed for the analytic endeavor.

On the basis of the business requirements outlined in the business case, it is possible to determine whether the business problems being addressed are indeed Big data problems. To be considered a Big data problem, a business issue must be directly related to one or more of the Big data characteristics like volume, velocity, or variety. Note that this phase also determines the base budget required to complete the analysis project. Any necessary purchase, including those for hardware, software, and training, must be comprehended in advance so that the intended investment can be weighed against the anticipated benefits of achieving the objectives. Initial iterations of the Big data analytics lifecycle will necessitate a larger up-front investment in Big Data technologies, tools, and training compared to later iterations, during which these previous expenditures can be routinely leveraged.

The goal of the *Data identification stage* is to locate the datasets and their sources that will be used in the analysis project. Finding hidden patterns and correlations may be more likely if a larger range of data sources are identified. For instance, when it is unclear exactly what to look for, it can be helpful to find as many different sorts of linked data sources as possible. The required datasets and their sources can be internal and/or external to the firm, depending on the business scope of the analysis project and the nature of the business problems being addressed.

In the case of internal datasets, a collection of available datasets from internal sources, such as data marts and operational systems, is frequently compiled and compared to a previously-defined dataset specification. For external datasets, an inventory of possible third-party data suppliers, such as data markets and publicly accessible datasets, is generated. Some external data may be embedded within blogs or other content-based websites, in which case they may need to be gathered using automated technologies.

All of the data sources that were identified during the previous step are gathered and filtered during the *Data Acquisition and Filtering stage*. Data that has been determined to be corrupt or to not be useful for the analysis goals is then removed from the acquired data using automatic filtering. Data may arrive as a collection of files, such as data acquired from a third-party data provider, or it may require API integration, such with Twitter, and this depends on the sort of data source.

When dealing with external, unstructured data, in particular, it is common for some or even all of the acquired data to be useless noise and may be eliminated throughout the filtering process. Corrupt data might include records with illogical or missing values as well as records with improper data types. Data that is excluded from one analysis could be useful for another sort of analysis. So, before starting the filtering, it is wise to store a verbatim copy of the original dataset. The verbatim copy can be compressed to reduce the amount of storage space needed.

Once it is generated or enters the enterprise border, both internal and external data need to be persistent. This data is initially saved to disc for batch analytics before being analyzed. When using real-time analytics, the data is first analyzed before being saved on disc. To enhance the classification and querying, metadata can be automatically added to data from both internal and external data sources. Dataset size and structure, source details, creation or collection dates and times, and language-specific information are a few examples of additional metadata. It is essential that metadata be machine-readable and transmitted to later stages of analysis. As a result, data accuracy and quality may be established and preserved throughout the Big Data analytics lifecycle, maintaining data provenance.

It is conceivable that some of the input data for the analysis will be in a format that the Big data solution cannot manage. It is more likely that externally sourced data will necessitate the handling of multiple data types. The objective of *the Data Extraction phase* is to extract dispersed data and convert it into a format that the underlying Big data solution can use for data analysis.

Depending on the types of analytics and capabilities of the Big Data solution, the required level of extraction and transformation will vary. For instance, it may not be necessary to extract the requisite fields from delimited textual data, such as web server log files, if the underlying Big data solution can already process those files directly. Similarly, text extraction for text analytics, which requires scanning entire documents, is facilitated if the underlying Big data solution can directly read the document in its native format. In order to divide the data into two distinct fields as required by the Big data solution, the data must endure additional transformation.

Using invalid data can distort and fabricate an analysis's results. Unlike traditional enterprise data, where the data structure is pre-defined and data is pre-validated, data input for Big data analysis may be unstructured and lack any indication of validity. Finding a set of appropriate validation constraints may be challenging due to its complexity. The establishment of frequently intricate validation rules and the elimination of any data that is known to be inaccurate are the goals of the *Data Validation and Cleaning stage*. Repetitive data from various datasets is frequently provided to Big data solutions. This redundancy can be used to investigate linked datasets in order to create validation parameters, and fill in gaps in valid data.

Data validation and cleaning can be accomplished for batch analytics via an offline (Extract, Transform, Load) ETL operation. A more complicated in-memory system is needed to validate and clean the data as it enters the system for real-time analytics. The accuracy and quality of disputed data can be determined likely by their provenance. Even data that seems erroneous may still be useful since it might include unobserved patterns and trends.

Data may be dispersed across various datasets, necessitating the joining of those databases via common attributes, like date or ID. In other instances, the identical data fields, such the date of birth, may occur in several databases. Either a method of data reconciliation is necessary, or it is necessary to identify the dataset that represents the correct value. The goal of the *Data Aggregation and Representation stage* is to combine various datasets into a single, cohesive perspective. The complexity of this stage can arise from variations in data structure and semantics.

Data aggregation can be a time-intensive and labor-intensive process due to the high volumes that Big data solutions process. Complex logic processing might be necessary to reconcile these discrepancies.

The actual analysis task, which often involves one or more types of analytics, is carried out during the *Data Analysis stage*. Iterative in nature, this stage can continue until the proper pattern or association is found, especially if the data analysis is exploratory.

This stage can be as easy as querying a dataset to generate an aggregation for comparison, depending on the type of analytical result required. On the other hand, finding patterns and anomalies or creating a statistical or mathematical model to represent correlations between variables can be as difficult as combining data mining and sophisticated statistical analysis approaches. Confirmatory analysis and exploratory analysis are two different types of data analysis, with the latter being related to data mining.

In a deductive method known as confirmatory data analysis, a potential reason of the phenomenon under investigation is released in advance. A hypothesis is the suggested explanation or speculation. The data is subsequently tested against the hypothesis, and conclusive responses to particular queries are then provided. Techniques for data sampling are typically utilized. Because a predetermined reason was suggested, unexpected findings or abnormalities are typically overlooked.

Machine learning is widely employed in a variety of real-world applications across several fields. *Machine learning* is used in situations where there is a large amount of structured and unstructured data. It has recently drawn experts from a variety of fields, including machine learning, which is utilized in plant sciences to analyze massive datasets. Data in biomedical and healthcare is generated on a daily basis, and it is critical to analyze it with greatest accuracy and minimal response time.

Machine learning and Big data are being utilized in healthcare to improve patient care and monitoring, early disease detection, and supporting doctors in forecasting patient health issues. Machine learning is being used to extract data for industries such as automotive, finance, intelligent transportation systems, national security, computer vision, and many more. In this digital age, where data is generated in massive quantities of varying quality and authenticity, organizations must prioritize efficient data management.

As a result, businesses are reorganizing infrastructures and migrating towards Big data to increase automation and the usage of smart devices to improve productivity and provide the best possible services to customers. Such services can be provided by machine learning systems with high computing and storage capacity, as well as intelligence, and major corporations have already merged machine learning with Big data.

Two areas of data science that receive a lot of attention are *Big data analytics* and *Deep learning*. Big data has grown in importance as a result of the large-scale collection of domain-specific information by both public and private organizations. This information can provide insight into issues like national security, cybercrime, fraud detection, marketing, and medical informatics. Large data sets are being analyzed by businesses like Google and Microsoft for business analysis and decisions, which affects both current and future technology. Through a hierarchical learning process, Deep Learning algorithms extract high-level, complex abstractions as data representations. Based on comparatively simpler abstractions created at the level above them in the hierarchy, complex abstractions are learned at that level.

Deep Learning is a significant technique for Big Data Analytics, because it can analyze and learn from enormous volumes of unsupervised data, even when the raw data is entirely unlabeled and uncategorized. In this work, how *Deep Learning* can be used to tackle certain significant problems in Big Data Analytics, needs to be explored, such as extracting complicated patterns from enormous amounts of data, semantic indexing, data tagging, quick information retrieval, and simplification of discriminative tasks.

It is necessary to *compare various Big data analysis techniques* in order to explore their strengths and weaknesses. Different perspectives are included in the comparison. Then, *new Big data analysis techniques* need to be suggested, along with an explanation of their characteristics.

If only the analysts can interpret the results, the ability to analyze large quantities of data and generate useful insights is meaningless. *The Data Visualization stage* is concerned with employing data visualization techniques and technologies to graphically present the outcomes of the analysis for business users' successful interpretation. Business users must comprehend the findings in order to derive value from the analysis and provide feedback.

Users are given the opportunity to conduct visual analysis as a result of completing the *Data visualization stage*, which enables them to find the answers to questions they haven't even thought to ask. There exist different visual analysis approaches.

The interpretation of the results may vary depending on how the similar results are presented in various ways. Therefore, it's crucial to employ the best visualization technique while keeping the context of the business domain in mind.

In addition, users must be able to filter down to relatively uncomplicated statistics in order to perceive how the generated results were aggregated or rolled up.

Once the analysis results have been made available to business consumers to aid in corporate decision-making, there may be additional opportunities to utilize them, such as through dashboards. In the *Utilization of Analysis Results stage*, the focus is on determining how and where processed analysis data can be utilized further.

Then, how organizations might use these strategies to maximize the value of analysis outcomes in the market. Real-time data analytics are made possible by Big data storage, a compute-and-storage architecture that gathers and maintains enormous data sets.

Big data analytics are applied by businesses to extract more intelligence from metadata. Although low-cost hard disc drives are typically used for *Big data storage and management*, the use of flash as the primary storage medium in servers and storage systems may now be feasible due to reduced flash prices. These systems can be hybrid systems that combine disc and flash storage or all-flash systems.

Big data's actual data is overwhelmingly unstructured, which primarily uses file-based and object-based storage. *Big data storage* typically refers to volumes that expand exponentially to terabyte or petabyte scale, even when a specific volume size or capacity is not formally defined.

One common misunderstanding concerning Big data is that it just relates to the size of the data set. Although generally speaking this is true, Big data science is more focused. The goal is to extract particular data subsets from numerous, sizable storage volumes. It's possible that these data are spread extensively across various systems and lack a clear correlation. The goal is to combine the data with intelligence and structure so that it can be quickly analyzed.

An organization can acquire knowledge that would not otherwise be apparent by being able to gather and handle varied data from many sources and place those associations in an intelligible context. The analysis is utilized to help in decision-making, for example, by looking into web browsing activity to customize products and services to a customer's interests or habits.

Then, *case studies in Big data* analysis must be provided, and how to use Big data analysis to provide market intelligence.

Finally, *Future expectations about Big data analytics* needs to be discussed, and how Big data implementation can be enhanced in the future by organizations and companies.

Big data analytics has been hailed as a game-changing technology that would redefine market intelligence, a field that uses data analytics to gather corporations' insights for better decision-making.

This book titled "Big Data Analytics Techniques for Market Intelligence" is focusing on Big data analytics techniques, and how can these Big data analytics provides Market Intelligence for organizations in different fields. The objective of this book is to present important concepts related to Big data analytics, then, explaining different stages for Big data Analytics lifecycle, and the role of each stage. Besides, this book clarifies the various Big data Analysis techniques, as well as, case studies for Big data analytics in market and industry, also, provides future research directions in this area. It is an emerging field that can implemented in enhancing market dynamics, providing better decision making. Besides, investing in market analytics can create value by proper allocation of resources. The implementation of Big data analytics software packages can be beneficial in diagnosing and improving performance.

This book is composed of nineteen chapters; ranging from introducing Big data analytics, implementation of Big data analytics for market intelligence, explaining different stages for Big data analytics lifecycle in details, with giving focus on various Big data analysis techniques, and, how machine learning and deep learning can be implemented in Big data analysis, and comparing the different Big data analysis techniques, besides, suggesting new techniques. Also, clarifying how organizations can maximize its benefit from Big data analysis results, and discussing means for storage and management of Big data. Finally, case studies about Big data utilization are discussed, and what are the future expectations from Big data analytics.

This book includes several topics related to Big data analytics and how it is used for market intelligence to help organizations for better decision making, and to increase their profits. Also, this book is targeting industry experts, researchers, students, practitioners and higher education institutions interested in Big data Analytics and its influence on Market, which is called "Market Intelligence".

Book Editor,

Dina Darwish
Ahram Canadian University, Egypt

Chapter 1
Introduction to Big Data Analytics

Dina Darwish
Ahram Canadian University, Egypt

ABSTRACT

Big data refers to data collections that are either too huge or too complex for traditional data-processing application software to manage. The three major concepts initially associated with big data are volume, variety, and velocity. The fourth major concept, veracity, is concerned with the accuracy or believability of the data. Big data analytics is the act of acquiring and analyzing massive volumes of data to discover market trends, insights, and patterns that may help firms in making better business decisions. Across all corporate sectors, improving efficiency results in more shrewd operations overall, more profits, and happy customers. This chapter gives an overview on how to store and manage big data, importance of big data analytics, how to apply big data analytics using different methods and tools to benefit businesses, and big data analytics applications in various fields, as well as challenges facing big data analytics.

INTRODUCTION

The creation of digital data is partially a result of the use of online-connected gadgets. Thus, information about their users is transmitted through cellphones, tablets, and desktops. Connected smart gadgets share data on how consumers utilize commonplace items.

Data originates from a variety of sources besides linked devices, including demographic data, climatic data, scientific and medical data, energy usage data, etc. The location of device users, their travels, their hobbies, their consumption patterns, their pastime activities, their projects, and other information are all provided by these data. But also details on how the tools, equipment, and infrastructure are utilized. The amount of digital data is continually expanding as more people utilize the Internet and mobile devices. We currently reside in an informational society that is transitioning to a knowledge-based society. We require more data in order to derive better information. Information is a key component of the political, cultural, and economic spheres in the society of information (Hilbert & Lopez, 2011).

DOI: 10.4018/979-8-3693-0413-6.ch001

The phrase "Big data" refers to the development and application of technologies that deliver the appropriate information from a vast amount of data that has been expanding exponentially in our society to the appropriate user at the appropriate moment. Along with handling the complexity of managing more varied forms and complicated and interrelated data, the problem is dealing with the continuously growing volumes of data. Its definition changes depending on the communities that are interested in it as a user or provider of services because it is a complicated polymorphic object. Big data, a technology developed by the web's titans, positions itself as a way to provide everyone real-time access to massive databases.

Big Data is highly challenging to define exactly because different fields have different ideas of what is considered to be a large amount of data. It identifies a class of techniques and technologies rather than a specific set of technologies. This is a new field, and the definition is evolving as we try to figure out how to use this new paradigm and capitalize on the benefits. Big data is a broad term for data that can be stored, processed, and computed more efficiently than traditional databases (Riahi & Riahi, 2015). Big Data as a resource necessitates the use of tools and techniques that may be used to examine and draw patterns from vast amounts of data (Najafabadi et al., 2015).

Because of the variety and velocity of the data manipulation, structured data analysis evolves. As a result, it is no longer sufficient to simply analyze data and generate reports; due to the variety of the data, the systems in place also need to be able to support data analysis. In order to aid in its exploitation, analysis entails automatically identifying, among a variety of quickly changing data, the correlations between the data.

The term "Big Data Analytics" refers to the procedure of gathering, compiling, and analyzing sizable data sets in order to identify various patterns and other pertinent data. Big data analytics is a collection of technologies and approaches that call for novel forms of integration in order to reveal significant hidden values from sizable datasets that are more complicated and huge in scale than typical datasets. It generally focuses on finding better and more efficient solutions to both new and old problems.

This chapter discusses the characteristics and ecosystem of Big data, as well as the types and applications of Big data analytics. The main topics to be covered in this chapter includes the following;

- The meaning of the term "Big data" and its characteristics
- Big data ecosystem
- Storage of Big data
- Big data management technologies
- Big data analytics
- Big data analytics life cycle
- Big data Analytics Processing
- Big data analytics and machine learning
- Key studies and trends in machine learning and Big data analytics
- Current research directions, developments and challenges in machine learning and Big data analytics
- Benefits of Big data analytics to businesses
- Types of Big data analytics
- Tools used in Big data analytics
- Applications of Big data analytics
- Ethical implications of Big Data
- Challenges and Barriers for Big data analytics

Also, this chapter is organized as follows; the first section includes the background, then, the second section contains the main focus of the chapter, including the main topics stated in the previous section, then finally, the conclusion section is provided.

BACKGROUND

Big data refers to data sets that are too large or complicated for typical data-processing application software to manage. Data with more entries (rows) has greater statistical power, while data with more characteristics (or columns) may have a higher false discovery rate. Despite the fact that it is frequently used imprecisely due to the absence of a formal definition, the definition of Big data that appears to best characterize it, is one connected to a massive body of information that we could not fathom when employed in smaller quantities.

Big data analytics is the process of acquiring, examining, and analyzing massive volumes of data in order to discover market trends, insights, and patterns that can help firms make better business decisions. Companies may use this information to make strategies quickly and efficiently, preserving their competitive advantage.

Just a few of the major data analysis issues include data collecting, data storage, data analysis, search, sharing, transfer, visualization, querying, updating, information privacy, and data source. The three key concepts related to Big data were volume, variety, and velocity. And, the fourth concept, veracity, is associated to the quality or depth of the data. The amount and diversity of data may result in costs and risks that surpass a company's capacity to use and benefit from Big data, if sufficient investment in Big data knowledge is not made.

Businesses can acquire structured and unstructured data from a number of sources using business intelligence (BI) tools and systems. User input (typically from employees) into these technologies aids in understanding organizational performance and operations.

Big data analytics is essential to the contemporary healthcare sector, since it can maintain hundreds of patients' records, insurance policies, medications, and vaccine-related data. It contains enormous volumes of structured and unstructured data, which, when analyzed, can provide crucial information. Big data analytics quickly and effectively does this so that medical professionals can use the data to make accurate, life-saving diagnoses.

Big data analytics are crucial because they enable businesses to use their data to find areas for growth and progress. Across all corporate sectors, improving efficiency results in more shrewd operations in overall, more profits, and happy customers. Big data analytics aids businesses in cost-cutting and the creation of superior, client-focused goods and services.

Big data analytics aids in delivering insights that enhance how our society operates. Big data analytics is essential to evaluate COVID-19 outcomes globally in addition to monitoring and analyzing individual patient records. It provides guidance to each country's health ministries on immunization strategies and develops plans for preventing pandemic breakouts in the future.

Machine learning-based business process decision-making can make computers smarter. Regression analysis in supervised machine learning predicts continuous-valued output by examining the relationship between a target and a predictor (Sarker, 2021; Shukla & Fricklas, 2018). Regression analysis predicts the dependent variable or causal impact for explanatory component experts. Clustering algorithms automatically classify homogeneous circumstances. Clustering organizes data for analysis. Retailers cluster data for customer purchasing behavior, sales campaigns, retention, anomaly detection, and more. Unsupervised association rule learning links variables. This descriptive approach reveals surprising patterns in large datasets. Association learning creates all user-specified connections (Witten & Frank, 2005). Association rules help data scientists uncover patterns, correlations, and co-occurrences in massive datasets.

Associations affect supermarket shoppers' buying habits and marketing. Physicians may utilize association guidelines. Association rules and machine learning help doctors assess sickness risk. Association rules predict consumer behavior, market research, bioinformatics, weblog mining, recommendation systems, and more. Dates or timestamps index time series (Sarker et al., 2018) can be utilized. Annual, quarterly, monthly, weekly, daily, hourly, minute-wise, or second-wise time-series are conceivable. Time series and analytical forecasting may be valuable.

Opinion mining or sentiment analysis is the computational study of people's views, sentiments, assessments, and attitudes towards goods, services, organizations, people, situations, events, topics, and their attributes (Liu, 2020). Anger, delight, despair, curiosity, and neutrality. Issue-related emotions are detectable.

Opinion mining and sentiment analysis are valuable yet challenging. Consumer feedback helps a company enhance its products and services. Brand social image may improve. Buyers seek product and service reviews. Document, phrase, aspect, and concept opinion mining is possible (Hemmatian & Sohrabi, 2019).

Behavioral analytics may improve e-commerce, online gaming, mobile and smartphone applications, IoT user behavior, and others (Sarker et al., 2020). Customer motivations predict behaviors. Marketers may target the finest customers. Behavioral analytics uses app, game, and website event data. Marketing response, clicks, social media, and purchases. Sarker et al. (Sarker, 2019; Sarker at al., 2018; Sarker & Kayes, 2020) explained how to deduce phone usage patterns from phone log data for several reasons.

Outlier analysis reveals anomalies. Anomalies include oddities, novelties, cacophony, inconsistency, irregularities, and outliers (Kwon et al., 2019; Sarker et al., 2020). Data patterns may reveal abnormalities. Anomalies can indicate financial fraud.

Factor analysis describes variable correlations (Cudeck, 2000). Variance classifies variables statistically. Factor analysis counts the fundamental effects underlying a collection of variables, studies the degree to which each variable is connected to the factors, and analyses which factors contribute to output on which variables to comprehend the factors (Yong et al., 2013). Factor analysis clarifies relationships (Young et al., 2013).

System administrators may just use logs (He et al., 2017). Computer log analysis requires knowledge. Event, audit trace, and audit record logs. Data archiving records them. Machine learning computations include input, hidden, and output layers (Han et al., 2011).

The temporal extent of neural networks' history surpasses the common perception held by the majority of individuals. This section will concentrate on the pivotal occurrences that have contributed to the development of cognitive frameworks concerning neural networks, whose prominence has experienced fluctuations throughout the years.

In 1943, Warren S. McCulloch and Walter Pitts (McCulloch & Pitts, 1943) released a scholarly work titled "A logical calculus of the ideas immanent in nervous activity." The objective of this study was to comprehend the mechanisms by which intricate patterns are generated by interconnected neurons within the human brain. A prominent concept that emerged from this study was the correlation between neurons possessing a binary threshold and Boolean logic.

In 1958, Frank Rosenblatt (Rosenblatt, 1958) is acknowledged for his contribution to the advancement of the perceptron, as evidenced by his scholarly work titled "The Perceptron: A Probabilistic Model for Information Storage and Organization in the Brain." The author extends the research of McCulloch and Pitt by incorporating weights into the equation. By utilizing an IBM 704, Rosenblatt achieved the feat of enabling a computer to acquire the ability to differentiate between cards that were marked on the left side versus those marked on the right side.

In 1974, the concept of backpropagation was explored by several researchers. However, Paul Werbos was the first individual in the United States to recognize its potential application in neural networks, as evidenced by his doctoral dissertation (Werbos, 1974).

In 1989, Yann LeCun authored a scholarly article that demonstrated the efficacy of incorporating constraints into backpropagation and integrating it into the neural network framework for algorithmic training purposes (LeCun et al., 1989). This study effectively utilized a neural network to identify hand-written zip code digits.

Artificial neural networks (ANN) are a subset of machine learning that are utilized in deep learning, a field of computational intelligence that has become increasingly significant. The capabilities of deep learning with ANN are noteworthy and have garnered attention. The efficiency of artificial neural networks in handling and analyzing large volumes of data has led to their increasing popularity in Big Data analysis.

Deep learning works well with large datasets (Sarker at al., 2020; Xin et al., 2018). MLP, CNN, and LSTM-RNN dominate deep learning.

In security-oriented fields, the primary characteristic of a fuzzy model is its interpretability. Historically, fuzzy models that rely on expert knowledge have exhibited strong interpretability, albeit with imprecise results. Fuzzy models that rely on numerical data exhibit high levels of accuracy, albeit at the expense of interpretability.

Big data is commonly used to represent the use of modern data analytics techniques to extract value from massive amounts of data, rather than a specific amount of data collection. These approaches include predictive analytics, user behavior analytics, and others. There is no doubt that the amount of data already available is considerable, but that is not the most crucial feature of this new data ecosystem. Data analysis, among other things, can discover new connections that can be used to identify market trends, combat disease, and prevent crime. In industries such as Internet searches, fintech, healthcare analytics, geographic information systems, urban informatics, and business informatics, vast data sets frequently present challenges to scientists, corporate executives, medical practitioners, advertising professionals, and government authorities. When conducting research in e-Science disciplines such as meteorology, genomics, connectomics, advanced physics simulations, biology, and environmental studies, scientists commonly encounter limitations.

MAIN FOCUS OF THE CHAPTER

The Term Big Data and Its Characteristics

The word "Big data" has been in usage since the 1990s, and some link it to John Mashey (Mashey, 1998). Big data is widely used to describe data volumes that are too enormous for standard software tools to acquire, manage, and process in a reasonable length of time (Lohr, 2013) (Snijaders, 2012). Unstructured, semi-structured, and structured data are all included in the Big data concept, although the focus is on unstructured data. According to a definition from 2018, "Big data" is defined as "where parallel computing tools are needed to handle data" and it adds that "This represents a clearly defined change in the computer science used, via parallel programming theories, and losses of some of the guarantees and capabilities made by Codd's relational model."(Fox, 2018)

Kitchin and McArdle revealed in a comparative investigation of enormous datasets that none of the frequently thought-of properties of Big data emerge consistently across all of the analyzed examples (Kitchin & McArdle, 2016). As a result, several research found reinterpretation of power dynamics in knowledge discovery as the distinguishing attribute (Balazka & Rodighiero, 2020). This alternate viewpoint develops a relational understanding of the object, claiming that none of the frequently assumed properties of Big data exist consistently across all of the analyzed situations.

Structured data are data organized in a particular format, such as a database or a spreadsheet. Customer relationship management (CRM), invoicing systems, product databases, and contact lists are examples of structured data. The sources of structured data include online forms, GPS sensors, network logs, web server logs, OLTP systems, and so on. The storage of structured data is performed in data warehouses. Unstructured data are data that are not organized according to a particular schema. Examples of unstructured data include documents, videos, audio files, posts on social media, and emails. Email messages, word processing documents, pdf files, and so on. The storage of unstructured data is done in data lakes. Also, Semi-structured data are data outside databases, but has certain structure, like XML and JSON file, and can be generated from data from various sensors, Geo graphical analysis, Context-relevant analysis, and Mobile visualization. Figure 1 shows how data evolved in size from Megabytes to Petabytes, in Big data, which is composed mostly from unstructured data.

Figure 1. Data evolution

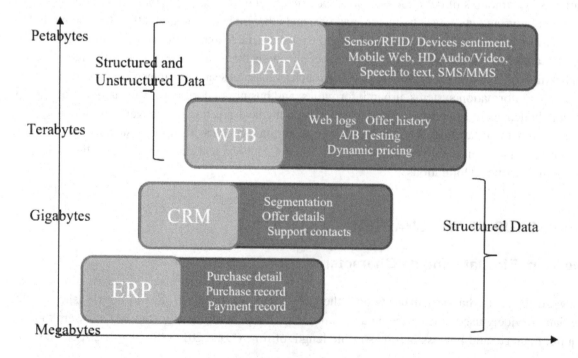

The following traits can be used to define Big data:

- *Volume*: is the volume of data created and kept. The value and potential insight of the data, as well as whether it qualifies as Big data, are all dependent on its quantity. Big data typically exceeds terabytes and petabytes in size (Sagiroglu, 2013).
- *Variety*: is information's nature and type. RDBMSs, one of the early systems, were effective and efficient at handling structured data. But the transition from structured to semi-structured or unstructured presented a difficulty for the available tools and technology. Big data technologies were developed with the primary goal of capturing, storing, and processing the semi-structured and unstructured (variety) data generated at a high rate and in large quantities. These techniques and technologies were later investigated and employed, mostly for storage but also for managing structured data. In the end, processing structured data—whether through Big data or conventional RDBMSs—was still preserved as an option. This aids in data analysis so that the hidden insights revealed from data acquired via social media, log files, sensors, etc. may be used effectively. Big data uses text, photos, audio, and video as well as data fusion to fill in the gaps.
- *Velocity*: is the rate at which data is produced and processed in order to fulfil the requirements and difficulties that stand in the way of growth and progress. Big data is frequently accessible right away. Big data is produced more frequently than little data. The frequency of generation and the frequency of handling, recording, and publication are two types of velocity associated with Big data (Kitchin & McArdie, 2016).
- *Veracity:* is the accuracy or dependability of the data, which relates to the data quality and value. Big data must not only be enormous in quantity but also be trustworthy in order to be useful in analysis. An accurate analysis can be hampered by the inconsistent quality of the data that has been collected.(Big data fourth V, 2023).
- *Value*: is the value of information that can be attained through the handling and examination of massive datasets. Big data's other attributes can also be evaluated to determine its value (IBM Big data & analytics, 2023). Value may also refer to how profitable the information is that is gleaned by big data research.
- *Variability*: is the trait of Big data's fluctuating formats, structures, or sources. Big data can consist of both organized and unstructured data, as well as both types combined. Big data analysis could incorporate unprocessed data from several sources. Unstructured data conversions into structured data may also be a part of the processing of raw data. Figure 2 illustrates the Big data characteristics.

The primary sources of big data encompass a wide range of data-generating entities. Three primary resources contribute significantly to the generation of Big data.

1.   Machine data
2.   Social data, and
3.   Transactional data.

Furthermore, corporations also generate data internally through direct customer engagement. The aforementioned data is typically stored within the organization's firewall. Subsequently, the data is externally imported into the management and analytics system. An additional crucial aspect to contemplate

Figure 2. Big data characteristics

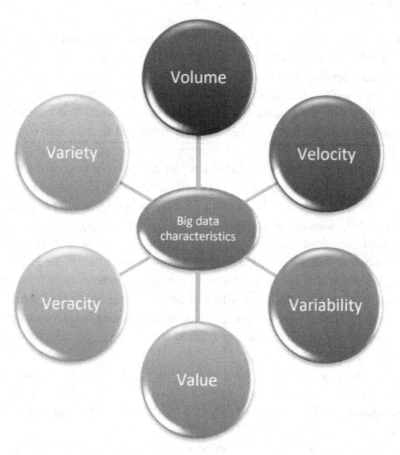

regarding Big data sources pertains to the categorization of data as either structured or unstructured. Unstructured data lacks a predetermined framework for storage and administration. Hence, a significantly greater allocation of resources is necessary for extracting significance from unstructured data and render it useful for business purposes. In this section, we will examine the three main sources that contribute to the generation of big data.

1. *Machine Data*

Machine data is generated in an automated manner, either in response to a particular event or according to a predetermined schedule. This entails that the data is derived from various sources, including smart sensors, SIEM logs, medical devices and wearables, road cameras, IoT devices, satellites, desktops, mobile phones, industrial machinery, and so forth. These sources facilitate the monitoring of consumer behavior by companies. The volume of data obtained from machine sources exhibits exponential growth in tandem with the dynamic external market environment. In a broader context, machine data also encompasses the information generated by servers, user applications, websites, cloud programs, and other related sources.

2. *Social data*

The data is sourced from various social media platforms, including but not limited to Twitter, Facebook, Instagram, YouTube, and LinkedIn. This includes content such as tweets, retweets, likes, video uploads, and comments. The vast amount of data produced by social media platforms and online channels provides valuable qualitative and quantitative information regarding various aspects of brand-customer interaction.

The dissemination of social media data occurs rapidly and reaches a wide-ranging audience. This analysis provides valuable insights into customer behavior and their sentiments towards products and services. The utilization of social media channels by brands enables them to establish a robust connection with their online demographic. Organizations have the ability to utilize this data in order to gain insights into their intended market and clientele. This ultimately improves their process of making decisions.

3. Transactional data

refers to the information generated and recorded during the course of business transactions. It encompasses the details of each transaction. Transactional data refers to the collection of information obtained from both online and offline transactions occurring at various points of sale. The dataset comprises essential information such as the time of transactions, their respective locations, the products that were purchased, the prices of these products, the payment methods employed, any discounts or coupons that were utilized, and any other pertinent quantifiable data associated with the transactions. The sources of transactional data encompass a variety of channels from which this type of data is derived. The documents that pertain to financial transactions include payment orders, invoices, storage records, and electronic receipts.

Transactional data plays a pivotal role as a primary source of business intelligence. One distinguishing feature of transactional data is its temporal dimension. Due to the inclusion of a timestamp in all transactional data, it can be inferred that such data is time-sensitive and subject to high volatility. Transactional data will diminish in both credibility and significance if it is not utilized promptly. Therefore, companies that effectively utilize transactional data can acquire a competitive advantage in the market. However, the processing, analysis, interpretation, and management of transactional data require a distinct group of experts. Furthermore, this particular kind of data presents the greatest difficulty in terms of interpretation for the majority of businesses.

Big Data Ecosystem

The primary elements and big data ecosystem are described as follows in a 2011 McKinsey Global Institute report (Manyika et al., 2011):

- A/B testing, machine learning, and natural language processing are methods for analyzing data.
- Databases, cloud computing, and business intelligence are examples of Big data technology.
- Data visualization through the use of graphs, charts, and other displays

Tensors and OLAP data cubes are two distinct mathematical methods for exhibiting vast quantities of multidimensional data. To store and query this type of data, array database systems have been developed. Big data technologies include Massively parallel processing (MPP) databases, search-based applications, data mining, distributed file systems, distributed cache (like burst buffer and Memcached), distributed databases, cloud and HPC-based infrastructure (applications, storage, and computing resources), the Internet, and efficient tensor-based computation. Nevertheless, the majority of these applications are still in their beginning.

Some Massively parallel processing (MPP) relational databases can manage and store petabytes of data. It is presumed that you are capable of loading, managing, backing up, and optimizing the use of the RDBMS's enormous data tables (Monesh, 2023). With the founding of the business "Ayasdi" in 2008, the technology behind DARPA's Topological Data Analysis program—which tries to understand the underlying structure of enormous data sets—went public (Ayasdi, 2013).

In general, Big data analytics practitioners dislike slower shared storage, (CNET, 2023) preferring instead direct-attached storage (DAS), which can take many different forms, from solid state drives (SSD) to large SATA discs hidden inside parallel processing nodes. Storage area network (SAN) and network-attached storage (NAS) are two common shared storage designs that have the reputation of being slow, complicated, and expensive. These characteristics are incompatible with Big data analytics systems, which rely on affordable, low-cost, and high-performing systems.

One of the defining features of Big data analytics is the dissemination of information in real-time or almost real-time. Therefore, latency is avoided whenever and wherever it is practicable. Data on memory or disc that is directly attached is good; however, data on memory or disc that is connected to a fiber channel storage area network (FC SAN) is not. When used at the scale required for analytics applications, SANs are substantially more expensive than other storage methods.

Storage of Big Data

When working with Big data, the data is uploaded to operational data stores using Extract, Transform, Load (ETL) or Extract, Load, Transform (ELT) technologies, which extract data from external sources, modify it to match operational needs, and load it into the database or data warehouse. As a result, the data is cleaned, processed, and categorized before being used in data mining and online analytic processes (Bakshi, 2012).

Magnetic, Agile, Deep (MAD) analysis abilities are required in the Big data environment, which is different from the features of a conventional Enterprise Data Warehouse (EDW) environment. First off, conventional EDW methods restrict the use of fresh data sources until they have been filtered and integrated. Big data settings must be magnetic in order to draw in all data sources, regardless of data quality, due to the prevalence of data nowadays (Cohen et al., 2009). Furthermore, given the increasing number of data sources and the sophistication of data analysis, Big data storage should enable analysts to swiftly and easily produce new data. This involves the use of a flexible database, the logical and real contents of which can change over time in response to the fast evolution of data (Herotou et al., 2009). Because contemporary data studies use complicated statistical procedures, and analysts must be able to study enormous datasets by digging up and down, a Big data repository must also be deep and operate as a powerful algorithmic runtime engine (Cohen et al., 2009).

As a result, a variety of technologies have been utilized for Big data, from non-relational or in-memory databases to distributed systems and Massive Parallel Processing (MPP) databases for delivering high query performance and platform scalability. Unstructured, or non-relational, data was developed for storage and management using non-relational databases, such as Not Only SQL (NoSQL). Massive scale, data model flexibility, and streamlined application development and deployment are all goals of NoSQL databases. NoSQL databases divide data management and data storage from relational databases. These databases place a greater emphasis on high-performance scalable data storage and permit data management functions to be implemented at the application layer as opposed to languages tailored specifically for databases (Bakshi, 2012).

In-memory databases, on the other hand, control the data in server memory, eliminating the need for disc input/output (I/O) and allowing the database to respond immediately. The primary database could be stored in semiconductor-based main memory as opposed to mechanical disc storage. This exponentially improves performance and enables the creation of entirely new applications.

Additionally, in-memory databases are used for advanced Big data analytics, specifically to accelerate access to and scoring of analytical models for analysis. This permits enormous scalability of data and rapid discovery analytics (Russom, 2011). Hadoop is an alternative framework for large-scale data analytics that integrates storage and analytics and provides MapReduce-based reliability, scalability, and administration. Hadoop is comprised of two major components: MapReduce for large data processing and HDFS for massive data storage (EMC, 2012). The HDFS storage function divides a single file into blocks and distributes them among cluster nodes, providing a redundant and durable distributed file system optimized for big files. A replication mechanism is also utilized to safeguard data among nodes, ensuring availability and dependability in the event of node failure (Bakshi, 2012).

The Data Nodes and the Name Nodes are the two different categories of HDFS nodes. The Name Node serves as a mediator between the client and the Data Node, assigning the client to the specific Data Node that contains the requested data (Bakshi, 2012). Data is stored in replicated file blocks among the many Data Nodes.

Big Data Management Technologies

Big data repositories, which come in various sizes and configurations, have existed for some time. In the 1990s, businesses began offering parallel database management technologies for Big data. WinterCorp has published the most exhaustive database investigation in recent years (eWeek, 2023).

Teradata Corporation introduced the DBC 1012 parallel processing system in 1984. Teradata systems were the first to analyze and store one terabyte of data in 1992. Since the introduction of the first 2.5 GB hard disc drives in 1991, the term "Big data" has evolved frequently. Teradata developed the first petabyte-capable RDBMS-based system in 2007. A few dozen petabyte-scale Teradata relational databases were in use in 2017, with the largest surpassing 50 PB. Until 2008, all system data was relationally structured. Since then, unstructured data formats including XML, JSON, and Avro have been introduced to Teradata.

Seisint Inc. (formerly LexisNexis Risk Solutions) developed the HPCC Systems platform in 2000 as a distributed data processing and querying platform. This system automatically partitions, stores, and delivers structured, semi-structured, and unstructured data across a network of commodity computers.

A declarative dataflow programming language called ECL allows users to create data processing pipelines and queries. Data analysts using ECL are not compelled to design data schemas in advance; instead, they can concentrate on the specific issue at hand, altering data as best they can as they come up with a solution. When LexisNexis bought Seisint Inc. in 2008 (The Washington Post, 2023), they also acquired their high-speed parallel processing platform, which they successfully used to integrate Choicepoint Inc.'s data systems (Bertolucci, 2023). In 2011, the HPCC systems platform was open-sourced under the Apache v2.0 Licence.

Big data sets have been gathered by CERN and other physics experiments for many years. These data sets are often analyzed using high-throughput computing rather than the map-reduce architectures typically associated with the current "Big data" structure.

A similar architecture-using procedure named MapReduce was the subject of a paper published by Google in 2004. A related solution was made available to process massive volumes of data, and the MapReduce concept offers a parallel processing methodology. In the "map" step of MapReduce, queries are divided, distributed across multiple parallel nodes, and processed simultaneously. Next, the information is gathered and presented (the "reduce" stage). Because the framework was so effective, other people desired to copy the algorithm (Bertolucci, 2023). As a result, an Apache open-source project called "Hadoop" adopted an implementation of the MapReduce framework (Dean & Ghemawat, 2004). In response to the limitations of the MapReduce paradigm, Apache Spark was created in 2012 and adds in-memory processing and the ability to set up many operations (not just map followed by reducing).

The article "Big Data Solution Offering" outlined the consequences of Big data, and MIKE2.0 is an open approach to information management that recognizes the need for changes (MIKE 2.0, 2013). The technique covers Big data management in terms of usable permutations of data sources, complexity in interrelationships, and difficulty in removing (or editing) individual records (MIKE 2.0, 2018).

Studies from 2012 indicated that one solution to the problems Big data poses was a multiple-layer design. Data is dispersed across several servers in a distributed parallel architecture, and these parallel execution settings can significantly speed up data processing. This kind of design uses the MapReduce and Hadoop frameworks to insert data into a parallel DBMS. By leveraging a front-end application server, this kind of architecture aims to make the processing power transparent to the end user (Boja et al., 2012).

An organization can respond to the shifting dynamics of information management by focusing less on centralized control and more on a shared model thanks to the data lake. This makes it possible to quickly separate data into the data lake, which cuts down on overhead time (hcltech, 2023) (Marynowski et al., 2015).

Big Data Analytics

Big data is a broad term for data that can be stored, processed, and computed more efficiently using data analysis methods compared to traditional databases. Big data is a resource. Big data analysis and pattern extraction require tools and techniques that can be used (Devi & Judith, 2018).

Because of the variety and velocity of the data manipulation, structured data analysis evolves. Therefore, just analyzing data and creating reports is no longer sufficient due to the vast array of data requires that the systems in place be able to support data analysis. In order to aid in its exploitation, analysis entails automatically identifying, among a variety of quickly changing data, the correlations between the data.

The term "Big data analytics" refers to the procedure of gathering, compiling, and analyzing sizable data sets in order to identify various patterns and other pertinent data. In order to reveal significant hidden values from massive datasets, a collection of technologies and methodologies known as "Big data analytics" needs new types of integration. Datasets that depart from the ordinary, are more complex, and span a vastly huge area. The primary point focuses on finding better and more efficient solutions to both new and old challenges (Verma & Agrawal, 2016).

Phases of Big Data Analytics Lifecycle

Big Data analytics lifecycle is divided into nine stages, as follows:

Stage One: Business Case Evaluation

During this phase, the team acquires knowledge regarding the business domain, which provides the impetus and objectives for conducting the analysis. Also, during this phase, the issue is identified, and suppositions are formulated regarding the potential benefits that a company may gain upon conducting the analysis. Crucial tasks in this stage involve formulating the commercial issue as an analytical predicament that can be tackled in subsequent stages. The process aids decision-makers in comprehending the business resources that must be utilized, thereby enabling the determination of the requisite budget to execute the project.

Furthermore, it is possible to ascertain whether the issue at hand constitutes a Big Data challenge by examining the business needs outlined in the corresponding business scenario. In order for a problem to be classified as a big data problem, it is imperative that the underlying business case is intrinsically linked to at least one of the defining features of volume, velocity, or variety.

Stage Two: Data Identification

After the identification of the business case, the next step involves the search for suitable datasets to utilize. During this phase, a comprehensive analysis is conducted to examine the strategies and approaches adopted by other companies in comparable scenarios.

The origin of datasets utilized in a project can vary depending on the business case and scope of analysis. These sources may either be internal or external to the organization. Regarding internal datasets, they may encompass data obtained from internal sources, such as feedback forms or pre-existing software. Conversely, in the case of external datasets, the aforementioned collection encompasses datasets sourced from providers external to the primary organization.

Stage Three: Data Acquisition and Filtering

After identifying the source of data, the next step involves the collection of data from the identified sources. The majority of this data is typically free of a predetermined structure, also, called "unstructured". Subsequently, the data undergoes a filtration process, wherein corrupt or extraneous data is eliminated as it does not contribute to the analysis objective. Corrupt data refers to data that may contain missing records or incompatible data types.

Following the filtration process, a duplicate of the filtered data is archived and subjected to compression, as it may hold potential utility for subsequent analyses.

Data can be gathered through various means, such as:

- Various forms such as web forms, client or customer intake forms, vendor forms, and human resources applications are frequently utilized by businesses to generate data.
- Surveys have been identified as a potentially efficacious method for collecting enormous quantities of data from a considerable pool of participants.

- Interviews and focus groups are valuable methods for collecting qualitative and subjective data that may be challenging to obtain through alternative means. These techniques involve engaging with customers, users, or job applicants to gain insights into their experiences and perspectives.
- Direct observation can serve as a valuable means of data collection that may not be attainable through aforementioned methods. This involves observing the manner in which a customer engages with a website, application, or product.

Stage Four: Data Extraction

Now that the data has been filtered, there is still the chance that some of the items in the data are incompatible with one another. In order to resolve this problem, a distinct step known as the data extraction phase has been developed. During this stage, the data that do not conform to the fundamental parameters of the study are identified, then removed and changed into the appropriate format.

Stage Five: Data Validation and Cleansing

The data are acquired from a wide variety of sources, as was described in phase III, which results in the data having no particular organization. There is a potential that the data contain restrictions that are inappropriate, which might result in inaccurate findings. This can be a cause for concern. As a result, it is necessary to clean up and check the accuracy of the data.

It entails getting rid of any data that is invalid and setting intricate validation criteria. Validating and cleaning the data may be done in a variety of ways. For instance, a dataset may just include a few rows that all have the value "null." If another dataset with a comparable structure already exists, then those rows' entries will be copied from that dataset; otherwise, those rows will be discarded.

Stage Six: Data Aggregation and Representation

The data is cleaned up and checked for validity according to the enterprise's predetermined standards. However, the data could be dispersed throughout a number of different datasets, and it is not recommended to deal with a number of different datasets at the same time. Consequently, the datasets are combined into a single one. For instance, if there are two different datasets, such as a Student Academic section and a Student Personal Details section, then those two datasets may be connected together using variables that are common to both of them, such as roll number.

Since the quantity of data that needs to be processed at this phase might be very substantial, significant labor is required. Consideration might be given to the use of automation in order to carry out the aforementioned activities free of any involvement from a human being.

Stage Seven: Data Analysis

The real action, which is doing the analysis, is coming up next. Analysis is performed in a manner that is dependent on the nature of the issue with the Big data. Analysis of data may be broken down into two categories: exploratory analysis and confirmatory analysis. The first step of a confirmatory analysis is to investigate and understand the phenomenon's underlying cause. The statement that is being made is known as the hypothesis.

The data are analyzed to determine whether or not the hypothesis is supported by the findings. This kind of study delivers conclusive responses to certain particular queries and establishes whether or not an assumption was correct. In an exploratory analysis, the data are investigated in order to get insight into the reasons behind the occurrence of a phenomena. The question "why" a phenomena happened is answered by this style of study. While the findings of this form of study are not definite, they do allow for the identification of trends.

Stage Eight: Data Visualization

With the knowledge that we obtained from the data in the datasets, we can now provide answers to some of the queries that we had. However, these responses are still stored in a format that cannot be made available to business users.

It is necessary to have some kind of representation in order to get any kind of value or conclusion from the study. Therefore, a variety of technologies are used so that the data may be visualized in the form of a graph, which can be simply understood by business users. It has been suggested that visualization has an effect on how one should perceive the data. In addition to that, it enables users to find solutions to problems that have not yet been defined in their minds.

Figure 3. Big data analytics lifecycle

Stage Nine: Utilization of Analysis Results

After the analysis has been completed and the findings have been visualized, it is time for the business users to make choices about how to make use of the results. The results may be used for process improvement and optimization in the company's operations. It is also possible to utilize it as an input into the systems in order to improve their performance. Figure 3 illustrates the Big data analytics lifecycle.

Processing of Big Data Analytics

Big data processing needs to meet four important criteria. The quickest data loading is the initial need. It is vital to speed up data loading because disc and network traffic interferes with query executions while the data is being loaded. Fast query processing is the second need. Many queries are response-time essential due to the demands of high workloads and real-time requests. As a result, as the number of inquiries grows fast, the data placement structure must be able to maintain high query processing speeds. The third prerequisite for Big data processing is the extremely effective use of storage space. Due to limited disc space, it is essential that data storage be carefully handled during processing and that questions regarding how to store the data so that space utilization is maximized be addressed. The quick expansion in user activities can require scalable storage capacity and computer power. The ability to adjust well to workload patterns that are extremely dynamic is the final need.

Because enormous data sets are analyzed by various applications and users for different goals and in diverse ways, the underlying system should be particularly adaptive to unexpected dynamics in data processing and not exclusive to certain workload patterns (He et al., 2011).

Map Reduce is a parallel programming model that is appropriate for huge data processing and is modelled after the "Map" and "Reduce" of functional languages. It serves as the foundation of Hadoop and handles data processing and analytics (Cuzzocrea et al., 2011). In other words, scaling out rather than scaling up, according to EMC, the MapReduce paradigm is predicated on adding more computers or resources as opposed to expanding the power or storage capacity of a single computer (EMC, 2012). The core concept of MapReduce is segmenting a task into stages and carrying out those parts concurrently to speed up task completion (Cuzzocrea et al., 2011).

The mapping of input values to a set of key/value pairs as output is the first stage of a MapReduce task. Accordingly, the "Map" function breaks up big computational jobs into smaller ones and allocates them to the right key/value pairs (Cuzzocrea et al., 2011). As a result, unstructured data, such as text, can be converted into a structured key/value pair, where the key might be a word from the text and the value might represent the word's frequency.

The "Reduce" function then takes this output as an input (EMC, 2012). The final output of the computing task is subsequently produced by Reduce by collecting and merging all of the values that share the same key value (Cuzzocrea et al., 2011). Hadoop's Job Tracker and Task Tracker nodes are two of the nodes that the MapReduce function depends on. The nodes in the Job Tracker are the ones that are accountable for allocating the mapper and reducer functions to the accessible Task Trackers and keeping track of the outcomes (EMC, 2012). The Job Tracker starts the MapReduce job by giving a map task running on a node a portion of an input file on the Hadoop Distributed File System (HDFS) (Lee et al. 2011). The Task Tracker nodes, on the other hand, carry out the tasks and report their outcomes to the Job Tracker. Inter-node communication is reduced because it is frequently done through files and directories in HDFS (EMC, 2012). Figure 4 illustrates the Namenode-Datanodes architecture, and Figure 5 shows the Hadoop Map Reduce Processes.

Processing of Big data can be performed in batch or stream mode.

A. *Batch processing*. is a critical component for organizations to efficiently handle large volumes of data. Batch processing is particularly advantageous for performing repetitive tasks, such as accounting, due to its inherent suitability. It is worth noting that the fundamental principles of batch processing remain consistent across various industries and projects. The utilization of this technology has gained significant recognition as a result of its multitude of advantages within the realm of enterprise data management. Batch processing offers numerous advantages for businesses. The availability of computing and other tools facilitates the processing of jobs, thereby enhancing efficiency.

Organizations have the ability to arrange batch operations for tasks that do not require immediate attention, while giving priority to time-sensitive tasks. Additionally, it has the capability to be processed in the background, thereby reducing the burden on the processor. In contrast to stream processing, batch processing is a less intricate system that does not necessitate specific hardware or system support for data input. Minimal maintenance is required. When conducting batch processing analysis, it is advisable to consider a range of tools such as Hadoop, Dryad, Mahout, Jaspersoft, Pentaho, Skytree Server, Tableau, Karmasphere, Talend, and MapReduce.

B.*Stream Processing*. A significant portion of data in contemporary times is generated and organized in the form of a continuous stream. Batch data refers to a discrete collection of low-level data that is captured at a particular moment in time. From this standpoint, data is transmitted expeditiously, presented sequentially, and algorithms are required to analyze it in a singular iteration while abiding by stringent constraints on both space and time. The utilization of algorithms incorporates the application of probabilistic assurance in order to expedite the generation of estimated outcomes.

One limitation of MapReduce is its lack of suitability for expressing streaming algorithms. In contrast, traditional online algorithms are limited by the memory and bandwidth capacity of a singular console. Distributed stream processing engines (DSPEs) are a novel category of technologies that draw inspiration from MapReduce and are designed to address the aforementioned issue.

The utilization of these engines allows for the representation of parallel computing in the form of streams, effectively merging the scalability of multiprocessors with the efficiency of streaming algorithm techniques. In the analysis of stream processing tools, the following tools were taken into consideration: Storm, S4, SQLstream s-Server, Splunk, Apache Kafka, SAP HANA, Samza, Flink, Samoa, Millwheel, Heron, cloud-based streaming, Amazon Kinesis, S2, Microsoft Azure, and IBM streaming analysis.

Big Data Analytics and Machine Learning

Data interpretation has characterized machine learning as prediction algorithms that are then followed by a learning algorithm in an unstructured program. Supervised, unsupervised, and reinforcement learning are the three main categories of machine learning (ML), which are carried out during the "data preprocessing," "learning," and "evaluation phase." Preprocessing is concerned with transforming raw data into the proper form that can be used in the learning phase, which includes some levels like cleaning the data, extracting it, transforming it, and combining it. In the evaluation phase, a data set will be chosen, and performance will be assessed along with statistical tests and error or deviation estimation. This might result in changing a few learning process parameters. The first one deals with examining crucial aspects for categorization using training data that has been provided. The data utilized in the

Figure 4. Namenode-Datanodes architecture

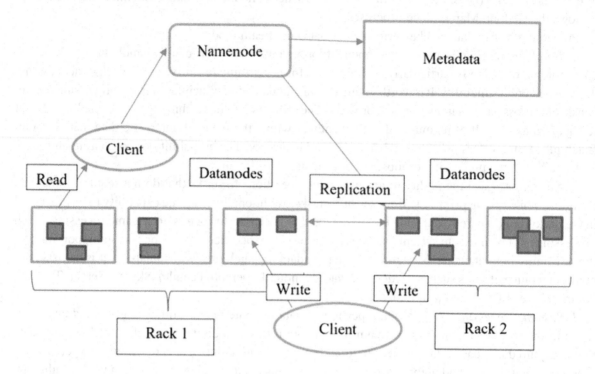

Figure 5. Hadoop map reduce processes

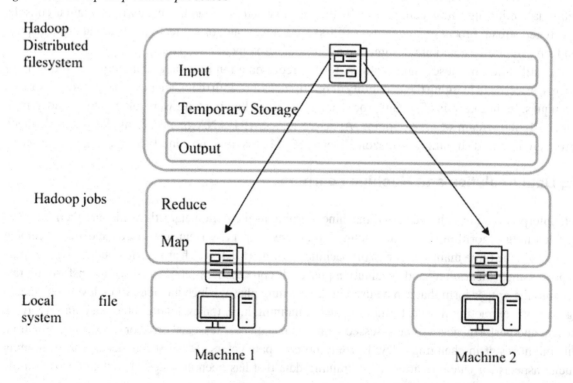

training algorithm will train, after which it will be tested using unlabeled data. Unlabeled data will be interpreted, and the output will be produced. If the result is continuous or discrete, it can be classed as regression. On the other hand, ML may be used to identify patterns without going through a training procedure; this is known as unsupervised ML. Cluster analysis is created in this category when patterns of features are utilized to group the data, and association is created when hidden rules in the data have been identified (Machine learning, 2023).

In other words, the basic goal of unsupervised machine learning (ML) or clustering is to identify natural grouping from unlabeled data. When comparing K cluster to other clusters in this process using the similarity measure, K cluster in a given batch of data is much more similar. The terms "hierarchical," "partitioned," and "overlapping" approaches refer to three forms of unsupervised ML. The terms "agglomerative" and "divisive" refer to two different types of hierarchical approaches. The first is an element that forms a distinct cluster and has a propensity to interact with a larger cluster, whereas the second is a complete collection that will split into a number of smaller clusters. Among all unsupervised learning techniques, K-means stands out. "Partitioned" methods start with creating several disjoint clusters from the data set without taking into account any hierarchical structure, and "overlapping" methods are defined as methods that try to find fuzzy or defuzy partitioning, which is done by "relaxing the mutually disjoint constraint." Unsupervised approaches primarily include "simplicity" and "effectiveness" (Zhou, 2019).

Machine learning and fuzzy logic Lofi Zadeh's (1965) fuzzy logic theory has been used in a wide range of industries, from engineering to data analysis and everything in between. Fuzzy logic has advantages for machine learning as well because it uses inductive reasoning. The changes took place in areas like "fuzzy rule induction," "fuzzy decision trees," "fuzzy nearest neighbor estimation," or "fuzzy support vector machines"(Cortes & Vapnik, 1995).

Classification is one of the most important aspects of ML (Urbanowicz & Moore, 2009), and it is the first stage of data analytics. Prior research identified new industries that may use this component, such as facial recognition or even handwriting recognition. Operating algorithms for categorization have been split into two groups, offline and online, according to (Urbanowicz & Moore, 2009). For training purposes, a static dataset is used in an offline manner. Once the training process is complete, classifiers will halt it and prevent any further modification of the data structure. While learning from fresh data, the online category is designated as a "one-pass" kind. The most important aspects of the data will be preserved in memory until the processed training data is deleted. The two primary techniques for online categorization are incremental and evolving processes (changing data patterns in unstable settings as a result of evolutionary system structure, and constantly updating meta-parameters) (Urbanowicz & Moore, 2009).

Due to its excellent learning performance, Cortes and Vapnik developed the support vector machine (SVM) in 1995 to solve challenges with multidimensional categorization and regression (Russell & Norvig, 2010). The main purpose of this strategy is to find the largest margin in binary categories while taking the hyperplane space into consideration. SVM does this by constructing a high-dimensional hyperplane that separates the input into binary categories (Mitchell, 1997). "Statistical learning theory," "Vapnik-Chervonenkis (VC) dimension," and "kernel method" are fundamental components in the creation of SVM, which uses a minimal number of learning patterns to achieve acceptable generalization while taking a risk minimization structure into consideration. K-nearest neighbor is one of the most prominent algorithms in classification issues in data mining and knowledge discovery, and it is used to categorize objects in the closest training class of characteristics (Hastie et al., 2001). Using this process, an item is allocated to its k-nearest neighbors. The efficiency of this strategy is determined by the weighted criteria of the characteristics. The approach is incapable of distinguishing between distant and close neighbors, and it is extremely dependent on the value of the K parameter, a gauge for determining neighborhood space. When neighbors are near, overlapping or noise might develop (Hall et al., 2008). KNN, one of the most significant data mining algorithms, was originally designed to solve classification difficulties before being expanded to pattern recognition and machine learning applications. KNN classification problems are used by expert systems.

Key Studies and Trends in Machine Learning and Big Data Analytics

In this section, an overview of a variety of advanced analytics methods based on machine learning modelling, which can make the computational process intelligent through intelligent decision-making in business processes is presented. A variety of methods, including regression and classification analysis, association rule analysis, time-series analysis, behavioral analysis, and log analysis, among others will be discussed.

Regression techniques (Han et al., 2011) are one of the most common statistical approaches used in data science for predictive modelling and data mining tasks. Regression analysis is a type of supervised machine learning that examines the relationship between a dependent variable (target) and independent variables (predictor) in order to predict output with continuous-valued values (Sarker, 2021; Shukla & Fricklas, 2018). Typically, regression analysis serves one of two purposes: to predict the value of the dependent variable for individuals with some knowledge of the explanatory variables, or to estimate the effect of an explanatory variable on the dependent variable, i.e., to determine the relationship of causal influence between the variables. Non-linear data cannot be fitted with linear regression, which may lead to an underfitting issue.

Clustering is a type of unsupervised machine learning technique and is well-known for statistical data analysis in many data science application domains (Han et al., 2011). Typically, clustering techniques seek for structures within a dataset and classify homogeneous groups of cases if the classification was not previously identified. This indicates that data points within a cluster are identical, but distinct from those in another cluster. Overall, the objective of cluster analysis (Sarker, 2021) is to classify various data points into groups (or clusters) that are internally homogeneous but externally heterogeneous. Clustering is frequently used to obtain insight into how data is distributed in a given dataset or as a preprocessing step for other algorithms. Data clustering, for instance, facilitates retail businesses with customer purchasing behavior, sales campaigns, consumer retention, anomaly detection, etc.

Association rule learning, also known as a rule-based machine learning system, typically employs an unsupervised learning technique to establish a relationship between variables. This is a descriptive technique that is frequently employed to analyze large datasets in order to discover intriguing relationships or patterns. The primary strength of the association learning technique is its exhaustiveness, as it generates all associations that satisfy user-specified constraints, such as minimal support and confidence value (Witten & Frank, 2005).

Association rules enable a data scientist to identify trends, relationships, and co-occurrences between data sets within large data collections. In a supermarket, for instance, associations infer information about the purchasing behavior of consumers for various products, which helps to modify the marketing and sales strategy. To better diagnose patients, physicians may utilize association guidelines in healthcare. Using association rules and data analysis based on machine learning, doctors can determine the conditional likelihood of a given disease by comparing symptom associations in the data from previous cases. Likewise, association rules are valuable for analyzing and predicting consumer behavior, customer market analysis, bioinformatics, weblog mining, recommendation systems, etc.

Typically, a time series is a sequence of data elements indexed in time order, specifically by date or timestamp (Sarker at al., 2018). Depending on the frequency, time-series can be of various types, such as annually, e.g., annual budget; quarterly, e.g., expenditure; monthly, e.g., air traffic; weekly, e.g., sales quantity; daily, e.g., weather; hourly, e.g., stock price; minute-wise, e.g., inbound calls in a call center; and even second-wise. Time-series analysis refers to the mathematical analysis of time-series data or the process of adapting a time series to an appropriate model. Relevant information can be extracted using a wide variety of time series forecasting algorithms and analysis techniques.

Sentiment analysis or opinion mining is the computational study of people's opinions, thoughts, emotions, assessments, and attitudes towards products, services, organizations, individuals, issues, events, topics, and their attributes (Liu, 2020). There are three types of emotions: positive, negative, and neutral, as well as more extreme emotions such as anger, happiness, sadness, interest, etc. According to the problem domain, more refined sentiments for evaluating the emotions of individuals in various situations can also be discovered.

Opinion mining and sentiment analysis are extremely challenging from a technical standpoint, but they are extremely useful in the actual world. For instance, a business always seeks public or customer feedback on its products and services in order to refine its business policy and make better business decisions. Understanding the social perception of a company's brand, product, or service can therefore be advantageous. In addition, potential customers are interested in the perceptions consumers have when they use a service or purchase a product. Document-level, sentence-level, aspect-level, and concept-level opinion mining are possible in this field (Hemmatian & Sohrabi, 2019).

Behavioral analytics is a recent trend that typically reveals new insights into e-commerce sites, online gaming, mobile and smartphone applications, IoT user behavior, and numerous other domains (Sarker et al., 2020). The objective of the behavioral analysis is to comprehend how and why consumers or users conduct, allowing for accurate predictions of their likely future behavior. For example, it enables advertisers to make the optimal offers to the appropriate client segments at the optimal time. Behavioral analytics utilize the large quantities of raw user event data collected during sessions in which people use apps, games, or websites. This includes traffic data such as navigation paths, clicks, social media interactions, purchase decisions, and marketing responsiveness. In previous papers, Sarker et al. (Sarker, 2019; Sarker at al., 2018; Sarker & Kayes, 2020), discussed how to extract users' phone utilization patterns from actual phone log data for a variety of purposes.

Anomaly detection, also known as Outlier analysis, is a phase in data mining that identifies data points, events, and/or findings that deviate from a dataset's regularities or typical behavior. Outliers, abnormalities, novelties, cacophony, inconsistency, irregularities, and exceptions are common terms for anomalies (Kwon et al., 2019; Sarker et al., 2020). By analyzing data patterns based on historical data, techniques for detecting anomalies may identify novel situations or cases as anomalous. Identifying financial misconduct or irregular transactions is one example of anomaly detection.

Factor analysis is a collection of techniques used to describe the relationships or correlations between variables in terms of more fundamental entities called factors (Cudeck, 2000). Variables are typically grouped into a small number of clusters based on their variance when mathematical or statistical methods are employed. The objectives of factor analysis are to determine the number of fundamental influences underlying a set of variables, to calculate the degree to which each variable is associated with the factors, and to learn more about the factors' existence by examining which factors contribute to output on which variables. The primary objective of factor analysis is to simplify the interpretation and comprehension of relationships and patterns (Yong et al., 2013).

Logs are frequently used in system management because they are frequently the only available data that record detailed system operational activities or behaviors (He et al., 2017). Log analysis is therefore the process of analyzing, interpreting, and comprehending computer-generated documents and messages, also known as logs. This can be a device log, a server log, a system log, a network log, an event log, an audit trace, or an audit record, among others. The creation of such recordings is known as data archiving.

Artificial Neural Networks

Neural networks, which are alternatively referred to as artificial neural networks (ANNs) or simulated neural networks (SNNs), constitute a subcategory of machine learning and serve as the fundamental building blocks of deep learning algorithms. The nomenclature and configuration of the aforementioned entities are derived from the human cerebral cortex, emulating the mechanism of inter-neuronal communication in biological systems.

Artificial neural networks (ANNs) are composed of multiple layers of nodes, including an input layer, one or more hidden layers, and an output layer. Every artificial neuron, also known as a node, establishes a connection with another neuron and is accompanied by a corresponding weight and threshold. In the event that the output of a given node surpasses the predetermined threshold value, stated node will become activated and transmit data to the subsequent layer within the network. In the absence of any data, transmission to the subsequent layer of the network does not occur.

Diverse learning techniques are employed in multi-layer networks. In 1965, Alexey Grigorevich Ivakhnenko and Valentin Lapa published the initial multi-layer perceptron (MLP) for deep learning (Ivakhnenko, 1973; Ivakhneneko et al., 1967; Schmidhuber, 2022). The authors incrementally added layers to their MLP and trained it in a layer-by-layer fashion until the remaining error reached an acceptable level. They employed a separate validation set to continuously prune any superfluous hidden units (Schmidhuber, 2022).

In 1967, Shun'ichi Amari published the initial deep learning MLP that was trained through stochastic gradient descent (Shun'ichi, 1967; Robbins & Monro, 1951). Saito, a student of Amari, conducted computer experiments wherein a multi-layer perceptron (MLP) consisting of five layers, two of which were modifiable, successfully acquired internal representations necessary for the non-linear classification of pattern classes (Schmidhuber, 2022).

The depicted architecture in Figure 7 is that of a multi-layer perceptron, which comprises numerous neurons distributed across distinct layers. The architecture of the aforementioned neural network holds resemblance to that of a single-layer perceptron, albeit with the incorporation of supplementary hidden layers. The various inputs are directed to an input layer. Subsequently, there exist one or multiple concealed strata contingent on the nature of the application. The input layer is responsible for receiving inputs, performing computations on them, and generating an output. The aforementioned result is utilized as an input for the subsequent layer, denoted as the hidden layer. The hidden layer comprises multiple neurons that exhibit distinct activation functions. The neural network will execute its designated operations on the input data it receives from the preceding layer. The output generated by the aforementioned layer is subsequently transmitted to the final layer, which is the output layer. This layer utilizes the received input to produce the ultimate output or response.

Backpropagation is the predominant algorithm employed for supervised training of a multi-layer perceptron. The aforementioned technique proves to be highly advantageous in determining the responsible node for the extent of loss incurred, owing to its ability to adeptly comprehend intricate multidimensional mappings, thereby reducing the loss function (Hetch-Neilsen, 1992). The phenomenon is characterized by two distinct phases or modes of propagation, namely forward and backward. During the process of forward propagation, the activation values originating from the input layer traverse through the neural network until they reach the output layer. During the process of backpropagation, the inputs undergo activation and are subsequently propagated to the output layer, where they produce a response or output. In the context of backward propagation, the generated response or output is compared with the intended output, and the discrepancy between the two is computed. The variation between the predicted output and the actual output is commonly referred to as the error. The backpropagation technique is designed to reduce this error by propagating it backwards through the neural network and modifying the weights and bias values accordingly. It is evident that this task may necessitate multiple iterations. Therefore, backpropagation serves as the foundation for computing the gradient of the error or loss function.

There exist various categories of neural networks. Neural networks can be categorized into distinct classifications that serve varying objectives. Although not exhaustive, the following list comprises the predominant types of neural networks encountered in typical use cases.

- *The perceptron*, which was developed by Frank Rosenblatt in 1958 (Rosenblatt, 1958), is considered to be the earliest form of neural network.
- *The multi-layer perceptrons* (MLPs), which are a type of feedforward neural networks. Neural networks are typically composed of three main layers: an input layer, one or more hidden layers, and an output layer. It is noteworthy that although these neural networks are frequently denoted as MLPs, they are essentially composed of sigmoid neurons rather than perceptrons, given that the majority of real-world predicaments exhibit nonlinearity. Typically, the models are trained by inputting data, which serves as the basis for neural networks, computer vision, natural language processing, and other related fields.
- *Convolutional neural networks (CNNs)* share similarities with feedforward networks, but are typically employed in the domains of image recognition, pattern recognition, and computer vision. The aforementioned networks utilize concepts from linear algebra, specifically the process of matrix multiplication, to detect and analyze patterns present in an image.
- The defining characteristic of *recurrent neural networks (RNNs)* is their utilization of feedback loops. Learning algorithms are predominantly utilized in the context of time-series data to forecast future outcomes, such as stock market predictions or sales forecasting.

The accuracy of neural networks is enhanced through the acquisition of knowledge from training data. After the optimization of these learning algorithms for precision, they become potent instruments in the fields of computer science and artificial intelligence, enabling us to rapidly classify and cluster data. The automation of tasks related to speech recognition or image recognition can significantly reduce the time required for completion, often taking only a few minutes as opposed to several hours that would be required for manual identification by human experts. Google's search algorithm is widely recognized as one of the most prominent neural networks.

Deep Learning

Deep learning is a specialized area within the broader field of machine learning, focused on the creation and improvement of algorithms capable of acquiring knowledge from data in a hierarchical fashion. Deep learning techniques employ artificial neural networks comprising interconnected nodes to analyze and process intricate data. Artificial neural networks are trained through the utilization of substantial quantities of labelled data and robust computational resources. Consequently, they are capable of acquiring the ability to identify patterns and generate predictions based on the data they are provided. The application of deep learning has been observed in diverse domains such as image and speech recognition, natural language processing, and autonomous vehicles.

Deep learning is a subfield that falls under the umbrella of machine learning. The fundamental distinctions between these algorithms pertain to their respective learning methodologies and the quantity of data utilized by each algorithmic type. Deep learning facilitates the automation of feature extraction, thereby reducing the need for manual human intervention. It was noted that the utilization of extensive data sets is made possible by this technology, thereby earning it the designation of "scalable machine learning." The aforementioned capability is of significant interest, especially in light of the increasing exploration of unstructured data. It is estimated that a substantial proportion of an organization's data, ranging from 80% to 90%, is unstructured.

Conventional machine learning, also known as classical or "non-deep" machine learning, relies more heavily on human intervention for the purpose of learning. Typically, in order to comprehend distinctions between data inputs, human experts employ a hierarchical approach to feature determination, which necessitates the utilization of more structured data for the purpose of learning.

Deep learning combines multiple processing layers, such as the input, hidden, and output layers, to construct a computational architecture that can learn from data (Han et al., 2011). Deep learning outperforms conventional machine learning techniques in a variety of situations, especially when learning from large datasets (Sarker et al., 2020, Xin et al., 2018). Multi-layer perceptron (MLP) (Pedregosa et al., 2011), convolutional neural network (CNN or ConvNet) (LeCun et al., 1998), and long short term memory recurrent neural network (LSTM-RNN) (Goodfellow et al., 2016) are the most prevalent deep learning algorithms.

The utilization of machine learning and neural networks has revolutionized the operational procedures of businesses by enabling them to optimize the utilization of available information. Recurrent neural networks aid enterprises in optimizing their workflow through their ability to facilitate report generation and text summarization. Recurrent neural networks (RNNs) are utilized by financial institutions such as banks and insurance companies to generate documents that are tailored to the specific needs of individual clients. Recurrent Neural Networks (RNNs) have found extensive application in machine translation, exemplified by their use in Google Translate, as well as in eCommerce platforms, where they serve to enhance the efficacy of search outcomes. In the past few years, scholars have conducted trials and formulated various categories of deep learning networks to address fundamental issues in the fields of engineering and science. Neural networks find application in various domains of engineering such as automotive control, chemical engineering, flight control, and power plants (Schumann et al., 2010; Gusmãoet al., 2020). The utilization of networks in scientific research has brought about a significant transformation in the fields of healthcare, medicine, chemistry, and food research.

Deep learning has been utilized to optimize advertising campaigns in the field of advertising. The healthcare industry is being transformed by deep learning, which is providing novel avenues for enhancing individuals' well-being. Convolutional neural networks (CNNs) have demonstrated significant efficacy in predictive analytics within the healthcare sector. Convolutional Neural Networks (CNN) are primarily utilized in the domains of image classification and facial recognition. However, they also have practical applications in other areas such as document or handwriting analysis, climate comprehension, and complicated duties such as the preservation of historical and environmental collections. The implementation of deep learning can be observed in various significant domains. There are various aspects of speech and image processing, including face recognition, face detection, image and speech recognition, image reconstruction, and noise removal. The field of healthcare and medicine encompasses various applications such as computer-aided disease detection, genome analysis, drug discovery, and medical imaging. The entertainment industry encompasses various sectors such as film production, music generation, and streaming services like Netflix and Amazon. The topic of discussion pertains to the utilization of unmanned aerial vehicles in defense, specifically in the context of automated target recognition. The automotive industry has witnessed significant advancements in recent times, particularly in the areas of self-driving cars, virtual sensors, and improved guidance systems. The field of sales and marketing involves the forecasting of commodity prices and the utilization of chatbots.

Fuzzy Models and Networks

The utilization of fuzzy models and networks is a prevalent topic in academic research. The application of a fuzzy model involves the utilization of logical reasoning and intelligent computation techniques to process imprecise information that lacks a precise mathematical model. The primary approach involves a procession based on IF-THEN rules, which is formulated using either expert knowledge or numerical data. Despite not relying on precise mathematical models, the fuzzy model is an effective methodology for logical inference, numerical computation, and approximating non-linear functions (Wang, 2021). The two primary steps involved in identifying a fuzzy model are the establishment of its structure and the estimation of its parameters (Tsekouras, 2005). The process of identifying structure is linked to the quantity of regulations following the selection of crucial input variables. The process of determining the parameters of a fuzzy set is a dependable method for approximating non-linear systems. The attribute of interpretability is a primary characteristic of a fuzzy model, particularly in specialized domains such as security-focused and military contexts. Experts possess a significant amount of knowledge and experience in their respective fields. The security of fuzzy logic (FL) models is crucial for military applications and the transparency and interpretability of knowledge when machine learning is utilized to handle such knowledge. The type of knowledge conveyed by FL is relatively straightforward to comprehend in terms of its concepts, accommodating of imprecise data, and conducive to human interaction. Expert knowledge-based fuzzy models are conventionally highly interpretable, as evidenced by the utilization of fuzzy logic in this approach.

It can be argued that fuzzy models based on expert knowledge have traditionally been inherently interpretable. The Mamdani rule-based architecture is well-suited for a fuzzy model that prioritizes interpretability. Fuzzy models that rely on numerical data may lack interpretability, but many of them exhibit high precision when coupled with computational methods.

It is recommended that the predictive fuzzy models incorporate both expert knowledge and numerical data in a synchronized manner. This approach has been supported by previous research (Ahmed, & Al-Jamimi, 2013; Wang, & Mendel, 1992; Wang et al., 2019). Historical data offers quantifiable measurements from prior projects concerning both internal and external quality attributes. Professionals draw upon their expertise to furnish imprecise data, or qualitative depictions of the association between the internal and external quality characteristics. Interpretability is a crucial aspect in developing a practical prediction model, as it enables practitioners to apply their own judgement to the linguistic predictors. The identification of structure and incorporation of expert judgements in black box prediction models, such as those based on artificial neural networks, pose significant challenges. The novel approach of FN demonstrates the ability to integrate rules derived from both knowledge-based and data-driven sources. The Fuzzy Network (FN) operates as either a Chained Fuzzy System (CFS) or a Hierarchical Fuzzy System (HFS), wherein it utilizes connections to map the inputs to the outputs. This has been documented in previous studies (Bucolo et al., 2004; Lee et al., 2003; Joo et al., 2005) and further elaborated through subsequent research (Gegov, et al., 2014; Yaakob et al., 2018; Gegov et al., 2016). The total quantity of regulations within the framework of Fuzzy Logic is a linear function that is contingent upon the quantity of inputs and the quantity of linguistic terms assigned to each input. In contrast to the Standard Fuzzy System (SFS), the Fuzzy Network (FN) entails a reduction and simplification of its rules. The transparency and interpretability of the structure in FN is higher. Figure 6 illustrates the perceptron model, and figure 7 shows the multi-layer perceptron model, while, figure 8 represents the deep neural network, and figure 9 shows the fuzzy model.

M11, J21 and *M12* are Boolean matrices

Figure 6. The perceptron model
(source amended from Rosenblatt perceptron by perceptron. Mitchell, machine learning p87, licensed under CC BY-SA 3.0, https://commons.wikimedia.org/w/index)

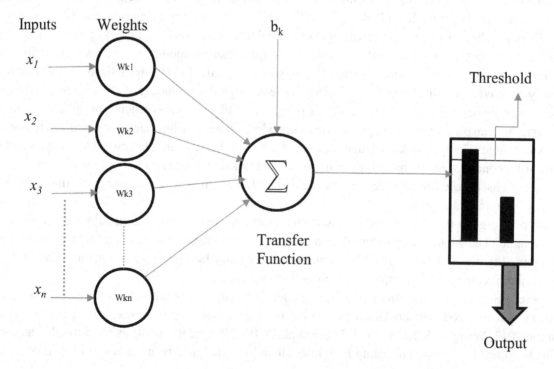

Figure 7. The multi-layer perceptron model

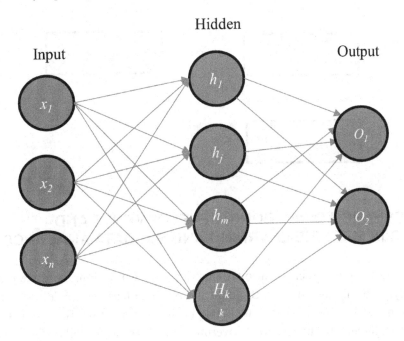

Figure 8. The deep neural network

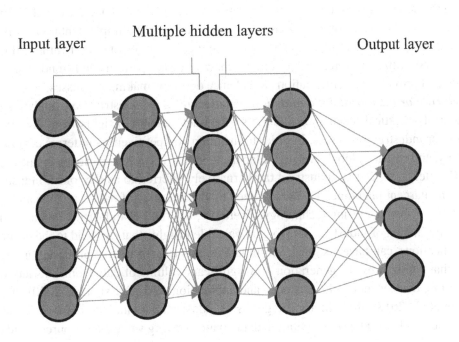

Figure 9. The fuzzy model

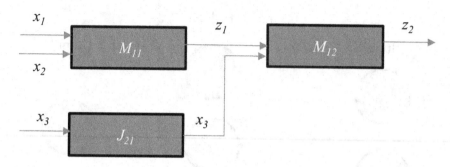

CURRENT RESEARCH DIRECTIONS, DEVELOPMENTS AND CHALLENGES IN MACHINE LEARNING AND BIG DATA ANALYTICS

The influence of data is pervasive across various industries and organizations, necessitating the utilization of advanced analytics techniques such as Big data and machine learning modelling. These techniques find applications in a wide range of sectors including business, marketing, finance, IoT systems, cyber-security, urban management, health care, and government policies, among others, where data generation is prevalent. This section presents a comprehensive analysis of the primary domains in which data sets and analytics are commonly applied.

Business or financial data analytics: business or financial data analytics encompasses the analysis and interpretation of data within the context of business and finance. Business data analytics is a broad field encompassing the examination of business or e-commerce data with the objective of extracting valuable insights that can inform intelligent decision-making and facilitate the implementation of high-quality actions (Provost et al., 2013). Data scientists possess the ability to create algorithms and data-driven models that can be utilized to forecast consumer behavior, detect patterns and trends using historical business data, and provide recommendations to enhance decision-making processes.

Manufacturing or industrial data analytics: manufacturing or industrial data analytics pertains to the application of analytical techniques and tools to extract valuable insights from data generated in manufacturing or industrial processes. In order to maintain competitiveness in terms of production capability, quality, and cost at a global level, manufacturing industries have experienced multiple industrial revolutions (Brettel et al., 2017). Industry 4.0, alternatively referred to as the fourth industrial revolution, denotes the nascent phenomenon characterized by the interplay of data exchange and automation within the realm of manufacturing technology. Therefore, the field of industrial data analytics, which involves the examination of industrial data to gain valuable insights that can lead to the optimization of industrial applications, can have a significant impact on this transformative process. The manufacturing sector is characterized by the generation of a significant volume of data from a variety of sources, including sensors, devices, networks, systems, and applications (Al-Abassi et al., 2020). According to a study (Wang et al., 2018), the primary categories of industrial data include large-scale data devices, life-cycle production data, enterprise operation data, manufacturing value chain sources, and collaboration data from external sources.

Medical or health information analytics: healthcare is experiencing notable advancements in data analytics, particularly in medical and health information analytics. Health data analytics is the process of deriving practical insights from aggregations of patient data, commonly obtained from electronic health records. The utilization of various data sources, including the electronic health record, billing claims, cost estimates, and patient satisfaction surveys, enables organizations to effectively evaluate and enhance the quality of healthcare provision, mitigate expenses, and augment the overall patient experience.

Internet of things (IoT) data analytics: Internet of Things (IoT) data analytics, as discussed by Atzori and his colleagues (Atzori et al., 2010), represents a groundbreaking area of technology that enhances the intelligence of electronic systems. It is widely recognized as a significant frontier with the potential to enhance various aspects of human life. The utilization of machine learning has emerged as an essential technological tool for Internet of Things (IoT) applications due to its ability to leverage expert knowledge in order to identify patterns and construct predictive models (Sarker et al., 2020). The primary application area of the Internet of Things (IoT) is the implementation of smart cities, which utilize technological advancements to improve municipal services and enhance the overall quality of life for residents.

Cybersecurity: cybersecurity, which involves safeguarding networks, systems, hardware, and data against digital attacks, holds significant importance within the context of Industry 4.0 (Sarker et al., 2020; Ślusarczyk, 2018). The utilization of data analytics techniques, specifically machine learning, has emerged as a pivotal cybersecurity technology. This technology exhibits the ability to continuously acquire knowledge and discern patterns through data analysis. Consequently, it enhances the detection of malware within encrypted traffic, identifies insider threats, predicts the presence of hazardous online environments, safeguards individuals during internet browsing, and fortifies data protection in cloud environments by unveiling suspicious user behavior (Sarker et al., 2020).

Behavioral data analytics: Behavioral data analytics refers to the analysis of information generated from various activities, primarily commercial behavior, conducted on Internet-connected devices such as personal computers, tablets, or smartphones (Sarker et al., 2020). Typical sources of behavioral data encompass various platforms such as websites, mobile applications, marketing automation systems, call centers, support offices, and billing systems. Behavioral data is considerably more complex than basic data, as it is not characterized by a fixed or unchanging nature (Sarker et al., 2019).

Smart cities or urban data analytics: The topic of discussion here revolves around the concept of smart cities and the utilization of urban data analytics. At present, a majority of the global population is concentrated in urban areas or cities (Nations, 2018). These urban areas are widely recognized as hubs of economic growth, wealth generation, improved quality of life, and social engagement (Resch & Szell, 2019; Schläpfer et al., 2014). In addition to urban centers, the term "urban area" can encompass various administrative divisions such as municipalities, conurbations, and suburbs.

Smart mobile phones: According to a study (Zheng & Ni, 2006), contemporary smart mobile phones are commonly recognized as advanced cellular devices that possess multiple functionalities, enabling efficient data processing and improved wireless connectivity. The study conducted by Sarker and his colleagues (Sarker et al., 2020) provides evidence of a growing consumer preference for "Mobile Phones" compared to other platforms such as "Desktop Computer," "Portable Computer," and "Tablet Computer" in recent years.

The investigation into big data analytics, advanced analytics methods, smart computing, and their practical applications in various domains prompts several research inquiries concerning data-driven business solutions and the development of data products. Consequently, this section will provide a summary of the challenges faced, along with the potential avenues for research and future prospects in the development of data-driven products.

The primary obstacle in the field of Big Data analytics modelling involves the comprehension of real-world business problems and the associated data. This includes understanding the characteristics of the data, such as its format, type, size, and identifiers. The primary objective of this task is to accurately identify, define, depict, and measure business problems and data that are specific to a particular domain, in alignment with the specified requirements.

One significant challenge that arises is the retrieval of relevant and precise information from the aforementioned gathered data. Data scientists are primarily focused on the exploration, explanation, representation, and acquisition of data-driven knowledge with the purpose of extracting practical insights from data. Nevertheless, the data gathered from real-world sources may encompass a multitude of uncertain values, absent values, extreme values, and data that lacks significance (Sarker, 2019).

Historically, data-driven models and systems have utilized substantial quantities of business data in order to generate decisions based on data analysis. In several application domains, it is more probable that newer trends will be captivating and valuable for the purpose of modelling and predicting future outcomes compared to older trends. Examples of areas that involve time-series data and the dynamic nature of human interests or preferences include the modelling of smartphone user behavior, Internet of Things (IoT) services, stock market forecasting, health and transportation services, job market analysis, and various other domains.

BENEFITS OF BIG DATA ANALYTICS TO BUSINESSES

When business executives hear the term "Big data," they immediately think of the vast amounts of data that are currently available. This data is generated by e-commerce and omnichannel marketing systems, IoT-connected devices, and business applications that generate ever-more-detailed transaction and activity information. These are merely a few examples. The mere volume of data is intimidating, and in some cases may even be overwhelming. However, there are significant commercial benefits to be obtained from analyzing large data sets. There are several advantages to incorporating Big data analytics into a business or organization:

- *Cost savings:* Because of Big data, storing all business data in one area can save money. Monitoring analytics also allows firms to find places where they might save money.
- *Product development:* Developing and marketing new goods, services, or brands is much easier when based on data acquired from customers' requirements and desires. Furthermore, Big data analytics assists firms in assessing product viability and trend tracking.
- *Strategic business decisions:* The ability to continually analyze data helps businesses to make faster, more accurate decisions such as supply chain and cost optimization.
- *Customer experience:* By improving the customer experience, data-driven algorithms help marketing objectives (for example, tailored commercials) and increase consumer happiness.
- *Risk management:* By evaluating data trends, firms may identify potential dangers and develop plans to mitigate them.
- *Entertainment:* The provision of personalized movie and music recommendations based on a customer's specific preferences has revolutionized the entertainment business.
- *Education:* Based on student needs and demand, Big data enables educational technology providers and institutions to create new curricula and enhance already-existing ones.

- *Health:* Keeping track of patients' medical history enables doctors to identify and stop diseases.
- *Government:* In order to better manage the public sector, Big data can be utilized to gather information from Closed Circuit Television (CCTV) and traffic cameras, satellites, body cameras and sensors, emails, calls, and more.
- *Marketing:* Targeted advertising campaigns with a high return on investment (ROI) can be developed using knowledge of customer information and preferences.
- *Banking:* Data analytics can be used to trace and keep an eye on unauthorized money laundering.

Types of Big Data Analytics

Big data analytics make it possible to make data-driven decisions with scientific support, allowing decisions to be based on true data rather than only on prior experience or intuition. The four main categories of analytics are: descriptive analytics, diagnostic analytics, predictive analytics, and prescriptive analytics. Each of these uses a different set of methodologies and analysis algorithms to achieve its results. This suggests that different sorts of analytic outputs may demand different amounts of data, storage, and processing. The complexity and expense of the analytic environment rise when high value analytic outcomes are produced. Big data analytics come in four primary categories and are used to assist and inform various business choices.

Descriptive Analytics

Data that is straightforward to read and analyze is referred to as descriptive analytics. With the use of this data, reports and information that can describe business sales and profits can be created. Descriptive analytics is used to provide information about already-occurring events. Data is contextualized in this type of analytics in order to produce information. What was the sales volume during the previous 12 months, for example, how many support calls were made, broken down by location and level of severity, or how much commission does each salesperson receive each month. Approximately 80% of data analytics that are produced are descriptive in nature. Descriptive analytics are the least valuable and call for only a small set of expertise. Ad hoc reporting or dashboards are frequently used to do descriptive analytics. The reports are typically static in nature and offer historical data in the form of graphs or data grids. From within an organization, such as a Customer Relationship Management system (CRM) or Enterprise Resource Planning (ERP) system, queries are run on operational data repositories. As an illustration, a top pharmaceutical corporation examined data from its offices and research facilities throughout the epidemic. They were able to find underused areas and divisions that were combined thanks to descriptive analytics, which helped the organization save millions of dollars.

One of the primary benefits of descriptive analytics is that it can help in monitoring and measuring the performance and progress of a certain business. key performance indicators (KPIs) can be monitored such as sales, revenue, customer satisfaction, retention, and loyalty using descriptive analytics. In addition, the results can be compared to required objectives, benchmarks, and competitors to identify strengths and weaknesses. Using charts, diagrams, dashboards, and reports, descriptive analytics can also help in communicating results and accomplishments to stakeholders, customers, and employees. It is simple to do; descriptive analysis does not necessitate extensive knowledge or experience with statistical methods or analytics. There are numerous available tools; there is an abundance of analytics tools to choose from, products that perform the majority of the heavy labor.

Concerning the limitations of descriptive analytics. First, descriptive analytics can only reveal what has occurred, not why or what will occur next. It cannot explain the causes or consequences of the observed patterns and trends, nor can it predict future outcomes or scenarios. Other categories of analytics, such as diagnostic, predictive, and prescriptive, are required for this purpose. Second, descriptive analytics may be deceptive or inaccurate if the data quality is inadequate, incomplete, or biased. It is essential to ensure that the data used for descriptive analytics is accurate, pertinent, and representative of the reality being analyzed. One of its main limitations is that it cannot ascertain the causes of a particular behavior, motivation, or event. In other words, it is unable to establish a causal relationship between variables in research.

The limitation of descriptive analytics is that they only enable to make generalizations about the people or things that have actually been measured. They can not generalize the collected data to other persons or objects (i.e., using sample data to infer the characteristics/parameters of a population).

Diagnostic Analytics

Business organizations can better grasp problems by using diagnostic analytics. Users of Big data technologies and tools can mine and retrieve data that aids in analyzing problems and preventing them in the future. Even though customers keep adding products to their shopping carts, a clothes store's revenues have fallen. Diagnostic analytics were useful in determining why the payment page had been malfunctioning for a few weeks.

Diagnostic analytics use queries that concentrate on the cause of the occurrence to try to identify the origin of a past phenomenon. This kind of analytics is to identify the data that is relevant to the phenomena in order to enable answering inquiries that aim to ascertain why something has happened, such as, why were Q2 sales lower than Q1 sales, for instance, or why do support calls from the Eastern region outnumber those from the Western region, or why have patient re-admission rates increased during the last three months. Despite requiring a more specialized skill set, diagnostic analytics are more valuable than descriptive analytics. Data from several sources must often be gathered for diagnostic analytics, and the data must be stored in a way that allows for drill-down and roll-up analysis. Users can spot trends and patterns by using interactive visualization tools to view the findings of diagnostic analytics. The queries are carried out on multidimensional data stored in analytical processing systems and are more complex than those of descriptive analytics.

Diagnostic analytics offers more specific insights than descriptive analytics (which solely summarizes data). Understanding the causes of business outcomes is crucial for a company's capacity to develop and avoid repeating past errors. Diagnostic analytics enable businesses to zero in on the factors that contribute to success or failure, including those that may not be immediately apparent. Diagnostic analytics can aid in instilling a data-driven analytical culture across the enterprise. Business executives are more likely to use diagnostic analytics in their decision-making when they recognize the company's capacity to investigate the root causes of problems. For instance, if a problem with on-time deliveries is identified and further analysis of the supply chain exposes disruptions and unpredictability in lead times, managers may decide to increase inventory to meet customer demand.

A disadvantage of diagnostic analytics is that they concentrate on historical data; they can only assist businesses in comprehending why past events occurred. In addition, it may be necessary to conduct additional research to determine whether the correlations disclosed by diagnostic analytics demonstrate cause and effect. To look into the future, businesses must employ additional analytic techniques, such as predictive analytics, which assess the potential future impact of trends and events, and prescriptive analytics, which suggest actions businesses can take to influence the outcome of these future trends. One disadvantage of diagnostic analytics is the possibility of mistaking correlation for causation, which can distort your conclusions.

Predictive Analytics

To develop forecasts, predictive analytics examines both historical and current data. Data mining, artificial intelligence (AI), and machine learning enable users to analyze the information to forecast market trends. A good example is the manufacturing industry, where businesses can forecast whether or when a piece of equipment will fail or break down using algorithms based on historical data. Predictive analytics is used to try and predict how an event that might happen in the future will turn out. With the use of predictive analytics, data is given meaning in order to provide knowledge that explains how the data is connected. Models that are used to produce future predictions based on past events are built upon the strength and amplitude of the associations. It is crucial to note that the predictive analytics models contain implicit dependencies on the circumstances of the historical occurrences. The models that produce predictions must be updated if these underlying factors change. For example, what are the chances that a customer will default on a loan if they have missed a monthly payment, or what percentage of patients would survive if drug B was used in place of drug A, or what are the possibilities that a consumer will buy Product C if they have already purchased Products A and B, are typical what-if questions.

Predictive analytics has broad advantages.

It boosts decision-making; the more data an organization possesses, the more predictive analysis can enhance its decision-making. This benefits numerous businesses. Predictive analytics helps companies analyze client buying trends, assess profit-boosting practices, and enhance company.

And it boosts efficiency; predictive maintenance keeps equipment running and reduces supply chain interruptions in many sectors. Operations disruptions hurt profitability and the sector. An oil and gas supply chain interruption might raise global gasoline costs.

Preventive maintenance; predictive analysis prevents equipment failure and boosts efficiency. It may also improve business processes, decrease waste, and help organizations adapt quicker.

Risk reduction; every industry faces daily risks. How firms manage these risks determines their success. Companies may expand with good risk management. Predictive analytics can identify fraud, vulnerabilities, and big financial losses from enormous data sets. Predictive analytics may help companies avoid previous errors.

Boosts sales; predictive analytics may enhance revenues by researching human behavior. This data analysis lets companies follow clients and adjust marketing to their interests. To make customers demand a product, companies may identify effective and failed marketing initiatives.

Predictive metrics give competitive information; A competitive advantage may make or break a firm that sells the same product as hundreds of others.

Enhances supply chain management; predictive analytics tracks resource consumption and predicts replenishment to simplify supply chain management. This research may reveal resource sending patterns to automate restocking.

Business executives should be mindful of the downsides of predictive analytics technologies.

Cannot forecast all human behavior; predictive analysis can properly forecast human behavior and transform many enterprises. However, human behavior cannot be predicted. Technology cannot predict all events, as shown by the 2008–2009 global financial crisis.

Need for update data regularly; predictive analysis requires updated data. Time affects forecast accuracy. An organization may lose significant money if it uses data from a year ago to forecast worldwide market developments.

Optimize data; an organization needs objectives or challenges to tackle before investing in predictive analytics. Without correlations, time and money may be wasted mining data. Some firms start prediction analysis by mining all their data, hoping to get insights that would transform their operations. Since prediction analysis relies on serious questioning about known situations, generalized thinking may be problematic.

Data gaps; predictive analysis assumes adequate data to provide relevant insights. What happens when data is incomplete? Incomplete data skews findings, increasing corporate risk.

Unreliable data; survey-based companies recognize that not all clients are honest. Personal biases may produce inaccurate data, not dishonesty. Inaccurate data always distorts results.

Prescriptive Analytics

Prescriptive analytics uses AI and machine learning to collect data and utilize it for risk management, offering a solution to a problem. To mitigate risk, utility companies, gas producers, and pipeline owners in the energy sector determine the variables that influence the price of oil and gas. By outlining the appropriate course of action, prescriptive analytics build on the findings of predictive analytics. The key is not just to choose the recommended course of action, but also to understand why. In other words, because they incorporate parts of situational information, prescriptive analytics produce findings that may be justified. As a result, using this kind of analytics can help you obtain an advantage or reduce your risk. Examples of questions might be; which of the following three medications gives the best results, or when is the most advantageous moment to trade a specific stock. Prescriptive analytics are the most valuable sort of analytics, and as a result, they call for the most sophisticated skill set, along with specialized software and tools. The optimum course of action is recommended for each outcome after various outcomes have been calculated. The strategy changes from explanatory to advisory, and it may involve simulating different scenarios.

Regarding the advantages, the ability to automate prescriptive analytics through machine learning is its primary benefit. Once you have predicted a set of prospective outcomes, prescriptive analytics helps you control those outcomes, which is ultimately advantageous for your business. It assists in comprehending how and which variables can be orchestrated to achieve the desired outcome. Predictive analytics enables a deeper comprehension of the competition, developing strategies to achieve a competitive advantage, optimization of existing products and services, improved comprehension of customer requirements, and reduced cost and time spent on efforts.

The benefits of implementing measures to prevent fraud, mitigate risk, and enhance efficiency, among other advantages are highlighted.

The simulation technique generates potential outcomes and presents their respective probabilities. However, its effectiveness is contingent upon the quality of the inputs. Furthermore, this method is not appropriate for long-term predictions or solutions. Additionally, certain providers of big data offer outcomes, while others do not.

Regarding disadvantages, a disadvantage of prescriptive analytics is that it requires a costly and time-consuming level of expertise. Even if a company has sufficient data, critics assert that computers and algorithms fail to take into account variables, such as altering weather, sentiments, and relationships, which may influence consumer purchasing patterns and human behavior.

Also, it should be noted that prescriptive analytics is not immutable. The efficacy of organizational efforts is reliant upon their ability to formulate appropriate inquiries and respond appropriately to the information obtained. Therefore, the effectiveness of the system is dependent upon the validity of its inputs. In the event that the fundamental presumptions are flawed, the resultant outcomes will lack precision.

The aforementioned data analytics methodology is exclusively appropriate for resolving issues of a temporary nature. Consequently, it is advisable for businesses to refrain from utilizing prescriptive analytics for making enduring decisions. The reliability of the data decreases as the duration of time required increases.

There exists variability among prescriptive analytics providers. It is imperative for enterprises to carefully contemplate the technology and its provider. Certain approaches yield tangible outcomes, whereas others offer the potential of utilizing large datasets but do not fulfil their claims.

Other disadvantages are:

- Distinguishing it from predictive analytics can be a challenge, thereby making it difficult to define the best practices.
- The excessive reliance on the predictive abilities of machine learning can result in individuals being influenced to adhere to its recommendations, irrespective of their accuracy.
- Likewise, the predictions of machine learning have the potential to influence individuals towards a state of passivity or contentment, which could be risky.
- If the foundational data utilized is inaccurate, the resulting suggestions will be skewed.
- Automated decision-making processes may pose a potential risk of inappropriate actions being taken by algorithms.
- The implementation of prescriptive analytics necessitates close monitoring by proficient analysts who possess expertise in machine learning, a process that is both resource-intensive and financially burdensome.

Figure 10 illustrates the different types of Big data analytics.

Tools Used in Big Data Analytics

There is a need to use tools to analyze all of that data effectively. Straightforward software programs are now widely available thanks to advancements in technology, such as:

- Hadoop: Big data collections are processed and stored using the open-source Hadoop platform. Both structured and unstructured data can be handled and analyzed with Hadoop.
- Spark: A cluster computing framework that is free and open source that processes and analyses data in real time.
- Software that streamlines the integration of Big data across several platforms, including MongoDB, Apache, Hadoop, and Amazon EMR.

Figure 10. Types of big data analytics

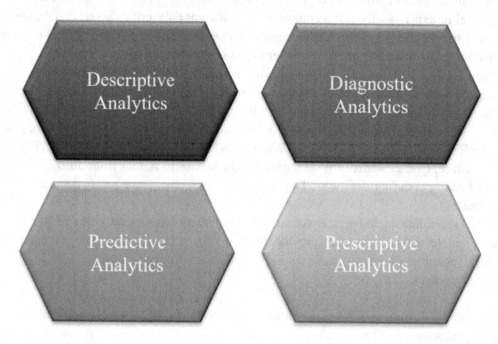

- Systems that filter, assemble, and analyze data that may be kept on several platforms and in various formats, like Kafka.
- Databases with the ability to distribute data over different servers and the capacity to spot lost or faulty data, like Cassandra.
- Systems that handle massive amounts of complicated data using machine learning and algorithms to forecast future results, such as fraud detection, marketing, and risk assessments, are known as predictive analytics hardware and software.
- Tools for data mining: Programs that let users search both structured and unstructured large amounts of data.

Non-relational data management systems, or NoSQL databases, are best suited for handling unstructured and unprocessed data. Storage for vast amounts of data gathered from numerous sources using preset schemas is done in data warehouses.

Applications of Big Data Analytics

Big data has raised demand for information management expertise, and Software AG, Oracle Corporation, IBM, Microsoft, SAP, EMC, HP, and Dell have invested over $15 billion in data management and analytics software businesses. In 2010, this market was valued over $100 billion and growing at over 10% per year, twice as fast as the software industry (The Economist, 2010). Industrialized countries use data-intensive technology. Over one billion individuals joined the middle class between 1990 and 2005, increasing literacy and knowledge. There are 4.6 billion mobile phone users and 1–2 billion internet users worldwide. One estimate sets one-third of all recorded data in alphanumeric text and still picture format, which is best for Big data applications. The world's effective capacity for transmitting information over telecommunication networks was 281 petabytes in 1986, 471 petabytes, 2.2 exabytes, and 65 exabytes in 2007 (Hilbert & Lopez, 2011). Underutilized data sources like audio and video records are important. If the company has the technical capability, experts propose building unique Big data platforms.

Government

The use of Big data in the legal system, in conjunction with analysis techniques, is currently one of the possible alternatives to expediting justice administration. The use and adoption of Big data in government operations improves cost, productivity, and innovation efficiencies, but it is not without downsides. Data analysis typically involves the collaboration of several government departments (both central and local) to get the desired outcome. A prominent example of a government organization that utilizes big data is the National Security Administration (NSA), which continually monitors Internet activity in search of any probable patterns of suspicious or criminal conduct that their system may detect. All birth-through-death certificate statuses are compiled by civil registration and vital statistics (CRVS). CRVS provides governments with access to massive amounts of data.

Media

According to Nick Couldry and Joseph Turow, media and advertising professionals should view Big data as a collection of actionable data points on millions of individuals. The company appears to be abandoning its previous approach of utilizing specialized media environments such as newspapers, journals, or television programs.

Consumer Targeting (For Marketing Purposes)

Publishers and journalists employ Big data technologies to create new and creative insights and info-graphics through data journalism. Channel 4, the United Kingdom's public-service television network, is home to prominent experts in Big data and data analysis.

Insurance

Although it is questionable if these predictions are presently utilized for pricing, health insurance companies are gathering data on social "determinants of health" such as food and television consumption, marital status, clothing size, and purchase behaviors in attempt to identify health concerns in their clients.

Healthcare

Big data analytics provided personalized medicine, prescriptive analytics, clinical risk intervention, predictive analytics, waste and care variability reduction, automated external and internal patient data reporting, standardized medical terms, and patient registries in healthcare. Some growing sectors are idealistic as opposed to pragmatic. The volume of data produced by healthcare systems is considerable. The volume of data will increase as more mHealth, eHealth, and wearable technologies are adopted. Data from electronic health records, imaging, patient-supplied data, sensor data, and other challenging-to-process data are included. These working conditions are now under greater stress to emphasize data and information quality. "Big data is frequently associated with 'dirty data,' and the proportion of inaccuracies increases as data volume increases." Human inspection is problematic due to the large data size, and there is an urgent need in health care for intelligent instruments for correctness and credibility management, as well as the processing of neglected information. Despite the fact that an enormous amount of healthcare information is now stored electronically, it is classified as Big data because it is unstructured and challenging to utilize. Big data in healthcare compromises human rights, privacy, autonomy, trust, and openness. Data-driven analysis may advance exploratory biomedical research faster than hypothesis-driven research (Copeland, 2017). Data trends may be used in hypothesis-driven biological and clinical research.

Development on a Global Scale

According to researches on the efficient use of information and communication technologies for development (commonly abbreviated "ICT4D"), Big data technology has the potential to greatly contribute to international development while generating distinct problems. Big data analysis improves decision-making in vital development sectors including health care, employment, economic productivity, crime, security, natural catastrophes, and resource management. User-generated data also allows the unheard to speak. However, underdeveloped countries' lack of technical infrastructure, economic, and human resources aggravate Big data challenges including privacy, methodology, and interoperability. "Big data for development" (Hilbert, 2016) is moving towards machine learning, often known as "Artificial Intelligence for development (AI4D)". (Mann & Hilbert, 2020)

Finance

Finance is rapidly adopting Big data to expedite processing and provide clients with better, more informed conclusions. Investment decisions and trading (processing quantities of accessible price data, limit order books, economic data, and more simultaneously), portfolio management (optimizing over an ever-expanding array of financial instruments, etc.), and risk management (optimizing over an ever-expanding array of financial instruments, etc.) are all financial applications of Big data.

Education

Private boot camps, such as The Data Incubator, which is free, and General Assembly, which is charged, have also built programs to meet this demand. According to a McKinsey Global Institute study, 1.5 million highly skilled data professionals and managers are needed (Manyika et al., 2011), and a number of universities have created master's courses to meet this need, including the University of Tennessee and UC Berkeley. In the field of marketing, one university has created a mascot.

Ethical Implications of Big Data

The concept of ethics pertains to the moral guidance of behavior and truth principles, as posited by Lewis (Lewis, 1985). This definition is rooted in the Kantian and utilitarian perspectives, as discussed by Mingers and Walsham (Mingers & Walsham, 2010) and Newell and Marabella (Newell & Marabella,

2015), which serve as the theoretical foundation for ethical conduct among economic agents. Kantian ethics posits that ethical conduct is predicated upon moral values and principles, such as veracity and responsibility.

The examination of the extant literature indicates several potential ethical consequences associated with the utilization of big data analytics. The utilization of algorithms to facilitate human decision-making is a fundamental aspect of big data analytics, as posited by Newell and Marabella (Newell & Marabella, 2015). Newell and Marabella posit that algorithmic decision-making involves the analysis of data from various sources to ascertain an individual's preferences and behavior, based on their current or past conduct. The foundation of algorithmic decision-making is based on the assumption that established correlations are significant and accurately reflect the objective causality of a particular phenomenon. An instance of this is the act of forecasting human conduct based on correlations found in a dataset, which fails to take into account the human element and the intrinsic errors and partialities in data, metrics, and examination (Clarke, 2016; Zuboff, 2015). The act of profiling individuals can lead to discrimination, which is considered as another form of unethical social impact, as stated by Zuboff (Zuboff, 2015).

The act of categorizing individuals into groups based on their race, ethnicity, gender, or socioeconomic status, and providing or withholding special treatments or services to them, may be considered as profiling, whether done deliberately or inadvertently (Martin, 2014; Newell & Marabella, 2015). The algorithms that enable such actions not only exhibit a disregard for outliers, such as through the utilization of mean reversion, but they also serve as a foundation for discriminating between various individuals or groups. Also, there may be a lack of sufficient information provided to individuals regarding the post-collection handling of their data. The primary data is transmitted from monitoring entities to data aggregators and subsequently to retailers through an information value chain. Data aggregators amalgamate data from various sources to generate a novel representation of individuals. At every stage of the value chain, ethical concerns may arise, as the final possessor of the data may employ it for purposes that diverge significantly from the original intention. Various components of the information value chain may present risks and dangers to the primary consumers who produced the data.

The recognition of Big Data as an industry with various stakeholders, including producers, distributors, and consumers, is imperative, as highlighted by Martin (Martin, 2015). It is important to acknowledge that Big Data is not solely a technological advancement. The utilization of extensive datasets has resulted in the monitoring and surveillance of individual conduct as an additional outcome. Entities that consistently monitor and scrutinize the conduct of persons can subsequently furnish tailored commodities and amenities, thereby limiting the exposure of said individuals to the entirety of market choices and substitutes. According to Zuboff (Zuboff, 2015), individuals are no longer governed by their inherent rights of autonomous decision-making and conduct. Instead, they are subjected to monitoring and regulation by algorithms that are specifically designed to shape their choices. According to Zuboff (Zuboff, 2015), the outcome is a form of capitalism centered on surveillance, which operates under distinct incentives and dynamics compared to conventional market-driven capitalism. Notwithstanding the aforementioned unfavorable instances of big data analytics, the repercussions on individuals, institutions, and the community at large remain insufficiently comprehended and under-researched.

Challenges and Barriers for Big Data Analytics

Organizations face challenges in adopting Big Data analytics due to managerial and cultural obstacles, such as inadequate comprehension of how to leverage it for enhancing business outcomes and insufficient management bandwidth amidst competing priorities. The hindrances posed by these factors outweigh those posed by data or technology. Research conducted across various industries has revealed that a significant proportion of structured data available to organizations is not utilized for decision-making purposes. Additionally, a little percentage of unstructured data is analyzed or exploited. It has been observed that a considerable number of employees have access to data that is not relevant to their roles, and a significant amount of analysts' time is spent on discovering and preparing data (DSI Big data, 2017). In contemporary times, leadership teams utilize data insights to establish objectives, adapt achievements, and pose relevant inquiries to tackle management obstacles. The potential of Big Data, despite its technological capabilities, necessitates a vision and insight.

As a consequence, company leaders who have vision and the ability to forecast future trends and possibilities will be able to act innovatively, motivate their employees to work efficiently, and achieve their objectives. Enterprises require human capital with sophisticated technical capabilities to use and leverage these technologies in order to provide useable information for end users, particularly the C-suite, in order to use data through Big data analytics. People's specialized talents include statistics, Big data mining, mastering visualization tools, a business-oriented approach, and machine learning. These are required to extract important insights from vast amounts of data and contribute to decision making. However, these professionals (data scientists, data analysts, and so on) are extremely difficult to find, and so there is a high demand for them. It is challenging to find data scientists that are proficient in both analytics and topic expertise.

In effective organizations, decision makers and information derived from data exploitation are located in the same area. Nonetheless, dealing with huge amounts of data presents challenges for decision makers. As a result, decision-makers with problem-solving talents and the ability to offer answers to issues using appropriate data or collaboration of diverse persons in problem solving through the use of Big data are necessary. The quality of decision making utilizing a data-driven approach is critical in capitalizing on Big data analytics prospects. Assuring decision-making quality in this context is connected to factors such as Big data source data quality, Big data analytics capabilities, personnel, and decision-maker quality.

The accuracy of Big data sources is important in offering high value in decision making and reducing erroneous actions, whereas Big data analytics capabilities are tied to the use of the proper methodologies and tools from Big data analytics professionals. Another important barrier to using a data-driven strategy is organizational culture. The ability to swiftly consolidate, analyze, and communicate critical company information to decision makers is the foundation for achieving a data-driven culture. That foundation is critical for improving company performance, and the creation and strengthening of such skills empower organizations, resulting in gains in all business sectors and improved returns on investments. In this setting, businesses must adopt data-driven decision making in all areas and cease relying primarily on gut feeling and hunches. As a result, management must thoroughly comprehend the importance of gaining insights from data exploitation. Furthermore, for a data-driven company, personnel participating in the process of data-driven decision making must satisfy certain qualifications. Managers must be able to manage effective data-analytics teams and projects, while marketers must grasp metrics and analytics in order to handle marketing operations properly.

Many businesses, seeing the importance of data, have acquired technical expertise in business intelligence and/or data warehousing, but Big data analytics solutions are distinct and novel. As a result, in order to derive value from Big data, businesses must employ current approaches and technology. Because these technologies are continually growing, IT departments should be able to expand their capacity and keep up with the constant innovation. Problems will arise, for example, if database software does not enable Big data analytics choices.

Collection of data worries a lot of people. Their privacy is invaded by Big data. Around 71% of consumers believe that brands with access to their personal data use it unethically, and 58% do not use any digital service due to privacy concerns, which affects the applications they download, the email addresses they share, and the social media sites they use to connect to websites (Kitchin & McArdle, 2016). Thus, firms must create protections to prevent consumer data from being utilized to breach privacy. To maximize Big data's advantages, privacy, security, intellectual property, and liability rules should be handled this way.

CONCLUSION

The widespread use of the Internet has made it simpler and less expensive for enterprises to gather vast amounts of data, and it has even increased the opportunities for external data collection. The term "Big data" refers to data quantities that are too large for ordinary software tools to obtain, manage, and handle in a reasonable amount of time. The idea of Big data encompasses unstructured, semi-structured, and structured data. Machine learning and natural language processing are ways for analyzing data, while databases, cloud computing, and business intelligence are examples of Big data technologies, in addition to data visualization. Traditional systems for storing and retrieving structured data include relational databases, data marts, and data warehouses. The HPCC Systems platform, in terms of Big data management technology, was created in 2000 as a distributed data processing and querying platform. K-means, KNN (K-nearest neighbor), and other machine learning algorithms can be employed in Big data analytics.

Incorporating Big data analytics into a business or organization has various advantages, including cost savings, product development, customer experience, and risk reduction. There are several forms of Big data analytics, including descriptive, diagnostic, predictive, and prescriptive analytics, each with its own set of applications. Big data analytics is carried out using a variety of technologies, including Hadoop, Kafka, Cassandra, and Spark, each with its own set of characteristics. Big data analytics may be used in a variety of industries, including government, banking, healthcare, education, and media. The biggest challenges to organizations embracing Big data analytics are managerial and cultural in nature rather than data and technology-related, with the main barriers being a lack of awareness of how to apply Big data analytics to benefit the business and a lack of management spectrum from conflicting goals. Big data analytics has the potential to assist organizations in better understanding their business environments, their customers' behavior and demands, and the actions of their rivals. Enterprises may use Big data analytics to shape their goods and actions in order to meet the demands of their consumers and innovate against competitors.

REFERENCES

Ahmed, M. A., & Al-Jamimi, H. A. (2013). Machine learning approaches for predicting sofware maintainability: A fuzzy-based transparent model. *IET Software*, 7(6), 317–326. doi:10.1049/iet-sen.2013.0046

Al-Abassi, A., Karimipour, H., Pajouh, H., Dehghantanha, A., & Parizi, RM., (2020). Industrial big data analytics: challenges and opportunities. In: Handbook of big data privacy; (pp. 37–61). Springer.

Shun'ichi, A. (1967). A theory of adaptive pattern classifier. *IEEE Transactions*, (16), 279–307.

Atzori, L., Iera, A., & Morabito, G. (2010). The internet of things: A survey. *Computer Networks*, 54(15), 2787–2805. doi:10.1016/j.comnet.2010.05.010

Ayasdi, (2023). *Resources on how Topological Data Analysis is used to analyze big data*. Avasdi.

Bakshi, K. (2012). Considerations for Big Data: Architecture and Approaches. In: *Proceedings of the IEEE Aerospace Conference*, (pp. 1–7). IEEE. 10.1109/AERO.2012.6187357

Balazka, D., & Rodighiero, D. (2020). Big Data and the Little Big Bang: An Epistemological (R) evolution". *Frontiers in Big Data*, 3, 31. doi:10.3389/fdata.2020.00031 PMID:33693404

Bertolucci, J. (2013). Hadoop: From Experiment To Leading Big Data Platform. *Information Week*.

Big Data's Fourth V. (2023). Spotless Data. https://web.archive.org/web/20180731105912/https:/spotlessdata.com/blog/big-datas-fourth-v

Boja, C., Pocovnicu, A., & Bătăgan, L. (2012). Distributed Parallel Architecture for Big Data. *Informações Econômicas*, 16(2), 116–127.

Bucolo, M., Fortuna, L., & Rosa, M. L. (2004). Complex dynamics through fuzzy chains. *IEEE Transactions on Fuzzy Systems*, 12(3), 289–295. doi:10.1109/TFUZZ.2004.825969

Clarke, R. (2016). Big data, big risks. *Information Systems Journal*, 26(1), 77–90.

CNET News. (2011). *Storage area networks need not apply*. CNet News.

Cohen, J., Dolan, B., Dunlap, M., Hellerstein, J. M., & Welton, C. (2009). MAD Skills: New Analysis Practices for Big Data. *Proceedings of the ACM VLDB Endowment*. ACM. 10.14778/1687553.1687576

Cortes, C., & Vapnik, V. N. (1995). Support-vector networks". *Machine Learning*, 20(3), 273–297. doi:10.1007/BF00994018

Cudeck, R. (2000). Exploratory factor analysis. In *Handbook of applied multivariate statistics and mathematical modeling* (pp. 265–296). Elsevier. doi:10.1016/B978-012691360-6/50011-2

Cuzzocrea, A., Song, I., & Davis, K. C. (2011). Analytics over Large-Scale Multidimensional Data: The Big Data Revolution! In: *Proceedings of the ACM International Workshop on Data Warehousing and OLAP*, (pp. 101–104). ACM. 10.1145/2064676.2064695

Dean, J., & Ghemawat, S. (2004). *MapReduce: Simplified Data Processing on Large Clusters*. Search Storage.

Devi, R., & Judith, D. (2018). Deep Learning Methods for Big Data Analytics. *IJRECE, 6*(4). https://www.researchgate.net/publication/354970200_Deep_Learning_Methods_for_Big_ Data_Analytics #fullTextFileContent.

EMC. (2012). *Data Science and Big Data Analytics*. EMC Education Services.

Eweek, (2023). Survey: Biggest Databases Approach 30 Terabytes. *Eweek.com.*

Fox, C. (2018). Data Science for Transport. Springer.

Gegov, A., Arabikhan, F., & Petrov, N. (2014). Linguistic composition based modelling by fuzzy networks with modular rule bases. *Fuzzy Sets and Systems, 269,* 1–29. doi:10.1016/j.fss.2014.06.014

Gegov, A., Sanders, D., & Vatchova, B. (2016). Mamdani fuzzy networks with feedforward rule bases for complex systems modelling. *Journal of Intelligent & Fuzzy Systems, 30*(5), 2623–2637. doi:10.3233/ IFS-151911

Goodfellow, I., Bengio, Y., Courville, A., & Bengio, Y. (2016). *Deep learning* (Vol. 1). MIT Press.

Gusmão, A., Horta, N., Lourenço, N., & Martins, R. (2020). Artificial Neural Network Overview. In *Analog IC Placement Generation via Neural Networks from Unlabeled Data* (pp. 7–24). Springer. doi:10.1007/978-3-030-50061-0_2

Han, J., Kamber, M., & Pei, J. (2011). *Data mining: concepts and techniques*. Elsevier Science.

HCLtech, (2023). *Solving Key Business Challenges With a Big Data Lake*. Hcltech.com.

He, P., Zhu, J., He, S., Li, J., & Lyu, M. R. (2017). Towards automated log parsing for large-scale log data analysis. *IEEE Transactions on Dependable and Secure Computing, 15*(6), 931–944. doi:10.1109/ TDSC.2017.2762673

He, Y., Lee, R., Huai, Y., Shao, Z., Jain, N., Zhang, X., & Xu, Z. (2011). RCFile: A Fast and Spaceefficient Data Placement Structure in MapReduce-based Warehouse Systems. In: *IEEE International Conference on Data Engineering (ICDE),* (pp. 1199–1208), IEEE. 10.1109/ICDE.2011.5767933

Hecht-Nielsen, R. (1992). Theory of the backpropagation neural network. In *Neural networks for perception* (pp. 65–93). Academic Press. doi:10.1016/B978-0-12-741252-8.50010-8

Hemmatian, F., & Sohrabi, M. K. (2019). A survey on classification techniques for opinion mining and sentiment analysis. Artificial intelligence review. doi:10.100710462-017-9599-6

Herodotou, H., Lim, H., Luo, G., Borisov, N., Dong, L., Cetin, F. B., & Babu, S. (2011). Starfish: A Self-tuning System for Big Data Analytics. In: *Proceedings of the Conference on Innovative Data Systems Research,* (pp. 261–272).

Hilbert, M., & López, P. (2011). The World's Technological Capacity to Store, Communicate, and Compute Information". *Science, 332*(6025), 60–65. doi:10.1126cience.1200970 PMID:21310967

IBM Big data & analytics, (2023). *Measuring the Business Value of Big Data Hub*. IBM. www.ibm-bigdatahub.com

Ivakhnenko, A. G. & Grigor'evich Lapa, V. (1967). *Cybernetics and forecasting techniques*. American Elsevier Pub. Co.

Ivakhnenko, A. G. (1973). *Cybernetic Predicting Devices*. CCM Information Corporation.

Joo, M. G., & Lee, J. S. A. (2005). class of hierarchical fuzzy systems with constraints on the fuzzy rules. *IEEE Transactions on Fuzzy Systems, 13*(2), 194–203. doi:10.1109/TFUZZ.2004.840096

Kitchin, R., & McArdle, G. (2016). What makes Big Data, Big Data? Exploring the ontological characteristics of 26 datasets". *Big Data & Society, 3*(1), 1–10. doi:10.1177/2053951716631130

Kwon, D., Kim, H., Kim, J., Suh, S. C., Kim, I., & Kim, K. J. (2019). A survey of deep learning-based network anomaly detection. *Cluster Computing, 22*(1), 949–961. doi:10.100710586-017-1117-8

LeCun, Y., Boser, B., Denker, J. S., Henderson, D., Howard, R. E., Hubbard, W., & Jackel, L. D. (1989). Backpropagation applied to Handwritten Zip Code recognition. *Neural Computation, 1*(4), 541–551. doi:10.1162/neco.1989.1.4.541

LeCun, Y., Bottou, L., Bengio, Y., & Haffner, P. (1998). Gradient-based learning applied to document recognition. *Proceedings of the IEEE, 86*(11), 2278–2324. doi:10.1109/5.726791

Lee, M.-L., Chung, H.-Y., & Yu, F.-M. (2003). Modeling of hierarchical fuzzy systems. *Fuzzy Sets and Systems, 138*(2), 343–361. doi:10.1016/S0165-0114(02)00517-1

Lee, R., Luo, T., Huai, Y., Wang, F., He, Y., & Zhang, X. (2011). Ysmart: Yet Another SQL-toMapReduce Translator. In: *IEEE International Conference on Distributed Computing Systems (ICDCS),* (pp. 25–36). IEEE.

Lewis, P. V. (1985). Defining 'business ethics': Like nailing jello to a wall. *Journal of Business Ethics, 4*(5), 377–383. doi:10.1007/BF02388590

Liu, B. (2020). *Sentiment analysis: mining opinions, sentiments, and emotions*. Cambridge University Press. doi:10.1017/9781108639286

Manyika, J.; Chui, M.; Bughin, J.; Brown, B.; Dobbs, R.; Roxburgh, C.; & Byers, A. H., (2011). *Big Data: The next frontier for innovation, competition, and productivity*. McKinsey Global Institute.

Martin, K. E., (2015). Ethical Issues in the Big Data Industry. *MIS Quarterly Executive, 14*(2), 67– 85.

Marynowski, J. E., Santina, A. O., & Andrey, R. P. (2015). Method for Testing the Fault Tolerance of MapReduce Frameworks. *Computer Networks, 86*, 1–13. doi:10.1016/j.comnet.2015.04.009

Mashey, J.R. (1998). *Big Data ... and the Next Wave of InfraStress. Slides from invited talk*. Usenix.

Mcculloch, W. S., & Pitts, W. (1943). A logical calculus of the ideas immanent in nervous activity. *The Bulletin of Mathematical Biophysics, 5*(4), 115–133. doi:10.1007/BF02478259

MIKE 2.0, (2013). *Big Data Solution Offering*. MIKE2.0.

MIKE 2.0, (2018). *Big Data Definition*. MIKE2.0.

Mingers, J., and Walsham, G., (2010). "Towards ethical information systems: The contribution of discourse ethics," (34:4), pp. 833–854.

Mitchell, T. (1997). *Machine Learning*. McGraw Hill.

Monash, C., (2009). eBay's two enormous data warehouses. EBay,

Najafabadi, M., Villanustre, F., Khoshgoftaar, T., Seliva, N., Muharemagic, E., & Wald, R. (2015). Deep learning applications and challenges in big data analytics. *Journal of Big Data, 2*(1), 1. doi:10.118640537-014-0007-7

Nations, U. (2018). *Revision of world urbanization prospects*. United Nations.

Newell, S., & Marabelli, M. (2015). *"Strategic opportunities (and challenges) of algorithmic decision making: A call for action on the long-term societal effects of 'datification,'" The Journal of Strategic Information Systems*. Elsevier B.V.

Pedregosa, F., Varoquaux, G., Gramfort, A., Michel, V., Thirion, B., Grisel, O., Blondel, M., Prettenhofer, P., Weiss, R., & Dubourg, V. (2011). Scikit-learn: Machine learning in python. *Journal of Machine Learning Research, 12*, 2825–2830.

Provost, F., & Fawcett, T. (2013). *Data science for business: what you need to know about data mining and data-analytic thinking*. O'Reilly Media, Inc.

Resch, B., & Szell, M., (2019). *Human-centric data science for urban studies*.

Riahi, A., & Riahi, S., (2015). The Big Data Revolution, Issues and Applications. *IJARCSSE, 5*(8).

Robbins, H., & Monro, S. (1951). A Stochastic Approximation Method". *Annals of Mathematical Statistics, 22*(3), 400–407. doi:10.1214/aoms/1177729586

Rosenblatt, F. (1958). The perceptron: A probabilistic model for information storage and organization in the brain. *Psychological Review, 65*(6), 386–408. doi:10.1037/h0042519 PMID:13602029

Russell, S. J., & Norvig, P. (2010). *Artificial Intelligence: A Modern Approach* (3rd ed.). Prentice Hall.

Russom, P. (2011). Big Data Analytics. In: TDWI Best Practices Report, (pp. 1–40). TDWI.

Sagiroglu, S. (2013). Big data: A review. *2013 International Conference on Collaboration Technologies and Systems (CTS)*. IEEE. 10.1109/CTS.2013.6567202

Sarker, I. H. (2019). A machine learning based robust prediction model for real-life mobile phone data. *Internet of Things: Engineering Cyber Physical Human Systems, 5*, 180–193. doi:10.1016/j.iot.2019.01.007

Sarker, I. H. (2021). Machine learning: Algorithms, real-world applications and research directions. *SN Computer Science, 2*(3), 1–21. doi:10.100742979-021-00592-x PMID:33778771

Sarker, I. H., Colman, A., & Han, J. (2019). Recencyminer: Mining recencybased personalized behavior from contextual smartphone data. *Journal of Big Data, 6*(1), 1–21. doi:10.118640537-019-0211-6

Sarker, I. H., Colman, A., Kabir, M. A., & Han, J. (2018). Individualized time series segmentation for mining mobile phone user behavior. *The Computer Journal, 61*(3), 349–368. doi:10.1093/comjnl/bxx082

Sarker, I. H., Hoque, M. M., Uddin, M. K., & Alsanoosy, T. (2020). Mobile data science and intelligent apps: Concepts, ai-based modeling and research directions. *Mobile Networks and Applications*, 1–19.

Sarker, I. H., & Kayes, A. S. M. (2020). Abc-ruleminer: User behavioral rule based machine learning method for context-aware intelligent services. *Journal of Network and Computer Applications*, *168*, 102762. doi:10.1016/j.jnca.2020.102762

Sarker, I. H., Kayes, A. S. M., Badsha, S., Alqahtani, H., Watters, P., & Ng, A. (2020). Cybersecurity data science: An overview from machine learning perspective. *Journal of Big Data*, *7*(1), 1–29. doi:10.118640537-020-00318-5

Schläpfer, M., Bettencourt, L. M. A., Grauwin, S., Raschke, M., Claxton, R., Smoreda, Z., West, G. B., & Ratti, C. (2014). The scaling of human interactions with city size. *Journal of the Royal Society, Interface*, *11*(98), 20130789. doi:10.1098/rsif.2013.0789 PMID:24990287

Schmidhuber, J. (2022). *Annotated History of Modern AI and Deep Learning*.

Schumann, J., Gupta, P., & Liu, Y. (2010). Application of neural networks in high assurance systems: A survey. In *Applications of Neural Networks in High Assurance Systems* (pp. 1–19). Springer. doi:10.1007/978-3-642-10690-3_1

Shukla, N., & Fricklas, K. (2018). *Machine learning with TensorFlow*. Manning.

Ślusarczyk, B., (2018). Industry 4.0: are we ready? Pol J Manag Stud., 17.

Snijders, C.; Matzat, U.; & Reips, U.-D. (2012). "'Big Data': Big gaps of knowledge in the field of Internet". International Journal of Internet Science. **7**: 1–5. Archived on 23 November 2019.

Steve, L. (2013). The Origins of 'Big Data': An Etymological Detective Story. *The New York* Times.

Tsekouras, G., Sarimveis, H., Kavakli, E., & Bafas, G. A. (2005). hierarchical fuzzy-clustering approach to fuzzy modeling. *Fuzzy Sets and Systems*, *150*(2), 245–266. doi:10.1016/j.fss.2004.04.013

Urbanowicz, R. J., & Moore, J. H. (2009). Learning Classifier Systems: A Complete Introduction, Review, and Roadmap". *Journal of Artificial Evolution and Applications*, *2009*, 1–25. doi:10.1155/2009/736398

Verma, J., & Agrawal, S. (2016). Big data analytics: challenges and applications for text, audio, video, and social media data. International Journal on Soft Computing, Artificial Intelligence and Applications (IJSCAI), 5(1).

Wang, G., Wang, H., & Long, Z. (2021). Norm approximation of mamdani fuzzy system to a class of integrable functions. *International Journal of Fuzzy Systems*, *23*(3), 833–848. doi:10.100740815-020-01008-3

Wang, J., Zhang, W., Shi, Y., Duan, S., & Liu, J., (2018). *Industrial big data analytics: challenges, methodologies, and applications*.

Wang, L.-X., & Mendel, J. M. (1992). Generating fuzzy rules by learning from examples. *IEEE Transactions on Systems, Man, and Cybernetics*, 22(6), 1414–1427. doi:10.1109/21.199466

Wang, X., Gegov, A., Farzad, A., Chen, Y., & Hu, Q. (2019). Fuzzy network based framework for software maintainability prediction. *International Journal of Uncertainty, Fuzziness and Knowledge-based Systems, 27*(5), 841–862. doi:10.1142/S0218488519500375

Werbos, P. J. (1974). Beyond Regression: New Tools for Prediction and Analysis in the behavioral sciences. PhD, Harvard University, Cambridge, Massachusetts.

Witten, I. H., & Frank, E. (2005). *Data mining: practical machine learning tools and techniques*. Morgan Kaufmann.

Yaakob, A. M., Gegov, A., & Rahman, S. (2018). Selection of alternatives using fuzzy networks with rule base aggregation. *Fuzzy Sets and Systems, 341*, 123–144. doi:10.1016/j.fss.2017.05.027

Yong, A. G., & Pearce, S. (2013). A beginner's guide to factor analysis: Focusing on exploratory factor analysis. *Tutorials in Quantitative Methods for Psychology, 9*(2), 79–94. doi:10.20982/tqmp.09.2.p079

Zheng, P., & Ni, L. M. (2006). Spotlight: The rise of the smart phone. *IEEE Distrib Syst Online., 7*(3), 3. doi:10.1109/MDSO.2006.22

Zhou, V., (2019). Machine Learning for Beginners: An Introduction to Neural Networks. *Medium.*

Zuboff, S., (2015). Big other: surveillance capitalism and the prospects of an information civilization. *Journal of Information Technology, 30*(1). Nature Publishing Group.

ADDITIONAL READING

Copeland, C.S. (2017). Data Driving Discovery (PDF). *Healthcare Journal of New Orleans* 22–27.

DSI Big data. (2017). *le Blog ANDSI, DSI Big Data.* ANDSI.

Hall, P., Park, B. U., & Samworth, R. J. (2008). Choice of neighbor order in nearest-neighbor classification. *Annals of Statistics, 36*(5), 2135–2152. doi:10.1214/07-AOS537

Hastie, T., Tibshirani, R., & Friedman, J. H. (2001). *The elements of statistical learning: data mining, inference, and prediction: with 200 full-color illustrations. (Jerome H.).* Springer.

Hilbert, M. (2016). Big Data for Development: A Review of Promises and Challenges. *Development Policy Review, 34*(1), 135–174.

Mann, S., & Hilbert, M. (2020). AI4D: Artificial Intelligence for Development. *International Journal of Communication, 14*(0), 21.

The Economist. (2010). Data, data everywhere. *The Economist.*

Xin, Y., Kong, L., Liu, Z., Chen, Y., Li, Y., Zhu, H., Gao, M., Hou, H., & Wang, C. (2018). Machine learning and deep learning methods for cybersecurity. *IEEE Access : Practical Innovations, Open Solutions, 6*, 35365–35381. doi:10.1109/ACCESS.2018.2836950

KEY TERMS AND DEFINITIONS

Customer Relationship Management System (CRM): is a technology for managing all your company's relationships and interactions with customers and potential customers.

Enterprise Data Warehouse (EDW): is a relational data warehouse containing a company's business data, including information about its customers. An EDW enables data analytics, which can inform actionable insights. Like all data warehouses, EDWs collect and aggregate data from multiple sources, acting as a repository for most or all organizational data to facilitate broad access and analysis.

Enterprise Resource Planning (ERP) System: is a type of software system that helps organizations automate and manage core business processes for optimal performance.

Magnetic, Agile, Deep (MAD) Analysis: Magnetic, Agile, Deep data analysis The authors define the MAD acronym as a re-imagination of the data warehouse concept such that: Magnetic: encourages (attracts) new data sources, has reduced sensitivity to cleanliness of data sources.

Massively Parallel Processing (MPP): is a way of processing large amounts of data by dividing it into parts and using many processors or computers to work on them at the same time.

Network Attached Storage (NAS): is dedicated file storage that enables multiple users and heterogeneous client devices to retrieve data from centralized disk capacity. Users on a local area network (LAN) access the shared storage via a standard Ethernet connection.

Return on Investment (ROI): is a popular metric because of its versatility and simplicity. Essentially, ROI can be used as a rudimentary gauge of an investment's profitability.

Solid State Drives (SSD): is a solid-state storage device that uses integrated circuit assemblies to store data persistently, typically using flash memory, and functioning as secondary storage in the hierarchy of computer storage.

Storage Area Network (SAN): is: a computer network that provides access to consolidated, block-level data storage.

Support Vector Machine (SVM): is a supervised machine learning algorithm used for both classification and regression.

Chapter 2
Big Data Analytics for Market Intelligence

Dina Darwish
Ahram Canadian University, Egypt

ABSTRACT

Market intelligence, a field that depends on data analytics to gather corporate insights for better decision-making, has embraced big data analytics as a disruptive technology that will transform it. It is necessary to talk about the big data analytics landscape from a market perspective. The idea of big data and its use in market intelligence have drawn a lot of attention in recent years due to their immense potential to have an impact on the market. Market intelligence (MI) involves obtaining and examining data on trends, rivalry, and customer monitoring that pertains to a company's market. Big data analytics tools can examine past marketing data to learn more about what occurred and why. There is a need to focus on the data sources, techniques, and applications associated with critical marketing perspectives. This chapter focusses on how big data analytics can be gathered and analyzed to benefit market intelligence.

INTRODUCTION

Market intelligence, a field that depends on data analytics to gather corporate insights for better decision-making, has embraced big data analytics as a disruptive technology that will transform it. It is necessary to talk about the big data analytics landscape from a market perspective. Big data analytics research currently faces a number of difficult problems, and its future paths are often market-related. Social media and other recent technical advances allow us to produce data much more quickly than in the past. The idea of big data and its use in market intelligence have drawn a lot of attention in recent years due to their immense potential to have an impact on the market.

Market intelligence (MI) is the gathering and analysis of data about a company's market, such as trends, competition, and customer (targeted, lost, and existing) monitoring. It is a subgenre of competitive intelligence (CI), which is data and information gathered by firms in order to give continual insight into market trends such as rivals' and consumers' values and preferences.

DOI: 10.4018/979-8-3693-0413-6.ch002

Marketing skills and MI in an organization collaborate to create a strategy for allocating resources and putting systems in place. It is used to offer ongoing strategic marketing planning for organizations in order to examine marketing positions in order for firms to get a competitive advantage and fulfil objectives more successfully.

Organizations can develop MI frameworks and models based on the four-step process of acquiring, verifying, processing, and presenting MI that are appropriate for their financial capabilities and target market sectors. MI data is collected in a variety of ways, including qualitative, quantitative, formal, informal, public, and unpublished data. MI is collected through both internal and external data sources.

Benefits of MI include the ability to obtain competitive edge in marketing strategies by providing customer, competitor, and market information. MI can cause problems by gathering data and information in an unethical or illegal manner, which can result in monetary loss and regulatory failures on the part of the government (Hedin et al.,2012).

Data that is pertinent to a company's markets is gathered and processed into insights that support decision-making in marketing intelligence, which places emphasis on the marketing-related parts of business intelligence. Market research has long been used by marketing intelligence to better understand consumer behavior and build better products. For instance, businesses utilize customer satisfaction surveys to research client attitudes. Important aspects for strategic marketing decisions, such customer perceptions of a product, service, or organization, can now be automatically tracked by mining social media data thanks to big data analytic technology.

To understand what happened in the past and why, big data analytics solutions can examine historical marketing data (such as client purchase histories from your customer relationship management (CRM) system). Focus needs to be placed on the data sources, techniques, and applications associated with the five critical marketing perspectives—people, product, place, price, and promotion—that serve as the cornerstone of marketing intelligence.

Additionally, they enable you to personalize your marketing, engage your audience, and enhance your social media strategy by giving you a complete picture of your customers across all platforms.

Additionally, they are able to forecast marketing outcomes, including customer response rates to various promotions.

This chapter discusses the importance of Big data analytics for Market intelligence, and how companies and organizations can benefit from Big analytics to improve their earnings. The main topics to be covered in this chapter includes the following;

- The meaning of the term "Market Intelligence"
- Processes for Market Intelligence Implementation
- Gathering data from different sources for use in Market Intelligence
- Impacts of utilizing Market Intelligence on companies
- Importance for analyzing data in Big Data Analytics
- Market Intelligence: Types and Methodologies with Examples
  - Market Intelligence for decision making
  - Business Intelligence and Big data Analytics
- Business Intelligence and Big Data theories and Models
- The role of Artificial Intelligence and Machine learning in Business Intelligence and Big Data Analytics

- The impact of Business Intelligence and Big Data Analytics on decision making processes and organizational performance
- The role of GIS in Business Intelligence and Big data Analytics
- The role of spatial data for Market Intelligence using examples
- The potential risks and limitations associated with business intelligence and big data analytics
- The issues and problems related to Market Intelligence and their solutions
  - Case studies to illustrate the trends in Market Intelligence
- Advantages of Market Intelligence
- Importance of Market Intelligence for businesses
- Ethical issues related to Market intelligence
  - Limitations of Market Intelligence
  - Forward looking perspective by discussing future trends and developments in the field

Also, this chapter is organized as follows; the first section contains the background, then, the second section includes the main focus of the chapter, including the main topics mentioned in the previous section, then finally, comes the conclusion section.

BACKGROUND

Market intelligence, a field that depends on data analytics to gather corporate insights for better decision-making, has embraced big data analytics as a disruptive technology that will transform it. It is necessary to talk about the big data analytics landscape from a market perspective. Big data analytics research currently faces a number of difficult problems, and its future paths are often market-related. Social media and other recent technical advances allow us to produce data much more quickly than in the past. The idea of Big data and its use in market intelligence have drawn a lot of attention in recent years due to their immense potential to have an impact on the market.

Market intelligence is recognized as an important instrument for organizations to compete and develop as a result of comprehending their business environment through the collection of information on strategically significant topics to support organization decision-making (Hedin, Hirvensalo, & Vaarnas, 2014). Despite the importance of market intelligence, there is a paucity of literature on the topic, and the term is defined in a variety of ways. Several researchers concur that market intelligence is not defined with sufficient precision in the academic literature. For instance, the ambiguity and interchangeability of market intelligence definitions was emphasized. In contrast, Market intelligence was determined as an ambiguous term and argue that it can be used interchangeably with other terms for data acquisition. Even though the definitional ambiguity was acknowledged, market intelligence and marketing intelligence are synonyms and should be used interchangeably throughout the literature. Market intelligence can be defined as business activities, which include public organizations participating in the markets and being active on various markets without engaging in any form of organization marketing. Others, such as Hedin, Hirvensalo, and Vaarnas (2014), however, referred to marketing intelligence as MI. Hedin, Hievensalo, and Vaarnas (2014) define market intelligence as "a tool for organizations to compete and grow as a result of understanding their business environment by gathering information on strategically important topics to support organization decision-making" This is confirmed by explaining that MI is comprised of information about the business environment in general, technology, competition, or research, as well as consumer needs, preferences, attitudes, and behaviors, as well as potential changes in the business environment that could affect buyers. Tan & Zaffar (1999) cite in their paper that defining market intelligence as not spying on competitors, but knowing what the competitors are doing and staying one step ahead of them through information gathering, and then by information gathering designing short- and long-term strategic plans. The difference between eavesdropping on competitors and market intelligence is that market intelligence involves ethical and legal information gathering (Tan & Zafar, 1999). In addition, market intelligence system was defined as a collection of procedures and sources that managers use to gather information about significant marketing environment developments. The definitions of market intelligence and marketing intelligence are ambiguous, according to the authors of this review. It is also common for authors of reviewed articles to not define clearly market intelligence or marketing intelligence with precision. For instance, literature mentioned that it is possible deriving market intelligence from microblogs.

Data that is pertinent to a company's markets is gathered and processed into insights that support decision-making in marketing intelligence, which places emphasis on the marketing-related parts of business intelligence. Market research has long been used by marketing intelligence to better understand consumer behavior and build better products. For instance, businesses utilize customer satisfaction surveys to research client attitudes. Important aspects for strategic marketing decisions, such customer perceptions of a product, service, or organization, can now be automatically tracked by mining social media data thanks to big data analytic technology.

Big data accessibility, although opening up previously unheard of possibilities for marketing intelligence, also presents difficulties for practitioners and scholars. Storage, administration, and processing are the three key difficulties that Big data analytics focuses on. Companies today have a wide range of methods (social media data, transactional data, survey data, sensor network data, etc.) to collect data from a variety of information sources for conventional marketing intelligence tasks, like consumer opinion mining. Different approaches can be used to find marketing intelligence depending on the features of the data that has been collected. Analysis models built using just one data source could only offer a few insights, which could result in biased business decisions. On the other hand, combining heterogeneous data from many sources results in a more accurate marketing intelligence and a holistic perspective of the domain. Unfortunately, it is not an easy operation to combine large data from various sources to produce marketing insight. In the area of marketing intelligence, this encourages investigation of novel approaches, applications, and frameworks for efficient Big data handling.

Business Intelligence aids decision-making via data, knowledge, and expertise (Alnoukari & Hanano, 2017). Big Data Analytics and Business Intelligence share decision-making tools. Interactive visualization helps Business Intelligence and BDA find data. More crucially, Big Data Analytics (BDA) as a service and technology complements Business Intelligence 's four cutting-edge technical pillars: cloud, mobile, big data, and social technologies (Passlick, Lebek, & Breitner, 2017; Sun, Zou, & Strang, 2015). Sun et al. (2015) recommend BDA for technology and data-driven Business Intelligence development. BDA improves Business Intelligence and business decisions. BDA and Business Intelligence systems seek knowledge (Sun, Zou, & Strang, 2015). Business Intelligence converted "raw data" into "Big Data." Business Intelligence /BD/BDA are interdependent. Data collection, analytics, insights, and decision-making benefit from an integrated DSS (Jin & Kim, 2018). It is found that BDA improves marketing intelligence via social media mining.

BD uses Block-Based storage models and Business Intelligence File-Based or Object-Based. SQL drives Business Intelligence, since traditional databases cannot store and analyze huge volumes of unstructured data, BD data models employ distributed storage and NoSQL databases (Faroukhi, El Alaoui, Gahi, & Amine, 2020). BD requires storage network infrastructure and virtualization, whereas Business Intelligence employs storage devices. BD requires distributed processing, but traditional Business Intelligence requires no distributed processing infrastructure (Faroukhi, El Alaoui, Gahi, & Amine, 2020). Finally, BD may provide prescriptive and diagnostic analytics, whereas BI traditionally provides descriptive and predictive analytics (Faroukhi, El Alaoui, Gahi, & Amine, 2020).

Passlick (2017) Business Intelligence /BDA architecture supports BDA and Business Intelligence analytical reporting. The architecture blends Business Intelligence and BD. Data processing handles ETL/BD EL(T). DWs, in-memory databases, and Hadoop clusters store and analyze data (Passlick, Lebek, & Breitner, 2017). Llave (2018) claims Data Lakes let Business Intelligence gather data without organization. Implicit data monetization improves data-based products, whereas explicit sells data. BD encourages data monetization, and Data-driven services evaluate data. Data sales generate knowledge. Faroukhi et al. (2020) suggest data extractors, suppliers, aggregators, and technological platform providers to monetize BD. Monetizing BD maximizes data-driven value (Faroukhi, El Alaoui, Gahi, & Amine, 2020).

The utilization of Big data analytics in business intelligence has the potential to aid companies in effectively leveraging big data for enhancing customer satisfaction, mitigating supply chain risk, producing competitive intelligence, furnishing real-time business insights to facilitate crucial decision-making, and optimizing pricing, as evidenced by scholarly works (Davenport, 2014; Erevelles et al., 2015; Narayanan, 2014; Wang & Alexander, 2015). Tankard (Tankard, 2012) reports that through the effective utilization of big data, a retailer has the potential to increase operating margins by 60% by gaining market share over competitors and leveraging detailed consumer data. In general, big data analytics offers five primary advantages. Initially, it enhances perceptibility by rendering associated information more readily obtainable. Secondly, it enables the enhancement of performance and exposure to variability by gathering precise performance data. Thirdly, customer segmentation aids in effectively addressing the genuine requirements of the customers. Furthermore, it enhances the process of decision-making through the utilization of automated algorithms, thereby providing significant insights. Fifthly, it results in the emergence of novel business models, principles, products, and services.

According to Ahmad and Quadri (Ahmed & Quadri, 2015) and Wang and Alexander (Wang & Alexander, 2015), a significant utilization of big data analytics is the generation of knowledge, development of novel management principles, and the establishment of an economy based on such principles. The utilization of big data analytics has the potential to enhance the management of supply chain operations across multiple dimensions, such as supply chain efficiency, supply chain planning, inventory control, risk management, market intelligence, and real-time personalized service. This assertion is supported by scholarly literature (Wang & Alexander, 2015; Vera-Baquero et al., 2015). The utilization of big data can facilitate the innovation of novel product and service development ideas within the supply chain, as well as enhance comprehension of how various sub-firms can collaborate to optimize operational processes in a cost-efficient manner (Tan et al., 2015). According to Kościelniak and Puto (Kościelniak & Puto, 2015), the utilization of big data analytics can aid in facilitating decision-making procedures. The optimal utilization of large-scale datasets is contingent upon an enhanced comprehension of varied decision-making scenarios and the associated mechanisms for information processing. Organizations seeking to integrate big data analytics into their decision-making processes must prioritize the reduction of equivocality and data variety.

The effective utilization of big data in decision making can be enhanced through collaboration between decision makers and data analysts. However, it is important to carefully manage the decision processes to minimize potential gaps in understanding, as noted by Kowalczyk and Buxmann (Kowalczyk & Buxmann, 2014). Efficient analytic methods are crucial for harnessing the vast amount of heterogeneous data contained in unstructured text, audio, and video formats, which constitute 95% of big data. Simultaneously, it is pertinent to employ novel techniques for conducting predictive analysis on organized voluminous data (Gandomi & Haider, 2015).

The article titled "Research on the Influence of Inter-user Relationships on Social Commerce Platforms on the Value Proposition of Electronic Commerce Enterprises" authored by Zheng et al. (Zheng et al., 2017) examines the effects of social commerce on various stakeholders, ranging from individual consumers to electronic commerce enterprises. The study provides theoretical insights into the impact of inter-user relationships on social commerce platforms on the value proposition of electronic commerce enterprises. The findings of this research are of practical significance for electronic commerce enterprises engaged in social network marketing. Huang et al. (Huang et al., 2017) have presented a research paper titled "Reliable and Efficient Big Service Selection" which outlines a big service selection strategy that utilizes the coefficient of variation and mixed integer programming to enhance the solution in two aspects: (1) minimizing the time cost and (2) maximizing the reliability. Empirical evaluation was conducted on authentic datasets to test the selection approach, and the findings of the experiment demonstrated that the approach outperforms alternative methods. Additionally, Chu and colleagues (Chu et al., 2017) have presented a scholarly article. This paper presents the design of a cloud-based tracker platform utilizing a system-of-systems service architecture. The authors, Chu et al., have introduced a novel, adaptable position tracking system, named CQtracker. The present platform is integrated with a cloud-based mechanism of sophisticated analytics. The CQtracker platform has been developed utilizing a system-of-systems service architecture framework, with the aim of providing a data-system-as-a-service. With regards to another scholarly article titled "Crowdsourcing Social Network Service for Social Enterprise Innovation," Tung and Jordann (Tung & Jordan, 2017) have proposed an integrated platform that combines social media and crowdsourcing services to facilitate business innovation within the context of Social Enterprise (SE). This particular social network service (SNS) is designed for crowdsourcing within the social entrepreneurship (SE) community, enabling individuals to access shared resources in order to advance their projects or even initiate a novel SE venture.

Market intelligence is closely related to market research and can be broken down into the following three components:

Competitor intelligence: is the practice of gathering information about your rival using lawful means, such as access to public databases and records. For instance, using competition data, Japanese automakers were able to seize and even dominate the US markets. They were able to successfully strategy and enter the US market because they recognized the demand for high-quality, fuel-efficient cars.

Product intelligence: is the process of acquiring information about competing or similar items on the market. For instance, a telecoms corporation must keep an eye on the costs of rival mobile phones in the same market. A competitive product's price reduction could indicate that the manufacturer is launching a new model. By having this knowledge, a business can deliberately introduce its models at the ideal timing and cost.

Market Understanding; Understanding the market entails being aware of your company's portion of the market, market trends, its size, and who your target customers are. A corporation can greatly benefit from knowing market demand and client preferences in order to boost sales and market share. A thorough market analysis, for instance, can provide a business with insightful information. Take the target market, for instance, which is made up of upper-middle-class families with children between the ages of 20 and

Figure 1. Market intelligence components

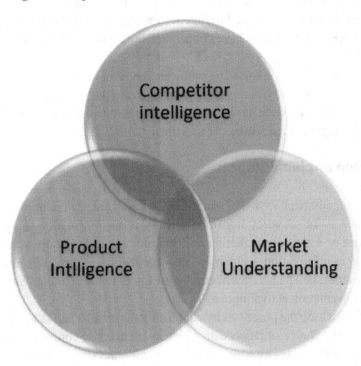

40, and Crossfit training is popular among this group as a way to stay healthy and active. With the help of this information and services tailored to this need, one gym in particular can expand considerably more quickly than other gyms do.

Many organizations have incorporated MI processes; collection, processing, validation and communication, in their strategic market planning, but it is still unclear what the hard and soft benefits of doing so are for an organization in general, a successful MI process can increase an organization's profitability and competitiveness. Its advantages can be divided into three categories: better and quicker choices, time and cost savings, and organizational learning and new ideas. An organization becomes more competitive when more MI is gathered because it enables organizations to innovate by enhancing current processes and expanding their capacity to discover and develop new goods. Figure 1 illustrates Market intelligence components.

MAIN FOCUS OF THE CHAPTER

Market Intelligence Term

According to Kelley's "Marketing Intelligence for Top Management," (Kelley, 1965) MI and its more general name, marketing intelligence, were originally used to give information that was analyzed, trustworthy, and consistent so that an organization could better develop policies and make commercial decisions.

R. Pinkerton follows Kelley by demonstrating the proactivity of organizations in "How to Develop a Marketing Intelligence System" (Kumar & Bagga, 2020) as marketing intelligence systems are implemented as the technological revolution develops. Professional organizations like "Global Intelligence Alliance" and "the Society of Competitive Intelligence Professionals (SCIP)" have made contributions to MI (Egan, 2001). These organizations have contributed both empirical and theoretical research in an effort to improve MI.

The fact that research into MI is conducted by academics and non-academics with various backgrounds has led to a dispersed state of study. As a result, terminology like competitive intelligence, business intelligence, and strategic intelligence are sometimes used interchangeably with MI (Egan, 2001). MI is still evolving to fulfil organizational needs at this time.

Market Intelligence Implementation

Depending on how an organization views MI, different strategies are used to implement it (Jamil, 2013). MI is composed of three major activities: information acquisition, information analysis, and information activation. The practice of acquiring marketing information required to address current and future client demands is known as information acquisition. The intelligence gathered by information analysis is known as information analysis. The practice of employing intelligence to implement and build marketing strategy is known as information activation.

Information acquisitions are the processes by which an actor obtains and stores the data that he or she will later use to identify the choice situation with which he is currently confronted. Information acquisition also encompasses the processes by which the actor obtains and stores the information that he or she uses when attending to and encoding actions conducted by others (or by himself or herself). Information Acquisition Techniques includes Sampling of concrete data; forms, applications, Background reading; reports, memos, etc, Interviewing entails visiting with individuals and asking inquiries, Questionnaires; disseminate a questionnaire to pertinent individuals, collect their responses and analyze them, and Observation, spending time witnessing the organizational context in which the new system will be deployed.

Information analysis is the process of examining, transforming, and modelling information by transforming unstructured data into actionable knowledge in support of decision-making. It requires the interpretation of processed data, and data and knowledge inputs from other sources. Information analysis is the systematic process of discovering and interpreting information, which may entail seeking for information from various sources. During analysis, the contents of the selected source(s) are examined in order to extract the most pertinent information conveyed by the source(s). Then, the pertinent data is extracted, evaluated, and confirmed. Finally, the extracted information is organized and classified into headings and subheadings based on a predetermined scheme. Information analysis tasks allows to:

- Define your processes, products, resources, and environments, or acquire an understanding of them.
- Evaluate your status in relation to your objectives by conducting an analysis.
- Predict by gaining an understanding of the relationships between processes and products, so that the values observed for some attributes can be used to predict others.
- Identify obstacles, fundamental causes, inefficiencies, and other opportunities for enhancement.

Information activation involves numerous stages and facets, but it is evident that digital transformation and information activation go hand in hand. Using digital transformation in its current context, the term was used in the context of digitization to refer to the transformation of information from digital to process. The term "information activation" is appropriate, as it is not merely how we manage information that is significant. Information activation can be used for the following purposes:

- Creating audience categories for customer segmentation.
- Implementing content personalization.
- Suggesting pertinent products to consumers.
- Implementing dynamic marketing campaigns.
- Selling audience information, including demographics, behavior, interests, and device data.
- Visualizing data through the creation of graphs, charts, and dashboards.
- Identifying a target market.

The Intelligence Organization

The intelligence organization is the "people and information resources who make the market intelligence process happen." An intelligence organization consists of five components: MI leadership, which manages and guides the MI process, a MI team, a portfolio of external information sources built by the MI team, an internal MI network comprised of MI users, and the personal information source network of each MI user.

The foundation upon which organizations model MI focuses around a four-step process: collection, validation, processing, and communication (Jamil, 2016). Data mining techniques are utilized throughout the operations to help in the collection and analysis of returned data and information. MI is a constant activity that businesses must analyze in order to enhance their strategic and tactical marketing plans (Fuller, 2023). Collection, validation, processing, and communication are examples of these processes.

Collection

The first step of the MI model is the collection of data and information about a certain market sector. External sources of such data and information include other companies and their market strategy, research organizations, and business publications.

It is claimed that 70% to 80% of intelligence is held by workers or the internal MI network of organizations, since they are the team that obtains information while engaging with suppliers, customers, and other industry connections (Tan & Zafar, 1999). The following consideration can be noted when involving employees into an intelligence program to gather data and information, which is developing a reward plan.

The selection of pertinent data and information is a barrier in the collection of data and information since organizations sometimes struggle to define a market sector. Here are some of the market intelligence collection examples:

Here are some examples of market intelligence collection:

- market research.
- surveys of customer satisfaction, interviews, ethnographic research, and product evaluation.
- monitoring social media and web analytics.
- competitive intelligence.
- Review of prices.

- competitor research.
- evaluating the strengths and shortcomings of your rivals.

Validation

illustrates how data duplication reduces data quality (Creative Commons, 2023). As data and information are gathered from a variety of sources, maintaining excellent data quality is critical (Ridzuan et al.,2019). Data and information collected from sources might be unclean, which means that it is incomplete, incorrect, unsuitable, or duplicated. This stage will allow data and information to be modified and understood by the organization.

Validation Methods

Validation is considered as the second step in the MI model, and can be referred to as data cleansing. The five steps of data cleansing include data analysis to discover mistakes, error elimination, verification to ensure error elimination is done properly, renewing the data in the data warehouse, and completing. Data cleaning is a complicated procedure that comprises numerous phases in order to provide high data quality for MI strategy usage (Ridzuan et al.,2019). Stages include determining the organization's degree of data quality, discovering faults in the data obtained, and finally fixing the defects (Ridzuan et al.,2019). Examples of market intelligence validation:

- Online polls
- Potential consumers' opinions on goods or services may be gathered via surveys from potential customers
- Competitor analysis
- Focus groups
- Usability tests
- A/B tests
- Customer interviews
- Social media monitoring
- Research on user experience

Processing

The third step in the MI model is processing, which comprises translating clean data into usable information, reports, and spreadsheets that enable the organization to learn specialized knowledge (Jamil, 2013). Because the interpretation of data into accessible information is complicated, it demands the employment of proper technology and considerable commitment from a senior organizational level to match data and information gaps.

MAG Industrial Automation Systems - Company serves as an example of MI processing. Background MAG is the third largest manufacturer of metal cutting machine tools in the globe. The company manufactures machines ranging from micromachining for medicinal applications to three-story-tall machines for large diameter cutting and milling. Aerospace, automotive, construction, mining, hydrocarbon regions, and power generation are customer industries. MAG is headquartered in New York.

MAG Industrial Automation Systems today have a comprehensive intelligence system in place that supports key processes in the organization, marketing and sales included. When Noam Sahbti, Director of Intelligence and Strategic Planning at MAG, took on the challenge of altering what was commonly referred to as a "Information Monster" in-house, the reality was quite different. (m-brain, 2023)

Also, publicly available information such as prominent financial figures, changes of key personnel, and senior management statements can be of great interest, as well as the majority of businesses conduct such research internally on a regular but unsystematic basis. On a more formal premise, a common endeavor conducted by external market research and intelligence agencies is marketing analysis of competitors. For instance, a precise estimate of a competitor's advertising budget can be derived from a combination of detailed monitoring of advertisements posted over a period of time and investigation of publications' advertising rates. Press analysis can also be used to assess the marketing strategy of competitors (by analyzing the messages behind the advertisements) and to obtain valuable intelligence on wage rates by examining employment advertisements. (b2binternational, 2023)

Communication

The MI model's ultimate step is communication. It comprises sharing, distributing, and transferring information gathered during the processing stage to personnel inside the organization who will utilize it in line with the market strategy (Heang, 2017). Because MI is a continually developing technology, managers with industry experience are required to evaluate the continued validity of the MI strategy and its execution (Heang, 2017). It is important to utilize a formalized approach to ensure that the MI strategy is communicated as effectively as feasible. Figure 2 shows major Market intelligence activities, and Figure 3 illustrates Market intelligence main processes.

De Telefoongids – Company provides an illustration of MI communication. In The Netherlands, De Telefoongids is the market leader for telephone directories. The company's database is the most comprehensive on the market, encompassing over 40 telecom operators and 6.1% of all phone numbers. 800 employees are employed by De Telefoongids, and its website receives 5.5 million unique visitors per month. Eric Knibbe, Marketing Intelligence and Research Manager at De Telefoongids, was interviewed to examine the case for how new business models and industry participants necessitate new MI measures from an established market participant. In the midst of industry change, sales and marketing require new tools and insights, and it is the responsibility of management intelligence to produce them.

MI provides sales personnel at DTG with information on a variety of topics, such as: Number of clicks on each heading in the online directory, Information on industry segments, Results from the direct ads system, Call tracking that reveals trends and the response to advertising, and Ad-hoc research in response to specific issues or problems.

Knibbe reminds us that in addition to deploying the common technical BI platform, we must also deliver BI presentations at sales team meetings, sales conferences, marketing planning meetings, and other events where the focus is on customer processes. "Pure facts are essential for supporting good business, but true intelligence is typically only generated when the facts are discussed and evaluated in a group," he mentioned. (m-brain, 2023)

Businesses now have greater access to information than ever before. However, information that can truly aid a company's decision-making is rare and valuable, and requires the services of an outsourced intelligence provider. Market entry and expansion studies provide information that can be applied when entering a new market or expanding an existing market presence. Information is typically gathered through

Figure 2. Market intelligence major activities

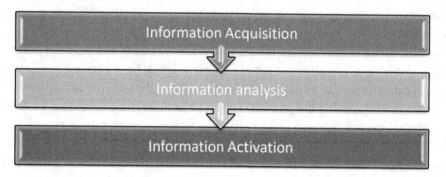

Figure 3. Market intelligence main processes

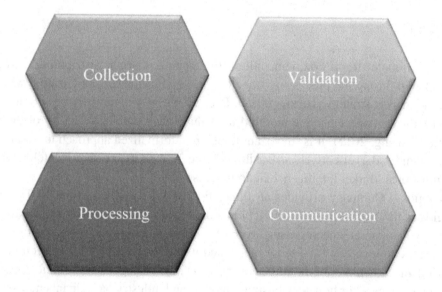

Figure 4. Visualizing results of big data analytics for market intelligence

interviews with buyers, intermediaries, competitors, and industry experts. Competitor intelligence studies are becoming increasingly popular; they are based on press analysis, pricing research, competitor interviews, customer interviews, interviews with other market participants, and online research (especially company websites) (b2binternational, 2023). Figure 4 illustrates visualizing results of Big data analytics to be used for market intelligence.

Gathering Market Intelligence Data

Utilizing Search Engines to Acquire MI

Various types of MI data are collected depending on an organization's financial capabilities. Data and information sources are classified as qualitative, quantitative, formal, informal, published, or unpublished. It entails using search engines and company websites to learn about competition strategies, as well as recognizing business trends through credible publications and current consumer base (Tsu & Zafar, 1999). Organizations gather MI using a variety of systems, one of which is the Open-source Intelligence system (SCIP, 1991).

OSINT (Open-Source Intelligence)

One of the most common methods of MI collecting used by organizations is open-source intelligence. OSINT is the scanning, gathering, exploitation, validation, analysis, and sharing of publicly accessible print and digital/electronic data from unclassified, non-secret, and grey literature with intelligence-seeking clients (Fleisher, 2008). It is widely used because its system is simple, affordable, and it processes a lot of raw materials that can be further processed (Sharma, 2020).

Intelligence Collection Using Information Systems

The use of marketing information systems, which employ artificial intelligence (AI) technology to facilitate the planning of strategic and tactical marketing strategies of MI while also sharing marketing expertise, enables organizations to continuously acquire, generate, and maintain both internal and external information.

Internal Intelligence Gathering

Customers, manufacturers, via R&D, workers, also known as salesforce, physical proof, sales quotations, sales records, trade exhibitions, and new recruits are just a few examples of internal intelligence collecting sources (Lackman et al., 2000). Organizations ranked these data sources on a scale of one to five, with five being very important and one being not important. Customers, manufacturers, and R&D were determined to be the three data sources that organizations value most highly, with 100% of organizations placing them at the four or higher level (Fleisher, 2008). It demonstrates that these data sources contributed the most value to organizations during the collection and gathering of MI data and information.

Figure 5. Methods for gathering market intelligence data

Gathering External Intelligence

External intelligence may be obtained from a variety of sources, including but not limited to client meetings, dealers/distributors, customers, business partners, market research projects, suppliers, web services, journals, and government publications (Lackman et al., 2000). When these data sources were compared to internal sources, the results demonstrated that customer meetings produced the most useful external intelligence for the organization. Figure 5 shows methods for gathering Market intelligence data.

Impacts of Market Intelligence

Using MI can assist or hurt an organization depending on how it is acquired, kept, and applied. Gaining a competitive edge in their marketing plans for companies is just one of the advantages that MI can bring. On the other hand, MI can also cause financial losses and regulatory failures on the part of the government. Acquiring MI data and information, as well as putting an organization's marketing strategy into practice, both provide challenges. If dirty data is not properly cleansed and problems are not mitigated or resolved, it may result in a variety of negative effects that cause the organization to lose money and its good name (Redman, 1998). Other problems include unethically and illegally obtaining intelligence.

Although many organizations have employed MI techniques in strategic market planning, it is still unclear what the hard and soft advantages are for an organization. The benefits of a successful MI process may be classified into three categories: better and quicker choices, time and cost savings, and organizational learning and new ideas. Overall, it can improve an organization's profitability and competitiveness.

Big Data Analytics

Intelligence and information are not the same. Information is useless unless it has some sort of meaning. Information is simply knowledge about a certain subject or product, whereas intelligence refers to significant information that may be put to use in making decisions. Analysis of the obtained data is necessary in order to convert the data into useful intelligence. Market intelligence software comes in a variety of forms. Such software enables you to collect data as well as analyze it using cutting-edge analytical techniques. An organization can better understand the thoughts, trends, and competitiveness of its target market as well as where adjustments or modifications are required by analyzing the material it has gathered and turning it into meaningful market intelligence. A corporation may accurately comprehend the market with the help of advanced analytical tools like Conjoint analysis, Maxdiff analysis, Gap analysis, Trend analysis, Text and Sentiment analysis, which helps them make smart business decisions.

In 2022, the global market size for Big data analytics (Fortune business insights, 2023) is projected to reach $271,83 billion. The market is anticipated to increase from USD 307.52 billion in 2023 to USD 745.15 billion by 2030, at a CAGR of 13.5% during the forecast period.

In defining the scope, some solutions were offered by market leaders, including Azure Databricks, SAP Analytics Cloud, SAP HANA Cloud, IBM Db2 Big SQL, and Background Data solutions.

Big data analytics assesses both unstructured and structured databases in order to comprehend and deliver insights based on correlation, concealed patterns, and other factors. By developing business intelligence, prominent industries intend to utilize analytical tools to gain consumer insights. For example, in December 2020, Amazon, Inc. introduced Amazon HealthLake, a HIPAA-compliant Big data analytics service for the healthcare industry that provides real-time patient data.

For instance, it is crucial for a business to continuously watch the market. A company can stay competitive and manage to grow its market shares, revenues, and customer base by analyzing and monitoring trends, assessing customer satisfaction scores, and using Net promoter scores. Depending on the situation or current trends, appropriate decisions may be made to alter or adapt the product.

Market Intelligence: Types and Methodologies With Examples

Using market information involves several steps, including reports and presentations. Reports and appealing infographics can help a business better understand the markets and provide answers to queries like "What do the metrics mean?" This stage is crucial in the market intelligence process since improper interpretation of such data might be dangerous for the organization. Utilizing dependable and potent market intelligence tools has made the entire process lot simpler. As a result, a corporation can efficiently penetrate a market, identify market segments, comprehend the competition, and comprehend the market as a whole by applying market intelligence.

Market Intelligence: Examples of the Different Kinds and Methodologies

Quantitative market research is a method that involves the collection of numerical data to facilitate the resolution of a research question or objective. Common quantitative research methodologies comprise surveys, polls, questionnaires, and demographic data obtained from primary and secondary sources. Quantification, comparison, and analysis of data can facilitate the identification of patterns, trends, and insights that can either support or refute a research inquiry.

Utilizing quantitative data can aid a corporation in obtaining solutions to strategic inquiries. Data analysis can assist organizations in identifying patterns, detecting trends, forecasting outcomes, and establishing means. Quantitative research is typically employed to address questions pertaining to the specifics of "how," "when," "what," and "where." Several of these comprise:

- What is the estimated size of the market?
- How have the demands of a given market evolved over time?
- What is the size of your target audience in terms of population?
- What is the estimated level of consumer interest in purchasing your product?
- Is there a viable market for the products in question?

- What is the primary online platform frequented by my target demographic?
- What is the frequency of consumer purchasing behavior for your product or service?
- What is the extent of the brand, product, or service awareness among the populace?
- What demographic or psychographic characteristics are most commonly exhibited by your most valuable clientele?
- What is the average duration of user engagement on your website?
- What is the proportion of satisfied customers with regards to your product or service?

The proportion of quantitative data available to most organizations may be as low as 20 percent, owing to the increasing number of sources from which data is generated. Relying solely on quantitative data may lead to an inadequate consideration of significant information, potentially leading to distorted insights and decision-making. It is imperative to have a solution that has the capability to access and analyze the remaining 80 percent (Entrepreneur, 2023).

It is imperative to acknowledge and consider alternative sources of information, even if they are not quantifiable. Qualitative data provides crucial insights into the perceptions and attitudes of customers towards both your products and your brand. The aforementioned data is of utmost importance in comprehending the optimal approach to effectively engage with individuals and attain triumph with one's enterprise. The process of analyzing qualitative data encompasses a range of methodologies such as narrative analysis, surveys, interviews, and user feedback. By utilizing these instruments, you will be able to comprehend the attitudes and beliefs towards your brand not only from consumers, but also from stakeholders and the wider audience who may have the potential to become customers.

The primary objective of qualitative research is to generate comprehensive and intricate portrayals of the subject matter under investigation, while also revealing novel perspectives and interpretations.

Quantitative data pertains to numerical information, whereas qualitative data pertains to descriptive information that pertains to phenomena that are observable but not measurable, such as language.

Qualitative research refers to the systematic approach of gathering, examining, and comprehending non-quantitative information, such as language. Qualitative research is a valuable approach for comprehending an individual's subjective perception and interpretation of their social reality.

Qualitative data refers to data that is not expressed in numerical form and can include various forms of media, such as text, video, photographs, or audio recordings. Diary accounts or in-depth interviews can be utilized to gather this category of data, which can then be subjected to analysis via grounded theory or thematic analysis.

While there are many different quantitative and qualitative approaches that can be used to gather market research. The following are some fundamental techniques for gathering data for Market intelligence:

Surveys

In order to obtain information from the target market and analyze it to provide useful market intelligence, survey research uses a set of simple questions. The results are more trustworthy the larger the sample size. Depending on the information that needs to be collected, surveys can be done using a variety of approaches.

Telephone Surveys

Telephone surveys are more expensive than mail surveys but are generally less expensive than in-person surveys. Although telemarketing is used by some businesses, the consumer does not respond favorably to the persistent pestering. As a result, it becomes increasingly harder to persuade the customer to participate in the survey, which lowers response rates and lowers the quality of results. Businesses, for instance, must comprehend consumer perceptions of particular products, such as laptops. The corporation can introduce the ideal product into the market by conducting a telephone survey with a set of questions about product characteristics, brand choice, pricing comfort, and many other topics.

Online Surveys

These are the best and among the most cost-effective ways to get data quickly. Such surveys have a reputation for producing incorrect data, but as newer technologies enter the market, this technique has gained popularity and proven to be a viable way to obtain real-time data quickly. Online surveys are the ideal way to obtain market data because the bulk of the target audience already prefers online contact. For instance, a mobile manufacturer needs to know where its rivals are in the market before launching its own product in the same niche. To learn about a rival's position in the market, their product features, and their market share, a competitor analysis survey can be carried out. With the aid of this information, the business will be able to choose the ideal customers, features, and prices in order to increase its market share.

In-Person Surveys

These surveys, which consist of one-on-one interviews, can be carried out to collect the necessary data in busy places like malls. Because you have the benefit of exhibiting a product or comparing products and gathering useful information, this also enables you to collect client feedback. Such a strategy offers good response rates, but it is relatively expensive because a professional person and an appropriate technology, such a tablet, are required at each location. For instance, a Fast Moving Consumer Goods (FMCG) business wishes to introduce a brand-new product to the female market. To learn the preferences of the target market and the trend for certain cosmetic items, in-person surveys can be carried out in malls. As a result, the product can be altered and introduced into the market to directly affect customer demand.

Mail Surveys

One of the least expensive ways to conduct surveys, especially with a wider population, is through mail. Since individuals no longer read paper mail due to technological advances, this strategy only receives 3–15% of responses. However, this approach is still widely used to collect the necessary data from the public in places where technology is still out of reach.

Questionnaires - A questionnaire is a list of questions used in research that can be printed out or submitted online. They can be used to collect information from a wide range of audiences and can be utilized for both qualitative and quantitative research.

Polls - A poll is similar to a survey, but there is only one question to be answered. The response rate is exceptionally high because it takes very little time to respond to these.

Forms - A researcher will use forms to ask a series of questions in order to gather the precise data needed to complete the work at hand. Questions intended to elicit opinions or responses from the respondent are not part of this methodology.

Focus groups - are made up of individuals who have been carefully chosen to reflect a target market. A business can assess client needs and preferences using focus group surveys, as well as solicit feedback from the group. This makes it possible to gather data that will help a business break into that market or introduce a new product into an already-existing industry. Usually, a moderator is needed to pose the question to a group of participants after a discussion reveals new information about the subject. However, focus group surveys can now also be conducted online, doing away with the requirement for a moderator. For instance, to find out what kind of phone would be best for them, a focus group is asked about their ideas. They will talk among themselves, and the company will learn which dimension is most popular on the market and why. Reasons such specific product features, screen size, phone color, operating system speed, pricing, etc. can give the business insights into which specific area they need to invest more in and help them use this knowledge to increase market share.

Observation - There are situations when the information obtained through other methods won't be accurate or insightful regarding consumer sentiments or purchasing patterns. In this situation, the observation approach gives you details about consumer behavior, shopping trends, and preferences for things like quality and price. An organization will be able to sell more effectively and alter their products in response to demand if they have this knowledge. For instance, to better understand the behavior of their customers, brands have cameras installed in their stores. These cameras continually record and may be examined later. A business can gain insight into the target market's unintentional buying habits or attitudes by making use of this observation.

Trials in the field - Trials in the field resemble running tests in real time. It entails putting a product in particular stores to gauge consumer reaction to the new item. A pilot run could be used to test the product on the market. For instance, a chocolate manufacturer wants to test a new product that they want to introduce. In order to test these chocolates with their intended customers, a few carefully chosen establishments are given access to them. These clients must represent the target market, so the corporation will be able to determine whether the product will succeed in the marketplace through their comments.

Personal interviews - are typically pricey affairs, but they yield useful, trustworthy information. This approach is utilized to comprehend a subject or a product thoroughly. They are unstructured, hour-long open-ended questions. Such a strategy is not chosen to acquire market data, however, as it will not represent the market as a whole because it is done on an individual basis. However, if you are unfamiliar with such business knowledge, interviews with subject matter experts can help you gain an awareness of the market trends in a specific area. For instance, a business needs to know what the market's current technical trends are. A corporation can learn useful information about what is popular right now and what might be anticipated in the near future by speaking with a subject matter expert in technology solutions. In light of this, it is possible to make strategic business decisions in order to direct investment.

Demographics refer to quantitative data that depict the attributes and traits of a given populace. Demographic analysis pertains to the examination of a population's characteristics, including but not limited to age, race, and gender. Demographic data pertains to socioeconomic information that is expressed statistically. This information encompasses various factors such as employment, education, income, marriage rates, birth and death rates, among others.

Demographics are utilized by governments, corporations, and non-government organizations to gain insights into the characteristics of a population for various objectives, such as policy formulation and economic market analysis. An enterprise specializing in the sale of luxurious recreational vehicles may aim to target individuals who are approaching or have reached the age of retirement, as well as the proportion of this demographic possessing the financial means to purchase their merchandise.

Demographic analysis pertains to the systematic gathering and examination of extensive features concerning populations and groups of individuals. Such data is highly advantageous for enterprises in comprehending how to effectively target consumers and devise strategic plans for upcoming shifts in consumer demand. The integration of the internet, big data, and artificial intelligence is significantly enhancing the efficacy and implementation of demographics as a marketing and business strategy tool.

Age or generation are commonly employed criteria for grouping market segments. The utilization of demographic data can facilitate the acquisition of insights into the characteristics of a given population.

The process of gathering and examining information pertaining to the overall attributes of particular groups of people is known as demographic analysis. The utilization of this tool is commonplace in the business industry for the purpose of ascertaining optimal methods of customer outreach and evaluating their behavioral patterns. The utilization of demographic segmentation enables organizations to ascertain the potential market size of a population.

Quantitative Market Research Designs

Quantitative market research uses secondary and primary data in mathematical form. Quantitative research design involves five methods.

I.   Descriptive research
     Quantitative research explores topics including population, situation, and phenomenon. It observes and analyses several factors. It describes qualities rather than why a research challenge exists. Appropriately, it outlines a study topic without analyzing why.
     Descriptive research examples:
     1.   A company's Black Friday advertising campaign.
     2.   A company's or consumers' service delivery difficulties.
     3.   Companies that provide gifts with internet purchases.
II. Experimental research
     True experimental research tests a hypothesis. It usually involves multiple unproven notions. This design controls variables to determine their causes and effects. Data types are modified and their effects examined. The investigation will identify how factors interact.
     1.   The impact of Black Friday marketing on company success.
     2.   Service delivery concerns and brand dependability.
     3.   Gift-with-purchase pleasure.
III. Relational research
     Correlational study often examines two strongly connected things. It examines their effects and changes. Multivariate quantitative research analyses data connections. It will compare their similarities and differences. It will not explore casual connections further.
     1.   Black Friday campaign performance and yearly income.
     2.   Delivery problems and brand reputation.
     3.   Freebies and loyalty.
IV. Quasi-experimental research

Experimental (casual comparative) research examines cause-and-effect relationships between variables. Using an independent and dependent variable distinguishes quasi-experimental research. This quantitative research approach uses a cause-and-effect technique to compare at least two data sets. Two groups are studied in a near-natural context. A naturally occurring group that closely matches the original environment. This establishes causality. Due to additional factors, not all casual connections are accurate.

1. How Black Friday's success affected staff productivity.
2. Service concerns affect brand impression.
3. Free gifts and consumer loyalty.

V. Market research quantitative data collecting

Quantitative research has many types. Choose a data gathering technique first. Three popular quantitative research data gathering methodologies are summarized here.

Interviews

Telephone, video, and in-person interviews apply. It's a great way to gather data from people, but it takes time to set up and run.

Market Research Surveys

provide quantitative data at low cost. Large groups of individuals may be surveyed fast and easily. For relevant survey results, carefully examine your survey questions. This style of market research requires closed-ended questions with yes/no or numerical answers.

QMR survey questions include:

1. Would you recommend a certain tool?
2. How would you evaluate your experience with a tool's customer care service today, from 1 to 10?
3. Did our site have what you needed today?
4. How simple was it to obtain the information you needed on our site today, from 1 to 10?
5. Did our help person answer your question?

Polls

Polls are shorter surveys. It gives researchers a snapshot of a huge group. In-person, phone, or internet data collection is possible. Figure 6 shows gathering data for market intelligence approaches.

Market Intelligence for Decision Making

The importance of big data, in the eyes of the decision maker, rests in its capacity to provide valuable knowledge and facts on which to base judgements. The managerial decision-making process has received significant attention. Big data is a resource that decision-makers are finding to be increasingly valuable. The ability to communicate with others via phones, loyalty cards, the web, and social media platforms provide organizations with important benefits. This is only achievable if the data is correctly analyzed to disclose insightful information that decision makers may use to their advantage.

Figure 6. Gathering data for market intelligence approaches

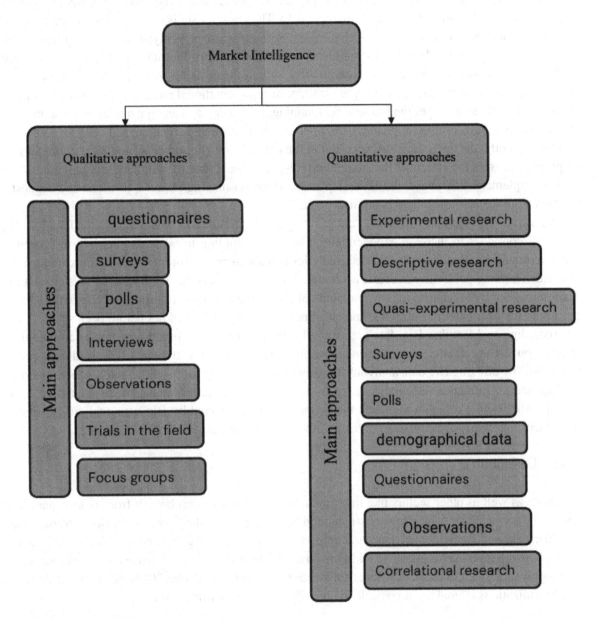

Additionally, organizations are already used to analyzing internal data, including as well as inventory, sales, and shipping. But the requirement for analyzing outside data, Supply chains and customer markets have emerged, and the usage of big data can deliver information and value throughout time. Making more educated decisions based on the growing volumes and varieties of unstructured data available makes sense.

The intelligence phase, where data are gathered, is the initial step in the decision-making process, which is gathered from internal sources and can be utilized to discover issues and opportunities as well as outside data sources. The sources of large data must be identified during this phase. And the information must be compiled from many sources, processed, stored, and transferred to the final user. Such large amounts of data must be handled appropriately. The chosen data is obtained and stored in any of the big data storage and management technologies, with the sources and types of data required for the analysis being determined. Following the collection and storage of big data, it is then prepared, organized.

The design phase, if applicable, is the following step in the decision-making process. Action plans are created and evaluated using a conceptualization, or representational model, of the issue. This phase is divided into three steps per the framework, planning, analyzing, and using a model. An example of a data analytics model, is chosen, planned, then put into practice, and lastly analyzed.

Consequently, the decision is the next step in the decision-making process, in which techniques are employed to assess the effects of the suggested fixes, or actions, starting with the design phase.

The implementation phase, the final step in the decision-making process, is where the suggested solution from the previous phase is put into practice.

Organizations from many industries are growing more interested in how to handle and analyze Big data as it continues to increase exponentially. They're scrambling to take advantage of the potential presented by Big data as a result. Big data analytics is implemented in order to get the maximum value, and understanding possibility to create economic value and to speed up and improve decision-making. Therefore, in order to analyze massive amounts of data, organizations are turning to Big data analytics quicker to uncover patterns, attitudes, and customer information that had not before been seen.

According to Manyika, Big data can allow businesses to Create brand-new goods and services, improve on already existing ones, and create wholly original business structures. These advantages can be attained by utilizing Big data analytics in many topics including supply chain intelligence, customer intelligence, performance, and quality as well as fraud detection and risk management (Manyika, 2011). Additionally, Cebr's research indicated the primary sectors affected by Big data analytics, including manufacturing, retail, central government, healthcare, telecom, and banking (Cebr, 2012).

Fraud Detection

Insurance as well as other sectors like investment or retail banking can benefit from risk management with Big data analytics. Since the assessment and consideration of the financial services industry must consider risk, and Big data analytics can compare the possibility of gains and the likelihood of losses when choosing investments losses. In addition, huge data from both internal and external sources may be thoroughly integrated, and risk exposures are dynamically evaluated (Cebr, 2012). Big data can therefore help organizations by making it possible to quantify hazards (Russom, 2011).

Customer Intelligence

The potential of Big data analytics to improve consumer intelligence is enormous. Businesses including retail, banking, and telecommunications stand to gain from this. Big data could lead to transparency, and stakeholders should have quicker access to pertinent data (Manyika, 2011). Organizations can profile customers using Big data analytics, and categorize clients according to several socioeconomic traits, as well as rise in client retention and satisfaction levels (Cebr, 2012). This could enable them to market to various segments based on better informed marketing decisions, recognizing sales and marketing opportunities while also taking into account their preferences (Russom, 2011). Additionally, businesses may utilize social media to learn what their clients appreciate in addition to what they dislike.

Businesses can use sentiment analysis to their advantage by be informed in advance when clients are leaving or switching to rivals products, and respond accordingly. Using the System of National Accounts (SNAs) to track consumer perceptions of brands, can assist organizations in responding to trends, and performing direct selling. Big data analytics can also make it possible to create prediction models. Models for consumer purchasing trends and behavior, increases total profitability (Cebr, 2012). Even businesses that have long embraced segmentation are nevertheless increasingly advanced. Big data techniques are starting to be used, such as real-time micro segmenting of clients, to target promotions and advertising (Manyika, 2011). Therefore, Big data analytics can be advantageous to businesses by providing better targeted Social influenced marketing, which defines and forecasts trends based on consumer attitude as well as researching and comprehending churn and other client behaviors (Russom, 2011).

Quality Control

Big data can be utilized for quality control, particularly in the industrial, energy and utilities, and tele-communications sectors, to boost profitability. and cut expenses by raising the caliber of the products and services delivered. Predictive analytics on big data, for instance, can be utilized in the manufacturing process to reduce performance variability and prevent quality concerns by early warning notifications. This can shorten the time to market and lower scrap rates. Preventing any production-related problems by identifying them in advance can have substantial outlays (Cebr, 2012). Furthermore, Big data analytics may enhance manufacturing lead times (Russom, 2011). Additionally, real-time data analysis and surveillance of Machine logs can help managers make judgements about quality control more quickly. The ability to monitor network demand in real-time is another benefit of Big data analytics. Healthcare IT solutions can also increase the effectiveness and caliber of care by transferring and integrating patient data between several institutions and departments while maintaining privacy restrictions (Cebr, 2012). Examining computerized medical records increase the continuity of care for patients while also building a huge dataset. This allows for the comparison and prediction of treatments and results. Therefore, electronic health information are being used more frequently, and improvements are made in the potential to mine the accessible de-identified patient data using analytics tools information for controlling illnesses and evaluating the standard of healthcare services for health (TechAmerica, 2012).

Additionally, the use of technology can enhance the standard of living for citizens. Sensors can be used in homes and hospitals for healthcare to ensure that the Patients are continuously monitored, and patient data are subjected to real-time analytics. This can be used to notify people and their medical professionals if any health irregularities are found in the analysis, the patient must seek medical attention and help (TechAmerica, 2012). Additionally, patients can be observed remotely by examining data from dispersed sensors on portable devices to assess their compliance with their enhance medication and treatment alternatives, and decrease prescriptions (Cebr, 2012). Additionally, transportation can be facilitated by real-time traffic information provided by roads and cars. It is possible to anticipate and avoid traffic congestion, and drivers may function more safely and without disrupting traffic as much. Such a novel kind transportation and the way roads are used could possibly be improved by the traffic ecosystem created by "intelligent" connected cars (TechAmerica, 2012). In light of this, Big data applications deliver intelligent routing based on personal, real-time traffic data local information. Additionally, these programs can automatically request assistance when the sensors identify problems and alert users in real-time about accidents, planned roadworks, and congested regions (Manyika, 2011). Big data can also be utilized to better comprehend locational changes, weather and climatic intensity and frequency.

This can help people and organizations who depend on the weather, like farmers, as well as industries like tourism and transportation. Additionally, new sensor technologies and analysis methods for long-m climate models and closer weather predictions can help predict weather-related natural disasters. Predictions allow for the taking of proactive, preventative or remedial measures (TechAmerica, 2012).

Supply Chain Management

Big data analytics can be used to forecast demand in supply chain management, and they adapt their supply accordingly. The manufacturing, retail, transportation, and logistics sectors can all gain from this to an increasing extent. Organizations are able to automate replenishment by analyzing stock utilization and geolocation data on delivery. Decisions that will minimize costs and delays, shorten lead times, and pauses in the procedure. Analyzing supplier data can be used to track performance, such as price competitiveness. Additionally, it is possible to rapidly run alternative price scenarios, which can lower inventories and boost profit margins (Cebr, 2012). Consequently, Big Data can help identify the underlying causes of cost and provide for better decision-making.

Performance management is another area where Big data analytics can be beneficial, where the public sector and healthcare sectors can both profit. The need to increase efficiency has made it possible to monitor worker performance information, and projected utilizing technologies for predictive analytics. Additionally, the use of predictive Key Performance Indicators (KPIs), availability of Big data, accessibility of performance information to operations managers improves corporate outcomes. By facilitating performance monitoring and enhancing transparency, goal-setting, and planning and management processes inside the organization, balanced scorecards and dashboards can bring about operational gains (Cebr, 2012).

Business Intelligence and Big Data Analytics

Platforms are displacing market share leaders in traditional Business Intelligence (BI), that increases analytics access, and produce better business value. Leaders in BI should monitor how traditionalists interpret their investments in forward-thinking products into a revitalized dynamism and better client service. The market for BI and analytics platforms is going through a fundamental modification. In the previous ten years, the majority of investments have gone towards IT-led consolidation and efforts to standardize extensive systems of record reporting. These have a history of being tightly regulated and centralized, where production reports created by IT were released to provide information to a wide range of information consumers analysts, too. A larger variety of corporate users are now insisting on having access to interactive analyses and insights, they can benefit from advanced analytics without needing IT or talents in data science. Considering the increase in business, users' data discovery capabilities are becoming more widespread, and IT Sector aims to meet this demand without making any sacrifices.

While system-of-record reporting is required to function, enterprises are still around, however there has been a big change in how Businesses are addressing this and other user-driven business needs. They are gradually moving away from employing the installed base, i.e., established and IT-focused platforms, to more decentralized data discovery using the enterprise standard enterprise-wide deployments that are currently becoming more common. There is the changeover to quickly implementable platforms. It is available for both analysts and business users to use either by IT to quickly generate analytics or to identify insights in order to deliver content that satisfies business criteria. According to Gartner, more than half of net new purchases are sparked by data discovery. With the adoption of a decentralized paradigm, More business users being empowered also increases the requirement for an approach to regulated data discovery.

Dashboards, visualizations, reporting, data mining, ETL, and OLAP are popular business intelligence technologies. Business Intelligence tools may include any combination of these features:

- Spreadsheets: tabular data that can be searched and formatted; accessible in web-based and downloadable software formats.
- Dashboards: real-time data visualizations.
- Data mining tools: AI, Machine Learning, statistics, and database systems show data patterns.
- Ad hoc data analytics: answering particular inquiries on the moment.
- Online analytical processing (OLAP) business intelligence technologies allow multi-dimensional analytical queries.
- Mobile BI optimizes desktop business information for mobile devices.
- Real-time BI: sophisticated corporate analytics that feeds business transactions into a real-time data warehouse to provide users with real-time information.
- Operational BI: real-time business analytics that automatically incorporate real-time data into an operational system for immediate usage.
- Software-as-a-service SaaS BI: cloud-based, subscription-based business intelligence software solutions.
- Open-source business intelligence (OSBI): software without a license.
- Collaborative BI: combining business information technologies with collaborative capabilities to simplify sharing.
- Location intelligence (LI) software links corporate data to spatial surroundings.
- Data visualization software: makes patterns and connections easier to see.
- Reporting, query, sort, filter, and display software
- Data cleaning and analysis software.
- Data warehousing tools: integrated data retrieval from several sources generates a consolidated data store that can be accessed later for analysis.
- Unified modelling language: natural language developers use to build, define, visualize, and describe software systems.
- Corporate performance management: evaluating techniques to fulfil corporate objectives.

BI Tools Comparison:
Some of the most popular business intelligence solutions:

HEAVY.AI-BI Tools: Heavy.AI boosts Big data analytics speed and scalability. Users may visually combine and cross-filter multi-dimensional data with clicks using interactive dashboards that query, visualize, and power billion-row databases.

Microsoft BI Tools: Power BI provides visualizations, analysis, and reporting for local or cloud-sourced data. Augmented analytics, data preparation, interactive dashboards, and visual exploration are included. Microsoft stores are targeted. Available in free desktop version for isolated users, Pro version for small teams, or Premium version for companies per dedicated cloud computing and storage resource.

Looker, a Google BI Tool, is a full-spectrum business intelligence and analytics platform that offers real-time visualizations, modelling, interactive dashboards, real-time business intelligence reporting tools, collaboration, data discovery, and can work on top of any analytical database. Designed to provide the team a 360-degree business picture.

AWS BI Tools: Amazon QuickSight is a cloud-based, serverless, embeddable, ML-powered BI solution. QuickSight enables dynamic BI dashboard publication, Machine Learning-powered insights, natural language query replies, huge scalability without infrastructure or capacity constraints, and mobile accessible. Pay-per-session is 30 minutes from sign-in. There exist Standard version, Enterprise version for writers with an annual subscription or month-to-month; Enterprise for readers or a per-session monthly or yearly plan.

SAP BI Tool: SAP BusinessObjects is a full Business Intelligence suite that offers a customizable dashboard where business users can access all of their BI tools in one place, real-time analytics, self-service reporting, streamlined workflow and full visibility, monitoring and security credential management for administrators, predictive modelling, cloud-based analytics, collaborative reporting, and more.

Business Intelligence and Big Data Theories and Models

Contemporary organizations engage in the ongoing collection of user data with the aim of enhancing their operational efficiencies and procedures. The utilization of vast amounts of stored data or electronic transaction data has become commonplace in facilitating decision-making processes. Technology is now widely adopted by managers, policymakers, and executive officers to convert these copious amounts of raw data into valuable and informative insights. The process of analyzing data can be intricate, however, a prevalent approach to data management known as "Big Data Analytics" (BDA) has emerged. BDA involves utilizing sophisticated analytical techniques such as data mining, statistical analysis, and predictive modelling on large datasets to generate new business intelligence practices. The field of Big Data Analytics (BDA) employs computational intelligence methodologies to convert unprocessed data into meaningful insights that can facilitate informed decision-making. The significance of analytical applications for evidence-based decision making has been amplified due to the growing dependence on Big Data in organizational decision-making processes.

Scholars contend that Business Intelligence (BI), BD, and BDA have a close relationship because BI provides the methodological and technological capabilities for data analysis (e.g. Llave, 2018; Sun, Zou, & Strang, 2015). BDA can be viewed as a subset of BI (Sun, Zou, & Strang, 2015). This is because BI supports firm decision-making with valuable data, information, and knowledge (Alnoukari & Hanano, 2017). In addition, BI and BDA share some decision-making process-supporting instruments. In addition, both BI and BDA emphasize valuable data, information, and knowledge. In addition, BI and BDA involve interactive data exploration and discovery via visualization. BI is also supported by BDA as a service and technology (Passlick, Lebek, & Bremner, 2017; Sun, Zou, & Strang, 2015). Furthermore, BI is currently based on the four cutting-edge technology pillars of cloud, mobile, big data, and social technologies (Passlick, Lebek, & Bremner, 2017; Sun, Zou, & Strang, 2015). Sun et al. (2015) argue further that BDA is an indispensable instrument for developing BI, at least from a technological and data perspective. BDA is data-driven and business-oriented techniques; therefore, it facilitates firm decision-making and enhances BI from a technological standpoint. Knowledge discovery is the core of BDA and BI systems from a data perspective (Sun, Zou, & Strang, 2015). Jin and Kim (2018) believe that BI's "raw data" have evolved into "Big Data" due to technological advancements. Therefore, it is reasonable to conclude that BI/BD/BDA are not distinct concepts. Therefore, it is advantageous to integrate them all into a unified DSS that encompasses all processes, from data collection to data analytics and insights to decision making (Jin & Kim, 2018). Fan et al. (2015) argue that BDA contributes to marketing intelligence by enabling the monitoring of consumer sentiments regarding a product, service, or company through social media mining techniques.

In their recent study, Faroukhi et al. (2020) identified several distinctions between BI and BD/BDA, including the following: BI is based on File-Based or Object-Based storage models, while BD is based on Block-Based storage models. BI is also founded on the conventional database data model, which includes SQL databases and data warehouses. For this reason, distributed storage and NoSQL databases are primarily used for the BD data model (Faroukhi, El Alaoui, Gahi, & Amine, 2020). Traditional databases are unable to meet the challenges of BD, which primarily involve storing and processing vast amounts of unstructured data. Similarly, the hardware storage infrastructure for BI is primarily comprised of storage devices, whereas BD requires additional storage infrastructure, including storage network infrastructure and storage virtualization. Additionally, BD requires a distributed processing infrastructure so that data, calculations, and processing can be shared across multiple interconnected nodes. Traditional BI, however, does not require such a distributed processing infrastructure (Faroukhi, El Alaoui, Gahi, and Amine, 2020). Lastly, and from an analytical standpoint, descriptive and predictive analyses were primarily developed by BI traditional systems, whereas BD provides the ability to develop and utilize additional analytics capabilities such as prescriptive and diagnostic analysis (Faroukhi, El Alaoui, Gahhi, and Amine, 2020).

The BI/BDA architecture paradigm proposed by Passlick et al. (2017) supports both traditional BI analytical reports and BDA. The proposed architecture paradigm incorporates BI and BD components. In addition to the standard ETL process, the data processing layer can also execute the BD EL(T) process. In addition, in the storage and analysis infrastructure layer, data integration can be performed using both the traditional DW and other BD technologies, such as in-memory databases or Hadoop clusters (Passlick, Lebek, & Breitner, 2017). Integration of the Data Lakes with BI is a second method proposed (Llave, 2018). Llave (2018) contends that Data Lakes have enabled BI to acquire data without regard to its structure. It is a tremendous capacity to store inexhaustible quantities of unprocessed data without data transformation. Data transformation is regarded as a bottleneck in ETL processes between data sources and data warehouses. Therefore, it is comparable to ELT, in which the transformation occurs in the final stage (Llave, 2018). The concept of data monetization has evolved significantly from the BI era to the BD era (Faroukhi, El Alaoui, Gahi, and Amine, 2020). Data monetization is a novel concept based on using an organization's data to generate profit. Explicit data monetization is the direct sale or sharing of data, whereas implicit data monetization is the indirect use of data to create value by improving one's own data-based products (Faroukhi, El Alaoui, Gahi, and Amine, 2020). During the era of business intelligence, data monetization was typically implicit and delivered by descriptive analytics. Typically, production data was utilized for internal purposes. During the BD era, data monetization gained in prominence and significance. In the era of BD, data monetization is becoming more appealing (Faroukhi, El Alaoui, Gahi, & Amine, 2020). The integration of external and internal data sources produces advanced analytical capabilities based on data-driven goods and services. This enables explicit data monetization and provides the agility necessary for creating and monetizing knowledge. Faroukhi et al. (2020) argue that monetizing BD can be articulated based on the following business model directions: extracting customer-based activities data (data extractors), collecting and selling data (data providers), aggregating services (data aggregators), and providing technical platforms that enable data processing, consumption, and sharing (technical platform providers). Monetizing BD enables companies to unleash value and maximize data-driven capability (Faroukhi, El Alaoui, Gahhi, and Amine, 2020).

The installed base, IT-centric systems are being supplemented, continuing a six-year trend. They were frequently relocated throughout 2014 for fresh deployments. Additionally, this is raising IT's issues with and demands for governance as deployments grow. The main objective of is to reach a wider range of people and use cases. Traditional BI platform providers have made a lot of effort to the market's requirements by providing their own capabilities for business users to drive data discovery and appealing by bundling and integrating it with the rest of their pile. However, their products have only been shoddy imitations. Their abilities could help them stand out and encourage adoption, but these options are still under development (for illustration, IBM Watson Analytics and SAP Lumira).

Additionally, organizations have integrated independent software vendors dashboards, interactive analysis, and traditional reporting business apps or processes. Furthermore, using more sophisticated and prescriptive analytics from the known statistical formulas and techniques, applications for analytics using the BI platform is implemented. This will produce missing insights to a larger group of analytics' users superior analytical abilities. As businesses adopt a more bimodal and decentralized controlled approach to data discovery for BI, and access to self-service capabilities by business users is also required by analysts. Beyond interactive visualization of data sources that have been selected by IT, this includes access to sophisticated, yet tools for data preparation that are usable by business users. Business Users seek out quicker and simpler methods to find important information.

As a result, business intelligence and analytics suppliers provide self-service data preparation (together with a number of firms such as ClearStory Data, Paxata, and Trifacta and Tamr), as well as clever data discovery and pattern recognition capabilities (an area in which are firms such as BeyondCore and DataRPM) to handle these increasing requirements and to create market distinctiveness. The intention is to broaden the usage of analytics, particularly advanced analytics insight, to a diverse group of consumers and non-traditional BI users, Mobile devices and cloud deployment are becoming increasingly popular. Interest in cloud BI fell marginally in 2015, to 42% in comparison to 45% a year before – of consumer survey responders, some are (28%) or plan to deploy (14%) BI in some kind of private, public, or hybrid cloud (Ruzgas & Bagdonavičienė, 2017). The focus has shifted to private clouds. As data gravity shifts to the cloud, and interest in putting BI on the cloud grows, Salesforce Analytics Cloud, for example, is a new market entry. On-premises cloud BI companies and cloud BI offers Vendors, that are rising to satisfy this need and provide more services.

Buyers of BI and analytics tools have several alternatives. While the majority BI suppliers now have a cloud strategy, as do many BI and analytics leaders. There is no plan for combining analytics activities, and link cloud services with their on-premises systems capabilities. Furthermore, businesses are increasingly investing in analytics. There are applications that make use of new multi-structured data sources that are both within and external to the organization and saved in the cloud and on-premises to undertake new sorts of experiments such as location analytics, sentiment analysis, and graph analysis analytics. The desire for direct access to multi-structured and streaming data paired with interactive visualization, early adopters are mostly responsible for exploring capabilities, as there exist more significant platform features.

The second group of literature delves into the application of Big Data Analytics (BDA) in organizational settings, specifically in enhancing the performance of firms within particular business domains (Akter et al., 2016). Researches that provide evidence for BDA have identified various dimensions of organizational performance (Mikalef et al., 2018; Wamba et al., 2017; Wang & Hajli, 2017; kwon et al., 2014; Kim & Park, 2017). A further investigation has been conducted on Big Data Analytics (BDA) with the aim of enhancing the efficacy of data utilization and decision-support capabilities. The development of Big data analytics capability (BDAC) for enhancing managerial decision-making processes was elucidated by the author in (Popovic et al., 2018), while (jha et al., 2020) performed a thematic analysis of 15 firms to ascertain the factors associated with the successful development of BDA capability in the context of supply chain management.

In order to facilitate decision-making for organizational expansion, it is imperative to establish efficient procedures that encompass ongoing assessment, strategic planning, and the execution and assessment of Big Data Analytics. According to Lewin's Organizational Development (OD) theory, the objective of processes is to impart knowledge and skills to an organization, primarily to enhance its problem-solving capabilities and effectively manage future changes.

According to Beckhard's definition (Beckhard, 1972), Organizational Development (OD) pertains to the internal workings of an organization, wherein a group of individuals collaborates to enhance the organization's effectiveness, capability, work performance, and adaptability to cultural, policy, practice, and procedural changes. According to scholarly literature, OD refers to the comprehensive implementation and utilization of behavioral science knowledge in order to facilitate the deliberate advancement, enhancement, and fortification of the tactics, frameworks, and procedures that culminate in organizational efficacy (Cummings & Worley, 2009). This approach encompasses three fundamental components, namely organizational climate, culture, and capability (Glanz, 2008). The concept of organizational climate pertains to the distinctive personality or mood of an organization, as per the definition provided by paper (Glanz, 2008). This encompasses the collective perceptions of the policies, practices, and procedures in place, as well as various climate features such as leadership, communication, participative management, and role clarity. The concept of organizational culture pertains to a collective set of fundamental assumptions, values, norms, behavioral patterns, and artefacts. As defined by paper (Shein, 1985), it refers to a discernible arrangement of shared basic assumptions that a group has acquired through addressing issues of external adaptation and internal integration. The concept of organizational capacity (OC) pertains to the operational aspects of an organization, including the production of goods or ser-

Figure 7. A traditional business intelligence system

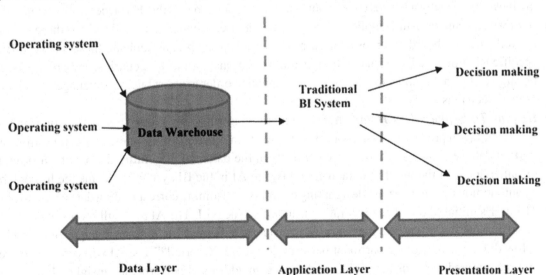

vices and the maintenance of organizational functions. It is comprised of four key components, namely resource acquisition, organization structure, production subsystem, and accomplishment, as outlined in previous research (Prestby & Wandersman, 1985). The capacity of an organization to operate effectively is influenced by its organizational culture and climate.

As a result of the market dynamics, Gartner's Magic Quadrant classifies BI and analytics as a software platform that provides thirteen important skills across three categories (to facilitate, create, and consume) in four BI and analytics use scenarios. These skills aid in the creation of an analytics portfolio that maps to moving obligations from IT to the business. From insight distribution to the analytics customer through an API IT frequently deploys an information portal centrally to an organization. Analysts who require interactive analytics workstation and sophisticated data exploration skills (Tapadinhas, 2014), enable BI executives to support a variety of roles and examples from system-of-record reporting and analytics applications to decentralized self-service data discovery. Figure 7 shows a traditional Business Intelligence system.

The Role of Artificial Intelligence and Machine Learning in Business Intelligence and Big Data Analytics

In this section, how BI's AI elevates and improves an organization's analysis and interpretation of its business' lifeblood will be examined.

1. *Transforming Business Users into Data Professionals:* Business analysts (BA) and IT officials typically control data access and interpretation. Despite the fact that these occupations are essential. Users of NLIs are no longer reliant on data science specialists to analyze their data, as modern BI tools, including LOB, contain AI tools. In order to "democratize" data, AI enables users to obtain immediate, actionable answers. In other words, it enables users to have a two-way communication with their data and to feel empowered to act with trustworthy responses. Here is an illustration of how AI operates in practice: A company is deploying a BI solution that employs an advanced NLI and Instead of relying on system administrators or data scientists to analyze data, the manager of a business unit directly accesses the BI solution. The manager makes the data accessible via telephone or download and uses uncomplicated language. The user then receives insight into these queries, as well as a dashboard and presentation-ready visuals to help communicate these answers. Even specific BI duties, such as visualization recommendations, "what-if" scenarios, and prognosis, can be targeted by an AI model that has been pre-trained in order to assist business managers in making crucial decisions.

2. *Helping To Explore Your Data:* There is something intrinsically gratifying about exploring your data with the appropriate AI-supported instrument. In a matter of minutes, you can go from importing data sets to uncovering concealed facts in the data and presenting the results in stunning visualizations. At the onset of data availability, the AI in the BI system performs the heavy labor by autonomously categorizing, designating columns, and joining corresponding data across groups. The user's initial step in data exploration is to access the NLI. The AI tool will propose potentially beneficial queries if you become confused. You can also begin with fundamental questions, such as "How did the retail store department perform during the X-period?" The AI will provide answers and recommend methods for exploring data to gain additional performance insights. Exploration is thrilling because you can continue to venture deeper into visions that can only be achieved by

artificial intelligence. What embodies the user's imagination is imagination. Visualizations are an integral component of all modern BI solutions; however, with AI-enabled AI solutions, users receive suggested, automated visualizations that best correspond to the answers to their queries.

3. *Modern Business Intelligence:* The more the user interacts with the BI tool, the better the AI will understand the user's presentation and analysis preferences. If the user routinely utilizes forecast data, the system will begin preparing and presenting the prediction model data via dashboards.

4. *Automatically Cleaning and Preparing Data:* To effectively interpret your data, it must be unified and searchable. Multiple datasets, as any business well knows, cause multiple difficulties. What if names are formatted in one spreadsheet as first name/last name and in another as last name/first name? What if duplicate records exist? What if one dataset contains records and the other does not? What if one set contains daily data and the other contains monthly data?

AI in BI reduces the amount of time spent on data purification and contact preparation, and provides enormous pain relief. By autonomously configuring data (one of the greatest time-saving applications of artificial intelligence), you can go from making data accessible to interacting with it in minutes, as opposed to hours or days. The future AI function will enable users to input both structured and unstructured data without missing a beat; a significant improvement given that the majority of data created today, including photos, videos, and audio, is unstructured. The advanced AI in BI tool assists users who are not data scientists in accessing and interpreting their data by, among other things, removing barriers to effective analysis.

5. *Gaining Competitive Advantage:* AI now makes a significant distinction between companies that enable its success and those who will soon be left behind. Gartner predicts that by 2021, 75% of pre-prepared reports, such as those used to extract data, will be supplanted by automated insights or enhanced by them. The robust AI in BI tools also improves the precision of reporting for crucial operational use. If they do not, data and analytics executives should promptly implement Enhanced Analyses (AI) in their businesses as the platform's capabilities mature. AI are currently available in BI solutions, and companies that adopt technology are more likely to succeed than those that do not. AI saves time and provides actionable insights to increase profitability and prevent potential problems by identifying trends and correlations in data, proposing ways to interpret results in natural language, and providing the best coordination for presenting these results.

The Impact of Business Intelligence and Big Data Analytics on Decision Making Processes and Organizational Performance

The driving force of artificial intelligence systems is machine learning. It improves models of artificial intelligence by analyzing large data sets. Machine learning improves models by analyzing complex data sets using a set of principles that it has automatically acquired.

The machine learning model learns from large amounts of data and frequent human interactions in order to provide information and answers pertinent to the user's interests or objectives. Big data refer to very enormous data collections, data that can be mathematically analyzed to disclose patterns, trends, and correlations, particularly pertaining to human behavior and interactions. Deep learning represents a substantial technological advance in the field of artificial intelligence. Programmers compose a code that instructs a device on how to interpret a sequence of words, images, or commands in order to reach a conclusion and execute an order.

The end-user then enters the data, while internal engineers may define more specific criteria for interpreting and analyzing the data. Finally, the system generates outputs (analysis) based on the inputs and principles specified. The authors of (Fahad & Alam, 2016) proposed a demand-forecasting model based on BI and machine learning.

Therefore, it is evident from the discussion that data management and big data analytics (Wael et al., 2013) are crucial to BI for the following four reasons:

Better decision making: Big data analytics can analyze current and historical data to make future predictions. Thus, businesses can not only make better judgements in the present, but also prepare for the future. Big data technologies, such as cloud-based analytics and Hadoop, offer significant cost savings when storing large data volumes. Moreover, they provided insight into the influence of numerous variables.

New products and services: With the ability to measure customer requirements and satisfaction via analytics, the strength lies in providing customers with what they desire. Therefore, more businesses are developing new products and services to satisfy customer demands.

Comprehend the market environment: By analyzing large amounts of data, we can gain a deeper understanding of current market conditions in order to retrieve vital information. In addition, the tools and techniques of Big data analytics must account for a number of characteristics and challenges, including scalability and defect tolerance (Kaisler et al., 2013; Zhou et al., 2014; Sivarajah et al., 2017).

The accelerated growth of business intelligence and analysis piqued the interest of scholars. As data increases exponentially, organizations can no longer rely on traditional technologies. This enormous volume of data necessitates the application of sophisticated analytic techniques in order to convert it into information that promotes organizational growth. BI&A is the modern methodology for extracting value from these enormous quantities of data, influencing strategic decision-making, and forecasting and capitalizing on future opportunities.

BI&A is required in the majority of organizations. BI&A has proven to be an effective decision-making aid. In addition, data and IT infrastructure are visibly impacted by the effective application of BI&A practices. Due to their value and benefits, business intelligence and analysis now play a crucial role in the majority of institutions and industries. BI&A assists organizations in gaining a better understanding of their confidential data, thereby enhancing fact-based decision-making. In addition to resolving technical and quality issues that will improve the performance and productivity of businesses (Lautenbach et al., 2017; Wang et al., 2019), these methodologies and data analyses also aid in maintaining a competitive advantage.

The Role of GIS in Business Intelligence and Big Data Analytics

The projected growth of the global market for geospatial data analytics is expected to be substantial, with an estimated increase from $69.9 billion in 2018 to $88.3 billion in 2020. In the given context, the revenue generated from geospatial analytics in the year 2018 can be considered through matched with the global market for Software-as-a-Service (SaaS), which amounted to $73.6 billion. It is worth noting that the SaaS market is considerably more established and encompasses a wider array of software offerings. With advancements in technology and a deeper understanding of analytics within organizations, this section aims to present a comprehensive overview of three disciplines and their potential applications of big data in Geographic Information Systems (GIS).

1.   GIS and Big Data facilitate humanitarian projects

The utilization of Geographic Information Systems (GIS) in conjunction with Big Data has proven to be instrumental in advancing humanitarian initiatives.

Geographic Information Systems (GIS) refer to a comprehensive system comprising a set of computational programs that integrate data, tools, and individuals to facilitate the aggregation, storage, retrieval, manipulation, visualization, and analysis of spatially referenced data (Li, 2016). This tool has the potential to serve as a cartographic instrument, a tool for spatial analysis, and a geographic information system. The authorized licensed use is limited to a database that is specifically designed for storing and retrieving spatial information. This database is intended for the purpose of geo-processing, which refers to a set of mathematical and computational techniques used to convert spatial data into meaningful spatial information (Cao, 2016). The process of obtaining geographic data involves the direct observation of the physical environment, and the level of information, accuracy, and precision must align with the objectives of the geographic information generated by the Geographic Information System (GIS). In order to achieve this objective, it is imperative to utilize the relevant scientific disciplines, technologies, methodologies, and instruments (Janelle, 2018).

The Sustainable Development Goals (SDGs) established by the United Nations serve as a comprehensive framework aimed at achieving a more equitable and environmentally sound future for global society. The proliferation of the Internet of Things, the emergence of open data platforms, the utilization of crowdsourced spatial data, and the advancement of big data technology have collectively facilitated the accessibility of an extensive volume of information that can aid nations in the pursuit of the United Nations' Sustainable Development Goals (SDGs). DigitalGlobe, an enterprise specializing in the acquisition of satellite data and its integration with diverse data sources including social media sentiment and aerial imagery, employs a geographic information system (GIS) machine learning algorithm to observe and detect irregularities within targeted areas.

DigitalGlobe is actively engaged in addressing a range of pressing global concerns, including but not limited to global poverty, child trafficking, and disaster response. Nevertheless, the substantial volume of data that operates in the background serves as a cohesive element in all of its undertakings. As of January 2018, the company had amassed nearly 100 petabytes of data, approximately equivalent to 100 million hours of Netflix streaming (or 33 million hours if streamed in high definition).

2.   Marketing Analysis Using Geospatial Data

The application of geospatial analytics in marketing is commonly observed in the practice of prospect or customer segmentation. For example, Under Armour has the ability to utilize data obtained from fitness monitors to categorize their target demographics according to their degree of physical activity. This enables them to strategically distribute promotional materials based on an individual's level of involvement with fitness and their affinity towards the brand.

However, with the increasing integration of spatial data from various sources, the utilization of geospatial analytics by marketers is expected to become more intricate. The utilization of social media platforms for the purpose of monitoring the public perception of a brand within specific geographical regions represents a burgeoning field of study that has garnered considerable attention. In the context of a corporation like Under Armour, the integration of this particular data with insights derived from their fitness tracking data has the potential to yield more precise and focused messaging strategies. This may involve addressing prevalent customer frustrations or aligning product descriptions with customers' actual usage and perceptions.

3. Using Big Data and GIS for Business Intelligence In Financial Services Organizations

The identification of branches to be consolidated has emerged as a prominent utilization of Geographic Information Systems (GIS) within the banking industry. Nevertheless, the integration of Geographic Information Systems (GIS) and big data is becoming more prevalent in order to tackle increasingly intricate problems. In the insurance sector, an effective approach involves integrating weather data with claim data to facilitate the identification of potential instances of fraudulent activity by companies.

Financial services firms, in conjunction with telecommunications companies and the government, are at the forefront of utilizing Geographic Information Systems (GIS) and business intelligence tools in a synergistic manner. The proliferation of startup companies in the financial industry is being facilitated by the utilization of geospatial big data. Numerous financial start-ups within this sector have emphasized their capacity to leverage unconventional data sources, such as satellite imagery, for the purpose of evaluating the prospective risk associated with providing insurance or loans. For example, the utilization of satellite imagery over a specific duration can enhance the precision of predicting the vulnerability of a property to flooding, thereby facilitating the assessment of appropriate insurance premiums.

The Role of Spatial Data for Market Intelligence Using Examples

Spatial intelligence refers to the utilization of data, tools, analysis, and visualization that are specific to particular locations, with the aim of enhancing the process of decision-making. It has the potential to aid governments, businesses, and non-governmental organizations in understanding, controlling, and overseeing their effects on nature, climate, and society.

In the foreseeable future, it is anticipated that businesses will have the capability to effectively trace their complete supply chains to their respective origins. This will enable them to estimate the environmental impacts resulting from their operations and quantify the risks associated with their supply chains.

A recommended initial approach for the private sector involves the identification of three key areas of action: commitment, capability, and collaboration. These areas will be further clarified, accompanied by concrete illustrations of immediate actions that businesses can undertake.

- Nature-positive commitments refer to actions and initiatives that aim to enhance and restore the natural environment, thereby promoting biodiversity, ecosystem health, and sustainable development. These commitments are intended to be integrated with net-zero objectives, which focus on achieving a balance between greenhouse gas emissions and their removal from the atmosphere. Nature-positive commitments need to be combined with net-zero objectives,
- Spatial intelligence is employed to effectively recognize, understand, and track advancements that are contingent upon geographical positioning.
- In order to evaluate progress towards objectives and identify potential hazards and opportunities, it is essential to establish a nature and climate baseline.
- Science-based objectives that are specific to the location should be established and monitored using spatial intelligence techniques.

Example: The disclosure of impacts and dependencies throughout value chains and the reporting of progress using established frameworks are essential components of academic research.

- The integration of spatial intelligence within financial decision-making processes can be employed to optimize funding allocation for initiatives related to integrated nature and climate action.
- A potential avenue for enhancing risk management and environmental, social, and governance (ESG) policies and procedures within enterprises and financial institutions is the integration of spatial intelligence.

Example: Allocate resources towards expanding internal capacity, while another option is to engage in collaborative partnerships with external specialists.

- Identify and rectify any deficiencies in data by collaborating with others to obtain and manage data that is compatible, easily accessible, reliable, and fair.

Example: Actors operating within a particular sector exhibit consensus regarding a predetermined collection of datasets and tools

- they collectively agree to utilize and allocate financial resources towards for the purpose of conducting specific analyses and assessments.

Example: Guarantee that individuals responsible for collecting and distributing data are compensated for their efforts, particularly with regard to the rights of Indigenous peoples and local communities (IPLCs).

- In order to effectively achieve nature and climate objectives, it is advisable to take proactive measures without hesitation. This can be accomplished by utilizing spatial intelligence to identify and execute nature-based solutions in regions where they will have the greatest impact.
- Implement collaborative water stewardship initiatives in specific geographical areas.

Example: Businesses and sector organizations engage in the practice of conducting a gap analysis.

- The researchers identify gaps in data across important metrics and indicators, and subsequently establish agreements with data providers and institutions to facilitate sustained data collection and monitoring efforts at a large scale.
- Financial institutions engage in innovative data collection activities, serving as a prime illustration.

Example: It is imperative to mandate the disclosure of the environmental and climate impacts associated with supply chains.

- It is recommended to allocate resources towards the acquisition of spatial intelligence data and the cultivation of expertise in order to consistently augment the depth and breadth of insights.
- Engage in collaborative efforts with others in order to establish systems that are regarded as respectable, credible, and open, while also conforming to social and cultural norms.

- The objective is to thoroughly utilize existing spatial data and expertise across various business units.
- Individual business units within an organization gather and organize their own spatial data, including information on site locations, environmental impact assessments, and greenhouse gas emissions monitoring. This data is then made available to other business units within the organization.

Example: It is advisable to refrain from obtaining resources from regions with high levels of biodiversity.

- The significance of location is evident in the utilization of spatial intelligence for environmental and climate-related business initiatives.
- Collaborate with local communities to effectively preserve and sustain the well-being of mangrove ecosystems, thereby enabling them to serve as a crucial defense mechanism against the destructive impacts of hurricane surges on coastal communities and associated economic activities.
- Engage in prototype initiatives.

Example: Businesses engage in the exchange of asset-level or location-specific data on a shared platform with the objective of accessing green financing, establishing credibility and transparency, and improving public accessibility to data of superior quality.

Example: The finance industry utilizes spatial data to offer privileged financing opportunities to projects that can effectively showcase positive efforts towards nature and climate through the application of spatial intelligence.

- Collaborate with both public and private sectors, as well as local communities, to promptly implement necessary measures.
- Meaningful and respectful collaboration necessitates the implementation of effective safeguards.

The Potential Risks and Limitations Associated With Business Intelligence and Big Data Analytics

The potential risks and limitations associated with business intelligence and big data analytics can be summarized as follows:

Storage Issue: Knowledge enhances marketing strategy (Katal et al.,2013). Experts argue enormous data is unorganized (Che et al., 2013). Massive data is crucial for company progress. One machine cannot handle many CDs, but cloud storage can be used to solve this situation. Since data is in terabytes and storage space is limited, businesses must determine which data to use and if it is more useful or better reflects the information. Thus, firms require customer-understanding tools and processes.

Management Issue: Unmanaged data is unwelcome. Processing heterogeneous big data demands high performance and complex management. Big data needs structures (Fan et al., 2014), and businesses need scalable data storage. Business people require clean, accurate, full, and evaluated data. Data management comprises cleaning, converting, clarifying, validating, dimension reduction, etc. Business intelligence can handle enormous data sets. Quantum computing and in-memory databases may cut processing expenses. However, outdated technologies may make company relocation costly and time-consuming. Businesses struggle with unmanaged huge data and try to update large data infrastructure.

Process Issue: Today, companies value on-time outcomes. Unsatisfactory, timely outcomes are least useful (Che et al., 2013). Most companies sell online to capture the market. Our equipment, infrastructure, and processes cannot handle such enormous data quantities in real time (Katal et al., 2013). The company must handle several data sources in real time. Many companies use MapReduce for long-running batches. Real-time S4 systems handle massive data. Companies want precise, real-time data processing. Hence, data processing must be improved to be precise and speedy. Data grows from bits to Yottabytes exponentially. Big data analysis requires smart tools and offers economic prospects, businesses must handle the aforementioned issues to compete.

Design/Interactivity: User recommendations, Big data mining, business system designers struggle with interaction. User involvement may find subjects in massive datasets. Marketers can mine huge amount of data, and subspace concentration increases processing speed and scalability. Heterogeneity hampers huge data. Interactivity shows massive data processing and mining outcomes. Also, designers must comprehend thousands of clients' wants to attract outstanding customers, using interfaces, images, conceptual models, and user feedback (Kaisler et al., 2013).

Big Data Issues: Challenges can accompany chances. Big data carries opportunity for society and business but has many obstacles (Chen & Zhang, 2013). Researchers have examined big data challenges such storage, transmission, management, processing, variety, heterogeneity, scalability, velocity, accuracy, privacy, data access and exchange, talent demands, technical or otherwise hardware, and analytical methods. New large data processing methods include Hadoop, Dryad, Apache Spark, and MapReduce. However, high-processing, sophisticated technology for massive data processing demands trained people to manage and administer a company. Big data specialists are naïve and need training. For educated decision-making, there is a need for huge number of data analysts and a lot of managers and trained analysts. Finally, big data analytics' organizations require frameworks, data scientists, and engineers for data architecture and administration to make good decisions. Also, competing companies require skilled data analysts. Big data and business intelligence boosted growth (Manyika et al., 2011).

Loading/Syncing: Data loading integrates many sources (Zaharia et al., 2010). Researchers and practitioners must resolve loading process difficulties, which process huge data should be accessible and offer data quickly. Loading and data source synchronization are difficulties. Big data systems load diverse data sources at different times, and, it may missynchronize. Data sync sources means synchronizing data sources in shared storage. Unsynchronized big data processing systems may provide incorrect mining results owing to inconsistent or faulty data. Commercial success demands data source synchronization. Companies eliminate analysis risks and get reliable results. Businesses struggle to transform and clean data before loading, and analysis (Hashem et al., 2015). Hadoop and MapReduce can handle unstructured data.

Visualization: Big data's volume, scalable methods cannot extract buried data. Researchers focus on enormous data visualization difficulties, but we must prepare for big data issues. Choice graphs show significant data visualization findings (Hashem et al., 2015). Consumer data visualizations are difficult and visual reports are twice as effective as text ones. Tableau, QlikView, and others boost data throughput (Sawant & Shah, 2013).

The Issues and Problems Related to Market Intelligence and Their Solutions

Problem One: Responses from unintended audiences

Accuracy is one of the most important characteristics of a reliable market research study. But what is "accurate" market research, and how can it be incorporated into your efforts? For businesses, market research is considered "accurate" when it includes data that reflects their customers (or target market) and contributes to the success of new campaigns, products, and services. Therefore, it would be disastrous if your market research questions were answered by the incorrect audiences. This is analogous to trying to load a container with water. You would have data after the exercise, but it would be meaningless and contradict the purpose of the research.

Solution to Problem One

The solution for preventing non-targeted respondents from completing a survey is screening queries. There are initial queries whose responses influence who completes the remainder of the survey. They are easy to ask, simple to complete, and have a substantial impact on the integrity of your data. A straightforward query would help you exclude respondents who do not need to continue with the survey, allowing you to continue with those who responded positively. They are your intended audience and can provide the necessary information.

Problem Two: Lack of Data Integrity or Invalid Data

Today's businesses regard market information as a commodity. With readily accessible data on customer preferences and behavior, market researchers can compile enormous data sets to mine for consumer insights. Indeed, a survey of recent market research industry papers reveals that data analysis has been the topic of conversation in the field. The majority of the time, however, the quality of the collected data impedes understanding of what matters most to consumers. Some market researchers equate data quality with sample size, believing that reliability, validity, and other "excellent measurement" characteristics result solely from the quantity of collected data. Obviously, this is not the situation.

Solution to Problem Two

Failure to evaluate the metrics that serve as the foundation for business decisions poses a substantial threat to the organization. Similarly, making data-driven decisions based on insufficient measurements can be significantly worse than taking no action at all. In order to acquire sufficient data, researchers must adhere to the predetermined demographic and psychometric evaluations of target respondents. This is to guarantee that survey respondents provide business-relevant insights. Data auditing and cleansing must also be taken seriously by researchers, as they have a significant impact on the integrity of the available data. In addition, research facilitated by AI can determine the precise IP addresses of respondents. This is to ensure that valid data is collected from the precise location/respondents you desire to target.

Problem Three: The Length of Time Required to Complete the Survey is Lengthy

Long questionnaires are fairly common. However, they have a negative impact on response rate, abandonment rate, sample representativeness, and data quality, which all have a negative effect on response rate. Every researcher wants to include all required survey questions and collect meaningful, compelling data. 60% of respondents do not desire to complete a survey that takes longer than 10 minutes, according to a study. If your survey takes too long, the implementation of data analysis, which is the purpose of the exercise, may be severely impacted. This may result in the accumulation of irrelevant data by day's end.

Solution to Problem Three

You can abbreviate the survey period and reach the deadline for data implementation due to technological advancements. The solution to the time-consuming nature of survey completion is to employ research specialists who can provide custom survey platforms. These platforms utilize mobile technology and permit the formulation of queries within one to two days. Moreover, as soon as the survey questions are published, you can begin observing insights in real time.

Problem Four: Your Surveys Are Administered by Unqualified Moderators or Facilitators

It is untenable to have incompetent moderators or facilitators administer your surveys. They are a nuisance for a market research project's success. Your survey facilitators/moderators have a substantial impact on the data that will result from your survey project, especially when the survey is conducted offline with illiterate or semi-literate respondents. Therefore, if they do not know what they are doing, they will undermine the entire activity, resulting in no duties being completed.

Solution to Problem Four

It is essential to provide personnel with the necessary instruments for success as well as ongoing training and recertification. For this reason, businesses must evaluate the market research teams they entrust with such a crucial responsibility. Employing a market research "expert" is not a decision that should be made carelessly. For optimal results, businesses must employ the finest market research firm. Offline facilitators and moderators are vital to the success or failure of a research endeavor. Therefore, they must be affable and skilled at obtaining information from responders in a professional manner. They have one-on-one conversations with respondents, who view them as brand ambassadors. Therefore, these significant parties must maintain their professionalism.

Problem Five: Not Asking Your Target Audiences In-Depth Follow-Up Questions

Expert researchers are the only ones who perceive the significance of and can effectively negotiate follow-up inquiries. Some researchers simply stick to the script, limiting the insights they are able to discern despite the fact that the respondent may be willing to share additional information. This diminishes the quality of Psychometric data that a researcher can collect.

Solution to Problem Five

After posing a query, follow-up inquiries should be posed based on the responses of the respondents. This will enable them to divulge concealed information that the researcher may overlook. The knowledgeable moderators will ask the appropriate follow-up question(s) to improve the quality of the insights you gain from your research project. This procedure, however straightforward it may appear, can only be carried out by industry experts. This is yet another reason why you must collaborate with people who have extensive survey experience.

In conclusion, business proprietors frequently form mental images of their markets. They believe they grasp the circumstance superior to any external. However, their individual and superficial research is replete with errors and inconsistencies. Consequently, the demand for market research services has grown substantially. Utilizing market research firms for problem identification and resolution is crucial for distinguishing out in the targeted industry. Additionally, you should always categorize your organization's problems before attempting to resolve them. Otherwise, you risk wasting vital resources on the incorrect problem (survey, 2023).

Case Studies to Illustrate Trends in Market Intelligence

The employment of big data and quantitative data analysis are commonly cited as prominent marketing strategies in contemporary business discourse. Several highly prosperous enterprises have established their business model on the basis of quantitative data analysis, encompassing numerical figures, computations, and algorithms.

The utilization of quantitative data analysis is prevalent to the extent that encountering a brand that does not employ it is an infrequent occurrence. Netflix is an example of a corporation that has leveraged data analysis to attain significant accomplishments.

Netflix acquires substantial quantities of data from its vast number of subscribers. The organization gathers information pertaining to the temporal aspects of users' viewing habits, such as the specific dates and times during which they engage with various shows. Additionally, the company records the genres or categories of programming that users consume, as well as the duration of time that they allocate to these viewing sessions. The aforementioned data is utilized to generate personalized suggestions for users, in addition to tailored promotional materials and sneak peeks of fresh content.

The utilization of quantitative data analysis has resulted in a remarkable customer retention rate for Netflix. The customer recommendation system that relies on data analysis is responsible for more than 80 percent of the streamed content. Netflix is considered to be one of the most valuable brands globally, with a net worth calculated by tens of billion dollars. The aforementioned numerical values are solely achievable through the utilization of quantitative data.

Another case study, Netscribes is a global data and insights company that satisfies the sales, marketing, product development, and innovation requirements of some of the world's largest organizations and assists them in adapting to market and technological shifts.

An international conglomerate that provides reinsurance solutions is renowned for its risk management expertise, innovative solutions, and exceptional client service. It partnered with Netscribes company to identify the fundamental causes of financial insecurity and the obstacles to accessing financial protection products. Assessing the economic, social, technological, and demographic factors that impeded access to high-quality financial protection products, the company sought to resolve these obstacles.

Safety is a top priority for all organizations, particularly the prestigious Fortune 500. Recognizing the importance of safety index and its impact on company performance, a leading enterprise sought to conduct a comprehensive market landscape analysis of safety practices among Fortune 500 firms. Recognizing the need to compare their safety standards to those of industry leaders, they collaborated with another company to conduct a comprehensive market research study. This exhaustive analysis cast light on critical factors including safety protocols, regulatory compliance, incident management, and more.

Netscribes company partnered with a global leader in information technology-enabled services (ITeS) to undertake a comprehensive market research study on the adoption of AI in the UK cyber insurance and security market. The objective was to assess the prospective scale of the market and analyze the prevalent trends, drivers, and obstacles in this segment.

The insights provided the client company with valuable information about the market landscape, including key actors and their products, to assist them in making strategic decisions. The market intelligence study assisted the client company in keeping abreast of the most recent advancements and emergent AI trends in the cyber insurance and security market, thereby positioning them for success in the competitive landscape. (netscribes, 2023)

Advantages of Market Intelligence

Market intelligence not only assists organizations in distinguishing their brand from competitors, but also in supplying essential information to stay in the game and improve at it. The following are some of the advantages that market intelligence gives. A comprehensive understanding of the market may propel a firm to success quickly. Market intelligence is the process of acquiring data from the market in real time and better understanding consumers, trends, behaviors, and so on, allowing a firm to stay competitive and satisfy market needs.

Customer retention - No matter how long a customer has been with a firm, they are always monitored and assaulted by the competitors. Understanding when a consumer is unsatisfied and the reasons for their dissatisfaction might help you avoid losing business. Market intelligence may assist you analyze and get insights into the areas of change that consumers require, allowing you to retain them and understand customer lifetime value.

Improve sales process - Businesses with a range of goods and a big number of clients frequently confront a dilemma, namely, which product to market to which groups? Market intelligence assists in determining market segmentation, allowing the organization to understand which product will succeed with which set of individuals.

Increase process efficiency - Market intelligence assists firms in increasing overall efficiency and productivity by detecting gaps, providing actionable insights to design critical strategies, and providing an organization with real-time data and analytics.

Gives a competitive edge - The phrase "first mover advantage" or "launching a product at the right time" is commonly used in business circles. These are only achievable with the use of market information. Market intelligence allows you to keep an eye on the competition, upcoming trends, and provides a complete picture of the market, allowing a company to penetrate or capture market share by launching a product or a new feature at the right time, giving them a competitive advantage.

Importance of Market Intelligence for Businesses

Market intelligence refers to information accumulated by a company about the market in which it operates or desires to operate. This information assists the company in identifying its target market segment, market penetration, and total opportunity. Marketing intelligence includes competitor intelligence, which concentrates on information about a company's specific competitors. This data may assist executives in making informed business decisions by indicating current market share, price levels, and consumer behavior. Market intelligence and business intelligence are very distinct.

Market intelligence provides businesses with a comprehensive understanding of their target market. In contrast, business intelligence pertains to internal data such as productivity, corporate sales, procedures, and other comparable data. Integrating market intelligence and business intelligence provides executives with a more comprehensive view of their target market.

For instance, a company must determine the best demographic target for a soon-to-be-released mobile phone. Based on the type of mobile device being released, a profiling survey can assist a business in narrowing its target demographic. For instance, if the phone's colors and features are designed to advertise it as a mobile gaming device, a survey will target individuals who appreciate gaming, are younger, and have a specific income level. This data enables the company to focus its efforts on the appropriate individuals, thereby saving money and time.

Market intelligence is essential to the success of any organization since it serves as the foundation for all marketing. The effective use of market intelligence include data gathering, analysis, and information application. Market intelligence allows you to become more customer-centric, understand market demands and consumer perspectives, collect real-time relevant data, increase upselling chances, decrease risks, grab larger market shares, and gain a competitive edge. These advantages are critical to the success of any organization, and hence market intelligence is one of the most important factors in implementing efficient plans for the profitability of any firm.

- Market intelligence can answer the following questions:
- What is the company's position in the market?
- Who are your target consumers? What are their requirements?
- Who are your primary competitors? What methods do they employ to entice new customers?
- How can your products be improved?
- How can launching new products or services generate profits for a business?
- What potential obstacles may arise in the future? How can we avoid these obstructions?

When a business discovers the answers to all of these questions, it will either modify its existing business strategies or develop new plans to ensure its success. The following are a few examples of why market information is essential for any organization.

- *To better grasp your market position* - Using surveys to gather market information helps you to have a thorough understanding of the market. It will inform you about what your rivals are doing, what the market demand is, and who your target audience will be, among other things. Analyzing this data will allow a firm to analyze its market position and develop appropriate plans.

- *To assess your product -* Marketing intelligence surveys can provide you with practical data into market product trends, demand for certain features, and product specifications. This information enables you to analyze your goods and make sound business decisions.
- *To know your market targe*t - Gathering market information will enable a firm to understand the demands of the audience, and through surveys, companies may shortlist their target demographic for specific products/services.
- *To perform competitive analysis* - Market intelligence is a huge field. In today's business world, conducting surveys to acquire intelligence about your competition is critical. Businesses may use this information to alter their goods as needed, understand rivals' failures and achievements, and design strategies depending on the competitor's position.

Ethical Issues Related to Market Intelligence

There are several possible ethical concerns in market intelligence. Every day, individuals exchange personal information via social media, workplace databases, and mobile devices. So, how can businesses ensure that they make ethical judgements when dealing with such huge amounts of research data? Marketers must weigh the advantages of having access to this data with the privacy and concern of all persons they may affect. Companies are hacked, personal information is shared or sold, and advertising is disguised as study. Each of these is potentially immoral.

Misleading Practices

First, consider various misleading practices that may be carried out via study. The first is to portray something as research when it is really an effort to promote a product. This is known as sugging. Suggesting occurs when a person identifies as a researcher, obtains data, and then utilizes the data to recommend certain products. Researchers should always separate product marketing from the research process, according to the Insights Association Code of Marketing Research Standards.

Other deceptive research practices include using persuasive language to encourage a participant to select a specific answer, presenting research data subjectively rather than objectively, and padding research data with fabricated answers to increase response rate or create a specific outcome.

Privacy Invasion

When it comes to marketing research data, another problem is privacy. For researchers, privacy means keeping study participants' data private and secret. Many participants are cautious to provide identifying information for fear of it leaking, being linked back to them personally, or being exploited to steal their identity. Researchers might identify the study as secret or anonymous to assist respondents overcome these fears.

When respondents give their identifying information with the researcher, the researcher does not share it with anyone else. In this case, the study may need an identification to match existing information with new stuff, such as a customer number or membership number. Anonymous data is obtained when a responder does not disclose any identifying information and hence cannot be identified. Personal information should always be kept behind a firewall, behind a password-protected screen, or physically locked away by researchers.

Confidentiality Breach

The issue of confidentiality of respondents' information is one of the most critical ethical concerns for market intelligence. Very personal information may be obtained in order to have a rich data collection of information. It is a violation of confidentiality when a researcher utilizes such knowledge unethically. Many research projects begin with a statement on how the respondent's information will be used and how the researcher will keep the information secret. Companies may sell personal information, exchange respondents' contact information, or link particular responses to a responder. All of them are violations of confidentiality for which researchers are held liable. (Openstax, 2023)

Limitations of Market Intelligence

Tracking markets and competitors is hard. Many MI practitioners struggle with data quality, organizational buy-in, and fast analysis and action. Five key issues facing MI workers this year.

Data Source Accuracy: Respondents struggled to "find the right and accurate information" to assess and interact with colleagues. MI personnel struggle to collect trustworthy data and stay "on top of numerous sources of info and data." Market activity and "handling 'hearsay' intel collected in the field" are ongoing issues. Track rivals' digital footprints. Use technology to automatically gather, arrange, and prioritize critical updates.

Data accuracy and timeliness: MI employees struggle. "Sometimes by the time we see it, it's already changed," making data fresh challenging. "Not enough real-time data" and "lots of people do small slices of it and it's hard to communicate findings in a timely way" were highlighted.

Automatically get MI data. Manual research gives obsolete data and limited time for analysis. Automate competitor monitoring and integrate real-time data with battlecards, opponent profiles, and customizable email alerts. Finally, combine field and automated competitive intelligence data.

Internal Buy-In: MI practitioners struggle to acquire data and convince colleagues to endorse their plan. Integration within the MI plan, "buy-in from the whole organization," and "internal acceptance" were challenges. MI "operates in a siloed environment," making corporate engagement hard. "Getting everyone on the same page" is crucial to using information. Internal buy-in links MI with department goals.

Intelligence Distribution: After buy-in, tell MI stakeholders. "Information and engagement" and "not enough visibility across the organization" were mentioned. "Developing battle cards and facilitating the sharing of competitive insights" using MI resources makes intel distribution harder.

MI drives more than information: Motivate the firm. "Getting actionable insights" and "translating intel into useful and impactful resources" were top problems. MI personnel struggle to "turn our research findings into actionable, bottom-line drivers." Need to focus on the "so what" and "what now" after collecting competitive knowledge. Do new competitive campaigns necessitate new messaging? Should a competitor's product investment trend effect your roadmap? Finally, rapidly share these findings with the right individuals so the company can act on them.

Forward Looking Perspective by Discussing Future Trends and Developments in The Field

Regarding how data and intelligence are collated, organized, disseminated, and analyzed to produce actionable insights, market intelligence must be reexamined for the next five years. Questions like How intelligence is delivered? Is the content interactive? Questions of increasing significance include: Does it enable collaboration and subsequent cohesive action based on the insight's delivery?

How does this empower and align the next generation of intelligence specialists? This is yet another question of crucial importance.

These requests from the new intelligence experience necessitate a substantial drive for a more inclusive, yet highly proactive, intelligent intelligence experience. Incorporating diverse perspectives, experiences, and origins into the research and analysis process, therefore employing a more inclusive and proactive market intelligence, satisfies these demands. This indicates that dynamic, ambitious, and forward-thinking topics must be covered. Tools used to gather and organize intelligence need to be more efficient. The veracity of the information and its predictive abilities are crucial, including the elimination of any bias that could have gone into building the artificial intelligence in some of these tools. Where inclusive market intelligence is the process of contemplating and integrating diverse perspectives, experiences, and origins in research and analysis.

In 2023, the top management of market research and consulting firms predicts that these challenges will result in a shift in the future delivery of market intelligence.

No longer are market intelligence and strategic recommendations based on actionable insights an investment based on return on investment (ROI). They are now a matter of survival and a factor of hygiene. The new intelligence experience should focus on analyzing data through an inclusive lens to unearth previously unnoticed market opportunities and insights and to gain a deeper understanding of their consumers and the market, leading to more effective decision-making and innovation.

In conclusion, current market signals and challenges suggest that future industry trends will necessitate a hyper-personalized, solution-focused future for MI in 2030. Contributing to the validation of conclusions and answering follow-up inquiries. While strategic technology and partnerships navigate data protection and innovation in market intelligence, market intelligence in 2030 will be transformed by the integration of advanced technologies such as natural language processing, predictive analytics, visualization tools, virtual reality, augmented reality, IoT, and blockchain. These technologies will enable organizations to gain a deeper understanding of the market, make more informed decisions, and stay ahead of the competition. The new intelligence will be an active-seeking, solution-based, actionable insight engine that delivers micro deliverables that are both predictive and prescriptive. Organizations that flourish on curiosity and view the proper intelligence as a superpower must embrace this new intelligence.

(The Future of Market intelligence, 2023)

CONCLUSION

Market intelligence has adopted Big data analytics as a disruptive technology that will revolutionize it, as it relies on Big data analytics to obtain business insights for improved decision-making. It is vital to discuss the Big data analytics environment from a market standpoint. "Marketing Intelligence for Top Management," MI and its more broad moniker, marketing intelligence, were originally designed to provide analyzed, trustworthy, and consistent information so that an organization could set policies and make business choices more effectively. Different ways are utilized to deploy MI depending on how an organization sees it. MI is made up of three key activities: data collection, data analysis, and data activation. The basis upon which organizations model MI is based on four steps: collection, validation, processing, and communication. Throughout the processes, data mining techniques are used to aid in the collecting and analysis of returning data and information. MI is a continuous activity that companies must assess in order to improve their strategic and tactical marketing initiatives.

These procedures include data collection, validation, processing, and transmission. Depending on an organization's financial capacity, many forms of MI data are gathered. Sources of data and information are characterized as qualitative, quantitative, formal, informal, published, or unpublished. Data may be obtained in a variety of ways, including internal intelligence gathering, external intelligence gathering, open-source intelligence, and other forms. The gathered data must be analyzed in order to be converted into meaningful intelligence. Market intelligence software is available in a variety of formats. This type of software allows you to collect data and analyze it using cutting-edge analytical techniques. There are several market intelligence kinds and procedures available, including questionnaires, surveys, observations, and others. In the viewpoint of the decision maker, the relevance of big data stems from its ability to supply important knowledge and facts on which to base decisions. The management decision-making process has gotten a lot of attention. The market for BI and analytics systems is undergoing fundamental change. In the preceding ten years, the majority of BI platform expenditures have gone towards IT-led consolidation and initiatives to standardize vast record reporting systems. Customer retention, improved sales processes, a competitive advantage, and other benefits are provided by market intelligence. Market intelligence is critical to every organization's success since it serves as the foundation for all marketing. Data collection, analysis, and information application are all important components of efficient market intelligence usage. Big data analytics has been discovered to present wide vistas of opportunity in a variety of applications and domains, including consumer intelligence, fraud detection, and supply chain management. Furthermore, its benefits may be applied to a variety of sectors and businesses, including healthcare, retail, telecommunications, manufacturing, and so on.

REFERENCES

Ahmad, W., & Quadri, B. S. M. K. (2015). Big Data promises value: Is hardware technology taken onboard? *Industrial Management & Data Systems, 115*(9).

Akter, S., Wamba, S. F., Gunasekaran, A., Dubey, R., & Childe, S. J. (2016). How to improve firm performance using big data analytics capability and business strategy alignment? *International Journal of Production Economics, 182*, 113–131. doi:10.1016/j.ijpe.2016.08.018

Alnoukari, M., & Hanano, A. (2017). Integration of business intelligence with corporate strategic management. *Journal of Intelligence Studies in Business, 7*(2), 5–16. doi:10.37380/jisib.v7i2.235

Beckhard, R. (1972). Organizational issues in the team delivery of comprehensive health care. *The Milbank Memorial Fund Quarterly, 50*(3), 287–316. doi:10.2307/3349351 PMID:5043084

Cao, Z. (2016). *Improving the accuracy and the efficiency of geo-processing through a combinative geo-computation approach* [Doctoral dissertation, UCL University College London].

Che, D., Safran, M., & Peng, Z. (2013). From big data to big data mining: challenges, issues, and opportunities. In *Database Systems for Advanced Applications* (pp. 1–15). Springer. doi:10.1007/978-3-642-40270-8_1

Chen, C. P., & Zhang, C. Y. (2013). *Data-intensive applications, challenges, techniques and technologies: A survey on big data.* IEEE.

Chu, V. W., Wong, R. K., Chi, C.-H., Zhou, W., & Ho, I. (2017). The Design of a Cloud-Based Tracker Platform based on system-of-systems service architecture. *Information Systems Frontiers, 19*(6), 1283–1299. doi:10.100710796-017-9768-9

Cummings, T. G., & Worley, C. G. (2009). Organization development and change. 8th ed. Mason: Thompson South-Western.

Davenport, T. H. (2014). How strategists use 'big data' to support internal business decisions, discovery and production. *Strategy and Leadership, 42*(4), 45–50. doi:10.1108/SL-05-2014-0034

Egan, M. P. (2001). Conclusion: Governance and Market-Building. In *Constructing a European Market* (pp. 260–272). Oxford University Press. doi:10.1093/0199244057.003.0011

Entrepreneur. (2023). Why Both Quantitative and Qualitative Data Are Vital for Results-Driven Businesses. *Entrepreneur.* https://www.entrepreneur.com/science-technology/why-both-quantitative-and-qualitative-data-are-vital-for/361314

Erevelles, S., Fukawa, N., & Swayne, L. (2016). Big Data consumer analytics and the transformation of marketing. *Journal of Business Research, 69*(2), 897–904. doi:10.1016/j.jbusres.2015.07.001

Fahad, S. A., & Alam, M. M. A. (2016). modified K-means algorithm for big data clustering. *International Journal of Computer Science and Engineering Technology, 6*(4), 129–132.

Fan, J., Han, F., & Liu, H. (2014). Challenges of big data analysis. *National Science Review, 1*(2), 293–314. doi:10.1093/nsr/nwt032 PMID:25419469

Faroukhi, A. Z., El Alaoui, I., Gahi, Y., & Amine, A. (2020). Big data monetization throughout Big Data Value Chain: A comprehensive review. *Journal of Big Data, 7*(1), 3. doi:10.118640537-019-0281-5

Fleisher, C. S. (2008). Using open source data in developing competitive and marketing intelligence. European Journal of Marketing, 42 (7/8), 853.

Fuller, C. J. (2023). *What is Tactical Marketing?* Marketing.

Gandomi, A., & Haider, M. (2015). Beyond the hype: Big data concepts, methods, and analytics. *International Journal of Information Management, 35*(2), 137–144. doi:10.1016/j.ijinfomgt.2014.10.007

Glanz, K., Rimer, B. K., & Viswanath, K. (Eds.). (2008). *Health behavior and health education: theory, research, and practice.* Wiley.

Hashem, I. A. T., Yaqoob, I., Anuar, N. B., Mokhtar, S., Gani, A., & Ullah Khan, S. (2015). The rise of "big data" on cloud computing: Review and open research issues. *Information Systems, 47*, 98–115. doi:10.1016/j.is.2014.07.006

Heang, R. (2017). *Book Review: The use of Market Intelligence in Competitive Analysis.* Digitala Vetenskapliga Arkivet.

Hedin, H., Hirvensalo, I., & Vaarnas, M. (Eds.). (2012). *The Handbook of Market Intelligence.* doi:10.1002/9781119208082

Huang, L., Zhao, Q., Li, Y., Wang, S., Lei, S., & Chou, W. (2017). Reliable and efficient big service selection. *Information Systems Frontiers*, *19*(6), 1273–1282. doi:10.100710796-017-9767-x

International, (2023). Market Intelligence, https://www.b2binternational.com/wp-content/uploads/2013/06/market_intelligence.pdf

Jamil, G. L. (2013). Approaching Market Intelligence Concept through a Case Analysis: Continuous Knowledge for Marketing Strategic Management and its Complementarity to Competitive Intelligence". *Procedia Technology*, *9*, 463–472. doi:10.1016/j.protcy.2013.12.051

Janelle, D. G., & Goodchild, M. F. (2018). Territory, Geographic Information, and the Map. In The Map and the Territory. Springer. doi:10.1007/978-3-319-72478-2_33

Jha, A. K., Agi, M. A., & Ngai, E. W. (2020). A note on big data analytics capability development in supply chain. *Decision Support Systems*, *38*, 113382. doi:10.1016/j.dss.2020.113382

Jin, D. H., & Kim, H. J. (2018). Integrated Understanding of Big Data, Big Data Analysis, and Business Intelligence: A Case Study of Logistics. *Sustainability (Basel)*, *10*(10), 3778. doi:10.3390u10103778

Kaisler, S., Armour, F., Espinosa, J. A., & Money, W. (2013). Big data: Issues and challenges moving forward. In *System sciences (HICSS), 2013 46th Hawaii international conference on* (pp. 995-1004). IEEE.

Katal, A., Wazid, M., & Goudar, R. (2013). Big data: Issues, challenges, tools and good practices. In: *Contemporary Computing (IC3), 2013 Sixth International Conference on*, (pp. 404-409). IEEE.

Kelley, W. T. (1965). Marketing Intelligence for Top Management". *Journal of Marketing*, *29*(4), 19–24. doi:10.1177/002224296502900405

Kim, M. K., & Park, J. H. (2017). Identifying and prioritizing critical factors for promoting the implementation and usage of big data in healthcare. *Information Development*, *33*(3), 257–269. doi:10.1177/0266666916652671

Kościelniaka, H., & Puto, A. (2015). BIG DATA in decision making processes of enterprises. *Procedia Computer Science*, *65*, 1052–1058. doi:10.1016/j.procs.2015.09.053

Kowalczyk, M., & Buxmann, P. (2014). Big Data and Information Processing in Organizational Decision Processes: A Multiple Case Study. *Business & Information Systems Engineering*, *5*(5), 267–278. doi:10.100712599-014-0341-5

Kumar, V. S., & Bagga, T. (2020). Marketing Intelligence: Antecedents and Consequences. Rochester, NY.

Kwon, O., Lee, N., & Shin, B. (2014). Data quality management, data usage experience and acquisition intention of big data analytics. *International Journal of Information Management*, *34*(3), 387–394. doi:10.1016/j.ijinfomgt.2014.02.002

Lackman, C., Saban, K., & Lanasa, J. (2000). The contribution of market intelligence to tactical and strategic business decisions". *Marketing Intelligence & Planning*, *18*(1), 8. doi:10.1108/02634500010308530

Lautenbach, P., Johnston, K., & Adeniran-Ogundipe, T. (2017). Factors influencing bussiness intelligence and analytics usage extent in south african organaisations. *South African Journal of Business Management, 48*(3), 23–33. doi:10.4102ajbm.v48i3.33

Li, D., Wang, H., Yuan, H., & Li, D. (2016). Software and applications of spatial data mining. *Wiley Interdisciplinary Reviews. Data Mining and Knowledge Discovery, 6*(3), 84–114. doi:10.1002/widm.1180

Llave, M. R. (2018). Data lakes in business intelligence: Reporting from the trenches. *Procedia Computer Science, 138,* 516–524. doi:10.1016/j.procs.2018.10.071

Mikalef, P., Pappas, I.O., Krogstie, J., & Giannakos, M. (2018). Big data analytics capabilities: a systematic literature review and research agenda. *Inf Syst e-Business Manage. 6*(3), 547–78.

Narayanan, V. (2014). Using Big-Data Analytics to Manage Data Deluge and Unlock Real-Time Business Insights. *Journal of Equipment Lease Financing., 32,* 1–7.

Passlick, J., Lebek, B., & Breitner, M. H. (2017). A Self-Service Supporting Business Intelligence and Big Data Analytics Architecture. In J. M. Leimeister & W. Brenner (Eds.), Proceedings der 13. Internationalen Tagung Wirtschaftsinformatik (WI 2017) (pp. 1126–1140). Academic Press.

Popovič, A., Hackney, R., Tassabehji, R., & Castelli, M. (2018). The impact of big data analytics on frms' high value business performance. *Information Systems Frontiers, 20*(2), 209–222. doi:10.100710796-016-9720-4

Prestby, J., & Wandersman, A. (1985). A. An empirical exploration of a framework of organizational viability: Maintaining block organizations. *The Journal of Applied Behavioral Science, 21*(3), 287–305. doi:10.1177/002188638502100305

Redman, T. C. (1998). The impact of poor data quality on the typical enterprise". *Communications of the ACM, 41*(2), 81. doi:10.1145/269012.269025

Ridzuan, F., Wan, Z., & Wan, M. N. (2019). A Review on Data Cleansing Methods for Big Data". *Procedia Computer Science, 161,* 731–738. doi:10.1016/j.procs.2019.11.177

Sawant, N., & Shah, H. (2013). Big Data Visualization Patterns. In Big Data Application Architecture Q & A, 79-90. Springer. doi:10.1007/978-1-4302-6293-0_7

Schein, E. H. (1985). *Organizational culture and leadership.* Jossey-Bass.

SCIP. (1991). SCIP Europe established. *Competitive Intelligence Review, 2*(1), 51–52.

Sharma, A. (2020). The organization of customer support services". *European Journal of Marketing, 54*(7), 1813–1814. doi:10.1108/EJM-07-2020-974

Sivarajah, U., Kamal, M. M., Irani, Z., & Weerakkody, V. (2017). Critical analysis of Big Data challenges and analytical methods. *Journal of Business Research, 70,* 263–286. doi:10.1016/j.jbusres.2016.08.001

Sun, Z., Zou, H., & Strang, K. (2015). Big Data Analytics as a Service for Business Intelligence. *14th Conference on e-Business, e-Services and e-Society (I3E),* (pp. 200-211). Springer. 10.1007/978-3-319-25013-7_16

Tan, W. T., & Zafar, U. A. (1999). Managing market intelligence: An Asian marketing research perspective". *Marketing Intelligence & Planning*, *17*(6), 39.

The Future of Market Intelligence. (2023). More Inclusive, More Proactive, More Personalized. *The Future of Market Intelligence*. https://gis.usc.edu/blog/how-gis-is-taking-advantage-of-big-data/

Vera-Baquero, A., Palacios, R. C., Stantchev, V., & Molloy, O. (2015). Leveraging big-data for business process analytics. *The Learning Organization*, *22*(4), 215–228. doi:10.1108/TLO-05-2014-0023

Wamba, S. F., Gunasekaran, A., Akter, S., Ren, S. J., Dubey, R., & Childe, S. J. (2017). Big data analytics and frm performance: Efects of dynamic capabilities. *Journal of Business Research*, *70*, 356–365. doi:10.1016/j.jbusres.2016.08.009

Wang, L., & Alexander, C. A. (2015). Big Data Driven Supply Chain Management and Business Administration. *American Journal of Economics and Business Administration*, *7*(2), 60–67. doi:10.3844/ajebasp.2015.60.67

Wang, Y., & Hajli, N. (2017). Exploring the path to big data analytics success in healthcare. *Journal of Business Research*, *70*, 287–299. doi:10.1016/j.jbusres.2016.08.002

Zaharia, M., Chowdhury, M., Franklin, M. J., Shenker, S., & Stoica, I. (2010). Spark: cluster computing with working sets. In: *Proceedings of the 2nd USENIX conference on Hot topics in cloud computing*, vol. 10

Zheng, C., Yu, X., & Jin, Q. (2017). How user relationships affect userperceived value propositions of enterprises on social commerce plat-forms. *Information Systems Frontiers*, *19*(6), 1261–1271. doi:10.100710796-017-9766-y

ADDITIONAL READING

Manyika, J., Chui, M., Brown, B., Bughin, J., Dobbs, R., Roxburgh, C., & Byers, A. H. (2011). Big Data: The Next Frontier for Innovation, Competition, and Productivity. In: McKinsey Global Institute Reports, pp. 1–156. McKinsey.

Russom, P. (2011). Big Data Analytics. In: TDWI Best Practices Report, pp. 1–40. TDWI.

Ruzgas, T. & Bagdonavičienė, J., (2017). Business Intelligence for Big Data Analytics. *International Journal of Computer Applications Technology and Research, 6*(01), 01-08.

Tan, K. H., Zhan, Y. Z., Ji, G., Ye, F., & Chang, C. (2015). Harvesting big data to enhance supply chain innovation capabilities: An analytic infrastructure based on deduction graph. *International Journal of Production Economics*, *165*, 223–233. doi:10.1016/j.ijpe.2014.12.034

Tapadinhas J., (2014). *How to Architect the BI and Analytics Platform.*

TechAmerica. (2012). Demystifying Big Data: A Practical Guide to Transforming the Business of Government. In: TechAmerica Reports, pp. 1–40. TechAmerica.

Tung, W.-F., & Jordann, G. (2017). Crowdsourcing social networkService for Social Enterprise Innovation. *Information Systems Frontiers*, *19*(6), 1311–1327. doi:10.100710796-017-9770-2

Wael, M. S. Yafooz., Abidin, S. Z., Omar, N., & Idrus, Z. (2013). Managing unstructured data in relational databases. In *Systems, Process & Control (ICSPC), 2013 IEEE Conference on* (pp. 198-203). IEEE.

Wang, T.-W. (2019). Depicting Data Quality Issues in Business Intelligence Environment Through a Metadata Framework. In S. J. Miah & W. Yeoh (Eds.), *Applying Business Intelligence Initiatives in Healthcare and Organizational Settings* (pp. 291–304). IGI Global. doi:10.4018/978-1-5225-5718-0.ch016

Zhou, Z. H., Chawla, N. V., Jin, Y., & Williams, G. J. (2014). Big data opportunities and challenges: Discussions from data analytics perspectives. *IEEE Computational Intelligence Magazine*, *9*(4), 62–74. doi:10.1109/MCI.2014.2350953

KEY TERMS AND DEFINITIONS

Business Intelligence (BI): refers to the procedural and technical infrastructure that collects, stores, and analyzes the data produced by a company's activities.

Competitive Intelligence (CI): sometimes referred to as **corporate intelligence**, refers to the ability to gather, analyze, and use information collected on competitors, customers, and other market factors that contribute to a business's competitive advantage.

Fast Moving Consumer Goods (FMCG) business: are: products that sell quickly at relatively low cost. These goods are also called consumer packaged goods. FMCGs have a short shelf life because of high consumer demand (e.g., soft drinks and confections) or because they are perishable (e.g., meat, dairy products, and baked goods).

Gartner's Magic Quadrant: A Gartner Magic Quadrant is a culmination of research in a specific market, giving you a wide-angle view of the relative positions of the market's competitors, and includes challengers, leaders, niche players and visionaries.

Information Technology (IT): is the use of computers to create, process, store, retrieve and exchange all kinds of data and information. IT forms part of information and communications technology (ICT).

Key Performance Indicators (KPIs): are a set of quantifiable measurements used to gauge the performance of a company.

Society of Competitive Intelligence Professionals (SCIP): formerly the Society of Competitive Intelligence Professionals, is a global non-profit best practice sharing community for experts from industry, academia, government, and non-profits in Strategic Intelligence: competitive intelligence, market intelligence, market research, strategic analysis, business intelligence, and strategy.

The System of National Accounts (SNA): is: the internationally agreed standard set of recommendations on how to compile measures of economic activity. The SNA describes a coherent, consistent and integrated set of macroeconomic accounts in the context of a set of internationally agreed concepts, definitions, classifications and accounting rules.

Chapter 3
Big Data Analytics Lifecycle

Smrity Prasad
https://orcid.org/0000-0002-8057-3612
Christ University, India

Kashvi Prawal
Penn State University, USA

ABSTRACT

Big data analysis is the process of looking through and gleaning important insights from enormous, intricate datasets that are too diverse and massive to be processed via conventional data processing techniques. To find patterns, trends, correlations, and other important information entails gathering, storing, managing, and analyzing massive amounts of data. Datasets that exhibit the three Vs—volume, velocity, and variety—are referred to as "big data." The vast amount of data produced from numerous sources, including social media, sensors, devices, transactions, and more, is referred to as volume. The rate at which data is generated and must be processed in real-time or very close to real-time is referred to as velocity. Data that is different in its sorts and formats, such as structured, semi-structured, and unstructured data, is referred to as being varied.

INTRODUCTION

Big data arose in recent years to fulfill the demands and challenges of expanding data volumes. Big data refers to the process of managing massive amounts of data from many sources such as DBMS, log files, social media posting, and sensor data (Bajaj et al. 2014). When we hear the term "big data," we immediately think of the massive amounts of data that must be stored and processed. Indeed, a large volume of data is a big data type feature that exceeds Exabyte (1018), necessitating unique storage solutions, high performance data processing, and particular analytics capacity (Kaisler et al., 2013). Big data is a collection of complex datasets (text, numbers, photos, and videos) in massive volumes that exceed the capabilities of typical database management systems (Govindarajan et al., 2014).

Big data, in particular, has three primary characteristics: volume, velocity, and variety. Aside from the three Vs, other big data traits included value and complexity (Kaisler et al., 2013; Katal et al., 2013).

DOI: 10.4018/979-8-3693-0413-6.ch003

The volume attribute denotes the amount of data. In general, big data has a vast volume of data that is beyond the capacity of typical storage systems. According to (Bajaj et al.,2014), 90 percent of the world's current data was created in the last two years, with an average of 2.5 quintillions of data bytes created everyday. The velocity aspect of big data relates to the rate at which data is generated and processed (Bajaj et al.,2014). Currently, data and information are generated and processed at a high pace, resulting in a massive amount of knowledge being contributed to the knowledge base; this velocity rate of big data necessitates more processing power than older systems. Furthermore, the term velocity alludes to the rapid movement of data between data storage locations via networks (Bajaj et al., 2014).

Variety is another important aspect of huge data. The term "variety" in big data refers to the various resources that generate data in various formats and types (Bajaj et al. 2014; Govindarajan et al. 2014; Kaisler et al., 2013; Katal et al., 2013). Digital photographs and videos, social media, sensor data, healthcare data records, text, log files, tweets, and purchase transaction records are all examples of data resources. In other words, big data is made up of several data forms, including structured, unstructured, and semi-structured data.

Value and complexity are two further big data properties (Kaisler et al., 2013). The value attribute in big data refers to the usefulness of information (knowledge) that may be derived from processing and analyzing big data. This newly produced information is beneficial and supportive of decision-making (Katal et al., 2013). The complexity attribute refers to the complexity of relationships and links in a large data structure. In this regard, we may understand how complex it is when only a few changes occur in enormous amounts of data, resulting in a significant number of modifications (Katal et al., 2013).

The Big Data process involves a number of processes, beginning with data collection and ending with decision-making. Researchers agree on a few key factors regarding the steps. As an illustration, (Bizer et al.,2012) list six (6) steps: data collection, storage, search, sharing, analysis, and visualization. (Marx, 2013) suggests five (5) phases to tackle a problem: problem definition, data searching, data transformation, data entity resolution, and query response/problem resolution. (Chen and Liu, 2014), in contrast, solely employ the three steps of data handling, data processing, and data movement. Building competences and capacity for data management is necessary for an efficient big data chain .The outcomes are influenced by the capacities of each business involved in the big data chain of information. Therefore, depending on the capacities of each entity, the capacity of organizations and enterprises to gather, prepare, and analyze big data may vary.

After analyzing number of authors, Following are the nine steps that make up the Big Data analytics lifecycle. Life cycle of big data analytics is shown in Figure 1.

1. Business Requirement Identification and Evaluation
2. Data Identification
3. Data Acquisition & Filtering
4. Data Extraction
5. Data Validation & Cleansing
6. Data Aggregation & Representation
7. Data Analysis
8. Data Visualization
9. Utilization of Analysis Result

Figure 1. Life cycle of big data analytics

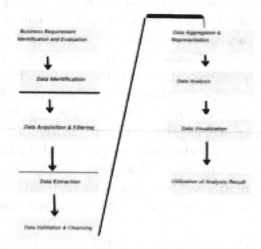

BUSINESS REQUIREMENT IDENTIFICATION AND EVALUATION

The Big Data Analytics lifecycle's first stage is the identification of business requirements and evaluation. Understanding the business objectives, ambitions, and challenges that an organization intends to address with big data analytics is the main focus at this stage. The main goal is to recognize and categorize the particular issues or possibilities where Big Data analytics can be useful.

IMPORTANT ACTIONS AT THIS PHASE INCLUDE:

Business grasp: To develop a thorough grasp of the organization's overall strategy, objectives, and pain points, the analytics team collaborates extensively with business stakeholders. They pinpoint areas where data analytics can improve performance and decision-making.

Specific challenges or opportunities are defined based on the knowledge gathered through the business understanding. These might have to do with enhancing operational effectiveness, comprehending consumer behaviour, enhancing marketing tactics, identifying fraud, foreseeing maintenance requirements, or any other pertinent business difficulty.

Setting Goals: The analytics project has definite, quantifiable goals. These goals assist determine the effectiveness of the analytics program and act as guides for the following phases.

Scoping and Feasibility: The team assesses the project's viability by taking into account variables including data availability, data quality, required technology, and probable difficulties. Setting realistic expectations and project scope is aided by this assessment.

Decision-makers can better understand the business concerns the analysis will address and the resources that will need to be used by evaluating the Big Data analytics business case.

It is possible to establish whether the business issues being addressed are indeed Big Data issues based on the business needs that are listed in the business case. A business issue must directly relate to one or more of the Big Data characteristics of volume, velocity, or variety in order to be considered a big data problem.

Also take note of the fact that this stage also determines the base budget needed to complete the analysis job. Any necessary purchase, including those for hardware, software, and training, must be understood beforehand in order to compare the planned investment to the expected advantages of attaining the goals. Compared to later iterations where these earlier expenditures can be regularly exploited, first iterations of the Big Data analytics lifecycle will demand a greater upfront investment of Big Data technologies, products, and training.

DATA RECOGNITION

The second stage of the Big Data analytics lifecycle is data identification.

The goal of the Data Identification step is to locate the datasets and their sources that will be used in the analysis project.

Finding hidden patterns and correlations may be more likely if a larger range of data sources are identified. For instance, when it is unclear exactly what to look for, it can be helpful to find as many different sorts of linked data sources as you can.

The required datasets and their sources can be internal or external to the firm, depending on the business scope of the analytic project and the nature of the business problems being addressed.

For internal datasets, a list of readily accessible datasets from internal sources, including data marts and operational systems, is often generated, and compared to a pre-defined dataset definition.

For external datasets, a list of potential third-party data suppliers is generated, including data markets and publicly accessible datasets. In cases when certain external data types are embedded in blogs or other content-based websites, automated techniques may be required to harvest the data.

DATA ACQUISITION AND FILTERING

All the data sources that were identified during the previous stage are gathered during the Data Acquisition and Filtering step, which is seen in Figure 1. Data that has been determined to be corrupt or to not be useful for the analysis goals is then removed from the acquired data using automatic screening.

The process of gathering data from multiple sources and storing it in a format appropriate for future analysis is known as data acquisition. Data can be obtained from a variety of sources in the context of data analytics, including databases, data warehouses, web servers, sensors, social media platforms, log files, and more. Since the quality and relevance of the data directly affect the precision and efficacy of the subsequent analysis, the data gathering step is extremely important.

Data may arrive as a collection of files, such as data acquired from a third-party data provider, or it may require API integration, such with Twitter. This depends on the sort of data source. The majority of the gathered data may be irrelevant (noise) in many situations, especially when external, unstructured data is involved, and can be eliminated as part of the filtering process.

The process of preparing the collected data for analysis by removing or correcting errors, inconsistencies, and extraneous information is known as data filtering, sometimes known as data cleaning or data preprocessing. This step makes that the data is correct, trustworthy, and appropriate for the particular analytics activities at hand.

Records having missing values, values that make no sense, or records with improper data types can all be considered "corrupt" data. Data that is excluded from one study could be useful for another sort of analysis. So, before starting the filtering, it is wise to store a verbatim copy of the original dataset. The verbatim copy can be compressed to reduce the amount of storage space needed.

Once it is generated or enters the enterprise border, both internal and external data need to be persistent. This data is initially saved to disk for batch analytics before being analyzed. When using real-time analytics, the data is first examined before being saved to disk.

EXTRACTION OF DATA

A critical phase of the Big Data Analytics lifecycle is data extraction. It alludes to the procedure of finding and gathering pertinent data from numerous sources so that it may be analyzed. Data extraction becomes a significant difficulty in the setting of Big Data, as data volumes are large and originate from several sources, and is a necessary step in getting the data ready for further analysis.

It's possible that some of the data designated as analysis input will arrive in a format that is incompatible with the Big Data solution. With data from outside sources, it is increasingly likely that the need to address various sorts of data will arise. Figure 2 depiction of the Data Extraction lifecycle stage illustrates how diverse data is extracted and converted into a format that the underlying Big Data solution can use for data analysis.

The sorts of analytics and capabilities of the Big Data solution determine how much extraction and transformation is necessary. For instance, if the underlying Big Data solution can already directly process those files, extracting the essential fields from delimited textual data, such as with webserver log files, may not be necessary.

Figure 2. Extraction of diverse data

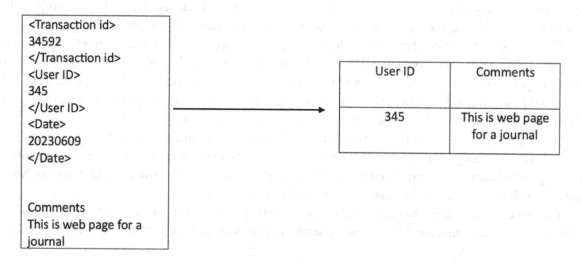

Similarly, if the underlying Big Data solution can read the document directly in its native format, text extraction for text analytics—which necessitates scans of entire documents -is facilitated.

VALIDATION AND CLEANUP OF THE DATA

Analyses can be skewed and falsified by using invalid data. Data input into Big Data analytics might be unstructured without any indication of validity, in contrast to traditional enterprise data, where the data structure is pre-defined, and data is pre-validated. Finding a set of appropriate validation constraints may be difficult due to its complexity.

The Data Validation and Cleansing stage is responsible for creating frequently intricate validation criteria and eliminating any data that is known to be invalid.

Multiple datasets frequently provide duplicate data to big data solutions. This redundancy can be used to investigate linked datasets, put together validation criteria, and fill in gaps with valid data.

For instance, as shown in this example.

Validating the age variable in a sizable collection of customer records is an illustration of data validation in the Big Data Analytics lifecycle.

Consider a situation where a business has built up a thorough client database by gathering information from a variety of sources, such as online forms, customer surveys, and purchase transactions. The "age" of the consumers, which represents their age at the time of data collection, is one of the fields in this dataset.

The age field may be subject to the following validation checks during the data validation phase:

1. Range Validation: The customer's age should be represented by numeric values in the age field. The values would be validated to ensure that they are within an appropriate age range (for example, 0 to 120 years). Values outside of this range could be a sign of poor data quality or data entry problems.

2. Data Type Validation: Making sure the age field only contains numeric information. Any text strings or non-numeric characters would be marked as invalid.

3. Consistency Validation: Checking the age field's agreement with other pertinent information. For instance, the calculated age should coincide with the age entered in the age field if another field has the customer's birth date.

4. Completeness Validation: Examining the age field for any missing values. If several records' age fields are empty or null, this may suggest incomplete data and call for additional research or imputation.

5. Logical Validation: Applying logical checks to make sure the age values are reasonable given the dataset's overall structure. Customers who are older than 120 years old, for instance, are unlikely to exist and could be an indication of inaccurate or fake data.

Detecting any extreme values in the age field that differ noticeably from the rest of the data distribution is known as Outlier Detection. Data input mistakes or other irregularities may be indicated by outliers.

Analysts can make sure that the age data is precise, dependable, and appropriate for analysis by performing these data validation procedures. Any discovered problems with the quality of the data can be fixed during the data cleaning or preprocessing stages, which will assist to increase the overall data quality and the confidence in the outcomes of the subsequent data analytics and modeling.

A more complex in-memory system is needed to validate and clean the data as it enters the system for real-time analytics. The accuracy and quality of disputed data can be determined in large part by their provenance. As demonstrated in Figure 1, data that initially seems erroneous may nevertheless be useful because it may include underlying patterns and trends.

DATA REPRESENTATION AND AGGREGATION

Data may be dispersed over various datasets, necessitating the joining of those databases via common attributes, like date or ID. In other instances, the identical data variables, such the date of birth, may occur in different databases. Either a method of data reconciliation is necessary, or it is necessary to identify the dataset that represents the true value.

The goal of the Data Aggregation and Representation stage is to combine various datasets into a single view.

Performing this stage can be challenging due to variations in:

Data Structure - The data model may change even though the data format may be the same.

Semantics - A value that has a different label in two separate datasets may yet signify the same thing, for instance, "surname" and "last name."

Data aggregation can be a time- and labor-intensive process due to the high volumes that Big Data solutions process. Conciliating these discrepancies may need for intricate logic to be carried out automatically without human involvement.

To promote data reuse, future data analysis requirements must be taken into account at this time. It's crucial to realize that the same data can be stored in a variety of ways whether or not data aggregation is necessary. For a specific kind of analysis, one form could be more appropriate than another. Data stored as a BLOB, for instance, would be of limited use if the analysis needed access to specific data fields.

A data format that has been standardized by the Big Data solution can serve as a base for a variety of analytical methods and initiatives.

EXAMPLE OF DATA AGGREGATION

Let's say a retailer has a ton of transactional data from all of its many outlets. Each transaction record contains information about that specific transaction, including the date of the sale, the item sold, the quantity sold, and the total amount of money received.

To determine daily sales revenue, the business would carry out the following aggregation process at the data aggregation stage:

1. Data Filtering: The dataset must first be filtered to exclude only the pertinent data needed to calculate daily sales income. In this filtering, records with a specific date range, such one day, are chosen.
2. Grouping: The filtered data is then categorized according to a shared characteristic, in this case, the selling date. This implies that all transactions that took place on the same day are combined.

Table 1. Aggregation of data

Date	Total Sales Revenue
2021-08-02	$22,000
2021-08-03	$29,500
2021-08-04	$16,800

3. Summation: The total revenue generated for each group (each day) is determined by adding the revenue from all of the group's individual transactions.
4. Result: The final output of the aggregate will be a dataset that offers the total revenue for each day, demonstrating how much sales revenue was produced on that day.

The output of the aggregation, for instance, would resemble this mentioned in the Table 1:

The corporation can acquire important insights into the daily operation of its stores by combining the individual sales transactions into daily sales income. This aggregated data can be used for many analytical tasks, including trend detection, sales performance tracking, and strategic corporate decision-making. In Big Data settings, where the sheer number of individual records makes interpreting the data in its raw form impossible, aggregating data is very crucial.

ANALYSIS OF DATA

The actual analysis task, which often comprises one or more types of analytics, is carried out at the Data Analysis step, Iterative in nature, this stage can continue until the proper pattern or association is found, especially if the data analysis is exploratory. We'll go into confirmatory analysis and the approach used for exploratory analysis shortly.

This stage can be as easy as querying a dataset to generate an aggregation for comparison, depending on the type of analytical output required. On the other hand, finding patterns and anomalies or creating a statistical or mathematical model to represent correlations between variables can be as difficult as combining data mining and sophisticated statistical analysis approaches.

Data analysis can be divided into two types: confirmatory analysis and exploratory analysis, the latter of which is related to data mining.

A logical method known as confirmatory data analysis involves putting up a potential cause for the event under investigation. A supposition or postulated cause is referred to as a hypothesis. The theory is subsequently tested against the data, and conclusive answers are given to queries. Techniques for data sampling are frequently employed. A predetermined reason was presumed, therefore unexpected discoveries or abnormalities are typically disregarded.

An inductive method known as exploratory data analysis is closely related to data mining. No preconceived notions or assumptions are made. Instead, the data is investigated through analysis to discover the reason for the behavior. Although it might not offer conclusive solutions, this approach offers a broad orientation that might aid in the identification of patterns or abnormalities.

VISUALIZATION OF DATA

If only the analysts are able to understand the results, then the ability to analyze enormous volumes of data and derive insightful conclusions is of little value.

The goal of the data visualization stage is to effectively interpret the analysis results for business users by employing data visualization techniques and tools.

The dashed line connecting stage 8 back to stage 7 shows that in order for business users to derive value from the research and later be able to offer feedback, they must be able to comprehend the outcomes.

Users are given the opportunity to undertake visual analysis as a result of finishing the data visualization step, which enables them to find the answers to questions they haven't even thought to ask. Later in this book, visual analysis approaches are discussed.

The interpretation of the results may vary depending on how the same results are presented in various ways. Therefore, it's crucial to employ the best visualization technique while keeping the context of the business domain in mind.

Another thing to bear in mind is that giving consumers a way to drill down to relatively simple information is essential if they are to comprehend how the results were rolled up or aggregated.

EMPLOYING ANALYSIS RESULTS

There may be additional chances to use the analysis results once they have been made available to business users to help corporate decision-making, for as through dashboards. Figuring out how and where to use the processed analysis data is the focus of the Utilization of Analysis Results stage.

It is possible for the analysis results to yield "models" that capture new insights and understandings about the nature of the patterns and relationships that exist within the data that was examined, depending on the nature of the analysis problems being addressed. A mathematical formula or a list of guidelines could be examples of models. Models can be used to enhance the logic of business processes and application systems, as well as serve as the foundation for new systems and software.

The following are typical topics that are covered at this stage:

Input for Enterprise Systems - To improve and optimize the operation of enterprise systems, the results of data analysis may be manually or automatically fed into such systems. For instance, processed customer-related analytical results could be supplied to an online retailer to influence how it makes product recommendations. New models may be used to enhance the programming logic in already-in-use business systems or as the foundation for brand-new systems.

Data analysis results in the identification of patterns, correlations, and anomalies that are then used to optimize business procedures. Consolidating transportation routes as part of a supply chain procedure is one example. Models may present chances to enhance the logic of business processes.

Data analysis findings may be included into already-existing alerts or may serve as the foundation for brand-new alerts. For instance, alerts may be developed to send users notifications via email or SMS text regarding an occurrence that necessitates their taking corrective action.

Case Study Illustration

The IT team at Smrity company works with business management to comprehend the goals of enhancing customer happiness and minimizing losses brought on by false claims. They understand that early business employees involvement is necessary to match expectations with what the Big Data solution can deliver.

The bulk of Smrity's IT staff believes that Big Data is the magic solution to all of their present problems. The qualified IT staff members point out that implementing Big Data is different from merely implementing a technology platform. Instead, a number of criteria must first be taken into account to ensure the successful implementation of Big Data. The IT team collaborates with the business managers to prepare a feasibility report in order to guarantee that the influence of business-related elements is completely understood. The early involvement of business personnel will further contribute to the development of a setting that narrows the gap between management's perceived expectations and what IT can really deliver.

Big Data adoption is widely acknowledged to be business-focused and to help Smrity accomplish its objectives. Big Data's capacity to mix various datasets and store and process enormous volumes of unstructured data will aid Smrity in understanding risk. By only selecting less hazardous applicants as clients, the corporation anticipates being able to reduce losses. Smrity forecasts that the capacity to examine a customer's unstructured behavioral data and identify anomalous behavior will further aid in loss reduction because fraudulent claims can be disregarded.

Smrity is now more prepared to adopt big data thanks to the decision to train the IT team in this area. The group thinks it currently possesses the fundamental knowledge needed to launch a Big Data endeavor. The team is in a good position to choose the necessary technologies thanks to the data that was earlier recognized and categorized. Business management's early involvement has also given them insights that enable them to foresee potential future changes that may be needed to maintain the Big Data solution platform in line with any new business requirements.

Only a small number of external data sources, including social media and census data, have been found at this early stage. The business staff has decided that a sufficient budget would be set aside for the purchase of data from outside data providers. Regarding privacy, business users are a little concerned that gathering more information about clients would make them less trusting. To win the approval and trust of clients, it is believed that an incentive-driven program, such as decreased premiums, can be implemented. The IT team points out that extra development work will be needed to guarantee that standardized, role-based access restrictions are in place for data kept within the Big Data solution environment when addressing security issues. For the open-source databases that will house non-relational data, this is extremely important.

Although the business users are thrilled to be able to undertake deep analytics using unstructured data, they raise concerns about how much they can trust the conclusions given that the study uses data from outside data sources. The IT team replies that a framework will be used to add and update metadata for each dataset that is saved and processed in order to ensure that provenance is maintained at all times and that processing outcomes can be traced back to the original data sources.

The current objectives of Smrity include reducing claim settlement times and identifying fraudulent claims. These objectives must be accomplished, and that means finding a solution that works quickly. The need for real-time data analysis support is not anticipated, nevertheless. The IT team thinks that by creating a batch-based Big Data solution that makes use of open source Big Data technology, these objectives can be achieved.

The IT infrastructure that Smrity currently uses uses very outdated networking standards. Similar to this, most server specifications—such as CPU speed, disk capacity, and disk speed—predict that they cannot deliver optimal data processing performance. Therefore, it is acknowledged that before a Big Data solution can be created and built, the current IT infrastructure needs to be upgraded.

Both the business and IT teams are adamant that a Big Data governance structure is necessary in order to enable them standardize the use of various data sources and completely comply with any legislation relating to data privacy. In addition, it is considered that an iterative data analysis approach including business professionals from the pertinent department is necessary due to the business focus of the data analysis and to ensure that meaningful analysis results are obtained. The marketing and sales teams, for instance, can be included in the data analysis process starting with the dataset selection stage to ensure that only the pertinent qualities of these datasets are chosen in the "improving customer retention" scenario. The business team can later offer insightful feedback regarding the interpretation and applicability of the analysis' findings.

The IT team notes that none of its systems are now hosted in the cloud and that the team does not have any skill sets relevant to cloud computing. The IT team decided to develop an on-premise Big Data solution in light of these facts and data protection issues. Because there is some speculation that their internal CRM system may someday be replaced by a cloud-hosted, software-as-a-service CRM solution, the group states that they will leave the option of cloud-based hosting open.

LIFECYCLE OF BIG DATA ANALYTICS

As part of Smrity's Big Data journey, its IT team now has the required expertise, and the management is persuaded of the potential advantages a Big Data solution may provide in support of the company's objectives. The CEO and the directors are excited to observe the use of big data. In response, the IT team undertakes the first Big Data project for Smrity in collaboration with the business staff. The "detection of fraudulent claims" objective is selected as the first Big Data solution following a careful evaluation procedure. The team then pursues attaining this goal by adhering to the Big Data Analytics Lifecycle's step-by-step methodology.

EVALUATION OF A BUSINESS CASE

Big Data analysis for "detection of fraudulent claims" directly correlates to a reduction in financial loss and, as a result, has full corporate support. Although there is fraud in each of Smrity's four business sectors, the scope of the big data analysis is only used to identify fraud in the building industry in order to keep the analysis simple.

Both personal and business customers can purchase building and contents insurance from Smrity. Although insurance fraud can be structured and opportunistic, the majority of occurrences involve opportunistic fraud, which takes the form of lying and exaggeration. One of the KPIs established is the 15% reduction in fraudulent claims, which is used to gauge the effectiveness of the Big Data solution for fraud detection.

The team determines that, given their budget, the purchase of new infrastructure suitable for creating an environment for a big data solution will represent their biggest outlay. They understand that they will be using open source technology to assist batch processing, therefore they don't think a sizable upfront investment in tooling is necessary. The team members recognize they should spend for the purchase of more data quality and cleansing tools as well as more modern data visualization technology when they take into account the larger Big Data analytics lifecycle. If the intended fraud-detecting KPIs can be achieved, a cost-benefit analysis shows that the investment in the Big Data solution can pay for itself several times over. The team thinks there is a compelling business case for leveraging Big Data for improved data analysis as a consequence of their investigation.

DATA RECOGNITION

There are both internal and external datasets found. Internal information comprises emails, call center agent notes, incident photos, policy data, insurance application paperwork, claim data, and claim adjuster notes. Social media data (such as Twitter feeds), weather reports, geospatial (GIS) data, and census data are examples of external data. Almost all datasets have a five-year history. The claim information consists of historical claim information with numerous fields, one of which indicates whether the claim was valid or fraudulent.

OBTAINING AND FILTERING DATA

The policy administration system provides the policy data, the claims management system provides the claim data, incident photos, and claim adjuster notes, and the document management system provides the insurance application paperwork. The claim data now contains the claim adjuster notes integrated inside it. So, to extract them, a different procedure is necessary. Emails and notes from call center agents are retrieved from the CRM system.

The remaining datasets are obtained from other data suppliers. Each dataset has an original version that is compressed and kept on disk. To document each dataset's provenance, the following metadata is tracked: the dataset's name, source, size, format, checksum, acquisition date, and number of records. Four to five percent of the records in Twitter feeds and weather forecasts appear to be corrupt, according to a brief review of their data quality. Two batch data filtering jobs are consequently created to eliminate the corrupt records.

EXTRACTION OF DATA

The IT team notices that pre-processing will be necessary for some of the datasets in order to extract the necessary fields. The tweets collection, for instance, is in JSON format. The user id, timestamp, and tweet text must be retrieved and transformed into tabular form in order to evaluate the tweets. Additionally, the weather dataset is delivered in a hierarchical style (XML), and fields like timestamps, temperature forecasts, wind speed forecasts, wind direction forecasts, snow forecasts, and flood forecasts are also retrieved and saved in a tabular format.

VALIDATION AND CLEANUP OF THE DATA

Smrity currently uses free copies of the weather and census datasets, which cannot be relied upon to be entirely accurate, in order to reduce expenditures. These datasets must therefore be verified and cleaned. The team can validate data type and range, examine the extracted fields for typographical errors and any incorrect data, and more based on the published field information. It has been established that records with some amount of significant information will not be deleted, even though some of their fields may contain erroneous data.

DATA REPRESENTATION AND AGGREGATION

It is chosen to combine policy data, claim data, and call center agent comments in a single dataset that is tabular in nature and where any field can be referred to via a data query in order to conduct relevant data analysis. This is expected to assist with a variety of data analytic activities, including risk assessment and quick claim settlement, in addition to the present role of identifying fraudulent claims. A NoSQL database houses the final dataset.

ANALYSIS OF DATA

The IT team consults data analysts at this point since it lacks the necessary expertise to analyze data in support of spotting false claims. The nature of fraudulent claims must first be investigated in order to determine the traits that set a fraudulent claim apart from a valid claim in order to be able to spot fraudulent transactions. The exploratory data analysis method is used for this. The data obtained after the initial pass are insufficient to fully understand what distinguishes a fraudulent claim from a legal one, so this stage is repeated several times. Aspects that are less likely to be used in a fraudulent claim are eliminated as part of this exercise, while those that have a direct connection are retained or added.

VISUALIZATION OF DATA

The team has made some intriguing discoveries, and it is now up to them to communicate the findings to the actuaries, underwriters, and claim adjusters. There are other visualization techniques employed, including as scatter plots, bar graphs, and line graphs. In order to assess groupings of fraudulent and valid claims in the context of several variables, such as customer age, policy age, number of claims made, and claim value, scatter plots are utilized.

EMPLOYING ANALYSIS RESULTS

The underwriting and claims settlement users now have a better grasp of the nature of fraudulent claims according to the results of the data analysis. However, a machine-learning-based model is created and then integrated into the current claim processing system to detect fraudulent claims in order to gain real-world benefits from this data analysis effort. In Chapter 8, the relevant machine learning method will be covered.

Example: Retail Analysis Using Sales Data Extraction

Step One: Identifying the Data Source

A retail business wants to examine its sales data to learn more about trends, consumer behavior, and product performance. Finding the pertinent data sources is the first stage in the data extraction process. These might include the company's customer relationship management (CRM) systems, point-of-sale systems, online sales platforms, and transactional databases.

Step Two: Connecting To and Retrieving Data

Data analysts or data engineers create links to these systems once the data sources have been identified in order to retrieve the necessary data. To extract data from numerous sources, they could use APIs, SQL queries, or data integration tools. For instance, they could utilize APIs to get information from an e-commerce platform and SQL to get transactional data from a database.

Step Three: Cleaning and Transforming Data

It's possible that the raw data you pull from several sources isn't in a uniform or practical format. The data must then be cleaned and transformed. Any missing or inaccurate values are taken care of, and data may need to be transformed into a standard format. To assure data accuracy, it could be necessary to standardize dates or eliminate duplication.

Step Four: Consolidating and Integrating Data

Data in a retail environment is frequently dispersed among several platforms. The data is then combined and integrated into a single data repository, similar to a data warehouse, after being extracted and cleansed. This makes it possible for analysts to carry out in-depth analysis on a centralized dataset.

Step Five: Validating the Data

To guarantee that the extracted and modified data truly represents the original source, data validation is essential. In order to find any differences between the raw data and the processed data, data analysts execute validation checks. By following this procedure, data quality and reliability are preserved for further analysis.

Step Six: Documentation and Data Storage

Data is securely saved and made available to the appropriate parties for analysis after successful validation. The relevant documentation is kept up to date, and it contains details on the data sources, extraction techniques, transformation procedures, and any data governance requirements.

Step Seven: Data Analysis

Data analysts can now use various analytics and data mining techniques to run on the extracted and prepared data to acquire insights into the retail industry. They might analyze sales trends, segment customers, assess the performance of products, and more.

Step Eight: Reporting and Data Visualization

Data visualization and reporting are used to present the findings from the data analysis to decision-makers and stakeholders. Charts, graphs, and dashboards are examples of visualizations that make it simpler for non-technical staff to comprehend and take action on the findings.

Step Nine: Continual Data Extraction and Refreshment

The data extraction stage is not a one-time occurrence because data analytics is an iterative process. For their assessments to remain current and pertinent, retail organizations regularly extract new data. To guarantee that the data utilized for analysis is current and accurate with regard to the most recent business situations, regular data refreshes are carried out.

In order for businesses to make data-driven decisions and obtain a competitive edge in the retail market, data extraction is an essential phase in the life cycle of data analytics, as demonstrated by the example given above.

STUDY OF FREQUENTLY USED DATA LIFE CYCLE

We show in this section the top five cycles from the twelve lifecycles analyzed in (Chen et al., 2014) based on the final ranking discovered in (El Arass et al.,2017), Hindawi DLC (Khan et al.,2014), Information DLC (Lin et al.,2014), USGS DLC (Demchenko et al.,2014) and Big Data Lifecycle (Faundeen et al.,2014). This allows us to place our DLC in relation to other lifecycles identified in the literature. After that, we provide examples from this work to show how our contribution relates to these pertinent cycles.

A.   Hindawi Lifecycle

The majority of businesses see their data as a valuable asset. They thus put up a great deal of work to ensure the growth and best application of this data. To get a consistent description between data and processes, a data lifecycle is modeled. (Khan et al.,2014) states that the steps of Hindawi DLC are as follows: data analysis, data storage, sharing & publishing, data retrieval & discovery, collection, filtering & categorization, and data analysis.

Based on the analysis done in (El Arass et al.,2017), Hindawi DLC was the best cycle. This lifecycle has been tailored to the Big Data environment and offers various benefits (Khan et al.,2014) Big Data is the source of the data. This cycle can handle both structured and unstructured data in a variety of formats. Data cleaning is done during the collection phase to prepare the data for better treatment later on. Data filtering is done prior to data analysis to narrow the focus to the needs of the company. Storage is handled intelligently because a management plan is put in place to conduct it with dependability, availability, and accessibility. Finally, a dedicated phase ensures data security. It includes guidelines and practices to safeguard lawful privacy, secrecy, and intellectual property.

B.   Information Lifecycle

This DLC is appropriate for a cloud setting. Data generation, data transmission, data storage, data access, data reuse, data archiving, and data disposal are the seven stages that make up this process (Lin et al.,2014).

The clever data management that occurs during the archiving and disposal stages is the benefit of this DLC in the context of big data.

The information lifecycle cycle addresses the drawbacks of the Hindawi cycle, including the lack of a data deletion phase and the cycle's restricted security. Security is introduced as a cross-cutting step in the information lifecycle that affects every other phase. The clever handling of the destruction and archiving stages is the best aspect of the Big Data environment for this cycle. The stages of data collection, planning, management, and quality control, which are essential for us to make the entire cycle intelligent, are, nevertheless, not very interesting to this cycle. Through the introduction of data restriction, filtering procedures for data that the company does not want, and their integration, Smart DLC contributes to the intelligence of data collecting. Additionally, Smart DLC intelligently provides data analysis results to decision-makers so they can act quickly and effectively.

C.   USGS Lifecycle

The collecting of pointless data cannot be justified or tolerated by USGS DLC. To satisfy a demand in science, data must be collected and kept up to date. The concept of data management across a lifespan becomes more pertinent as a result. This cycle concentrated on all matters related to ownership, quality control, storage, and documentation (Faundeen et al.,2014)

Plan, Acquire, Process, Analyze, Preserve, Publish/Share, Describe, Manage quality, and Backup & secure are the phases that make up USGS DLC.

This DLC adds new phases, such as planning, quality, security, and metadata description, that don't directly affect data. The cross-sectional existence of data description, quality, and security is another benefit of this DLC.

The cross-sectional presence of the quality and security phases is the USGS cycle's main benefit (Faundeen et al.,2014). As the planning phase is the first to be completed in this cycle, it is unrelated to the remaining phases in any manner.

D.   Big Data Lifecycle

This DLC, which has been modified for Big Data (Demchenko et al., 2014), is essentially the same as other conventional data lifecycles. The new phase of filtering and enriching data after it is collected seems interesting, but storing data throughout its lifecycle seems incompatible with big data because it doesn't address the volume issue related to big data; instead, the redundancy of the data makes managing it more difficult.

The Big Data cycle has incorporated new techniques to enhance the gathering process since it was first presented by Yuri Demchenko in (Demchenko et al., 2014) and featured in (Manyika, et al.,2011),

(Reeve,2013), (Chen et al., 2014), (Davis,2012). To lessen the amount of data that was initially gathered, a filtering and enrichment phase was implemented following collection. This model's unique selling point is its storage phase, where data is kept for the duration of its lifecycle, enabling reformatting and reuse of the data. Despite being established in the context of big data, this data lifecycle lacks intelligence because it lacks planning, security, and quality phases. Data deletion is not possible.

Smart DLC makes the end-to-end cycle smarter by addressing its flaws and reaping the rewards of this lifetime.

REFERENCES

Bajaj, R. H., & Ramteke, P. P. L. (2014). Big data–the New Era of data. *International Journal of Computer Science and Information Technologies*, *5*(2), 1875–1885.

Bizer, C., Boncz, P., Brodie, M. L., & Erling, O. (2012). The meaningful use of big data: Four perspectives — Four challenges. *SIGMOD Record*, *40*(4), 56–60. doi:10.1145/2094114.2094129

Chen, M., Mao, S., & Liu, Y. (2014). Big data: A survey. *Mobile Networks and Applications*, *19*(2), 171–209. doi:10.100711036-013-0489-0

Chen, M., Mao, S. M. Y., & Liu, Y. (2014). *Big data: A survey. Mobile Networks and Applications. Computing.* IEEE Publications. https://ieeexplore.ieee.org/xpls/abs_all.jsp?arnumber=6612229, doi:10.1007/s11036-013-0489-0

Davis, K. (2012). *Ethics of Big Data: Balancing risk and innovation.* O'Reilly Media, Inc.

Demchenko, Y., De Laat, C., & Membrey, P. (2014). Defining architecture components of the Big Data Ecosystem. In *Collaboration technologies and systems (CTS) International Conference on*, (pp. 104–112). IEEE. 10.1109/CTS.2014.6867550

El Arass, M. E., Tikito, I., & Souissi, N. (2017). *Data lifecycles analysis: Towards intelligent cycle.* In Fès Proceeding of The second International Conference on Intelligent Systems and Computer Vision, Fès, Morocco. 10.1109/ISACV.2017.8054938

Faundeen, J. L. (2014). *The United States Geological Survey science data lifecycle model.* United States Geological Survey.

Govindarajan, P., & Panneerselvam, S. (2014). Issues and challenges in big. In *Proceedings of the 2nd International Conference on Science* (pp. 265–272). Engineering and Management. http://www.ijaert.org/wp-content/uploads/2014/04/42.pdf

Kaisler, S., Armour, F., Espinosa, J. A., & Money, W. (2013). Big data: Issues and challenges moving forward. In *Proceeding of the 46th Hawaii International Conference on System Sciences*. IEEE. 10.1109/HICSS.2013.645

Katal, A., Wazid, M., & Goudar, R. (2013). Big Data: Issues, challenges, tools and Good practices. *Proceeding of the Sixth International Conference on Contemporary Computing*. IEEE. https://ieeexplore.ieee.org/xpls/abs_all.jsp?arnumber=6612229

Khan, N., Yaqoob, I., Hashem, I. A., Inayat, Z., Ali, W. K., Alam, M., Shiraz, M., & Gani, A. (2014). Big data: Survey, technologies, opportunities, and challenges. *The Scientific World Journal, 712826,* 1–18. doi:10.1155/2014/712826 PMID:25136682

Kim, S.-H., Kim, N.-U., & Chung, T.-M. (2013). Attribute relationship evaluation methodology for big data security. *International Conference on IT Convergence and Security (ICITCS),* (pp. 1–4). IEEE. 10.1109/ICITCS.2013.6717808

Krishnan, K. (2013). *Data warehousing in the age of big data.* Newnes.

Lin, L., Liu, T., Hu, J., & Zhang, J. (2014). A privacy-aware cloud service selection method toward data life-cycle. In *Parallel and Distributed Systems (ICPADS) 20th IEEE International Conference on,* (pp. 752–759). IEEE. 10.1109/PADSW.2014.7097878

Manyika, J. et al. (2011). *Big data: The next frontier for innovation, competition, and productivity.*

Marchal, S., Jiang, X., State, R., & Engel, T. (2014). A big data architecture for large scale security monitoring. In *Proceeding of the International Congress on Big Data.* IEEE. 10.1109/BigData.Congress.2014.18

Marx, V. (2013). Biology: The big challenges of big data. *Nature, 498*(7453), 255–260. doi:10.1038/498255a PMID:23765498

Miloslavskaya, N., Senatorov, M., Tolstoy, A., & Zapechnikov, S. (2014). Big data information security maintenance. In *Proceedings of the 7th International Conference on Security of Information and Networks—SIN,* (pp. 89–94). ACM Press. 10.1145/2659651.2659655

Reeve, A. (2013). Managing data in motion: Data integration best practice techniques and technologies. Research Gate.

KEY TERMS AND DEFINITION

Big Data: The term "big data" pertains to data sets that are characterized by their vast size and intricate nature, posing challenges for processing and analysis by conventional data processing techniques. The primary attributes associated with big data encompass: The generation of data from diverse sources has resulted in a substantial volume. In the realm of big data, data sets are typically characterized by their substantial size, sometimes measured in terabytes and petabytes. Diverse Range - Big data encompasses a diverse array of data sources and formats. The data may be organized in a structured format, such as databases, or in an unstructured format, encompassing emails, images, videos, and similar content. The velocity of data generation and processing in the context of big data is characterized by a high rate of speed. Streaming data plays a key role within the realm of big data. The veracity of data can be compromised by inconsistencies, noise, and irregularities. The task of maintaining the high quality and integrity of data presents significant challenges. The primary attribute of big data is in its capacity to reveal insights that contribute to company value, impact, and improved decision-making capabilities. The extraction of value from intricate data is of paramount importance.

Data Acquisition: Data acquisition refers to the systematic procedure of collecting, obtaining, or retrieving pertinent organized and unstructured data from diverse sources. The collection of this unprocessed data is necessary prior to conducting any analysis.

Data Analysis: Data analysis is the systematic examination, manipulation, and modelling of data in order to uncover valuable insights, propose valid conclusions, and facilitate informed decision-making. This process entails the utilization of analytical and statistical methodologies and algorithms to analyse and assess data.

Data Extraction: It's the process of obtaining particular data from various sources and formats, with the intention of utilizing it for subsequent analysis or manipulation. This entails undertaking activities such as data cleansing in order to eliminate extraneous elements and discrepancies.

Data Generation: Data generation refers to the process of generating data from diverse sources, including but not limited to social media platforms, sensors, and mobile devices. Ongoing generation of new data necessitates its collection and analysis.

Data Pre-Processing: Data pre-processing involves the necessary steps to prepare raw data for analysis. The process encompasses many techniques such as data cleansing, data integration, data reduction, data transformation, and data discretization, which are employed to ensure that the data aligns with the analysis prerequisites.

Data Security and Privacy: The protection of data from unauthorized access, use, disclosure, disruption, modification, or destruction. The practice of safeguarding large-scale datasets from unlawful access, utilization, disclosure, disturbance, alteration, or eradication. The process of safeguarding individuals' rights to exercise control over their personal data.

Data Visualization: Data visualization involves the creation of visual representations, such as graphs, charts, plots, or infographics, with the purpose of facilitating comprehension and interpretation of data and analytical outcomes, hence enabling the extraction of practical insights.

Chapter 4
Business Case Evaluation and Data Identification

Jignesh Patil
Rajiv Gandhi Institute of Technology, India

Sharmila Rathod
ⓘ https://orcid.org/0000-0003-1757-1419
Rajiv Gandhi Institute of Technology, India

ABSTRACT

Businesses need all data to be controlled centralized, and most corporations utilize analysis to learn where their company stands in the market. Big data tools and approaches are being used by researchers and practitioners to compute performance utilizing various algorithms. It is obvious that organisations require strong understanding of their consumers, commodities, and laws; nevertheless, with the aid of big data, organisations may find new methods to compete with other organizations. This study will focus on big data techniques and algorithms to find patterns to apply on the business cases which are lagging. Technology is simply a tool used by the business elite to keep their clientele close by. It has successfully aided the organisation in achieving cost savings, making quicker, better decisions using business big data cycle and collaborative filtering.

INTRODUCTION TO BUSINESS FACTOR

Business need that all data be controlled centralized, and most corporations utilize analysis to learn where their company stands in the market. We recognize that big data tools and approaches are being used by researchers and practitioners to compute performance utilizing various algorithms. Organization's typically have a large number of departments, and the risk analysis utilizes computations of the administrative flow and erroneous tests.

It is possible to link and dissociate distinct data assets from different big data sources using metadata. During the search process, metadata may be utilised to filter out irrelevant information, which helps search engines provide results with a high degree of confidence.

DOI: 10.4018/979-8-3693-0413-6.ch004

Despite the vast volume of content stored in these repositories, big data and analytics users may find the correct information fast by using metadata. Additionally, metadata establishes and preserves data consistency. Organisations can establish a uniform definition or business rule for a certain data attribute by using metadata. (Anuja Kulkarni, 2016).

Big data is the process of collecting and analyzing large data sets from traditional and digital sources to identify trends and patterns that can be used in decision-making. These large data sets are both structured (e.g. sales transactions from an online store) and unstructured (e.g. posts) on social media. Organizations are grappling with what big data is and how it effects their organizations and how it makes benefits to their organizations. A survey is conducted in which found that the only 12 percent organizations are implementing or executing the big data strategy and 71 percent organizations are going to begin the planning stage ("2013 Big

Data Survey Research Brief," n.d.) It is clear that organizations need good knowledge of customers, goods and rules, with the help of big data organizations can find new ways to compete with other organizations. The organizations of the world are using the big data for their future decisions. Types of decisions that organizations can make from big data are smarter decisions, future decisions and decisions that make the difference (M. Schroeck et al,2012)

Organizations are making business decisions on the basis of the transactional data in past and in present but there is another kind of data which are nontraditional, less structured data for example weblogs, social media, Email and photographs that can be used for effective business decisions making. (J. P. Dijcks,2012).

So big data has imparted golden opportunity to the universal market, every part of industry is trying to evaluate the higher possibilities to gain and analyze information to take better decisions, much data means much more use-cases, more use-cases leads to more illustration of business evaluation which ultimately leads to best business decision making.

This scenario will lead to much profit, by changing the traditional approach of managing data into helpful new approaches.(Sosna, M., Trevino Rodríguez, R. N. &Velamuri, S.R., 2010).

Big data is the process of collecting and analyzing large data sets from traditional and digital sources to identify trends and patterns that can be used in decision-making. These large data sets are both structured (e.g. sales transactions from an online store) and unstructured (e.g. posts) on social media. Organizations are grappling with what big data is and how it effects their organizations and how it makes benefits to their organizations. A survey is conducted in which found that the only 12 percent organizations are implementing or executing the big data strategy and 71 percent organizations are going to begin the planning stage ("2013 Big

Data Survey Research Brief," n.d.) It is clear that organizations need good knowledge of customers, goods and rules, with the help of big data organizations can find new ways to compete with other organizations. The organizations of the world are using the big data for their future decisions. Types of decisions that organizations can make from big data are smarter decisions, future decisions and decisions that make the difference (M. Schroeck et al,2012)

Organizations are making business decisions on the basis of the transactional data in past and in present but there is another kind of data which are nontraditional, less structured data for example weblogs, social media, Email and photographs that can be used for effective business decisions making. (J. P. Dijcks,2012).

So big data has imparted golden opportunity to the universal market, every part of industry is trying to evaluate the higher possibilities to gain and analyze information to take better decisions, much data means much more use-cases, more use-cases leads to more illustration of business evaluation which ultimately leads to best business decision making.

This scenario will lead to much profit, by changing the traditional approach of managing data into helpful new approaches.(Sosna, M., Trevino Rodríguez, R. N. &Velamuri, S.R., 2010).

Big data is the process of collecting and analyzing large data sets from traditional and digital sources to identify trends and patterns that can be used in decision-making. These large data sets are both structured (e.g. sales transactions from an online store) and unstructured (e.g. posts) on social media. Organizations are grappling with what big data is and how it effects their organizations and how it makes benefits to their organizations. A survey is conducted in which found that the only 12 percent organizations are implementing or executing the big data strategy and 71 percent organizations are going to begin the planning stage ("2013 Big

Data Survey Research Brief," n.d.) It is clear that organizations need good knowledge of customers, goods and rules, with the help of big data organizations can find new ways to compete with other organizations. The organizations of the world are using the big data for their future decisions. Types of decisions that organizations can make from big data are smarter decisions, future decisions and decisions that make the difference (M. Schroeck et al,2012)

Organizations are making business decisions on the basis of the transactional data in past and in present but there is another kind of data which are nontraditional, less structured data for example weblogs, social media, Email and photographs that can be used for effective business decisions making.

The act of gathering and analyzing massive data sets from conventional and digital sources in order to uncover trends and patterns that may be utilized in decision-making is known **as big data**. These huge data sets are both organised (for example, sales transactions from an online retailer) and unstructured (for example, social media posts). Organizations are wrestling with what big data is, how it affects their organisations, and how it helps their organisations.

Big Data is a popular phrase these days. This concept altered the definition of data, what can be mined from it, and how it may be used to help a firm flourish. There's a lot more; the modern individual interacts through a variety of channels, including emails, SMS, Twitter, and writing comments, all of which leave a permanent mark. (Jiwat Rama et al., 2016).

And it is this trace that has commercial possibilities. It can aid in getting to know the consumer better by using advanced analytical approaches on unstructured data. The goal of this project is to give an overview of the Big Data industry, as well as information regarding Big Data in general, technology used to process it, potential legal and ethical problems, and Big Data management.

It is obvious that organisations require strong understanding of their consumers, commodities, and laws; nevertheless, with the aid of big data, organisations may find new methods to compete with other organisations. (OGREAN Claudia, 2018).

The world's organisations are leveraging big data to make future judgements. Recent economic conditions, in which information is the most valuable resource, impose new techniques to assessing organisational success, as opposed to old performance measurement systems, which evolved only financial and accounting indicators.

One of the more recent techniques focuses on monitoring organisational performance using KPIs. KPIs are financial and non-financial measurements used by organisations to determine how effective they were in achieving long-term goals. To create an efficient system of performance assessment, all processes within the organisation must be identified and standardised. (Bhatti et al., 2014).

Figure 1. Phases of KPI

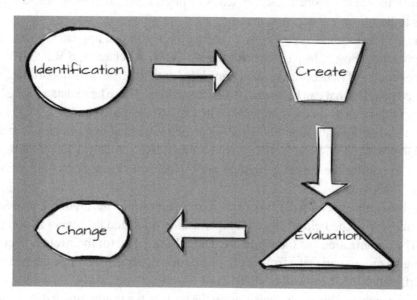

Professional performance evaluations involve the qualitative and quantitative representation of some results using predetermined indicators. Performance assessment enables successful organisations to quantify their performance. A very significant job is choosing the proper indicators that will be used to assess and evaluate the performances. It is vital to select a few key figures from the available information that best reflect the entire firm.

Figure 1 elaborates phases KPI system examines the consistency of the chosen activities with the goal and gives information for activity improvement.

KPIs and big data are two distinct sources that help businesses discover where they are falling short in business measures.

a. Financial Metrics
b. Process Metrics
c. Risk Metrics

Big data enhances business by applying numerous approaches and algorithms to departments, making it simpler to obtain information on the company's quality. In Figure 2, we can see which business factors are crucial and where big data is helping the firm.

In order to analyse a significant amount of data produced by various business organisations, big data and business analytics methodologies have recently been created and put into practise. Therefore, every firm need quicker access to the expanding amounts of transactional data. Real-time data analysis enables businesses to observe the past and predict the future. This is the appeal of streaming analytics, which may provide information on what happened (descriptive), why it happened (diagnostic), what could happen in the future (predictive), and, finally, how to change the course of events (prescriptive). (Ifeyinwa Angela Ajah et al., 2019).

Figure 2. Big data improvements in business

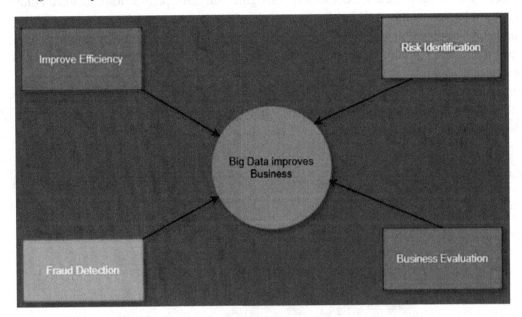

Big Data Business Phases

Big data analytics typically have five main benefits. It first improves visibility by making linked data easier to obtain. By gathering precise performance data, it promotes performance enhancement and variability exposure. Thirdly, by segmenting the population, it helps to better address the actual demands of clients.

Fourth, it adds important insights to the automated algorithms' decision-making. Fifthly, it produces fresh company models, guiding principles, goods, and services. (Wiener et al., 2021).

Big data analytics may enhance the management of the supply chain in a number of ways, including supply chain effectiveness, planning, risk management, inventory control, market information, and real-time personalised service.

Big data may also help the supply chain to understand how various sub-firms might work together to optimise the operating process in a way that is both efficient and innovative for the creation of new products and services. An increased knowledge of the many decision contexts and necessary information processing processes is the foundation for the efficient use of big data.(Wani et al., 2019).

Since the efficacy of decision-making is influenced by the quality of marketing information, marketing intelligence is crucial. No matter what market or sector of the economy a company works in, there is always competition among the different players (the companies), and each company needs to find strategies to survive, grow, and become a major force in its industry. It is still encouraged to make effective use of marketing intelligence, which involves watching marketing operations for important and crucial data. (Vossen & G, 2014).

Organisations want data on the efficacy of their marketing strategy instruments as they face increased competition. Managers nowadays must have access to current information in order to make prompt decisions in a fast changing environment.

An open system that includes specific sorts of significant information flows inside a company organisation and its surroundings might also be thought of as a marketing information system.

A marketing information system is described as an organised process for the routine collecting of unprocessed data from both internal and external sources and the translation of that data into information for choices.

A major company's top management invests a lot of time and money to realise that information management is just as important as managing people, materials, plants, and money. This process is known as the **Marketing Information System**.

Figure 3. Big data life cycle

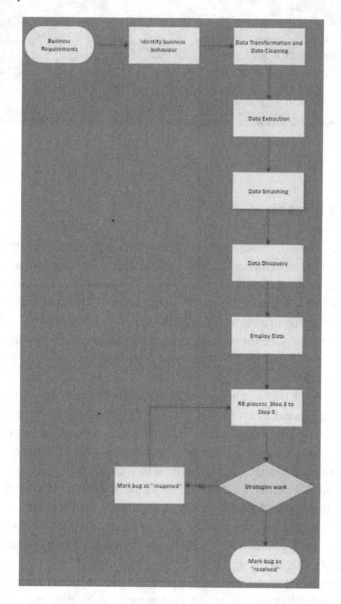

For a higher-quality outcome, every system has a set of procedures that must be followed. The business and big data relationships are discussed in Figure 3 of the big data life cycle. How each phase's data is transform.

1. Business Requirements: The business needs process is the initial step in the real business process, followed by meetings with clients and vendors to discuss the project needs. The questions that will satisfy the business criteria are as follows:
   a. What is the need basic need of the project?
   b. Whom will be project benefits?
   c. What will be project standard in the market?
   d. What are the competitive advantage to the project?
   e. Which technologies will beneficial to the project?

2. Data Identification: A data life cycle is required to assess the impact of data on expensive and plentiful data. Data sensing might result from any of the data processing, analysis, or exchange processes. During the search for meaningful data, it would be feasible to combine data from several sources. For the creation, development, and distribution of analytics, augmented analysis, which integrates IoT and machine learning, is now popular in addition to big data analytics.

3. Data Transformation and Data Cleaning:

   Analysing the data to find mistakes and inconsistencies in the database is the first stage in **data cleaning**. In other words, this stage is known as data inspection, and it is at this stage that all kinds of irregularities inside the database will be discovered.

   In addition, data analysis will be used to uncover issues with data quality by obtaining information about the data attributes.

   Data mining and data profiling are two methods used in data analysis

   a. Data profiling places a focus on the examination of specific instances of particular attributes.
   b. Data mining, on the other hand, focuses on identifying a specific data trend in a vast dataset.

   A series of actions on data is what is referred to as a **data transformation**, which includes the discovery and removal of abnormalities.

   After data analysis to learn more about the current abnormalities, it is stated. The number of sources, degree of heterogeneity, and "dirtiness" of the data all affect how many transformation processes are necessary.

   The schema-related transformation and the purification stages must be provided using a declarative query and mapping language in order to enable the automated development of the transformation code.

4. Data Extraction: Sinking various sources of data with the aim to extract data from them is the process of data extraction. In the majority of instances, it is done to move the data to a location that permits additional data processing or analysis. Given the technically advanced capabilities of data warehouses in terms of storage, processing, and reporting, this location is frequently a data warehouse.
   a. Operational Data: Data that is used to examine daily market trends and business progress from day-to-day organisation reports. For example: Inventory Management.
   b. Transactional Data: Businesses require a code of ethics to sustain their behaviour. In this case, database storage is used for data that was transferred between two parties. For example: Transaction ID

Figure 4. Data extraction

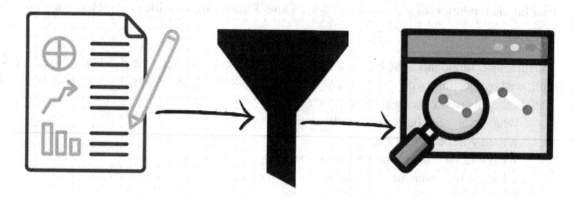

c.   Customer Data: The data analyst or the system keeps track of the customer's behaviour in order to suggest new items to them.

d.   Product Data: Involvement of new product, current product and future product to analyze the product standard in the market.

e.   Marketing Data: The marketers have the ability to access actual market data, which they utilise to sell the product by selecting a demographic target group.

Figure 4 emphasis modern enterprises, data extraction is a very valuable and crucial tool. It gives businesses the ability to swiftly gather specific information from websites, databases, and other online sources, enabling them to understand patterns and make wise decisions.

5.   Data Smashing: Leveraging the information that has been gathered through the business pipeline. Unwanted data should be deleted or destroyed until we find genuine patterns that can be applied to another process.

6.   Data Discovery: The knowledge which is obtained through data smashing process is used for implementation on actual project. The process where the patterns is used for projectis called data discovery. A comprehensive set of machine learning and data mining techniques is typically used to do data and business analytics. With the use of these technologies, business decision-makers can analyse data on a small to large scale. The data mining tools and algorithms for data analytics can be roughly divided into:

a.   Clustering and Segmentation: Here the process of evaluating an assortment of clients to discover more specific customer segments for customised marketing.
     For example: Categorize customers data according the surveys conducted by the team

b.   Classification: To determine the group into which a brand-new client would be assigned.
     For example: Data abstraction which leads to hiding information from the employees according their designation.

c.   Regression: To forecast future mobile money payment penetration, use mobile money subscription data, usage level, transaction type, transaction amount, and geographic area.
     For example: Statistical Analysis of data to navigate user's behavior and company behavior.

d.   Association: This could enable lead officials of electronic currency to provide personalised incentives to customers of mobile payment apps based on usage level, transfer value, and number of transactions.

Figure 5. Transmission data cubes into statistics analysis or different visualize method

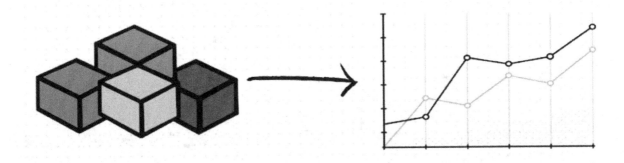

For example: Use of the data to recommend offers to users.

7.   Data Visualization: Enhancement of data through numerous views that provide day-to-day reports, such as: subscription sales.

We understand that a data mart is constructed up of subjects, and that OLAP procedures can be used to convert or analyse each subject. Data cubes are transformed into a graphical representation for data visualisation, as seen in Figure 5.

8.   Employ Data: Utilize data and fix the bugs of business, if bug is not fix repeat the step 3 to 7.

Case Study on Business Analysis Using Big Data

In the context of analytics, it refers to technique analysis. Examining whether predicted sales, costs, and profits satisfy the company's objectives is part of business analysis. Only after all objectives have been met can the product concept be advanced to the product development stage. In other words, query, report, OLAP, and alert tools can answer queries like "what occurred" and "what exactly is expected to occur in the future." Actually, business data analysis (BA) can answer deeper questions than BI.

It can anticipate what will happen in the future, why it will happen (i.e. forecast), what we should do and why. In the age of big data, data-driven decision-making will undoubtedly take the lead in enterprise. Businesses utilise BA to adopt data-driven decision-making, with the ultimate objective of defeating competitors and becoming leaders of comparable businesses. (Christian Janiescha et al., 2022).

For instance, by examining consumer data, marketers might provide various discounts or coupons to distinct client. For improved acquisition, customers who are new to the product or service may receive larger discounts. Personalization helps businesses better understand the needs of each unique consumer, which boosts sales and customer loyalty. As a consequence, the company guarantees customer acquisition and retention.

Predictions about sales, risks, human resources, and other aspects of the business are among the common factors that affect every part of the company. Figure 6 highlights a case study of the company process, including which day is the busiest for sales, etc.

Figure 6. Business case evaluation for Store to increase the sales and predication of the products

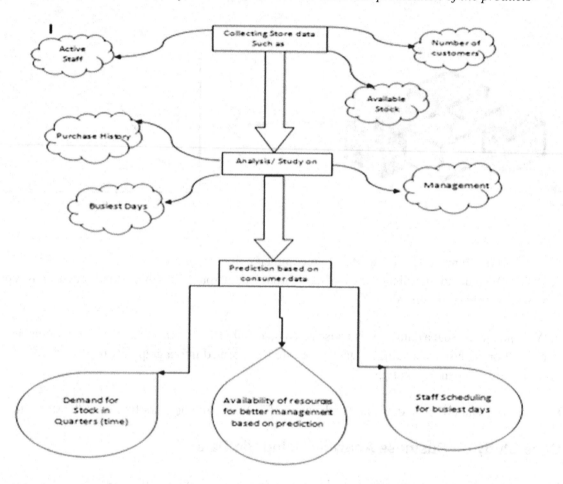

Common problems in business include product loss, product risk in the market, and inferior product quality. It is often known that big data may make forecasts and recommendations for products to improve their performance or answer product queries by examining customer behavior, market value, and important product surveys that boost sales. We have facts and statistical data to analyze product performance utilizing customer criteria, ranging from query analysis to visualizations. Additionally, there may be regular customers as well as seasonal ones. Seasonal, recurring, and predictable consumers can occasionally supply information to help users make product recommendations based on historical data and consistent clients, which offers data for product recommendations to the user through historical analysis. For example, be as follows there may be incidents where there is inadequate inventory in the warehouse as a result of worker strikes or a shortage of raw materials. This condition is caused by a lack of data and inconsistent information, which makes it difficult for the organization to provide the right answers in moments of need. Through the analysis or identification of business KPIs and indicators, decision-making and big data analytics technologies provide accurate answers regarding the overall structural system in this situation. These KPIs will produce accurate and precise data that big data will use to conduct operations on the most vulnerable sets in the organization.

Performance Analysis and Utilizing Results

OTT is often understood to refer to content, a service, or an application that is made available to end users through an open network. It follows that there are no joint ownership arrangements with content, broadband, or Internet service providers and that there is no integration or association with them. As a result, its business models have changed how consumers consume media by enabling them to freely access whatever material they like. The diffusion of innovation theory or the technology acceptance framework have been used by academic research to analyse consumer adoption of OTT as a novel service built on cutting-edge technology.

Figure 7 says Market intelligence for OTT platforms that illustrates how market intelligence impacts a business's operation. Engaging users based on their internet-based behaviour can assist you offer more video content on OTT.

The term "collaborative filtering" describes the practise of matching individuals based on their shared interests. The scores that each user has previously earned for the item are utilised to determine how similar the two users are. User-based filtering and item-based filtering are two categories of collaborative filtering. Collaborative filtering says that the suggestion of people-to-people correlation relates to the relevance of users' purchases on e-commerce websites and seeks to locate other users who share target consumers' tastes.

The recommender system suggests similar content to each other by using collaborative filtering, as illustrated in Figure 8, when two similar users watch the same feature content on OTT.

Figure 7. Market intelligence for OTT

Figure 8. Collaborative filtering

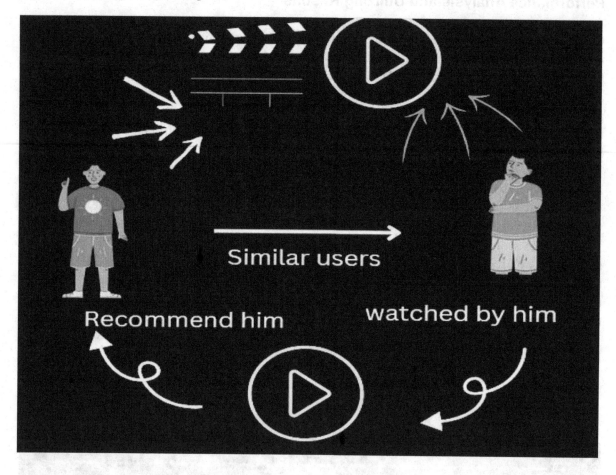

One of the most extensively studied recommender system strategies is collaborative filtering. The goal of collaborative filtering is to identify members of a community who have similar tastes. When two people rank the same or almost the same products, it indicates that their tastes are comparable. These users establish a community or so-called neighbourhood.

A user receives suggestions for products that he or she hasn't yet reviewed but that have previously received favourable reviews from other users in the area. Users of CF-based systems, which may be further divided into item-based CF and user-based CF, receive suggestions based on others who share their interests and preferences. The goods that the user has already evaluated play a significant part in the user-based approach when looking for a group of people who share his appreciations. In item-based systems, the anticipated rating is based on the user's ratings of related things.(Manisha Khileri & Prof. RiyaGohil, 2019).

Analysis of Collaborative Filtering Using Coefficient Pearson and User Similarity Matrix

Step 1: Import important libraries (Figure 9)

Step 2: Dataset that includes just a few subscribers and a few series (Figure 10)

Figure 9. Step 1

```
[35]:  import pandas as pd
       import numpy as np
       from math import sqrt
```

Figure 10. Step 2

```
[76]:  dataset={
              'OM':{'Guns & Gulaabs': 4,
                    'Scoop': 5,
                    'Kohra': 4,
                    'Class': 2,
                    'Delhi Crime': 3,
                    'Betaal': 3},
              'Sanjay':{'Guns & Gulaabs': 5,
                    'Scoop': 4,
                    'Kohra': 3,
                    'Betaal': 3},
              'Mayur':{'Guns & Gulaabs': 4,
                    'Scoop': 3,
                    'Kohra': 4,
                    'Class': 3,
                    'Delhi Crime': 1,
                    'Betaal': 2},
              'Yugesh':{'Guns & Gulaabs': 5,
                    'Scoop': 2,
                    'Delhi Crime': 1,
                    'Betaal': 3},
              'Shashikant':{'Guns & Gulaabs': 5,
                    'Scoop': 4,
                    'Kohra': 3,
                    'Class': 2,
                    'Delhi Crime': 3},
              'Bhupendra':{
                    'Delhi Crime': 4,
                    'Betaal': 2},

              'Sagar':{'Guns & Gulaabs': 4,
                    'Scoop': 5,
                    'Kohra': 4,
                    'Class': 2,
                    'Delhi Crime': 3,
                    'Betaal': 3},

              'Viru':{'Guns & Gulaabs': 4,
                    'Scoop': 3,
                    'Kohra': 4,
                    'Class': 3,
                    'Delhi Crime': 4,
                    'Betaal': 3},

              'Shubham':{ 'Guns & Gulaabs': 4,
                    'Delhi Crime': 3,
                    'Betaal': 2}}
```

Figure 11. Step 3

```
[ ]:  dataset_df=pd.DataFrame(dataset)
      dataset_df.fillna("Not Seen Yet",inplace=True)
      dataset_df

      C:\Users\user\AppData\Local\Temp\ipykernel_3244\4855286488.py:2: FutureWarning: Setting an item of incompatible dtype is deprecated and will raise in a
      future error of pandas. value 'Not Seen Yet' has dtype incompatible with float64, please explicitly cast to a compatible dtype first.
        dataset_df.fillna("Not Seen Yet",inplace=True)
```

	OM	Sanjay	Mayur	Yugesh	Shashikant	Bhupendra	Sagar	Viru	Shubham
Guns & Gulaabs	4	5.0	4	5.0	5.0	Not Seen Yet	4	4	4.0
Scoop	5	4.0	3	2.0	4.0	Not Seen Yet	5	3	Not Seen Yet
Kohra	4	3.0	4	Not Seen Yet	3.0	Not Seen Yet	4	4	Not Seen Yet
Class	2	Not Seen Yet	3	Not Seen Yet	2.0	Not Seen Yet	2	3	Not Seen Yet
Delhi Crime	3	Not Seen Yet	1	1.0	3.0	4.0	3	4	3.0
Betaal	3	3.0	2	3.0	Not Seen Yet	2.0	3	3	2.0

Figure 12. Step 4

```
[..]:  def unique_items():
           unique_items_list = []
           for person in dataset.keys():
               for items in dataset[person]:
                   unique_items_list.append(items)
           s=set(unique_items_list)
           unique_items_list=list(s)
           return unique_items_list

[..]:  unique_items()

[..]:  ['Kohra', 'Delhi Crime', 'Scoop', 'Class', 'Guns & Gulaabs', 'Betaal']
```

Figure 13. Step 5

```
[..]:  def person_corelation(person1,person2):
           both_rated = {}
           for item in dataset[person1]:
               if item in dataset[person2]:
                   both_rated[item] = 1

           number_of_ratings = len(both_rated)
           if number_of_ratings == 0:
               return 0

           person1_preferences_sum = sum([dataset[person1][item] for item in both_rated])
           person2_preferences_sum = sum([dataset[person2][item] for item in both_rated])

           person1_square_preferences_sum = sum([pow(dataset[person1][item], 2) for item in both_rated])
           person2_square_preferences_sum = sum([pow(dataset[person2][item], 2) for item in both_rated])

           product_sum_of_both_users = sum([dataset[person1][item] * dataset[person2][item] for item in both_rated])

           numerator_value = product_sum_of_both_users - (
           person1_preferences_sum * person2_preferences_sum / number_of_ratings)
           denominator_value = sqrt((person1_square_preferences_sum - pow(person1_preferences_sum, 2) / number_of_ratings) * (
           person2_square_preferences_sum - pow(person2_preferences_sum, 2) / number_of_ratings))
           if denominator_value == 0:
               return 0
           else:
               r = numerator_value / denominator_value
               return r
```

Figure 14. Step 6

```
[..]:  def most_similar_users(target_person,no_of_users):

           scores = [(person_corelation(target_person,other_person),other_person) for other_person in dataset if other_person !=target_person]

           scores.sort(reverse=True)

           return scores[0:no_of_users]

[..]:  most_similar_users('OM',6)

[..]:  [(1.0, 'Sagar'),
        (0.6741998624463242, 'Shashikant'),
        (0.42640143271122803, 'Sanjay'),
        (0.40779543587027256, 'Mayur'),
        (0.17407765595568785, 'Viru'),
        (0.15289415743128707, 'Yugesh')]
```

Step 3: Create data frames for the data set (Figure 11)

Step 4: Create function to identify the unique sets from the dataset (Figure 12)

Step 5: Create function Pearson Coefficient (Figure 13)

Utilising Pearson A recommendation system's coefficient focuses on neighbourhood users and correlates their behaviour. The system will propose things to users whose behaviour matches.

Step 6: Create function to match similar user's (Figure 14)

Step 7: Function for knowing the seen and unseen movies (Figure 15)

Figure 15. Step 7

```
[73]: def target_movies_to_users(target_person):
          target_person_movie_lst = []
          unique_list =unique_items()
          for movies in dataset[target_person]:
              target_person_movie_lst.append(movies)

          s=set(unique_list)
          recommended_movies=list(s.difference(target_person_movie_lst))
          a = len(recommended_movies)
          if a == 0:
              return 0
          return recommended_movies,target_person_movie_lst

[77]:
      unseen_movies,seen_movies=target_movies_to_users('Shubham')

      dct = {"Unseen Movies":unseen_movies,"Seen Movies":seen_movies}
      pd.DataFrame(dct)
```

[77]:

	Unseen Movies	Seen Movies
0	Kohra	Guns & Gulaabs
1	Class	Delhi Crime
2	Scoop	Betaal

Figure 16. Step 8

```
def recommendation_phase(person):
    totals = {}  #empty dictionary
    simSums = {} # empty dictionary
    for other in dataset:

        if other == person:
            continue
        sim = person_corelation(person, other)

        if sim <= 0:
            continue
        for item in dataset[other]:

            if item not in dataset[person]:

                totals.setdefault(item, 0)
                totals[item] += dataset[other][item] * sim

                simSums.setdefault(item, 0)
                simSums[item] += sim

    rankings = [(total / simSums[item], item) for item, total in totals.items()]
    rankings.sort(reverse=True)
    # returns the recommended items
    recommendations_list = [(recommend_item,score) for score, recommend_item in rankings]
    return recommendations_list

print("Enter the target person")
tp = input().title()
if tp in dataset.keys():
    a=recommendation_phase(tp)
    if a != -1:
        print("Recommendation Using User based Collaborative Filtering: ")
        for webseries,weights in a:
            print(webseries,'---->',weights)
else:
    print("Person not found in the dataset..please try again")

Enter the target person
Shubham
Recommendation Using User based Collaborative Filtering:
Scoop ----> 3.8629123419504348
Kohra ----> 3.6192456027807105
Class ----> 2.3575771602393294
```

Step 8: Recommend web series on the basis of user behavior (Figure 16)

Most OTT platforms employ collaborative filtering to provide goods or products that are compatible with the same human behaviour as one another. This is one of the main association techniques used to improve company sales. When a user exhibits the same behaviour but is unable to subscribe to read the most recent material, the recommender system notifies him of the subscription. Because of user similarities, we may suggest previously unwatched series and films to the targeted person as seen in the study of the above result set.

CONCLUSION

Big data analyses business by using numerous tools and algorithms to maximise profits. In this study, we learned about KPIs, metrics, and several fundamental business ideas that evaluate businesses and identify market circumstances based on user and content behaviour by evaluating user history.

REFERENCES

Al-Dulaimi, A. H. (2020). Big data: Definition, characteristics, life cycle, applications, and challenges. *IOP Conference Series. Materials Science and Engineering, 769*(1), 012007. doi:10.1088/1757-899X/769/1/012007

Bhatti, M. (2014). The key performance indicators (KPIs) and their impact on overall organizational performance. *Quality & Quantity, 48*(6), 3127–3143. doi:10.100711135-013-9945-y

Ifeyinwa, A. (2019). Review Big Data and Business Analytics: Trends, Platforms, Success Factors and Applications. *Big Data Cogn. Comput.* . doi:10.3390/bdcc3020032

Christian Janiescha, C., Dinterb, B., Mikalefc P., & Tona, O. (2022). Business analytics and big data research in information systems. *Journal of business analytics, 5*(1), 1–7. https://doi.org/. doi:10.1080/2573234X.2022.2069426©

Jiwat, R. (2016). *The implications of Big Data analytics on Business Intelligence: A qualitative study in China*. ICRTCSE. doi:10.1016/j.procs.2016.05.152

Manisha, K. (2017). Recommender System. In *Big Data Environment, 3*(6).

Kulkarni, A. (2016). A Study on Metadata Management and Quality Evaluation. *Big Data Management, 4*(7).

Vossen, G. (2014). Big data as the new enabler in business and other intelligence. *Vietnam J ComputSci, 1*(1), 3–14. doi:10.100740595-013-0001-6

Wani, M., & Jabin, S. (2018). *Big Data: Issues*. Challenges, and Techniques in Business Intelligence. doi:10.1007/978-981-10-6620-7_59

Wiener, M., Saunders, C., & Marabelli, M. (2020). Big-data Business Models: A Critical Literature Review and Multi-perspective Research Framework. *Journal of Information Technology*, *35*(1), 66–91. doi:10.1177/0268396219896811

KEY TERMS AND DEFINITIONS

Big Data Cycles: These plug in spaces in business or solve issues that contain bugs or faults by defining solutions to real-world situations.

Big Data: The act of gathering and analyzing massive data sets from conventional and digital sources in order to uncover trends and patterns that may be utilized in decision-making.

Collaborative Filtering: This describes the practise of matching individuals based on their shared interests.

Data Transformation: A series of actions on data which includes the discovery and removal of abnormalities.

Key Performance Indicators: (KPIs): These gauge how well your teams are working together to accomplish the overarching goals and objectives of the company. KPIs can be used to monitor the effectiveness of individual team members as well as the various departments that make up an organisation.

Marketing Information System: A major company's top management invests a lot of time and money to realise that information management is just as important as managing people, materials, plants, and money.

User History: A term used to describe data that is used for user analysis or prediction. We are aware that historical data can be used to forecast actual statistical analysis, which in turn provides business solutions.

Chapter 5
Big Data Collection, Filtering, and Extraction of Features

Ganesh B. Regulwar
iD https://orcid.org/0000-0001-9320-7040
Vardhaman College of Engineering, India

Ashish Mahalle
G.H. Raisoni College of Engineering, Nagpur, India

Raju Pawar
G.H. Raisoni College of Engineering, Nagpur, India

Swati K. Shamkuwar
G.H. Raisoni College of Engineering, Nagpur, India

Priti Roshan Kakde
iD https://orcid.org/0000-0002-5951-8723
G.H. Raisoni College of Engineering, Nagpur, India

Swati Tiwari
iD https://orcid.org/0009-0006-1063-5538
G.H. Raisoni College of Engineering, Nagpur, India

ABSTRACT

Big data is a term used to describe data sets that are too large or intricate for traditional data processing systems to handle. Big data collection, filtering, and feature extraction are significant procedures in data science that enable organizations to scrutinize vast amounts of data to obtain insights and make well-informed decisions. Following filtration, feature extraction is executed to identify vital patterns and relationships in the data using techniques such as clustering, principal component analysis, and association rule mining. The primary objective of big data collection, filtering, and feature extraction is to identify valuable information that can aid in decision-making, enhance operations, and develop new products and services. These processes are essential for organizations that aspire to remain competitive and at the forefront of the constantly changing data landscape.

DOI: 10.4018/979-8-3693-0413-6.ch005

1. INTRODUCTION

In today's digital era, we find ourselves immersed in an unprecedented flood of data. This overwhelming abundance of information is commonly referred to as "big data." To tap into the immense potential of this data ocean, it's crucial to understand how to effectively collect, filter, and extract valuable features from it.

his chapter delves into the essential aspects of handling big data, focusing on three vital stages: data collection, data filtering, and feature extraction. We will explore the methodologies and techniques used to gather data from diverse sources, refine it by eliminating noise and irrelevant details, and uncover valuable insights by extracting meaningful features (Ray, 2019).

Whether you are an enthusiastic data explorer, a researcher, or a professional seeking to harness big data's power for your organization, this chapter will provide you with a solid groundwork to navigate through the realm of abundant data effectively. Let's embark on this enlightening journey to unveil the hidden treasures concealed within big data!

1.1 Overview of Big Data

The concept of big data in the rapidly evolving digital world. Big data refers to massive volumes of both structured and unstructured data, produced at a high speed and encompassing various data types. It is characterized by three fundamental attributes known as the three Vs: Volume, Velocity, and Variety. The exponential growth of big data is driven by factors such as the proliferation of connected devices, social media platforms, and the Internet of Things (IoT).

Organizations across industries recognize the potential value hidden within big data. By analyzing and extracting insights from these vast datasets, businesses can make data-driven decisions and gain a competitive edge. Governments and research institutions also utilize big data for critical applications, ranging from healthcare advancements to urban planning (Perer, 2019).

However, managing big data comes with challenges as traditional data processing tools struggle to cope with the scale and complexity of these datasets. Scaling storage, processing capabilities, and ensuring data privacy and security become vital concerns (Desai, 2020).

The chapter aims to delve into the methodologies and techniques employed for big data collection, filtering, and feature extraction, empowering researchers and organizations to unlock the potential of big data and drive innovations in today's data-centric world.

1.2. Importance of Data Collection, Filtering, and Feature Extraction

Data collection, filtering, and feature extraction hold immense significance in the domain of big data analytics. Each stage plays a vital role in transforming raw data into valuable insights and actionable knowledge. Here are the key reasons that underscore the importance of these processes:

Data Collection: High-quality and comprehensive data collection is crucial for accurate and reliable analysis. Incomplete or biased data can result in erroneous conclusions and flawed decision-making. Data collection from diverse sources enables the identification of hidden patterns, trends, and correlations, leading to a deeper understanding of complex phenomena. Well-executed data collection empowers organizations to make informed decisions based on evidence rather than intuition or guesswork.

Data Filtering: Filtering out irrelevant data and noise improves data quality and enhances the precision and dependability of subsequent analyses. Reducing data volume and eliminating unnecessary details streamlines the analytical process, leading to faster processing times and improved computational efficiency. Data filtering also enables the detection and handling of outliers, ensuring the robustness of analytical results by addressing their potential impact on analysis outcomes.

Feature Extraction: Feature extraction involves reducing data dimensionality for better analysis. High-dimensional data can be computationally challenging and negatively impact model performance. Extracting relevant features enhances machine learning and statistical models' performance, fosters interpretability, and enables valuable insights from unstructured data like text or images by converting them into a structured format (Sahu, 2023).

Data collection, filtering, and feature extraction are integral to the success of big data analytics. These processes ensure that the data used for analysis is of high quality, relevance, and manageability. They empower organizations and researchers to draw meaningful conclusions, make data-driven decisions, and extract valuable insights from the vast pool of data available today.

2. BIG DATA COLLECTION

Big data collection marks the initial and crucial step in managing extensive and diverse datasets. As the volume, velocity, and variety of data continue to surge, efficient data collection becomes imperative to extract valuable insights and facilitate informed decision-making. Below are the key aspects of big data collection:

Data Sources: Big data originates from diverse sources, including social media platforms, IoT devices, sensors, transaction logs, and mobile applications. Identifying and understanding relevant data sources is essential to acquire comprehensive and varied datasets.

Data Collection Techniques: Depending on data nature and velocity, different data collection techniques are utilized. Batch processing handles large datasets collected at intervals, while real-time streaming deals with continuous data ingestion in real-time.

Scalability and Distributed Systems: Managing big data requires scalable solutions, often involving distributed systems like Apache Hadoop or Apache Spark. These distributed frameworks enable parallel processing, facilitating efficient data collection and storage across multiple nodes.

Data Quality: Ensuring data quality is vital for drawing accurate and dependable conclusions. Data cleaning, validation, and enrichment processes are necessary to eliminate errors, inconsistencies, and duplicates from the collected data.

Data Privacy and Ethics: Big data collection raises concerns about data privacy and ethical considerations. Organizations must adhere to regulatory frameworks and implement privacy measures to safeguard sensitive information.

Cloud-Based Solutions: Cloud computing offers scalable and flexible solutions for big data collection. Cloud-based platforms provide resources for storing and processing massive datasets without extensive infrastructure investments.

Web Scraping and APIs: Web scraping techniques and Application Programming Interfaces (APIs) enable organizations to gather data from websites and online platforms, extracting pertinent information for analysis.

Data Integration: Data collected from various sources may require integration to create a unified and coherent dataset. Data integration techniques help combine diverse data streams into a single, manageable format.

Real-Time Data Collection: Some applications demand real-time data collection and processing for immediate decision-making. This approach is prevalent in areas like financial trading, supply chain management, and healthcare monitoring.

10. Internet of Things (IoT): With the proliferation of IoT devices, data collection now includes information from sensors and connected devices, providing real-time insights for numerous applications.

Big data collection lays the groundwork for subsequent data processing and analysis. By implementing effective data collection strategies and leveraging appropriate technologies, organizations can unlock the vast potential of big data, gaining valuable insights that drive innovation, efficiency, and competitive advantage. However, it is vital to ensure data privacy, maintain data quality, and adhere to ethical standards while harnessing the power of big data for responsible and meaningful applications.

2.1 Sources of Big Data

Sources of big data are varied and continually expanding as our digital world evolves. These sources generate extensive volumes of structured and unstructured data, offering valuable insights for various applications. Here are key sources contributing to big data:

Social Media: Platforms like Facebook, Twitter, Instagram, and LinkedIn generate vast user-generated content, including posts, comments, images, and videos.

Internet of Things (IoT) Devices: IoT devices such as sensors, wearables, smart appliances, and industrial machinery continuously collect and transmit data, significantly contributing to the growth of big data.

Web and E-commerce: Websites, e-commerce platforms, and online services generate substantial data through user interactions, clicks, online purchases, and browsing behavior.

Mobile Applications: Mobile apps collect data on user behavior, location, preferences, and interactions, adding to the pool of big data.

Transaction Logs: Financial institutions, online payment systems, and businesses generate significant data on transactions, purchases, and customer behavior through transaction logs.

Sensors and IoT Networks: Various industries use sensors to monitor real-time data on environmental conditions, traffic, weather, and more.

Healthcare and Medical Devices: Electronic health records, medical imaging, and wearable health devices contribute to significant data accumulation in the healthcare sector.

Genomics and Bioinformatics: DNA sequencing and bioinformatics research generate massive datasets in genomics and life sciences.

Government and Public Data: Government agencies collect and publish data on demographics, transportation, education, crime, and public services, enriching big data sources.

Research and Scientific Data: Scientific experiments, simulations, and research studies generate extensive datasets across various fields, such as physics, astronomy, and climate research.

Surveillance and Security: Video surveillance, security cameras, and facial recognition systems contribute to big data through continuous monitoring and data collection.

Machine and System Logs: Log files from computer systems, servers, and applications record activities, errors, and performance metrics, creating substantial data streams.

Text and Documents: Large volumes of unstructured text data, including emails, documents, and web pages, contribute to big data sources.

Geospatial Data: Geographic Information System (GIS) data, satellite imagery, and geolocation information contribute significant spatial data.

Social Networks and Online Forums: Online forums, discussion boards, and social networking sites generate vast textual data reflecting public opinions and sentiments.

These examples highlight the multitude of sources that contribute to big data. As technology advances and our interconnectedness grows, new data sources will likely emerge, further enriching the landscape of big data and opening doors to innovative insights and applications.

2.2 Challenges in Big Data Collection

Big data collection presents numerous challenges due to the vast amount, rapid pace, and diverse formats of data being generated. Addressing these challenges is crucial to ensure the collected data is of high quality, relevant, and suitable for analysis. Here are the key challenges in big data collection:

Scale and Scalability: Managing the sheer volume of data requires scalable infrastructure and distributed computing to handle the data efficiently.

Velocity of Data: Real-time data sources demand rapid data collection and processing to keep up with the continuous flow of information.

Data Variety: Dealing with data in various formats, such as structured, unstructured, and semi-structured, requires integration and processing capabilities.

Data Privacy and Security: Protecting sensitive data and complying with privacy regulations are critical considerations during data collection.

Data Quality: Ensuring data is accurate and reliable is vital to obtain meaningful insights from the collected data.

Heterogeneous Data Sources: Integrating data from different platforms and systems with varying data schemas can be complex.

Cost Management: Collecting and storing large datasets can be costly, necessitating cost-efficient data collection strategies.

Data Governance and Compliance: Establishing proper data governance frameworks and adhering to legal requirements are important aspects of big data collection.

Data Extraction Complexity: Extracting data from unstructured sources, like websites, poses technical challenges.

Addressing Data Bias: Overcoming biases in data collection is crucial to avoid skewed analysis results.

Real-Time Processing: Handling real-time data for immediate decision-making requires low-latency and high-performance systems.

Data Ownership and Sharing: Establishing clear data ownership and sharing agreements is essential for collaborative data collection efforts.

Tackling these challenges in big data collection involves deploying advanced technologies, robust data management practices, and ethical data handling procedures. Organizations must invest in scalable infrastructure, data integration tools, and data quality assurance mechanisms to harness the full potential of big data responsibly. By addressing these challenges, organizations can effectively collect and utilize big data to gain valuable insights and drive innovation.

3. DATA FILTERING AND PREPROCESSING

Data filtering and preprocessing are vital initial steps in big data analysis, aiming to refine and cleanse raw data to ensure its quality, consistency, and suitability for further exploration. These processes play a significant role in preparing data for analysis and modeling. Here are the key points regarding data filtering and preprocessing:

1. Data Filtering:

Noise Reduction: Filtering out irrelevant or noisy data improves the accuracy and reliability of analysis results. Noise, arising from errors or outliers, can distort the overall findings.

Feature Selection: Data filtering identifies the most relevant features or variables, reducing data dimensionality, enhancing computational efficiency, and boosting model performance.

Data Reduction: By eliminating unnecessary data points or subsets, data filtering reduces the data volume, making it more manageable for analysis and storage.

Data Imputation: Handling incomplete or missing data is crucial. Data filtering may involve imputing missing values using various techniques to maintain data completeness.

2. Data Preprocessing:

Data Cleaning: Data preprocessing involves cleaning data to rectify errors, inconsistencies, and duplicates that might occur during data collection.

Data Transformation: Data may require normalization, scaling, or transformation to ensure uniformity and comparability between different variables.

Handling Categorical Data: Categorical variables may need to be encoded or converted into numerical values to be used effectively in machine learning algorithms.

Dealing with Outliers: Outliers, extreme values, can significantly impact analysis results. Data preprocessing techniques may include handling outliers to mitigate their influence.

Handling Unstructured Data: Unstructured data, like text or images, requires specialized preprocessing techniques, such as text tokenization or image feature extraction, for effective analysis.

Data Integration: When dealing with multiple data sources, data preprocessing involves integrating data into a unified format to create a comprehensive dataset.

Benefits of Data Filtering and Preprocessing:

Improved Data Quality: Filtering and preprocessing enhance data quality by eliminating noise, errors, and inconsistencies.

Enhanced Analysis Accuracy: High-quality data leads to more accurate and reliable analysis outcomes, providing better insights.

Efficient Computing: Data reduction and normalization improve computational efficiency, speeding up analysis and modeling processes.

Robust Models: Cleaned and preprocessed data helps create more robust and effective machine learning and statistical models.

Data filtering and preprocessing are crucial steps in big data analysis. By refining and cleansing raw data, organizations can ensure the data is of high quality, relevant, and well-suited for advanced analytics, enabling them to derive meaningful insights and make informed decisions (Hariharakrishnan, 2017).

3.1 Data Cleaning Techniques

Data cleaning, an essential part of data preprocessing, involves various techniques to rectify errors, inconsistencies, and inaccuracies in datasets. These techniques aim to improve data quality and enhance the reliability of analysis results. Here are some common data cleaning techniques:

Duplicate Removal: Identifying and eliminating duplicate records or entries to avoid redundancy and ensure data integrity.

Handling Missing Values:

Imputation: Filling in missing values using statistical methods like mean, median, or regression.

Deletion: Removing rows or columns with missing values, with caution to avoid data loss.

Outlier Detection and Treatment: Identifying and addressing outliers, extreme data points that deviate significantly from the majority, to prevent skewing of results.

Data Normalization: Scaling numerical data to a standardized range, such as between 0 and 1, for fair comparisons.

Data Standardization: Transforming numerical data to have a mean of 0 and a standard deviation of 1 for better model convergence.

Encoding Categorical Data: Converting categorical variables into numerical representations, like one-hot encoding or label encoding, suitable for machine learning algorithms.

Handling Inconsistent Data: Correcting inconsistent data entries that do not adhere to defined rules or constraints.

Data Formatting: Ensuring consistent data formats, such as date formats, to facilitate analysis and prevent errors.

Parsing and Tokenization: Breaking down unstructured data, such as text, into meaningful components like words or phrases for analysis.

Data Integration and Deduplication: Integrating data from various sources and removing duplicate entries merged from different datasets.

Addressing Spelling and Typographical Errors: Using fuzzy matching or spell-checking algorithms to correct spelling mistakes.

Handling Incomplete or Inaccurate Data: Identifying and correcting data that appears incomplete or inaccurate based on predefined rules.

Handling Irrelevant Data: Removing irrelevant or unrelated data that does not contribute to the analysis.

Data Verification and Validation: Verifying and validating data against predefined rules or external sources to ensure accuracy.

Data Sampling: Taking a representative sample from excessively large datasets to reduce computational load and processing times.

Each data cleaning technique serves a specific purpose in enhancing data quality, and their selection depends on the dataset's characteristics and specific requirements. Diligent data cleaning is essential to ensure accurate and reliable data analysis and modeling results.

3.2 Data Transformation

Data transformation is a crucial step in data preprocessing, involving the conversion or modification of original data into a suitable format for analysis, modeling, or visualization. The primary objectives of data transformation are to enhance data quality, reduce noise, handle outliers, and make the data compatible with various statistical methods and algorithms. Below are the key aspects of data transformation:

1. Data Scaling:

    Normalization: Scaling numerical data to a standardized range, typically between 0 and 1, to ensure equal weightage for all features during analysis.
    Standardization: Transforming numerical data to have a mean of 0 and a standard deviation of 1, facilitating comparisons and model convergence.

2. Data Encoding:

    One-Hot Encoding: Converting categorical variables into binary vectors to represent different categories, making them suitable for machine learning algorithms.
    Label Encoding: Assigning integer values to categorical data for simplified representation.

3. Data Binning:

    Binning: Grouping continuous numerical data into discrete bins or intervals, simplifying data analysis and handling outliers.

4. Log Transformation:

    Logarithmic Transformation: Applying logarithm functions to compress large value ranges, making data suitable for certain analyses.

5. Data Discretization:

    Discretization: Converting continuous data into discrete intervals, making data analysis more manageable.

6. Handling Outliers:

    Clipping: Capping extreme values (outliers) to predefined upper or lower thresholds to prevent their undue influence on analysis.

7. Power Transformation:

    Square Root Transformation: Applying square root functions to data to reduce the impact of extreme values and stabilize variance.

8. Data Aggregation:

Aggregation: Combining individual data points into summary statistics or averages for higher-level analysis.

9. Feature Engineering:

Creating New Features: Deriving new features or variables from existing ones to improve model performance.

10. Handling Skewed Data:

Box-Cox Transformation: Adjusting data distribution to a more symmetrical shape using power transformations.

11. Data Inversion:

Data Inversion: Inverting data values to reverse the direction of the relationship between variables, if necessary for analysis.

Data transformation plays a vital role in data preprocessing, ensuring that data aligns with the assumptions of statistical methods and algorithms. By employing appropriate data transformations, researchers and data scientists can enhance data analysis quality and achieve better performance in machine learning models, leading to more accurate and reliable insights.

4. FEATURE EXTRACTION

Feature extraction is a fundamental technique in data preprocessing and machine learning, with the aim of identifying and selecting the most important and informative aspects of raw data. Its purpose is to transform the original data into a condensed and manageable representation, called features, while preserving its essential information. Feature extraction plays a vital role in various data analysis tasks, such as pattern recognition, classification, and clustering. Here are the main points about feature extraction:

1. **Reducing Dimensionality:** Feature extraction helps in reducing the number of variables or dimensions in the data, particularly when dealing with high-dimensional datasets. This simplifies analysis and improves computational efficiency.
2. **Selecting Informative Features:** The technique focuses on identifying features with significant discriminative power, filtering out noise and irrelevant attributes, and concentrating on the most relevant information.
3. **Transformation Approaches:** Feature extraction often involves mathematical transformations to derive new features or data representations. Common methods include Principal Component Analysis (PCA), Linear Discriminant Analysis (LDA), and Singular Value Decomposition (SVD).
4. **Image and Signal Processing:** In computer vision and signal processing applications, feature extraction identifies essential patterns or characteristics in images or signals, enabling tasks like object detection, facial recognition, and speech recognition.

5. **Text and Natural Language Processing:** In NLP, feature extraction converts raw text data into numerical representations, such as Bag-of-Words or Word Embeddings, making it usable in machine learning algorithms.

6. **Feature Engineering:** Feature extraction is often part of a broader process known as feature engineering, where domain knowledge and creativity are applied to generate meaningful and relevant features from the original data.

7. **Data Compression:** Feature extraction can lead to data compression as the new feature representation typically requires fewer bits to accurately represent the same information.

8. **Overcoming Multicollinearity:** In situations where features are highly correlated (multicollinearity), feature extraction can help reduce redundancy and multicollinearity issues in the data.

9. **Improving Model Performance:** By selecting informative features and reducing noise, feature extraction enhances model performance, resulting in more accurate predictions and better generalization.

10. **Visualization:** Feature extraction aids in visualizing high-dimensional data by projecting it into a lower-dimensional space, making it easier to explore and interpret.

Feature extraction is a crucial step in data analysis and machine learning, as it enables efficient and effective data representation, reduces complexity, and enhances the performance of predictive models. Through the extraction of meaningful features from raw data, researchers and data scientists can uncover critical insights and patterns that inform decision-making across various domains and applications.

4.1 Traditional Feature Extraction Techniques

Traditional feature extraction techniques are well-established methods used in data analysis and machine learning for many years. These techniques aim to transform raw data into a more concise and informative representation suitable for various modeling and analysis tasks. Here are some common traditional feature extraction techniques:

1. **Principal Component Analysis (PCA):** PCA is a widely used method for dimensionality reduction, identifying new features (principal components) that capture the most significant variance in the data while reducing the number of dimensions.

2. **Linear Discriminant Analysis (LDA):** LDA is employed for supervised dimensionality reduction and feature extraction. It finds linear combinations of features that maximize class separability, making it useful for classification tasks.

3. **Singular Value Decomposition (SVD):** SVD is a matrix factorization technique used in various applications, including feature extraction. It breaks down the data matrix into three matrices to identify important features.

4. **Independent Component Analysis (ICA):** ICA is a statistical technique that aims to find statistically independent components in the data, making it suitable for blind source separation and feature extraction from mixed data.

5. **Wavelet Transform:** This technique is valuable for analyzing signals and images. It decomposes the data into different frequency components, capturing localized features in both time and frequency domains.

6. **Histogram of Oriented Gradients (HOG):** HOG is commonly used in computer vision for object detection. It describes object shapes by capturing the distribution of gradient orientations in an image.

7. **Bag-of-Words (BoW):** BoW is a feature extraction technique widely used in natural language processing (NLP). It represents text data numerically by counting word frequencies in a document.

8. **Term Frequency-Inverse Document Frequency (TF-IDF):** TF-IDF is another popular NLP feature extraction technique that quantifies word importance in a document relative to a corpus.

9. **Mel-Frequency Cepstral Coefficients (MFCC):** MFCC is commonly used in speech and audio signal processing to extract relevant features from audio data.

10. **Local Binary Patterns (LBP):** LBP is a texture analysis technique used in image processing to describe local patterns in an image.

Although more complex feature learning methods, like deep neural networks, have gained popularity with advancements in deep learning, traditional feature extraction techniques remain valuable and often serve as essential steps in the overall data preprocessing process.

4.2 Advanced Feature Extraction Techniques

Advanced feature extraction techniques utilize sophisticated algorithms and deep learning models to automatically learn and derive complex and abstract representations from raw data. These techniques have become prominent in recent years due to their ability to capture intricate patterns and relationships within the data. Here are some examples of advanced feature extraction techniques:

Convolutional Neural Networks (CNNs): CNNs are extensively used in computer vision tasks, excelling at feature extraction from images. They employ convolutional layers to automatically detect relevant features like edges, textures, and shapes.

Recurrent Neural Networks (RNNs): RNNs are designed to handle sequential data, making them suitable for tasks such as natural language processing and time-series analysis. They can capture temporal dependencies and extract meaningful features from sequences.

Transfer Learning: This involves using pre-trained deep learning models, such as VGG, ResNet, or BERT, and fine-tuning them on specific tasks or datasets. These models have learned rich features from vast amounts of data, making them useful for various applications with limited data.

Autoencoders: Autoencoders are unsupervised neural networks that reconstruct input data at the output layer. The hidden layers serve as compressed representations of the data, effectively extracting important features.

Word Embeddings: Word embeddings like Word2Vec, GloVe, and FastText are dense vector representations of words in a language. These embeddings capture semantic relationships between words and facilitate feature extraction for NLP tasks.

Generative Adversarial Networks (GANs): GANs consist of a generator and a discriminator that compete against each other. The generator learns to create realistic data, while the discriminator aims to differentiate between real and generated data. GANs can learn and generate complex and meaningful data representations.

Long Short-Term Memory (LSTM): LSTM is a specialized RNN architecture that effectively captures long-term dependencies in sequential data, making it suitable for tasks like sentiment analysis and speech recognition.

Attention Mechanisms: Attention mechanisms focus on specific parts of the input data, enabling the model to concentrate on relevant features during processing. They are particularly useful for tasks with variable-length inputs, such as machine translation.

Capsule Networks: Capsule networks address the limitations of traditional CNNs by capturing hierarchical relationships between features, potentially leading to more robust feature representations.

Graph Neural Networks (GNNs): GNNs are designed to handle data represented as graphs, such as social networks or molecular structures. They can learn meaningful features from graph-structured data.

Advanced feature extraction techniques provide powerful tools for data scientists and researchers to automatically learn intricate and informative representations from raw data. By leveraging these techniques, they can address complex tasks and achieve state-of-the-art performance in various domains, including computer vision, natural language processing, and graph analysis.

4.3 Feature Engineering

Feature engineering involves the process of crafting and selecting pertinent features from raw data to improve the performance of machine learning algorithms. It includes transforming and manipulating data to create informative and meaningful representations that are crucial for accurate predictions and insightful data analysis. Feature engineering plays a pivotal role in data preprocessing and significantly impacts the success of a machine learning model. Here are the key aspects of feature engineering:

1. **Leveraging Domain Knowledge:** Feature engineering relies on domain knowledge to identify and create features that align with the underlying problem. A good understanding of the data and the problem domain helps in selecting the most relevant and informative features (Sughasiny, 2018).
2. **Extracting and Selecting Features:** Feature engineering involves extracting features from raw data using techniques like statistical measures, text processing, image analysis, and more. Additionally, it entails selecting the most significant features to avoid overfitting and improve model efficiency.
3. **Dealing with Missing Data:** Feature engineering includes handling missing data through techniques like imputation, where missing values are replaced by estimated ones based on other data points or external information.
4. **Managing Categorical Data:** Categorical variables need to be transformed into numerical representations to be effectively utilized in machine learning algorithms. Feature engineering commonly employs techniques like one-hot encoding or label encoding.
5. **Ensuring Feature Scaling:** Scaling numerical features to a consistent range prevents certain features from dominating the model. Common scaling techniques include normalization and standardization.
6. **Addressing Outliers:** Outliers can negatively impact model performance. Feature engineering techniques may involve outlier detection and treatment to minimize their influence on the model.
7. **Creating Interaction Features:** Feature engineering allows the combination of existing features to create interaction or polynomial features, which can capture complex relationships within the data.
8. **Time-Series Features:** For time-series data, feature engineering might include creating lag features or calculating rolling window statistics to capture temporal patterns.
9. **Analyzing Feature Importance:** Analyzing the importance of features helps identify irrelevant or redundant ones, leading to a more efficient and effective feature set.

10. **Reducing Dimensionality:** Feature engineering might employ dimensionality reduction techniques like PCA or LDA to compress the data into a lower-dimensional space while retaining essential information.

11. **Handling Skewed Data:** For skewed data distributions, feature engineering techniques like logarithmic or power transformations can help normalize the data and improve model performance (Zhou, 2019).

Feature engineering is a blend of art and science, requiring creativity, domain knowledge, and data analysis skills. By crafting meaningful features from raw data, feature engineering significantly enhances the predictive power and generalization capabilities of machine learning models, leading to more accurate and valuable insights for decision-making.

5. BIG DATA ANALYTICS AND APPLICATIONS

Big data analytics involves the examination and extraction of valuable insights from large and complex datasets, which often surpass the capabilities of traditional data processing methods. In today's digital era, where data grows exponentially, big data analytics has become crucial for organizations to gain valuable insights, make informed decisions, and uncover hidden patterns and trends. Below are the diverse applications of big data analytics:

1. **Business** Intelligence and Decision Making: Big data analytics empowers businesses to analyze vast volumes of data from diverse sources, including customer interactions, sales data, and market trends. This analysis facilitates data-driven decision-making, process optimization, and overall efficiency improvement.

2. **Customer Behavior Analysis:** Big data analytics enables businesses to understand customer preferences, behavior, and purchasing patterns. By analyzing customer data, companies can customize marketing strategies, enhance customer experiences, and offer personalized product recommendations.

3. **Predictive Analytics:** Utilizing historical data, big data analytics can predict future outcomes and trends. This is particularly valuable in financial modeling, risk assessment, and demand forecasting.

4. **Healthcare and Life Sciences:** Big data analytics plays a vital role in healthcare and life sciences by analyzing vast amounts of medical data, genomic information, and patient records. It facilitates disease diagnosis, drug discovery, and personalized medicine.

5. **Internet of Things (IoT) Analytics:** With the proliferation of IoT devices, big data analytics processes and analyzes real-time data from sensors and connected devices. This enables applications like smart cities, industrial automation, and remote monitoring.

6. **Social Media and Sentiment Analysis:** Big data analytics is employed to analyze social media data to understand public sentiment, opinions, and trends. This information is valuable for brand reputation management, market research, and targeted advertising (Hande, 2023).

7. **Fraud Detection and Cybersecurity:** Big data analytics is used to identify anomalies and patterns in vast datasets, aiding in fraud detection, cybersecurity, and threat prevention.

8. **Natural Language Processing (NLP):** Big data analytics is utilized in NLP applications to process and analyze vast amounts of textual data, enabling sentiment analysis, language translation, and chatbot development.

9. **Environmental Monitoring:** Big data analytics supports environmental monitoring by analyzing large datasets from sensors and satellites, facilitating climate modeling, pollution tracking, and disaster management.

10. **Supply Chain Optimization:** Big data analytics optimizes supply chain management by analyzing data from various stages of the supply chain. This aids in inventory management, demand forecasting, and logistics optimization.

11. **Sports Analytics:** Big data analytics is employed in sports to analyze player performance, game strategies, and fan engagement, assisting coaches, teams, and sports organizations in data-driven decision-making.

12. **Government and Public Policy**: Big data analytics is used in the public sector for policy planning, social welfare programs, and urban planning, helping governments make informed decisions for their citizens.

Big data analytics is revolutionizing industries and driving innovation across diverse sectors. By harnessing the potential of big data, organizations can gain a competitive edge, enhance operational efficiency, and develop better products and services to meet the dynamic demands of the data-centric world.

5.1 Data-driven Decision Making

Data-driven decision making is a strategic approach that relies on the analysis and interpretation of data to guide choices, strategies, and actions. This method empowers organizations to use data analytics and evidence-based insights to inform decision-making processes across various domains. By embracing data-driven decision making, businesses, governments, and individuals can make more informed and objective choices, leading to enhanced outcomes and increased efficiency. Here are the key aspects of data-driven decision making:

1. **Data Collection and Analysis:** The initial step in data-driven decision making involves gathering relevant data from diverse sources, such as customer interactions, market trends, or operational metrics. Analyzing this data reveals valuable patterns, trends, and correlations.

2. **Evidence-Based Decisions:** Instead of relying solely on intuition or gut feelings, data-driven decision making emphasizes using data and statistical analysis to support choices. This approach reduces biases and enhances objectivity.

3. **Key Performance Indicators (KPIs):** Defining KPIs is crucial in data-driven decision making. These metrics represent critical business objectives and help measure progress towards goals.

4. **Predictive Analytics:** Leveraging historical data and predictive analytics, organizations can forecast future trends and potential outcomes, aiding in proactive decision making.

5. **Continuous Monitoring and Evaluation:** Data-driven decision making involves continually monitoring the impact of decisions and evaluating their effectiveness. This iterative process enables organizations to adjust strategies and tactics as needed.

6. **Personalization and Customer Experience:** Data-driven insights allow businesses to personalize customer experiences, tailor products or services, and address individual needs more effectively.

7. **Operational Efficiency:** By analyzing operational data, organizations can identify inefficiencies and optimize processes to improve overall efficiency and resource allocation.

8. **Risk Management:** Data-driven decision making helps in identifying potential risks and uncertainties, enabling better risk management strategies.

9. **Data-Driven Cultures:** Organizations that embrace data-driven decision making foster a culture of data literacy and encourage employees to base their actions on evidence rather than assumptions.

10. **Agility and Adaptability:** Data-driven decision making provides organizations with the agility to respond quickly to changes in the market or business environment.

11. **Transparency and Accountability:** Relying on data for decision making increases transparency and accountability within an organization, as decisions are based on objective evidence.

12. **Enhanced Innovations:** By analyzing data, organizations can uncover insights that drive innovations and foster creativity in product development or process improvements.

Data-driven decision making has become a cornerstone of modern business and governance. By harnessing the power of data, organizations can gain a competitive edge, optimize operations, and deliver better products and services that meet the evolving needs of their customers and stakeholders. Moreover, data-driven decision making fosters a culture of learning and improvement, driving continuous growth and success.

5.2 Predictive Analytics

Predictive analytics is a potent data analysis technique that utilizes historical data and statistical algorithms to forecast forthcoming outcomes and trends. By scrutinizing past patterns and relationships within the data, predictive analytics aids organizations in making proactive decisions, identifying potential risks, and capitalizing on opportunities before they materialize. This invaluable tool finds extensive application across various industries, empowering them to gain a competitive edge and enhance their decision-making processes. The key aspects of predictive analytics include:

1. **Historical Data Analysis:** Predictive analytics commences with the examination of historical data, identifying patterns, and comprehending relationships between variables. This historical information serves as the basis for predictive models.

2. **Data Preparation and Cleaning:** Before constructing predictive models, data must be cleansed and prepared to ensure accuracy and dependability. This process involves handling missing values, outliers, and other data anomalies.

3. **Selection of Predictive Models:** Various predictive modeling techniques, such as regression analysis, time series analysis, and machine learning algorithms, are employed to make accurate predictions based on data characteristics and the nature of the problem.

4. **Feature Engineering:** Feature engineering plays a pivotal role in predictive analytics, encompassing the selection of pertinent features and the creation of new ones to enhance the predictive power of the model.

5. **Training and Testing:** Predictive models are trained using historical data, and their performance is evaluated using test datasets to gauge their accuracy and generalization capabilities.

6. **Forecasting Future Trends:** Once the predictive model is validated, it is applied to new or unseen data to forecast future outcomes or events. This enables organizations to anticipate trends and potential scenarios.

7. **Risk Assessment and Management:** Predictive analytics is extensively used in risk assessment and management across diverse sectors, such as finance, insurance, and healthcare. It aids in identifying potential risks and assessing their likelihood of occurrence.

8. **Customer Behavior Prediction:** In marketing and customer analytics, predictive analytics helps forecast customer behavior, enabling personalized marketing strategies and targeted campaigns.

9. **Demand Forecasting**: Predictive analytics facilitates demand forecasting for businesses, allowing them to optimize inventory levels, production schedules, and supply chain management.

10. **Predictive Maintenance**: In industrial settings, predictive analytics is utilized for predictive maintenance, enabling organizations to detect and address potential equipment failures before they transpire, thereby reducing downtime and maintenance costs.

11. **Fraud Detection:** Predictive analytics is deployed to detect fraudulent activities in financial transactions and other domains, mitigating potential losses and ensuring security.

12. **Healthcare and Medical Diagnosis:** Predictive analytics assists in medical diagnosis and patient risk assessment, helping healthcare professionals make informed decisions and design personalized treatment plans.

Predictive analytics empowers organizations to gain valuable insights from data, anticipate future trends, and make data-driven decisions with confidence. By harnessing the power of predictive analytics, businesses and institutions can optimize operations, improve customer experiences, and maintain a competitive advantage in today's dynamic and fast-paced world.

5.3 Recommender Systems

Recommender systems are intelligent algorithms designed to offer personalized recommendations to users based on their preferences, behaviors, and past interactions. These systems aim to assist users in discovering relevant items, products, or content, leading to a more satisfying and tailored user experience. Recommender systems have become ubiquitous in today's digital landscape, powering various online platforms and services. Here are the key aspects of recommender systems:

1. **Collaborative Filtering:** Collaborative filtering is one of the fundamental techniques used in recommender systems. It analyzes user-item interactions and identifies patterns of similarity among users or items to suggest relevant recommendations.

2. **Content-Based Filtering:** Content-based filtering relies on the attributes or features of items to make recommendations. It suggests items that are similar in content to those preferred by the user in the past.

3. **Hybrid Recommender Systems:** Hybrid recommender systems combine collaborative filtering and content-based filtering to leverage the strengths of both approaches, providing more accurate and diverse recommendations.

4. **Matrix Factorization:** Matrix factorization is a popular method used in collaborative filtering. It decomposes user-item interaction matrices to discover latent features and preferences, enabling better recommendation accuracy.

5. **Item-Based and User-Based Filtering:** In item-based filtering, similar items are recommended to a user based on their interactions with other items. User-based filtering suggests items based on the preferences of users with similar tastes.

6. **Implicit and Explicit Feedback:** Recommender systems can use both implicit feedback (e.g., clicks, views) and explicit feedback (e.g., ratings, reviews) to learn user preferences and make personalized recommendations.

7. **Context-Aware Recommender Systems:** Context-aware recommender systems consider additional contextual information, such as time, location, or user context, to provide more relevant and timely recommendations.

8. **Real-Time and Batch Processing:** Recommender systems can be designed to provide recommendations in real-time, such as in streaming services, or in batch mode for offline processing.

9. **Long-Tail Recommendations:** Recommender systems are effective in suggesting niche or long-tail items that might be of interest to users but are less popular or well-known.

10. **Cross-Domain Recommendations:** Some recommender systems offer cross-domain recommendations, where preferences from one domain (e.g., books) are used to make recommendations in another domain (e.g., movies).

11. **Serendipity and Diversity:** Recommender systems can be optimized to introduce serendipity and diversity in recommendations, exposing users to novel and unexpected items.

12. **Evaluation Metrics:** Various evaluation metrics, such as precision, recall, and mean average precision, are used to assess the performance and accuracy of recommender systems.

Recommender systems have revolutionized the way users interact with digital platforms, leading to personalized and engaging experiences. By leveraging user data and sophisticated algorithms, these systems help businesses and platforms improve customer satisfaction, increase user engagement, and enhance overall user retention and loyalty.

5.4 NLP and Image/Video Processing

Natural Language Processing (NLP) and Image/Video Processing are two distinct yet interconnected fields within artificial intelligence and computer science. NLP focuses on the interaction between computers and human language, encompassing tasks like text analysis, sentiment analysis, machine translation, and speech recognition. On the other hand, Image/Video Processing deals with analyzing and manipulating visual data, including image recognition, object detection, video summarization, and facial recognition.

These fields often converge in various applications, where the combination of language and visual information leads to a more comprehensive understanding of data. Here are the key aspects of NLP and Image/Video Processing and their collaborative applications:

1. **Multimodal AI:** Multimodal AI is a burgeoning area that combines NLP and Image/Video Processing to understand and process information from multiple modalities, such as language and vision. This allows AI systems to analyze both textual and visual content in a unified manner.

2. **Image Captioning:** Image captioning is an example of synergy between NLP and Image Processing. It involves generating descriptive captions for images using NLP techniques, enhancing image understanding and context.

3. **Visual Question Answering (VQA):** VQA is another collaborative application where a system can answer questions related to an image or video using both visual information and language comprehension (Çelik, 2019).

4. **Sentiment Analysis on Visual Data:** Sentiment analysis can be applied to visual data, such as analyzing emotions in facial expressions, detecting sentiments in images or videos, and understanding reactions to visual content.

5. **OCR (Optical Character Recognition):** OCR is a classic illustration of combining NLP and Image Processing, where text is extracted from images or scanned documents, making it accessible for language-based applications.

6. **Medical Imaging and NLP:** In healthcare, NLP can be used to extract information from medical reports or records, while Image Processing aids in diagnosing medical conditions from visual data like X-rays or MRI scans.

7. **Video Summarization with NLP:** NLP techniques can be employed to summarize video content, providing textual summaries for a more efficient understanding of lengthy videos.

8. **Human-Robot Interaction:** Integrating NLP and Image Processing enables robots to comprehend and respond to both language-based and visual cues from humans, enhancing human-robot interaction.

9. **Visual Emotion Recognition with NLP:** The combination of visual data and language allows systems to recognize and describe emotions present in images or videos, enabling more nuanced analysis.

10. **Social Media Analysis:** NLP and Image/Video Processing can be combined to analyze social media content, extracting insights from both textual posts and visual media shared by users.

By integrating language and visual data, NLP and Image/Video Processing form a powerful synergy that enhances the capabilities of AI systems. They enable the processing and understanding of information from diverse sources, encompassing language, images, and videos. This convergence paves the way for more sophisticated AI applications, enriching our interaction with technology and unlocking innovative solutions across various domains.

6. ETHICAL CONSIDERATIONS

As NLP and Image/Video Processing technologies continue to advance and find widespread applications, it is essential to address the ethical implications that arise from their use. These technologies have the potential to significantly impact individuals, communities, and society as a whole. Here are key ethical considerations related to NLP and Image/Video Processing:

1. **Privacy and Data Protection:** NLP and Image/Video Processing involve the collection and analysis of vast amounts of personal data. Ensuring privacy and protecting this data is crucial to prevent unauthorized access or misuse that could infringe upon individuals' rights.

2. **Bias and Fairness:** Data used to train NLP and Image/Video Processing models may contain biases that reflect societal prejudices. This can lead to biased recommendations or decision-making, causing unfair or discriminatory outcomes. Addressing and mitigating bias is essential for ensuring fairness.

3. **Consent and Informed Use:** Ethical considerations demand that individuals provide informed consent for the use of their data in NLP and Image/Video Processing applications. Users must be aware of how their data will be utilized and have the option to opt out if they choose.

4.   **Transparency and Explainability:** AI models, especially those in NLP and Image/Video Processing, can be complex and difficult to interpret. Ensuring transparency and explainability in the decision-making process is crucial for users to understand how recommendations or outcomes are generated.

5.   **Accountability and Responsibility:** Organizations and developers working with NLP and Image/Video Processing technologies must be accountable for their creations. Clear guidelines and protocols should be established to ensure responsible use and mitigate potential harm.

6.   **Cultural and Social Impact:** NLP and Image/Video Processing can influence cultural perceptions, public opinion, and social norms. Considering the broader impact of these technologies on cultural diversity and societal values is essential.

7.   **Deepfakes and Misinformation:** The ability to manipulate audio, images, and videos raises concerns about deepfakes and misinformation. Ensuring the authenticity and integrity of media content is critical to prevent the spread of false or misleading information.

8.   **Security and Adversarial Attacks:** NLP and Image/Video Processing models can be vulnerable to adversarial attacks, where malicious actors manipulate inputs to produce incorrect or harmful outputs. Robust security measures must be in place to safeguard against such attacks.

9.   **Human-AI Collaboration:** As AI technologies become more pervasive, ethical considerations include the impact on human labor, employment, and job displacement. Ensuring AI systems work in harmony with humans and enhance human capabilities is crucial.

10. **AI in Critical Applications:** In applications such as medical diagnosis or autonomous vehicles, the ethical implications of errors or failures in NLP and Image/Video Processing can have life-altering consequences. Rigorous testing, validation, and safeguards are essential in such critical domains (Barse, 2023).

11. **End-User Empowerment:** Ethical considerations also involve empowering end-users with a clear understanding of how AI systems work, their limitations, and the implications of their decisions.

12. **Regular Ethical Reviews:** Ongoing ethical reviews and audits of NLP and Image/Video Processing applications can help identify and address potential ethical challenges as technology evolves.

Addressing these ethical considerations is crucial to ensure the responsible and ethical deployment of NLP and Image/Video Processing technologies. Striking the right balance between innovation and safeguarding human values and rights will be vital for the long-term positive impact of these powerful AI tools on society.

6.1 Privacy and Data Protection

In the realm of NLP and Image/Video Processing, as well as broader technology applications, privacy and data protection stand as vital ethical considerations. In today's digital age, where extensive personal data is gathered and processed, ensuring the privacy and security of individuals' information is paramount. Here are key aspects of privacy and data protection:

1.   **Data Collection and Consent:** Organizations must obtain explicit and informed consent from individuals when collecting personal data for NLP and Image/Video Processing purposes. Users should be fully aware of the data's intended use and any potential sharing with third parties.

2. **Anonymization and Pseudonymization:** Sensitive data handling can involve anonymization and pseudonymization techniques to remove or replace personally identifiable information, minimizing the risk of direct identification.

3. **Data Minimization:** Limiting the collection and retention of personal data to what is strictly necessary helps reduce potential exposure of sensitive information.

4. **Data Security and Encryption:** Employing robust data security measures and encryption protocols ensures data protection against unauthorized access and breaches.

5. **User Control and Transparency:** Providing users with control over their data and clear visibility into its use fosters trust and enables informed decisions about their privacy.

6. **Data Breach Response:** Having a well-defined plan for responding to data breaches is essential to minimize impact and mitigate potential harm.

7. **Compliance with Regulations:** Organizations must adhere to relevant data protection regulations and standards, such as GDPR or CCPA, depending on the jurisdiction.

8. **Cross-Border Data Transfer:** When handling data crossing international borders, compliance with data protection laws in different jurisdictions is crucial.

9. **Third-Party Data Sharing:** If sharing data with third-party providers or partners, ensuring they maintain the same privacy and data protection standards is critical.

10. **Children's Privacy:** Special attention should be given to protecting the privacy of children, with explicit parental consent required for data processing involving minors.

11. **Privacy Impact Assessments (PIAs):** Conducting PIAs helps identify and address potential privacy risks and implications of data processing activities.

12. **Ethical AI Use:** Integrating privacy and data protection principles into the design and development of AI systems ensures that ethical considerations are foundational.

Respecting individuals' privacy rights and safeguarding their data is not only a legal and ethical duty but also crucial for building trust with users and maintaining a positive reputation. Privacy and data protection measures should be ingrained in NLP and Image/Video Processing applications, and any technology dealing with personal information. Striking a balance between data utilization and individual privacy rights is essential for a responsible and sustainable digital future (Bhave, 2023).

6.2 Bias and Fairness in Big Data

Big Data, with its vast scale and diverse origins, holds immense potential for driving innovation and insights across various industries. However, it is not immune to biases and fairness issues that may arise during data collection, processing, and analysis. These biases can lead to unjust or discriminatory outcomes, perpetuating existing inequalities. Addressing these ethical challenges is crucial to ensure responsible and equitable use of Big Data. Here are key aspects of bias and fairness in Big Data:

1. **Data Collection Bias:** Bias can be introduced during data collection if the data does not represent the entire population or if certain groups are underrepresented. Biased data can lead to skewed analyses and reinforce stereotypes.

2. **Algorithmic Bias:** Big Data algorithms can inherit biases present in the data used to train them. If historical data reflects discriminatory practices, the algorithm may perpetuate these biases when making decisions or recommendations.

3. **Unintended Correlations**: Big Data may reveal unexpected correlations between variables, some of which might be spurious or irrelevant. These correlations can lead to biased conclusions if not carefully analyzed and understood.

4. **Fairness Metrics:** Developing fairness metrics is essential to assess the impact of Big Data applications on different demographic groups. Fairness metrics can help identify and mitigate biases in algorithms and decision-making processes.

5. **Explainability and Transparency**: Big Data algorithms can be complex and difficult to interpret. Ensuring explainability and transparency in these algorithms is crucial for understanding how decisions are made and identifying potential biases.

6. **Mitigating Algorithmic Bias:** Techniques like adversarial testing, fairness-aware learning, and data augmentation can be employed to mitigate algorithmic bias and promote fair outcomes.

7. **Diverse Representation:** Ensuring diverse representation in the teams working with Big Data can help identify and address potential biases during the development and implementation stages.

8. **Regular Audits:** Regular audits of Big Data applications can help assess fairness and identify any bias that may have emerged over time.

9. **Data Bias Mitigation**: Pre-processing data to remove sensitive attributes or using differential privacy techniques can help mitigate data bias without compromising the utility of the data.

10. **Fair Data Collection Practices:** Ensuring that data collection practices are fair and comply with relevant regulations can help prevent biases at the source.

11. **Responsible Use of Big Data:** Encouraging responsible use of Big Data involves promoting ethical awareness and ensuring that the insights gained are used for the betterment of society, avoiding harm to individuals or communities.

12. **Ethical Guidelines:** Developing and adhering to ethical guidelines for Big Data usage can help guide organizations in making fair and unbiased decisions.

Addressing bias and fairness in Big Data requires a multifaceted approach, encompassing data collection, algorithm design, and ethical considerations. By prioritizing fairness and transparency, Big Data can be harnessed as a powerful tool to drive positive change and enhance decision-making processes in an inclusive and just manner.

6.3 Transparency and Explainability

Transparency and explainability are vital principles in the realm of AI systems, including those driven by Big Data, NLP, and Image/Video Processing. As AI technologies advance, understanding how these systems reach their decisions becomes increasingly critical. The goal of transparency and explainability is to demystify AI decision-making processes, fostering trust among users, developers, and stakeholders. Let's explore why transparency and explainability are essential:

1. **Building Trust:** AI systems significantly impact individuals' lives, from personalized recommendations to critical decisions. When users comprehend how AI reaches its conclusions, they are more likely to trust the system and rely on its outputs.

2. **Ethical Considerations:** In sensitive domains like healthcare, finance, or criminal justice, transparency and explainability are essential to ensure that AI-based decisions align with ethical guidelines and avoid biases.

3. **Accountability and Responsibility:** Transparency empowers developers and organizations to take responsibility for AI system behavior. If a mistake occurs or inappropriate behavior arises, transparent models facilitate debugging and accountability.

4. **Compliance and Regulations:** As AI becomes prevalent in various industries, compliance with regulations may require AI models to provide understandable explanations for their decisions, ensuring regulatory adherence.

5. **Avoiding Black-Box AI:** Transparency and explainability help steer clear of "black-box" AI models, where decisions occur without clear insights into the reasoning. This is crucial in critical applications that demand interpretability.

6. **User Empowerment:** Transparent AI systems empower users by enabling them to understand the factors influencing AI recommendations, making informed decisions based on comprehensible outputs.

7. **Identifying and Mitigating Bias:** Transparent AI allows developers to identify and address bias in data or algorithms, leading to fair and equitable decision-making.

8. **Effective Communication:** Transparent AI fosters effective communication between AI systems and users, minimizing misunderstandings and enhancing the overall user experience.

9. **Interpretability for Experts:** In domains where domain experts collaborate with AI systems, interpretability is crucial for experts to verify model outputs and integrate AI into their decision-making process.

10. **Insights and Learning:** Transparent AI models offer insights into how the system interprets and processes information, enabling learning and continuous improvement.

11. **Balancing Complexity and Interpretability:** Striking a balance between model complexity and interpretability is vital, ensuring that AI models remain understandable without compromising accuracy.

By emphasizing transparency and explainability, AI development aligns with ethical and responsible practices, enabling users and stakeholders to make well-informed decisions. Transparent AI deployment embraces the augmentation of human intelligence with technology while upholding ethical principles and ensuring accountability.

REFERENCES

BarseS.BhagatD.DhawaleK.SolankeY.KurveD. (2023). Cyber-Trolling Detection System. SSRN 4340372.

Bhave, R., Thakre, B. P., Kamble, V., Gogte, P., & Bhagat, D. (2023). BMSQABSE: Design of a Bioinspired Model to Improve Security & QoS Performance for Blockchain-Powered Attribute-based Searchable Encryption Applications. *International Journal on Recent and Innovation Trends in Computing and Communication, 2023*(11), 527–535. doi:10.17762/ijritcc.v11i5s.7114

Çelik, O., Hasanbaşoğlu, M., Aktaş, M. S., Kalıpsız, O., & Kanli, A. N. (2019, September). Implementation of data preprocessing techniques on distributed big data platforms. In *2019 4th International Conference on Computer Science and Engineering* (UBMK) (pp. 73-78). IEEE. 10.1109/UBMK.2019.8907230

Desai, V., & Dinesha, H. A. (2020, November). A hybrid approach to data pre-processing methods. In *2020 IEEE International Conference for Innovation in Technology (INOCON)* (pp. 1-4). IEEE. 10.1109/INOCON50539.2020.9298378

Hariharakrishnan, J., Mohanavalli, S., & Kumar, K. S. (2017, January). Survey of pre-processing techniques for mining big data. In *2017 international conference on computer, communication and signal processing (ICCCSP)* (pp. 1-5). IEEE.

Perer, A., & Liu, S. (2019). Visualization in data science. *IEEE Computer Graphics and Applications, 39*(5), 18–19. doi:10.1109/MCG.2019.2925493 PMID:31442962

Ray, S. (2019, February). A quick review of machine learning algorithms. In *2019 International conference on machine learning, big data, cloud and parallel computing (COMITCon)* (pp. 35-39). IEEE. 10.1109/COMITCon.2019.8862451

Sahu, M., Dhawale, K., Bhagat, D., Wankkhede, C., & Gajbhiye, D. (2023). Convex Hull Algorithm based Virtual Mouse. *Grenze International Journal of Engineering & Technology (GIJET), 9*(2).

Sughasiny, M., & Rajeshwari, J. (2018, August). Application of machine learning techniques, big data analytics in health care sector–a literature survey. In *2018 2nd International Conference on I-SMAC (IoT in Social, Mobile, Analytics and Cloud)(I-SMAC) I-SMAC (IoT in Social, Mobile, Analytics and Cloud) (I-SMAC), 2018 2nd International Conference on* (pp. 741-749). IEEE. 10.1109/I-SMAC.2018.8653654

Zhou, T., Li, B., Wu, C., Tan, Y., Mao, L., & Wu, W. (2019, November). Studies on big data mining techniques in wildfire prevention for power system. In *2019 IEEE 3rd Conference on Energy Internet and Energy System Integration (EI2)* (pp. 866-871). IEEE. 10.1109/EI247390.2019.9061901

Chapter 6
Big Data Preprocessing, Techniques, Integration, Transformation, Normalisation, Cleaning, Discretization, and Binning

Pranali Dhawas

https://orcid.org/0009-0003-4276-2310

G.H. Raisoni College of Engineering, Nagpur, India

Abhishek Dhore

MIT School of Computing, MIT ADT University, Pune, India

Dhananjay Bhagat

https://orcid.org/0009-0009-1100-3219

G.H. Raisoni College of Engineering, Nagpur, India

Ritu Dorlikar Pawar

G.H. Raisoni College of Engineering, Nagpur, India

Ashwini Kukade

G.H. Raisoni College of Engineering, Nagpur, India

Kamlesh Kalbande

G.H. Raisoni College of Engineering, Nagpur, India

ABSTRACT

"Unleashing the Power of Big Data: Innovative Approaches to Preprocessing for Enhanced Analytics" is a groundbreaking chapter that explores the pivotal role of preprocessing in big data analytics. It introduces diverse techniques to transform raw, unstructured data into a clean, analyzable format, addressing the challenges posed by data volume, velocity, and variety. The chapter emphasizes the significance of preprocessing for accurate outcomes, covers advanced data cleaning, integration, and transformation techniques, and discusses real-time data preprocessing, emerging technologies, and future directions. This chapter is a comprehensive resource for researchers and practitioners, enabling them to enhance data analytics and derive valuable insights from big data.

DOI: 10.4018/979-8-3693-0413-6.ch006

Figure 1. Objectives of big data preprocessing

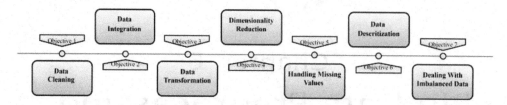

1. INTRODUCTION TO BIG DATA PREPROCESSING

Big data preprocessing plays a critical role in the data analysis process by converting raw and unprocessed data into a structured and clean format suitable for analysis. As the volume, velocity, and variety of data continue to grow exponentially, preprocessing becomes increasingly vital for extracting valuable insights and knowledge from large datasets.

The process of big data preprocessing involves employing various techniques and operations to enhance data quality, reduce noise and inconsistencies, handle missing values, and prepare the data for subsequent analysis tasks as shown in figure 1. It significantly contributes to improving the efficiency, accuracy, and effectiveness of data analysis (O. Çelik, 2019).

The main objectives of big data preprocessing include:

Data Cleaning: Raw data often contains errors, outliers, duplicates, or inconsistencies. Data cleaning aims to identify and rectify these issues to ensure high data quality. By eliminating noise and irregularities, the resulting clean data provides a reliable foundation for analysis.

Data Integration: Big data originates from diverse sources such as databases, sensors, social media, or IoT devices. Data integration involves combining data from different sources and formats into a unified representation. This step ensures data consistency and compatibility for analysis (Z. Cai-Ming, 2020).

Data Transformation: Data transformation techniques are applied to convert data into a suitable format for analysis. This may involve scaling numerical data, normalizing values, encoding categorical variables, or deriving new features through mathematical or statistical operations. Transformation facilitates data standardization and simplifies subsequent analysis tasks.

Dimensionality Reduction: Dealing with high-dimensional data can pose computational challenges and introduce noise or overfitting problems. Dimensionality reduction techniques help decrease the number of variables or features while preserving crucial information. This simplifies the analysis process and improves computational efficiency (H. S. Obaid, 2019).

Handling Missing Values: Missing data is a common issue in large datasets. Preprocessing techniques include imputing missing values using statistical methods or leveraging imputation algorithms to fill in the gaps. Proper handling of missing data ensures that the analysis is not compromised by incomplete information (T. A. Alghamdi, 2022).

Data Discretization: Discretization involves converting continuous data into categorical or discrete representations. This technique simplifies analysis by reducing the complexity associated with continuous variables. It allows for the application of methods specifically designed for categorical data (P. Gao, 2020).

Dealing with Imbalanced Data: Imbalanced data refers to situations where one class or category is significantly more prevalent than others. Preprocessing techniques address this imbalance by employing methods such as oversampling, under sampling, or generating synthetic samples to achieve a balanced representation of the data.

Big data preprocessing is indispensable for extracting valuable insights from complex datasets. By effectively cleaning, transforming, and organizing the data, preprocessing ensures that subsequent analysis tasks are more accurate, efficient, and reliable. The specific techniques utilized may vary based on the data's nature, analysis objectives, and the challenges posed by the dataset at hand.

1.1 Definition and Significance of Big Data Preprocessing

Big data preprocessing involves transforming raw data into a structured and usable format suitable for analysis, mining, and machine learning tasks. It employs a range of techniques to enhance data quality, eliminate noise and inconsistencies, handle missing values, and reduce data dimensionality. Its purpose is to ensure that the data is reliable, relevant, and well-suited for subsequent analysis and decision-making processes (G. S. Krishna, 2022).

Big data preprocessing holds immense importance in extracting meaningful insights and knowledge from large-scale datasets. Here are key reasons highlighting its significance:

Data Quality Improvement: Preprocessing techniques address data quality issues like missing values, outliers, and inconsistencies. By cleaning and enhancing the data, preprocessing ensures accurate and reliable results in subsequent analysis and modelling (S. Pradha, 2019).

Noise and Outlier Removal: Big data often contains irrelevant and noisy information that can impact the accuracy and performance of analytical models. Preprocessing helps identify and eliminate such noise and outliers, improving data quality and reliability.

Data Integration and Fusion: In big data scenarios, data originates from diverse sources and formats. Preprocessing techniques enable the integration and fusion of heterogeneous data, facilitating a unified view for analysis and decision-making (T. A. Alghamdi, 2022).

Dimensionality Reduction: Big data often has a high dimensionality, with numerous features or attributes. Preprocessing techniques like dimensionality reduction and feature selection simplify the data by extracting the most informative features. This enhances computational efficiency and model performance.

Handling Missing Values: Big data can suffer from missing values, introducing biases and affecting analysis validity. Preprocessing techniques offer strategies, including imputation methods, to handle missing data and preserve valuable information.

Scalability and Efficiency: Big data preprocessing techniques are designed to efficiently handle the volume and velocity of large-scale datasets. Methods like distributed processing and parallelization enable scalable and high-performance preprocessing operations.

Enhanced Analysis and Decision Making: Preprocessing prepares the data for analysis, enabling the extraction of meaningful patterns, correlations, and insights from big data. This empowers data-driven decision-making, giving organizations a competitive edge through actionable intelligence.

Big data preprocessing is a critical step in unlocking the value of large-scale datasets. By addressing data quality issues, integrating heterogeneous data, reducing dimensionality, and enhancing analysis efficiency, preprocessing ensures robust, accurate, and reliable subsequent analysis and modeling processes.

1.2 Key Challenges Associated With Preprocessing Big Data

Preprocessing big data poses several challenges due to the unique characteristics of large-scale datasets.

Figure 2 illustrates the key challenges associated with preprocessing big data which includes:

Volume: The massive volume of big data requires specialized techniques and infrastructure capable of processing and managing such vast amounts of data efficiently.

Variety: Big data comes in diverse formats, including structured, unstructured, and semi-structured data, necessitating preprocessing techniques that can handle and extract insights from different data types.

Velocity: The high speed at which big data is generated requires preprocessing techniques that can handle real-time or near real-time data processing, ensuring timely analysis and insights.

Veracity: Big data is prone to data quality issues such as inaccuracies, noise, and inconsistencies. Preprocessing must address these issues, including handling missing values, outliers, and correcting errors to ensure reliable analysis outcomes.

Scalability: Processing large-scale datasets requires preprocessing techniques that can scale horizontally across distributed systems, utilizing parallel processing frameworks to handle the computational demands efficiently.

Computational Complexity: The complexity of preprocessing operations increases with the size and complexity of the data. Efficient algorithms and techniques are necessary to optimize processing time and memory usage.

Privacy and Security: Preprocessing big data involves handling sensitive information, requiring adherence to privacy regulations and security measures to protect data privacy during transformation and integration processes.

Resource Constraints: Preprocessing big data may face limitations in terms of memory, processing power, and storage capacity. Optimizing preprocessing techniques to make efficient use of available resources becomes crucial.

Figure 2. Key challenges associated with preprocessing big data

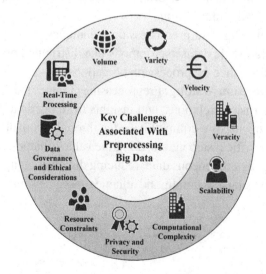

Data Governance and Ethical Considerations: Big data preprocessing should adhere to data governance policies, ethical guidelines, and legal regulations to ensure responsible data handling and compliance.

Real-Time Processing: Some big data applications require real-time or near real-time processing for time-sensitive ana lysis and decision-making. Preprocessing techniques must be designed to handle streaming data and enable real-time analytics.

Effectively addressing these challenges entails employing advanced algorithms, scalable processing frameworks, efficient infrastructure, and domain-specific expertise to preprocess big data efficiently and derive meaningful insights from the complex and vast datasets.

2. DATA CLEANING TECHNIQUES

Data cleaning techniques are essential in preprocessing to ensure data quality and reliability. Commonly employed techniques include handling missing values through deletion or imputation using mean, median, mode, or advanced machine learning algorithms. Outlier detection involves univariate or multivariate methods and winsorization to handle extreme values. Inconsistent data is addressed through standardization or data transformation. Data deduplication techniques include record linkage and fuzzy matching. Inconsistent or erroneous data is handled through data validation and error correction. Skewed data can be addressed through data transformation or binning. The selection of techniques should consider dataset characteristics and analysis requirements, and combining multiple techniques can enhance the data cleaning process for high-quality subsequent analysis.

2.1 Handling Missing Values and Outliers

2.1.1 Handling Missing Values

Addressing missing values is a critical step in data preprocessing to maintain data integrity and mitigate biases. Here are techniques commonly used for handling missing values:

Deletion: Eliminate instances or variables with missing values as shown in figure 3. This approach is suitable when missingness is random and has minimal impact on the analysis. However, it can result in data loss.

Mean/Median/Mode Imputation: Replace missing values with the mean, median, or mode of the respective variable as its shown in figure 4. This simple method assumes no relationship between missing values and other variables.

Regression Imputation: Estimate missing values by regressing the variable with missing values on other variables. This technique utilizes variable relationships but assumes linearity and may introduce bias.

Multiple Imputation: Generate multiple imputed datasets using predictive models to estimate missing values. Each dataset represents plausible values, allowing for uncertainty estimation in subsequent analyses.

Hot Deck Imputation: Assign missing values by randomly selecting values from similar instances in the dataset. This method preserves variable relationships but introduces randomness.

Figure 3. Elimination of instances

```
demo1_df = emp_test_df.dropna(thresh=7) # 7 non-null values
demo1_df
```

	Emp ID	First Name	Age in Yrs	Weight in Kgs	Age in Company	Salary	City
4	193819	Benjamin	40.31	58.0	4.01	117642.0	Fremont
8	477616	Frances	58.18	42.0	23.27	121587.0	Delmita
9	162402	Diana	29.73	60.0	3.44	43010.0	Eureka Springs
10	231469	Ralph	42.50	80.0	8.29	118457.0	Sabetha
11	153989	Jack	22.21	61.0	0.56	82965.0	Las Vegas
...	...	...	...	...	...	...	...
95	639892	Jose	22.82	89.0	1.05	129774.0	Biloxi
96	704709	Harold	32.61	77.0	5.93	156194.0	Carol Stream
97	461593	Nicole	52.66	60.0	28.53	95673.0	Detroit
98	392491	Theresa	29.60	57.0	6.99	51015.0	Mc Grath
99	495141	Tammy	38.38	55.0	2.26	93650.0	Alma

Figure 4. Null value imputation with mean

```
df["Age in Company"].mean()
```

```
8.801868131868131
```

```
df["Age in Company"].fillna(8.801868131868131,inplace=True)
df
```

	Emp ID	First Name	Age in Yrs	Weight in Kgs	Age in Company	Salary	City
0	677509	Lois	36.36	60.0	13.68	168251	Denver
1	940761	Brenda	47.02	60.0	9.01	51063	Stonewall
2	428945	Joe	54.15	68.0	0.98	50155	Michigantown
3	408351	10000	39.67	51.0	18.30	180294	Hydetown
4	193819	Benjamin	40.31	58.0	4.01	117642	Fremont
...	...	...	...	...	...	...	...
95	639892	Jose	22.82	89.0	1.05	129774	Biloxi
96	704709	Harold	32.61	77.0	5.93	156194	Carol Stream
97	461593	Nicole	52.66	60.0	28.53	95673	Detroit
98	392491	Theresa	29.60	57.0	6.99	51015	Mc Grath
99	495141	Tammy	38.38	55.0	2.26	93650	Alma

2.1.2 Handling Outliers

Effectively addressing outliers is crucial to prevent their undue influence on analysis results. Consider these techniques for handling outliers:

Removal: Exclude instances that contain outliers. However, caution must be exercised as this approach may result in information loss.

Winsorization or Capping: Replace extreme values with predetermined values at a specific percentile. This method reduces outlier impact while maintaining the overall data distribution.

Transformation: Apply mathematical transformations like logarithmic, square root, or Box-Cox transformation to lessen the influence of outliers and achieve a more balanced data distribution as shown in figure 5.

Binning: Group data into intervals or bins, treating outliers as extreme values within a bin. This approach helps mitigate outlier effects and handle skewed distributions (V. Desai,2020).

Robust Statistical Methods: Utilize statistical techniques less sensitive to outliers, such as robust regression or robust estimation methods like the median absolute deviation (MAD) or interquartile range (IQR) which is shown in figure 6 using boxplot and figure 7 using matplotlib(Hande, 2023).

Careful consideration should be given to the nature of missing values or outliers and the specific analysis requirements when selecting the most appropriate technique as its shown in figure 8. This ensures

Figure 5. Log transformation method

```
df['nprice']=np.log(df['price'])

sns.distplot(df['nprice'])

<matplotlib.axes._subplots.AxesSubplot at 0x25ccced3518>
```

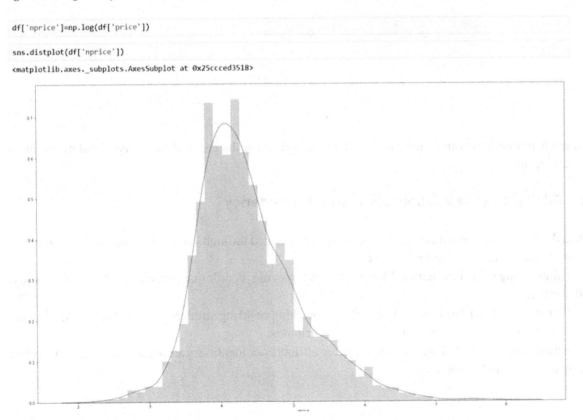

Figure 6. Detection of outliers

```
sns.boxplot(array1)
```

```
C:\ProgramData\Anaconda3\lib\site-packages\seaborn\_decorators
arg: x. From version 0.12, the only valid positional argument
keyword will result in an error or misinterpretation.
  warnings.warn(
```

```
<AxesSubplot:>
```

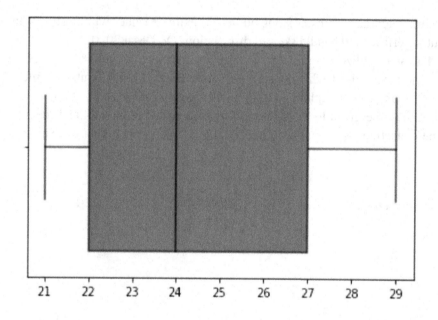

proper handling of missing values and outliers while meeting the goals of the analysis and maintaining data integrity.

2.2 Addressing Data Duplication and Redundancy

Data duplication and redundancy can be effectively managed through various techniques during the data cleaning process. These methods include:

Eliminating exact duplicates: Identifying and removing records that are completely identical across all attributes.

Handling partial duplicates: Using fuzzy matching or string similarity algorithms to identify and manage records with similar values in specific attributes.

Employing record linkage: Comparing key attributes or identifiers across different datasets to link related records and merge them.

Figure 7. Outlier detection using Matplotlib

```
import matplotlib.pyplot as plt

plt.figure(figsize=(20,10))
df.boxplot()

<AxesSubplot:>
```

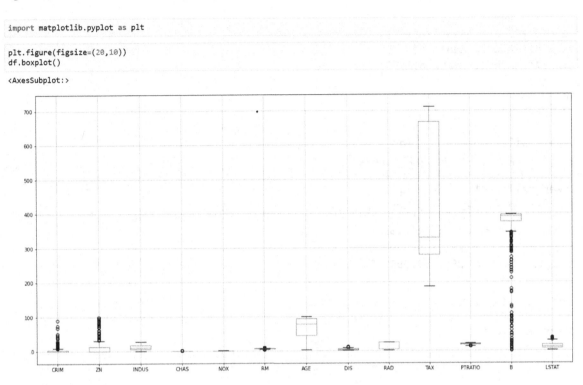

Utilizing de-duplication algorithms: Employing algorithms like Levenshtein distance or Jaccard similarity to detect and eliminate duplicates based on similarity measures(Barse, 2023).

Normalizing data: Standardizing data formats to remove redundancy and ensure consistency, such as converting different date formats into a common format or unifying units of measurement.

Implementing data governance policies: Establishing guidelines for data entry, unique identifiers, and data quality standards to prevent duplication and redundancy.

Conducting regular data monitoring: Continuously monitoring data quality, implementing data quality checks, and performing periodic audits to identify and address duplication and redundancy issues.

By applying these techniques and following data management practices, data duplication and redundancy can be effectively addressed, resulting in cleaner and more reliable datasets.

2.3 Removing Noise and Irrelevant Information

The text discusses various techniques used in data preprocessing to remove noise and irrelevant information, thereby improving data quality and relevance. The techniques mentioned are as follows:

Data Filtering: Filters are applied to eliminate noise and irrelevant data points by setting thresholds or excluding instances with low signal-to-noise ratios.

Feature Selection: The most significant features that contribute meaningfully to the analysis or model performance are identified and selected, reducing dimensionality and removing irrelevant or redundant features.

Figure 8. Outlier treatment using IQR method

```
q1 = df["AGE"].quantile(0.25)
q2 = df["AGE"].quantile(0.50)
q3 = df["AGE"].quantile(0.75)

iqr = q3 - q1
print(f"The IQR = {iqr}")

upper_tail = q3 + 1.5 * iqr
print(f"Upper Tail = {upper_tail}")

lower_tail = q1 - 1.5 * iqr
print(f"Lower Tail = {lower_tail}")
```

```
    The IQR = 49.04999999999999
    Upper Tail = 167.64999999999998
    Lower Tail = -28.54999999999999
```

```
df[["AGE"]].boxplot()
```

```
<AxesSubplot:>
```

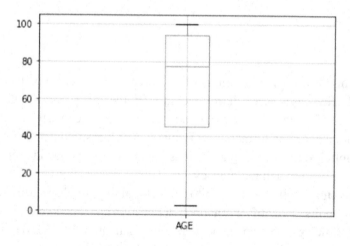

Text Mining Techniques: For textual data, methods like stop-word removal, stemming, or lemmatization are employed to eliminate noise and irrelevant words that do not contribute to the analysis.

Data Smoothing: Smoothing techniques such as moving averages or Gaussian smoothing are applied to reduce random noise or fluctuations in time series or signal data, revealing underlying trends and patterns.

Outlier Detection: Outliers, which significantly deviate from the majority of the data, are identified and removed to prevent distortion of analysis results and introduction of noise.

Domain Knowledge and Expertise: Leveraging domain knowledge and subject matter expertise helps identify noise or irrelevant information specific to the dataset or analysis objectives.

Data Sampling: Sampling techniques like random or stratified sampling can be used to reduce data size while preserving its representativeness, eliminating irrelevant information while retaining overall dataset characteristics.

Quality Assessment: Thorough assessments of data quality are conducted to identify and address errors, inconsistencies, or inaccuracies, resolving noise and irrelevant information stemming from data quality issues.

It is crucial to consider the unique characteristics of the data, analysis goals, and domain context when selecting and applying these techniques. By doing so, data preprocessing optimally enhances data quality and relevance for subsequent analysis.

3. DATA INTEGRATION AND FUSION

Data integration and fusion involve the process of combining data from multiple sources to create a unified dataset with a cohesive view. This process includes aligning data structures, resolving conflicts, and merging information. Here are some key elements and techniques related to data integration and fusion:

Identification of data sources: Identify the various data sources that need to be integrated, such as databases, files, APIs, or external streams.

Mapping and aligning data schemas: Understand the structure and format of data from different sources and map them to a common schema or data model to ensure compatibility.

Data transformation: Convert data from different formats or representations into a consistent format by adjusting data types, standardizing units of measurement, or normalizing values.

Entity resolution: Resolve inconsistencies and conflicts by identifying and matching records that refer to the same entity across different sources. Techniques like record linkage, fuzzy matching, or probabilistic matching can be used for accurate entity resolution.

Addressing data quality issues: Tackle data quality problems during integration by applying data cleaning techniques such as removing duplicates, correcting errors, and imputing missing values.

Integration methods: Choose appropriate integration methods based on data characteristics and requirements, including batch processing, real-time integration, or incremental updates.

Data fusion techniques: Merge data from different sources to create a unified dataset, incorporating aggregation, combining overlapping information, and resolving conflicts using data fusion algorithms.

Data synchronization: Establish mechanisms to keep the integrated dataset up to date by ensuring synchronization with the source systems. This can involve periodic updates, event-driven triggers, or real-time data replication.

Metadata management: Maintain comprehensive metadata, including data definitions, lineage, and transformations applied during integration, to facilitate understanding and management of the integrated dataset.

Security and privacy considerations: Implement appropriate security measures and privacy protocols to protect data during the integration process, including access controls, anonymization techniques, and compliance with data protection regulations.

Data integration and fusion play a vital role in enabling data-driven decision-making and gaining insights from diverse data sources. By effectively integrating and fusing data, organizations can maximize the value of their data assets and gain a holistic understanding of their information.

3.1 Techniques for Integrating Data From Multiple Sources

Integrating data from multiple sources is a common challenge in data preprocessing. Here are various techniques for effectively integrating data from diverse sources:

Concatenation: Merge datasets by appending rows or columns together. This method is suitable when the datasets have a consistent structure and can be easily aligned.

Joins and Merging: Combine datasets based on shared key attributes through join operations. Inner joins, outer joins (left, right, or full), and cross joins can be used depending on the desired merging behavior.

Union: Stack datasets vertically to create a single dataset. This technique is useful when the datasets have similar structures and share common variables or attributes.

Data Linkage: Establish connections between records or entities across datasets using shared identifiers or key attributes. Techniques like record linkage or entity resolution help integrate data by linking related records.

Entity Matching: Apply matching algorithms to identify and merge records representing the same entity across datasets. This technique is valuable when datasets contain overlapping or duplicate information.

Data Integration Platforms and Tools: Utilize specialized tools or platforms designed for data integration. These tools offer functionalities for mapping, transforming, and integrating data from various sources, simplifying the integration process.

Extract, Transform, Load (ETL) Processes: Employ ETL processes to extract data from multiple sources, transform it into a standardized format, and load it into a target destination. ETL frameworks and pipelines streamline the integration and transformation of data.

Application Programming Interfaces (APIs): Utilize APIs provided by data sources to programmatically access and integrate data. APIs offer standardized methods for retrieving data, facilitating seamless integration with other datasets.

Semantic Integration: Employ semantic technologies like ontology matching or semantic mapping to integrate data based on shared semantics or meaning. This approach aligns the underlying concepts and relationships across datasets.

Data Warehousing: Establish a data warehousing strategy where data from multiple sources is consolidated into a centralized repository. This enables efficient querying, analysis, and reporting on integrated data.

The choice of integration techniques depends on factors such as data structure, compatibility, complexity, and integration goals. By combining different techniques and leveraging appropriate tools, the data integration process can be streamlined, resulting in unified and comprehensive datasets for further analysis.

3.2 Handling Data in Different Formats and Structures

Managing data in diverse formats and structures requires specific approaches to ensure compatibility and efficient data handling. Consider the following techniques:

Data format conversion: Convert data from one format to another, such as converting between file formats (e.g., CSV, JSON, XML) or database formats (e.g., MySQL, PostgreSQL), enabling smooth integration and processing.

Data extraction and parsing: Extract relevant data from various sources and parse it into a consistent structure. Understand the source-specific syntax or markup language to transform it into a standardized format for further use.

Schema mapping and alignment: Map data elements from different structures to a common schema or data model. Establish relationships and identify corresponding attributes or fields across diverse formats, ensuring interoperability.

ETL (Extract, Transform, Load) processes: Implement ETL workflows to extract data from different sources, transform it into a unified structure, and load it into a target system. Apply necessary data transformations like aggregation, filtering, or merging to maintain data consistency.

Data integration tools and platforms: Utilize specialized tools or platforms designed for data integration, offering capabilities to handle various formats and structures. These tools often provide connectors and parsers for seamless data processing.

APIs and data connectors: Leverage APIs or pre-built connectors provided by data sources or platforms to simplify data retrieval and integration. These interfaces facilitate accessing data in different formats and structures.

Custom data mapping and scripting: Develop custom data mapping and scripting solutions to handle unique data formats or structures. Create scripts or code to parse, transform, and align data according to specific requirements.

Data virtualization: Implement data virtualization techniques to create a logical layer that abstracts underlying data formats and structures. This enables unified access and querying of diverse data sources without physical integration.

Data preprocessing and normalization: Apply preprocessing techniques like data cleaning, filtering, and standardization to ensure consistency and compatibility across various formats and structures.

Metadata management: Maintain comprehensive metadata describing the structure, format, and meaning of data elements across different sources. This metadata facilitates understanding and manipulation of data in diverse formats and structures.

By utilizing these techniques, organizations can effectively manage data in different formats and structures, enabling smooth integration and analysis of diverse data sources.

4. DATA TRANSFORMATION

Data transformation is a crucial step in preprocessing big data, involving the conversion of raw data into a standardized format suitable for analysis and modeling. The following techniques are commonly used in data transformation:

Data Normalization: Adjusts the scale of features to prevent any single feature from dominating the analysis. Techniques like min-max scaling, z-score normalization, and decimal scaling are used to ensure fairness in downstream analysis.

Discretization: Converts continuous variables into discrete intervals or categories, reducing complexity. Common methods include equal-width binning, equal-frequency binning, and entropy-based binning.

Attribute Construction: Creates new attributes based on existing ones, extracting more meaningful information. Operations like mathematical calculations and feature extraction methods such as PCA are employed to enhance data representation.

Data Encoding: Converts categorical variables into numerical or binary representations suitable for analysis. Techniques like one-hot encoding, label encoding, and ordinal encoding enable algorithms to interpret and extract patterns from categorical data.

Outlier Handling: Identifies and treats data points that significantly deviate from the general pattern. Statistical methods like z-score, box plots, and robust measures are used for outlier handling, including removal, transformation, or replacement.

Textual Data Processing: Transforms unstructured text into structured information for analysis. Techniques like tokenization, stop word removal, stemming, lemmatization, and sentiment analysis enable the extraction of meaningful features for text mining and natural language processing.

When selecting data transformation techniques, it's important to consider dataset characteristics, analysis requirements, and scalability. Exploratory data analysis and domain knowledge play a crucial role in determining appropriate transformations. Additionally, leveraging distributed processing frameworks ensures efficient execution of transformations for big data (R. Mo, 2019).

4.1 Standardization and Normalization Techniques

Standardization and normalization techniques are widely used in data preprocessing to bring variables to a standardized or normalized scale for fair comparison and analysis. The techniques discussed are:

Standardization (Z-Score Normalization): Transforms data to have a mean of 0 and a standard deviation of 1, making it suitable for Gaussian-distributed variables or algorithms requiring standardized data which is shown in figure 9.

Min-Max Normalization (Rescaling): Maps data to a specific range, typically between 0 and 1, preserving the order of the data while scaling it to the desired range.

Robust Scaling: Normalizes data using the median and interquartile range (IQR), making it robust to outliers and skewed distributions.

Unit Vector Normalization: Scales each sample to have a unit norm (magnitude of 1), commonly used in algorithms relying on distance measures.

The choice between standardization and normalization techniques depends on the data's characteristics and analysis requirements. Standardization is suitable for Gaussian-distributed variables or when standardized data is expected. Normalization techniques like min-max normalization or robust scaling are useful for scaling data to a specific range or handling outliers and skewed distributions.

4.2 Handling Skewed and Imbalanced Data Distributions

The text explains the importance of addressing skewed and imbalanced data distributions during data preprocessing to ensure accurate analysis results as its shown in figure 10. It outlines several techniques commonly used to handle these distributions:

Logarithmic Transformation: This technique compresses the range of high values and stretches the range of low values by taking the logarithm of the data, making the distribution more symmetric and reducing the impact of extreme values.

Power Transformation: Figure 11 illustrates the power transformation method where, Square root or cube root transformations normalize the data distribution and reduce the influence of extreme values, helping to mitigate skewness. The choice of power depends on the data's characteristics and degree of skewness.

Figure 9. Z-Score normalization

```
outliers_list = get_outliers_list(array2,2.5)

print(f"Outliers List = {outliers_list}")

  Array = [ 27  27  29 250  23 280  22  22  23  27  21  27  25  21  21  29  23  22
    27  22]
  Mean of an array = 48.4
  STD of an array = 72.40400541406534
  Outliers List = [250, 280]
```

```
from scipy.stats import zscore
```

```
z_score_val = zscore(array1)
z_score_val
```

```
array([ 0.88594414,  0.88594414,  1.60916385,  0.16272443, -0.56049527,
        1.247554  , -0.92210513, -0.92210513, -0.56049527,  0.88594414,
       -1.28371498,  0.88594414,  0.16272443, -1.28371498, -1.28371498,
        1.60916385, -0.56049527, -0.92210513,  0.88594414, -0.92210513])
```

```
np.where(z_score_val >= 3)
```

```
(array([], dtype=int64),)
```

```
array1[np.where(z_score_val >= 3)[0]]
```

```
array([], dtype=int32)
```

```
z_score_val = zscore(array2)
z_score_val
```

```
array([-0.29556376, -0.29556376, -0.26794098,  2.78437635, -0.35080932,
        3.19871806, -0.36462071, -0.36462071, -0.35080932, -0.29556376,
       -0.3784321 , -0.29556376, -0.32318654, -0.3784321 , -0.3784321 ,
       -0.26794098, -0.35080932, -0.36462071, -0.29556376, -0.36462071])
```

Box-Cox Transformation: An advanced technique that optimizes the power transformation to achieve the best possible normality. By selecting the power parameter lambda, this method is particularly useful for highly skewed data distributions.

Resampling Techniques: Employed for imbalanced data, oversampling replicates minority class samples, while under sampling randomly removes instances from the majority class. Both approaches aim to create a more balanced dataset for effective learning by models, but potential information loss or bias introduction should be carefully considered.

Synthetic Minority Over-sampling Technique (SMOTE): A popular algorithm that generates synthetic samples for the minority class by interpolating between existing instances, increasing its representation and improving the model's ability to learn patterns from it.

Figure 10. Skewed data

```
sns.distplot(df['price'])

<matplotlib.axes._subplots.AxesSubplot at 0x25ccce41748>
```

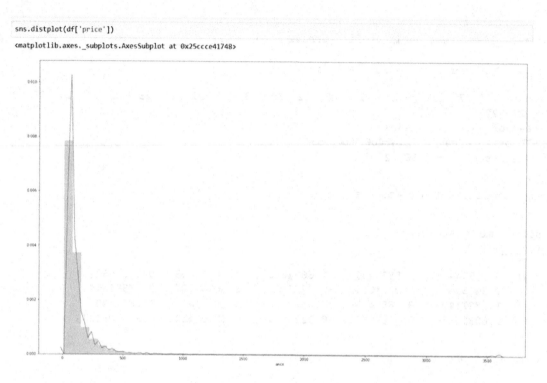

Figure 11. Power transformation

```
df['nprice1']=df['price']**(1/6)
```

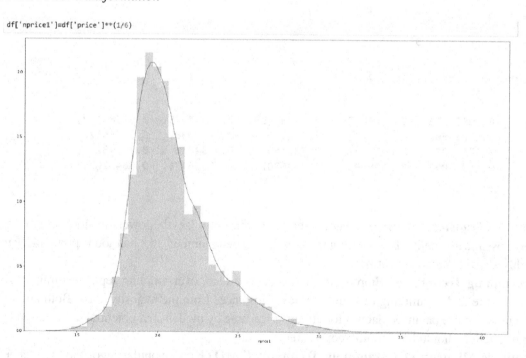

Ensemble Methods: Techniques like bagging and boosting combine multiple models or assign weights to give more emphasis to the minority class, effectively handling imbalanced data distributions and reducing bias towards the majority class.

Algorithmic Techniques: Certain algorithms have mechanisms to handle imbalanced data, such as weighted loss functions or cost-sensitive learning, assigning higher weights or penalties to minority class instances during training.

Appropriate techniques should be chosen based on the specific characteristics of the data and analysis objectives. Understanding the data distribution and potential impacts of preprocessing techniques is crucial for obtaining valid and reliable results. Evaluation metrics should also consider the inherent imbalance when assessing model performance on imbalanced datasets.

4.3 Dimensionality Reduction Methods

Dimensionality reduction techniques are employed in data preprocessing to reduce the number of features while preserving important information. Common methods include:

Principal Component Analysis (PCA): Identifies uncorrelated variables capturing maximum variance, transforming data to a lower-dimensional space and minimizing information loss.

Singular Value Decomposition (SVD): Decomposes a data matrix into three matrices, allowing for rank truncation and effective dimensionality reduction.

t-distributed Stochastic Neighbor Embedding (t-SNE): Nonlinear technique for visualizing high-dimensional data, preserving local relationships and revealing clusters or patterns.

Linear Discriminant Analysis (LDA): Supervised technique maximizing class separability to find a lower-dimensional representation, commonly used in classification tasks.

Non-negative Matrix Factorization (NMF): Decomposes non-negative data matrices into parts-based representations, useful for non-negative data like text or spectrograms.

Feature Selection: Identifies relevant features based on correlation, mutual information, or statistical tests, reducing dimensionality while preserving informative features.

When selecting a dimensionality reduction technique, it's important to consider data characteristics, analysis objectives, exploratory data analysis, domain knowledge, and evaluation metrics. Additionally, assessing the impact on downstream tasks like classification or clustering helps ensure the reduced representation retains necessary information..

4.4 Feature Extraction and Selection Techniques

The text discusses feature extraction and selection techniques used in data preprocessing to identify relevant and informative features for analysis or modeling. These techniques aim to reduce dimensionality, improve computational efficiency, and enhance machine learning algorithm performance. The commonly employed techniques are:

Principal Component Analysis (PCA): Identifies uncorrelated variables (principal components) that capture maximum variance in the data, enabling dimensionality reduction while preserving essential information.

Linear Discriminant Analysis (LDA): Maximizes separability between classes in supervised learning scenarios by projecting features onto a lower-dimensional space. Particularly useful for classification tasks.

Independent Component Analysis (ICA): Extracts statistically independent components from original features, separating mixed underlying factors.

Factor Analysis: Identifies latent factors underlying observed variables, revealing influential factors driving the data and enabling dimensionality reduction.

Recursive Feature Elimination (RFE): Iteratively eliminates less important features based on their impact on model performance, selecting the optimal subset.

SelectKBest: Evaluates statistical relationship between each feature and target variable, selecting K features with the highest scores based on a specific statistical metric.

L1 Regularization (Lasso): Promotes sparsity in the feature space by shrinking less important feature weights towards zero, automatically selecting a subset of relevant features.

Tree-based Feature Importance: Determines feature importance by analyzing the tree structure of decision tree-based algorithms, assigning scores based on their contribution to overall tree performance.

The selection of appropriate techniques depends on dataset characteristics, problem nature, and analysis goals. Evaluating technique performance using suitable metrics and validating selected features on independent datasets ensures enhanced accuracy and interpretability of models.

5. DATA DISCRETIZATION AND BINNING

The text explains data discretization, also known as binning, as a preprocessing technique that converts continuous variables into categorical or ordinal formats. It offers advantages such as simplifying data complexity, handling outliers, and facilitating analysis. The commonly used data discretization and binning techniques are:

Equal-Width Binning: Divides the value range into equal-sized bins. Each bin covers a specified interval width or an equal number of values, simplifying the approach but potentially ineffective for unevenly distributed data.

Equal-Frequency Binning: Divides the data into bins with an equal number of data points. It ensures equal representation in each bin, accommodating skewed data distributions and mitigating the impact of outliers.

Custom Binning: Allows manual definition of bin boundaries based on domain knowledge or specific requirements. It provides flexibility in creating bins aligned with criteria or meaningful thresholds.

Adaptive Binning: Dynamically determines bin boundaries based on data characteristics, utilizing statistical measures or algorithms. It can handle data with varying distributions and adjust bin boundaries to capture significant patterns or variations.

Information-Based Binning: Aims to maximize information gain or minimize information entropy within each bin. Measures like entropy, information gain, or Gini index help identify optimal bin boundaries, ensuring informative and discriminative bins.

Target-Driven Binning: Divides data into bins based on the relationship between input variables and the target variable. It considers the target variable's distribution within each bin, capturing nonlinear relationships and enhancing predictive modeling.

The selection of a suitable data discretization and binning technique depends on data characteristics, analysis objectives, and modeling requirements. It is important to carefully consider the data nature and the potential impact of binning on subsequent analyses.

5.1 Discretization Methods for Continuous Variables

The text explains that discretization methods transform continuous variables into categorical or ordinal formats, simplifying data analysis, handling outliers, and improving interpretability. Common discretization techniques include:

Equal-Width Binning: Divides the value range into bins of equal size, based on a specified number of bins. However, it may not handle unevenly distributed data effectively.

Equal-Frequency Binning: Divides the data into bins with an equal number of data points in each bin, addressing skewed distributions and reducing the influence of outliers.

K-Means Clustering: Uses an unsupervised learning algorithm to group similar data points into clusters, which can represent distinct categories or bins.

Custom Discretization: Allows manual specification of bin boundaries based on domain knowledge or specific requirements, providing flexibility to align with business rules or expert knowledge.

Information-Based Discretization: Maximizes information gain or minimizes information entropy within each bin, considering the relationship between the target variable and the continuous variable.

Entropy-Based Discretization: Uses information theory concepts to identify bin boundaries that minimize information entropy within each bin, maximizing homogeneity. The ChiMerge algorithm is a common method for entropy-based discretization.

When selecting a discretization method, it is important to consider the data characteristics, analysis objectives, and problem requirements. Additionally, evaluating the impact of discretization on subsequent analyses or modeling tasks is recommended to ensure alignment with the intended goals.

5.2 Binning Approaches for Handling Large-Scale Data

The text discusses binning approaches specifically designed to handle large-scale data efficiently:

Sampling-Based Binning: Randomly samples a subset of the data and performs binning on the sampled subset, applying resulting bin boundaries to the entire dataset. Reduces computational requirements while providing reasonable binning results.

Histogram-Based Binning: Estimates data distribution by constructing histograms, dividing data into fixed-width or dynamically adjusted bins based on the histogram structure. Can be done in parallel or distributed settings using techniques like MapReduce or Spark.

Stream-Based Binning: Handles data in a streaming fashion, processing one data point at a time or in small chunks. Updates bin boundaries incrementally as new data arrives, adapting to changes in data distribution over time.

Distributed Binning: Distributes computation across multiple computing nodes or clusters, partitioning data and processing it in parallel. Results from each partition are combined to obtain final bin boundaries. Utilizes frameworks like Apache Hadoop or Apache Spark.

Approximate Binning: Trades off accuracy for computational efficiency. Uses sampling, approximation algorithms, or statistical summaries to estimate bin boundaries instead of exact calculations on the entire dataset. Reduces computational overhead while providing slightly less precise results.

When choosing a binning approach for large-scale data, it's important to consider the trade-off between accuracy and computational efficiency. The selection should be based on data characteristics, available computing resources, and analysis goals. Evaluating the quality and reliability of the binning results is crucial to ensure the chosen approach meets the desired requirements for large-scale datasets.

6. HANDLING STREAMING AND REAL-TIME DATA

Managing streaming and real-time data requires specialized approaches and techniques to process and analyze data as it arrives. Traditional batch processing methods are not suitable for streaming data. Here are strategies for handling streaming and real-time data:

Stream Processing Frameworks: Utilize frameworks like Apache Kafka, Apache Flink, or Apache Storm designed for scalable and fault-tolerant processing of continuous data streams.

Data Ingestion and Collection: Implement efficient mechanisms to capture and receive streaming data from various sources using messaging systems, data integration platforms, or APIs.

Real-time Data Pipelines: Design pipelines that ensure seamless flow of data from source to processing layer, maintaining data integrity, reliability, and low-latency processing.

Event Time Processing: Handle out-of-order events and event time delays accurately by assigning timestamps, aligning events based on their event time, and managing time-based operations.

Windowing and Time-Based Operations: Analyze data over specific time intervals or sliding windows to enable real-time aggregations, calculations, and analysis.

Real-time Analytics and Visualization: Incorporate components for real-time insights and monitoring through dashboards, visualizations, and anomaly detection algorithms.

Scalability and Parallel Processing: Ensure the infrastructure can handle high data volumes by distributing the workload across multiple processing nodes for parallel processing.

Continuous Model Training and Updating: Implement techniques for dynamic model adaptation and learning from streaming data in real time.

Fault Tolerance and Data Resilience: Design the infrastructure with fault tolerance mechanisms like data replication, distributed processing, and checkpointing to recover from failures and maintain data integrity.

Effective management of streaming and real-time data requires robust and scalable systems tailored to their unique characteristics. These systems enable real-time analysis and decision-making while handling the continuous and time-sensitive nature of streaming data.

6.1 Techniques for Preprocessing Streaming Data

Preprocessing streaming data involves applying techniques to prepare the data for analysis or downstream tasks. These techniques need to be designed to handle the dynamic nature of streaming data. Commonly used techniques for preprocessing streaming data include:

Data Cleaning: Handling missing values, outliers, and noisy data in real time using techniques like imputation, filtering, or smoothing.

Data Transformation: Converting streaming data into a suitable format for analysis by normalizing, standardizing, scaling, or encoding features.

Feature Extraction: Extracting relevant features from the data stream using techniques such as dimensionality reduction or time-series and text feature extraction.

Windowing and Sliding Windows: Processing streaming data in fixed time intervals or sliding windows to perform calculations, aggregations, or statistical operations.

Online Learning: Updating models continuously as new data arrives to adapt and learn from the latest observations using techniques like online clustering or concept drift detection.

Data Deduplication: Handling duplicate data instances in real time using deduplication techniques like hashing, clustering, or similarity measures.

Outlier Detection: Identifying and handling outliers in streaming data using real-time outlier detection algorithms.

Data Integration and Fusion: Integrating and fusing multiple data streams or sources into a unified representation to gain a comprehensive view.

Stream Filtering and Sampling: Applying filtering techniques to reduce noise or focus on specific subsets of the data stream, and using sampling techniques for computational efficiency or storage limitations.

When preprocessing streaming data, it is important to consider timeliness, efficiency, adaptability, real-time processing capabilities, fault tolerance, and scalability to handle the continuous influx of streaming data effectively.

6.2 Real-Time Data Cleansing and Normalization

Real-time data cleansing and normalization involve applying data cleaning and normalization operations to streaming data as it is received in real time. The goal is to ensure that the data is accurate, consistent, and ready for immediate analysis or use. The key steps in real-time data cleansing and normalization are:

Data Validation: Validate incoming data by checking data types, identifying missing or invalid values, and validating against predefined rules or constraints.

Data Standardization: Standardize the format, structure, and units of incoming data to achieve consistency. Convert data to a common format, harmonize units of measurement, and apply standard naming conventions.

Data Deduplication: Detect and handle duplicate data instances as they arrive in real time. Use techniques like hashing, clustering, or similarity measures to identify and eliminate duplicate records.

Outlier Detection and Handling: Identify and address outliers or unusual data points in real time. Utilize outlier detection algorithms, statistical methods, or machine learning techniques to handle outliers as they occur.

Missing Data Handling: Address missing data in real time to prevent gaps in analysis. Employ imputation techniques like mean imputation, regression imputation, or nearest-neighbour imputation.

Data Transformation and Normalization: Normalize data values to a consistent scale or range for accurate analysis. Rescale numerical data, such as normalizing to a [0, 1] range or standardizing with zero mean and unit variance.

Real-time Error Handling: Implement error handling mechanisms to deal with errors or exceptions during data cleansing and normalization. Log errors, capture error statistics, and define strategies to handle errors.

Continuous Monitoring and Feedback: Continuously monitor the quality of the data cleansing and normalization process. Use monitoring techniques, real-time dashboards, or anomaly detection algorithms to identify data quality problems and initiate corrective actions.

7. EVALUATION AND VALIDATION OF PREPROCESSING TECHNIQUES

The text emphasizes the importance of evaluating and validating preprocessing techniques to ensure the quality and effectiveness of the data preparation process. It provides ten key aspects to consider when evaluating and validating preprocessing techniques:

Define Evaluation Metrics: Establish appropriate metrics aligned with preprocessing objectives, such as accuracy, precision, recall, F1-score, or mean squared error.

Split Data for Evaluation: Divide the dataset into training, validation, and test sets to develop, optimize, and evaluate preprocessing techniques.

Establish Baselines: Compare the performance of preprocessing techniques against raw data, minimal preprocessing, or established techniques.

Measure Impact on Downstream Tasks: Assess how preprocessing techniques affect the performance of classification, clustering, or regression tasks.

Consider Computational Efficiency: Evaluate the time and resource requirements of preprocessing techniques, particularly for large-scale or real-time applications.

Cross-Validation and Robustness: Use cross-validation to validate the generalization capability and stability of preprocessing techniques across different data subsets.

Compare Different Techniques: Conduct controlled experiments to compare the performance of multiple preprocessing techniques and identify the most effective approach.

Sensitivity Analysis: Perform sensitivity analysis to evaluate how changes in preprocessing parameters impact outcomes.

Reproducibility and Documentation: Document all steps, techniques, parameters, metrics, and results to ensure reproducibility and facilitate knowledge sharing.

Iterative Improvement: Continuously evaluate and refine preprocessing techniques based on feedback and real-world performance.

By following these practices, one can enhance the reliability, effectiveness, and capability of preprocessing techniques to improve data quality for downstream analysis tasks.

8. FUTURE TRENDS AND DIRECTIONS

The text discusses future trends and directions in the field of big data preprocessing. Here's a summary of the key points:

Automation of Preprocessing: Machine learning and AI algorithms will automate preprocessing steps, improving efficiency and reducing manual effort.

Streaming Data Preprocessing: Techniques will focus on real-time data cleansing, normalization, and feature extraction to handle streaming data sources.

Integration of Domain Knowledge: Preprocessing techniques will incorporate domain-specific knowledge to improve accuracy and relevance.

Privacy-Preserving Preprocessing: Methods like differential privacy will protect sensitive information while maintaining data utility.

Preprocessing for Unstructured and Semi-Structured Data: Specialized techniques will handle text, images, and multimedia using NLP, computer vision, and deep learning.

Preprocessing for Edge Computing: Techniques will optimize for resource-constrained edge devices, limited bandwidth, and low-latency requirements.

Integration of Preprocessing with Data Quality Assessment: Data quality assessment algorithms will be integrated into preprocessing to identify and rectify quality issues.

Preprocessing for Explainable AI: Methods will enable explainability and interpretability in AI models, reducing bias and increasing transparency.

Preprocessing for Context-Aware Analysis: Techniques will adapt to the specific context or environment of the data, improving relevance and accuracy.

Integration of Preprocessing with Data Governance: Preprocessing will align with data governance practices, enhancing transparency and accountability.

By embracing these future trends, practitioners and researchers can enhance the efficiency, accuracy, and reliability of big data preprocessing for analytical applications.

REFERENCES

Alghamdi, T. A., & Javaid, N. (2022). A survey of preprocessing methods used for analysis of big data originated from smart grids. *IEEE Access : Practical Innovations, Open Solutions*, *10*, 29149–29171. doi:10.1109/ACCESS.2022.3157941

BarseS.BhagatD.DhawaleK.SolankeY.KurveD. (2023). Cyber-Trolling Detection System. Available at SSRN 4340372.

Çelik, O., Hasanbaşoğlu, M., Aktaş, M. S., Kalıpsız, O., & Kanli, A. N. (2019, September). Implementation of data preprocessing techniques on distributed big data platforms. In *2019 4th International Conference on Computer Science and Engineering (UBMK)* (pp. 73-78). IEEE. 10.1109/UBMK.2019.8907230

Desai, V., & Dinesha, H. A. (2020, November). A hybrid approach to data pre-processing methods. In *2020 IEEE International Conference for Innovation in Technology (INOCON)* (pp. 1-4). IEEE. 10.1109/INOCON50539.2020.9298378

Hande, T., Dhawas, P., Kakirwar, B., & Gupta, A. (2023, August) Yoga Postures Correction and Estimation using Open CV and VGG 19 Architecture. In *2023 International Journal of Innovative Science and Research Technology*.

Krishna, G. S., Supriya, K., & Rao, K. M. (2022, September). Selection of data preprocessing techniques and its emergence towards machine learning algorithms using hpi dataset. In 2022 IEEE Global Conference on Computing, Power and Communication Technologies (GlobConPT) (pp. 1-6). IEEE. 10.1109/GlobConPT57482.2022.9938255

Gao, P., Han, Z., & Wan, F. (2020, October). Big Data Processing and Application Research. In 2020 2nd International Conference on Artificial Intelligence and Advanced Manufacture (AIAM) (pp. 125-128). IEEE.

Cai-Ming, Z., & Hao-Nan, C. (2020, December). Preprocessing method of structured big data in human resource archives database. In 2020 IEEE International Conference on Industrial Application of Artificial Intelligence (IAAI) (pp. 379-384). IEEE.

Gawhade, R., Bohara, L. R., Mathew, J., & Bari, P. (2022, March). Computerized Data-Preprocessing To Improve Data Quality. In *2022 Second International Conference on Power, Control and Computing Technologies (ICPC2T)* (pp. 1-6). IEEE. 10.1109/GlobConPT57482.2022.9938255

Mo, R., Liu, J., Yu, W., Jiang, F., Gu, X., Zhao, X., & Peng, J. (2019, August). A differential privacy-based protecting data preprocessing method for big data mining. In *2019 18th IEEE International Conference On Trust, Security And Privacy In Computing And Communications/13th IEEE International Conference On Big Data Science And Engineering (TrustCom/BigDataSE)* (pp. 693-699). IEEE. 10.1109/TrustCom/BigDataSE.2019.00098

Obaid, H. S., Dheyab, S. A., & Sabry, S. S. (2019, March). The impact of data pre-processing techniques and dimensionality reduction on the accuracy of machine learning. In *2019 9th Annual Information Technology, Electromechanical Engineering and Microelectronics Conference (IEMECON)* (pp. 279-283). IEEE. 10.1109/IEMECONX.2019.8877011

Pradha, S., Halgamuge, M. N., & Vinh, N. T. Q. (2019, October). Effective text data preprocessing technique for sentiment analysis in social media data. In *2019 11th international conference on knowledge and systems engineering (KSE)* (pp. 1-8). IEEE. 10.1109/KSE.2019.8919368

KEY TERMS AND DEFINITIONS

Data Cleaning: Data Cleaning involves the identification and correction of errors, outliers, duplicates, or inconsistencies in raw data to improve its quality, aiming to eliminate noise and irregularities and establish a reliable foundation for subsequent analysis.

Data Discretization: Data Discretization involves converting continuous data into categorical or discrete representations, simplifying analysis by reducing complexity associated with continuous variables and enabling the application of methods designed for categorical data.

Data Integration: Data Integration is the process of merging data from various sources and formats (databases, sensors, social media, IoT devices) into a unified representation, ensuring data consistency and compatibility for analysis.

Data Transformation: Data Transformation includes applying techniques to convert data into a suitable format for analysis, such as scaling numerical data, normalizing values, encoding categorical variables, or deriving new features through mathematical or statistical operations. This standardization simplifies subsequent analysis tasks.

Dealing with Imbalanced Data: Dealing with Imbalanced Data focuses on situations where one class or category is significantly more prevalent than others. Preprocessing techniques, such as oversampling, undersampling, or generating synthetic samples, aim to achieve a balanced representation of the data.

Dimensionality Reduction: Dimensionality Reduction entails employing techniques to reduce the number of variables or features in high-dimensional data while preserving essential information. This simplifies analysis, addresses computational challenges, and enhances efficiency by minimizing noise and overfitting problems.

Handling Missing Values: Handling missing values are the process of addressing missing data in large datasets. Techniques involve imputing missing values using statistical methods or leveraging imputation algorithms to fill gaps, ensuring that analysis is not compromised by incomplete information.

Chapter 7

Big Data Analysis Techniques:
Data Preprocessing Techniques, Data Mining Techniques, Machine Learning Algorithm, Visualization

Pranali Dhawas
 https://orcid.org/0009-0003-4276-2310
G.H. Raisoni College of Engineering, Nagpur, India

Minakshi Ashok Ramteke
G.H. Raisoni College of Engineering, Nagpur, India

Aarti Thakur
G.H. Raisoni College of Engineering, Nagpur, India

Poonam Vijay Polshetwar
CSMSS College of Polytechnic, India

Ramadevi Vitthal Salunkhe
Rajarambapu Institute of Technology, India

Dhananjay Bhagat
 https://orcid.org/0009-0009-1100-3219
G.H. Raisoni College of Engineering, Nagpur, India

ABSTRACT

Big data analysis techniques are the methods and tools utilized for extracting insights and knowledge from vast and intricate datasets. Due to the increasing velocity, volume, and variety of data being produced, conventional data analysis methods have become inadequate. Therefore, big data analysis techniques employ advanced computational and statistical methods to extract treasured information from big data. There are several big data analysis techniques, including data mining, natural language processing, machine learning, predictive analytics, and deep learning. For example, data mining involves identifying patterns and relationships within data sets, while machine learning enables systems to learn from data without explicit programming. Additionally, natural language processing focuses on analyzing human language, and predictive analytics utilizes statistical modeling techniques to predict future outcomes. Deep learning, which uses neural networks to model complex data patterns, is also a common big data analysis technique.

DOI: 10.4018/979-8-3693-0413-6.ch007

1. INTRODUCTION

Big data analysis is a process of examining and interpreting massive and complex datasets to extract valuable insights, enabling decision-makers to make informed decisions. "Big data" describes datasets too large or complicated for conventional data processing tools to handle. Advanced software and hardware tools are used in big data analysis to collect, store, process, and analyze large datasets using various analytical techniques, which includes statistical analysis, machine learning, data mining, and natural language processing.

The insights obtained through big data analysis which can be used to inform decision-making in multiple industries and applications, such as healthcare, finance, marketing, and manufacturing. For example, healthcare providers can identify patterns in patient data, leading to more effective diagnosis and treatment. Retailers can analyze customer purchase patterns and create better marketing strategies.

Big data analysis has become prevalent as a result of the substantial increase in data volume originating from digital technologies like mobile devices, social media and Internet of Things (IoT). By utilizing these massive datasets, organizations can obtain a deeper understanding of their customers, operations, and markets, resulting in better decision-making and improved business outcomes.

Big data analytics involves identifying problem, gathering relevant data from diverse sources, storing it in scalable infrastructures, cleaning and preprocessing the data, integrating multiple datasets, exploring and analyzing the data using statistical and machine learning techniques, evaluating and validating models, interpreting and visualizing insights, and utilizing those insights for decision making and value creation as shown in below Figure1.

Figure 1. Process of big data analytics

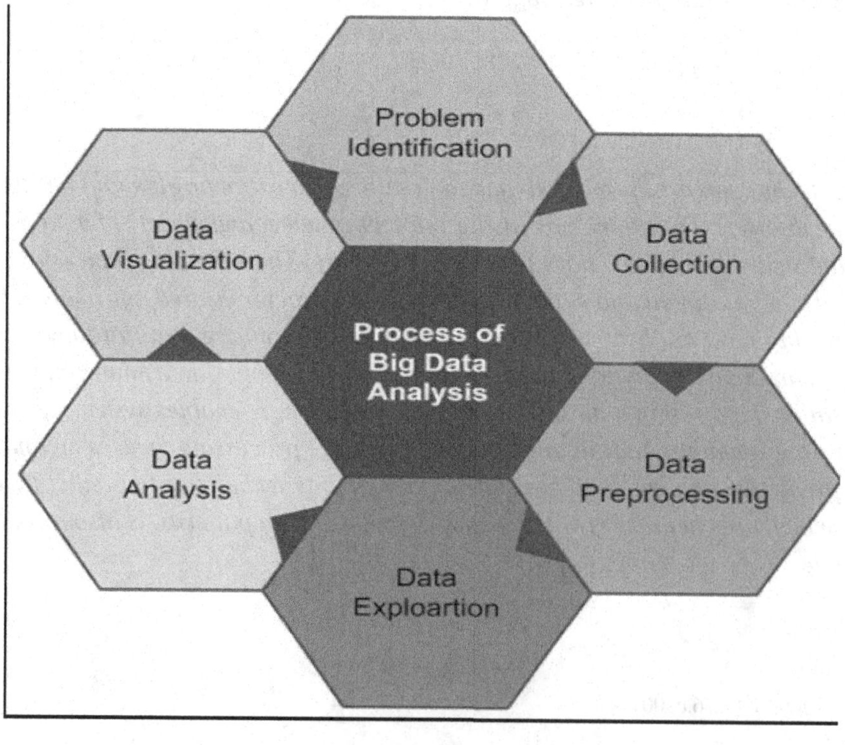

In today's data-driven economy, big data analysis serves as a powerful tool for organizations aiming to extract the value from their data and secure a competitive edge.

1.1 Definition and Overview of Big Data Analysis

The term "big data analysis" refers to the procedure of analyzing and interpreting datasets that are too large, complex, or heterogeneous for traditional data processing tools to handle. This process involves using advanced software and hardware tools to collect, store, process, and analyze large datasets with a variety of analytical techniques, like statistical analysis, data mining, machine learning, and natural language processing.

The insights gained from big data analysis can inform decision-making across many industries, including healthcare, finance, marketing, and manufacturing. As an example, healthcare providers can employ big data analysis to recognize patterns within patient data, aiding in improved disease diagnosis and treatment approaches. Similarly, retailers can use big data analysis to evaluate customer purchasing patterns and develop more effective marketing strategies.

The advent of big data analysis is due to the explosion of data produced by digital technologies like social media, mobile devices, and the Internet of Things (IoT). By analyzing these massive datasets, organizations can gain deeper insights into their customers, operations, and markets, which can enhance decision-making and improve business outcomes.

1.2 Importance of Big Data Analysis

Big data analysis plays a vital role in the current data-centric world, and its significance cannot be emphasized enough. The following are some reasons why big data analysis is essential:

Enhanced decision-making: Big data analysis gives businesses the information they need to make wise decisions by providing insights into consumer behaviour, market trends, and operational inefficiencies. It enables businesses to leverage data for driving innovation and enhancing overall business outcomes.

Improved customer experience: Through the analysis of extensive datasets, organizations can acquire a more profound understanding of the requirements and preferences of their customers. This will help businesses provide more personalized products and services, resulting in an enhanced customer experience and increased customer loyalty.

Increased efficiency: Big data analysis can help businesses optimize their operations by identifying bottlenecks and inefficiencies. It can also help automate routine tasks and reduce manual labor, leading to increased efficiency and cost savings.

Innovation: Big data analysis can assist businesses in identifying new opportunities and avenues for growth. By analyzing large datasets, businesses can identify emerging trends and new markets, enabling them to develop new products and services.

Competitive advantage: The utilization of big data analysis can provide businesses with a competitive edge through the provision of unique insights that may not be accessible to their rivals. By making informed decisions based on data, businesses can maintain a competitive advantage and outperform their competition.

1.3 Challenges Associated With Big Data Analysis

While big data analysis offers numerous benefits, it also presents several challenges as shown in Figure 2. Here are some of the primary difficulties associated with big data analysis (Bagga, 2018):

Data quality: Large, complex datasets can be challenging to handle, with inaccurate, inconsistent, or missing data making it hard to draw meaningful insights.

Data privacy and security: As the amount of data being collected increases, so do the risks associated with data breaches and cyber-attacks. Organizations must protect their data from unauthorized access, theft, and misuse.

Scalability: The velocity, volume and variety of big data often surpass the capabilities for traditional data processing tools. Consequently, organizations must allocate resources to acquire advanced software and hardware tools capable of effectively managing large datasets.

Skill gap: Big data analysis requires specialized skills in data analysis, statistics, and machine learning, which are in high demand. The shortage of skilled professionals in this field makes it difficult for organizations to find and retain talent.

Cost: Collecting, storing, processing, and analyzing large datasets can be costly. Organizations must invest in infrastructure, software, and personnel to conduct big data analysis.

Ethical considerations: Big data analysis raises ethical concerns around data privacy, discrimination, and bias. Organizations must ensure that their data analysis practices are transparent, fair, and unbiased.

Figure 2. Challenges associated with big data analysis

Technical Challenges

- Data Storage and Management
- Data Processing & Analysis
- Data Integration

Security and Privacy Challenges

- Data Security
- Data Privacy

Challenges in Big Data Analysis

Resource Challenges

- Computing Resources
- Human Resources
- Financial Resources

Quality Challenges

- Data Quality
- Data Validity

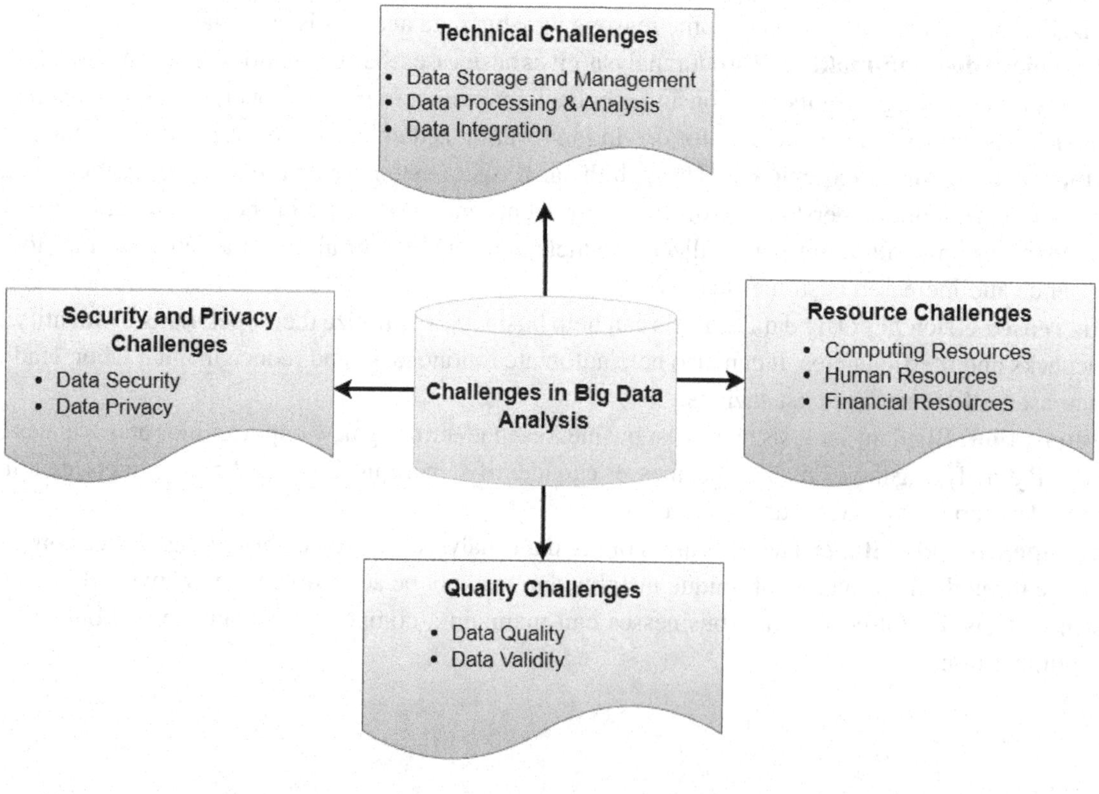

2. DATA PREPROCESSING TECHNIQUES FOR BIG DATA

A critical component of large data analysis is data preparation, which includes preparing raw data for further analysis by cleaning, transforming, and organizing it. To accomplish this, data cleaning, data normalization, data reduction, data transformation, data integration, data discretization, and data aggregation are commonly used techniques (Perer, 2019). These techniques help eliminate errors, inconsistencies, and missing data, convert data into appropriate formats, reduce data size, combine data from multiple sources, standardize data scales, discretize continuous data, and group data into subsets. Utilizing these techniques enables big data to be made ready for further analysis, which results in improved accuracy and efficiency in data analysis (Dwivedi, 2015).

When it comes to large data analysis, data preprocessing assumes a vital role as it encompasses the tasks of cleaning, transforming, and preparing raw data to ensure its suitability for subsequent analysis. Below are a few widely employed data preprocessing techniques in big data analysis:

2.1 Data Cleaning

Data cleaning is an essential stage in data preprocessing for big data, as significant datasets can be vulnerable to errors, discrepancies, and gaps, which can harm the analysis's accuracy and dependability (Hariharakrishnan, 2017). Below are some frequently used methods for cleaning data in big data analysis:

Removing duplicates: Eliminating duplicates is a vital data cleaning technique in data preprocessing for big data analysis, as they can arise from various sources, such as data entry errors or data merging. Duplicates can cause inaccurate analysis results and require unnecessary computing resources, making it crucial to identify and address them in the data cleaning phase. To identify and remove duplicates in large datasets, techniques such as data profiling and data deduplication can be employed. Data profiling can be used to detect potential duplicates by analyzing patterns in the data, while data deduplication involves identifying and eliminating duplicate records or data points. By removing duplicates, the data becomes more accurate, efficient, and suitable for further analysis.

Handling missing values: Dealing with missing values is a crucial technique in data cleaning for data preprocessing in big data analysis. Missing values can happen for a number of reasons, including incorrect data entry, technical problems, or insufficient data. Ignoring missing values can lead to inaccurate analysis results, making it essential to address them in the data cleaning stage. Techniques such as imputation, deletion, or interpolation can be used to manage missing values in large datasets. Imputation involves swapping missing values with estimated values based on the available data, while deletion involves eliminating the entire row or column containing missing values. Interpolation involves estimating missing values based on nearby values. By handling missing values, the data becomes more complete, reliable, and suitable for further analysis.

Handling outliers: Handling outliers is a crucial data cleaning technique in the data preprocessing stage for big data analysis. Missing values can happen for a number of reasons, including incorrect data entry, technical problems, or insufficient data. Outliers may arise from measurement errors, data entry mistakes, or rare events and can skew analysis results. Data scientists use various techniques such as clustering, regression analysis, and decision trees to identify and handle outliers. Clustering is a group of similar data points together, while regression analysis identifies and removes outliers based on statistical tests. By handling outliers, the data can be made more accurate, reliable, and suitable for further analysis.

Standardizing data formats: converting data into a consistent and uniform format for accurate analysis. This may involve transforming different types of data, such as dates, times, and currencies, into a standardized format to facilitate comparison and identification of inconsistencies. Standardizing data formats is a necessary step in preparing big data for analysis as it ensures data cleanliness, consistency, and suitability for further processing.

Correcting inconsistent values: In data preprocessing, correcting inconsistent values is an essential technique in data cleaning. Inconsistent values can originate from multiple sources such as human errors in data entry, diverse data sources, or software problems, and can cause inaccurate or unreliable results during data analysis. To address this, techniques such as data profiling, data parsing, and regular expressions can be employed to identify and rectify inconsistent values in large datasets. The correction of inconsistent values results in more reliable, accurate, and appropriate data for further analysis.

Handling data incompatibilities: Data cleaning for data preprocessing involves handling data incompatibilities, which can arise from various factors such as differences in units of measurement, conflicting data types, and languages. These incompatibilities can lead to errors in analysis, making it essential to address them in the data cleaning stage. Data normalization, data conversion, and data integration are some of the techniques that can be used to handle data incompatibilities. For instance, data normalization can standardize units of measurement, and data conversion can convert data types. Handling data incompatibilities is crucial in making the data more consistent, reliable, and suitable for further analysis.

2.2 Data Integration

Data integration is a fundamental aspect of data preprocessing for big data analysis that involves merging data from diverse sources into a single, unified dataset. This can include combining data from various file formats, databases, and even external sources such as APIs or web scraping.

Data integration plays a crucial role as it allows analysts to acquire a comprehensive perspective of the data, facilitating the identification of patterns and relationships that may remain concealed when examining individual datasets. Nevertheless, merging data from various sources can present challenges, potentially leading to inconsistencies in data formats or conflicting values.

To address these challenges, analysts can use techniques like data mapping and data transformation. Data mapping includes identifying common fields between datasets and mapping them with a standardized format, while data transformation involves converting data into a standardized format.

2.3 Data Transformation

Data transformation is a crucial data preprocessing technique for big data analysis, involving the conversion of data from one format to another to make it more suitable for analysis. Data transformation may include altering the data type, scaling the data, or creating new features from existing data.

The importance of data transformation lies in standardizing the data, removing any inconsistencies or outliers that may be present in the original data, and enlightening the accuracy of analysis results. Techniques like normalization, scaling, and feature engineering can be utilized to transform data. For example, normalization involves scaling data to a common range such as between 0 and 1, scaling involves adjusting the range of data to a specific range like -1 to 1, and feature engineering includes creating new features from existing data, such as calculating the average of multiple columns.

2.4 Data Reduction

One of the frequently used data preprocessing techniques in big data analytics is data reduction. Its purpose is to decrease the data set's size while still retaining its crucial features. There are various methods available for data reduction, which include:

Principal component analysis (PCA): It is a data reduction technique used for data preprocessing, aims to transform large datasets into lower-dimensional spaces while still preserving the most crucial information. It achieves this by identifying the essential variables or features that capture the highest variation in the data and then creating a new set of variables or principal components that summarize the data's variability. By doing so, it can significantly decrease the computational resources required for analysis, making it a valuable tool for handling large data sets. Additionally, PCA can assist in identifying correlations between variables and can be employed for data visualization and pattern recognition. However, it is crucial to ensure that the reduced data set retains the most important characteristics of the original data to avoid compromising the analysis outcomes.

Feature selection: Feature selection is a powerful data preprocessing technique that simplifies analysis by identifying and eliminating irrelevant variables or features from a dataset. By doing so, it reduces the data's dimensionality while preserving the necessary information for analysis. Feature selection methods can include statistical techniques like correlation analysis and mutual information, or machine learning algorithms like decision trees or gradient boosting. Feature selection offers many benefits, including improved model performance, reduced overfitting, faster training times, and better interpretability of analysis results. However, it's critical to ensure that the reduced dataset still retains the most important characteristics of the original data to avoid negatively affecting the analysis outcomes.

Sampling: Sampling is a data preprocessing technique that includes selecting a representative subset of data from a larger dataset for analysis, with the aim of reducing computational and time resources required for analysis while retaining critical information. To select data points from the dataset, various sampling methods like simple random sampling, stratified sampling, or cluster sampling can be employed. Simple random sampling involves randomly selecting data points without any specific criteria, while stratified sampling includes distributing the dataset into homogeneous subcategories and randomly selecting data points from each subgroup. Cluster sampling involves dividing the dataset into clusters and randomly choosing some clusters for analysis. Sampling can improve analysis accuracy, increase efficiency, and reduce computational resources, but it's important to guarantee the selected sample is representative of the original dataset and that any biases or errors introduced during the sampling process are minimized by choosing an appropriate sampling method.

Data compression: Data compression is an important technique in data reduction and processing that enables large datasets to be compressed into a smaller form while still retaining crucial information for analysis. Its primary aim is to reduce storage space and enhance the efficiency of data transmission and processing.

Data compression can be categorized into two types: lossless and lossy. Lossless compression guarantees that the compressed data can be restored to its original form without any loss of information. On the other hand, lossy compression sacrifices a portion of the data to achieve a higher level of compression.

Various techniques are used to achieve data compression, like run-length encoding, Huffman coding, and arithmetic coding. Run-length encoding is simple method that substitutes repetitive data with a shorter code, while Huffman coding and arithmetic coding are more complex algorithms that assign codes to data based on their frequency.

The advantage of data compression is that it can considerably reduce the storage space needed for a dataset, making it easier to store and transmit. However, it is crucial to ensure that the compression algorithm used does not significantly affect the essential information necessary for analysis. Therefore, it is essential to evaluate the data compression technique used and its effect on data quality and analysis results carefully.

2.5 Data Normalization

To ensure accurate analysis outcomes by minimizing the impact of inconsistent data scales and units, data normalization is a fundamental data preprocessing technique in big data analytics that standardizes data into a consistent format.

The rescaling of data values to fit within a particular range, typically between 0 and 1 or -1 and 1, is achieved in data normalization by dividing the result of subtracting the minimum value from each data point by the range of values. Alternatively, data normalization can be accomplished by converting data into z-scores, where each data point is subtracted from the mean and divided by standard deviation of data set.

By transforming data into a standardized format, data normalization avoids problems arising from differing units of measurement, scales, and distributions when comparing and analyzing data. It also makes it easier to recognize patterns and relationships within the data, improving the accuracy of analytical tools such as machine learning models.

2.6 Data Discretization

Data discretization is an essential data preprocessing technique that converts continuous data into a discrete format, making it easier to analyze and process (Ray, 2019). This technique is particularly important in big data analytics, as many data mining algorithms can only handle discrete data.

To achieve data discretization, continuous data is divided into number of smaller intervals, and each interval is assigned a discrete value or label. There are various methods for partitioning the data, including equal width binning, equal frequency binning, and clustering. With equal width binning, the range of values are divided into a fixed number of intervals with equal widths. In contrast, equal frequency binning creates intervals with the same number of data points in each interval, and clustering groups data points into clusters based on resemblance and assigns labels to each cluster.

Data discretization simplifies data analysis and enables the use of data mining algorithms that can only handle discrete data, which helps minimize the number of unique values in a dataset, making data storage and processing more efficient.

However, data discretization can result in information loss due to the loss of precision in continuous data. Thus, choosing an appropriate discretization method and interval width is crucial to minimize information loss while preserving the essential features of the original data.

2.7 Data Aggregation

Data aggregation is a technique used in data preprocessing for big data analytics that enables analysts to combine multiple data points into a single, more manageable data point. The purpose of this technique is to simplify the data set while retaining critical information.

Data aggregation involves combining data points based on a specific attribute or characteristic. For instance, time-series data can be aggregated by hour, day, or week, and summary statistics such as average, minimum, or maximum values can be computed for that time period. Similarly, data can be aggregated based on location, category, or other attributes to generate summary statistics for these groups.

The benefits of data aggregation are numerous, including simplifying the data set, reducing the number of unique values, and improving the efficiency of data storage and processing. Additionally, data aggregation aids in identifying trends and patterns by presenting the data in a more manageable format.

Data aggregation can result in information loss, particularly when using summary statistics that do not capture the entire range of values in the data set. Therefore, it is necessary to choose an appropriate aggregation method and ensure that the summary statistics accurately reflect the data.

3. DATA MINING TECHNIQUES FOR BIG DATA

Data mining techniques as shown in figure 3 are essential for analyzing large and complex datasets in big data analytics (Sowmya, 2017). These techniques allow analysts to identify relationships, patterns, and anomalies in the data. Commonly used data mining techniques include classification, regression, clustering, association rule mining, text mining, anomaly detection, and neural networks. Classification groups data into predefined categories, clustering groups similar data points, association rule mining identifies patterns of co-occurring items, regression models relationships between variables, anomaly detection identifies outliers, text mining extracts insights from unstructured text data, and neural networks recognize complex patterns. Using a combination of these techniques, analysts can extract valuable insights from the data for informed business decisions (Desai, 2020).

Figure 3. Data mining techniques for big data

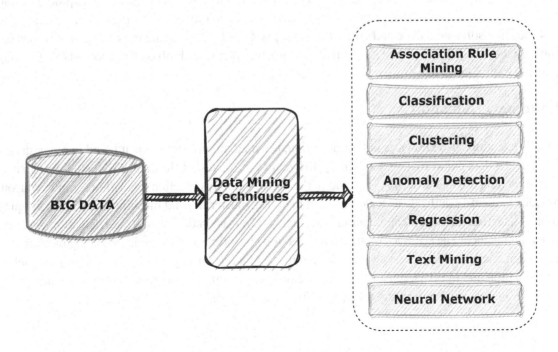

3.1 Association Rule Mining

Association rule mining is a powerful data mining technique used in big data analytics to uncover patterns of co-occurring items in a dataset. This technique is employed to find associations or correlations between variables based on their frequency of occurrence. For example, it can be used to identify which items are commonly purchased together in a shopping cart, allowing businesses to optimize their product recommendations or marketing strategies. By using association rule mining, companies can extract valuable insights from their data and gain a competitive benefit in the marketplace.

3.2 Classification

In big data analytics, classification is a commonly utilized data mining technique that includes assigning data points to predefined categories based on their attributes. The technique is particularly useful in predicting the category of new data based on the patterns detected in the training data. Classification algorithms find various applications in areas like fraud detection, sentiment analysis, and image recognition. Evaluation metrics like precision, recall, and F1 score are used to assess the accuracy of classification models, and the models can be further optimized with techniques like hyperparameter tuning and cross-validation. By applying classification, businesses can automate processes and make informed decisions based on the predicted categories of new data points.

3.3 Clustering

Clustering is a technique utilized in big data analytics to group data points with similar attributes into clustersData analysis entails the identification of patterns and relationships within the data, which may not be readily apparent in its raw form. Various methods like distance metrics or density-based clustering can be used to measure similarity between data points. Clustering can be useful for exploratory data analysis, customer segmentation, and anomaly detection. The quality of clustering can be evaluated using metrics like silhouette score and cohesion and separation. By leveraging clustering, businesses can obtain valuable insights into their data and make data-driven decisions built on patterns and relationships discovered within the data.

3.4 Anomaly Detection

Anomaly detection, also known as outlier detection, is a data mining technique utilized in big data analytics to detect data points that are knowingly different from the rest of the data. The technique can help identify potential anomalies, errors, or fraud in the data. Anomaly detection algorithms employ various techniques to identify outliers, such as statistical methods, clustering, and machine learning techniques. Anomaly detection has several applications, like network intrusion detection, fraud detection, and predictive maintenance. The accuracy of anomaly detection algorithms can be evaluated using metrics such as precision, recall, and F1 score, and the algorithms can be further improved using techniques such as cross-validation and hyperparameter tuning. By employing anomaly detection, businesses can identify potential problems in their data and take corrective actions to minimize their impact.

3.5 Regression

Regression is a key statistical method used in big data analytics to model the connection between one or more independent variables and a dependent variable. Regression analysis' main objective is to predict the value of the dependent variable based on the values of the independent variables. There are numerous regression models, including logistic regression, polynomial regression, and linear regression, each of which is intended to address a particular use case. Regression is useful in various applications, such as predicting sales, optimizing prices, and assessing risks. The accuracy of regression models can be measured by evaluating metrics like root mean square error (RMSE), mean absolute error (MAE), and R-squared. By leveraging regression, businesses can make data-driven decisions, improve operational efficiency, and optimize their strategies to achieve their goals.

3.6 Text Mining

Text mining is a data mining technique used in big data analytics to extract meaningful information and insights from unstructured text data. It involves analyzing large volumes of text data, like customer reviews, emails, social media posts, and news articles, to identify patterns, trends, and relationships. Text mining algorithms use various methods, including natural language processing (NLP), sentiment analysis, and topic modeling, to extract relevant information from the text data. Text mining has various applications, such as market research, customer feedback analysis, and social media monitoring. The accuracy of text mining results can be evaluated using metrics such as precision, recall, and F1 score, and optimization techniques such as feature selection and model tuning can further enhance them. By using text mining, businesses can gain valuable insights into their products, customers, and markets and make data-driven decisions accordingly.

3.7 Neural Networks

Neural networks are a powerful data mining technique used in big data analytics to model complex relationships between inputs and outputs. They simulate the structure of the human brain with interconnected layers of nodes that can learn to identify patterns and make predictions based on input data. Neural networks have a wide range of applications, including image and speech recognition, as well as natural language processing. They are also useful for predictive modeling and forecasting. Metrics like accuracy, precision, recall, and F1 score are utilized to assess the performance of neural network models. While neural networks require significant computational resources and may take longer to train than other machine learning techniques, they can be highly accurate and effective for complex tasks. By leveraging the power of neural networks, businesses can make more informed decisions and gain valuable insights from their data.

3.8 Applications of Data Mining in Various Industries

Data mining shown in figure 4 is widely used across different industries for various purposes. The following examples demonstrate some of the applications of data mining:

Figure 4. Applications of data mining in various industries

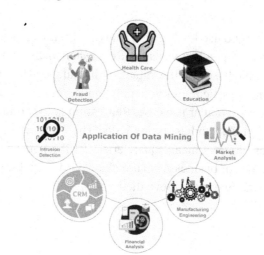

Healthcare: Healthcare providers can use data mining to analyze patient data, classify patterns and trends in disease diagnosis, treatment, and outcomes, and make more informed decisions on treatment plans and drug development (Hande, 2023).

Education: In the Education Industry, data mining plays a crucial role in educational analytics, predicting student performance, and facilitating personalized learning. It aids in the examination of student data, the identification of students at risk, the provision of personalized learning trajectories, and the assessment of the effectiveness of educational programs.

Market Analysis: Marketers can analyze customer data using data mining to create targeted marketing campaigns, identify patterns and preferences, and optimize advertising spend. Retailers can utilize data mining techniques to analyze customer purchase patterns, preferences, and behaviors, and make informed decisions on pricing, inventory management, product recommendations, and marketing strategies.

Manufacturing Engineering: In the manufacturing industry, data mining can be employed to optimize production processes, improve quality control, reduce waste and identify potential equipment failures for preventive maintenance scheduling.

CRM: Data mining techniques are employed within CRM systems to extract valuable insights and patterns from customer data, empowering businesses to improve their management of customer relationships. Through the analysis of customer interactions and behaviors, data mining enables businesses to uncover customer preferences, forecast purchasing trends, customize marketing approaches, and optimize customer service. This leads to the cultivation of stronger customer relationships, fostering business growth and success.

Intrusion Detection: Data mining is instrumental in intrusion detection as it detects and addresses unauthorized access and malicious activities within computer networks. By employing advanced analytical techniques on network data, data mining identifies patterns, anomalies, and suspicious behaviors that indicate possible intrusions. This proactive approach enables organizations to protect network security, prevent unauthorized breaches, and uphold the integrity of their systems and data.

Fraud detection: Utilizing advanced analytical techniques, data mining plays a vital role in detecting and preventing fraudulent activities. Through the analysis of extensive datasets, organizations can identify patterns, anomalies, and suspicious behaviors that may signify potential fraud. This proactive approach enables businesses and financial institutions to mitigate risks, safeguard assets, and uphold operational integrity, thereby preventing financial losses and protecting their reputation.

Finance Analysis: Financial institutions can analyze customer data using data mining techniques to detect fraud, predict credit risk, and optimize investment portfolios, among other things.

Transportation: Data mining can be employed by transportation companies to enhance route optimization, safety improvements, fuel consumption reduction, maintenance predictions, and scheduling optimization.

As data continues to grow in volume and complexity, the significance of data mining in decision-making processes across various industries will undoubtedly rise.

3.9 Strengths and Limitations of Data Mining Techniques

Data mining techniques possess numerous strengths, but also exhibit some limitations. Below are some of the key strengths and limitations of data mining techniques:

3.9.1 Strengths

Scalability: Data mining techniques can handle large datasets, allowing the analysis and extraction of useful information from massive volumes of data.

Automation: Data mining algorithms can automate the data analysis process, saving time and reducing errors that could occur with manual analysis.

Prediction: Data mining techniques can predict future trends and behaviors based on historical data, enabling pattern identification and informed decision-making.

Customization: Data mining techniques can be customized to meet specific industry needs, allowing the algorithms to be tailored to specific requirements.

Efficiency: Data mining techniques can quickly and accurately identify patterns and trends in large datasets, allowing for real-time data-driven decisions.

3.9.2 Limitations

Data quality: Data mining techniques rely heavily on the quality of the data analyzed. If the data is inaccurate or incomplete, the analysis results may be unreliable.

Overfitting: Data mining algorithms may suffer from overfitting, where the algorithms are too specific to the training data and cannot generalize well to new data.

Interpretation: Data mining algorithms may identify patterns or trends that are difficult for humans to interpret, making it challenging to understand the results and make informed decisions.

Ethics: Data mining techniques may raise ethical concerns, particularly with privacy and data ownership issues.

Technical expertise: Data mining techniques require a high level of technical expertise and may be difficult for non-experts to understand and implement effectively.

4. MACHINE LEARNING ALGORITHMS FOR BIG DATA ANALYSIS

Machine learning algorithms as shown in figure 5 are essential for analyzing big data due to their capability to handle large and complex datasets (Singh, 2017). Commonly used algorithms for big data analysis include Random Forest, Gradient Boosting, Deep Learning (utilizing neural networks like CNNs and RNNs), K-Means Clustering, Support Vector Machine and Principal Component Analysis. Random Forest and Gradient Boosting are effective for classification and regression, while Deep Learning excels in tasks like image recognition and natural language processing. SVM finds optimal hyperplanes for classification, K-Means Clustering identifies clusters based on similarity, and PCA reduces dimensionality while preserving important information. Choosing the right algorithm depends on the specific task, dataset characteristics, and desired analysis outcomes.

Figure 5. Machine learning algorithms for big data analysis

4.1 Decision Trees

Decision trees are a eminent supervised machine learning technique utilized in both classification and regression scenarios. Their simplicity and comprehensibility have made them extensively employed across diverse domains.

A decision tree is akin to a flowchart, where internal nodes signify features or attributes, branches represent decisions based on those features, and leaf nodes represent outcomes or class labels. The root node initiates the tree, while branches indicate possible feature values or ranges.

To construct a decision tree, the dataset is partitioned iteratively based on feature values, with the goal of maximizing information gain or minimizing impurity at each stage. The objective is to generate partitions or subsets that are as homogeneous as possible concerning the target variable.

For classification tasks, decision tree leaves correspond to class labels. For instance, in an email spam classification tree, leaves can be labeled as "spam" or "not spam." The decision tree employs features like keyword presence, sender information, or other attributes to make decisions at each node.

In regression tasks, decision trees estimate continuous values instead of discrete class labels. The predicted output is represented by the value assigned to each leaf node. For example, a decision tree could predict the price of a house based on features like bedroom count, location, and square footage.

Decision trees effectively handle categorical and numerical features, including missing values. They exhibit relatively fast training speed and scalability to large datasets. However, decision trees are prone to overfitting, wherein the model becomes overly tailored to the training data, leading to poor performance on unseen data. Concerns related to overfitting can be addressed through techniques such as pruning, constraining tree depth, or employing ensemble methods like random forests.

4.2 Random Forests

Random Forest is a hugely utilized and potent machine learning algorithm extensively employed in the analysis of large-scale data. It falls under the category of ensemble learning methods and combines numerous decision trees to make predictions.

Random Forest is highly effective when confronted with extensive and intricate datasets due to its capacity to handle high-dimensional data and noisy features. This algorithm is applicable to both classification and regression tasks.

The functioning of Random Forest entails the creation of numerous decision trees, with each tree being trained on a random subset of the data and features. During the prediction phase, the algorithm consolidates the predictions made by individual trees to arrive at the final prediction.

An inherent advantage of Random Forest lies in its ability to handle high-dimensional data without succumbing to overfitting. The algorithm automatically performs feature selection by identifying the most informative features for accurate prediction. Moreover, Random Forest possesses the capability to handle missing values and sustain high accuracy, even when confronted with a substantial number of input variables.

Parallelizability is a notable attribute of Random Forest, rendering it suitable for distributed computing frameworks and facilitating efficient processing of big data. It exhibits commendable scalability with large datasets and demonstrates efficient performance in parallel and distributed computing environments.

The extensive adoption of Random Forest spans various domains, including finance, healthcare, marketing, and image processing.

4.3 Neural Networks

Neural networks, vital in machine learning, play a key role in analyzing large datasets for big data applications, excelling in image and speech recognition, natural language processing, and recommendation systems. Comprising interconnected artificial neurons in layers, neural networks, particularly in Deep Learning, uncover intricate patterns in data through multi-layered networks.

Convolutional Neural Networks (CNNs) specialize in image recognition, automatically learning and detecting complex visual features, while Recurrent Neural Networks (RNNs) analyze sequential data, capturing dependencies across sequences.

Neural networks automatically learn and extract relevant features from data, reducing the need for manual engineering. Despite computational demands, advancements in hardware and parallel computing enable training deep neural networks on extensive datasets. Techniques like transfer learning and model optimization simplify the application of pre-trained models to new domains, reducing resource requirements.

Across computer vision, natural language processing, and recommendation systems, neural networks have achieved breakthroughs, establishing them as invaluable tools for big data analysis.

4.4 Support Vector Machines

Support Vector Machines (SVM) play a crucial role in big data analysis, particularly for classification and regression tasks. SVM determines an optimal hyperplane with maximum margin to separate data points of different classes, acting as a decisive boundary for precise predictions on new data. Known for its proficiency in handling complex, high-dimensional datasets, SVM effectively manages multiple input variables, making it well-suited for big data scenarios and competent even with limited training samples. Through the use of kernel functions, SVM transforms data into higher-dimensional spaces, capturing intricate patterns and ensuring high prediction accuracy. With robustness against outliers, SVM prioritizes points near the decision boundary, guaranteeing reliable predictions. Despite computational demands in dealing with large datasets, improvements in parallel computing enhance the efficiency of SVM. Its success in domains such as image classification and finance, coupled with its resilience to outliers and adaptability, establishes SVM as an indispensable tool in the realm of big data analysis.

4.5 Applications of Machine Learning in Various Industries

Machine learning has revolutionized numerous industries by transforming processes, decision-making, and insights. Below are examples illustrating the application of machine learning in different sectors:

Healthcare: Machine learning contributes to disease diagnosis, patient outcome prediction, and treatment identification. It facilitates personalized medicine, assists in analyzing medical images, and aids in drug discovery and development.

Finance: Machine learning algorithms are utilized for fraud detection, credit scoring, algorithmic trading, and risk management. They analyze extensive financial data to identify patterns, make predictions, and automate financial decision-making.

Retail and E-commerce: Machine learning is employed for personalized product recommendations, demand forecasting, inventory management, and customer segmentation. It enhances the customer experience, optimizes pricing strategies, and improves supply chain operations.

Manufacturing: Machine learning techniques improve quality control, predictive maintenance, and supply chain optimization. They enable real-time monitoring of production processes, detect anomalies, and enhance operational efficiency.

Transportation and Logistics: Machine learning assists in route optimization, fleet management, and predictive maintenance of vehicles. It optimizes logistics operations, reduces delivery times, and enhances overall transportation efficiency.

Marketing and Advertising: Machine learning is applied in targeted advertising, customer segmentation, and sentiment analysis. It aids businesses in understanding customer behavior, optimizing marketing campaigns, and delivering personalized experiences.

Energy and Utilities: Machine learning algorithms optimize energy consumption, predict equipment failures, and facilitate smart grid management. They enhance energy efficiency, reduce costs, and facilitate the integration of renewable energy.

Agriculture: Machine learning is used for crop yield prediction, disease detection, and precision farming. It enables optimized resource allocation, improves crop quality, and assists in implementing sustainable agricultural practices.

Education: Machine learning supports personalized learning, adaptive tutoring, and educational analytics. It tailors educational content to individual students, provides insights for curriculum development, and assists in analyzing student performance.

Government and Public Services: Machine learning aids in fraud detection, cybersecurity, predictive policing, and public health analysis. It enhances decision-making processes, improves public safety, and enables data-driven policy-making.

These examples showcase the diverse application of machine learning across industries. As technology progresses, the potential for machine learning applications continues to expand, driving innovation and transforming various sectors.

4.6 Strengths and Limitations of Machine Learning Algorithms

Machine learning algorithms possess a range of strengths and limitations that demand careful consideration when applying them across different contexts. Here, we outline some principal strengths and limitations of machine learning algorithms:

4.6.1 Strengths

Proficiency in handling complex and extensive datasets: Machine learning algorithms excel at processing and analyzing substantial amounts of data, including high-dimensional and unstructured data, which may pose challenges for traditional statistical techniques.

Pattern recognition and prediction: Machine learning algorithms can identify intricate patterns and relationships within data, enabling accurate predictions and informed decision-making.

Adaptability and flexibility: Machine learning algorithms can adapt and learn from new data, empowering them to improve over time and adjust to evolving environments or circumstances.

Automation and efficiency: Machine learning algorithms automate processes and tasks, diminishing human effort and time required for analysis. They prove highly efficient in handling repetitive and computationally demanding tasks.

Scalability: Machine learning algorithms can scale effectively with large datasets, enabling efficient analysis and processing of big data.

4.6.2 Limitations

Data quality and bias: Machine learning algorithms deeply depend on the quality and representativeness of the training data. Biased or incomplete data can lead to biased or inaccurate predictions.

Overfitting: The unique patterns and noise in the training set may be captured by machine learning algorithms too precisely, which leads to poor generalisation to new, unforeseen data.

Interpretability: Some complex machine learning algorithms, such as deep neural networks, lack interpretability. Understanding and explaining the underlying reasoning or decision-making process of the algorithm can prove challenging.

Computational resources and complexity: Certain machine learning algorithms, particularly deep learning models, necessitate substantial computational resources, including processing power and memory, for training and inference.

Need for labeled data: Supervised machine learning algorithms typically require labeled data for training, which can be costly and time-consuming to obtain, especially in certain domains or specialized tasks.

Ethical considerations: Machine learning algorithms can amplify biases present in the data or unintentionally discriminate against certain groups if not thoughtfully designed and monitored. Ensuring fairness and ethical considerations in algorithmic decision-making is of utmost importance.

To choose an appropriate machine learning approach and address potential challenges, it is vital to evaluate these strengths and limitations within the context of the specific problem, dataset, and analysis objectives.

5. VISUALIZATION TECHNIQUES FOR BIG DATA ANALYSIS

Visualization techniques shown in figure 6 are essential for analyzing and interpreting big data as they present complex information visually, facilitating understanding and insight extraction. Commonly used techniques include scatter plots and bubble charts for visualizing relationships and correlations, heat maps for displaying patterns and trends, line charts and area charts for tracking time-based data, histograms and bar charts for understanding data distribution, tree maps for hierarchical visualization, network graphs for depicting relationships, geospatial visualization for mapping data, parallel coordinates for visualizing multivariate data, word clouds and word trees for text analysis, and interactive dashboards for comprehensive data exploration (Zhou, 2019). These techniques enable analysts and decision-makers to comprehend complex patterns, outliers, and relationships, leading to informed decision-making and actionable outcomes.

5.1 Scatter Plots

Scatter plots are widely used in the visualization of big data analysis. They depict data points as individual dots on a two-dimensional plane, where each dot represents a specific data instance. Scatter plots are effective for visualizing the relationships and correlations between variables (Sughasiny, 2018).

Figure 6. Visualization techniques for big data analysis

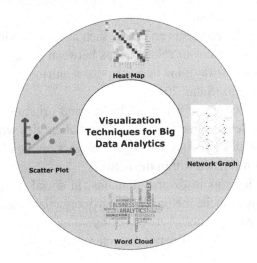

In a scatter plot, one variable is typically represented on the horizontal axis, while another variable is represented on the vertical axis. By plotting the data points, one can observe patterns, clusters, and trends. The position of each dot indicates the values of the two variables for that particular data instance.

To enhance scatter plots, additional information can be incorporated, such as the size or color of the dots, to represent a third variable. This variation is known as a bubble chart, where the size or color of the bubbles conveys an additional dimension of information.

Scatter plots are particularly valuable when working with large datasets because they can accommodate a high volume of data points. They assist in identifying relationships, outliers, and clusters within the data, enabling analysts to extract insights and make informed decisions.

By visually representing data in scatter plots, analysts can quickly grasp the distribution and trends, and evaluate the strength and nature of the relationship between variables. This facilitates the identification of patterns, comparisons, and detection of anomalies or unusual behavior within the dataset.

5.2 Heatmaps

Heatmaps are a widely used visualization method in big data analysis, employing color gradients to represent data values on a two-dimensional grid. They are particularly useful for visualizing patterns and trends in extensive datasets, such as geographical, time series, or multivariate data. Each cell in a heatmap corresponds to a specific combination of variables or categories, with color intensity indicating the associated magnitude. This visualization method is effective for highlighting patterns and relationships, whether in geographical analysis, time series analysis, or variable/category comparisons. Heatmaps can handle large datasets, making them suitable for big data analysis, but it's crucial to recognize their limitations, especially in terms of careful interpretation and consideration of color scale choices to avoid potential misinterpretations.

Network graphs

Network graphs, also referred to as network visualizations or network diagrams, are an invaluable visualization method employed in the analysis of big data. They depict the connections between entities as nodes (vertices) interconnected by edges. Network graphs are particularly effective when dealing with intricate networks or interconnected data.

In a network graph, each node represents an entity, such as an individual, organization, or concept, while the edges signify the connections or relationships between them. These connections can be directed (one-way) or undirected (two-way), and they can possess attributes or weights that offer additional information about the relationships (Sahu, 2013).

Network graphs aid in the discovery of patterns, clusters, and structures within the data. They enable the identification of central nodes, communities, or influential entities within the network. By analyzing the connectivity and properties of nodes and edges, insights can be obtained regarding the flow of information, collaboration, or influence within the network.

Network graphs find applications in diverse domains. In social network analysis, they visualize connections among individuals in social media platforms or organizational structures. In transportation and logistics, they illustrate the connections between different locations or transportation routes (Barse, 2023). They are also utilized in biological networks, internet networks, and numerous other interconnected datasets.

The visualization of network graphs can be enhanced by incorporating attributes such as node size, color, or edge thickness, which can represent additional variables or measures. By including such attributes, it becomes possible to gain insights into the characteristics or significance of nodes and edges within the network.

One of the challenges associated with network graphs lies in their complexity. When dealing with large datasets, the number of nodes and edges can become overwhelming, making it challenging to interpret and analyze the graph effectively. However, advanced techniques like community detection algorithms or interactive filtering can help address this challenge and enable focused exploration of specific areas of interest within the network (Çelik, O, 2019).

5.3 Word Clouds

Word clouds, also referred to as tag clouds, are a widely employed visualization method in the analysis of big data. They visually represent the frequency and importance of words in a text document or dataset. In a word cloud, words are presented in varying sizes, where larger fonts indicate higher frequency or importance.

Word clouds serve as a convenient tool for obtaining a rapid overview of the prominent terms or topics within extensive collections of text data. They can be generated from diverse sources like customer reviews, social media sentiment, or text mining outcomes.

Creating a word cloud involves several steps. Initially, the text data undergoes processing to eliminate common stop words such as "the," "and," or "is." Subsequently, the remaining words are analyzed based on their frequency or importance. The most frequent or important words are then exhibited in the word cloud, with their size being proportionate to their frequency or importance.

By visually portraying word frequencies, word clouds facilitate the identification of crucial themes, trends, or sentiments present in the text data. Analysts can quickly discern the most significant terms without necessitating an exhaustive textual analysis.

5.4 Importance of Visualization in Big Data Analysis

The significance of visualization in the analysis of big data cannot be emphasized enough. Here are some essential reasons highlighting the importance of visualization in handling extensive and intricate datasets:

Understanding the data: Visualization simplifies the comprehension of complex data by representing it visually. It allows analysts to easily grasp the underlying patterns, trends, and relationships, making the information more intuitive and accessible.

Detecting patterns: Visualizations enable the identification of patterns and outliers that may go unnoticed with other analytical methods. By visually exploring the data, analysts can quickly identify anomalies, correlations, and trends that provide valuable insights.

Generating insights: Visualization facilitates the generation of meaningful insights and discoveries from big data. By visually exploring the data, analysts can uncover hidden patterns, relationships, and dependencies that contribute to informed decision-making and actionable outcomes.

Effective communication: Visualizations are powerful tools for effectively communicating insights and findings to stakeholders and decision-makers. By presenting data visually, complex information can be conveyed in a compelling and easily understandable manner, enhancing understanding and engagement.

Exploratory analysis: Visualization supports exploratory analysis, enabling analysts to interactively explore and navigate through large datasets. Interactive features such as filtering, zooming, and drill-down capabilities allow analysts to delve into specific aspects of the data, revealing new perspectives and driving further analysis.

Decision-making support: Visualizations provide decision-makers with a clear and concise representation of the data, facilitating informed decision-making. By presenting data visually, decision-makers can quickly grasp complex information, evaluate options, identify trends, and assess potential risks and opportunities.

Data validation and quality assessment: Visualizations assist in assessing data quality and identifying potential errors or inconsistencies. By visually examining the data, analysts can detect outliers, missing values, or inconsistencies that may require further investigation or data cleansing.

5.5 Applications of Visualization in Various Industries

Visualization finds wide-ranging applications in numerous industries, empowering professionals across different fields to gain valuable insights, make well-informed decisions, and effectively communicate complex information. Here are some instances showcasing how visualization is utilized in various industries:

Healthcare: Visualization assists medical professionals in interpreting and analyzing medical scans like MRI or CT scans, aiding surgical planning, patient data monitoring, and identification of disease patterns for diagnosis and treatment.

Finance: Visualization plays a crucial role in finance for data analysis, risk assessment, and portfolio management. It helps visualize market trends, stock performance, and financial indicators, enabling investors to make informed decisions.

Marketing and Advertising: Visualization supports marketers in comprehending customer behavior, market segmentation, and campaign performance analysis. It helps visualize customer demographics, social media sentiment, website traffic, and the effectiveness of advertising campaigns.

Manufacturing and Supply Chain: Visualization optimizes manufacturing processes, supply chain management, and logistics. It aids in visualizing production data, inventory levels, delivery routes, and resource allocation, leading to enhanced efficiency and cost savings.

Energy and Utilities: Visualization is employed in monitoring and analyzing energy consumption, grid management, and renewable energy sources. It helps visualize power usage patterns, network infrastructure, and real-time energy production, facilitating resource planning and energy efficiency.

Transportation and Logistics: Visualization assists in route optimization, fleet management, and supply chain logistics. It aids in visualizing transportation networks, tracking shipments, planning delivery routes, and managing warehouse operations, thereby enhancing operational efficiency and customer satisfaction.

Environmental Science: Visualization aids scientists in studying and monitoring environmental data such as climate patterns, pollution levels, and ecosystem changes. It helps visualize geographic data, satellite imagery, and sensor data, enabling a better understanding of environmental issues and their mitigation.

Education: Visualization enhances learning by presenting complex concepts and data in a visual format. It helps students grasp abstract ideas, comprehend scientific phenomena, and analyze data sets, thereby promoting engagement and facilitating knowledge retention.

Government and Public Policy: Visualization assists policymakers in analyzing public data, demographic trends, and socioeconomic indicators. It aids in visualizing public health statistics, crime rates, transportation patterns, and urban planning, thereby facilitating evidence-based decision-making.

Sports Analytics: Visualization is employed in sports analytics to analyze game strategies, player performance and match statistics. It helps visualize player movements, team formations, and performance metrics, enabling coaches and analysts to make data-driven decisions.

6. FUTURE OF BIG DATA ANALYSIS

The upcoming of big data analysis is poised for significant advancements and holds tremendous potential. Here are some key trends and possibilities that may shape its trajectory:

Automation: As data volume and complexity continue to grow, automation will play a critical role in data analysis. Machine learning algorithms and artificial intelligence will automate tasks such as data preprocessing, analysis, and visualization, enabling faster and more accurate insights.

Real-time Analytics Integration: The prevalence of real-time analytics will increase, allowing organizations to process and analyze streaming data in real-time. This capability will facilitate quicker decision-making, proactive problem-solving, and immediate response to changing conditions.

Advanced Data Visualization Techniques: Data visualization will evolve with the emergence of new techniques and tools. Interactive and immersive visualizations, including virtual reality, augmented reality, and 3D visualizations, will provide more engaging and intuitive ways to explore and comprehend complex data.

Integration of Structured and Unstructured Data: The seamless integration of structured data and unstructured data analysis will permit organizations to extract insights from diverse data sources such as text, images, audio, and video. Technologies like natural language processing and image recognition will play a vital role in extracting insights from unstructured data.

Enhanced Privacy and Security Measures: Heightened concerns regarding data privacy and security will lead to the implementation of robust measures. Techniques such as differential privacy, secure multi-party computation, and blockchain technology will ensure data security while enabling secure data sharing and collaboration.

Edge Computing for Real-time Analysis: Edge computing, which facilitates data analysis at or near the data source, will gain prominence. This approach reduces latency associated with transmitting large volumes of data to central servers and enables real-time analysis and decision-making at the network edge.

Emphasis on Ethical and Responsible Data Analysis: Ethical and responsible data analysis practices will receive greater attention. Organizations will prioritize transparency, fairness, and accountability in their data analysis processes to minimize biases and discrimination.

Integration of Big Data with Internet of Things (IoT): The integration of big data analysis with IoT devices will enable organizations to leverage data generated by interconnected devices. This integration will lead to improved predictive analytics, better resource management, and enhanced decision-making in domains like healthcare, transportation, and smart cities.

Collaboration and Data Sharing: The future of big data analysis will involve increased collaboration and data sharing among organizations and industries. Data marketplaces and federated learning approaches will facilitate secure data sharing while preserving privacy, enabling organizations to leverage diverse datasets for comprehensive analysis.

Ethical AI and Responsible Data Governance: With the growing prevalence of AI algorithms in big data analysis, there will be a heightened focus on ethical AI and responsible data governance. Ensuring transparency, fairness, and accountability in AI algorithms will be crucial for building trust and addressing ethical concerns.

7. IMPLICATIONS FOR BUSINESSES AND INDUSTRIES

The implications of big data analysis for businesses and industries are significant and far-reaching. Here are some key implications that organizations can anticipate:

Enhanced Decision-making: Big data analysis offers organizations valuable insights and predictive analytics, elevating their decision-making processes. By leveraging extensive and diverse datasets, businesses can make evidence-based, data-driven decisions that lead to better outcomes and more informed choices.

Improved Customer Understanding: Big data analysis enables organizations to advance deeper insights into their customers. Through the analysis of customer behaviour, preferences, and feedback, businesses can personalize their offerings, tailor marketing campaigns, enhance customer service, and identify new growth opportunities.

Increased Operational Efficiency: By analyzing vast datasets, organizations can identify operational inefficiencies within their operations and supply chains. Big data analysis helps optimize processes, streamline workflows, reduce costs, and improve overall productivity, thereby boosting operational efficiency and enhancing competitiveness.

Enhanced Risk Management: Big data analysis empowers businesses to identify and mitigate risks more effectively. By analyzing historical and real-time data, organizations can detect patterns, anticipate potential risks, and develop proactive strategies for risk management and mitigation.

Improved Product Development: Big data analysis provides valuable insights into market trends, customer preferences, and emerging needs. Organizations can leverage this information to develop new products and services that align with customer demands, stay ahead of competitors, and foster innovation.

Optimized Marketing and Sales Strategies: Big data analysis helps businesses optimize their marketing and sales approaches. By analyzing customer data, market trends, and competitor insights, organizations can target their marketing efforts more effectively, improve customer engagement, optimize pricing strategies, and increase sales conversions.

Streamlined Supply Chain Management: Big data analysis plays a crucial role in optimizing supply chain operations. By analyzing data linked to demand patterns, inventory levels, supplier performance, and logistics, organizations can optimize inventory management, reduce costs, minimize disruptions, and improve overall supply chain efficiency.

Enhanced Fraud Detection and Security: Big data analysis aids in the identification and prevention of fraud and security threats. By analyzing large volumes of data in real-time, organizations can detect anomalies, identify patterns of fraudulent activity, and proactively take measures to safeguard their assets and customer data.

Personalized Customer Experiences: Big data analysis enables businesses to deliver personalized customer experiences. By leveraging customer data and preferences, organizations can tailor their products, services, and marketing efforts to individual customers, fostering loyalty and satisfaction.

Competitive Advantage: Organizations that effectively harness big data analysis gain a competitive edge in the marketplace. By leveraging data-driven insights, businesses can differentiate themselves, innovate rapidly, respond promptly to market changes, and outperform competitors.

REFERENCES

Bagga, S., & Sharma, A. (2018, August). Big data and its challenges: a review. In *2018 4th International Conference on Computing Sciences (ICCS)* (pp. 183-187). IEEE. 10.1109/ICCS.2018.00037

BarseS.BhagatD.DhawaleK.SolankeY.KurveD. (2023). *Cyber-Trolling Detection System.* SSRN 4340372.

Çelik, O., Hasanbaşoğlu, M., Aktaş, M. S., Kalıpsız, O., & Kanli, A. N. (2019, September). Implementation of data preprocessing techniques on distributed big data platforms. In *2019 4th International Conference on Computer Science and Engineering (UBMK)* (pp. 73-78). IEEE. 10.1109/UBMK.2019.8907230

Desai, V., & Dinesha, H. A. (2020, November). A hybrid approach to data pre-processing methods. In *2020 IEEE International Conference for Innovation in Technology (INOCON)* (pp. 1-4). IEEE. 10.1109/INOCON50539.2020.9298378

Dwivedi, S. K., & Rawat, B. (2015, October). A review paper on data preprocessing: a critical phase in web usage mining process. In *2015 International Conference on Green Computing and Internet of Things (ICGCIoT)* (pp. 506-510). IEEE. 10.1109/ICGCIoT.2015.7380517

Hande, T., Dhawas, P., Kakirwar, B., & Gupta, A. Yoga Postures Correction and Estimation using Open CV and VGG 19 Architecture.

Hariharakrishnan, J., Mohanavalli, S., & Kumar, K. S. (2017, January). Survey of pre-processing techniques for mining big data. In *2017 international conference on computer, communication and signal processing (ICCCSP)* (pp. 1-5). IEEE.

Perer, A., & Liu, S. (2019). Visualization in data science. *IEEE Computer Graphics and Applications, 39*(5), 18–19. doi:10.1109/MCG.2019.2925493 PMID:31442962

Sahu, M., Dhawale, K., Bhagat, D., Wankkhede, C., & Gajbhiye, D. (2023). Convex Hull Algorithm based Virtual Mouse. Gre*nze International Journal of Engineering & Technology (GIJET), 9*(2).

Singh, D., & Srivastava, V. M. (2017, January). Triple band regular decagon shaped metamaterial absorber for X-band applications. In *2017 International Conference on Computer Communication and Informatics (ICCCI)* (pp. 1-4). IEEE.

Sowmya, R., & Suneetha, K. R. (2017, January). Data mining with big data. In *2017 11th International Conference on Intelligent Systems and Control (ISCO)* (pp. 246-250). IEEE. 10.1109/ISCO.2017.7855990

Sughasiny, M., & Rajeshwari, J. (2018, August). Application of machine learning techniques, big data analytics in health care sector–a literature survey. In *2018 2nd International Conference on I-SMAC (IoT in Social, Mobile, Analytics and Cloud)(I-SMAC) I-SMAC (IoT in Social, Mobile, Analytics and Cloud) (I-SMAC),* (pp. 741-749). IEEE. 10.1109/I-SMAC.2018.8653654

Zhou, T., Li, B., Wu, C., Tan, Y., Mao, L., & Wu, W. (2019, November). Studies on big data mining techniques in wildfire prevention for power system. In *2019 IEEE 3rd Conference on Energy Internet and Energy System Integration (EI2)* (pp. 866-871). IEEE. 10.1109/EI247390.2019.9061901

KEY TERMS AND DEFINITIONS

Application Context: The passage briefly alludes to the application context of each technique. For instance, natural language processing is explicated as concentrating on the analysis of human language, while predictive analytics is mentioned to leverage statistical modeling techniques for predicting future outcomes.

Big Data Analysis Techniques: The passage furnishes a clear and succinct elucidation of big data analysis techniques, portraying them as methods and tools meticulously crafted to extract insights and knowledge from vast and intricate datasets.

Connection to Data Challenges: The text establishes a clear correlation between the challenges presented by the characteristics of big data (velocity, volume, and variety) and the imperative to employ sophisticated analysis techniques.

Emphasis on Deep Learning: The passage particularly underscores deep learning as a prevalent big data analysis technique. It clarifies that deep learning employs neural networks to model intricate data patterns.

Examples of Techniques: Concrete instances and functionalities of big data analysis techniques are provided. For example, data mining involves discerning patterns and relationships within datasets, whereas machine learning enables systems to learn from data without explicit programming.

Increased Complexity of Data: The text underscores the inadequacy of traditional data analysis methods in the face of escalating data velocity, volume, and variety. This underscores the imperative need for deploying advanced computational and statistical methods.

Utilization of Advanced Methods: Big data analysis techniques are characterized by the incorporation of advanced computational and statistical approaches. This implies that these techniques surpass conventional methods, addressing challenges posed by extensive and diverse datasets.

Chapter 8
Machine Learning and Deep Learning for Big Data Analysis

Tarun Pradhan
Manipal University Jaipur, India

Prathamesh Nimkar
Manipal University Jaipur, India

Kavita Jhajharia
iD https://orcid.org/0000-0002-6424-2127
Manipal University Jaipur, India

ABSTRACT

As data plays a role in machine learning and provides insights across various sectors, organizations are placing more emphasis on collecting, organizing, and managing information. However, traditional methods of analysing data struggle to keep up with the increasing complexity and volume of big data. To extract insights from datasets, advanced techniques like machine learning and deep learning have emerged. In the field of self-driving cars, analysing sensor data relies on methodologies developed from data analytics. These trends extend beyond cases; big data and deep learning are driving forces supported by enhanced processing capabilities and the expansion of networks. Managing the complexities involved in processing amounts of data requires scalable architectures that leverage distributed systems, parallel processing techniques and technologies such as GPUs. This development is particularly relevant for industries like banking, healthcare, and public safety, which have pressing demands, for transparency and interpretability in models.

1. INTRODUCTION

Big Data is a kind of data that is so vast and complex that it cannot be handled by standard systems or data-warehousing technology. Big data is unable to stored using a relational database management system or processed using standard SQL-style queries (Ishwarappa & Anuradha, 2015). Due to the develop-

DOI: 10.4018/979-8-3693-0413-6.ch008

ment of technology and services, massive amounts of structured, unstructured and semi-structured data have been generated from a variety of sources (Ishwarappa & Anuradha, 2015). Big data is originated from various sectors like agriculture, medical, IOT. In healthcare sector big data is produced by medical equipment, automated medical tools, such as sensor devices and high-throughput instruments, etc (Mohammed Alqahtani, 2023). By attaching IOT devices to fields, soil, and plants to collect data in real time directly from the ground, the agriculture industry creates big data.

Big Data can be identified using 7 Vs includes Velocity, Volume, Variety, Veracity, Variability, Visualization, and Value. Keep in mind that these Vs are provisional and could go up or down in the near future (Tyagi & G, 2019).

- " Volume" is a term used to refer to the quantity of Big Data. The IOT, medical devices, cloud computing traffic, and other variables all play a part in the rapid increase in data volume. Many big companies like Google, Apple etc. have a large amount of information or data in the form of logs (Ishwarappa & Anuradha, 2015).
- "Velocity" describes the rate with which data is gathered and the rate with which it is processed, stored, and evaluated by databases.
- "Variety" is a term that describes the range of data types. Different form of data can be gathered from numerous sources. Data might be structured, unstructured or semi-structured.
- "Variability" refers to the inconsistencies in the data that gets generated. This is mostly due to varied data sources, distinct data layouts, or errors in data filling.
- "Veracity" reflects on the accuracy as well as data quality. when coping with massive amount of data. It might not be entirely accurate or it might. Missing information may be present in the accumulating data. (Ishwarappa & Anuradha, 2015)
- "Visualisation" refers to the ability to convert data into pictorial representations that are easy to understand and analyse.
- "Value" is discussing the potential value of big data, which directly affects how organizations might use the information obtained.

Different sensor technologies used in various industries are producing a tremendous amount of data. But traditional data mining methods, however, were not powerful enough to manage huge data or uncover hidden patterns. As a result, Arthur Samuel invented the name "Machine Learning" (Weiss, 1992), and according to Samuel, " The discipline of machine learning equips computers with the ability to learn without being explicitly programmed" (Weiss, 1992). Classification and prediction are the core focuses of machine learning (ML) (Tyagi & G, 2019). Deep learning algorithms are very effective for learning from massive amounts of unsupervised data. Usually, they adopt a greedy layer-wise learning strategy to pick up data representations (Najafabadi et al., 2016). A Google-Brain Project member said, " The deep learning models might be thought of as a rocket engine, and the massive amounts of data we must feed these (exiting) algorithms as fuel (Tyagi & Rekha, 2020)." The Graphical Processing Unit (GPU) has emerged as a crucial component in the Deep Learning algorithm's execution. GPU is utilized to handle enormous amounts of data where parallel processing is used (Tyagi & Rekha, 2020). Deep learning has been used to improve the performance of classification models in some Big Data fields, like speech recognition and computer vision (Najafabadi et al., 2016). In the classification of biomedical images, Machine Learning and Deep Learning algorithms have achieved exceptional results. A wide range of procedures, including the structuring of databases of biomedical image to picture classifications before diagnostics, are aided by classification methods. Several studies have been carried out in the past to enhance the accuracy of biomedical image classification (Mohammed Alqahtani, 2023). Deep learning can be used for every stage of processing and analysing remote sensing data, from the classic tasks of object detection and image registration to the more modern and difficult ones of multitemporal analysis and high-level semantic segmentation (Zhang et al., 2022). Additionally, deep learning has been successfully used in commercial goods that benefit from the abundance of digital data. Projects linked to deep learning have been vigorously promoted by companies like Google, Meta and Apple which regularly collect and analyse enormous amounts of data (Xue-Wen Chen & Xiaotong Lin, 2014).

The objective of the book chapter is to give a clear and thorough summary of the fundamentals, challenges, and potential applications of these techniques in the context of big data. The purpose of this chapter is to familiarize readers with the fundamentals of these technologies and demonstrate how to use them efficiently to manage and analyse large datasets. It will examine big data-specific feature engineering, scalability, model selection, and data preprocessing. In addition, it will explore future directions, ethical issues, and useful case studies, giving readers a comprehensive grasp of how to use these methods for data-driven decision-making in the big data era.

2. FOUNDATIONS OF MACHINE LEARNING AND DEEP LEARNING

The field of artificial intelligence includes machine learning. Machine learning enables the computer to study a dataset and learn how to tackle related issues. A subset of machine learning known as "deep learning" aims to create an artificial neural network that automatically finds patterns from the features selected (Kaur et al., 2020). This network is motivated by the information processing in biological systems (Kaur et al., 2020). The machine learning algorithms make prediction for upcoming or unknown properties based on previously known properties from the training data (Tyagi & G, 2019). It is a highly multidisciplinary field that takes encouragement from several different fields of study, including artificial intelligence, information theory, optimization theory, cognitive science, statistics, optimal control, also many other domains in the mathematics, engineering, and sciences (Qiu et al., 2016). Numerous problems have been solved using machine learning, including those involving, autonomous control systems recognition systems, recommendation engines, and informatics and data mining (Qiu et al., 2016).

Typically, there are three subdomains of machine learning which includes Supervised Machine learning, Unsupervised Machine learning, and Reinforcement Machine learning.

Supervised Learning: In supervised learning, the data is trained using labelled data, and a function allocates or maps an input dataset to an output dataset based on examples of input-output pairs (Kaur et al., 2020). Learning by examples is another name for supervised learning (Alzubi et al., 2018). When specific objectives are identified to be achieved from a specific group of inputs, supervised learning is used, i.e., a task-driven technique (Sarker, 2021). The two most common supervised activities are classification, and regression. Classification separates the data, whereas regression fits the data. Like, text classification (sentiment analysis) is the process of determining the class label or mood of a piece of text, such as a product review or a tweet (Sarker, 2021). Support Vector Machine Decision Tree, and Naive Bayes are the most often used supervised learning algorithms (Kaur et al., 2020).

Unsupervised Learning: Unsupervised learning focuses on finding unknown patterns in data and using those patterns to deduce rules. This method is appropriate when the categories of data are ambiguous/uncertain. (Alzubi et al., 2018). This is frequently used to extract generative characteristics, find significant structures and trends, organize results, and conduct exploratory work (Sarker, 2021). Anomaly detection, clustering, dimensionality reduction, density estimation, finding association rules, feature learning, etc. are the most popular unsupervised learning tasks (Sarker, 2021). Principal Component Analysis and K-means clustering are the key algorithms used in this learning (Kaur et al., 2020).

Reinforcement Learning: Reinforcement learning is an special kind of machine learning algorithm, which allows software agents and computers to automatically determine the optimal conduct in a specific setting or circumstance to enhance its effectiveness (Sarker, 2021). Reward- based learning is the another name of reinforcement learning (Tyagi & Rekha, 2020). Through interactions with the external environment, reinforcement learning enables learning via feedback (Qiu et al., 2016). It is an effective technique for building artificial intelligence (AI) models that can boost automation or improve the operational effectiveness of complex systems including manufacturing, autonomous driving, robots, and supply chain logistics, however, it is not recommended to utilise it to solve straightforward or fundamental problems. (Sarker, 2021). Reinforcement Learning is essentially be divided into Model-based and Model free approaches. Model-based Learning includes taking actions and watching the outcomes, such as the subsequent state and the immediate reward, in order to infer the most optimal course of action from a model of the environment (Sarker, 2021). Some of the most prominent instances of model-based strategies are Alpha Zero and AlphaGo. On the other hand, a model-free approach does not employ the distribution of the reward function and transition probability associated with the Markov Decision Process (MDP). Deep Q Network, Q-learning, Monte Carlo Control, and other model-free algorithms are examples of model-free algorithms (Sarker, 2021).

"Deep learning" is a group of machine learning techniques that trains deep architectures with several levels of representation (Xue-Wen Chen & Xiaotong Lin, 2014). Deep learning techniques automatically extract complex representation from a large amount of unstructured input. These algorithms are mostly inspired by the study of artificial intelligence, which aims to mimic the human brain's capacity for observation, analysis, learning, and decision-making, particularly for issues that are exceedingly complex (Najafabadi et al., 2016). Deep Learning uses neurons or the idea of hidden layers in its operation to tackle complicated problems. Each neuron is a mathematical processing unit that works in concert with every other neuron to figure out how to relate the input features to the output (Georgevici & Terblanche, 2019). It produces findings far more quickly than machine learning techniques. However, a drawback of deep learning is that it does not reveal the method by which an output is produced, as opposed to machine learning, which reveals the process by which an output is formed by having all the inputs or processing steps.

Deep learning algorithms includes Neural Networks, and Deep Neural Networks.

Neural Network: Neural Networks (NNs) are computational processing systems that derive a significant portion of their functionality from biological nerve systems, like the human brain (O'Shea & Nash, 2015). The human brain, the most complex entity in the universe, serves as the model for neural networks. A substantial amount of interconnected computing nodes, often referred to as neurons, serve as the fundamental component of neural networks. These nodes work together in a dispersed manner to learn from the input and maximize the final output (O'Shea & Nash, 2015). Mathematicians Warren McCulloch and Walter Pitts designed a simple algorithm based system to simulate human brain activity in the early 1940s, opening the door for investigation into the use of neural networks in artificial intelligence (Thakur, 2021). A neural network is composed of three layers, first one is the input layer, second is the hidden layer, and last is the output layer (Zhang et al., 2022). Perceptron is the basic unit of Neural Networks. The perceptron, which first appeared in the 1960s, served as the foundation for the initial neural networks (Zhang et al., 2022). It serves as a paradigm for binary classification that draws inspiration from biology and seeks to formally codify how a biological neuron functions (Zhang et al., 2022). A neuron with one output and two inputs makes up the perception system (Thakur, 2021). Unfortunately, nonlinear classification cannot be done by a perceptron. Neural Networks offer effective answers to issues in a variety of fields, such as filtering, classification, pattern recognition, prediction, optimization, and function approximation (Thakur, 2021).

Deep Neural Network: A neural network that have three or more layers, which includes the inputs and outputs, is considered to be a deep neural network (Thakur, 2021). Most deep neural networks operate in a feed-forward manner, which means that data flows from input to output exclusively in this case (Thakur, 2021). As an alternative, you might train your model using backpropagation, which entails going backwards from input to output (Thakur, 2021). Backpropagation enables us to quantify and attribute the mistake related to each neuron, allowing us to appropriately adjust and fit the algorithm. A deep neural network, in comparison, features input and output layers as well as multiple hidden layers in place of a single hidden layer. The deep neural network (DNN) has a deep architecture that allows it to learn feature representations from labelled and unlabelled input (Xue-Wen Chen & Xiaotong Lin, 2014). Deep neural network architecture includes Recursive Network, Autoencoders, Deep Belief Network and Convolutional Neural Network. The kind of data utilized to train a DNN is an important consideration. If the data needed to train the DNN is labelled, the outcome is known, and supervised learning can take place (Georgevici & Terblanche, 2019). Unsupervised methods must be used if the output label is uncertain and to enhance the output of unsupervised learning, semi-supervised learning makes use of labelled data sets (Georgevici & Terblanche, 2019).

3. CHALLENGES AND OPPORTUNITIES IN BIG DATA ANALYTICS

As was previously mentioned, multiple industries or businesses generate enormous amounts of data, most of it is generated by machines. As a result, there will be an unprecedented rise in the difficulties associated with big data, including data processing, data mining, data querying, and data indexing (Bhattarai et al., 2019). High data quantities are a very difficult problem for machine learning as well as deep learning. Without a doubt, the amount of data that we are currently surrounded by is too large and it is frequently impractical to train a machine learning and deep learning algorithm using a central processor and storage (Qiu et al., 2016; Xue-Wen Chen & Xiaotong Lin, 2014). Therefore, the preferable alternative is distributed frameworks with parallelized machines (Qiu et al., 2016; Xue-Wen Chen & Xiaotong Lin, 2014). Some deep learning techniques can become quite expensive to compute when working with high-dimensional data, such as photographs. This is presumably due to the learning process being slow on a regular basis and having a deep tiered hierarchy of learning data interpretations and abstractions from a lower-level layer to a higher-level one (Najafabadi et al., 2016).

Recently, noteworthy improvements have been made to reduce the difficulties brought on by huge volumes of data. Model parallelism or data parallelism strategies, or even both, have been produced (Xue-Wen Chen & Xiaotong Lin, 2014). Powerful programming framework MapReduce allows automatic parallelization and distribution of processing applications on huge clusters of commodity appliances (Qiu et al., 2016; Xue-Wen Chen & Xiaotong Lin, 2014). The use of cloud computing to facilitate learning is another important development for data systems to manage the volume challenge of big data (Qiu et al., 2016).

Big data is problematic due to its huge diversity of data, which is the second factor. Various sources can be used to collect different types of data. Rapidly expanding collections of audio and video streams, images, unstructured text, and graphics and animations, all with unique properties, are among the multimedia data arriving from the mobile and web devices (Xue-Wen Chen & Xiaotong Lin, 2014). Only specific types of input, such text, numbers, or images, may be used with the majority of classical ML techniques (Zhou et al., 2017). In many circumstances, the types and formats of the data that could be used for a particular ML objective may vary. It is sometimes referred to as a "Big Dimensionality" challenge and will cause an explosion of features to be learnt (Zhou et al., 2017). Data integration is a crucial strategy for handling large variety which aims to aggregate data from several sources and give the user a consistent view of all these data (Qiu et al., 2016; Xue-Wen Chen & Xiaotong Lin, 2014). High velocity presented additional challenges for Big Data learning since data are being generated at an incredibly fast rate and must be handled quickly. Online learning strategies are one way to learn from such high velocity data (Qiu et al., 2016; Xue-Wen Chen & Xiaotong Lin, 2014). Instead of learning in an offline or batch mode, which requires gathering all of the training data, Online learning is an established technique for learning that uses the one instance at a time approach (Qiu et al., 2016; Xue-Wen Chen & Xiaotong Lin, 2014).

3.1 Opportunities in Big Data Analytics

In order to expand their potential, organizations have engaged on data analytics and interpretation. Big data analytics provides ample of opportunities in various sectors (Shukla et al., 2015) mentioned in figure 1.

Figure 1. Big data opportunities

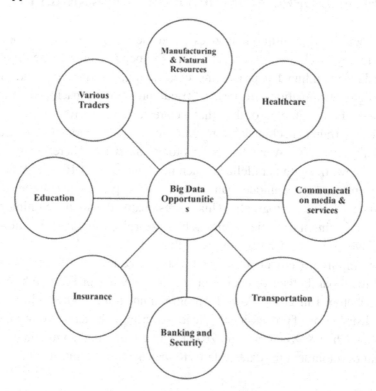

Healthcare is one notable industry where big data analytics has demonstrated its value. Healthcare practitioners may see patterns, anticipate illness outbreaks, and create treatment regimens specifically for individual patients by analysing massive datasets of patient records, clinical trials and medical histories (Et Al., 2023). Big data analytics are becoming essential in the retail industry. Retailers personalize marketing campaigns, improve inventory control, and estimate demand with customer data (Et Al., 2023). In order to make planning and operational choices, all stakeholders, including grid operators, electric utilities, customers, etc., can benefit from the cross-fertilization of diverse data sources. Big data from various sources is used in smart grids to carry important information (Bhattarai et al., 2019). Unprecedented amounts of educational data are being gathered as a result of the use of e-learning and the popularity of social networks on large scale. Big Data analytics makes it possible to effectively mine and analyse educational data, use technologies from statistics, computer science, and machine learning to extract relevant information from amassed educational data, gain insightful knowledge of learning, and identify ways to enhance student performance and teacher effectiveness, which has various advantages for the education sector (Cen et al., 2015). Another industry where big data analytics has had a significant impact is manufacturing. Manufacturers can predict equipment breakdowns, cut downtime, and enhance product quality by evaluating data from sensors integrated into machinery and manufacturing lines. Predictive maintenance, a proactive approach to maintenance, has the ability to prevent expensive production interruptions and save millions of dollars in maintenance expenditures (Et Al., 2023). Moreover, Big data analytics is also used by government organizations for a variety of objectives, including strengthening public safety, optimizing resource allocation, and urban planning. For instance, in order to minimize traffic congestion and enhance traffic flow, city planners can benefit from the analysis of traffic data. Likewise, the analysis of crime data can assist law enforcement organizations allocate their resources more effectively in order to deter and address criminal activity.

4. PREPROCESSING AND FEATURE ENGINEERING FOR BIG DATA

The enormous volume of data gathered may reveal insightful trends and patterns. As a result, it needs to be processed and maintained. Big Data preparation is a difficult task since the size of the data streams makes it difficult to use the previous methods directly. If we want to learn from large-scale datasets, standard algorithms for big data preprocessing and analytics must also be modified (García et al., 2016). It is not a simple task and poses a significant difficulty for researchers. More advanced methods are needed to analyse larger amounts of data. Data preprocessing makes it possible to process data that would otherwise be impractical by adjusting the data to the demands of each data mining technique (García et al., 2016). Despite being a powerful tool that can assist the user in handling and analysing complicated data, data preparation can be quite time-consuming. It includes a variety of topics such as data preparation and data reduction methods (García et al., 2016). Data preprocessing is not just used for conventional data mining activities, such as regression or classification, but is used by researchers working in cutting-edge data mining domains as a tool to enhance their models (García et al., 2016).

Most of data mining techniques rely on an allegedly noise-free or complete data collection. However, real-world data is rarely accurate or full. It is common practice in data preprocessing to use strategies to either eliminate noisy data or impute missing data (García et al., 2016). It is challenging to treat missing values when missing data are managed improperly, bad information may be gathered and false conclusions may be drawn. The knowledge extraction method has reportedly reduced efficiency as a result of missing values. There are numerous methods available to *handle the missing value* (García et al., 2016). Typically, the initial step is to get rid of all occurrences that might have a missing value. However, this strategy hardly works because removing data may create bias in the learning and cause critical information to be missed (García et al., 2016). *Data imputation* is another crucial technique in statistics and data analysis. This includes estimating or filling in missing data points with suitable values to ensure the completeness of the dataset (García et al., 2016). Using MLE, one can determine which distribution's parameters best suit the observed data and then use those parameters to impute missing values. Machine learning techniques are increasingly in demand today since they may be used without any previous information because the actual probability model for a particular data collection is typically not known (García et al., 2016).

Dealing with the issue of *noisy data* is essential since the quality of the outcomes produced by a data mining technique depends on the quality of the data used. The input features, the output values, or both can be impacted by noise (García et al., 2016). Two basic strategies are frequently employed to deal with noise in data mining. One is to eliminate the noise using *data polishing* techniques, especially if it interferes with an instance's labelling (García et al., 2016). The other is to utilize *noise filters*, which can be used to find and eliminate noisy instances in training data without modifying the data mining technique (García et al., 2016).

The curse of *dimensionality* problem affects data mining techniques when data sets have a large number of predictor variables or occurrences (García et al., 2016). Many data mining algorithms will struggle to function as a result of this critical issue as the cost of computation increases. The most important *dimensionality reduction algorithms*, classified into space transformation and Feature Selection based approaches (García et al., 2016).

Feature Selection (FS) is the method of locating and removing as much redundant and irrelevant data as feasible (García et al., 2016). The objective is to extract a subset of the original problem's attributes that still adequately describes it. It is also recognized that using FS reduces the chance of over-fitting in ensuing algorithms (García et al., 2016). The learning process will be quicker and use less memory as a result of FS's reduction of the search space dictated by the features. The use of Feature Selection during gathering of data can save the costs associated with labour, sampling, sensing, and personnel (García et al., 2016).

Space transformation approaches combine the original features to create a completely new collection of features rather than picking the most promising ones. Different criteria can be used to create this combo (García et al., 2016). The first methods used linear techniques, such as factor analysis. Recent methods aim to take advantage of nonlinear relations between the variables. LLE, ISOMAP, and derivatives are a few of the most significant space transformation techniques in terms of both applicability and utility (García et al., 2016). They concentrate on reducing the number of projections from the initial set of variables while occasionally taking into account the geometrical characteristics of patches or clusters of instances on the underlying manifolds (García et al., 2016).

5. MACHINE LEARNING TECHNIQUES FOR BIG DATA

Regression problems help to extract information from enormous volumes of data in order to make a prediction effect, which is why more people are paying attention to regression problems as machine learning technology develops quickly. Data prediction is currently a common practice among people.

The technology is currently widely used in many different fields, including weather forecasting, disease diagnosis, and economic forecasting. As a result, one of the most active areas of research in the field of machine learning in recent years has been the study of machine learning algorithms in regression problems. On the other hand, classification is a supervised machine learning technique in which the model aims to anticipate the proper label of some input data, determining whether an email is spam or ham (not-spam).

1. Linear Regression: The linear regression algorithm, which belongs to the family of regression algorithms, looks for dependencies and correlations between variables (Nasteski, 2017). Using a linear function, it demonstrates the link between a dependent variable (y) and one or more independent or explanatory variables (X) (Nasteski, 2017). A linear regression line has an equation of the form as shown in Eq. 1:

$$y = mx + c \tag{1}$$

where x = independent variable, y = dependent variable and the m = slope of the line.

The multiple regression model that uses a linear combination of input variables has the following structure as represented in Eq. 2 (Nasteski, 2017):

$$y = m_0 + m_1 x_1 + m_2 x_2 + \ldots + c \tag{2}$$

2. Logistic Regression: By fitting data to a logistic function, this particular sort of regression can determine the likelihood that an event will occur. Logistic regression uses a variety of predictor variables, which may be categorical or numerical, just like other regression analysis approaches (Nasteski, 2017). The logistic regression hypothesis is given as in Eq. 3 (Nasteski, 2017):

$$h_\theta = g\left(\theta^T x\right) \tag{3}$$

Where 'g' is a sigmoid function {range: [0, 1]} defined as in Eq. 4 (Nasteski, 2017):

$$g(z) = \frac{1}{1 + e^{-z}} \tag{4}$$

Values in the [0, 1] range are produced by the sigmoid function's unique properties.

Cost function is a method for evaluating how effectively a machine learning model operates given a collection of data. The error between the predicted and expected values is simply calculated and presented by the Cost Function as a single real number.

Figure 2. A typical decision tree

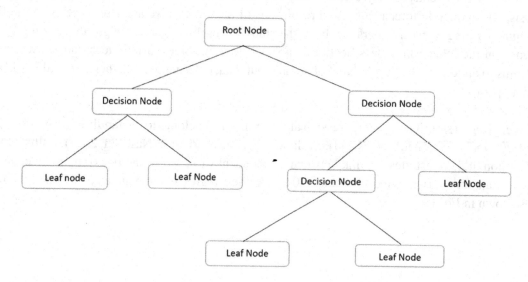

3. <u>Decision Trees</u>: Decision tree can be used by both regression and classification. Sorting instances using the values of their features allows decision trees to categorize them. Every node represents a feature in an instance that needs to be classified in a decision tree, and each branch provides a potential value for the node (Babcock University et al., 2017). In data mining and machine learning, a decision tree is used as a prediction model that connects observations about an object to estimates the expected value of the item. The following fields include those where the Decision Tree Classifier can be applied: Customer Relationship Management, Energy Consumption, Error Diagnosis, Health Management, Fraud Declaration Detection, etc (Department of Electrical Engineering, IIT Roorkee, Roorkee, India. et al., 2022), represented in Figure. 2.

4. <u>Naive Bayes</u>: The Naive Bayes classifier is made up of many algorithms which can be summarised as a widely utilized and simple to construct classification algorithm. It is typically used for huge dataset types (Department of Electrical Engineering, IIT Roorkee, Roorkee, India. et al., 2022). It is a classification method that uses the Bayes Theorem and the independent predictors presumption (Mahesh, 2019). Evey feature is independent of every other feature in the classifier, according to the premise this particular classification method follows to (Department of Electrical Engineering, IIT Roorkee, Roorkee, India. et al., 2022). In contrast to the numerical data, it works well with textual and categorical data. Its foundation is probability theory, and it determines probabilities using a mathematical method Bayes theorem, shown in Eq. 5 which states (Department of Electrical Engineering, IIT Roorkee, Roorkee, India. et al., 2022):

$$P(class \mid Features) = \frac{P(Features \mid class \times P\left(class\right)}{P\left(Features\right)} \tag{5}$$

5. Support Vector Machine (SVM): One of the most popular learning algorithms in machine learning is the support vector machine. SVM can be used for regression and classification (Department of Electrical Engineering, IIT Roorkee, Roorkee, India. et al., 2022). SVM is mostly used for dealing with classification-related problems. SVM is typically used to handle complex and small datasets. In contrast to other machine learning algorithms, SVM uses a unique methodology (Department of Electrical Engineering, IIT Roorkee, Roorkee, India. et al., 2022). The dataset's classes are divided up by SVM to an n-dimensional space called a hyperplane, which also helps identify any data points that are already present. Whether or not to create a hyperplane depends on the magnitude of the input features. If there are two or less input features, the hyperplane will be viewed as a single line, and if there are more than two characteristics, then it will be viewed as a two-dimensional plane (Department of Electrical Engineering, IIT Roorkee, Roorkee, India. et al., 2022). The current emphasis is on optimized hyperplane search that can effectively separate classes. Margin gap can be used to determine this. Support vectors are the data points that are most closely spaced from the hyperplanes. The likelihood of selecting an optimum hyperplane increases with the size of the margin gap between the support vectors (Department of Electrical Engineering, IIT Roorkee, Roorkee, India. et al., 2022). There are two types of SVM, A linear classifier is one that classify the data into only two classes using a straight-line hyperplane and a nonlinear SVM classifier, which is used when the data cannot be classified into two categories (Department of Electrical Engineering, IIT Roorkee, Roorkee, India. et al., 2022).

6. Random Forest: The most popular and often applied machine learning algorithm is the random forest classifier. It frequently used in various computer vision and computer applications (Department of Electrical Engineering, IIT Roorkee, Roorkee, India. et al., 2022). The Random Forest classifier is built on an ensemble technique known as Bagging or Bootstrap aggregation. In the ensemble method, 'n' samples are chosen at random from the dataset; these samples are referred to as bootstrap samples. To create 'n' decision trees, these samples are utilized (Department of Electrical Engineering, IIT Roorkee, Roorkee, India. et al., 2022). The results or forecasts from each decision tree are then integrated to get the final outcome. Random forest is utilized in a number of applications, including the detection of credit card fraud, the prediction of diabetes and breast cancer, price optimization in e-commerce, stock market analysis, etc (Department of Electrical Engineering, IIT Roorkee, Roorkee, India. et al., 2022).

7. K-Means Clustering: K-means, a most straightforward unsupervised learning methods for dealing with the common clustering problem (Mahesh, 2019). The technique uses a suitable number of clusters to categorize a given data set simply and clearly. To define k centres, one for each cluster, is the main concept. Because different places produce different results, these centres need to be strategically located, thereby would be wise to place them as much apart as possible from one another (Mahesh, 2019).

8. Principle Component Analysis: It is used as a dimensionality reduction technique. It is a statistical method that converts a set of observations of variables with potential correlation to a set of principal component values, corresponding to values of variables with linear uncorrelation. The computations are sped up and made easier by reducing the dimension of the data. It is used to clarify the variance-covariance arrangement of a collection of variables using linear combinations (Mahesh, 2019).

9. K-Nearest Neighbour Classifier: The K-Nearest Neighbour classifier, sometimes known as KNN. It is a supervised machine learning method renowned for its ease of use, effectiveness and adapt-

ability (Department of Electrical Engineering, IIT Roorkee, Roorkee, India. et al., 2022). This classifier, usually referred to as a lazy algorithm, delivers results with a very high degree of accuracy. Since KNN functions as a non-parametric classifier, it makes no assumptions regarding the data set (Department of Electrical Engineering, IIT Roorkee, Roorkee, India. et al., 2022). The KNN learns during the experimental phase; it does not learn anything while storing data points in its learning phase. The K nearest neighbours, or feature space data points closest to the proposed new data point, are taken into consideration while using the method (Department of Electrical Engineering, IIT Roorkee, Roorkee, India. et al., 2022). This algorithm's goal is to process samples whose classes are ambiguous in order to determine the classes they are intended for. The following are some applications for KNN classifier: face recognition, weather and climate forecasting, audio recognition, assistance with agriculture by calculating soil and water levels, handwriting detection, stock market, etc (Department of Electrical Engineering, IIT Roorkee, Roorkee, India. et al., 2022).

Using ensemble learning, a machine learning technique, predictions from several models are combined to boost prediction accuracy (Mahajan et al., 2023). Reducing prediction generalization error with the use of ensemble models. In comparison to predictions provided by a single classifier, ensemble techniques mix several machine learning algorithms (Mahajan et al., 2023). The generalization error is to be minimized by the usage of ensemble models. When the base models varied and independent, this method lowers model prediction error. The four main classes of ensemble learning algorithms are boosting, bagging, stacking, and voting (Mahajan et al., 2023).

1. Bagging: Combining predictions from numerous decision trees that have been fitted to various samples of the same dataset is known as bagging (Mahajan et al., 2023). In order to lower the variance and overfitting of the classifier, bagging, often referred to as bootstrapping, resamples data from the training set with the same cardinality as the starting set (Mahajan et al., 2023). Compared to a single model, the final model ought to be less overfitted. A high variance model implies that the outcome depends on the provided practice data. Therefore, the model may still perform poorly even with extra training data and its variance might not even decrease (Mahajan et al., 2023). The entire structure of bagging is shown in figure. 3.

2. Boosting: Weighted averages are used by boosting algorithms to convert weak learners into strong learners. The initial dataset is divided into a number of subgroups during boosting (Mahajan et al., 2023). The classifier is trained using the subset, producing a series of models with mediocre performance. The items that the previous model misclassified are used to create new subsets (Mahajan et al., 2023). In order to integrate the weak models, the ensemble technique uses a cost function, which helps it perform better. Boosting is a technique that can be used to resolve issues with regression and identification, like bagging, shown in figure 4. (Mahajan et al., 2023).

3. Stacking: Stacking is an assembly technique in which a MetaLearner classifier is stacked on top of one or more base-level classifiers. In stacking, the original data is fed into a variety of unique models (Mahajan et al., 2023). The weights of each model, along with their input and output, are then estimated using the metaclassifier. Models that perform the best are chosen, while the others are disregarded (Mahajan et al., 2023). By utilising a metaclassifier, stacking combines numerous basic classifiers that were learned on a single dataset using various learning techniques. Because all data are blended together to provide a forecast or categorization, ensemble stacking is also known as mixing. The most sophisticated methods are multilinear response and probability distribution stacking (Mahajan et al., 2023), stacking approach represented in figure 5.

Figure 3. Followed steps in bagging technique

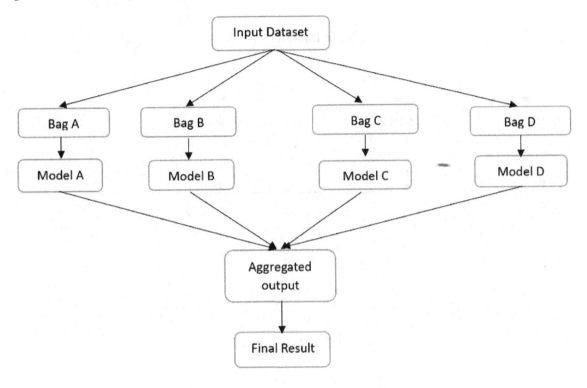

Figure 4. Boosting technique framework

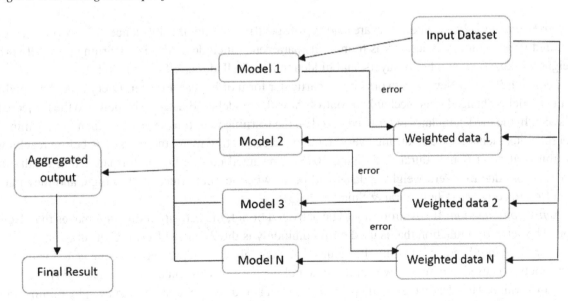

Figure 5. Stacking approach framework

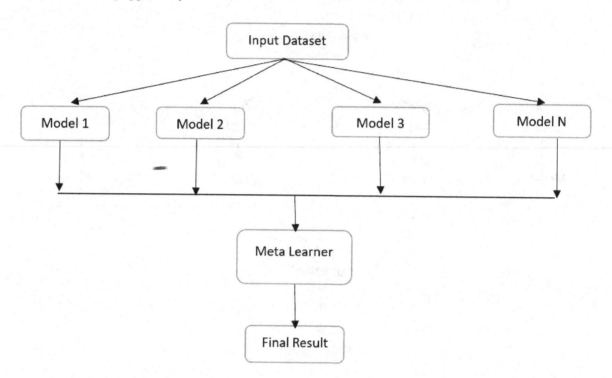

6. DEEP LEARNING MODELS FOR BIG DATA

6.1 Basic Concepts Involved in Deep Learning

Hyper-Parameter: Hyper-parameters are made up of specific variables that influence the network's structure and regulate how the network is trained. Its parameters include batch size, learning rate, network weight initialization, number of layers, and hidden units (Chelladurai & Sujatha, 2023).

Learning Rate: In Neural Networks it is a particular form of hyperparameter. Every time the weight of the model is changed, this mechanism controls how the model is adjusted in response to the projected mistake. In the model, updates are trained based on the learning rate. If it is very less, then merely minor weight adjustments are made during every iteration, necessitating many modifications before reaching the minimal point (Chelladurai & Sujatha, 2023). Unwanted conflicting performance that results in function loss due to severe weight updates will occur when learning rates are too high, and they may even flop to converge (Chelladurai & Sujatha, 2023).

Activation Function: If a neuron should be activated or not, the activation function makes that decision. The activation function that is used most commonly is the Rectified Linear Unit function.

Cost Function: When comparing the values that a neural network predicts with the actual values, a cost function is used to assess how useful the neural network is. Cost function's primary purpose is to maximize value. The ideal weights and parameters for a neural network can be achieved by minimising its cost function, which in turn maximizes the model's performance (Chelladurai & Sujatha, 2023).

Backpropagation: Using a backpropagation iterative technique, neural networks analyse vast volumes of data to investigate the selected function. This has a close connection to the cost function. The backpropagation uses a technique known as chain rule to efficiently train the neural network. After every forward pass, backpropagation does a reverse pass over the network, changing the neural network's weights and biases in the process.

6.2 Artificial Neural Network (ANN)

A neural network is a group of algorithms that replicates how the brain of a human works in order to discover the undetected links in an instance of data. Recently, there has been a tremendous increase in interest in how the brain functions across the globe. According to Haykin, an ANN is a machine created to work similarly to how the human brain does a certain task of interest (Abiodun et al., 2018). An artificial neural network act similarly. Without the assistance of a programmer, artificial neural networks learn to carry out tasks by analysing samples and drawing conclusions about rules (Thakur, 2021). ANNs have found extensive use in different sectors, such as three-dimensional object recognition, speech recognition, texture analysis, the diagnosis of hepatitis, recovering data from malfunctioning software in telecommunications, deciphering multilingual messages, undersea mine detection, and recognition of handwritten words, facial recognition (Abiodun et al., 2018).

An artificial neural network composed of a several artificial neurons, organised in a hierarchy of layers. Three layers make up a neural network: the input layer, the hidden layer, and the output layer (Zhang et al., 2022). The input layer aids in obtaining the data/values. The hidden layer that may consists of one or more than one layer is present between the input layer and the output layer (Kukreja et al., 2016). The last and final layer of artificial neural network is the output layer which produces the output. Typically, single neuron is present in the output layer and the result is between 0 and 1 including 0 and 1. However, there may also be a number of outputs (Kukreja et al., 2016). The collection of values known as inputs are those for which an output value must be predicted. They can be thought of as properties or features in a dataset. Each input is associated with the values called weights. weights serve to convey the importance of a particular input or trait in predicting an outcome. Weights may be zero, positive, or negative (Kukreja et al., 2016). A weight with negative value indicates the blocked or decreased signal. There is no link between the two neurons if there is zero weight (Kukreja et al., 2016). Weights are modified accordingly to obtain the required results. To move the activation function left or right bias is employed. When given the appropriate input vector, a single layer neural network known as a perceptron trained its biases and weights to output the correct target vector, single layer neuron shown in figure 6.

The weights and inputs are bound together and their sum is computed by the summation function, computed as Eq. 6. X1...Xm are the inputs to the neuron. W0...Wn are the weights. 'b' is the bias(Kukreja et al., 2016).

$$Sum = \sum_{i=1}^{n} Wi * Xi + b \tag{6}$$

To restore the neuron's output to normal, the "activation function" is used. The activation functions are the mathematical formulas that determine the neural network's output (Thakur, 2021). The primary objective of the activation function is to increase the nonlinearity to the neuron's output (Chelladurai &

Figure 6. A single layer neural network

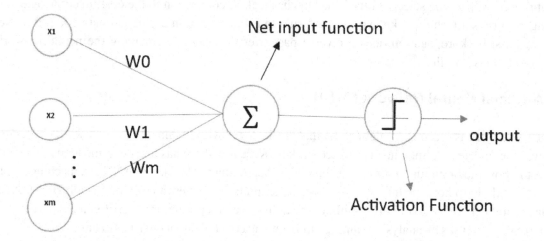

Sujatha, 2023). A 0 mean and a 1 standard deviation are applied to the data during conversion (Thakur, 2021). This is referred to as standardization. Every neuron has a different activation mechanism (Thakur, 2021). The sigmoid activation function is most frequently utilized, which is provided by Eq. 7. (Kukreja et al., 2016).

$$F(x) = \frac{1}{1 + e^{-sum}} \tag{7}$$

linear function, hyperbolic tangent function or tanh, Step function, and ramp function are some more functions that are used (Kukreja et al., 2016). The most popular technique for training neural networks is the back propagation algorithm (Abiodun et al., 2018). Here, the layers impacted by the difference between the desired and actual output, and the weights are changed (Kukreja et al., 2016). The supervised learning approach and feed-forward architecture is uses by Backpropagation Neural Network. For prediction and classification, backpropagation is considered as the most prevalent neural network method (Kukreja et al., 2016).

6.3 Convolutional Neural Network (CNNs)

A multilayer perceptron variation serves as the foundation for a convolutional neural network (CNN) (Thakur, 2021). CNNs are most frequently used to assess visual images and are intended to minimize pre-processing. It is a type of feed-forward neural network (Thakur, 2021).The grid structure with multiple dimensions of the input image is something that CNNs are made to take use of (Zhang et al., 2022). The primary use of CNNs is the identification of patterns in images (O'Shea & Nash, 2015), whereas traditional ANN models unable to handle the complexity of the computation needed to compute image data, is considered to be one of their biggest disadvantage (O'Shea & Nash, 2015).

Convolution, pooling, and fully connected layers are the three primary types of neural layers that make up standard CNNs (Zhang et al., 2022). The input of a CNN is transformed into a more abstract representation by a convolutional layer, which is a crucial component of the algorithm (Zhang et al., 2022). As it moves through the input image using convolutional kernels, it conducts a convolution process between every input section and the kernel to create feature maps (Zhang et al., 2022). To create the whole output volume from the convolutional layer, there will be layering along the depth dimension for each kernel's activation maps (O'Shea & Nash, 2015). By optimizing model's output, convolutional layers can also considerably decrease the complexity of the model. Three hyperparameters that are tuned for these are the stride, depth, and zero-padding(O'Shea & Nash, 2015). One can manually alter the depth of the output volume produced by the convolutional layers by altering the number of neurons in every layer to the same region of the input (O'Shea & Nash, 2015). How many units/pixels by which the filter is moved over the input image is known as the "stride." (O'Shea & Nash, 2015). Zero-padding, which is the straightforward process of padding the boundary of the input image, helps to regain the size of the tensor (O'Shea & Nash, 2015). Pooling layers seek to reduce the dimensionality of the feature map while maintaining depth, hence lowering the computational complexity of the model and parameter count. The most well-liked type of pooling is called max pooling, which selects the highest value across all pooling regions (O'Shea & Nash, 2015; Thakur, 2021). Global and average pooling are other forms of pooling. Between the penultimate layer and the output layer, a fully connected layer is frequently added to further describe the nonlinear interactions of the input characteristics or a fully connected layer is the layer which is present after the pooling layer (Zhang et al., 2022). Fully connected layer contains neurons that have direct associations to the neurons in the two adjacent layers (O'Shea & Nash, 2015). Fully connected layers then convert the 2D feature maps into a 1D feature vector. This 1D feature vector can either be used as a feature vector for additional processing or it can be fed into a set of fully connected layers to generate output (Zhang et al., 2022).

In addition to these three fundamental layers, other blocks were created to enhance the efficiency of the neural networks. For example, a residual block was created to address the deep network underfitting issue, a bottleneck block was created to lighten the load, the internal covariate shift reduced by a normalization layer, and the connection weight was dynamically changed by an attention block (Zhang et al., 2022). Convolutional neural networks excel at image and video recognition, natural language processing, the identification of paraphrases, semantic parsing, and recommender systems. Additionally, they are utilized in signal processing and image classification (Thakur, 2021).

6.4 Recurrent Neural Network (RNNs)

Recurrent neural networks (RNNs), which are Artificial Neural Network (ANNs) with recurrent connections and which are able to simulate sequential input for sequence recognition and prediction (Salehinejad et al., 2018). At each time step, an RNN computes a new memory or hidden state depending upon the previous state of memory and the input (Thakur, 2021). This structure enables the RNNs to retain, recall, and process complicated signals from the past over an extended period of time. RNNs are able to predict the sequence in the next timestep and map an input sequence to an output sequence in the present timestep. That's why RNNs is referred as Memory based model (Salehinejad et al., 2018; Thakur, 2021). The input, recurrent hidden, and output layers make up the three layers of a simple RNN (Kasongo, 2023). Simple RNN structure is represented in figure 7.

Here, Xp represents the input, hp denotes the output and NN represents the basic neural network. The architecture of RNN is typically characterized by cyclic connections, that provide the RNN the ability

Figure 7. Simple RNN

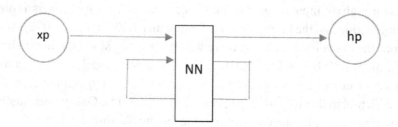

to modify its present state based on previous states and current input data. So, for the sequential data, RNNs have been employed a lot (Zhang et al., 2022).

RNNs made up of sigma or tanh cells are not able to understand or learn and connect the pertinent data when there is a wide input gap (Zhang et al., 2022). Despite its effectiveness in a variety of prediction applications, standard RNNs do struggle with a vanishing gradient. Gated Recurrent Unit (GRU) and Long-Short Term Memory (LSTM) are two other forms of RNNs that were developed to address this problem (Kasongo, 2023). Long short-term memory (LSTM), in which gates were established to govern dependencies, was proposed to handle "long-term dependencies" (Zhang et al., 2022). Every LSTM block is made up of three gates, that are, an input gate, a forget gate, sometimes known as a keep gate, and an output gate, together with a cell that serves as the memory component of the unit (Zhang et al., 2022). These gates regulate how information moves throughout the cell. Compared to a conventional recurrent cell, the LSTM is more capable of learning. However, adding more parameters makes the computation more difficult (Zhang et al., 2022). The LSTM cell's input gate and keep gate (forgot gate) are combined by the GRU cell to form an update gate. The GRU cell consists of a reset gate and a update gate (Zhang et al., 2022). Consequently, it could save a single gating signal along with its related properties. Due to the absence of one gate, a single GRU cell is less efficient than the original LSTM gate (Zhang et al., 2022).

A forward-backward propagation technique is used to carry out the standard RNN model's training procedure. Every unit of a simple RNN uses a nonlinear activation function. However, if a simple structure is properly trained using timesteps, it can simulate complex dynamics (Salehinejad et al., 2018). A significant issue is efficient RNN training. The challenge is in properly initializing the weights in the network and the optimization algorithm to adjust them in order to minimize the training loss. It is crucial to initialize the weights and biases in RNNs. As a general rule, weights should be given low values. Though the biases are typically set to zero, the output bias can also be set to a very low value (Kasongo, 2023). A simple and most popular optimization technique in deep learning is gradient descent (GD). Applications of RNN include operating robots, composing music, and recognizing human actions, to name a few (Thakur, 2021).

7. SCALABLE ARCHITECTURES FOR BIG DATA PROCESSING

Numerous tools have been released in past few years for the study of big data. Apache Hadoop, Spark, Flink are the tools available for big data analysis. These tools place a strong emphasis on stream processing and batch processing. Real-time analysis typically employs data stream analysis programs. Examples of systems for data flow analysis include Spark and Flink (Nazari et al., 2019).

7.1 Distributed Computing Paradigms: MapReduce, Spark, and Flink

Applications for data processing are developed using the Apache HADOOP framework and operate in a distributed computing environment. Within the Hadoop environment, data is stored using the distributed file system known as Hadoop Distributed File System (HDFS), which is similar to the local file system of a personal computer.

MapReduce

The Hadoop MapReduce engine relies on the MapReduce algorithm as its primary method of allocating work among a cluster (Shukla et al., 2015). MapReduce is a Big Data processing programming model created by Google that uses the divide and conquer technique (Nazari et al., 2019). The parallel processing of a lot of data is made possible via MapReduce programming. According to this approach, each piece of software is a series of operations of MapReduce that uses a map step and a reduce step to process a lot of different independent data (Nazari et al., 2019).

Map function: An input data row with key and value can be transformed into an output key/value row using the map transform function (Nazari et al., 2019; Shukla et al., 2015).

- Map(key1, value1) -> list<key2, value2>

This means that for a given input, it produces a list with 0 or more key-value pairs. A different key than the input can be used for the output. Several entries with the same key can show up in the output (Shukla et al., 2015).

Reduction function: A reduction transform can be used to create a new list of the reduced output by taking all values for a given key (Shukla et al., 2015).

- Reduce(key2, list<value2>) -> list<value3>

For the successful completion of a Hadoop work, there are three nodes for every MapReduce task, the Name node, the job submission node, and the Slave node. MapReduce tasks are tracked using task and job trackers, and all work is done on Data nodes under Namenode control. The Slave node is where these operations are carried out (Ketu et al., 2020).

MapReduce has several benefits, includes:

- parallel processing
- Data locality
- large files processing
- Minimal hardware cost
- maximum operating capability
- High scalability (Nazari et al., 2019)

Disadvantages of MapReduce includes:

- ability to optimize the system is hampered by the ambiguous nature of the Map and Reduce functions.
- Custom programs are written, causing issues with reuse and maintenance, even for common functions like filtering and projection.
- There is no streaming data support (Nazari et al., 2019)

Spark

In 2009, University of Berkeley, a text based framework called Apache Spark was introduced (Nazari et al., 2019). The open-source platform Apache Spark was created for fast distributed big data processing. Spark mainly refers to a parallel computing architecture which provides a number of cutting-edge services, including real-time stream processing and machine learning methods (Saeed et al., 2020). Due to its superiority to competing frameworks like Hadoop MapReduce, researchers attracted towards Spark for processing of big data (Saeed et al., 2020). The processing performance is greatly accelerated by spark as it follows in-memory computing. As opposed to Hadoop, which only supports one programming language or model, Spark supports three different languages includes Java, Scala, and Python. It contains algorithms that can be created with the help of these programming languages (Ketu et al., 2020).

Different components of spark include Spark Core, Spark streaming, spark GraphX, spark MLlib, spark SQL. *Spark Core* is considered as the building block of Apache Spark, comprises crucial features, such as memory management, components for task scheduling, storage system interaction, and fault recovery (Saeed et al., 2020). API located in Spark Core, defines resilient distributed datasets (RDDs), which are Spark's original programming abstraction (Nazari et al., 2019; Saeed et al., 2020). Its import features include, responsible for the essential I/O capabilities, playing a crucial role in planning and monitoring Spark cluster, solving MapReduce's complexity by recovering from failures by using calculations in memory (Nazari et al., 2019). The streaming component of Spark provides scalable, high-throughput APIs for processing real-time stream data from many sources (Saeed et al., 2020).

Apache Spark has the following benefits: It is simple to install; Open-source experts including IBM, Cloudera, Intel, Databricks, and MapR have publicly stated their support for Apache Spark as the industry standard engine for huge data analysis; can be integrated with various storage systems, such as Casendra, the Hadoop Distributed File System (HDFS) and Hbase, removes the requirement for large format processing with different types of data such as data charts, text data, etc.) and effectively maintains sources of data.

Flink

At the Technical University of Berlin, under the name Stratosphere, Flink was created. In January 2015, it completed the Apache incubation phase and became a top-level project (Landset et al., 2015). With the exact same objectives as Spark in the Hadoop Ecosystem, Flink was developed as a substitute to the MapReduce Hadoop framework. Apache Flink is freely accessible. Flink offers efficiency, speed, and accuracy for bulk processing and can handle the direct and stream processing as well as the batch processing (Nazari et al., 2019). Instead of being based on MapReduce, flink has its own runtime. As a result, it can function entirely independently of the Hadoop ecosystem or be integrated with HDFS and YARN (Landset et al., 2015). The core, the APIs (such as Table & SQL, DataSet, DataStream), and the libraries make up the Apache Flink architecture (Ceballos et al., 2021). The core, which is a streaming dataflow engine, offers data distribution, communication, and fault tolerance for distributed computations over streams of data. The Table & SQL API enables the synthesis of queries using relational operators, the DataSet API processes limited datasets (batch processing), and the DataStream API handles potentially unbounded data streams (Ceballos et al., 2021). These APIs provide the foundation of the libraries (Ceballos et al., 2021). The processing model used by Flink transforms parallel data sets. These modifications encompass the map and reduce procedures in addition to join, group, iterate, and other operations. A cost-based optimizer is also present, which chooses the ideal execution plan for each work automatically (Landset et al., 2015). Flink uses multiple programming language includes Java, Scala, Python and R (Nazari et al., 2019). Performance-wise, Flink outperforms all other information processing systems. Flink accelerates machine learning and graph processing by using repeated closed loop operators (Nazari et al., 2019).

7.2 Parallel Processing and GPU Acceleration

Due to their parallel processing abilities and high bandwidth memory, which meet the needs of many workloads, mostly analytical ones, GPUs have become an increasingly common processing unit for data management systems (Raza et al., 2020). Since the beginning of general-purpose computing on Graphics Processing Units, analytical activities have been identified as a target for acceleration due to their data-parallel nature. Since that time, analytics on GPUs have gained a lot of attraction, and research in this area has expanded significantly. There are many academic and commercial GPU-accelerated analytical DBMSs available. The hardware and topology of CPU-GPU servers with multiple CPUs and multiple GPUs are closely coupled with the design principles of existing GPU-accelerated DBMS.

The manner in which GPU-accelerated Data transfers and the GPU programming model are two things that DBMS takes into account. The kernels used by GPUs are a collection of data-parallel operations. The execution model used by the first generation of GPU-accelerated DBMS is operator-at-a-time. They execute the plan bottom-up by mapping each operator in the query plan to a kernel. The execution of queries is sped up by modern GPU-accelerated systems by interleaving it with data transfers. One method involves using the shared address space shared by the GPU memory and main memory to access the main memory directly from the kernels across the connection. Asynchronous data transfers are a different strategy that may be used to pipeline the utilization of the interconnect and the GPU and is compatible with the vector-at-a-time execution model. A data vector is processed by the GPU, and the subsequent vector is transferred instantly (Raza et al., 2020).

7.3 Stream Processing for Real-Time Analysis of Streaming Data

Stream processing is in higher demand. Because of this, not only must a large amount of data be handled, but also must process the data quickly to allow organizations or enterprises to respond in real-time to changing conditions (Kolajo et al., 2019). It is a new paradigm that is necessary due to new data-generating scenarios, such as the widespread usage of location services, mobile devices, and sensors (Kolajo et al., 2019). A real-time, large volume of data from various sources must be handled by stream processing solutions, taking availability, scalability, and fault tolerance into account. Incorporation of data as an infinite tuple, analysis, and creation of results that can be used to take action are all components of big data stream analysis (Kolajo et al., 2019). Due to its suitability for handling data that requires a real-time response, stream processing is required as the data processing framework that can achieve minimal latency (J. Wang et al., 2020). Storm is a distributed real-time stream data processing system that is freely accessible. Storm may reduce processing latency because it is analogous to a real-time Hadoop computing system and does not require complex job scheduling (J. Wang et al., 2020).

The following traits of Storm are present:

- an easy programming models
- scalability
- High fault tolerance (if an exception occurs while processing messages, Storm reassigns the problematic processing units)
- high reliability (in contrast to real-time systems like S4, Storm guarantees that data may be processed completely) (J. Wang et al., 2020).

Apache Samza is a stream processing framework that has the ability to process massive volumes of data effectively. The largest LinkedIn Samza implementation can process millions of messages per second during peak times (J. Wang et al., 2020). Samza and Kafka together, however, can better capitalize on the benefits of the two frameworks. Samza can benefit from Kafka's fault tolerance, data buffering, state storage, and other technologies in a way similar to how the MapReduce engine depends on HDFS (J. Wang et al., 2020).

8. INTERPRETABLE MACHINE LEARNING AND EXPLAINABLE AI FOR BIG DATA

8.1 The Need for Transparency in Complex Models

Various application sectors are being transformed by artificial intelligence (AI) technology. These technologies, which are ML and DL-powered, are demonstrating their dominance as they are used in everything from self-driving cars to computerized chess players (Hassija et al., 2023). Keeping into account the remarkable success of AI led researchers to forecast that its market worth will soar over the coming years, reaching $190.61 billion in 2025 (Hassija et al., 2023). As a result, the rise of AI has prompted people to ask themselves, " How accustomed are we to relying mindlessly on outcomes produced by AI? When something goes wrong, who will be responsible? (Hassija et al., 2023) It is crucial to note that Deep Neural Networks, that are formed from incredibly complex non-linear statistical models and countless parameters, are what produce the highly accurate predictions of AI models (Hassija et al., 2023). This compromises the transparency of the aforementioned algorithms. As a result, AI algorithms experience opacity, a situation which occurs when a system cannot provide a justification or explanation that is appropriate for the factors that led to its judgments, often known as "the black-box problem" (Hassija et al., 2023). When discussing AI models, the term "black-box" is generally used to describe systems whose underlying processes for making decisions are opaque or excessively large or complex for a human to comprehend easily. The degree of a model's black-boxiness is frequently described by the technical term "opacity" (Panigutti et al., 2023).

The AI Act1, a proposal for a regulation in the European Union (EU) establishing standardized standards for AI systems, was offered by the European Commission in 2021 (Panigutti et al., 2023). The AI Act uses a risk-based methodology. Certain requirements are made of AI systems based on the level of risk, which is related to the context of use and the potential effects on health, safety, or fundamental rights of the people. Particularly, a series of rules that include, among others, human monitoring and transparency, are applied to high-risk AI systems (Panigutti et al., 2023). As an illustration, in medical sector, the analysis of electronic health records (EHRs) using machine learning algorithms to spot people at risk for delirium, these algorithms can estimate a patient's risk of delirium by considering a wide range of patient-specific details, such as demographic details, laboratory test results, and drug use (Hassija et al., 2023). Even though these models have been greatly enhanced using the training data set, user acceptability is still in question. Thus, it was determined that the healthcare industry is one among the ones where user acceptance of AI algorithms depends on both accuracy and understandability (Hassija et al., 2023).

8.2 Techniques for Interpreting Black-Box Models in Big Data Scenarios

LIME: One of the most favourite interpretability techniques for black box models is LIME (local interpretable model-agnostic explanations). using an intuitive yet effective methodology, LIME can provide explanations for any classifier's single prediction score (Linardatos et al., 2020). LIME's objective is to build a straightforward, understandable model that replicates the black-box model's behaviour close to the instance being described. Through that, LIME provides a trustworthy and correct explanation for the black-box model's predictions without necessitating a thorough comprehension of its inner working (Hassija et al., 2023). A brief explanation of LIME's operating theory is provided below:

- An instance of interest whose explanation is needed is selected from the black box's predictions.
- Using modified samples, a new dataset is created, and the black-box model's related predictions are taken out.
- The new samples are weighted based on their closeness to the relevant occurrence.
- The black-box model is understood by an interpretable model trained on the modified dataset using the following equation 9, (Hassija et al., 2023).

$$Explanation\left(x\right) = \arg\min_{g \in G} L\left(f, g, \pi_x\right) + \left(g\right) \tag{8}$$

SHAP: Shapley Additive explanations, a method based on game-theory, calculates the significant values for each attribute for each prediction in an effort to increase interpretability (Linardatos et al., 2020). In order to develop a deep learning model that can predict whether a medication would cause depression, the researchers used the Shapley Additive Explanations (SHAP) technique (Hassija et al., 2023). The most significant parameters influencing each patient's predictions made by the model were found by the researchers using SHAP. These parameters included demographic details like age and gender as well as genetic markers linked to treatment response (Hassija et al., 2023).

Anchors: The same creators' anchor proposals might be seen as an extension of LIME. LIME is used in a method called Anchor to better explain the forecasts provided by machine learning algorithms (Hassija et al., 2023). Precomputing interpretations for a portion of the dataset's instances is the main idea behind Anchors, and after that then use these explanations to come up with explanations for other instances (Hassija et al., 2023). The predictions of enormous, sophisticated models can be explained using this method at a reduced computing cost (Hassija et al., 2023). Using a bottom-up methodology, the anchors are built incrementally. More particular, an empty rule that is applicable to every instance is initialized for each anchor. After creating new candidate rules repeatedly, the candidate rule with the highest estimated accuracy substitutes the prior for that specific anchor (Linardatos et al., 2020). The iterative procedure comes to an end when the current candidate rule satisfies the criteria for an anchor, indicating that the required anchor has been found (Linardatos et al., 2020).

9. CASE STUDIES AND APPLICATIONS IN BIG DATA ANALYTICS

9.1 Healthcare: Disease Prediction and Patient Monitoring

The entire healthcare sector depends on accuracy and it is crucial to guarantee prediction accuracy. Predictive analysis pinpoints the patient population that is more susceptible to specific diseases and makes recommendations for early preventive action. The majority of chronic diseases account for 75% of healthcare spending. Cancer, diabetes, kidney disease and heart disease are a few of them. Particularly in countries with low and moderate incomes, many diseases are on the rise ("BIG DATA ANALYTICS FOR CHRONIC DISEASE PREDICTION," 2022).

Big Data technologies are crucial for managing and adjusting cardiovascular disease treatment. Acute myocardial infarction known as heart attack is among the most lethal conditions that people can suffer from. Comparing, contrasting, and mining vast amounts of data for information that may be utilized to recognize, handle, and treat chronic illnesses like heart attacks is the key to treating cardiovascular disease ("BIG DATA ANALYTICS FOR CHRONIC DISEASE PREDICTION," 2022). Diabetes is a metabolic illness that essentially causes an increase in the body's blood sugar levels ("BIG DATA ANALYTICS FOR CHRONIC DISEASE PREDICTION," 2022). If you have diabetes, your body either produces insufficient insulin or is unable to utilise the insulin that is made. There are both modest and large risks that could be fatal. As a result of advances in technology, various researches have been conducted to apply data analytics technology in the prediction of diabetes in healthcare industry ("BIG DATA ANALYTICS FOR CHRONIC DISEASE PREDICTION," 2022). Predictive analytic algorithms in the Hadoop/Map Reduce environment can be used to predict the common types of diabetes, its consequences, and the type of medication to be administered. Hadoop can process large volumes of health data, mostly by distributing partitioned data sets to a number of servers in the form of clusters, each of which addresses a distinct aspect of the overall problem before integrating the results ("BIG DATA ANALYTICS FOR CHRONIC DISEASE PREDICTION," 2022). It is necessary to examine patterns for the treatment of diabetes, such as plasma glucose concentration and serum insulin. Another method of applying big data analytics with different dataset sizes and different processing core counts using Apache Spark has also been demonstrated to be highly effective ("BIG DATA ANALYTICS FOR CHRONIC DISEASE PREDICTION," 2022).

There are numerous telemonitoring products available on the market right now, the most of which are designed for use in homes. Numerous monitoring sensors and application host equipment collect the observations that are made (Morales-Botello et al., 2021). The monitoring data is often collected using specialist software and stored in multiple databases. In addition to their own record-keeping systems, health professionals must have access to a variety of software platforms in order to get a comprehensive understanding of the patients' situations (Morales-Botello et al., 2021; Rana & Bhushan, 2023). Considering the current state of situations, high-performance computing infrastructure and scalable data storage are still required in order to efficiently store, process, and share health data (Morales-Botello et al., 2021). Oxygen consumption, heart rate, blood pressure, inhaled/exhaled CO_2, respiratory rate and effort, blood oxygenation, cardiac output, and glucose can all be tracked by wellness and health monitoring devices at the moment (Morales-Botello et al., 2021).

9.2 Finance: Fraud Detection and Credit Risk Assessment

The number of publicly traded companies worldwide is rising annually as a result of the booming global economy. Additionally, more and more businesses are experiencing financial difficulties than before (Zhao & Bai, 2022). When a company's accountant or senior manager intentionally manipulates, falsifies, or modifies papers, this is referred to as financial fraud. They occasionally even fail to notice or remove crucial information from financial documents, which can have a big effect on how the firm is managed (Zhao & Bai, 2022). In China, Luckin Coffee raised sales income and falsely recorded coffee cup prices. Muddy Waters released a report about financial fraud behaviour in February 2020. The business later admitted to financial crime and left the stock market on May 19. Currently, a number of factors influence how financial fraud is detected (Zhao & Bai, 2022). We must create feature selection and classification models utilizing an extensive variety of samples and indicators in order to improve prediction accuracy in comparison to earlier work and offer actionable advice to policymakers and investors (Zhao & Bai, 2022).

The expansion of Internet finance has become irreversible because of the extensive use of big data technologies and financial sector's ongoing innovation (Pichler & Hartig, 2023). Big data offers information query services that include operator data, credit card data, travel data and social security data, and then criminal inquiries and vehicle inquiries, information verification services, verifying academic credentials, identity transactions (H. Wang, 2021). Big data technology enables detailed information mining and accurate data analysis. The virtual representation of the data can be represented as accurately as possible with the aid of scientific methodologies and model findings, and it can provide real-world examples and increase the area of its applicability (H. Wang, 2021).

9.3 E-Commerce: Recommender Systems and Personalization

Due to the rapid advancement of the web and smart electronic gadgets, e-commerce systems have become more accessible and widely used in everyday life. Because there are so many different types of products present on sites like Amazon, Flipkart etc. it is not easy for customers to choose one that is right for them. This reduces customers' interest in making purchases, which lowers sales for merchants (Abdul Hussien et al., 2021). The users and businesses of a sophisticated e-commerce website would therefore benefit greatly from a good recommender system. The usage of recommendation systems, which are frequently based only on purchasing data, improves the operational efficiency of e-commerce systems. A recommender system gathers information from a consumers and suggests items among available goods that it thinks the consumer will value the best (Abdul Hussien et al., 2021).

Recommendation Systems are thought of as software tools and procedures that automatically offer things to customers based on their preferences. The offered suggestions were intended to give customers a wide range of decision-making options (Abdul Hussien et al., 2021). Various domains, including machine learning, knowledge recovery, text classification, and decision support systems, all incorporate recommendation systems. Different types recommendation systems are: *Content-based recommendation systems* aim to provide recommendations for content that is similar to that which the user has earlier loved. The determination of how similar the things are is established based on the characteristics of the similar goods (Abdul Hussien et al., 2021). *A demographic-based recommender system* makes product recommendations based on the demographic profile of the customer. The idea is that various demographic records can receive different suggestions. Many demographically based solutions. Customers are sent to particular sites based on information like their language or origin (Abdul Hussien et al., 2021). *Knowledge-based systems* generate product recommendations using specific information about how particular items qualities satisfy clients' preferences and needs, also ultimately, how the client uses these items (Abdul Hussien et al., 2021). By integrating two or more approaches that aim to lessen their flaws, a *hybrid recommendation system* created with a combination of the aforementioned techniques. A hybrid technique has been employed to try and alleviate the drawbacks of both collaborative and content-based methods (Abdul Hussien et al., 2021). There are several other types of recommendation systems are also present (Praful Bharadiya, 2023).

9.4 IoT: Predictive Maintenance and Anomaly Detection

The Internet of Things has experienced tremendous growth recently. Real-time machine communication over the Internet is made possible by IoT (Kamat & Sugandhi, 2020). Many different kinds of data, such as pressure, temperature, humidity, vibration, location, and others, are continuously collected by IoT devices and sensors. These sensors produce enormous amounts of data streams. IoT is essential to predictive maintenance since it provides real-time data for analysis while continuously monitoring the state of the equipment (Kamat & Sugandhi, 2020). Real-time data analysis is done using tools like Apache Spark Streaming, Apache Flink, or dedicated stream processing platforms (Nazari et al., 2019).

By reducing equipment downtime, eliminating malfunctions, increasing overall operational efficiency, and enhancing security, IoT-based predictive maintenance and anomaly detection have the potential to save enterprises significant expenditures. In-depth research is required to create efficient anomaly detection (A set of significant approaches identification aims to find abnormal patterns that differ from typical behaviour) methods that prevent manufacturers from performing superfluous maintenance activities that waste resources in addition to warning them well in advance of those activities (Kamat & Sugandhi, 2020). Deep learning and Machine learning models are used by big data analytics platforms for interpreting the data from IoT devices (Kamat & Sugandhi, 2020). These models examine past IoT data to forecast when equipment failure is most likely to occur.

9.5 Agriculture: Crop Yield Prediction, Soil Management, Pest Management

Food production and crop yield are influenced by a number of variables. The concept of "big data" in agriculture aids in recognizing the necessity for significant expenditures in platforms for the storage and analysis of agricultural data (Research Scholar, Department of Computer Science and Engineering, B.M.S. College of Engineering, Bangalore, India. et al., 2019). Big data guarantees efficient storage, processing, and analysis of data which was formerly difficult to achieve using traditional methods. It allows for the discovery, fusion, and connection of numerous agricultural statistics to produce the finest farming findings (Research Scholar, Department of Computer Science and Engineering, B.M.S. College of Engineering, Bangalore, India. et al., 2019). Relationships between elements such as data from remote sensors such as soil mapping, health of the crop, Leaf Area Index and statistical information such as temperature, and rainfall, encourage decisions regarding fertilizer suggestions, price prediction, handling pest, crops yield predictions, suggestions for policy (Research Scholar, Department of Computer Science and Engineering, B.M.S. College of Engineering, Bangalore, India. et al., 2019).

Data produced by machines, data generated by processes, and data produced by people are the three types of agricultural data that are gathered. Sensor, drone, and GPS data are examples of *machine-generated information* (Research Scholar, Department of Computer Science and Engineering, B.M.S. College of Engineering, Bangalore, India. et al., 2019). These new technology data could be anything from sounds to pictures. Data gathered from fields, includes monitoring, details on planting, and recording the agricultural activities, like applying fertilizer to seeds, are included in *process-generated data* (Research Scholar, Department of Computer Science and Engineering, B.M.S. College of Engineering, Bangalore, India. et al., 2019). *Human-sourced* refers to previously documented human experiences. Experiences that were formerly preserved as books are now digitally preserved and made accessible (Research Scholar, Department of Computer Science and Engineering, B.M.S. College of Engineering, Bangalore, India. et al., 2019).

For site-specific crop management systems, taking into account soil qualities and their effect on crop yield is a key component. Chemical and physical characteristics of the soil are present. Physical characteristics include the soil's texture, rooting depth, slope, ability to hold water, structure (Research Scholar, Department of Computer Science and Engineering, B.M.S. College of Engineering, Bangalore, India. et al., 2019). The chemical parameters that are primarily taken into account are potassium, organic carbon, electrical conductivity, total nitrogen, accessible phosphorus, acidity (pH), and cation exchange capacity (Research Scholar, Department of Computer Science and Engineering, B.M.S. College of Engineering, Bangalore, India. et al., 2019). The agriculturists can select the crop that best fits the soil conditions with the use of a model that links the favourable soil features for the various crops. But because of the high cost of manual soil surveys, comprehensive information regarding soil conditions is only available in few places (Research Scholar, Department of Computer Science and Engineering, B.M.S. College of Engineering, Bangalore, India. et al., 2019). Accurate soil maps are being produced recently as a result of the acceptance of the Global Information System to investigate properties of the soil. Acceptable values of soil parameters can be obtained using modern substitutes like remote sensing, Global Positioning System (GPS), and digital evolution models (Research Scholar, Department of Computer Science and Engineering, B.M.S. College of Engineering, Bangalore, India. et al., 2019). Recording the locations where the pest has been seen, connecting those observations to the surrounding environment, and generating a geographic map of the pest data are frequently the first steps in the pest mapping process. The geographic distribution of agricultural pests is likely to shift in the near future. It facilitates recognizing pest risk factors and raises the likelihood of future practical pest remedies (Research Scholar, Department of Computer Science and Engineering, B.M.S. College of Engineering, Bangalore, India. et al., 2019).

10. FUTURE DIRECTIONS

10.1 Ethical Implications of Machine Learning and Deep Learning in Big Data

Numerous improvements have been made thanks to machine learning (ML) in a number of sectors, such as transportation finance, and healthcare. However, as the usage of these technologies increases, it becomes more crucial to consider their potential social and ethical implications (Tiwari, 2023). One of the main ethical concerns with Machine Learning and Deep Learning is the chance for algorithmic bias. Because AI and ML systems are generally trained on collections of data that reflect these biases, there is a possibility that societal biases will be reinforced and retained in the choices made by the technology (Tiwari, 2023). Concerns regarding privacy and the loss of autonomy have also been highlighted by the potential of machine learning and deep learning systems to collect and analyse vast volumes of personal data (Rahmaty, 2023). Another major social concern is the potential loss of jobs as a consequence of deep learning and Machine Learning systems' ability to perform tasks that were previously done by humans (Tiwari, 2023). Furthermore, concerns exist around the power being concentrated in a small number of powerful technology companies that control the development and use of Machine learning and deep learning systems. Experts in the field have put out a variety of solutions to address these issues, including the creation of fair and transparent artificial intelligence systems, the application of laws to safeguard autonomy and privacy, and the promotion of retraining and upskilling initiatives to reduce job displacement (Tiwari, 2023). Furthermore, there is a need for improved transparency in the decision making procedures of Machine Learning and deep learning systems, for example, through the usage of explainable AI, which would enable people to comprehend the justification for a system's conclusions (Tiwari, 2023). Future studies might look at the societal and ethical effects of AI and ML in certain sectors or settings, such finance or healthcare. Future studies might also concentrate on the effects of AI and ML on various marginalized groups and consider potential solutions that can help to advance justice and equality in the application of AI and ML (Tiwari, 2023).

10.2 Emerging Trends and Future Research Directions in Big Data Analytics

It becomes clear that creating Big Data technologies to analyse more, real-time data from more devices than ever will be the norm going forward, despite experts' views that it would merely be an extension of the current strategy. Researchers are eager to use data at a deeper level to obtain more insightful conclusions than the typical data points that are being now extracted. It is obvious that the Big Data era is still in its infancy and that there are still a lot of things to learn.

The use of Big Data Analytics could create a dynamic and revolutionary environment that will redefine industries and transform the ability to make decisions (Et Al., 2023). certainly the most noticeable trends on the rise is the effortless incorporation of artificial intelligence and machine learning technologies in big data analytics processes (Et Al., 2023). With the help of this integration, businesses will be able to glean deeper insights from huge datasets, improving the precision and applicability of predictive and prescriptive analytics (Et Al., 2023). Businesses will be able to adapt quickly to changing trends and seize opportunities as they arise thanks to real-time data, which will eventually become the norm (Et Al., 2023). Big data analytics are becoming more and more popular, which raises questions about data privacy and ethics. To deal with these problems, it is necessary to have strong governance structures and to follow any additional regulations that may be in effect (Et Al., 2023). Natural Language Processing (NLP) will advance through leveraging conversational interfaces, ensuring data available to user without technical backgrounds. At the same time, enhanced analytics tools will automate the preparation of data and the generation of insights (Et Al., 2023).

Ontology and semantic web technologies can aid in the analysis of huge amounts of data, they are still in their infancy. As a result, it will be important to conduct research on how to incorporate these two technologies into machine learning techniques for handling large amounts of data (Qiu et al., 2016). Another future research trend will be how to combine various big data processing-related approaches with machine learning (Qiu et al., 2016). Despite being in its infancy, quantum computing has the potential to solve difficult problems quickly. The use of blockchain technology may also help to improve data security and traceability (Et Al., 2023). To guarantee fairness and transparency in analytics outputs, ethical AI and bias prevention efforts will be crucial. Cross-domain collaborations will grow and encourage sharing of data between businesses for mutual gain (Et Al., 2023). In conclusion, The big data analytics' future lies in the union of technological advancement, ethical concerns, and the democratization of data, enabling enterprises to fully exploit their data assets and achieve an edge over the competition in a world that is increasingly data-driven (Et Al., 2023).

REFERENCES

Abdul Hussien, T., Rahma, A. M. S., & Abdul Wahab, H. B. (1897). Recommendation Systems For E-commerce Systems An Overview. *Journal of Physics: Conference Series*, *1897*(1), 012024. doi:10.1088/1742-6596/1897/1/012024

Abiodun, O. I., Jantan, A., Omolara, A. E., Dada, K. V., Mohamed, N. A., & Arshad, H. (2018). State-of-the-art in artificial neural network applications: A survey. *Heliyon*, *4*(11), e00938. doi:10.1016/j.heliyon.2018.e00938 PMID:30519653

Alzubi, J., Nayyar, A., & Kumar, A. (2018). Machine Learning from Theory to Algorithms: An Overview. *Journal of Physics: Conference Series*, *1142*, 012012. doi:10.1088/1742-6596/1142/1/012012

Babcock University. (2017). Supervised Machine Learning Algorithms: Classification and Comparison. *International Journal of Computer Trends and Technology*, *48*(3), 128–138. doi:10.14445/22312803/IJCTT-V48P126

Bhattarai, B. P., Paudyal, S., Luo, Y., Mohanpurkar, M., Cheung, K., Tonkoski, R., Hovsapian, R., Myers, K. S., Zhang, R., Zhao, P., Manic, M., Zhang, S., & Zhang, X. (2019). Big data analytics in smart grids: State-of-the-art, challenges, opportunities, and future directions. *IET Smart Grid*, *2*(2), 141–154. doi:10.1049/iet-stg.2018.0261

Ceballos, O., Ramírez Restrepo, C. A., Pabón, M. C., Castillo, A. M., & Corcho, O. (2021). SPARQL-2Flink: Evaluation of SPARQL Queries on Apache Flink. *Applied Sciences (Basel, Switzerland)*, *11*(15), 7033. doi:10.3390/app11157033

Cen, L., Ruta, D., & Ng, J. (2015). Big education: Opportunities for Big Data analytics. *2015 IEEE International Conference on Digital Signal Processing (DSP)*, (pp. 502–506). IEEE. 10.1109/ICDSP.2015.7251923

Chelladurai, K., & Sujatha, N. (2023). A Survey on Different Algorithms Used in Deep Learning Process. *E3S Web of Conferences*, *387*, 05008.

Chen, X.-W., & Lin, X. (2014). Big Data Deep Learning: Challenges and Perspectives. *IEEE Access : Practical Innovations, Open Solutions*, *2*, 514–525. doi:10.1109/ACCESS.2014.2325029

García, S., Ramírez-Gallego, S., Luengo, J., Benítez, J. M., & Herrera, F. (2016). Big data preprocessing: Methods and prospects. *Big Data Analytics*, *1*(1), 9. doi:10.118641044-016-0014-0

Georgevici, A. I., & Terblanche, M. (2019). Neural networks and deep learning: A brief introduction. *Intensive Care Medicine, 45*(5), 712–714. doi:10.100700134-019-05537-w PMID:30725133

Hassija, V., Chamola, V., Mahapatra, A., Singal, A., Goel, D., Huang, K., Scardapane, S., Spinelli, I., Mahmud, M., & Hussain, A. (2023). Interpreting Black-Box Models: A Review on Explainable Artificial Intelligence. *Cognitive Computation*. doi:10.100712559-023-10179-8

Ishwarappa & Anuradha, J. (2015). A Brief Introduction on Big Data 5Vs Characteristics and Hadoop Technology. *Procedia Computer Science, 48*, 319–324.

Jain, N., & Kumar, R.Department of Electrical Engineering. (2022). A Review on Machine Learning & It's Algorithms. *International Journal of Soft Computing and Engineering, 12*(5), 1–5. doi:10.35940/ijsce.E3583.1112522

Kamat, P., & Sugandhi, R. (2020). Anomaly Detection for Predictive Maintenance in Industry 4.0- A survey. *E3S Web of Conferences, 170*, 02007.

Kasongo, S. M. (2023). A deep learning technique for intrusion detection system using a Recurrent Neural Networks based framework. *Computer Communications, 199*, 113–125. doi:10.1016/j.comcom.2022.12.010

Kaur, G., Goyal, S., & Kaur, H. (2020). Brief Review Of Various Machine Learning Algorithms. SSRN *Electronic Journal*. doi:10.2139/ssrn.3747597

Ketu, S., Kumar Mishra, P., & Agarwal, S. (2020). Performance Analysis of Distributed Computing Frameworks for Big Data Analytics: Hadoop Vs Spark. *Computación y Sistemas, 24*(2). doi:10.13053/cys-24-2-3401

Kolajo, T., Daramola, O., & Adebiyi, A. (2019). Big data stream analysis: A systematic literature review. *Journal of Big Data, 6*(1), 47. doi:10.118640537-019-0210-7

Kukreja, H., N, B., & S, K. (2016). AN INTRODUCTION TO ARTIFICIAL NEURAL NETWORK. *International Journal Of Advance Research And Innovative Ideas In Education, 1*(5), 27–30.

Landset, S., Khoshgoftaar, T. M., Richter, A. N., & Hasanin, T. (2015). A survey of open source tools for machine learning with big data in the Hadoop ecosystem. *Journal of Big Data, 2*(1), 24. doi:10.118640537-015-0032-1

Linardatos, P., Papastefanopoulos, V., & Kotsiantis, S. (2020). Explainable AI: A Review of Machine Learning Interpretability Methods. *Entropy (Basel, Switzerland), 23*(1), 18. doi:10.3390/e23010018 PMID:33375658

Mahajan, P., Uddin, S., Hajati, F., & Moni, M. A. (2023). Ensemble Learning for Disease Prediction: A Review. *Health Care, 11*(12), 1808. PMID:37372925

Mahesh, B. (2019). Machine Learning Algorithms -. *RE:view, 9*(1).

Mohammed Alqahtani, T. (2023). Big Data Analytics with Optimal Deep Learning Model for Medical Image Classification. *Computer Systems Science and Engineering, 44*(2), 1433–1449. doi:10.32604/csse.2023.025594

Morales-Botello, M. L., Gachet, D., De Buenaga, M., Aparicio, F., Busto, M. J., & Ascanio, J. R. (2021). Chronic patient remote monitoring through the application of big data and internet of things. *Health Informatics Journal, 27*(3), 146045822110309. doi:10.1177/14604582211030956 PMID:34256646

Najafabadi, M. M., Villanustre, F., Khoshgoftaar, T. M., Seliya, N., Wald, R., & Muharemagc, E. (2016). Deep Learning Techniques in Big Data Analytics. In B. Furht & F. Villanustre, Big Data Technologies and Applications (pp. 133–156). Springer International Publishing. doi:10.1007/978-3-319-44550-2_5

Nasteski, V. (2017). An overview of the supervised machine learning methods. *HORIZONS.B, 4*, 51–62.

Nazari, E., Shahriari, M. H., & Tabesh, H. (2019). BigData Analysis in Healthcare: Apache Hadoop, Apache spark and Apache Flink. *Frontiers in Health Informatics, 8*(1), 14. doi:10.30699/fhi.v8i1.180

O'Shea, K., & Nash, R. (2015). *An Introduction to Convolutional Neural Networks.*

Panigutti, C., Hamon, R., Hupont, I., Fernandez Llorca, D., Fano Yela, D., Junklewitz, H., Scalzo, S., Mazzini, G., Sanchez, I., Soler Garrido, J., & Gomez, E. (2023). The role of explainable AI in the context of the AI Act. *2023 ACM Conference on Fairness, Accountability, and Transparency*, (pp. 1139–1150). ACM. 10.1145/3593013.3594069

Pichler, M., & Hartig, F. (2023). Machine learning and deep learning—A review for ecologists. *Methods in Ecology and Evolution, 14*(4), 994–1016. doi:10.1111/2041-210X.14061

Praful Bharadiya, J. (2023). A Comparative Study of Business Intelligence and Artificial Intelligence with Big Data Analytics. *American Journal of Artificial Intelligence.*

Qiu, J., Wu, Q., Ding, G., Xu, Y., & Feng, S. (2016). A survey of machine learning for big data processing. *EURASIP Journal on Advances in Signal Processing, 2016*(1), 67. doi:10.118613634-016-0355-x

Rahmaty, M. (2023). Machine learning with big data to solve real-world problems. *Journal of Data Analytics, 2*(1), 9–16. doi:10.59615/jda.2.1.9

Rana, M., & Bhushan, M. (2023). Machine learning and deep learning approach for medical image analysis: Diagnosis to detection. *Multimedia Tools and Applications, 82*(17), 26731–26769. doi:10.100711042-022-14305-w PMID:36588765

Raza, A., Chrysogelos, P., Sioulas, P., Indjic, V., Ailamaki, A., & Anadiotis, A. (2020). GPU-accelerated data management under the test of time. *Conference on Innovative Data Systems Research.*

Saeed, M. M., Al Aghbari, Z., & Alsharidah, M. (2020). Big data clustering techniques based on Spark: A literature review. *PeerJ. Computer Science, 6*, e321. doi:10.7717/peerj-cs.321 PMID:33816971

Salehinejad, H., Sankar, S., Barfett, J., Colak, E., & Valaee, S. (2018). *Recent Advances in Recurrent Neural Networks.*

Sarker, I. H. (2021). Machine Learning: Algorithms, Real-World Applications and Research Directions. *SN Computer Science, 2*(3), 160. doi:10.100742979-021-00592-x PMID:33778771

Shukla, S., Kukade, V., & Mujawar, S. (2015). Big Data: Concept, Handling and Challenges: An Overview. *International Journal of Computer Applications, 114*(11), 6–9. doi:10.5120/20020-1537

Thakur, A. (2021). Fundamentals of Neural Networks. *International Journal for Research in Applied Science and Engineering Technology*, 9(VIII), 407–426. doi:10.22214/ijraset.2021.37362

Tiwari, R. (2023). Ethical And Societal Implications of AI and Machine Learning. *Interantional Journal Of Scientific Research In Engineering And Management*, 07(01).

Tyagi, A. K., & G, R. (2019). Machine Learning with Big Data. *SSRN Electronic Journal*.

Tyagi, A. K., & Rekha, G. (2020). Challenges of Applying Deep Learning in Real-World Applications. In R. Kashyap & A. V. S. Kumar (Eds.), (pp. 92–118). Advances in Computer and Electrical Engineering. IGI Global. doi:10.4018/978-1-7998-0182-5.ch004

Wang, H. (2021). Credit Risk Management of Consumer Finance Based on Big Data. *Mobile Information Systems*, *2021*, 1–10. doi:10.1155/2021/7054016

Wang, J., Yang, Y., Wang, T., Sherratt, R. S., & Zhang, J. (2020). Big Data Service Architecture: A Survey. *Journal of Internet Technology*, *21*, 393–405.

Zhang, X., Zhou, Y., & Luo, J. (2022). Deep learning for processing and analysis of remote sensing big data: A technical review. *Big Earth Data*, *6*(4), 527–560. doi:10.1080/20964471.2021.1964879

Zhao, Z., & Bai, T. (2022). Financial Fraud Detection and Prediction in Listed Companies Using SMOTE and Machine Learning Algorithms. *Entropy (Basel, Switzerland)*, *24*(8), 1157. doi:10.3390/e24081157 PMID:36010821

Zhou, L., Pan, S., Wang, J., & Vasilakos, A. V. (2017). Machine learning on big data: Opportunities and challenges. *Neurocomputing*, *237*, 350–361. doi:10.1016/j.neucom.2017.01.026

KEY TERMS AND DEFINITIONS

Big Data: Big data refers to enormous and complex datasets that exceed the capacity of typical data.

Data Mining: Finding relevant patterns, trends, and information inside huge databases by statistical, mathematical, or computational methods is known as data mining.

Deep Learning: Deep learning is a subfield of machine learning that uses neural networks with numerous layers (deep neural networks) to learn and represent complicated patterns in data.

Machine Learning: Machine learning is a computational method that enables systems to automatically learn and improve from experience without being explicitly programmed.

Reinforcement Learning: In the machine learning paradigm known as reinforcement learning, agents are trained to make decisions by interacting with their surroundings, taking feedback in the form of rewards or penalties, and modifying their behavior over time to maximize the cumulative reward.

Supervised Learning: In the supervised learning paradigm, a model is trained on a labeled dataset to determine the correlation between the input data and the associated output, allowing the model to be used for classification or prediction.

Unsupervised Learning: Unsupervised learning, which is frequently used for clustering, dimensionality reduction, or anomaly detection, is a machine learning paradigm in which a model investigates and finds patterns in unlabeled data without explicit direction.

Chapter 9
Comparing Big Data Analysis Techniques

Santosh Ramkrishna Durugkar

https://orcid.org/0000-0002-5079-2224

Independent Researcher, India

ABSTRACT

Big data refers to the large volume of data which can be processed to get the relevant, required, and meaningful data within less time. It is required to apply sophisticated methods and techniques to process big data. There are many methods and techniques available, like regression analysis, time series analysis, sentiment analysis, descriptive analysis, predictive analysis, association analysis with sampling, machine learning, visualization techniques, classification, and qualitative and quantitative analysis. In the future, there is a need to enhance the performance of these techniques due to increasing size of data. Many applications are based on any of these techniques to process the large volume of data in order to retrieve the meaningful data. It is expected, big data analysis techniques will filter and process the large volume and find the relevant one. Analysis of big data is very helpful in many areas like businesses, industries, and other sectors.

1. INTRODUCTION

Analyzing the big data is nothing but processing *raw data* to get meaningful and relevant data. Retrieved meaningful data can be useful in many applications which are based on different approaches like decision making, probabilistic analysis, and deterministic analysis. With the help of existing data analysis techniques, one can form the business strategies like *identifying customer segments, customer retention, possible future business growth etc.* However, it is suggested one can use data analysis technique as per the requirement i.e. type of input data and insights to uncover.

With the increasing size of users and applications data size is also increasing & in future it could be more than expected. Therefore, in future there would be a requirement of machines with good configurations & best analysis techniques. There are many existing analysis techniques available like *regression analysis, time series analysis, sentiment analysis, descriptive analysis, predictive analysis, diagnostic*

DOI: 10.4018/979-8-3693-0413-6.ch009

analysis, association analysis with sampling, ensemble method for analysis, machine learning, visualization techniques, classification, and genetic algorithms and qualitative & quantitative analysis.

Big data refers to the large volume of data and can be characterized on the basis of *volume, variety and velocity* (V3 model of big data). Volume refers to the quantity of data and keeping the storage as per the requirement. Variety refers to the different data i.e. structured and unstructured data and can have different forms. Velocity refers to the keeping an eye on incoming data with the ever increasing size of users and applications. Big data analysis techniques must deal with the metadata i.e. data about data. Metadata reveals the quality, and characteristics about the data. To process and retrieve the meaningful data, it is expected that analysis techniques must be capable enough to process the metadata too. Identifying the '*relevance*' among the different segments (different variables) data is very important & known as '*association rule*' mining. It is also expected to process the real time data (RT data), qualitative and quantitative data in order to get the relevant data from large volume. Big data refers to processing the 'n' large datasets & more sophisticated big data analysis techniques can be applied to extract the relevant data with less processing time. Examples of big data are as follows – *server web logs, patient records in hospitals, data related to surveillance, institutional data, large time series data, audio and video archives, and the most popular datasets from 'e-commerce' industries.*

1.1 Challenges in Big Data Analysis

Following are the challenges in big data analysis –

- *Storage*
- *Security*
- *Quality*
- *Scalability*
- *Analysis issues*
- *Selection of appropriate tool to analyze the large volume of data*
- *Lack of trained people*

2. LITERATURE REVIEW

In the research paper (Khurana 2014; Berisha et al. 2022) author has pointed the change in technological era i.e. use of cloud computing and big data and these two technologies are discussed in this paper. As the term define bi data, it deal with few steps such as, collecting the raw data, processing it, forming and handling the queries etc. These technologies are rapidly changing the face and pace of data driven applications. Cloud computing which refers to the infrastructure, hardware, software where the data will reside. There are public and private cloud service providers and this technology can be divided into the infrastructure as a service, platform as a service, and software as a service. Nowadays, AWS amazon web services are changing the face of data driven applications. Along with Amazon there are many cloud service providers such as Google, Microsoft etc. In this paper (Cheng et al. 2015; Attaallah et al, 2022) authors have focused on integrity and security of the data stores on the cloud. To protect this data one can divide it in multiple parts and store on multiple locations. Securing the big data on cloud authors have proposed a trapdoor function using various data elements to analyze, compare and simulate the responses. In recent era and future applications the data sensitivity will be an important aspect in the cloud computing as big data is being used in many data sensitive applications such as data mining, real time data analysis etc. To store and handle all the queries industries are establishing the data centers – a platform to store and process the data. Authors (Wang et al. 2017) recognized the big data characteristics such as – volume i.e. large volume of data, variety – data from multiple sources and heterogeneous data, veracity – accuracy of the data or correctness of the data and last velocity – in response to handle the query and returning the relevant results within either the stipulated time or least time than expected. By recognizing these characteristics authors reviewed these technologies i.e. big data and storing this data on clouds. Authors have proposed a framework, known as big data as a service based on the three layers (1) sensing plane (2) cloud plane, (3) application plane. A bicycle sharing system example is illustrated in this paper and the proposed framework gives some suggestions to improve the effectiveness of this system.

In the research paper (Wu et al. 2017) authors have discussed optimization of big data processing by using job sequences and pipelining. A HDM concept is proposed in this paper – hierarchically distributed data matrix. Authors also focused MapReduce framework and Hadoop with advantages and limitations. Important point discussed in this paper, big data processing should be fault tolerant which should be managed by these frameworks. Spark, Flink, Pregel Storm are the few available framework can be used for big data processing. However, when we talk about real world scenario, system must deal with multiple jobs. System deals with the multiple jobs where one can apply pipelining and integration. Feature extraction and classification trainer could be the important modules in this system. Pipelining concept is very useful in handling multiple data streams or multiple components. Only the concern is evolving process where components/data can be re-developed, updated or new components is added. Hence it is not an easy task to manually optimize the performance of each component as this component may have gone through evolving process. One point is clear when system deals with the real time scenario, a chain of operations i.e. pipelining is required. In the paper (Hababeh et al. 2018) authors have discussed the impact of cloud technology in our day to day life and keenly pointed the security issues in this regard too. A methodology is proposed in this paper suggests that, one can classify the secure data before using it for analysis or using it in redundancy operations. Hadoop a distributed file system can be used for managing, storing and use of stored data for analysis purpose in decision making operations etc. Important features of any big data projects including redundancy, handling the scalability, executing multiple tasks parallel can be achieved using Hadoop. Authors also mention the use of Map-reduce in scheduling the jobs in distributed file system. Ultimate objective discussed in this paper is securing the big data over the cloud. Authors concern is to secure the data when it is stored on the storage devices, when someone is using it for analysis and when data is in transmission. Along with security paper focuses on access control mechanism (ACL).

This paper (Salloum et al. 2019; Benatia et al. 2022; Fournier-Viger et al. 2022) focuses on the data partition as the volume could be so large to handle. Therefore, authors have suggested, strategies needs to be designed to partition the data. This partition could be in terms of consistent data blocks. A model proposed in this paper is based on random sample partition and the blocks generated will be known as RSP blocks. These blocks will acts as a representative block of the data set and can be used for predictive modeling. Block level sampling is proposed in this paper supports data analysis. As discussed earlier, RSP blocks are the representative blocks for the entire data set. Hence, these RSP blocks are quite similar to record level sampling. During data analysis samples from these RSP blocks will be selected and analysis phase completes. This process is executed in parallel to every selected RSP blocks. Integration phase, which will integrates all the outputs by producing desired result for the entire data. Authors have used data sets up to 1TB, executed the proposed algorithm using RSP blocks and concluded that only few RSP blocks are required to represent the entire data set. This idea can be termed as cluster computing as 'n' RSP blocks are used in parallel and estimation will be done.

Authors (Leung et al. 2014) also suggested using frequent pattern mining could be a useful solution implemented with the MapReduce tool. Authors have also surveyed big data analytics & tools involved in this process, quantitative processes involved were used to mine required data from the large volume. Few cloud computing techniques are also surveyed by the authors.

1.   Data analytics
2.   Machine learning

A Deep Learning DL approach is proposed by the authors (Kanagasabai et al. 2016; Rohini, P. et al, 2022) to process the big data in the telecommunication sector. The objective is to identify the mobile user's behavior by analyzing the web log data and the authors have stated it applies to other industries too. The use of the internet is rapidly increasing for many years and almost many applications are being used by the end-users e.g. e-commerce, web search engines etc. These tremendous uses of the internet and internet-based applications (ONLINE applications) have increased the traffic over the internet. Authors have noted one can analyze this big data to identify the insights. These insights are nothing but identifying the frequent patterns available in the web log data. Its main purpose is to know the customers, what they are searching, how they are searching, which relevant items they are frequently searching etc. Once these issues get sorted one can focus on the similar or associated patterns.

Authors (Sukhobok et al. 2017) have discussed data cleaning & its importance in effective and efficient retrieval. This paper describes the data anomalies & steps to handle these anomalies. Authors have considered these anomalies for improving the quality of software products. Dealing with the large volume of data requires processing it in the earlier phases as maximum time and effort are required in executing the data cleaning. A large volume of data could be in an unstructured, structured format or in a semi-structured format. Once the user identifies and processes this type of data then can perform the classification, clustering etc. steps suggested in the data mining. In this process, it seems easier to process the structured and semi-structured data. However, it becomes quite difficult to process the unstructured data. This unstructured data may be documents, may be audio & video files etc. Authors (Koehler et al. 217) have discussed data wrangling, and ETL (extraction, transform & load). The authors also focused on a cost-effective way for the execution of this data wrangling process. ETL plays an important role in data wrangling. Nowadays we are dealing with big data where the data is large, its nature is heterogeneous. Big data processing requires time & effort, to reduce the same there is a need to develop a cost-effective model. This cost-effective model deals with the variety and veracity of big data. In this paper, the authors have focused on automating the wrangling process. In this automation, context data, reference data & main data will be considered. In this process, contextual data plays an important role which helps in better data retrieval. Authors (Ajayan et al. 2018; Bharadiya J.P., 2023) have noted, that big data can be processed & required important information can be aggregated to visualize. Once this aggregated information is collected & trained, using the same pattern other emerging patterns could be compared to find abnormal patterns. In this way, authors have suggested one can develop a visualization framework. Authors have also suggested developing uniform architecture to handle the heterogeneous data, avoiding complexity in processing such data. This framework can avoid the data redundancy &

unbalanced data structures. Outlier detection generally processed in batch modes and based on threshold to identify the outlier in the data stream can be detected. A paper (Chen et al. 2020) referred to by the author suggests a distance-based outlier detection method. It is based on a concept, that if the object 'O' doesn't lie within distance then it (object) could be treated as an outlier. The same concept is applicable in distinguishing the features using a threshold. If the feature/s is not satisfying the condition then it could be treated as an outlier and the remaining features processed in the next phases. An important point, in this paper, is drift detection. If we predict the 'n' conditions and if the system fails to behave according to these conditions then new patterns can be observed. These new patterns are different from the regular patterns and are known as drift in output.

3. DIFFERENT APPROACHES OF BIG DATA ANALYSIS

3.1 Prescriptive Analytics

In future to process the large volume advanced tools and techniques are required. Many applications are developed for the businesses, industries and institutes require processing the large volume of data in order to filter, personalize and recommend meaningful relevant data. Therefore, prescriptive analytics suggests what should users do? To achieve this, it is necessary to apply rules, methods, and techniques collecting, process and accurately predicting the desired results. One can say, this process is the combination of '*what', 'when' and 'why*' questionnaires. Hence, it is the anticipatory process finding the answers of these questions. Carefully finding the answers/feedbacks of the 'what', 'when' and 'why' questionnaires help avoiding any future risk. There are many applications based on the prescriptive analytics like healthcare applications, finance, retail industry, hospitality industries and manufacturing etc. Datasets, image data, video & audio data can be given as an input to the applications based on prescriptive analysis. Next step is train and test the data to deploy & take automated decisions in the later step. As an automated decision can be taken by the model eliminating the human intervention & therefore final step could have few 'biases'. As discussed earlier there are many applications where prescriptive analysis is helpful are –

- *Finance – identifying the possible credit risk associated with any account.*
- *Healthcare- taking care of the patients and monitoring their specific parameters to forecast the possible risks.*
- *Manufacturing – perfectly managing the supply & demand curve.*
- *Marketing & Sales – helps analyzing the customer data and deciding the business strategies.*
- *Transportation – prescriptive analysis helps optimizing the delivery routes and reducing the package delivery time.*

3.2 Descriptive Analysis

Descriptive Analysis is a big data analysis technique based on statistical analysis. As its name suggests descriptive analysis finds the desired data. With the help of the descriptive analysis, it is possible to translate the queries into mathematical model. Once successfully applied it is possible to visualize the data used to improve the decision-making process. *Dashboards and results are the output of descriptive analysis* helps taking the better business decisions and understanding the customer base. This approach consists of few steps like collecting the data, preparation of the data, exploring to get better insights, analyzing the data, visualizing the data, representing the dataset with statistical analysis, and final step is prediction. It also allows users understanding different trends and patterns in the given dataset. With the help of descriptive analytics, businesses can process the large volume of data helps retaining the customers, identifying the popular products etc. It also helps personalizing the customer's data, identify their purchasing habits, spending analysis etc. There are few metrics (as a result) generated by descriptive analytics includes the following:

1. *Reports*: It provides the abstract view or one can say initial level indicator in different organizations. Reports are very useful to strengthen different areas of businesses as it can represent the business performance.
2. *Visualizations*: With the help of different visualizations (charts, graphs etc.) effective presentation can be given and communicated to the different stakeholders of the organizations.
3. *Dashboards*: Many recent applications use '*Dashboards*' to keep track of progress in different departments and sections etc. Even it is possible to manage the workload among different persons of the organization.

3.2.1 Learning management system (LMS)

LMS platform an example of descriptive analytics which keeps track student's & teacher's participation, student's attendance, and student's test results etc. Descriptive analytics can provide an overview about overall working of the LMS. Teachers can monitor student's attendance, test results, can examine grade distributions. LMS also helps them designing the curriculum of subjects undertaken. Therefore, LMS could be a perfect example of descriptive analysis to report, visualize and prepare the dashboard of required data. Advantages of LMS are as follows-

- *Customized experience*
- *Continuous learning experience*
- *User can track progress & learning experience*
- *Unlimited access anywhere*
- *Reduced cost*
- *Saves time*

3.3 Quantitative Data Analysis

As its name indicates, it involves numerical variables like statistics, calculations, measurements etc. The nature of quantitative data is typically numerical & processes it with the algorithms, mathematical analysis tools to process the input data and uncover in depth insights which helps increasing the business values.

E.g. A financial data analyst can use one or more variables to track their employee's performance. Data analyst can use quantitative data to project the possible future growth of business. With the help of existing data analyst can do feasibility study before launching any specific product. Study of quantitative data helps in many areas like assessing ratings given by the customers, assessing the qualities of company's products, evaluating the staff performance, predicting the future growth of business etc.

3.4 Qualitative Data Analysis

Qualitative data focuses on 'qualities' which are typically non-numerical values. Hence, qualitative data analysis focuses on *specific unique identifiers of the products or services* like labels and properties. Reviews and feedbacks play important roles in both the approaches i.e. qualitative and quantitative analysis. Customers, users and different stakeholders give their opinions about specific products or services which must be noted and processed by the organizations.

E.g. Qualitative data analysis techniques are integral part of the software development life cycle (SDLC). Every stage of the SDLC focuses on quality i.e. preparation of good quality software requirement specification document (SRS), generating good quality design phase, detecting errors, bugs etc. Hence, it is expected to maintain the quality at each stage which contributes in the final good quality software product.

4. DIFFERENT BIG DATA ANALYSIS TECHNIQUES

4.1 Association Rule Learning

It suggests processing the large volume of data to find the possible '*associations*' among different variables. E.g. *for a grocery shop identifying the customer segment who purchase the milk & bread in one transaction*. This data analysis technique helps discovering correlations between the different variables. Association rule learning helps businesses knowing the customer segment and their choices. Once successfully implemented this technique could help businesses to grow rapidly. *There are few popular algorithms which are based on association rule mining like F-P growth algorithm, Apriori algorithm and Eclat algorithm etc.* Based on this technique, one can use it to personalize the data, manage the large inventory, managing the customer relations etc.

E.g. Association rule mining can be applied on the grocery shop data where relation could be {milk, bread} ⇒ {butter} it means if a customer buys milk and bread together then customer can also buy butter (it means there are maximum chances that customer could buy butter). Therefore, association rule mining helps processing the large volume of data and extracts co-occurrences of the data. Another best example of this technique is doctor treating patients by studying different symptoms. If the patients have different diseases then doctor can study those symptoms with the help of *conditional probabilities*. To process the data minimum threshold and support needs to be applied. Minimum threshold helps filtering the dataset. Only those itemsets will be considered for next step in processing which satisfies the minimum threshold. Confidence decides the strategy defining the 'rules' & selects the 'transactions' from the dataset which satisfies 'X' also satisfies 'Y'. Association rule mining is predicting the occurrence of a specific item based on the occurrences of other items.

Association rule mining is very valuable method to discover different patterns and relationships within data. In programming languages like Python and R, there are several libraries available to implement the association rule mining. These libraries also help visualizing the results & enables association rule mining in multiple contexts so that better insights and understanding the structure of dataset becomes possible. It is suggest selecting an appropriate algorithm and dataset with required parameters. Effectiveness of the association rule mining can be evaluated using *minimum support* and *confidence* to obtain meaningful, relevant and accurate results. Apriori algorithm helps discovering *frequent itemsets* by executing a process known as *candidate itemset generation*.

Suppose a grocery store's retail transactions for a month includes the following data:

- *Total number of transactions: 700,000*
- *Transactions containing milk: 8,500 (1.21 percent)*
- *Transactions containing bread: 50,000 (7.14 percent)*
- *Transactions containing both milk and bread: 8,000 (1.14 percent)*

However, if the transactions are more it could have 'n' items & need to process these transactions in multiple steps. This is an *iterative approach* where k-itemsets to explore (k+1) itemsets. This process results in different frequent itemsets found in multiple steps until no more frequent k-itemsets can be found. In this way Apriori algorithm, reduces the search space through multiple steps & improves the efficiency at each level. In this analysis, support is nothing but finding the item's popularity by comparing it with the total transactions. E.g. one wish to find the support for an item 'x' among the total transactions 'n' then support can be defined as –

Support = (transactions of the item 'x') / (total transactions 'n')

Similar to the support, association rule mining 'confidence' needs to be calculated for the 02 or more items. E.g. it is nothing but for a grocery shop finding the customers purchasing item 'x' and item 'y' collectively. It means getting the 'confidence' for likelihood i.e. finding the transactions which consists of both the items 'x' & 'y'. Confidence can be defined as follows –

Confidence (xy) = (Transactions with both (x and y))/ (Transactions containing x)

4.2 Regression Analysis

It is a statistical technique measuring the tentative relationship between variables like dependent and independent variables. This technique is mainly use in prediction, forecasting and finding the possible trend in data. Figure 1 illustrates the line fit plot for the sales compare to advertisements. Table 1 contains the sample data illustrating the advertisement impact on the sales of the organization. Table 2 gives regression analysis of the data shown in table 1. In table 2, multiple R & R-square helps user understanding the relationship between different variables.

Table 1. Regression analysis

advertisement	sales
90	1000
120	1300
150	1800
100	1200
130	1380
200	1900

Table 2. Summary output of regression analysis

Regression Statistics	
Multiple R	0.995557
R Square	0.991134
Adjusted R Square	0.791134

Figure 1. Line fit plot

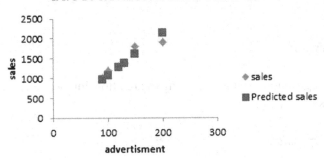

Figure 2. Residual plot

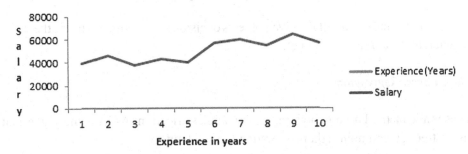

Figure 2, shows the residual plot for the table 1 data. As mentioned earlier, regression analysis technique mainly used in prediction forecast and analyze trend of the continuous variables. Applications such as weather forecast, predicting the possible sales, and processing the customer data to know the market trend can use regression analysis technique. Given data may contain dependent, independent variables and regression technique helps getting the relationship between these variables. One can easily identify how variables interact with each other.

There are different types of regression

- *Linear Regression*

It is used to predict the value by processing different variables. Value to be predicted of the variable is known as 'dependent' variable.

- *Logistic Regression*

It estimates the occurrence of the variable and predicts the value of dependent variable using independent variable.

- *Polynomial Regression*

It is a form of linear regression technique finding the relationship between independent & dependent variable by modeling as n^{th} polynomial.

- *Support Vector Regression*

It helps finding the optimum 'hyperplane' by processing the given dataset. It is capable enough to process the large volume of data & separates different hyperplane and predicts the target feature value.

- *Decision Tree Regression*

By observing different features of the given objects decision tree regression trains the model to predict the data to generate the continuous output.

- *Random Forest Regression*

It is an ensemble method used in both regression & classification. As its name suggests it forms different decision trees and combines them to predict the final output.

- *Ridge Regression*

With the availability of 'n' variables model could be over fitted. To reduce the overfitting proposed model considers all the variables from the given dataset. It is a special method which analyzes multiple regression data where 'Multicollinearity' occurs.

- *Lasso Regression*

It is known as 'Least Absolute Shrinkage Selector Operator' and helps reducing the complexity of the model. It is also known as L1 regularization technique. Lasso regression is good for those models which have high level of Multicollinearity and accurately predicts the desired value for the dependent variable.

Table 3. Linear regression

Experience(Years)	Salary
1.1	39300
1.3	46200
1.5	37700
2	43500
2.2	39890
2.9	56640
3	60150
3.2	54445
3.2	64445
3.7	57189
3.9	63218
4	55794
4	56957
4.1	57081
4.5	61111
4.9	67938
5.1	66029
5.3	83088
5.9	81363
6	93940
6.8	91738
7.1	98273
7.9	101302
8.2	113812
8.7	109431
9	105582
9.5	116969
9.6	112635
10.3	122391
10.5	121872

Example of Simple linear regression

Table 3 consists of sample data with 02 variables i.e. experience & salary of the employees. This data will be used to calculate the simple linear regression. Simple linear regression divides the data into 'training' and 'testing' sets and processes it as shown in the figure 3 & figure 4.

Figure 3. Training set (linear regression)

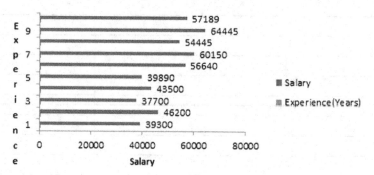

Figure 4. Test set (linear regression)

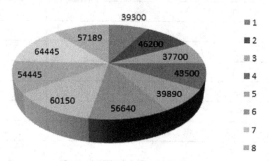

4.3 Sentiment Analysis

Sentiment analysis is the key concept in recent machine learning applications. It became necessary for the industries to know the interest of customers i.e. customer segmentation, sentiments can also be used in staff retention and hospitality industries etc. Growth of the businesses are totally depends on the customer's feedback which plays a vital role. Machine learning is the new trend to be applied on the big data (large volume) and extracting the different patterns is the crucial and important step. In this process natural language processing (NLP) plays an important role to process the reviews/feedbacks and emotions etc. It is expected that to process the large volume of data systems (machines) must be capable enough to process and extract the meaningful, relevant words to be used for prediction. One can apply classification methods such as naïve bayes to classify the given data used for prediction (segmentation). Systems can help the users to extract the polarity of words/sentences by categorizing in different classes like –

a.   Positive
b.   Very positive
c.   Neutral / can't say
d.   Negative

Even it is also possible to apply the scale like 10 – best and 01- worst (scaling). This type of rating can be very useful in retrieving the feedback from customers for a particular service. E.g. Banking – how was an overall experience in net banking portal? Giving feedback for the ATM service provided by the bank, etc.

4.3.1 Challenges in Sentiment Analysis

There are some challenges in the sentiment analysis listed below-

- **Tone** - it is hard to identify the tone of the sentences and therefore more sophisticated tools are required to identify the correct meaning. e.g. Mobile is really good but costs a lot. One can interpret that mobile is good but the cost of mobile makes it unaffordable to the customer.
- **Polarity**- if the customer gives rating such as "Good", "Bad" or "Average" it is known as feedback with different polarities. Therefore, it is expected that big data processing applications must carefully process the large volume of data in order to avoid any discrepancy.
- **Comparison** – if the customer gives feedback such as *"product A is good than B"* then system should carefully compare these two products. It is expected system should differentiate these products based on specific parameters.
- **Handling sentiment analysis in multilingual environment** – a statement/word used in expressing interest or feedback can lost the whole meaning if translated in other language. In such cases in-depth training must be given to the model and rigorous testing of all the variables are required.
- **Audio/visual feedback**- model must be capable enough to handle the audio / visual data by interpreting the correct meaning.

Part of speech (POS) tagging is the example of sentiment analysis to identify the given documents for verbs, nouns, adverbs and adjectives. Low-level tokenization, syntax analysis can be a part of sentiment analysis process.

Example of sentiment analysis -

positive_vocab = ['excellent', 'good', 'enjoyed', 'nice', 'outstanding', 'awwsome', 'very good', 'great'] .... (1)

negative_vocab = ['bad','poor','disappointed'] .... (2)

neutral_vocab = ['average', 'reasonable'] .... (3)

Sentence = "movie is good. However the action scenes are average and music is average"

Positive: 0.6923076923076923

Negative: 0.0

Neutral: 0.3076923076923077

4.4 Factor Analysis

Datasets may have 'n dimensions and data analytics techniques can be known as *factor analysis* in order to reduce the dimensions for better prediction. Factor analysis helps analyzing the variations among connected variables based on known factors. Idea of applying facto analysis is to know the tentative relationship between a set of variables. Once successfully applied next step in this technique is grouping and classifying the processed variables. Factor analysis helps dividing the large volumes into smaller, easier-to-understand sets. With the help of factor analysis new independent variables or patterns can be retrieved and finds the relationship between other dependent variables. It is a kind of statistical analysis method can be used in analyzing the big data. As its name suggests goal is to reduce the variables and parameters for analysis purpose. One can say it is filtering and processing the required values for analysis purpose. It is also suggested to differentiate the values in terms of unobserved and observed variables. It states that processing the observed values can give unobserved values (factors) in the analysis stage. These unobserved (retrieved) values can be used to interpret & reduce the number of variables. Reducing the variables can helps in better visibility of patterns in the dataset.

E.g. Marketing professionals can use many variables and selects required variables which are most important like for any product 'price' plays very important role which is most attractive to any customers and every organization always thinks about this 'price' factor before launching any product.

4.5 Cluster Analysis

It is necessary to know the structure of the variables available in the datasets. A method to explore this structure i.e. grouping of variables based on some similarity is known as cluster analysis as shown in the figure 5. If there are multiple datasets then grouping of variables from intra as well as inter datasets becomes an essential task. Therefore, sorting needs to be applied to classify and group the variables from different datasets. Cluster analysis helps identifying distinct variables and data points from one

Figure 5. Clustering

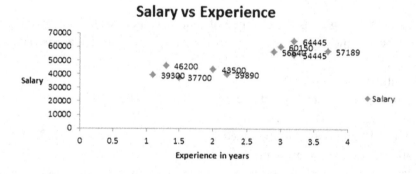

Table 4. Time series analysis

Timestamp	Price of the stock
2023-09-08 09:15:00 AM	100
2023-09-08 09:25:00 AM	101
2023-09-08 09:40:00 AM	99
2023-09-08 10:15:00 AM	100.5
2023-09-08 10:30:00 AM	101
2023-09-08 11:00:00 AM	102

Figure 6. Time series analysis

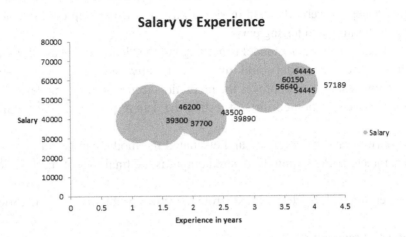

cluster and compares it with other clusters. It also involves 'labeling' and 'grouping' of the variables which helps in categorization.

4.6 Time Series Analysis

As its name indicates it analyzes the data over time as shown in the table 4. Data of a specific time period can be processed & analyzed to get the different patterns. Actually it is a large volume time series data & objective to process this data is to derive meaningful data, different possible patterns. Processing of the time series data involves modeling and presenting the dependent series of data if any. Table 4 illustrates the example of time series data for the stock market with timestamp & price of the stock & helps identifying different trends for the stock in terms of price, volume and lower & upper circuits.

Other examples of time series data are rainfall data, census data, temperature data, stock market data etc. Following figure 6 shows how temperature raised over the years.

4.7 Other Machine Learning Methods for Big Data Analysis

Machine Learning (ML) has very popular methods and techniques used in many areas listed below. ML helps in automated data processing and decision-making processes. ML methods and techniques improve themselves (self-learning) based on past experience. This approach improves from past experiences without being explicitly programmed.

4.7.1 Important Steps in Big Data Analysis

- *Data Collection*: integration of data from different sources is the initial step of the machine learning applications. Relevant, reliable data can be collected from different sources which can impact the outcome of machine learning model. It is also possible to select the required data from the integrated dataset and train the proposed data model.
- *Data Preparation*: this step prepares the data for further processing i.e. applying filters, cleansing the data and processing the same are the few basic steps in data analysis. Data cleaning step

ensues the erroneous data, abnormal data is removed and data is ready to use in next steps. Data standardization step converts the data in single format. Further step of data analysis divides the dataset into the training and testing parts.

- *Training the Model*: training the model is nothing but the "learning" phase. It predicts the desired output value. If necessary model could involve 'n' iterative steps and trained data can be used to test the remaining test data & improves the prediction accuracy of the model.
- *Model Evaluation*: evaluation consists of testing the data & predicting the accuracy of proposed model.
- *Prediction*: once the model is trained and evaluated the model can be further improved by fine-tuning the parameters. Predicting the desired output is the final step of machine learning.

As data size is increasing, ML has to play a key role in critical problem solving in different areas like:

- *Facial expression recognition*
- *Speech Recognition*
- *Healthcare industry*
- *Finance and Banking industry*
- *Natural Language Processing (NLP)*
- *Biological applications*
- *Automated vehicles*
- *Marketing*

ML has effective methods, techniques, and automated tools which integrate data from different sources, analyze it and provide the desired results. It is also possible to store the data on cloud and make it available to the users and when required. ML can process large volume of data with the application of classification, regression, clustering, ensemble modeling, dimensionality reduction, reinforcement learning etc.

4.7.2 Classification

Important class of supervised machine learning is *classification* which predicts a class value. E.g. Classification helps predict whether or not the customers will buy a product? E.g. a classification method helps assessing whether a given image contains a bicycle or a car. In this case after successful application of classification the output will have 03 different values: 1) the image contains a bicycle 2) the image contains a car and 3) the image may contain neither both the vehicles.

Types of ML Classification Algorithms

Classification Algorithms can be further divided into the mainly two categories:

- **Linear Models**
- Logistic Regression
- Support Vector Machine (SVM)
- **Non-linear Models**
- K-Nearest Neighbor
- Naïve Bayes classification

Figure 7. Formation of clusters

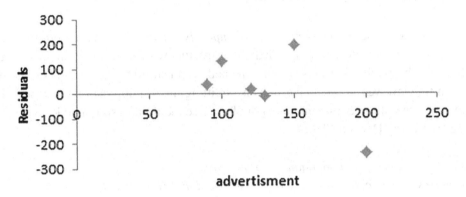

- Decision Tree Classification
- Random Forest Classification

Classification algorithms can be used in different applications as listed below:

- Speech Recognition
- Detecting the spam emails
- Identifications of Cancer tumor cells.
- Biometric Identification in different industries etc.

4.7.3 Clustering

It is the task of dividing the given data points into a number of 'n' groups based on some similarity as shown in the figure 7. The groups will be formed based on similarity and data points which are not similar into other groups. Clustering is important to form the intrinsic groups among the unlabeled data points. Predetermined criteria can be defined to form different clusters. Following figure elaborates the cluster formation process.

Applications of Clustering in different fields:

1. **Marketing**: marketing professionals can divide customers based on area, spending capacities etc. which could be very useful in marketing.
2. **Biology**: with the help of clustering it became possible to classify different plants and animals.
3. **Libraries**: clustering helps grouping different books, novels and magazines on the basis of branches, topics and relevant information.
4. **Finance, Banking and Insurance**: customer segmentation is possible with the help of clustering and defining policies accordingly.
5. **Image Processing**: grouping similar images, classifying given input images based on relevant contents is possible with the help of clustering.

6.   **Customer Service**: very important in every business to integrate different customers based on their similar inquiries, complaints, and other common issues.

4.7.4 Decision Tree in Machine Learning

A decision tree is one of the powerful methods of *supervised learning* used in both the *classification and regression* tasks. Tree represents a flowchart-like structure where each internal node indicates a test on an attribute. Each branch represents an outcome and each leaf node (terminal node) holds the class label. Decision tree involves 'n' recursive steps by splitting the training data into subsets. These steps have certain stopping criteria & maximum depth of the tree required to split a node.

Advantages of Using Decision Trees

*   *Decision trees are easy to understand and interpret.*
*   *Decision tress can effectively handle both numerical and categorical data.*
*   *Decision trees can determine all the possible expected values for different scenarios.*
*   *Decision trees involve data preparation and data normalization.*

4.7.5 Long Short Term Memory (LSTM)

LSTM – Long Short Term Memory a deep learning method used in many applications. It helps increasing the prediction accuracies in the proposed model. With the help of *LSTM* it is possible to process the complex data & consists of a *"memory unit"* to store information for long period of time. Memory units helps model to learn further dependencies. *LSTM* based models can be used in *forecasting* & can deliver results with better accuracy. It consists of 03 gates namely *forget gate, Input & output gate.* *Sigmoid layer* available in the LSTM helps binding the input & output. With this approach a **BiLSTM** can be developed to train the sequences (input) is given in both the direction i.e. backward & forward directions. *BiLSTM uses 02 LSTMs to train the input data i.e. first LSTM processes the input & second*

Table 5. Sample data

Experience(Years)	Salary
1.1	39300
1.3	46200
1.5	37700
2	43500
2.2	39890
2.9	56640
3	60150
3.2	54445
3.2	64445
3.7	57189

works on the reverse of the input data. Benefit of the second LSTM brings the additional context to the processing, increases speed & accuracy of the proposed model.

4.8 Data Visualization Techniques

- Box plots
- Histograms
- Heat maps
- Charts
- Tree map
- Network diagram

To illustrate different visualization methods sample data is used as shown in the table 5.

4.8.1 Box Plots

A box plot is a graph which indicates how the values in the data are spread out. Box plots may seem primitive in comparison to a histogram or density plot. These plots are useful in comparing the distributions between many datasets as shown in the figure 8.

Population size: 20
Median: 18851.85
Minimum: 1.1
Maximum: 64445
First quartile: 2.375
Third quartile: 52383.75
Interquartile Range: 52381.375
Outliers: none

Figure 8. Box plot

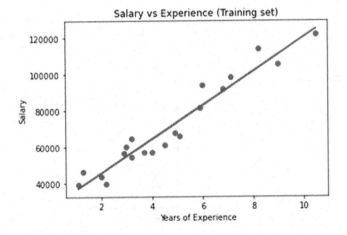

Figure 9. Histogram

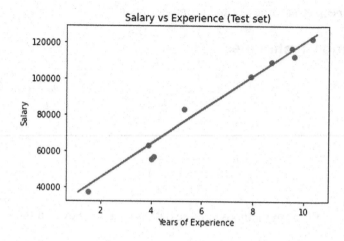

4.8.2 Histogram

As shown in below figure 9, a histogram displays data using bars of different heights. In a histogram, each bar groups numbers into different ranges. Taller bars represents more data falls in the specified range. A histogram exhibits the shape and spread of continuous sample data.

4.8.3 Heat Map

A heat map represents a visual way to integrate and make decisions from different data values. It is a graphical representation of data where the individual values contained in a matrix are represented as different colors.

4.8.4 Line Chart

A line plot can be used to plot the relationships between variables. To plot the relationship between the two variables, one can call the plot function and draw the line chart as shown in the below figure 10.

Figure 10. Line chart example

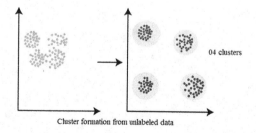

Figure 11. Bar chart example

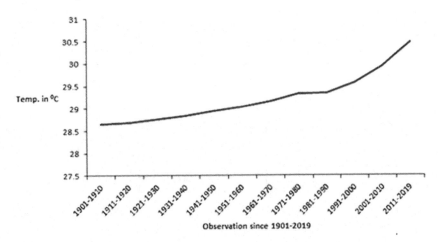

4.8.5 Bar Charts

Bar charts are simple and can be used to compare the quantities of different categories. Values of a categories are represented with the help of bars as shown in the below figure 11 and can be configured with vertical or horizontal bars.

4.8.6 Pie Chart

As shown in the below figure 12, it represents different slices to illustrate numerical proportion. The *arc* length of every slide is proportional to the quantity it represents. Pie charts are used to compare the parts of a whole and most effective when there are limited components.

However, in few cases it can be difficult to interpret because the human eye has a hard time estimating areas and comparing visual angles as shown in above figure 12.

Figure 12. Pie chart

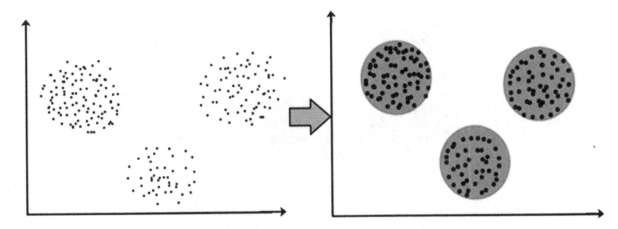

Figure 13. Scatter chart

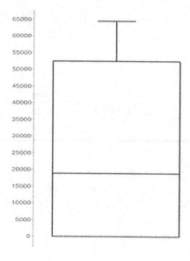

4.8.7 Scatter Charts

A scatter plot is a 2-D plot representing the joint variation of two data items as shown in the below figure 13.

When assigned more than two measures to the scatter, a matrix is produced that is a series of scatter plot displaying every possible pairing. Scatter plots are used to examine the relationship between X and Y variables.

4.8.8 Bubble Charts

It is a variation of scatter chart in which data points are replaced with bubbles, and an additional dimension of data is represented in the size of the bubbles as shown in the figure 14.

Figure 14. Bubble chart

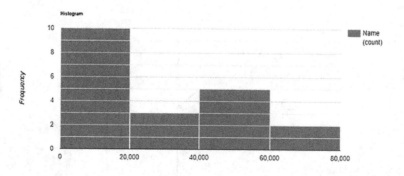

4.8.9 Timeline Charts

Timeline charts as its name indicates events, tasks etc. in the chronological order. E.g. progress of the project, any acquisition process etc. It considers the time periods in terms of weeks, months, years, and quarters.

4.8.10 Tree Map

A tree map a visualization which displays hierarchically organized data. Tree map consists of rectangles, parent elements and child elements. The sizes and colors of rectangles are proportional to the values of the data points. A *leaf node* rectangle has an area proportional to the specific dimension of the data. Depending on the choice, the leaf node is colored, sized or both according to chosen attributes. They make efficient use of space, thus display thousands of items on the screen simultaneously for the better visualization.

CONCLUSION

Chapter explains different approaches of big data analysis. There are different techniques & methods which can be used to analyze the large volume of data. Recent technologies like artificial intelligence (AI), machine learning (ML) and deep learning it is possible to develop big-data driven applications. Big data analysis techniques can process heterogeneous data i.e. structured, unstructured and semi-structured data. In future big data analysis existing techniques and methods must process the large volume of data. 'Big data' would be the next primary requirement for many businesses, institutes, and organizations. Hence, to analyze the big data a team of experts and data analyst will be high in demand and therefore more technical as well as non-technical persons must be trained accordingly.

REFERENCES

Attaallah, A., Alsuhabi, H., Shukla, S., Kumar, R., Gupta, B. K., & Khan, R. A. (2022). Analyzing the Big Data Security through a Unified Decision-Making Approach. *Intelligent Automation & Soft Computing, 32*(2), 1071–1088. doi:10.32604/iasc.2022.022569

Benatia, M. A., Baudry, D., & Louis, A. (2022). Detecting counterfeit products by means of frequent pattern mining. *Journal of Ambient Intelligence and Humanized Computing, 13*(7), 3683–3692. doi:10.100712652-020-02237-y

Berisha, B., Mëziu, E., & Shabani, I. (2022). Big data analytics in Cloud computing: An overview. *Journal of Cloud Computing (Heidelberg, Germany), 11*(1), 24. doi:10.118613677-022-00301-w PMID:35966392

Bharadiya, J. P. (2023). A Comparative Study of Business Intelligence and Artificial Intelligence with Big Data Analytics. *American Journal of Artificial Intelligence, 7*(1), 24.

Chen, R. C., Dewi, C., Huang, S. W., & Caraka, R. E. (2020). Selecting critical features for data classification based on machine learning methods. *Journal of Big Data, 7*(1), 52. doi:10.118640537-020-00327-4

Cheng, H., Rong, C., Hwang, K., Wang, W., & Li, Y. (2015). Secure big data storage and sharing scheme for cloud tenants. *China Communications*, *12*(6), 106–115. doi:10.1109/CC.2015.7122469

Fournier-Viger, P., Gan, W., Wu, Y., Nouioua, M., Song, W., Truong, T., & Duong, H. (2022, April). Pattern mining: Current challenges and opportunities. In *International Conference on Database Systems for Advanced Applications* (pp. 34-49). Cham: Springer International Publishing.

Hababeh, I., Gharaibeh, A., Nofal, S., & Khalil, I. (2018). An integrated methodology for big data classification and security for improving cloud systems data mobility. *IEEE Access : Practical Innovations, Open Solutions*, *7*, 9153–9163. doi:10.1109/ACCESS.2018.2890099

Khurana, A. (2014). Bringing big data systems to the cloud. *IEEE Cloud Computing*, *1*(3), 72–75. doi:10.1109/MCC.2014.47

Leung, C. K. S., & Jiang, F. (2014, December). A data science solution for mining interesting patterns from uncertain big data. In *2014 IEEE Fourth International Conference on Big Data and Cloud Computing* (pp. 235-242). IEEE.

Rohini, P., Tripathi, S., Preeti, C. M., Renuka, A., Gonzales, J. L. A., & Gangodkar, D. (2022, April). A study on the adoption of Wireless Communication in Big Data Analytics Using Neural Networks and Deep Learning. In *2022 2nd International Conference on Advance Computing and Innovative Technologies in Engineering (ICACITE)* (pp. 1071-1076). IEEE. 10.1109/ICACITE53722.2022.9823439

Salloum, S., Huang, J. Z., & He, Y. (2019). Random sample partition: A distributed data model for big data analysis. *IEEE Transactions on Industrial Informatics*, *15*(11), 5846–5854. doi:10.1109/TII.2019.2912723

Sukhobok, D., Nikolov, N., & Roman, D. (2017, August). Tabular data anomaly patterns. In *2017 International Conference on Big Data Innovations and Applications (Innovate-Data)* (pp. 25-34). IEEE. 10.1109/Innovate-Data.2017.10

Wang, X., Yang, L. T., Liu, H., & Deen, M. J. (2017). A big data-as-a-service framework: State-of-the-art and perspectives. *IEEE Transactions on Big Data*, *4*(3), 325–340. doi:10.1109/TBDATA.2017.2757942

Wu, D., Zhu, L., Lu, Q., & Sakr, S. (2017). HDM: A composable framework for big data processing. *IEEE Transactions on Big Data*, *4*(2), 150–163. doi:10.1109/TBDATA.2017.2690906

KEY TERMS AND DEFINITIONS

Access Control List (ACL): Nothing but a list of privileges assigned to different users.

Clustering: Clustering is grouping the objects based on similarity.

Deep Learning: A subset of machine learning used for performing complex tasks.

Natural Language Processing (NLP): As its name suggest, it interprets, breaks and analyzes the human languages.

Parts of Speech: Processing a sentences based on nouns, verbs, adverbs, etc.

Random Sample Partition (RSP) Blocks: Random sample partition data blocks used in sampling.

Real Time Data: Data which is available to process as soon as it is generated.

SDLC: Software development life cycle – consists of steps must be followed for the development of a good software product.

Chapter 10
Suggesting New Techniques and Methods for Big Data Analysis:
Privacy–Preserving Data Analysis Techniques

Puneet Gangrade

https://orcid.org/0009-0008-1149-7282

Fordham University, USA

ABSTRACT

New privacy rules and responsible data use are pushing companies to find clever ways to learn from data without exposing personal details. This chapter explains different techniques that protect privacy while still gaining insights. They provide strong privacy guarantees so organizations can use and share data safely. Real-world examples show how companies in marketing, healthcare, banking, and other industries apply these techniques to drive business value through secure collaboration and accelerated innovation. Recommendations help teams choose and test the right privacy tools for their needs. With the proper privacy toolbox, market intelligence can thrive in an era of ethical data analysis. Organizations that embrace privacy-first practices will gain a competitive advantage and consumer trust. This chapter equips teams to adopt modern privacy-preserving approaches to tap hidden insights in data while respecting user confidentiality.

INTRODUCTION

The digital age has ushered in an unprecedented era of data generation and collection, offering a treasure trove of insights for organizations across sectors. According to IDC, the global datasphere is expected to grow to 175 zettabytes by 2025 (Reinsel, 2018). While this abundance of data presents immense opportunities for market intelligence, it also poses significant challenges in safeguarding sensitive in-

DOI: 10.4018/979-8-3693-0413-6.ch010

formation. The stakes are high; mishandling data can lead to severe financial penalties and irreparable damage to the brand's reputation.

In this complex landscape, privacy-preserving data analytics has emerged as a cornerstone for responsible data utilization. It is no longer a matter of choice but a business imperative driven by regulatory pressures, technological advancements, and evolving consumer expectations. According to a Gartner report, by 2023, 65% of the world's population will have its personal information covered under modern privacy regulations, up from 10% today (Gartner, 2020)

Privacy-preserving data analytics techniques serve as the linchpin that allows organizations to unlock the value of data without compromising privacy. These techniques transform raw data into a format that retains its analytical utility but obscures individual identifiers. This dual capability enables multi-party data analytics, where insights can be derived from combined datasets without exposing each party's sensitive information. A seminal paper by Cynthia Dwork introduced the concept of differential privacy in 2006, marking a significant milestone in the field (Dwork Cynthia, 2006).

The journey of privacy-preserving analytics has been transformative. What began as cryptographic protocols in academic circles in the late 1990s has evolved into mature technologies like differential privacy, federated learning, and secure multi-party computation. These technologies have practical applications across industries, from healthcare and finance to marketing and supply chain management. With the right strategies and tools, organizations can comply with stringent privacy regulations, gain a competitive edge, foster partnerships, and build consumer trust.

LITERATURE REVIEW

The interplay among computerized databases, big data analytics, and privacy has been an evolving area of research and discussion over the past few decades. The U.S. Privacy Act of 1974 was enacted in an era where the growth of computerized databases raised significant concerns about personal data privacy (DOJ, 2020). This period saw the rapid expansion of government databases, leading to fears about the potential misuse of personal information. The Act was influenced by earlier studies and reports, such as the Secretary's Advisory Committee on Automated Personal Data Systems (1973) report, highlighting the risks of automated data systems to personal privacy (U.S. Department of Health & Human Services, n.d.). The Act restricted the disclosure of personal data by federal agencies, requiring consent from individuals for most disclosures. The Privacy Act of 1974 contributed to a societal and academic environment and played a significant role in raising awareness about the importance of data privacy, both among the public and within the academic and technical communities. The Act's heightened awareness likely influenced the direction of research in fields related to data privacy, including cryptography. One of the seminal works is the paper "Cryptographic Approaches to Privacy" by Yao in 1982, which proposed protocols for secure computation between two parties without revealing their inputs (Yao, A. C, 1982). This laid the foundations for secure multi-party computation, a core privacy-preserving technique. The U.S. Privacy Act and Yao's research represent parallel developments in addressing privacy concerns - one through policy and regulation, the other through technological innovation. In the late 1990s and early 2000s, key research emerged on privacy-preserving data mining and statistical databases. Agrawal and Srikant proposed data perturbation techniques like additive noise for privacy in data mining (Rakesh Agrawal & Ramakrishnan Srikant, 2000). These works highlighted the privacy risks in data mining and the need for privacy-enhancing solutions. The concept of differential privacy, which today is one of the most influential privacy frameworks, was introduced in a 2006 paper by Dwork (Dwork Cynthia, 2006). It provides strong mathematical guarantees of individual privacy in statistical databases. Follow-on work expanded differential privacy for various applications like analysis of social networks and genomic data. Also, in 2009, Craig Gentry developed the first fully Homomorphic Encryption scheme that could perform unlimited numbers of addition and multiplication operations on encrypted data (Gentry, 2009).

Federated learning was proposed in 2016 by Google researchers to enable collaborative machine learning without centralizing data (McMahan, B., 2017). This protects user privacy while benefitting from global data. Further research has enhanced the efficiency, robustness, and privacy of federated learning. In parallel, cryptography research advanced privacy-enhancing cryptographic protocols. Yao et al. proposed garbled circuits for secure two-party computation (Yao, A. C, 1986). New tools like homomorphic encryption, mixnets, and zero-knowledge proofs emerged, laying the technical foundations for privacy-preserving analytics.

Rapid advancements in digital technology have enforced the implementation of The General Data Protection Regulation (GDPR) in 2018 (GDPR Info, n.d.). GDPR kicked in after increased public awareness and concern over data privacy, fueled by high-profile data breaches, thereby driving the demand for stricter data protection laws. GDPR aims to unify varying data protection laws across EU member states and provide a consistent framework. Similarly, the California Consumer Privacy Act (CCPA) was passed in the USA in 2018 to empower consumers with the rights to the personal information businesses collect (Office of the Attorney General of California, n.d.). As regulations like GDPR and CCPA took effect, the adoption of privacy-preserving techniques increased across healthcare, finance, marketing, and human resources (Kupwade Patil, Harsh & Seshadri, Ravi, 2014). This multi-disciplinary evolution shows that privacy protection and data analytics can synergistically co-exist. On the industry side, major technology companies like Google, Apple, and Microsoft have integrated differential privacy and federated learning into their offerings. Open-source libraries like TensorFlow Privacy (TensorFlow (2023, October 7)), PyTorch Privacy (PyTorch. (2023, October 7)) and OpenMined (OpenMined. (2023, October 7)) are accelerating development. Leading conferences like ACM CCS, IEEE S&P, and PETS highlight cutting-edge advancements. Also, the Digital Personal Data Protection Act 2023 received assent in India (International Association of Privacy Professionals, n.d.). This Act will strengthen how personal data is collected and used digitally and offline.

Factors Driving Adoption of Privacy-Preserving Data Analysis Techniques for Market Intelligence

Many regulatory, technological, organizational, and competitive market forces are catalyzing the growing adoption of privacy-enhancing technologies and techniques for extracting insights from data while protecting confidentiality. These key factors are propelling the privacy-preserving data analytics movement. We first examine how new regulations like GDPR and CCPA grant individuals more control over their personal data and restrict how companies can collect, store, process, and share this data. Non-compliance can lead to steep fines, forcing companies to re-evaluate practices.

Next, we explore how advances in cryptographic protocols, algorithms, and machine learning make privacy-preserving analysis commercially viable. Technologies like homomorphic encryption, multi-party computation, and differential privacy have matured from academic research into practical applications. Improvements in efficiency and turnkey offerings are also lowering adoption barriers. Beyond regulatory compliance, privacy preservation also serves critical organizational needs. Keeping data encrypted enables new big data collaborations between companies to combine proprietary data for richer insights securely. It allows utilizing third-party cloud services without exposing raw data. Reducing data exposure also limits liability in case of breaches while enabling tighter control against insider threats.

Finally, market forces like consumer demands for transparency and control over personal data usage, expectations of privacy-conscious business customers, and competitive dynamics are also strong drivers. Proactive adoption of privacy techniques can burnish brand reputation and trust.

Regulatory Drivers

Privacy regulations have evolved due to growing public concern over how personal data is being collected, used, and shared by organizations. A few high-profile data breaches and scandals drew attention to risky practices by companies and underlined the need for more stringent rules and enforcement around individuals' data privacy rights.

Regulators responded with comprehensive new legislations like GDPR and CCPA that require explicit consent, disclosure, and access mechanisms while restricting indiscriminate usage and sharing of personal information. Non-compliance can lead to heavy fines proportionate to company revenues. Sector-specific rules have also tightened to safeguard sensitive data categories like financial, health, and telecom records.

These regulations represent society's push to restore greater control over individuals over their personal data. The evolution also aims to compel organizations to implement strong privacy disciplines by creating significant compliance risk incentives. We will explore specific regulatory developments and requirements in the following sub-sections.

- *New Privacy Laws*

The EU's General Data Protection Regulation (GDPR) went into effect in 2018 and established stringent requirements around companies' collection and processing of EU residents' personal data. GDPR mandates unambiguous consent from users, collecting only data required for specified purposes, allowing users access to their data, and restricting the sharing or transfer of data outside the EU. Importantly, GDPR levies severe financial penalties for non-compliance - up to 4% of a company's global revenue or €20 million, whichever is higher. This created a strong incentive for companies globally to re-examine their data policies and implement privacy safeguards when handling EU citizen data.

California's Consumer Privacy Act (CCPA), which went into effect in 2020, created similar obligations around the personal data of California residents. It requires businesses above a certain size to disclose what categories of personal information they collect, why they need it, how they use it, with whom they share it, and to delete consumer data upon request. CCPA violations can lead to fines of $2,500 per incident and up to $7,500 per intentional violation. The CCPA is widely seen as a precursor to a comprehensive federal privacy law in the US. Its passage sparked a wave of new state-level consumer data privacy laws, such as in Virginia, Colorado, Utah, and Connecticut. Many other countries are also drafting legislation similar to GDPR.

These pioneering regulations established unprecedented guardrails and consumer rights around private data usage, compelling organizations to implement privacy-by-design principles and technologies. Non-compliance risks hefty fines and reputational damage.

- *Enhanced Enforcement*

Alongside establishing new data privacy regulations, authorities have also taken enforcement actions against violations in recent years. Huge fines over high-profile data breaches, improper data handling, and non-compliance with new laws have put companies on notice. For instance, British Airways was fined a record £183 million ($230 million) by the UK's data protection authority in 2019 over a 2018 data breach that compromised the personal and payment information of over 400,000 customers. Marriott International was fined £18.4 million by the UK regulator in 2020 after a breach exposed approximately 339 million guest records (TechCrunch, 2019)

In the US, the Federal Trade Commission and state attorneys general have brought enforcement actions against tech giants like Facebook and Google for privacy violations, mandating reforms. Facebook paid a record $5 billion fine in 2019 to settle FTC charges over Cambridge Analytica data misuse (Reuters, 2019). The specter of fines in the tens or hundreds of millions for privacy failures has compelled companies to re-evaluate their data infrastructure, policies, and practices through the lens of regulatory compliance. Adopting privacy-enhancing technologies is seen as a risk mitigation necessity.

- *Sector-Specific Regulations*

In addition to broad consumer privacy laws, regulations in certain industries restrict how companies can collect, store, share, and analyze specific categories of confidential data. This necessitates privacy techniques. For instance, the healthcare industry must comply with strict protections on patient medical records enshrined in laws like HIPAA in the US and analogous legislation in other countries. These limit the sharing of identifiable health data without consent. Technologies like homomorphic encryption enable healthcare organizations to analyze medical images and genetic data to develop treatment insights while encrypting the underlying patient information.

The financial services sector must comply with regulations like the Gramm–Leach–Bliley Act in the US and EU payment data directives that greatly restrict the sharing of customer transactional data. Secure multi-party computation methods allow banks to collaborate on fraud analytics across their datasets without exposing raw transaction data. Various laws prohibit Telecom companies from sharing customers' call detail records. Using differentially private mechanisms, telecom can share aggregated mobility analytics to aid urban planning while obscuring individual user data. By mandating privacy safeguards tailored to sensitive data types, sector-specific rules nudge organizations towards privacy-preserving analysis techniques that enable extracting insights from regulated data while maintaining confidentiality.

Technology Enablers

While regulatory compliance is a crucial driver for adopting privacy-enhancing data analysis, progress in underlying cryptographic techniques, algorithms, hardware capabilities, and cloud platforms has also been a pivotal enabler. Advances in homomorphic encryption, secure multi-party computation, zero-knowledge proofs, and differential privacy have taken these technologies from theoretical research topics just a decade ago to mature solutions ready for real-world deployment today. Companies like Microsoft, IBM, and Google now offer homomorphic and confidential computing capabilities on their cloud platforms. Startups like Partisia and Sepior provide turnkey, secure multi-party computation solutions tailored to sectors like finance and pharmaceuticals. Leading data science frameworks like TensorFlow integrate differential privacy.

Improvements in efficiency and scalability have encouraged the progress. Computationally intensive cryptographic techniques have become orders of magnitude faster, making them viable for large datasets and complex analytics. More importantly, solutions have become more accessible for data science teams without deep cryptography expertise. Availability as managed services on cloud platforms and integration with popular data science toolkits is commoditizing access to these formerly exotic technologies. As the capability-complexity gap narrows, privacy-preserving analysis evolves from a niche advantage to a broadly available best practice.

For organizations, these developments alleviate the technical hurdles towards adopting privacy-enhancing techniques. Compliance teams see a path to meeting new regulatory obligations around data confidentiality. Data science teams gain new tools to collaborate, innovate, and build trust. Together, these technology enablers are unlocking the next generation of privacy-first analytics.

- *Cryptographic Advances*

Advanced cryptography is making privacy-preserving data analysis more accessible for marketers. Recent developments have made these techniques more straightforward to apply to marketing data.

- Fully homomorphic encryption allows doing analytics on encrypted data without decrypting it first. This is like having a locked box that one can still do calculations without unlocking. Marketers can analyze sensitive customer data without exposing it.
- Secure multi-party computation enables different organizations to jointly analyze data sets without sharing the actual data. It is like securely combining secret ingredients from different parties to bake a cake. It helps marketers collaborate.
- Differential privacy adds controlled noise to data to prevent the identification of individuals. It is like blurring out faces in photos before sharing them publicly. Helps share aggregated marketing metrics privately.
- Trusted execution uses secure hardware to isolate data analysis. It is like having a private computer in a locked vault to analyze sensitive data. It prevents exposure even from internal staff.
- Frameworks simplify integrating these techniques with marketing tools. It is like plug-and-play privacy modules for business intelligence software. It makes adoption easier.
  - *Machine Learning and AI Capabilities*

The rapid advancement of machine learning and artificial intelligence algorithms has made powerful data analysis capabilities available to organizations. However, traditional ML/AI methods generally require centralizing data into large corpora for training models. This raises significant privacy concerns. In response, researchers have developed innovative ways to conduct ML training and statistical analysis while preserving privacy:

Federated learning allows collaborative model development without sharing raw data. Models are trained locally on decentralized datasets; only model updates are shared. This enables collective learning without centralizing sensitive data. Privacy-preserving ML techniques like differential privacy and federated transfer learning can produce aggregate insights from datasets containing personal information without revealing individual-level data. New ML algorithms optimized for encrypted data can unlock insights from sensitive datasets while maintaining end-to-end encryption. Homomorphic encryption enables this by allowing computations on ciphertexts. Trusted execution environments leverage secure hardware to isolate ML model training on sensitive data. This prevents exposure of raw data to third parties.

These methods allow organizations to utilize powerful AI for market intelligence while aligning with privacy best practices and regulations. As ML/AI continues advancing, we can expect further techniques that promote privacy in data analysis.

- *Trusted execution environments (TEEs)*

Trusted execution environments (TEEs) are secure areas within computer chips where sensitive data can be processed in an isolated environment. TEEs act like a "safe bubble" where the rest of the system protects code and data from being accessed. TEEs are enabling more privacy-preserving analytics by creating these secure enclaves for data processing. Organizations can use TEEs to extract insights from sensitive data while protecting it.

For example, banks use TEEs for secure multi-party computation to detect fraud across institutions without exposing customer transaction data. The analysis happens within the secure TEEs, so banks get insights into fraud without sharing raw data. Healthcare organizations also leverage TEEs to run analytics on patient records while maintaining privacy. One hospital used TEEs to train AI models to provide personalized care without accessing identifiable patient data. Retailers are looking at using TEEs to safely pool sales data from franchises and gain market insights while preventing leaks of proprietary data. TEEs allow running analytics code on decentralized data sources without transferring raw data. As data analytics becomes more integral, TEEs will see increased adoption to address privacy concerns. Their ability to isolate sensitive data allows organizations to extract insights while maintaining confidentiality. TEEs also provide security against emerging threats like quantum computing.

- *Cloud Computing Platforms*

Cloud computing platforms enable more organizations to adopt privacy-preserving data analytics techniques for market intelligence. The scalability and flexibility of cloud platforms allow companies to efficiently implement solutions like differential privacy, secure multi-party computation, and federated learning. For example, retailers like Walmart and Amazon use differential privacy techniques on cloud platforms to analyze customer purchase data without compromising individual privacy. The large computing resources available via the cloud make it feasible to add carefully calibrated noise to mask individual data points. Banks are also turning to secure multi-party computation on cloud platforms to jointly analyze financial transaction datasets from multiple institutions without exposing sensitive data. The cloud facilitates securely outsourcing computation to untrusted third parties. In the healthcare sector, federated learning on cloud platforms enables different hospitals to collaboratively train AI models on patient data without sharing the raw data. This improves model accuracy while maintaining patient privacy.

Overall, the scalability, accessibility, and cost-effectiveness of cloud computing are encouraging the adoption of privacy-enhancing techniques for extracting insights from data while protecting sensitive information. However, proper access controls, encryption, and security measures are essential to safeguard privacy in the cloud.

- *New tools and solutions from vendors*

A range of technology vendors globally are providing packaged solutions to enable the adoption of privacy-enhancing techniques for data analytics across industries. In the adtech and media intelligence space, major players like Google, Amazon, and Meta offer products like data clean rooms and secure multi-party computation services. Specialist vendors like LiveRamp, InfoSum, Habu, and Eyeota provide data collaboration solutions using cryptographic methods. In the healthcare sector, vendors like HiFi, Cosmian, and Anonos provide tools for analytics on encrypted data or secure multi-party computation among hospitals and research institutes to enable collaborative insights while preserving patient privacy. Financial services institutions are leveraging analytic solutions from vendors like Privitar, Secure Multi-Party Computation (MPC) technologies from Unbound Tech, and hardware-based secure enclave offerings from the cloud service providers. Banks and insurance companies can extract insights from consumer data without compromising privacy.

Organizational Needs

While regulations and new technologies are accelerating the development of privacy-preserving analytics, organizations are demanding these capabilities for various business needs. Companies want to derive insights from data while maintaining confidentiality and limiting liability. Specifically, organizations across sectors have four fundamental needs driving adoption:

First, companies want to collaborate on proprietary datasets without exposing sensitive information. For example, two banks may want to jointly analyze customer credit patterns without sharing raw data. Privacy-preserving techniques like differential privacy and secure multi-party computation enable this controlled data sharing.

Second, organizations must utilize third-party analytics services without handing over raw data. For instance, a hospital can get insights from a cloud provider using homomorphic encryption to analyze encrypted patient data. The cloud provider never sees the unencrypted data.

Third, limiting data exposure reduces risk and liability for organizations. Retailers can analyze shopping patterns without collecting personal data that could be exposed in a breach. Privacy-preserving approaches like anonymization and synthetic data generation can analyze patterns while protecting individual identities.

Finally, companies want to selectively share data with partners to enable collaboration while preventing misuse. Through access controls and query-based analysis, organizations can provide controlled external data access rather than full extracts. Partners can get results from queries without direct access to the underlying data.

- *Enable Collaboration on Proprietary Data*

Organizations have several key needs that drive them to collaborate on proprietary data in a privacy-preserving manner:

- Access a more comprehensive dataset to improve analytics and insights. For example, banks can gain more predictive signals by combining transaction data from multiple institutions while maintaining customer privacy.

- Share costs and risks of data acquisition and management. Automakers can jointly build datasets for training autonomous vehicle systems, spreading the overhead needed for large-scale data collection.
- Gain insights not visible in own data. Pharma companies can detect potential drug interactions and side effects by analyzing adverse event data across multiple organizations.
- Leverage shared benchmarks and standards. Tech firms can establish AI testing benchmarks by collaborating on proprietary metric data in a privacy-safe way.
- Attain the scale needed for initiatives enabled by shared data. Retailers can effectively combine supply chain datasets to achieve the required volume to train demand forecasting algorithms.
- Maintain privacy and IP protection. Manufacturers can jointly analyze proprietary production data to optimize processes while keeping sensitive data anonymous.

- *Utilize Third-Party Services Securely*

Organizations increasingly seek to leverage public cloud platforms' convenience, scalability, AI capabilities, and third-party analytics services for their data analytics needs. However, sharing proprietary data with external parties raises significant privacy concerns. Privacy-preserving techniques allow organizations to benefit from third-party services while maintaining data confidentiality.

For example, a retail company can securely upload sales data to a cloud analytics platform to gain insights into purchasing patterns without exposing sensitive customer information. The data is encrypted before sharing so that even the cloud provider cannot view the raw data. Similarly, a healthcare provider can utilize a third-party AI model to analyze medical images to detect anomalies while keeping patient data private. The images are transformed into an encrypted format that retains the essential features needed for analysis but hides patient-identifiable details. In the financial services sector, banks can detect fraud by running analytics on transaction datasets pooled from multiple institutions. Cryptographic methods allow searching for fraud patterns across institutions without revealing each bank's raw transaction data.

Market Forces

In addition to regulatory, technology, and organizational factors, market forces are equally crucial in propelling demand for privacy-preserving data analytics. After breaches like Cambridge Analytica's misuse of Facebook data, consumer activism has increased calls for ethical data practices (The Guardian, 2019). Competitive dynamics rewarding privacy protection, like Apple's differential privacy techniques, have shifted market share to more privacy-focused companies. Strategic partners like healthcare providers require confidential collaboration models before sharing data assets, as seen in partnerships between hospitals and big tech firms like Microsoft. Litigation and fines over violations, such as the $5 billion fine against Facebook (Federal Trade Commission, 2019), exemplify the financial risks of inadequate data protection. Rising national regulations like GDPR, CCPA, and standards from groups like IEEE compel businesses to implement privacy-enhancing technologies - market stakeholders, from consumers to regulators, pressure businesses to analyze data while preserving confidentiality.

- ***Growing consumer demand for privacy and transparency in data practices.***

Today's consumers are increasingly vocal about wanting companies to take a privacy-first approach to data and provide more transparency in data practices. Surveys consistently show that people are more likely to trust and spend money with businesses that offer visibility into how they collect, use, and share personal information. This growing customer demand forces organizations to rethink their data strategies and prioritize privacy.

Examples:

- In 2020, Apple introduced detailed privacy nutrition labels on the App Store, providing summaries of how each app handles user data, including contact info, location, browsing history, financial data, and more. This feature directly meets consumer demands for plain-language transparency around data use. App developers are now accountable to users in accessing and managing sensitive information.
- In 2021, over 90% of U.S. Apple users chose to opt into Apple's App Tracking Transparency restrictions, demonstrating a growing demand for individual control over how personal data is accessed and monetized. This shift benefited consumers by reducing invasive ad targeting while compelling apps to be transparent on data collection.
  ○ *Avoiding brand damage from data breaches*

While data breaches are becoming more common, their consequences seem only to intensify - from viral outrage and calls for accountability to plummeting stock prices and massive legal liability. Implementing privacy protections before a breach occurs is imperative to reduce the now-predictable fallout of lost consumer trust, lawsuits, and substantial financial costs. When sensitive data is exposed externally, brands rarely walk away unscathed.

Examples:

- In 2013, Target faced public condemnation and calls for boycotts after a breach exposed 70 million customers' personal and payment card information. Their brand perception and sales plunged during the 2013 holiday season, and they agreed to pay $18.5 million to 47 states in a consumer protection settlement.
- In 2014, Sony Pictures suffered devastating embarrassment and operational disruption when hackers spilled sensitive company information like employees' medical records, social security numbers, and embarrassing executive emails across the internet. Sony faced lawsuits from employees and criticism for their poor response.

Types of Privacy-Preserving Data Analysis Techniques

This section dives into the technical details of how various techniques for privacy-preserving data analysis are used to extract valuable insights from data while maintaining robust privacy protections. The goal is to provide an overview of how methods like differential privacy, homomorphic encryption, multi-party computation, and so on work at a high level and explain the technical concepts of each technique.

K-anonymization:

This technique protects data by ensuring that each data entry cannot be distinguished from a minimum of 'k-1' other entries within the identical dataset. This is typically done by generalizing, removing, or encrypting specific identifiers. In other words, it works by suppressing or generalizing identifiable

Figure 1. Sample data containing age, gender, and purchase product of individuals

Age	Gender	Purchased_Product
25	M	Laptop
26	F	Smartphone
25	M	Smartwatch
30	F	Laptop
29	M	Headphones
27	F	Laptop
31	M	Smartphone
32	F	Smartwatch
28	M	Laptop
28	F	Headphones

attributes in a dataset until each record maps to at least k other records. This method prevents linking specific records to individuals. Analysis can then be performed on the anonymized data to derive insights while protecting privacy. Here is a step-by-step guide to K-anonymization.

Step 1: Obtain and Understand the Dataset

Consider an extended dataset from a business containing customer data: Age, Gender, and Purchased_Product (Figure 1) of each individual.

Step 2: Identify Quasi-Identifiers

Quasi-identifiers are attributes in the dataset that can indirectly identify an individual.

In our dataset, the attributes "Age" and "Gender" are quasi-identifiers.

Step 3: Determine the Desired 'k' Value

Let us use k=3 for this example. This means each unique set of quasi-identifiers should appear with at least three records in the dataset.

Step 4: Modify the Dataset for K-anonymization

To achieve k=3, generalize the quasi-identifiers so that at least three records share the same generalized values. We can generalize the 'Age' attribute into age ranges, as shown in Figure 2.

Step 5: Ensure Anonymity

After generalization, each combination of quasi-identifiers should have at least 'k' entries in the dataset. Here, the combination (25-30, M) appears five times, (25-30, F) appears four times, and (30-35, F/M) appears three times. Thus, ensuring k=3 anonymity.

Step 6: Analyze and Use the Dataset

Figure 2. Grouped data at the age level

Age	Gender	Purchased_Product
25-30	M	Laptop
25-30	F	Smartphone
25-30	M	Smartwatch
30-35	F	Laptop
25-30	M	Headphones
25-30	F	Laptop
30-35	M	Smartphone
30-35	F	Smartwatch
25-30	M	Laptop
25-30	F	Headphones

The k-anonymized dataset can now be used for various business analyses without risking individual privacy. The business can gauge which products are popular within specific age and gender brackets without depending on individual customers.

Business Scenarios for K-anonymization:

- Marketing Analysis: Gauge the purchase behaviors of age and gender cohorts without breaching individual data privacy.
- Customer Segmentation: Formulate generalized customer groups for specific targeting without pinpointing exact individuals.
- Product Recommendation: Discern patterns in generalized data to suggest products to broader customer segments.

Always be aware that while k-anonymization aids in preserving privacy, there is a balance between data utility and privacy that businesses must assess depending on context and data sensitivity.

Private set intersection:

In an increasingly collaborative business environment, companies often find themselves at a crossroads - wanting to combine insights from datasets without exposing sensitive individual data. Enter Private Set Intersection (PSI), a technique that offers a solution to this very challenge, enabling collaborative data insights without compromising individual data points. Private Set Intersection (PSI) is a cryptographic method that enables two parties to find the common elements in their datasets without revealing other information about their respective sets. It ensures that each party learns only about the shared elements and nothing else.

Here is an example: Imagine two people, Alice and Bob, having a list of numbers. They want to find out their common numbers without revealing the other numbers in their lists. PSI would allow them to do just that – determine the common numbers without showing the entire list to the other person.

- PSI uses complex cryptographic protocols, but here is a simplified representation

    ○ Let us denote Alice's set as A and Bob's as B.
    ○ Through PSI protocols, Alice and Bob can compute C, where C=A∩B (the intersection of A and B).
    ○ The key here is that neither Alice nor Bob learn any other values from A or B apart from the common elements in C.

Value Proposition

- Secure Collaboration: PSI facilitates safe inter-party collaborations, enabling mutual insights without risking data exposure.
- Enhanced Data Privacy: Only the intersection of datasets is revealed, ensuring that all other data remains confidential.
- Flexibility: PSI can be integrated into various data analytics workflows, ensuring privacy in many collaborative scenarios.

Examples in Data Analytics

- Marketing Analytics: Let us say an e-commerce company (Company A) has a list of its customers' email addresses. A digital advertising company (Company B) has its list of email addresses of users who clicked on a particular ad.

    ○ Objective: Company A wants to find out how many of its customers clicked on that ad without revealing its entire customer list to Company B. Similarly, Company B wants to keep its entire list of users who clicked on the ad private from Company A.
    ○ Using PSI: Both companies can use PSI to find the intersection of the two datasets, i.e., the list of Company A's customers who also clicked on the ad, without exposing additional email addresses to each other. This allows privacy-preserving targeted marketing and performance measurement without compromising user data.

Differential Privacy

Differential Privacy (DP) stands as a cornerstone in data privacy. In an era where data breaches are increasingly common, and the demand for personal data protection is louder than ever, DP offers a mathematical framework to obtain valuable insights from a dataset without revealing the specifics about individual entries. A technique that injects random noise into the data or query mechanism to ensure that the removal or addition of a single database entry does not significantly affect the output of a query, thereby protecting individual data entries. It is a system for publicly sharing information derived from a dataset while withholding information about whether any individual's data was included. It adds mathematically calibrated noise to queries before results are returned.

Value Proposition

- Robust Privacy Guarantees: DP provides robust and provable privacy assurances, unlike other techniques susceptible to auxiliary or background knowledge attacks.
- Flexibility: DP is not tied to a specific type of data or analysis, making it versatile across various data analytics tasks.
- Adaptability: As more data gets added, DP mechanisms can be adjusted to provide consistent privacy protection.

Mathematical Function: Differential Privacy is often implemented using a "privacy budget" denoted by ε (epsilon). A smaller ε represents stronger privacy. The formal definition is:

For a function f and any datasets D1 and D2 that differ in one entry, and for any possible subset of outputs, f satisfies ε-differential privacy if: $\Pr [f(D1) \in S] \leq e^{\varepsilon} \times \Pr [f(D2) \in S]$

Where Pr denotes probability, this equation ensures that the probability of a specific output, given any two almost identical datasets, remains close.

Mathematically, a query satisfies ε-differential privacy if the probability of any outcome changes by, at most, a small multiplicative factor ε when any single record is added or removed from the input dataset. Lower epsilon values enforce stricter privacy.

Here are a few examples of DP:

- A hospital can release differentially private statistics about success rates for procedures. By adding calibrated noise, the published aggregate rates do not allow deducing outcomes of any given patient, preserving their privacy.
- Imagine a database that holds the ages of people in a town. While we want to know the average age, we do not want to identify or infer any individual's age. With differential privacy, noise is added to the results, ensuring that the exact age of any specific individual cannot be determined, but the overall average remains approximately accurate.
- A streaming service wants to know the most popular genres without identifying individual users' viewing habits. Using differential privacy, the service can analyze data and determine, for instance, that 35% of users prefer drama and 40% prefer comedy. While noise might alter these percentages slightly, individual users' exact preferences remain private, and the service still gets a near-accurate understanding of general viewing trends.

Differentially private analysis retains overall utility for business insights from population-level data while guaranteeing provable privacy for individuals. It is gaining adoption in data products across technology, healthcare, finance, and other sectors handling sensitive data.

Federated Learning

Federated Learning emerges as a revolutionary approach in a world where data remains distributed across multiple devices and platforms. Instead of centralizing data to train models, Federated Learning brings the model to the data, ushering in a new era of privacy-focused and efficient machine learning.

It is a machine-learning approach where a model is collaboratively trained across multiple devices or servers while keeping the data localized. Rather than sending data to a central server, model updates and learnings are shared, and the central model aggregates these updates, improving over time without direct access to individual data points.

Imagine a classroom where each student reads a unique book. Instead of collecting all the books to write a summary, the teacher asks each student to provide a summary of their book. The teacher then compiles a comprehensive summary from these individual summaries. Here, the students' books are the data, the individual summaries are the model updates, and the comprehensive summary represents the updated central model in Federated Learning.

Value Proposition

- Empower Edge Devices: Devices, even if they are not powerful, can participate in model training, leveraging their local data.
- Real-time Learning: With decentralized training, models can learn and adapt in real time without waiting for centralized data updates.
- Holistic Model Improvement: As data remains diverse and distributed, Federated Learning ensures that the central model benefits from various information sources.

Examples in Data Analytics

- Healthcare Analytics: Hospitals can collaborate on medical research without sharing patient data directly. Each hospital trains local models on patient data and only shares model updates, ensuring patient confidentiality while improving diagnostic models.
- Smart Devices & IoT: Devices like smart thermostats or wearables can use Federated Learning to improve user experience. Each device learns from user behaviors and sends these learnings as model updates, refining the overall model without compromising individual user data.

Federated Learning paves the way for a future where devices learn and collaborate while ensuring user privacy and data security. It is a testament to how innovation can balance the increasing demand for data insights and the imperatives of data protection.

Homomorphic Encryption

Executes calculations on coded data without deciphering it first. This process creates an encoded outcome which, upon decryption, aligns with the result obtained from operations conducted on the unencrypted data. For example, a hospital can analyze encrypted medical records with third-party analytics services. Retail companies encrypt customer data, perform analytics on the encrypted data to segment customers, and tailor promotions, all without accessing the actual data, thereby preserving customer privacy. In the quest for extracting value from encrypted data without ever decrypting it, Homomorphic Encryption emerges as a groundbreaking solution. This encryption paradigm reimagines how we approach data security and analytics, fostering computations on encrypted data and ensuring the results remain encrypted.

Homomorphic Encryption is a form of encryption that allows computation on ciphertexts, generating an encrypted result that matches the result of the operations as if they had been performed on the plaintext.

Imagine a locked treasure chest (encrypted data), and you want to know the value of the jewels inside without opening the lock. Homomorphic Encryption is like magic, allowing one to estimate the worth of those jewels while they are still inside the locked chest, and the result (the estimated value) itself is given to you in a smaller locked box (encrypted result).

Value Proposition

- Data Privacy Assurance: Even during computations, the data remains encrypted, ensuring its confidentiality at all stages.
- Versatility: Enables a wide range of computations on encrypted data, from simple arithmetic to complex machine learning algorithms.
- Enhanced Cloud Security: When using cloud platforms, businesses can ensure their data remains encrypted, even during processing, thus mitigating potential security risks.

Examples in Data Analytics

- Healthcare Analytics: Hospitals can analyze encrypted patient records to derive insights about disease outbreaks or treatment efficacy without accessing raw, sensitive patient data.
- E-commerce: E-commerce platforms can analyze encrypted customer data to derive purchasing trends, preferences, and forecast demands, all the while ensuring that individual customer data is never exposed.

Secure Multi-Party Computation

Enables joint computation on combined datasets while keeping each party's data private. It ensures that no party learns more about the other parties' inputs than what can be inferred from the function's output. Banks can detect fraud by jointly analyzing financial transactions without sharing customer data. In the modern data-centric world, multiple entities often need to collaborate on computational tasks without unveiling their private inputs to each other. Secure Multi-party Computation (SMPC) emerges as a potent technique, ensuring that parties can jointly compute a function over their inputs while keeping those inputs private.

Imagine multiple chefs (the parties) trying to make a secret sauce. Each chef knows one ingredient but wants to keep it private from the others. Using SMPC, they can all contribute to the sauce without ever unveiling their specific ingredient. In the end, they all taste the sauce (the result) but remain unaware of the individual ingredients.

Value Proposition

- Joint Computation without Data Exposure: Enables collaborative computation tasks without any party exposing their raw data.
- Enhanced Trust: Parties can engage in collaborative tasks with the assurance that their data remains confidential.

- Versatile Applications: SMPC can be applied across a broad spectrum of tasks, from simple computations to complex algorithms.

Examples in Data Analytics

- Medical Research: Medical institutions worldwide engage in collaborative research, especially during global health crises like the COVID-19 pandemic. They want to derive insights from combined data (like patient outcomes, drug efficacy, etc.) without violating patient privacy norms or revealing data that might be proprietary to a particular institution. SMPC serves as a method to achieve this. For instance, institutions should collectively determine the efficacy of a treatment without revealing specific patient data.
- Supply Chain Optimization: In complex supply chains, where multiple vendors, manufacturers, and logistics providers collaborate, there is a need to optimize processes based on collective data. However, businesses might be wary of revealing data that could give away competitive advantages, such as inventory levels, demand forecasts, or supplier contracts. SMPC allows these entities to optimize the supply chain processes based on collective data without revealing specifics to each other.

Trusted Executed Environments (TEE)

This represents a secure processor area that guarantees that code and data loaded inside the TEE are protected for confidentiality and integrity. It uses secure enclaves to process data in an isolated environment. Credit card companies can run fraud detection models within enclaves to preserve transaction privacy. As the digital world grapples with escalating cybersecurity threats and the dire need to protect sensitive data, Trusted Execution Environments (TEE) have emerged as a pivotal solution. These secure areas within a main processor guarantee that the code and data loaded inside them are protected for confidentiality and integrity.

Imagine a fortified vault within a bank. While the bank has security, this vault provides an extra layer of protection for the most valuable items. In the digital realm, a TEE functions similarly, offering a protected space within a device's main processor where data can be processed securely, shielded from potential threats.

Value Proposition

- Robust Security: Provides a strong layer of protection against software attacks and physical tampering.
- Integrity Assurance: Ensures that the data and the operations on the data (computations) remain untampered and maintain their integrity.
- Enhanced Privacy: Processes sensitive data in isolated, secure environments, ensuring that data remains confidential even during computations

Examples in Data Analytics

- Healthcare Data Analysis:

- Scenario: Medical institutions must analyze patient data to derive insights about disease patterns, treatment efficacy, etc. This data is highly sensitive and requires maximum protection.
- Applicability: Hospitals can process this sensitive data using TEE, ensuring it remains confidential during computations. For instance, when running predictive analytics to determine disease outbreaks or the effectiveness of a new treatment regime, the data is processed within the TEE, keeping it shielded from potential breaches or tampering.
- **Financial Transaction Analysis:**
  - Scenario: Banks and financial institutions often run algorithms to detect fraudulent activities. These algorithms need to process vast amounts of transaction data, which is highly sensitive.
  - Applicability: With TEE, these algorithms can operate within a secure environment, ensuring the confidentiality and integrity of each transaction processed. For example, a bank might use machine learning models within a TEE to flag suspicious transactions, ensuring that transaction data remains uncompromised during the analysis.
- **E-commerce Personalization Algorithms:**
  - Scenario: E-commerce platforms utilize user behavior data to personalize shopping experiences. This involves analyzing user preferences, past purchases, browsing history, etc.
  - Applicability: TEE ensures that such personalization algorithms can operate on user data without exposing the data or the insights derived from it. An e-commerce giant might use TEE to run recommendation algorithms, ensuring that individual user data remains private and secure while offering tailored product suggestions.

Business Use Cases

Illustrate real-world examples and use cases of privacy-preserving data analysis techniques relevant to market intelligence teams across different industries. Discuss applications in areas like collaborative filtering, data sharing with partners, creating aggregated datasets, targeted marketing, testing analytical models, and so on, and showcase these techniques' actionable insights and business value for short-term and long-term business goals.

- *Marketing Use Cases*
  - Ad Targeting Without Revealing User Interests:
    - Major online advertising platforms like Google and Facebook face the situation where they must provide advertisers with meaningful user insights. Their task is to facilitate targeted ad campaigns without compromising user privacy. By employing differential privacy, their action is to share aggregate user behaviors or interests without individual data exposure. As a result, advertisers craft tailored campaigns based on broad trends, preserving user confidentiality. Use Case: Collaborative Consumer Insights
    - Leading e-commerce entities, such as Amazon and eBay, find themselves in a situation where they aim to mutually benefit from broader market insights without unveiling proprietary data. Tasked with this delicate balance, they turn to Secure Multi-party Computation. In doing so, they collaboratively analyze overarching consumer purchasing patterns without revealing specifics. This action subsequently results in refined marketing strategies for both, ensuring a competitive edge remains intact.

- *Finance Use Cases*
  - ○ Fraud Detection Across Banks: Facing the widespread situation of potential fraud, banking institutions like Bank of America and Wells Fargo are tasked with enhancing their detection mechanisms. They collaboratively identify patterns shared between their databases by employing Private Set Intersection. This action effectively pinpoints fraudulent activities, bolstering security and customer trust.
  - ○ Secure Financial Forecasting: Investment giants such as Goldman Sachs and J.P. Morgan are in a situation where they need to make secure market predictions while ensuring data privacy. Their task is to employ proprietary forecasting algorithms without exposing client data or the algorithmic intricacies. Utilizing Trusted Execution Environments, their action is to run these computations in a secure enclave. This strategy results in accurate market forecasts, all while safeguarding vital data and proprietary methodologies.
- *CPG (Consumer Packaged Goods) Use Cases*
  - ○ Collaborative Demand Forecasting: CPG titans like Procter & Gamble and Unilever are in a competitive market demanding efficient production based on precise demand forecasting. Tasked with this challenge, they employ federated learning for collaborative model enhancement without direct data sharing. Through this action, they optimize their production and inventory, reducing overheads and waste.
  - ○ Supply Chain Optimization: In the complex world of supply chain management, leaders such as Nestle and PepsiCo face the task of coordinating seamlessly with suppliers and distributors. Given the situation of maintaining operational efficiency without compromising business-sensitive details, they employ homomorphic encryption. This action lets them process encrypted transactional data to optimize supply chain mechanisms, resulting in timely deliveries and reduced operational costs.
- *Automotive*
  - ○ Vehicle Telematics Analysis: Automotive innovators like Tesla and General Motors are in a rapidly evolving market where continuous vehicle improvement is paramount. They apply differential privacy when gleaning insights from telematics data without compromising user privacy. Through this action, they anonymously analyze vehicle data, enhancing vehicle performance and robust safety features while ensuring driver privacy.

Case Studies

Unlocking Healthcare Insights With Privacy-Preserving Data Collaboration: A LynxCare and Decentriq Case Study (Decentriq. (2023, October 1))

- Introduction: LynxCare provides a healthcare data mining platform using advanced NLP and analytics to uncover insights from siloed clinical data sources. They were founded to address challenges around fragmented healthcare data and ineffective patient follow-up.
- Challenge: Vast amounts of patient health data hold value for improving care through analytics. However, regulations impose strict use/sharing standards to protect privacy. Granular data carries a higher risk of re-identification. LynxCare needed to fully utilize detailed data to drive healthcare improvements without compromising privacy.

- Solution: LynxCare leveraged Decentriq's confidential computing platform for privacy-preserving analytics. Decentriq uses encryption techniques to keep data protected during processing/analysis. Healthcare data computations occur encrypted within trusted execution environments. This enabled LynxCare to derive insights from sensitive data while guaranteeing privacy. In summary, Decentriq's cryptographic privacy technologies allowed LynxCare to overcome regulatory limitations and tap into the full potential of detailed healthcare data to improve patient outcomes while preserving privacy.

Mastercard Uses Anonymization to Enable Compliant Data Insights (Truata (2023, October 1))

- Abstract: Mastercard provides a merchant business intelligence solution leveraging transaction data to enable benchmarking, growth opportunities, and new revenue streams. This platform generates significant recurring revenue but faces challenges under new privacy regulations like GDPR.
- Challenge: GDPR and similar privacy laws imposed new requirements around legal basis for processing and analytics on personal data that would limit Mastercard's ability to derive insights from its data. This put over $30M in annual recurring revenue at risk. Mastercard needed a scalable anonymization solution to comply with regulations while conducting valuable analytics.
- Solution: Mastercard partnered with Trūata and leveraged their privacy-preserving analytics platform. Trūata applied proprietary anonymization techniques to Mastercard's data to make it non-identifiable per GDPR. This allowed Mastercard to continue detailed analytics and insights for merchants while ensuring regulatory compliance. The platform was migrated to Trūata's cloud solution to enable scalable, compliant data analytics and protect Mastercard's revenue stream.

Privacy-First Innovation for CPG Brands in CTV Advertising (Infosum (2023, October 1))

- Abstract: Channel 4 and loyalty data provider Nectar360 partnered to offer CPG brands retail audience targeting and measurement for CTV advertising without sharing data.
- Challenge: CPG brands needed access to retailer first-party data to target and measure CTV ad campaigns sold via third parties effectively. Brands needed to leverage high-value retail audiences at scale while preserving privacy.
- Solution: Channel 4 and Nectar used InfoSum's data clean rooms for privacy-safe data collaboration. Nectar shared audience segments for targeting, while Channel 4 measured sales uplift without exposing raw data. This enabled scaled targeting and closed-loop incrementality measurement for CPGs.
- Results: CPG brands saw up to 122% sales uplift from targeted campaigns, proving the impact of data-driven CTV ads. The privacy-preserving clean room model created value for brands, media owners, and retailers.

Data Partnerships in the Privacy Era: An Indeed and Disney Case Study (Adweek (2023, October 1))

- Abstract: Indeed leveraged Disney's privacy-preserving data clean room to reach new audiences and drive incremental revenue for its job site.

- Challenge: Indeed's business model relies on growing its audience of active job seekers and employer accounts that advertise open positions. To increase these critical user bases, Indeed needed to find ways to reach incremental users beyond its owned channels. However, acquiring users across third-party sites and platforms required collaborating on audience data in privacy-compliant ways. Regulations like GDPR and CCPA imposed strict standards for data sharing and usage. Indeed needed to do more than transfer its first-party data to media partners like Disney to activate audiences. They needed a framework that enabled data collaboration for targeting and measurement without exposing raw user-level data. This presented a significant challenge for Indeed to access new media audiences while respecting data privacy.

- Solution: To overcome this challenge, Indeed partnered with Disney to leverage their interoperable data clean room powered by Snowflake's technology. The clean room provided a privacy-preserving environment for Indeed and Disney to collaborate on data securely. Indeed input encrypted first-party audience data, which allowed Disney to create privacy-safe lookalike audiences for Indeed to target advertisements on Hulu. Disney used their first-party data to measure incremental lift to create exposed and holdout groups. Indeed, then input conversion data to match back to users in the clean room without sharing any raw data. User-level data was never exposed outside of the encrypted clean room environment. This enabled Indeed to expand its reach to new audiences across Disney's properties while upholding stringent privacy standards. Indeed, it was able to drive significant incremental revenue thanks to the privacy-preserving data clean room solution.

Platforms/Softwares That Companies Use for Privacy-Preserving Data Analysis

- For Marketing Intelligence: Google Ads Data Hub (ADH), Amazon Marketing Cloud (AMC), and Facebook Advanced Analytics (FBAA) are used for digital advertising use cases. This includes planning, measurement, optimization, and activation.
  - Google Ads Data Hub (ADH) explains how the data from multiple data sources such as Google Campaign Manager, Display & Video 360 (DV360), Google Ads, and YouTube is used for market intelligence in a privacy-preserving manner.
  - Amazon Marketing Cloud (AMC) explains the significance of AMC in the context of e-commerce advertising analytics and what different ad placement types help various advertisers optimize media spending.
  - Facebook Advanced Analytics (FBAA) explains the importance of how social advertising analytics can be explored by small, medium, and enterprise organizations for better ROAS.
- For Enterprise Data Collaboration: Habu, Liveramp's Safe Haven, Infosum, Google Cloud Platform BigQuery Clean Rooms, Snowflake Media Data Cloud, Amazon AWS Clean Rooms, and so on are used by publishers, advertisers, and other data owners.

Practical Limitations for the Adoption of Privacy-Privacy Data Analytics Platforms

While privacy-preserving analytics platforms provide privacy-safe methods of collaborating to share and infer data between business partners in the data ecosystem, certain constraints and limitations must be considered while operating.

- Working with a Privacy-Preserving Data Analytics Platform requires trust and careful checking between partners.
  - Those using the platform must understand and follow different legal rules depending on privacy laws and how they work together. Getting legal advice is essential to ensure they follow these rules correctly.
  - Usually, everyone must trust both the platform provider and the cloud service being used. Sometimes, this means trusting the same cloud service for all parties.
  - It is also essential for all users to trust that no one will try to break the platform's privacy protections or advanced privacy technologies. This can be ensured through contracts, careful checks, and regular monitoring.
- Common Matching Mechanism: A shared matching mechanism or a set of established criteria is essential for aligning two or more datasets. Without an existing mechanism, collaboration with an identity partner or a third party is advisable to develop a suitable matching or overlap process, adhering to permissible guidelines. For instance, using a hashed email address as a matching criterion is prevalent.
- These platforms are expensive. In 2022, according to IAB and Ipsos, nearly two-thirds (62%) of the organizations using these platforms spent a minimum of $200K on the technology, with a quarter (23%) spending $500K+ (Interactive Advertising Bureau, n.d.). This indicates that smaller brands and publishers might need help to afford these tools due to their high costs.

Figure 3. Challenges faced by organizations

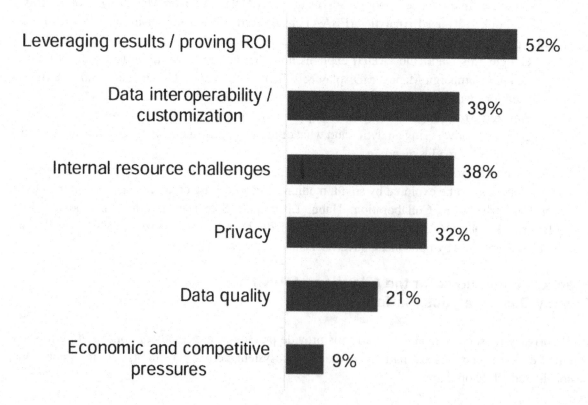

- The setup of these platforms could be lengthy and complex. This includes reviewing privacy and governance settings internally and with external partners, evaluating data use cases and ownership rights, and working with product and tech teams on deeper privacy, security, and compliance requirements (Interactive Advertising Bureau, n.d.).
- 52% of the organizations highlight that it is difficult to prove the ROI of using these privacy-safe platforms, whereas 38% of the respondents accept the limitation on their internal resources, as shown in Figure 3 (Interactive Advertising Bureau, n.d.)

Best Practices for Privacy-Preserving Data Analytics Techniques in Market Intelligence

Conduct Comprehensive Needs Assessments

- Before selecting specific privacy-preserving techniques, market intelligence teams must understand their organizational needs thoroughly. This includes the nature of the data they handle, its specific privacy concerns, and the analytics objectives. By starting with a deep-dive assessment, teams can ensure that the chosen techniques align with their operational needs and privacy objectives.

Stay Abreast of Regulatory Developments

- With privacy regulations continually evolving globally, teams must maintain a current understanding of both local and international laws. Regularly reviewing and updating knowledge about privacy-related regulations ensures that chosen analytical methods remain compliant, minimizing legal risks.

Prioritize Vendor Evaluation and Due Diligence

- A rigorous vendor assessment process is essential when exploring tools or solutions for privacy-preserving analytics. Look for vendors with a strong track record in privacy, transparent methodologies, and positive feedback from similar industries. This ensures that the tools or techniques implemented are robust and trustworthy.

Implement Robust Training and Change Management

- Introducing new privacy-preserving techniques can represent a significant shift in how analytics is performed. As such, ensure a comprehensive training program is in place for all users. A structured change management process can smoothly transition to these new methods while addressing any concerns or resistance.

Regularly Measure and Review Implementation Success

- Post-implementation, it is crucial to continually measure the success and efficiency of the privacy-preserving techniques in place. This involves technical evaluations (like accuracy and performance metrics) and organizational assessments (like user feedback and compliance checks). Regular reviews ensure that the techniques remain relevant, efficient, and compliant.

Foster a Culture of Privacy

- Beyond just techniques and tools, fostering a culture that values privacy is essential. This involves leadership buy-in, regular privacy-awareness campaigns, and creating an environment where privacy is viewed as both a responsibility and an asset. Such a culture ensures long-term adherence to best practices and positions the organization as a trusted player in the market.

CONCLUSION

Privacy-preserving analytics has come a long way from its cryptographic roots to become an integral capability for responsible data utilization. As regulations and consumer expectations around ethical data practices continue to evolve, adopting privacy-enhancing techniques is no longer just a compliance checkbox but a competitive necessity. Companies that embed privacy by design in their analytics workflows will thrive through enhanced trust, collaboration opportunities, and innovation.

We can expect rapid advances in federated learning and confidential computing to make privacy-preserving analysis even more scalable and versatile. As 5G and edge computing proliferate, federated learning will unlock new localized learning paradigms. Hardware-based security mechanisms like trusted execution environments (TEEs) will become ubiquitous. Frameworks like TensorFlow Privacy and PySyft will continue democratizing access to differential privacy and secure computation methods.

However, technology alone cannot guarantee responsible data practices. Organizations must foster a culture of privacy and ethics through leadership, training, and governance. Privacy should be valued as an asset, not a burden. Compliance must go hand-in-hand with transparency and accountability. With the exponential growth in data generation, market intelligence teams must stay attuned to the privacy imperative, building consumer trust and brand reputation through privacy-first analytics. The next era of data science must balance ever-deeper insights with ever-stronger privacy protection.

REFERENCES

Adweek. (2023, October 9). How Indeed Is Growing Audience and Revenue With Disney's Data Clean Room. *Adweek.* https://www.adweek.com/programmatic/how-indeed-is-growing-audience-and-revenue-with-disneys-data-clean-room/

Agrawal, R., & Srikant, R. (2000, June). Privacy-preserving data mining. *SIGMOD Record, 29*(2), 439–450. doi:10.1145/335191.335438

CIGI and Ipsos. (2019). *CIGI-Ipsos Global Survey on Internet Security and Trust.* IPSOS. https://www.ipsos.com/en/2019-cigi-ipsos-global-survey-internet-security-and-trust

Decentriq. (2023, October 1). *Case Study: LynxCare* Decentriq. https://www.decentriq.com/request/case-study/lynxcare

DOJ, United States Department of Justice, Office of Privacy and Civil Liberties. (2020). *Overview of the Privacy Act of 1974 (2020 Edition)*. US DoJ. https://www.justice.gov/opcl/overview-privacy-act-1974-2020-edition

Dwork, C. (2006). Differential Privacy. *Automata, languages, and programming*, 1–12. https://doi.org/doi:10.1007/11787006_1

Federal Trade Commission. (2019, July 24). *FTC Imposes $5 Billion Penalty, Sweeping New Privacy Restrictions on Facebook*. FTC. https://www.ftc.gov/news-events/news/press-releases/2019/07/ftc-imposes-5-billion-penalty-sweeping-new-privacy-restrictions-facebook

Gartner, S. (2020). *65% of the World's population will have personal data covered under modern privacy regulations*. Gartner. https://www.gartner.com/en/newsroom/press-releases/2020-09-14-gartner-says-by-2023--65--of-the-world-s-population-w

Gentry, C. (2009). Fully homomorphic encryption using ideal lattices. In *Proceedings of the forty-first annual ACM symposium on Theory of computing (STOC '09)*. Association for Computing Machinery, New York, NY, USA. 10.1145/1536414.1536440

Infosum. (2023, October 9). *Case Study: Retail, Nectar360, and Channel 4 Deliver Up to 122% Sales Uplift for CPGs*. Infosum. https://www.infosum.com/case-studies/ret4il-nectar360-and-channel-4-deliver-up-to-122-sales-uplift-for-cpgs

Interactive Advertising Bureau. (n.d.). *State of Data 2023*. IAB. https://www.iab.com/insights/state-of-data-2023/

International Association of Privacy Professionals. (n.d.). *5 Steps to Prepare for India's Digital Personal Data Protection Act*. IAPP. https://iapp.org/news/a/5-steps-to-prepare-for-indias-digital-personal-data-protection-act/

McMahan, B., Moore, E., Ramage, D., Hampson, S. & Arcas, B. (2017). Communication-Efficient Learning of Deep Networks from Decentralized Data. *Proceedings of the 20th International Conference on Artificial Intelligence and Statistics*. MLR Press. https://proceedings.mlr.press/v54/mcmahan17a.html.

Office of the Attorney General of California. (n.d.). *California Consumer Privacy Act (CCPA)*. OAG. https://oag.ca.gov/privacy/ccpa

Patil, K. & Seshadri, R. (2014). Big Data Security and Privacy Issues in Healthcare. *Proceedings - 2014 IEEE International Congress on Big Data, BigData Congress 2014*, (pp. 762–765). IEEE. . https://ieeexplore.ieee.org/document/6906856 doi:10.1109/BigData.Congress.2014.112

PyTorch. (2023, October 7). *PyTorch Opacus*. GitHub. https://github.com/pytorch/opacus

Reinsel, D. (2018, November 27). *The Digitization of the World from Edge to Core*. Seagate Technology. https://www.seagate.com/files/www-content/our-story/trends/files/idc-seagate-dataage-whitepaper.pdf

Reuters. (2019, July 24). *Facebook to pay a record $5 billion U.S. fine over privacy, faces antitrust probe.* Reuters. https://www.reuters.com/article/us-facebook-ftc/facebook-to-pay-record-5-billion-u-s-fine-over-privacy-faces-antitrust-probe-idUSKCN1UJ1L9

TensorFlow. (2023, October 7). *TensorFlow Privacy.* GitHub. https://github.com/tensorflow/privacy

The Guardian. (2019, March 17). *The Cambridge Analytica scandal changed the world but did not change Facebook.* The Guardian. https://www.theguardian.com/technology/2019/mar/17/the-cambridge-analytica-scandal-changed-the-world-but-it-didnt-change-facebook

Truata. (2023, October 9). Case Study: Mastercard Business Intelligence Platform. https://www.truata.com/resources/case-study/case-study-mastercard-business-intelligence-platform/

U.S. Department of Health & Human Services. (n.d.). *Records, Computers and the Rights of Citizens.* US DHH. https://aspe.hhs.gov/reports/records-computers-rights-citizens

Yao, A. C. (1982). Protocols for secure computations. *23rd Annual Symposium on Foundations of Computer Science.* IEEE. 10.1109/SFCS.1982.38

Yao, A. C.-C. (1986). How to generate and exchange secrets. *27th Annual Symposium on Foundations of Computer Science.* IEEE. 10.1109/SFCS.1986.25

KEY TERMS AND DEFINITIONS

Audience: A group of people with a standard set of characteristics used to create profiles and affinity categories, such as demographics, interests, and intents, whom an advertiser wants to show an ad. Specifically, for example, this could be a list or group of customers or individuals most likely to purchase a given product or service from an advertiser or a list of individuals or households with a well-defined set of attributes with common interests.

CCPA: This law provides California residents with enhanced privacy rights and consumer protection regarding their personal data. It includes the right to know about and delete the data held by businesses and the right to opt out of the sale of their personal information. The CCPA sets a precedent for stronger privacy legislation in the United States, focusing on consumer rights and corporate responsibility.

Cryptography: Cryptography protects information by transforming it into a secure format known as encryption. This process ensures that only authorized people can read and process the information. It is used to secure communication from outsiders, often called adversaries.

Data Clean Room: This is a secure digital environment for handling sensitive data, ensuring that raw data is not directly accessed or exposed. Data clean rooms are designed to allow for the analysis and processing of data under strict privacy controls, often used in contexts where data sharing needs to comply with stringent data protection laws and regulations.

Differential Privacy: This technique adds a specific kind of 'noise' or random variation to the data, making identifying individuals in a dataset difficult. It allows the helpful sharing of aggregate information about groups while ensuring the confidentiality of individual data points, balancing data utility with privacy protection.

Federated Learning: This approach enables the creation of a shared model from multiple decentralized data sources, like smartphones or computers, without transferring the data itself. It enhances privacy by keeping sensitive data localized while allowing collective learning and model improvement from diverse datasets.

First-Party Data: Data acquired by an organization as a result of an individual's interaction with the organization, either online on their website, mobile app, or connected device, or offline in their physical locations, by mail or phone.

GDPR: This is a comprehensive privacy regulation in the European Union that sets guidelines for collecting and processing personal information. It gives individuals more control over their data and imposes strict rules on data handlers, with significant penalties for non-compliance. The GDPR emphasizes transparency, security, and accountability in data management.

Homomorphic Encryption: This advanced encryption method allows data to remain encrypted during processing, supporting computations on the encrypted data to generate encrypted results. When these results are decrypted, they match the outcome of operations as if they were performed on the original, unencrypted data, offering high data security during processing.

K-anonymization: This process involves modifying personal data so that an individual's information blends with others', preventing identification. It is about adjusting data so that each person's details are indistinguishable from at least k−1 others in the same dataset, creating a form of anonymity that protects personal identity.

Privacy-enhancing technologies (PETs): Privacy-enhancing technologies (PETs) are technology solutions, such as differential privacy, secure multi-party computing, confidential computing, and federated learning. These technologies enable complex data processing functions for sharing and analysis without revealing individual, household, or device-level personal information to parties that do not already have it. PETs protect personal information and data from unauthorized access, use, and disclosure.

Secure Multi-party Computation: This cryptographic method enables multiple parties to collaboratively compute a function over their inputs while keeping those inputs private from each other. It is a way of ensuring that each party's data contributions remain confidential, even as they contribute to a collective outcome.

Third Party: A party to an interaction without a direct relationship with the individual involved.

Trusted Execution Environments (TEEs): These are designated secure areas within a computer's central processor, designed to execute sensitive tasks safely. They protect sensitive data and code from the rest of the system, ensuring this information remains confidential and unaltered, even in system vulnerabilities.

Chapter 11
Big Data Visualization:
KPI Dashboards for Big Data Visualization

Dishant Banga
https://orcid.org/0009-0008-8373-3408
Bridgetree, USA

ABSTRACT

In today's data-driven world, organizations across industries are grappling with vast amounts of data, and the realm of market intelligence is no exception. The explosive growth of big data has created both opportunities and challenges for businesses seeking to gain valuable insights from their data assets. This chapter proposes to explore the significance of big data visualization with key performance indicator (KPI) dashboards as a powerful technique to visualize and extract actionable intelligence from complex datasets in the context of market intelligence. This chapter provides a comprehensive overview of KPI dashboards as these are essential tools for monitoring and analyzing business performance and to make data-driven decisions. The chapter explores the importance of KPIs, the design and implementation of KPI dashboards in big data. Additionally, it discusses the benefits and challenges associated with these tools, along with real-world examples of their successful implementation.

INTRODUCTION

In the dynamic and competitive business environment and with huge volume of Big data, organizations strive to monitor their performance effectively and make informed decisions to drive success. Key Performance Indicators (KPIs) play a crucial role in this process, providing measurable metrics that enable businesses to evaluate their progress towards strategic objectives using Big data. However, manually tracking and analyzing KPIs can be laborious and error-prone, leading to a need for efficient tools that can streamline the process when it comes to big data.

DOI: 10.4018/979-8-3693-0413-6.ch011

Background and Literature Review

The concept of using KPIs to study Big data has gained widespread recognition across various industries as a means of evaluating performance. KPIs are specific metrics that provide organizations with quantifiable insights into their performance in relation to their strategic goals (Parmenter, 2015) These indicators span different dimensions of business performance, including financial, operational, customer-centric, and employee-related aspects. By tracking KPIs metrics, businesses can assess their progress, identify areas for improvement, and make data-driven decisions to enhance overall performance. Traditionally, organizations relied on manual processes and static reports to track KPIs metrics, often involving complex spreadsheets and time-consuming data analysis. However, with advancements in technology and the exponential growth of data, businesses have shifted towards automated KPI dashboards that offer real-time visibility and interactive visualizations of performance metrics (Kiron, 2018). KPI dashboards provide executives and managers with a consolidated view of critical indicators, facilitating quicker and more informed decision-making. Building visualizations can yield several benefits for businesses. They enhance transparency and accountability, promote a data-driven culture, facilitate early identification of performance gaps, and support proactive decision-making (Wixom, 2010). However, challenges exist in the design, implementation, and utilization of these tools, such as data quality issues, integration complexities, and ensuring user adoption and engagement. Ensuring the quality and accuracy of Big Data is paramount. Researchers such emphasize KPIs related to data cleansing efficiency, error rates, and consistency across datasets as essential in assessing the reliability of Big Data analytics outcomes (Smith, 2017). Operational KPIs assess the efficiency of processes involved in collecting, storing, and processing Big Data. Response time, system downtime, and resource utilization are vital indicators in evaluating the operational performance of Big Data system (Brown, 2018). In the realm of business intelligence, KPIs focus on how well Big Data insights align with strategic goals. Metrics like customer acquisition cost, customer lifetime value, and market basket analysis are crucial in evaluating the effectiveness of Big Data-driven decision-making processes (Chen L. e., 2019).

Objective of Chapter

This chapter will explore the design principles and best practices for implementing KPI visualizations, the considerations for selecting relevant metrics, and the potential benefits and challenges associated in shaping marketing intelligence strategies. Real-world marketing and business examples to explain and highlight successful implementations of KPI dashboards and share valuable insights into their practical application and impact on business performance. Readers can use the tools and technologies covered in this chapter based on various marketing related problems to work on and answers business questions.

KEY PERFORMANCE INDICATORS (KPIS) FOR BIG DATA

Key Performance Indicators (KPIs) are measurable metrics that organizations use to evaluate their performance and progress towards achieving their strategic objectives. KPIs provide quantifiable evidence of an organization's success or failure in meeting its goals and can be used to track progress over time (Parmenter, 2015). KPIs serve as a valuable tool for businesses as they provide a clear and objective assessment of performance, enabling organizations to identify areas for improvement, make informed decisions, and align their efforts with their strategic direction. KPIs are essential for several reasons. Firstly, they provide a common language and framework for communicating performance across different levels of an organization, facilitating a shared understanding of goals and objectives (Eckerson, 2010). KPIs ensure that everyone within the organization is working towards the same targets, promoting alignment and focus. Secondly, KPIs enable organizations to monitor and measure progress objectively, allowing for timely interventions and adjustments to strategies and tactics (Parmenter, 2015). By providing real-time insights into performance, KPIs help identify deviations from targets and prompt corrective actions. Lastly, KPIs foster a culture of accountability and continuous improvement within an organization. They create a sense of ownership and responsibility for performance outcomes, driving individuals and teams to strive for excellence (Eckerson, 2010).

Types of KPI's

There are various types of KPIs metrics that organizations can utilize to measure different aspects of their performance. Some common types of KPIs include:

1. Financial KPIs

These KPIs assess an organization's financial health and performance, including metrics such as revenue growth, profitability, return on investment (ROI), sales and cash flow.

2. Operational KPIs

These KPIs focus on the efficiency and effectiveness of operational processes. Examples include production cycle time, quality metrics, on-time delivery, and inventory turnover.

3. *Customer KPIs*

These KPIs measure the satisfaction and loyalty of customers, reflecting the organization's ability to meet customer expectations. Examples include customer satisfaction scores, customer retention rates, and net promoter scores.

4. Employee KPIs

These KPIs assess employee performance, engagement, and development. They can include metrics such as employee turnover, productivity, training participation, and employee satisfaction.

5. Strategic KPIs

These KPIs align with the organization's strategic goals and objectives. They measure progress towards the desired outcomes and can vary depending on the organization's specific strategic priorities.

Selection and Alignment of KPI's

Selecting and aligning KPIs is a critical process that requires careful consideration to ensure they accurately reflect the organization's objectives and provide meaningful insights into performance. The following steps can help in the selection and alignment of KPIs:

1. Understand organizational goals

Start by clearly defining the organization's strategic goals and objectives. This understanding will provide a foundation for selecting relevant KPI metrics that align with the desired outcomes.

2. Identify critical success factors

Identify the key factors that contribute significantly to the achievement of organizational goals. These factors should be measurable and have a direct impact on performance.

3. Define measurable indicators

Determine specific metrics that reflect the identified critical success factors. Ensure that the selected indicators are measurable, relevant, and can provide actionable insights.

4. Prioritize and balance KPIs

Prioritize the selected KPIs based on their importance and relevance to the organization's strategic goals. Strike a balance between leading and lagging indicators to provide a comprehensive view of performance.

5. Ensure alignment and cascading

Align the selected KPIs across different levels of the organization to ensure a cohesive and interconnected measurement framework. Cascading KPIs from the organizational level to departmental and individual levels helps align efforts towards common objectives.

BIG DATA VISUALIZATION DASHBOARD DESIGN AND IMPLEMENTATION

Overview of Visualization Dashboards

Dashboards provide visual representations of key KPI metrics in a concise and user-friendly format. These dashboards consolidate relevant data and present it in a visually appealing manner, allowing users to monitor and analyze performance briefly. KPI visualization dashboards offer real-time insights into critical metrics, enabling organizations to make informed decisions and take timely actions to drive performance improvement.

Effective KPI visualization dashboards go beyond merely displaying data; they provide actionable information, foster data-driven decision-making, and enhance transparency and accountability within an organization. By leveraging big data visualization techniques, dashboards simplify complex information, highlight trends and patterns, and facilitate a deeper understanding of performance metrics by visualizations.

Design Principles for Effective KPI Visualization Dashboards

Designing an effective KPI visualization dashboard requires careful consideration of various factors. Here are some key design principles to keep in mind:

1. *Clarity and simplicity*

Ensure that the dashboard design is clean, uncluttered, and easy to understand. Use clear labels, concise descriptions, and intuitive icons or symbols to represent KPI metrics. Avoid information overload by focusing on the most relevant and actionable metrics.

2. *User-centric approach*

Tailor the dashboard design to the needs and preferences of the target users. Understand their roles, objectives, and the specific insights they require. Design the dashboard layout and navigation in a way that allows users to access the information they need quickly and effortlessly.

3. *Visualization techniques*

Utilize effective data visualization techniques to present information in a visually appealing and understandable manner. Choose appropriate chart types (such as bar charts, line graphs, or pie charts) that best represent the KPIs and support data interpretation. Use colors, icons, and visual cues to highlight important trends or performance thresholds.

4. *Contextual information*

Provide contextual information alongside KPI metrics to enhance understanding and interpretation. Add benchmarks, targets, historical trends, or comparative data to provide context and enable users to gauge performance against set standards or goals.

5. *Interactivity and drill-down capability*

Incorporate interactive elements into the dashboard design to allow users to explore data in more detail. Provide drill-down functionality that enables users to access granular information or navigate to related reports or dashboards for deeper analysis.

6. *Responsive design*

Ensure that the dashboard is responsive and compatible with different devices and screen sizes. This flexibility allows users to access and interact with the dashboard seamlessly across desktops, laptops, tablets, and mobile devices.

Data Visualization Techniques

Data visualization plays a crucial role in presenting KPI metrics effectively. Here are some commonly used data visualization techniques for KPI dashboards:

1. *Charts and graphs*

Bar charts, line graphs, area charts, pie charts, and scatter plots are commonly used to visualize KPI data. Each chart type has its strengths in conveying specific types of information. For instance, bar charts are useful for comparing multiple categories, while line graphs can show trends over time. Figure 1 represents a single-color bar graph of sample data and sorted from highest to lowest.

2. *Gauges and meters*

Gauges and meters provide a visual representation of a single KPI against a target or threshold. They offer a quick and intuitive way to assess performance briefly, with indicators such as needles, dials, or progress bars. Figure 2 represents Guage chart for sales of a company.

3. *Heat maps*

Heat maps use color gradients to represent the intensity or magnitude of a KPI. They are useful for visualizing patterns, identifying outliers, or displaying geographic data. Figure 3 represents heat map for sales, profit and order per month per year of a company

Figure 1. Sample bar graph chart

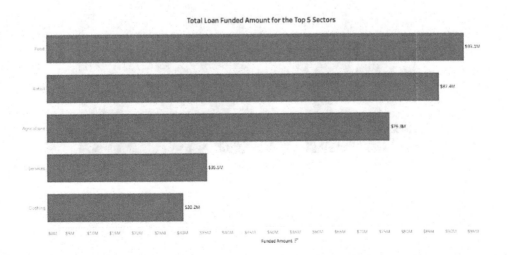

Figure 2. Sample gauge chart for sales of a company

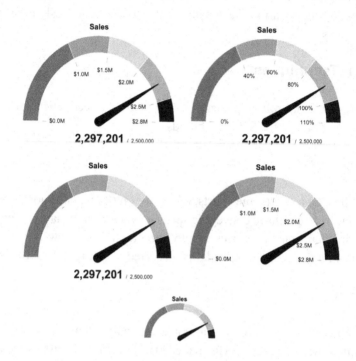

Figure 3. Sample heat map for sales, profit, and order per month per year of a company

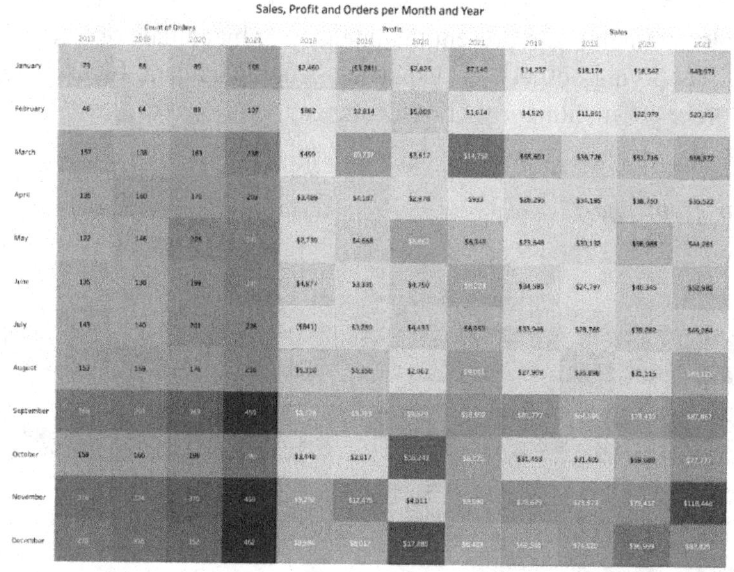

Figure 4. Sample Sparklines of a dataset to identify the outliers

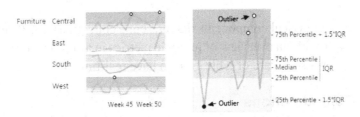

Figure 5. Sample scorecard of a business to have real-time insights

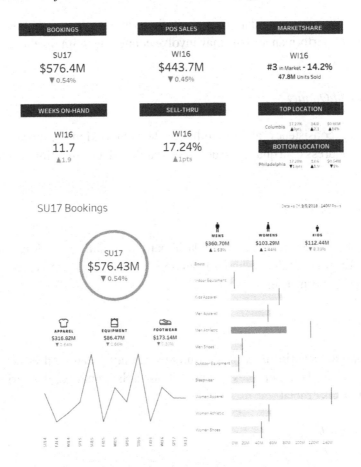

4.   Sparklines

Sparklines are small, condensed line graphs that represent the trend of a single KPI within a limited space. They are often used to provide historical context or show trends alongside the actual value. Figure 4 represents sparklines of a dataset to identify the outliers.

5. *Dashlets and scorecards*

Dashlets or scorecards are visual components that present a collection of KPIs in a summarized and organized manner. They provide an overview of multiple metrics in a compact format, often using grids or tables. Figure 5 represents scorecard of a business to have real-time insights.

Implementation Considerations

Implementing a visualization dashboard requires careful planning and consideration of various factors. Here are some key implementation considerations to ensure a successful deployment:

1. *Data Integration*

Establish a process for integrating data from multiple sources to ensure that the dashboard presents a comprehensive view of performance. This may involve connecting with databases, APIs, or other data sources.

2. *Data Accuracy and Quality*

Ensure the accuracy, consistency, and reliability of the data used in the dashboard. Implement data governance practices, address data quality issues, and establish data validation mechanisms to maintain data integrity.

3. *Scalability and Performance*

Consider the scalability requirements of the dashboard, especially if dealing with large datasets or a growing user base. Ensure that the dashboard can handle increasing data volumes and user demands without compromising performance.

4. *Security and Access Controls*

Implement appropriate security measures to protect sensitive data and ensure that access to the dashboard is controlled based on user roles and permissions. Safeguarding data privacy and complying with relevant regulations is crucial.

5. *User Training and Adoption*

Provide comprehensive training to users to familiarize them with the dashboard's features, functionality, and navigation. Encourage user adoption through effective communication, demonstrating the value of the dashboard, and addressing user concerns or feedback.

UTILIZING KPI VISUALIZATION DASHBOARDS FOR BUSINESS PERFORMANCE IN BIG DATA

KPI visualizations dashboards serve as powerful tools for monitoring and improving business performance. They provide real-time visibility into KPI metrics and enable organizations to track progress, identify trends, analyze anomalies, and make data-driven decisions. This section explores how KPI dashboards can be effectively utilized to enhance business performance in various ways.

1.   Monitoring and Tracking KPI metrics

One of the primary functions of KPI dashboards is to monitor and track KPIs regularly. By displaying KPI metrics in a visual and accessible format, dashboards allow stakeholders to monitor performance in real-time and keep a pulse on the organization's progress towards its goals. Regular monitoring helps identify performance gaps and enables timely interventions to address issues. It also promotes accountability and fosters a culture of continuous improvement. Visualization dashboards provide a comprehensive view of KPI metrics across different departments and levels of the organization. This facilitates transparency and promotes alignment by ensuring that everyone has access to the same performance information. Monitoring KPIs on dashboards can drive healthy competition among teams, as well as collaboration and knowledge sharing to improve overall performance.

2.   Identifying Performance Trends and Anomalies

KPI dashboards are instrumental in identifying performance trends and anomalies. By visualizing historical data and trends, dashboards enable users to spot patterns and understand the trajectory of performance over time. This insight helps organizations identify positive trends that indicate success and areas of improvement that require attention. In addition, KPI visualization dashboards allow for the detection of performance anomalies or outliers. By comparing current performance against historical data or established benchmarks, organizations can identify unusual spikes or dips in KPI metrics. Anomalies may signal problems or opportunities that require further investigation and action. Timely identification of anomalies can help organizations mitigate risks, optimize processes, or capitalize on emerging opportunities.

3.   Analyzing Root Causes of Performance Issues

KPI dashboards facilitate the analysis of root causes behind performance issues. When a KPI indicates underperformance, dashboards provide a starting point for exploring the factors influencing that performance. By combining KPI data with other relevant data sources, such as customer feedback, operational metrics, or market trends, organizations can gain deeper insights into the root causes of performance issues. Analyzing root causes helps organizations understand the drivers behind poor performance and supports the development of targeted improvement strategies. It enables organizations to take corrective actions, allocate resources effectively, and address underlying issues that may be impacting multiple KPIs. By drilling down into the data and identifying causative factors, organizations can make informed decisions on how to enhance performance.

4.   Improving Decision-Making with KPI Dashboards

KPI dashboards play a vital role in improving decision-making processes within organizations. By providing real-time, accurate, and actionable information, dashboards empower decision-makers to make informed choices based on data-driven insights. The availability of up-to-date KPI data on dashboards eliminates reliance on outdated reports or manual data gathering processes. KPI visualization dashboards facilitate evidence-based decision-making by presenting relevant KPIs alongside contextual information, such as targets, benchmarks, or historical trends. This allows decision-makers to assess performance against predefined standards or goals and evaluate the impact of potential decisions on different KPIs. Dashboards also enable stakeholders to collaborate and share insights, aligning decision-making across departments and ensuring a holistic view of performance.

By utilizing KPI dashboards in decision-making processes, organizations can enhance agility, increase efficiency, and improve outcomes. They can respond quickly to emerging trends, identify strategic opportunities, and address performance gaps promptly.

BENEFITS AND CHALLENGES OF KPI DASHBOARDS FOR BIG DATA

KPI dashboards provide real-time visibility into key performance indicators, facilitating monitoring and decision-making processes. Understanding the benefits and challenges of these tools is crucial for organizations to leverage their full potential. This section discusses the benefits of KPI dashboards, challenges in implementing them, and challenges in utilizing them. Real-world examples and references support the discussion and provide comprehensive insights into the topic.

Benefits of KPI Dashboards

KPI dashboards offer numerous benefits to organizations:

1.   Real-time Monitoring

KPI dashboards provide real-time visibility into key performance indicators, enabling organizations to monitor performance briefly. This allows for timely interventions, quick, and proactive decision-making (Few, S. 2006).

2.   Data-driven Decision-making

KPI dashboards facilitate data-driven decision-making by presenting critical information in a clear and concise manner. The visual representations of KPIs aid in understanding complex data, identifying trends, and making informed decisions based on accurate and up-to-date information (Few, S. 2013).

3.   *Enhanced Accountability*

KPI dashboards foster a culture of accountability by making performance data transparent and accessible. Employees and teams become more aware of their performance and take ownership of their goals, driving improvements and aligning efforts with organizational objectives (Rosenfeld, 2006).

4.   *Performance Insights and Gap Analysis*

KPI dashboards provide valuable insights into performance trends and enable the identification of performance gaps. By comparing actual performance against targets or benchmarks, organizations can pinpoint areas that require improvement and allocate resources effectively.

Challenges in Implementing Big Data Visualization Dashboards

Building and implementing big data visualization dashboards comes with its own set of challenges:

1.   *Data Quality and Integration*

Ensuring data accuracy, consistency, and integration from multiple sources can be challenging. Organizations need to establish data governance practices, address data quality issues, and integrate data from disparate systems to provide a unified view of performance (Few, 2006).

2.   Selecting Relevant KPIs

Selecting the right KPI metric that aligns with organizational goals and provide actionable insights is crucial. It requires a deep understanding of the business context, identification of meaningful metrics, and alignment with the strategic objectives (Few, S. 2013).

3.   User Adoption and Engagement

Encouraging user adoption and engagement with KPI dashboards can be challenging. Proper training, effective communication, and demonstrating the value of dashboards to end-users are essential to foster acceptance and utilization (Rosenfeld, 2006).

TOOLS AND TECHNOLOGIES FOR BIG DATA VISUALIZATION

In the dynamic landscape of big data, the ability to effectively visualize complex datasets is essential for extracting actionable insights. To address this need, a plethora of tools and technologies have emerged, offering diverse capabilities to handle, analyze, and visualize large-scale data. These tools empower businesses to make informed decisions, identify patterns, and uncover hidden trends within the vast sea of information. This section explores some of the prominent tools and technologies used for big data visualization, highlighting their features, benefits, and contributions to the field of market intelligence.

Open-Source Visualization Tools

Open-source tools have gained significant traction for their accessibility, customizability, and community-driven development. Among these, D³.js (Data-Driven Documents) stands out as a powerful JavaScript library for creating dynamic and interactive visualizations in web browsers (Bostock, 2011). Its flexibility allows developers to control every aspect of visualization, making it suitable for creating tailored visualizations aligned with market intelligence needs.

Another noteworthy tool is Matplotlib, a popular Python library that offers a wide range of static, interactive, and animated visualizations (Hunter, 2007). Matplotlib's simplicity and compatibility with various data formats make it a preferred choice for data scientists and analysts.

Commercial Visualization Platforms

Commercial platforms provide comprehensive solutions for data visualization, offering user-friendly interfaces and advanced features. Tableau is a widely adopted platform that allows users to create interactive dashboards, reports, and charts without extensive coding knowledge. Its drag-and-drop interface enables rapid visualization creation, making it suitable for professionals seeking quick insights from their data.

Power BI by Microsoft is another robust platform that seamlessly integrates with other Microsoft products. It offers a range of data connectors, advanced analytics capabilities, and AI-driven insights. Power BI's integration with cloud-based services facilitates real-time collaboration and sharing of visualizations.

Integration With Big Data Analytics Platforms

The integration of visualization with big data analytics platforms enhances the seamless flow of data analysis and visualization. Apache Hadoop, a widely used framework for distributed storage and processing of large datasets, has evolved to incorporate visualization tools such as Hue. Hue provides an intuitive web interface for interacting with Hadoop components, enabling data exploration and visualization. Apache Spark has also embraced visualization through libraries like Spark SQL, which enables data analysts to create interactive visualizations directly from Spark data. This integration minimizes data movement between platforms, streamlining the visualization process.

Selecting the appropriate tool or technology depends on factors such as data complexity, user expertise, and specific market intelligence requirements. As the field of big data visualization continues to evolve, staying informed about these tools and their capabilities is crucial for deriving valuable insights from the ever-expanding universe of data.

BIG DATA VISUALIZATION FOR MARKET INTELLIGENCE

In the era of big data, where information flows ceaselessly from numerous sources, the art of visualization has emerged as a critical tool for turning data into insights. In the realm of market intelligence, where the ability to decipher trends, patterns, and opportunities is paramount, effective visualization practices play a pivotal role. This section delves into the best practices that elevate big data visualization for market intelligence, encompassing data preprocessing, visualization technique selection, interactive dashboard design, and the integration of storytelling and narrative elements.

Data Preprocessing and Cleaning for Visualization Tools

Data, in its raw form, is often riddled with noise, inconsistencies, and gaps. These imperfections can distort the visual representation of insights and lead to misguided conclusions. Hence, the initial step in the big data visualization process is data preprocessing and cleaning (Wang, 2018). This practice involves detecting and rectifying outliers, handling missing values, and addressing inconsistencies. Before data can be effectively visualized, it needs to be transformed into a structured, coherent format. Cleansing data ensures that the visualization accurately portrays the underlying market intelligence. Neglecting this step can result in misinterpretations and poor decision-making.

Choosing the Right Visualization Technique for Data Exploration

Selecting the appropriate visualization technique is akin to choosing the right tool for a task. Different visualization types excel at revealing distinct aspects of data. In the context of market intelligence, understanding the nature of the data and the insights sought is crucial in choosing the right visualization method (Steele, 2010).

For instance, line graphs are ideal for showcasing trends over time, while scatter plots help identify correlations between variables. By aligning the visualization technique with the data's characteristics, market intelligence professionals can unlock insights that might remain hidden in raw data.

Designing Interactive Dashboards for Real-time Monitoring

Market intelligence is a dynamic field where timely insights are paramount. Interactive dashboards provide an avenue for real-time monitoring and exploration of data (Satyanarayan, 2016). Tools like Tableau and Power BI empower users to navigate through data, apply filters, and drill down into specific details.

Designing interactive dashboards involves crafting user-friendly interfaces, organizing visualizations coherently, and providing intuitive controls. Such dashboards offer the advantage of on-demand exploration, enabling market intelligence professionals to make swift decisions based on the latest data.

Security and Privacy

In the era of big data, where vast amounts of information are harnessed for marketing intelligence, ensuring the security and privacy of this data is paramount. Key Performance Indicators (KPIs) specific to security and privacy serve as vital metrics, guaranteeing the integrity of customer data and the trust of clients and stakeholders. One crucial Security KPI in the realm of marketing intelligence is Data Encryption Effectiveness, measuring the strength of encryption algorithms used to protect sensitive customer information. It ensures that data remains confidential during transmission and storage, building customer trust (Li, 2020)

Another essential KPI is Access Control Effectiveness, indicating how well the system restricts unauthorized access to marketing data. Effective access controls guarantee that only authorized personnel can view or manipulate specific datasets, safeguarding customer privacy (Chen L. e., 2019).

Incorporating Storytelling and Narrative in Visualizations

Data is more than just numbers; it tells a story. Incorporating storytelling and narrative elements into visualizations humanizes the data, providing context and guiding the audience through the insights (Hullman, 2011). This practice goes beyond presenting charts and graphs which helps create a narrative structure that highlights key points, fosters engagement, and influences decision-making.

In the realm of market intelligence, storytelling can contextualize trends, explain anomalies, and offer strategic recommendations. By integrating narrative elements, visualizations become more impactful tools for communication and persuasion.

The art of storytelling elevates visualizations to a level where they transcend data and become persuasive tools for decision-makers. By interweaving narratives, market intelligence professionals can provide context, evoke emotions, and guide actions based on insights derived from data. In the intricate world of big data, these best practices offer a roadmap to transform raw information into a compelling narrative, arming businesses with the insights needed to navigate the ever-evolving market landscape.

REAL-WORLD EXAMPLES OF BIG DATA KPI DASHBOARDS

This section provides real-world examples of the successful implementation and utilization of KPI dashboards. Case studies from different industries showcase the practical applications and benefits of these tools. Additionally, key lessons learned from these implementations are discussed, providing insights into best practices and considerations for organizations seeking to implement KPI dashboards References support the examples and lessons learned, ensuring a comprehensive understanding of the topic.

Case Study One: KPI Dashboard Implementation in Manufacturing Industry

In this case study, a manufacturing company implemented a KPI dashboard to monitor and improve its production processes. The company faced challenges in tracking key metrics and identifying bottlenecks that affected productivity and quality. By implementing a KPI dashboard, they aimed to gain real-time visibility into their operations and make data-driven decisions.

The KPI dashboard included metrics such as production cycle time, equipment downtime, defect rate, and on-time delivery. Real-time data from production machines and systems were integrated into the dashboard, providing a holistic view of performance. The dashboard utilized data visualization techniques such as line graphs, bar charts, and color-coded indicators to present the KPIs in an easily understandable format. Figure 6 shows a sample KPI dashboard of manufacturing industry to measure productivity. (Kinsey, 2023). The implementation of the KPI dashboard had several benefits for the manufacturing company. It enabled them to monitor performance at various levels, from individual machines to entire production lines. The real-time visibility allowed them to identify and address production inefficiencies promptly. By analyzing the KPIs, the company reduced downtime, improved cycle times, and enhanced overall productivity. The dashboard also facilitated effective communication among teams, as performance data was easily accessible and transparent.

Figure 6. Sample dashboard of manufacturing industry to measure productivity

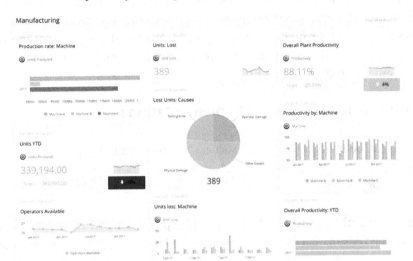

Case Study Two: Visualization Dashboard for Sales Trend and Distribution in Retail

In this case study, a retail company goal is to optimize inventory management and build a dashboard to study the same. The company faced challenges in accurately predicting customer demand and optimizing their inventory levels. By leveraging historical sales data, market trends, and external factors such as promotions and weather patterns, they aimed to improve their sales performance.

The prediction tools will utilize advanced analytics techniques, including time series models and machine learning algorithms, to forecast future sales at different levels, such as individual stores and product categories. The dashboard provided insights into demand patterns, allowing the company to optimize their inventory management strategies. Figure 7 shows the dashboard of sales along different demographics along with trend and sub-category information. (Anthonysmoak, 2018).

Figure 7. Sample dashboard of sales along different demographics with trend and sub-category

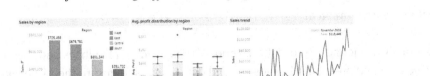

The visualization dashboard had significant benefits for the retail company. Accurate sales forecasting study enabled them to proactively adjust inventory levels, optimize replenishment cycles, and minimize stockouts or excess inventory. By aligning inventory with customer demand, they improved operational efficiency, reduced costs associated with overstocking or understocking, and enhanced customer satisfaction through improved product availability.

Lessons Learned from Successful Implementations

Several key lessons can be learned from these successful implementations:

1. *Clearly Define Objectives*

Clearly define the objectives and desired outcomes of implementing KPI dashboards. Align them with organizational goals and ensure that the selected metrics and models support these objectives effectively.

2. *Involve Stakeholders*

Engage stakeholders from various levels of the organization during the implementation process. Their input and feedback will ensure that the dashboards and tools meet their specific needs and provide valuable insights for decision-making.

3. Data Quality and Integration

Place emphasis on data quality, accuracy, and integration. Implement data governance practices, establish data quality controls, and integrate data from different sources to ensure the reliability and consistency of the information presented on dashboards.

4. Training and Support

Provide comprehensive training and ongoing support to end-users. Educate them on how to interpret and use dashboards effectively. Regular communication and support will encourage user adoption and maximize the value derived from these tools.

5. *Continuous Improvement*

Continuously refine and improve the dashboards based on user feedback and changing business needs. Regularly review and update KPIs, models, and data sources to ensure their relevance and accuracy.

CONCLUSION

In the swiftly evolving terrain of contemporary business, data has emerged as a strategic asset, and the capacity to translate this data into actionable insights holds paramount importance. Big data visualization emerges as a robust ally in this pursuit, serving as a vital link between intricate, extensive datasets and decision-makers seeking to harness their latent potential within the realm of market intelligence.

The exploration across the preceding sections has illuminated the intricate and multifaceted role that big data visualization assumes in the domain of market intelligence. Ranging from the unveiling of concealed patterns through cognitive and perceptual principles to the creation of interactive dashboards that empower real-time decision-making, the significance of proficient visualization techniques remains incontrovertible. Among the most profound revelations is the recognition that data surpasses the boundaries of numerical values – it encapsulates a narrative eager to be unveiled. The integration of storytelling and narrative components into visualizations adds a human dimension to data-driven insights. By providing contextual understanding, accentuating pivotal aspects, and adeptly guiding audiences through the data, visualizations evolve beyond being mere tools; they morph into instruments of communication and persuasion, endowed with the potential to significantly influence strategic decisions.

Furthermore, the potential of big data visualization extends to democratizing data-driven insights. In an era where proficiency in data interpretation is increasingly coveted, visualizations dismantle the complexities that data often presents. They empower a diverse array of stakeholders – ranging from top-tier executives to front-line analysts – to effectively engage with and interpret data. This democratization process ensures that valuable insights are not restricted to a privileged few; instead, they are disseminated throughout an organization, fostering a culture firmly rooted in data-driven decision-making.

As technology forges ahead with relentless momentum, the future of big data visualization in the sphere of market intelligence is brimming with promise. Advancements in machine learning and artificial intelligence are poised to amplify the capabilities of visualization tools. The convergence of virtual and augmented reality is revolutionizing how users interact with data, ushering in immersive experiences that transcend traditional two-dimensional representations.

However, this expedition is not devoid of challenges. Ethical considerations, including data privacy and bias, must remain at the forefront of visualization endeavors. Ensuring that insights are not merely accurate but also ethically sound is imperative to uphold public trust and drive conscientious decision-making.

In summation, big data visualization stands as a cornerstone of contemporary market intelligence. It metamorphoses raw data into a language that resonates with decision-makers, equipping them with the confidence to navigate the intricate contours of the market landscape. From uncovering trends and seizing opportunities to mitigating risks, visualizations serve as a navigational compass that steers businesses through the tumultuous waters of data. By adhering to the tenets of effective visualization, embracing the advancements of technology, and steadfastly upholding ethical standards, organizations can harness the full potential of big data, fostering innovation, growth, and triumphant strides in the ever-evolving realm of market intelligence.

REFERENCES

Banga, D. &. (2023). Emotion Detection in Speech. *11th International Symposium on Digital Forensics and Security (ISDFS)*, (pp. 1-4). Chattanooga, TN, USA.

Banga, D., & Peddireddy, K. (2023). Artificial Intelligence for Customer Complaint Management. *International Journal of Computer Trends and Technology*, *71*(3), 1–6. doi:10.14445/22312803/IJCTT-V71I3P101

Bostock, M. O., Ogievetsky, V., & Heer, J. (2011). D³ Data-Driven Documents. *IEEE Transactions on Visualization and Computer Graphics*, *17*(12), 2301–2309. doi:10.1109/TVCG.2011.185 PMID:22034350

Brown, A. (2018). Operational Efficiency in Big Data Management: A Comparative Study. *International Journal of Information Management*, *36*(5), 690–701.

Chen, H. C., Chiang, & Storey. (2012). Business intelligence and analytics: From big data to big impact. *Management Information Systems Quarterly*, *36*(4), 1165–1188. doi:10.2307/41703503

Chen, L. e. (2019). Leveraging Big Data for Competitive Advantage: A Case Study in E-commerce. *Journal of Business Analytics*, *2*(1), 45–56.

Eckerson, W. W. (2010). *Performance dashboards: Measuring, monitoring, and managing your business*. John Wiley & Sons.

Few, S. (2006). *Information dashboard design: The effective visual communication of data*. O'Reilly Media.

Few, S. (2009). *Now you see it: Simple visualization techniques for quantitative analysis*. Analytics Press.

Few, S. (2013). *Information dashboard design: Displaying data for at-a-glance monitoring*. O'Reilly Media.

Hullman, J., & Diakopoulos, N. (2011). Visualization rhetoric: Framing effects in narrative visualization. *IEEE Transactions on Visualization and Computer Graphics*, *17*(12), 2231–2240. doi:10.1109/TVCG.2011.255 PMID:22034342

Hunter, J. D. (2007). Matplotlib: A 2D graphics environment. *Computing in Science & Engineering*, *9*(3), 90–95. doi:10.1109/MCSE.2007.55

Kelleher, J. D. (2015). *Fundamentals of machine learning for predictive data analytics: Algorithms, worked examples, and case studies*. MIT Press.

Kinsey, S. (2023, February 24). *KPI Dashboards: A comprehensive guide*. Simple KPI. https://www.simplekpi.com/Blog/KPI-Dashboards-a-comprehensive-guide

Kiron, D. P. (2018). *Data-driven: Creating a data culture*. MIT Sloan Management Review Research Report.

Li, W. (2020). Enhancing Big Data Security: A Comprehensive Approach. *Journal of Cybersecurity*, *5*(3), 201–215.

Makridakis, S. S., Spiliotis, E., & Assimakopoulos, V. (2018). Statistical and Machine Learning forecasting methods. *Concerns and ways forward. PLoS One*, *13*(3), e0194889. doi:10.1371/journal.pone.0194889 PMID:29584784

Milgram, P. (1994). A taxonomy of mixed reality visual displays. *IEICE Transactions on Information and Systems*, *77*(12), 1321–1329.

Parmenter, D. (2015). *Key performance indicators: Developing, implementing, and using winning KPIs.* John Wiley & Sons. doi:10.1002/9781119019855

Rosenfeld, L. (2006). *Information architecture for the World Wide Web: Designing large-scale web sites.* O'Reilly Media.

Satyanarayan, A. M. (2016). Vega-Lite: A grammar of interactive graphics. *IEEE Transactions on Visualization and Computer Graphics*, 341–350. PMID:27875150

Segel, E., & Heer, J. (2010). Narrative visualization: Telling stories with data. *IEEE Transactions on Visualization and Computer Graphics*, *16*(6), 1139–1148. doi:10.1109/TVCG.2010.179 PMID:20975152

Smith, J. (2017). Data Quality in Big Data: A Review. *Journal of Data Analysis14(2)*, 112-125.

Steele, J. (2010). *Designing data visualizations.* O'Reilly Media.

Wang, S. (2018). Data cleaning in big data: A survey. *Data Science and Engineering*, *3*(1), 15–30.

Witten, I. H. (2016). *Data mining: Practical machine learning tools and techniques.* Morgan Kaufmann.

Wixom, B. H. (2010). The BI-based organization. *MIS Quarterly Executive*, *9*(2), 61–80.

KEY TERMS AND DEFINITIONS

Dashboard: It is useful for monitoring, measuring, and analyzing relevant data in key areas. They take raw data from many sources and clearly present it in a way that's highly tailored to the viewer's needs.

Data Accuracy: Refers to the correctness and reliability of the data. It indicates the overall data quality It helps businesses to make smart and strategic decisions.

Data Analysis: the process of systematically applying statistical and/or logical techniques to describe and illustrate, condense and recap, and evaluate data.

Data Anomalies: It refers to the faults or defects in the data caused whenever there is unclean data. This can affect the analysis and alter the business decisions.

Data Variables: Any characteristics or features about the data. A variable can be a number, quantity, or text. Examples: Age, sales amount, Address.

Key Performance Indicator (KPI): Refers to the measured to measure the success of any business activities.

Segmentation: It is the process of dividing the data in homogeneous groups so that similar data group together based on the chosen parameters so that it can be use more efficiently for marketing and operations purposes.

Chapter 12
Apollo Hospital's Proposed Use of Big Data Healthcare Analytics

Shahanawaj Ahamad
University of Hail, Saudi Arabia

S. Janani
Periyar Maniammai Institute of Science and Technology, India

Veera Talukdar
https://orcid.org/0000-0002-9204-5825
D.Y. Patil International University, India

Tripti Sharma
https://orcid.org/0009-0003-4122-4481
Rungta College of Engineering and Technology, India

Aradhana Sahu
Rungta College of Engineering and Technology, India

Sabyasachi Pramanik
https://orcid.org/0000-0002-9431-8751
Haldia Institute of Technology, India

Ankur Gupta
https://orcid.org/0000-0002-4651-5830
Vaish College of Engineering, Rohtak, India

ABSTRACT

This chapter describes how one may stock clinical data in digital forms, such as patient reports as an electronic health record, and how one may create meaningful information from these records utilizing analytics methods and tools. Apollo Hospital is the biggest hospital in West Bengal. It collects a huge quantity of heterogeneous data from various sources, including patient health records, lab test results, digital diagnostic supplies, healthcare insurance data, social media data, pharmaceutical data, gene expression records, transactions, and data from MY hospital's Mahatma Gandhi Memorial Medical College. Data analytics could be used to organise this data and make it retrievable. As a result, the term "big data" may be used. Big data is defined as exceptionally big datasets which may be analysed computationally to uncover trends, patterns, and relationships, as well as visualisation, querying, information privacy, and predictive analytics on a huge dataset.

DOI: 10.4018/979-8-3693-0413-6.ch012

1. INTRODUCTION

Today's healthcare business creates a vast quantity of data from patient records, health and medical device records, pharmaceutical experimentation data, healthcare insured data, medical data, patient feedback data lab findings, images (like CT scan and X-ray), health policy data audio and video data. The data which are produced may be unstructured or structured. In this modern digital world, digitization of this data is required. In exchange, the digitalization of healthcare data will aid in the provision of higher-quality treatment at lower costs. Healthcare companies may leverage current tools and technology to evaluate data in digital form and provide significant insights in treating patients. Big data is characterised as a high amount of structured (RDBMS) and un-structured (multimedia, text and web pages) data that is challenging to manage utilizing standard databases and software (MySQL, MongoDB and Oracle). Big data denotes a technique which consists of both tools and procedures that a company needs to manage massive amounts of data and storage. To enhance the standard of medical treatment, it is required for extraction of hidden facts and statistics from a vast amount of acquired data in order to address new difficulties such as lowering healthcare costs. Similarly, hospitals like the Apollo hospital in Kolkata that is taken into granted to be Kolkata's largest hospital in Kolkata, generate huge volumes of data that may be classified as "Big data" because millions of people are served every day, the majority of who are below the poverty-level and mostly work as daily-earners. If these persons go to the hospital, they would have to stand in a lengthy line for medication, wasting the entire day and losing their income for the whole day, leaving them hungry. So, to get out of this predicament, we may save patient information in electronic medium such as the EHR (Mahajan, H.B., et al. 2023) that will retain both money and time for patients and healthcare providers, and the government. An electronic health record (EHR) is a standardised assemblage of a patient's e-health record that may be exchanged across multiple hospital branches in a network. Demographics, medical history, medications, prior lab test reports, radiology-based records, major organ reports, and individual record may all be stored in EHRs.

With the utilization of decision tree (Chellam, V. V. Et al. 2023), clustering, association, sequence analysis, classification, segmentation, regression, and web mining techniques, big data analysis aids in the discovery of important judgments by identifying data patterns and their relationships. Hadoop is an open-source software architecture stores data that enables massive repository of various data, tremendous computation power having the capacity for executing almost unlimited parallel operations or tasks.

2. REVIEW OF THE LITERATURE

It has been discovered that digitalizing denotes a necessary in medical organisations since a great quantity of record is created connecting a patient's wellbeing data to its genomic investigation, and effective storage is sought utilising big data and analytics to maintain track of this information.

Doctors may produce profound insights, according to (Won *et al* 2021), via the digitalization of health records, which may expedite clinical processes, enhance treatment, build-patient associations, save expenditures, and better things.

In a research published in (Bi, H. et al. 2021) showed how big data analysis consists of having the ability for altering sophisticated technology for getting insight from healthcare and other datasets and making judgments.

(Mahajan, H.B. 2020) explained that attaining good results at reduced costs is critical for medical care, and that this may be accomplished by using MapReduce and Hadoop HDFS to unearth the knowledge hidden in large health datasets.

According to (Bi, H. et al. 2021) analysis by Mackinsey & Company, big data analytics may save the US $300 billion per year in costs, with $165 billion saved in medical operations and billions saved in Research & Development wastage. Indian government spends around 5.3% of the GDP on medical research, necessitating the utilization of technologies such as big data analysis to provide good medical treatment to the citizens.

3. APOLLO HOSPITAL HEALTHCARE

Apollo hospital is the name of a private hospital in Kolkata, India. Kolkata is a health-care centre as well as a pharmaceutical powerhouse in eastern India. Among both government and private hospitals in West Bengal, Apollo hospital is the biggest. Since 1952, it has been eastern India's 1st computerised private hospital. It has 2300 beds and most of the main clinical departments, including a 20-bed Medical Intensive Care Unit, an 8-bed ICCU, five haemodialysis machines, an endoscopic unit, and ventilators, among others. It is an eight-story government hospital with sub-hospitals on its site, including a 600-bed COVID-19 Hospital, a 160-bed cancer Hospital, and a 180-bed Coronary Artery Disease hospital. This hospital is also connected to a medical school. Under a federal government programme, underprivileged people are given preferential treatment at this hospital. Millions of persons from all across eastern region of the country visit this facility on daily means. It also serves as an emergency centre for the majority of West Bengal's rural and district hospitals. This hospital has all of the current healthcare services. It also consists of a Blood Bank, that promotes young people to give blood and, during a crisis, this mobile blood bank may be utilised as a lifesaver.

In the country's countryside public clinical system, there are 3 categories of medical access. Health care is divided into three categories: a) primary b) secondary and c) tertiary. During the most basic phase, one has primary health centres (PHCs) (Praveenkumar S. et al. 2023) that are basic branches with basic amenities servicing the village population in India. An individual PHC oversees six sub centres, with the most vital category of health in communities with the initial place of contact for the village people with public health care. Secondary medical care refers to the 2nd layer of the health-care framework, when patients from 3rd level are sent for specialist care. Health centres and Community health centres provide secondary health care. Fig 1 shows the various levels of healthcare in India.

The initial and most frequent level of care for health issues, diseases, illnesses, symptoms, or non-life-threatening situations is primary care. A family doctor or general practitioner is a common representation of basic care, and you visit them when you're ill or have health problems. During annual physicals or scheduled appointments, primary care professionals (PCPs) evaluate your general health to identify prevalent ailments and disorders and to address other personal healthcare issues like:

- A skin rash
- Bone fractures
- Colds
- Flu
- Allergies

Figure 1. Various levels of healthcare in the country

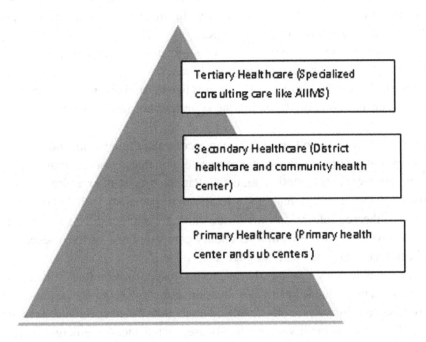

- Weight management problems
- Virus and bacterial infections

Primary healthcare practitioners are crucial because they frequently give better access to healthcare services, more well-being education, and frequently lower the frequency of emergency room visits or hospitalizations in a community. In some cases, usually through referrals, they assist in coordinating your care with experts or higher levels of care. Primary care physicians provide treatment for minor ailments, conduct routine examinations and tests, respond to your medical inquiries, and maintain records pertaining to your overall health and welfare. PCPs can be generalists in healthcare or those that focus on a single population group, and they can include:

- Doctors
- Pediatricians
- Geriatricians
- Obstetrician

Secondary care is a far special degree of care, regularly taken care of by physicians having a basic area of expertise. This may be for a particular body organ or framework, or a basic illness, disease, or state. Oncologists, for instance, are medical professionals trained in the treatment of cancers. Most of them also have additional specializations in certain cancer types, like breast cancer, lung cancer, or skin cancer. Heart specialists only treat diseases and anomalies of the heart. Dermatologists also treat conditions like eczema, psoriasis, acne, and other skin conditions. Various such instances of secondary care physicians include:

- Asthma, hives, and other allergic disorders and ailments are all treated by allergists.
- Doctors of infectious diseases are experts in treating infectious conditions like pneumonia, cellulitis, influenza, and infections following surgery.
- Ophthalmologists are medical professionals with a focus on vision and eye care, such as regular eye exams, eye operations, and eye illnesses or diseases.
- Endocrinologists: Endocrinologists treat problems like thyroid disorders, infertility, and hormonal imbalances by concentrating on the endocrine system of hormones and glands.

Both primary care physicians and specialists can recommend treatments and provide medications. When a patient's medical condition necessitates more attention than a primary care practitioner can supply, secondary care reviews are frequently conducted. Patients frequently require a recommendation, or referral, from their primary care physician in order to see a specialist. To help coordinate overall care and make sure all healthcare professionals are aware of what the other doctor is handling and guiding, patients who are receiving treatment from a secondary care supplier—or from several secondary care dealers—often keep their main care supplier engaged.

In the healthcare area, tertiary care mostly denotes to hospitalization that calls for expert tools and knowledge for a significant or unique healthcare situation. For some patients, it represents the third point of contact after visits to a primary care physician and a secondary care specialist. Transferring a patient to a larger metropolitan medical facility or one that focuses on advanced or emergent care is occasionally necessary for tertiary care. Tertiary care examples include:

- Aneurysmal dissections
- Hemodialysis or the kidney
- heart bypass surgery
- Neurosurgery
- remedies for severe burns

Although some patients may require tertiary care, most patients can anticipate using primary and secondary care throughout their lifespan. A patient could require tertiary care more than once, depending on their illness or their particular medical circumstance. To make certain optimum uses and outcomes for long-goal and continuing nursing or self-management for persistent illnesses and ailments, patients getting tertiary care again frequently have contact with their primary care doctor all through the techniques. Fig 2 shows the flow diagram of the activities of Apollo Hospital.

Apollo Hospital's Treatment Procedure

To get treatment, patients visiting the hospital must complete a number of tasks.

1. To obtain an appointment, patients must first register at the OPD and pay a nominal fee of Rs 10.
2. Patients are sent to a certain division or sub-hospital of the hospital after registering at the OPD, based on the medical-based information provided by the patients.
3. Patients are treated by professional physicians who prescribe medications or send them to a laboratory for testing.
4. Patients then go to the lab for testing and get their results.

Figure 2. Flow diagram of the activities of Apollo Hospital

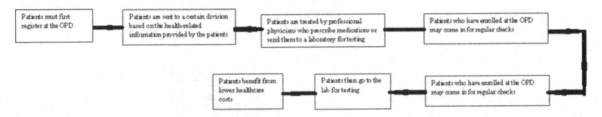

5.   Doctors treat patients based on the findings of their tests.

6.   The majority of drugs, including those for disorders like as cancer, are freely accessible. In this facility, Ebola is offered at a lower cost.

7.   Patients who have enrolled at the OPD may come in for regular checks without incurring any additional charges.

8.   A team of professional physicians is always accessible in the event of an emergency.

9.   Patients benefit from lower healthcare costs for sophisticated surgery like as knee replacement, heart surgery, and other procedures that would otherwise be prohibitively expensive in a private hospital. Even ICCU is fairly inexpensive per bed.

The flow diagram is shown below.

4. RESEARCH CONDUCTED IN HOSPITAL

For our study, we wanted to investigate how the existing health system in Apollo Hospital operates, what services are provided to patients, and what challenges they encounter. We performed a survey of 150 employees at Apollo Hospital and attempted to establish a link between Apollo hospital's present operations and current healthcare technology accessible in the market, as well as how we might enhance the hospital's healthcare facilities utilizing big data analytics.

We enquired many questions in our survey, including their name, age, city, if they have health insurance, if they patients have to wait in a long line to see a consultant, what are the difficulties they face when they visit the hospital, their existing health issue or disease, and their previous health matters, as well as their annual salary and healthcare expenditures. Additionally, we enquired them if they utilize a smart phone or the internet, and if they would prefer to purchase their health records in the form of an EHR. We also enquired them regarding the "future research work," that will be an appendix of this research, and if they have a "one touch" facility, that would mean building an application through which a patient could access all of his current and historical healthcare records in one place.

The findings of this study conducted at Apollo Hospital illustrate a number of issues that patients and clinicians encounter, including 1.

1.   Patients must line for extended periods of time at the OPD, the physicians' waiting room, the laboratory, and the medicine department, among other places.

2.   Patients sometimes misplace their prescription papers, making it harder for physicians to treat them.

Figure 3. Percentage of respondents who agree that they must wait in a lengthy line

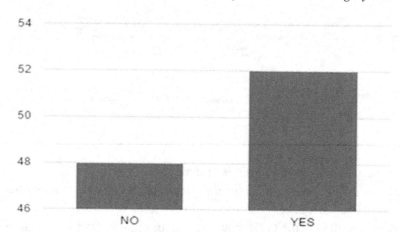

3. Thousands of patients visit this facility, and occasionally their labs and health records are out of sync, which may be disastrous.
4. Doctors must treat thousands of individuals on a daily basis without knowing their medical history, evaluating their condition, which is a time-consuming and error-prone task.
5. This patient's therapy takes a long time, which inhibits everyday wagers to complete medication on time.

The utilization of big data analytics to digitise the present system might be a solution to all of the problems outlined above.

We questioned individuals in this poll whether they had to stay in large lines for consultant's appointments or if they have to submit a sample at a laboratory. Yes, they had to stand in large lines and it is a time-engaging procedure, according to the majority of them. Fig 3 represents the percentage of respondents who agree that they must wait in a lengthy line

This issue may be handled at Apollo hospital by implementing an electronic health record (EHR), which will aid in the electronic storage of patient records and enable retrieval, reducing patient wait times.

Another question we had was about the facility provided at APOLLO HOSPITAL., and most people said they are average, emphasising the need for improvement in this area. Patient's management (Pramanik, S. et al. 2023), according to people, is the most important area for improvement because they are frequently ported from one zone to the other extreme zone of the hospital, wasting plenty of time needlessly, and in situations of emergency, patients face calamity, giving up their soul. The pie chart here depicts the issue as well as the survey results. Figure 4 shows the results of a survey of Apollo Hospital hospital's services.

The financial history of the patient arriving to APOLLO HOSPITAL was the third part of our survey. We inquired about their medical bills on a yearly basis. Because of their background, the individuals who attend Apollo Hospital are impoverished and unable to pay private hospitals, according to the results of this poll. When patients and attainders come to the hospital, they are mainly everyday gamblers who can't afford to remain and eat for days on end owing to their bad financial situation; therefore wasting time at the hospital is a restraint for them. We believe that big data analytics might be a solution to this

Figure 4. Results of a survey of Apollo Hospital hospital's services

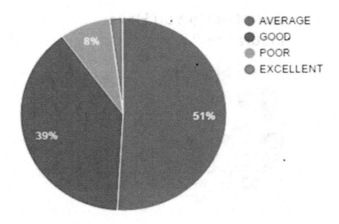

issue since when a patient returns for follow-up, he will need to spend the least amount of time feasible in therapy. The graph below depicts the link between an individual's yearly income and medical expenses. Fig 5. Shows the survey outcomes for earning and yearly costs.

Another financial component of health insurance is the premiums. We discovered that few persons had healthcare coverage and were also ignorant of current programmes such as the "PM Fund Relief" indicating that government initiatives are moreover failing to reach the poor and underprivileged owing to a need of knowledge among this demographic. The pie chart depicts the results of our insurance survey. Figure 6 shows the number of persons with health insurance.

Figure 5. Survey outcomes for earning and yearly costs

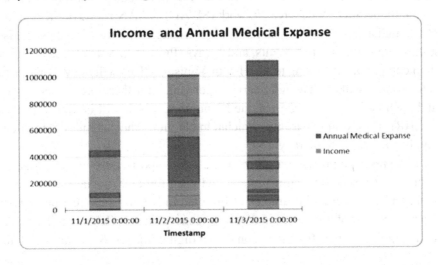

Figure 6. Number of persons with health insurance

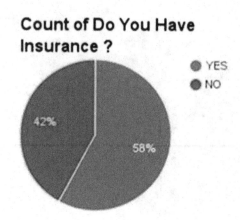

5. PROPOSED ELECTRONIC HEALTH RECORD AND BIG DATA IMPLEMENTATION IN APOLLO HOSPITAL'S MEDICINAL

Apollo hospital creates a vast quantity of data, and storing it electronically using computers, EHRs, and other technologies will make it easier to run analytics on it. We can record patient data and produce a special quantity exclusive to him using EHR, and patient information may be accessed simply using this unique number. The data may be kept in data warehouses, and we may utilise data mining, data classification, and data clustering to extract meaningful information from the vast data. The problems identified in the study may be rectified by physicians and patients using computers in hospitals.

Hospitals have altered as a consequence of engineering progress, allowing nurses and physicians to become effective with patients. Big Data (Bansal, R. et al. 2021) analytics methodologies and future technologies can be implemented at Apollo Hospital because, according to the Indian government's health department, Madhya Pradesh, where Apollo medical centre is situated, will be the foremost state in the nation to have complete computerised healthcare facilities, and Apollo Hospital can be digitally mastered with this future plan. Another feather in the cap is the government of India's announcement that it would computerise health facilities, 20 health centres, and three medical institutions in the future years by connecting them to the State Wide Area Network (SWAN). SWAN is one of the core infrastructural components of the Indian government's national e-governance initiative. Patients' registration slips, healthcare histories, prescriptions, test results, and X-rays (Pramanik, S. et al. 2021) will be accessible online via post on computers, according to the Health Minister. "This will allow patients to get therapy in any other state hospital without having to carry paperwork." Furthermore, patients who attend government hospitals will be issued a single Unique ID number, which will be linked to their Electronic Health Record (EHR). This would assist the clinician in obtaining the patient's comprehensive medical history and providing appropriate therapy."

Patient data, like prescriptions, laboratory reports, x-ray reports, case history, food chart, pool of physicians and nurses at a specific health centers, and drug research, social media, genetic research, transactional data, and so on, are all examples of big data in health-care. Healthcare businesses have been keeping a large quantity of transactional data in various databases (Khanh, P. T. et al. 2023), forms, and systems for a long time. Apart from traditional, and digital images (Samanta, D. Et al. 2021), non-

Figure 7. Sources of healthcare data

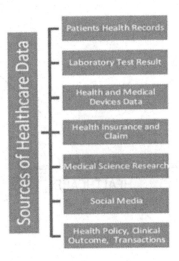

traditional, less structured data from web blogs, social media, call centres, group chats, videoconferencing, e - mail, hardware sensors (Ghosh, R. et al. 2020), and digital images may be mined for decision taking. Data collecting has become possible due to lower storage and computational power costs. The following are examples of big data in healthcare:

Traditional business data: For example, insurance transactional data, patient admittance, laboratory test information, and so on. Fig. 7 shows the sources of healthcare data

Data from health equipment like CT digitized scanners, backup systems, and telemetry data and telemedicine data.

Patients' feedback streams, blogs on Twitter or Facebook are all examples of social media data.

Drug analysis, genetic research, healthcare and transaction research are all examples of medical science study.

Big Data Characteristics

There are six features of big data.

Volume: As previously said, healthcare companies create large amounts of data from many sources of medical data. This capability afforded by big data may aid in the storage of cell sequence structures of massive persons, which can then aid in the detection of future genetic disorders like as diabetes and cancer, which can then be proactively managed and prevented from occurring.

Velocity: Different units at a hospital produce significant amounts of data at the same time. Social media generates a lot of opinions and relationships. This data is useful for monitoring patient comments, payments, adverse effects in medication trials, and well-being conversations in hospitals. The immediate availability of data may be utilised to seek advice from physicians in far-flung locations in order to treat a patient in any area.

Variety: It denotes to a wide range of structured and unstructured data sources, including databases, emails, photos, videos, monitoring equipment, telemedicine, sensors (Pramanik, S. et al. 2019), and EHRs, among others. Structured data types, such as excel spreadsheet, datasets, emails, photos, videos,

Figure 8. Six V's of big data

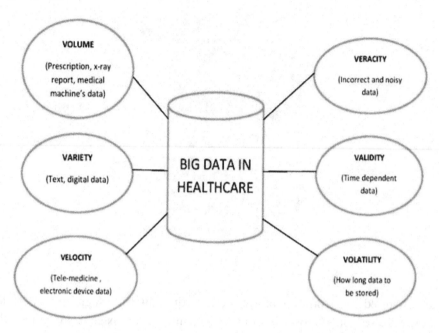

monitoring equipment, telemedicine, sensors, and electronic health records, are examples of structured data, whereas unstructured data poses challenges for data storage, mining (Pramanik, S. et al. 2022), and analysis. All previous patient treatment experiences and lessons acquired may be saved and referenced later. Fig. 8. Shows the six V's of big data

The term "veracity" refers to the noise (Jayasingh, R. et al. 2022) and inaccuracy in healthcare data. All outmoded data connected to medications and pharmaceuticals must be cleansed on a regular basis by deleting this "dirty data."

Validity: In healthcare, it relates to time-based data, such as in telemedicine, where the data of every second is critical in treatment. If data is not received in a timely manner, the patient's life may be jeopardised. For instance, there are various tests that are impossible to detect locally; as a consequence, samples are transferred to major cities, where reports take 3 to 7 days to arrive in India. Big data analytics may have a key role in making reports or findings accessible in seconds. Fig. 9. Shows the Hadoop Architecture.

Volatility relates to the length of time that data is valid and storable, as well as whether or not it should be removed. Small health concerns, such as normal temperature and discomfort, may be phased out over time since they become outdated and, at times, do not help to making long-term choices for major illnesses.

Big Data's Benefits at Apollo Hospital

Healthcare services at Apollo Hospital may be enhanced by digitising, consolidating, and properly exploiting big data. Using EHR, patients' information may be maintained electronically, allowing for faster access to health records. The usage of electronic health records (EHRs) will considerably expand

Figure 9. Hadoop architecture

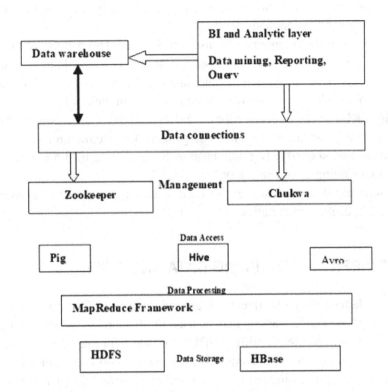

healthcare data. Detecting diseases at a timely stage while they may be handled more eagerly and successfully, supervising specific person and population health, and identifying insurance fraud faster and easily are all fruitful advantages of big data. Big data analytics may provide answers to a variety of issues. Certain developments or outcomes, like duration of stay in health centres, patients who will choose elective surgery, patients who will likely not profit from surgical procedure, patients at threat for health problems, patients at threat for various clinic disease; disease extension; doctors at risk for progress in disease states; causal factors of disease progress can be estimated dependent on huge quantity of past data. At Apollo hospital, we're monitoring hospital quality and upgrading treatment procedures. At Apollo Hospital big data and analytics may assist in the areas:

Clinical Forms of treatment: Big data will permit for the effective repository of organised and unstructured medical data, as well as the efficient and correct treatment of patients at a lower cost and time by doing analytics on this data.

Administration: Big data will aid in the maintenance of all transactional records, financials, and the tracking of patient EHRs, feedback, and schedules of physicians and nurses, as well as assisting administration in making decisions.

Apollo hospital is the biggest government hospital in central India, and thousands of people visit it on a daily basis for treatment. Big data will aid in the extraction of hidden information (Pramanik, S. 2023) from massive data sets, allowing the government to develop health policy and allocate health budgets based on the findings of large data sets.

Clinical investigation and advancement: Apollo Hospital will serve as a testing ground for its affiliated medical schools. Medical students may use big data analytics to do investigation in therapy, genetics, semantics, and medication analysis.

Public health: Using big data to monitor disease outbreaks, analyse patterns (Ngoc, T. H. et al. 2023), and spread can help improve monitoring and response. It may be possible to design vaccinations that are quickly and precisely targeted. As an example, discovering new harmful illnesses, as well as their prevention and treatment, allowing individuals to be proactive in their cure.

Device/remote tracking: Big data can capture and analyse massive amounts of fast-moving data in real time, like data from in-healthcare and in-house gadgets, for safe monitoring.

Healthcare result and security: Big data enables fast access to health records in the event of an emergency while maintaining complete safety.

Fraud Detection: Big data analytics can be used to identify and eradicate insurance claim fraud (Pramanik, S. 2023) in healthcare organisations.

6. TOOLS AND APPROACHES IN BIG DATA ANALYSIS

Hadoop and HDFS (Hadoop file system) technologies might be utilised to do analytics on massive data created by APOLLO HOSPITAL. Hadoop may be used for data processing and storage since it is scalable, open source, and fault tolerant. It utilizes HDFS, that has fault tolerance, higher bandwidth, and a clustered storage design, and it works on commodity hardware. MapReduce (Pramanik, S. et al. 2021) is used for decentralized data processing of both structured and unstructured data. Fig 8 depicts the layers included in a Hadoop stack's software architecture.

HDFS, a decentralized file system in which every file seems to be extremely big, continuous, and addressable randomly, is shown at the bottom. The Hadoop Map Reduce system that acts on data in HDFS partitions, sorts and disburses the outcomes depending on key values for the output data, and thereby lowers the groupings of O/P data items utilizing match keys from the map phase of the job, is the middle tier of the stack. A key value layer exists in the Hadoop architecture for basic key-dependent record management activities. HBase may be accessed directly or controlled using declarative languages by a client application. Clients use the higher language compiler, which is the topmost layer in Hadoop.

Big data analytics is becoming more affordable because to new developing technologies such as the Apache Hadoop framework.

Other Big Data Analytics Tools and Approaches

Cloud computing is a less expensive technique. Many leading companies, such as Intel and IBM, provide SaaS to analyse data stored in cloud-dependent databases (Software as a Service) facility. Google Analytics is also used in our study. Cloud computing is a less expensive option.

OpenRefine: It's being used to improve the validity of massive data by cleaning a database. For instance, GoogleRefine allows us to prepare everything for examination.

At Apollo hospital, other technologies such as ML, A/B testing, visualisation, and search-dependent applications may be employed for healthcare data analytics.

Big Data Processing for Medical Imaging: A Viewpoint

Anatomical information is crucially provided by medical imaging in addition to identifying disease stages, and organ function. Moreover, it's utilized for organ delineation, detecting lung cancers, diagnosing spinal deformities, finding artery stenosis, finding aneurysms, and other things. These techniques merge machine learning techniques with image processing approached as enhancement, segmentation, and denoising. Newer computer-aided approaches and platforms are needed when data quantity and complexity rise in order to understand data relationships and construct successful, accurate, and computationally successfully approaches. The use of computer-aided medical diagnostics and decision support systems in clinical settings has enhanced as a consequence of the rapid growth of both the quantity of hospitals and patients. By using computational intelligence, various facets of medical, including diagnosis, prognosis, and screening, may be enhanced.

The merger of suitable care and computer analysis has the prospects to help doctors in performing diagnostic precision. Diagnostic accuracy and turnaround time may be increased by merging medical imaging with various forms of electronic health record data and genetic information.

Applications of Big Data in Genomics

As the human genome has been fully sequenced, the development of high-throughput sequencing techniques has allowed scientists to study genetic markers spanning a huge range of populations, increase productivity by more than huge orders of magnitude, and associate genetic causes of the phenotype in disease states. Microarray-based genome-wide analyses have proved effective in evaluating population-wide features and in aiding in the treatment of complex chaos including Crohn's disease and age-related muscle degeneration.

Given that the human genome contains 28,000–35,000 genes, analytics of higher-throughput sequencing methods in genomics is essentially a large data challenge. The integration of medical data from the genetic level to the physiological level of a human being is now surveyed over a number of years. These programs will help in helping every patient with individualized treatment.

To provide suggestions in a therapeutic environment, genome-scale large data can be easily and accurately surveyed. Because of the high cost, labour-intensive nature of this large data issue analysis, this topic is in its early stage with applications in certain target areas, like cancer.

Applications of big data in genomics span a broad span of areas. Here, we concentrate on pathway analysis, that examines the functional consequences of genes which are differentially denoted in an experiment or gene set of particular interest, and network reconstruction that examines the signals obtained utilizing higher-throughput approaches in order to reconstruct underlying regulatory networks. These networks have a result on a various cellular functions which have an impact on a person's physiological condition.

7. CONCLUSSION

Apollo Hospitalcreates a large amount of data, called as big data. Because Apollo hospital operates on a conventional system, it is important to turn paper work into paperless labour utilising digitization tools such as computers and electronic health records (EHRs), which will allow for the electronic storage of healthcare data. Big data analytics at this clinic will assist to deliver contemporary medical services at a lower cost and in less time, which will benefit the whole population of central India, since the majority of those who attend, are poor. This article discusses the issues that patients and clinicians confront, as well as potential remedies. It also goes into how big data analytics could be used to change people's healthcare by providing insight into healthcare choices. It also covers big data analytics technologies and methods such as Hadoop, cloud, and OpenRefine, as well as HDFS for large data storage. With using big data analytics, Apollo hospital may be able to reduce patient wait times in various lines, as well as providing clinicians with patient information via a unique number that can be used anytime and anywhere. The main benefit would be in an emergency scenario, saving more lives and enhancing patient and doctor satisfaction at Apollo hospital.

FUTURE DEVELOPMENT

Our research can be expanded by utilising cloud computing to allow for the portability of EHRs across the country or around the world for decent healthcare anywhere, at any time, without the need to carry an individual's previous treatment records, trying to make it more cost-effective, timely, and paperless.

REFERENCES

Bansal, R., Obaid, A. J., Gupta, A., Singh, R., & Pramanik, S. (2021). Impact of Big Data on Digital Transformation in 5G Era. *2nd International Conference on Physics and Applied Sciences (ICPAS 2021).* IOP. 10.1088/1742-6596/1963/1/012170

Bi, H., Liu, J., & Kato, N. (2021). Deep Learning-based Privacy Preservation and Data Analytics for IoT Enabled Healthcare. IEEE Transactions on Industrial Informatics. IEEE. doi:10.1109/TII.2021.3117285

Chellam, V. V., Veeraiah, V., Khanna, A., Sheikh, T. H., Pramanik, S., & Dhabliya, D. (2023). *A Machine Vision-based Approach for Tuberculosis Identification in Chest X-Rays Images of Patients, ICICC 2023.* Springer.

Ghosh, R., Mohanty, S., Pattnaik, P. K., & Pramanik, S. (2020). Performance Analysis Based on Probablity of False Alarm and Miss Detection in Cognitive Radio Network. *International Journal of Wireless and Mobile Computing*, 20(4), 2020. doi:10.1504/IJWMC.2021.117530

Jayasingh, R., Kumar, R. J. S., Telagathoti, D. B., Sagayam, K. M., & Pramanik, S. (2022). Speckle noise removal by SORAMA segmentation in Digital Image Processing to facilitate precise robotic surgery. *International Journal of Reliable and Quality E-Healthcare*, 11(1). 10.4018/IJRQEH.29508

Khanh, P. T., Ngọc, T. H., & Pramanik, S. (2023). Future of Smart Agriculture Techniques and Applications. In A. Khang & I. G. I. Global (Eds.), Advanced Technologies and AI-Equipped IoT Applications in High Tech Agriculture. Springer. doi:10.4018/978-1-6684-9231-4.ch021

Mahajan, H. B., Rashid, A. S., Junnarkar, A. A., Uke, N., Deshpande, S. D., Futane, P. R., Alkhayyat, A., & Alhayani, B. (2023). Integration of Healthcare 4.0 and blockchain into secure cloud-based electronic health records systems. *Applied Nanoscience, 13*(3), 2329–2342. doi:10.100713204-021-02164-0 PMID:35136707

Ngọc, T. H., Khanh, P. T., & Pramanik, S. (2023). Smart Agriculture using a Soil Monitoring System. In A. Khang & I. G. I. Global (Eds.), *Advanced Technologies and AI-Equipped IoT Applications in High Tech Agriculture*. doi:10.4018/978-1-6684-9231-4.ch011

Pramanik, S. (2022). An Effective Secured Privacy-Protecting Data Aggregation Method in IoT. In M. O. Odhiambo, W. Mwashita, & I. G. I. Global (Eds.), *Achieving Full Realization and Mitigating the Challenges of the Internet of Things.*, doi:10.4018/978-1-7998-9312-7.ch008

Pramanik, S. (2023). An Adaptive Image Steganography Approach depending on Integer Wavelet Transform and Genetic Algorithm. *Multimedia Tools and Applications, 2023*(22), 34287–34319. Advance online publication. doi:10.100711042-023-14505-y

Pramanik, S., Galety, M. G., Samanta, D., & Joseph, N. P. (2022). Data Mining Approaches for Decision Support Systems, *3rd International Conference on Emerging Technologies in Data Mining and Information Security*. IOP.

Pramanik, S., & Obaid, A. J., N M, & Bandyopadhyay, S. K. (2023). Applications of Big Data in Clinical Applications. *Al-Kadhum 2nd International Conference on Modern Applications of Information and Communication Technology*. AIP. 10.1063/5.0119414

Pramanik, S., Samanta, D., Ghosh, R., & Bandyopadhyay, S. K. (2021). A New Combinational Technique in Image Steganography. *International Journal of Information Security and Privacy, 15*(3). doi:10.4018/IJISP.2021070104

Pramanik, S., Singh, R. P. and Ghosh, R. (2019). A New Encrypted Method in Image Steganography. *International Journal of Electrical and Computer Engineering, 14*(3), 1412- 1419. DOI: , 2019. doi:10.11591/ijeecs.v13.i3.pp1412-1419

Praveenkumar, S., Veeraiah, V., Pramanik, S., Basha, S. M., Lira Neto, A. V., De Albuquerque, V. H. C., & Gupta, A. (2023). Prediction of Patients' [Springer]. *Incurable Diseases Utilizing Deep Learning Approaches, ICICC*, 2023.

Samanta, D., Dutta, S., Galety, M. G., & Pramanik, S. (2021). A Novel Approach for Web Mining Taxonomy for High-Performance Computing. *The 4th International Conference of Computer Science and Renewable Energies (ICCSRE'2021), 2021*. ACL. 10.1051/e3sconf/202129701073

Won, J. Y. (2021). Development and Initial Results of a Brain PET Insert for Simultaneous 7-Tesla PET/MRI Using an FPGA-Only Signal Digitization Method. IEEE Transactions on Medical Imaging. IEEE. . doi:10.1109/TMI.2021.3062066

KEY TERMS AND DEFINITIONS

Big Data: Big data is the term used to describe data sets that are too big or complicated for conventional data-processing application software to handle. While data with more complexity may result in a higher false discovery rate, data with more entries give better statistical power.

Electronic Health Record: The organised gathering of population- and patient-specific electronically stored health data in a digital format is called an electronic health record. These documents are interchangeable across various healthcare environments.

Genomics: The analysis of an organism's whole or partial genetic or epigenetic sequence information, known as genomics, aims to comprehend the composition and operation of these sequences as well as the biological products that follow.

Hadoop: A set of free and open-source software tools called Hadoop makes it easier to use a large computer network to address challenges requiring enormous volumes of data and processing. It offers a software framework for the MapReduce programming paradigm, which is used for distributed massive data processing and storage.

Healthcare Analytics: Within the health care sector, health care analytics is a subset of data analytics that leverages historical and contemporary data to provide actionable insights, enhance decision-making, and maximise results.

Patient Management: It also involves managing patients in the sense of identifying their issues, monitoring their development, and offering the most effective course of therapy. Stated differently, we are discussing the clinical treatment of the person rather than relationship management.

Primary Health Centres: In developing nations, the fundamental structural and operational component of public health services is the primary healthcare centre (PHC). As per the Alma Ata Declaration of 1978, PHCs were formed to provide people with primary health care that is accessible, inexpensive, and readily available. This was done in compliance with the World Health Organization's member states.

Chapter 13
Connecting the Dots:
Harnessing OpenStreetMap for Big Data Analytics and Market Insights

Munir Ahmad
ⓘ https://orcid.org/0000-0003-4836-6151
Survey of Pakistan, Pakistan

ABSTRACT

OpenStreetMap (OSM) emerges as a dynamic asset for market intelligence, opening a plethora of possibilities for businesses and organizations to enrich their strategies and decision-making processes. By tapping into the geospatial wealth offered by OSM, enterprises can glean valuable insights into market dynamics, consumer preferences, and competitive landscapes. This information can equip them to refine supply chain logistics, make well-informed choices about expansion initiatives, and seamlessly amalgamate diverse data sources to gain a holistic market perspective. OSM's utility can be extended to analyzing market share and extracting invaluable consumer behavior insights. Its adaptability can lend itself to tailor-made data amalgamation, facilitating bespoke market intelligence solutions. Additionally, OSM can be proved instrumental in amplifying digital marketing endeavors, fine-tuning SEO tactics, and delivering accessible public datasets, catering to businesses seeking seamless geospatial data integration.

INTRODUCTION

In an era dominated by the imperative of data-driven decision-making, the significance of accessible and current geospatial data has evolved into a foundational element for well-informed strategies. OpenStreetMap (OSM), a vibrant Volunteered Geographic Information (VGI) platform, occupies a distinctive position in this landscape, continually evolving as a dynamic repository of geospatial knowledge. The collaborative power of crowdsourcing lies at the heart of OSM, rallying a global community to collectively contribute to creating, organizing, and disseminating geographical data. Its inclusive nature sets OSM apart, embracing both seasoned cartographers and individuals without specialized expertise, fostering widespread engagement in mapping initiatives (Goodchild, 2007).

DOI: 10.4018/979-8-3693-0413-6.ch013

Ahmad, (2023) delved into the impact of VGI on community growth and trust-building, while Sarretta et al., (2023) further underscored OpenStreetMap's utility as a data input for official governmental datasets, especially in its integration with the National Summary Database (DBSN) of the Italian Military Geographic Institute (IGM). OSM's Points of Interest (POI) data, as demonstrated by Zhang & Pfoser, (2019), finds application in urban analytics research, facilitating the understanding and modeling of urban change. Additionally, the potential of OSM data for calculating attractiveness in travel demand models is highlighted by Klinkhardt et al., (2021). This emphasizes OpenStreetMap's role as a versatile source of geospatial data with significant implications across various applications, as Wichmann et al., (2023). they are elaborated on in their research on marketing research.

Market intelligence, functioning as a linchpin in today's data-driven landscape, plays a pivotal role in the strategic decision-making processes across various industries. Its essential nature lies in enabling businesses to secure a competitive edge by providing actionable insights derived from a deep understanding of market dynamics, consumer behavior, and industry trends. The ascendance of Geospatial Artificial Intelligence (GeoAI) is deemed vital for organizations seeking a competitive advantage, as highlighted by Ansari & Binninger, (2022). Moreover, the significance of data sources as a catalyst for market-oriented tourism organizations is underscored in the research by Vidal et al., (2023).

Against this backdrop, this chapter offers a comprehensive investigation into OpenStreetMap's status as an invaluable wellspring of geospatial data for extensive market intelligence. The chapter outlines its objectives and boundaries, laying the groundwork for a thorough exploration of OSM's multifaceted applications in market analysis.

BACKGROUND

In this section, fundamental insights concerning market intelligence and OpenStreetMap are presented.

Market Intelligence

Market intelligence forms the very foundation of the marketing philosophy. Ideally, each decision made within an organization pivot on a profound comprehension of how the target markets of that organization are anticipated to respond to diverse value offerings and the configurations of marketing elements (Gebhardt et al., 2019; Kotler & Keller, 2021). Market Intelligence encompasses the vital process of acquiring and analyzing information pertinent to a company's market, playing a pivotal role in aiding organizations to make well-informed decisions and gain a competitive advantage. The roles and significance of market intelligence in the realm of marketing are presented as follows:

Cornerstone of Marketing

Market intelligence serves as the bedrock upon which modern marketing strategies are built. It encompasses the systematic process of gathering, analyzing, and interpreting a wide spectrum of data. This data includes insights into markets, customer behavior, competitive landscapes, and the broader business environment. The data collected through market intelligence activities is not just an asset; it's an indispensable resource that empowers organizations to formulate and implement effective marketing strategies. Without this foundation of knowledge, marketing decisions would be akin to navigating in the dark.

Informed Decision-Making

Informed decisions, in the context of marketing, are those made with a profound understanding of market dynamics. Market intelligence equips organizations with the insights required to anticipate how their target markets will react to various marketing approaches, product launches, pricing strategies, and promotional efforts. Armed with this understanding, organizations can make calculated decisions that are more likely to yield positive outcomes. It can reduce the element of guesswork and minimize the risk of marketing initiatives that fall flat.

Target Markets

Effective marketing begins with a crystal-clear identification of target markets. Market intelligence plays a pivotal role in this process by assisting organizations in segmenting and defining these markets. It can provide the means to categorize customers into specific groups based on demographics, psychographics, and behaviors. By delineating target markets accurately, organizations can tailor their marketing efforts to cater to the unique needs and preferences of each customer group. This can enhance the precision and effectiveness of marketing campaigns.

Value Propositions

Understanding what customers value and what propositions resonate with them is paramount in marketing. Market intelligence shines a spotlight on customer needs, preferences, and pain points. It can enable organizations to unearth valuable insights that inform the development of compelling value propositions. Armed with this knowledge, organizations can craft products, services, and messaging that align closely with what customers seek, thereby increasing the likelihood of customer engagement and loyalty.

Marketing Mix Configurations

The marketing mix, often represented as the 4Ps (Product, Price, Place, and Promotion), is the nucleus of marketing strategy. Market intelligence guides organizations in optimizing these elements. By analyzing market data, organizations can make informed decisions about product features, pricing strategies, distribution channels, and promotional tactics. This ensures that their marketing strategy is finely tuned to meet customer expectations and align with prevailing market conditions.

Adaptation and Agility

Markets are not static; they are dynamic and subject to constant change. Customer preferences can shift rapidly due to evolving trends, technological advancements, or unforeseen external factors. Market intelligence equips organizations with the agility to adapt swiftly to these shifts. This adaptability is crucial for maintaining relevance and effectiveness in the marketplace. Without market intelligence, organizations may find themselves ill-prepared to respond to changes in consumer behavior or market trends.

Competitive Advantage

Having a superior understanding of the market provides a significant competitive advantage. Organizations armed with comprehensive market intelligence can identify market gaps, identify emerging trends, and stay one step ahead of competitors. This advantage can enable organizations to be proactive rather than reactive in their marketing efforts. They can seize opportunities and address challenges with a heightened level of strategic insight.

Market intelligence encompasses the collection, analysis, and interpretation of data related to markets, customers, competitors, and the broader business environment. Its significance is underscored by several factors depicted in Figure 1 and elaborated below:

Enhanced Strategic Decision-Making

Market intelligence provides organizations with the insights needed to formulate informed and data-driven strategies. This enables them to make decisions that align with market trends, customer preferences, and competitive dynamics (Kumar & Rajan, 2016).

Competitor Analysis

Understanding competitor behavior and market positioning is essential for sustained success (Grèzes, 2015). Market intelligence equips organizations with the tools to monitor competitors' activities, strengths, and weaknesses, aiding in the development of effective counterstrategies.

Customer-Centric Approach

In a data-driven landscape, customer preferences and behavior are continually changing. Market intelligence can allow organizations to track these changes, enabling them to tailor their products, services, and marketing efforts to meet evolving customer needs (KÖYLÜOĞLU et al., 2021; Mahmoud et al., 2020).

Risk Mitigation

By analyzing market conditions and potential risks, organizations can proactively identify and address challenges. Market intelligence helps in risk assessment, allowing businesses to develop contingency plans and reduce vulnerabilities.

Opportunity Identification

Market intelligence uncovers new opportunities for growth and expansion. It can enable organizations to identify emerging markets, niche segments, and untapped customer needs that might otherwise go unnoticed.

Resource Allocation

In a data-driven landscape, efficient allocation of resources is crucial. Market intelligence can guide organizations in allocating their budget, human resources, and efforts to areas with the highest potential for return on investment (ROI) (Fleisher & Bensoussan, 2007).

Innovation and Product Development

Staying competitive requires innovation. Market intelligence can offer insights into market gaps, unmet needs, and emerging trends, providing a foundation for innovative product and service development (Paradza & Daramola, 2021).

Global Expansion

For organizations eyeing global markets, market intelligence can help navigate cultural, regulatory, and economic differences. It assists in identifying the most suitable international markets and tailoring strategies accordingly.

Sales and Marketing Effectiveness

Market intelligence can aid in optimizing marketing campaigns and sales efforts by targeting the right audience with the right message. This results in increased conversion rates and revenue ((Morgan & Hunt, 1994).

Figure 1. Significance of market intelligence

Continuous Improvement

In a dynamic business environment, organizations must adapt continually. Market intelligence can foster a culture of continuous improvement by providing feedback on past strategies and outcomes, enabling organizations to refine their approaches (Mentzer & Gundlach, 2010).

OpenStreetMap

OpenStreetMap (Figure 2) had its genesis in the United Kingdom back in 2004 under the visionary leadership of Steve Coast. This pioneering endeavor was born out of a desire to forge an open and freely accessible platform for cartographic data. Steve Coast's vision was simple yet profound: to craft a global map driven by the collective efforts of a burgeoning community, one that would be accessible and editable by anyone with an inclination to contribute (openstreetmap, 2023a; Wiki, 2023b). The nascent OpenStreetMap swiftly gained ground among aficionados of maps and advocates for open data. It wasn't long before a vibrant community of contributors rallied around the project. This collective assembly of minds worked in unison to fashion an all-encompassing and meticulously updated global map. This community-centric approach emerged as a linchpin in OpenStreetMap's triumphant journey and its sustained evolution (openstreetmap, 2023a; Wiki, 2023b).

OpenStreetMap's progress has been marked by a continuous cycle of technological and infrastructural evolution. Within its ambit, various subprojects such as OpenHistoricalMap and OpenRailwayMap have emerged, each dedicated to refining specific facets of mapping and historical data (Wiki, 2023b). As the years unfolded, OpenStreetMap metamorphosed into one of the most triumphant exemplars of crowdsourced geographic information on a global scale. Its applications have traversed a wide spectrum, serving as an invaluable resource for navigation, disaster response, urban planning, and environmental surveillance, among others (Minghini & Frassinelli, 2019). OSM can play a pivotal role in promoting

Figure 2. Snapshot of OpenStreetMap

sustainable development across various sectors, encompassing the economy, environment, and society (Ahmad, 2023b; Ahmad & Ali, 2023). Even OSM green space data has great value for fostering business development (Ahmad, 2023c).

Main Structure of OpenStreetMap

The fundamental structure of OpenStreetMap hinges on a data model meticulously designed to portray the physical world. Within this construct, several key elements play pivotal roles in shaping and organizing geographical data:

Elements

At the core of OSM's conceptual data model are elements, the building blocks that give form to the representation of the physical world. These elements come in three primary flavors:

Nodes: They stand as solitary points in space, each firmly anchored in a specific geographic location. They serve as the cartographic equivalent of pins on a map, storing precise latitude and longitude coordinates to mark exact positions.

Ways: They emerge as sequences of nodes woven together to create linear or area features. They are versatile in their capacity to depict various geographical phenomena, from roads and rivers to territorial boundaries. Ways serve as the means by which nodes are connected, shaping lines or polygons on the map.

Relations: They step in to elucidate how other elements collaborate and interact. They can orchestrate nodes and ways into intricate compositions, giving rise to sophisticated structures like bus routes or multipolygon boundaries.

Tags

To enhance the descriptive power of elements, OSM employs tags, which come in the form of key-value pairs. These tags, like informative labels, can be affixed to nodes, ways, and relations, providing crucial supplementary information about the geographical features they represent. For instance, a way embodying a road may bear tags that detail its name, surface texture, and prescribed speed limit. For example, a road might be tagged as "highway=residential" to indicate it's a residential street.

OpenStreetMap Functions

OpenStreetMap's open data model and the synergy of its collaborative spirit render it a prized asset across diverse applications. Its utility spans realms such as navigation, urban planning, disaster response, and environmental surveillance. It empowers individuals and organizations to both contribute to and access a rich trove of geographical data. It offers a diverse array of functions and features that facilitate the handling of maps and geographic information. Here are some noteworthy OpenStreetMap functions:

Mapping Physical Features

Within OpenStreetMap's purview, users wield the capability to chart tangible elements on the Earth's surface. This encompasses an array of physical entities such as roads, structures, waterways, green spaces, and more. These features find representation through tags, affixed to fundamental data structures known as nodes.

API Access

OpenStreetMap can extend an Application Programming Interface (API) that serves as a conduit for developers to engage with map data elements dynamically. This API is the linchpin for programmatically interfacing with and manipulating OpenStreetMap data.

Creating and Editing Maps

A distinctive facet of OpenStreetMap lies in its provision for users to craft and refine maps within its domain. This collaborative editing ethos engenders an environment of perpetual enhancement, with a global collective of mappers actively contributing to geographical data refinement.

Extracting Connectivity Information

The richness of OpenStreetMap data makes it a potent source for unearthing connectivity insights. This encompasses critical data like road networks and pathways, a boon for routing and navigation applications.

Viewing Maps

OpenStreetMap offers an inviting and intuitive interface for map exploration. Users traverse maps laden with diverse layers, including data pertaining to roadways, edifices, natural terrain, and much more.

Community Collaboration

The bedrock of OpenStreetMap's success resides in its expansive and engaged community of contributors. This dynamic cohort diligently perpetuates the refinement and evolution of map data. Notably, OpenStreetMap is an inclusive platform where anyone, upon registering an account on the OpenStreetMap website, can seamlessly join the ranks of contributors.

Data Validation

The OSM community actively reviews and validates edits to maintain data accuracy and quality. Quality control mechanisms include user discussions, automated tools, and periodic data validation efforts.

Rendering and Usage

OSM data can be used to create maps, navigation apps, location-based services, and more. Various software tools and libraries, including Mapbox, Leaflet, and Mapnik, allow developers to access and display OSM data.

Key Benefits of OpenStreetMap

OpenStreetMap offers a host of advantages that set it apart from other mapping services like Google Maps. Some of the key benefits are depicted in Figure 3 and elaborated below:

Open and Community-Driven

OSM operates as an open-source project, drawing upon contributions from a global community of mappers. This open ethos empowers anyone to participate in editing and enhancing map data, resulting in maps that are continually updated and enriched.

Flexibility

OSM's inherent flexibility is a standout feature, owing to its robust tagging system. This adaptability allows it to accommodate a wide spectrum of geographic features, rendering it suitable for an extensive array of applications, ranging from navigation to urban planning.

Local Knowledge

OSM places a premium on local knowledge, granting individuals the authority to incorporate region-specific information into the map. This approach yields maps that exhibit enhanced accuracy and detail, especially in areas where commercial mapping services may exhibit gaps in coverage (openstreetmap, 2023b).

Free and Open Data

OSM is distinguished by its unwavering commitment to providing free and unrestricted access to its comprehensive dataset. This open accessibility makes it an invaluable resource for developers, researchers, and businesses seeking unencumbered access to geographical data (openstreetmap, 2023b).

Privacy

In a landscape where concerns about privacy loom large, OSM stands out by not tracking users' locations or collecting personal data. This privacy-conscious stance renders it a more user-friendly choice for mapping and navigation, especially for those who value data privacy.

Customization

OSM extends a canvas for developers to craft custom maps and applications utilizing its data. This opens up possibilities for greater control and flexibility in map design and functionality, catering to specific needs and preferences.

Global Scope

OpenStreetMap sets its sights on the ambitious goal of mapping the entirety of the world. This all-encompassing approach transforms it into an invaluable resource, catering to both localized and international cartographic needs (openstreetmap, 2023b).

Multifaceted Repository

OpenStreetMap boasts a vast repository of geographical information. Within its confines, one can uncover an extensive array of data, including but not limited to roads, structures, addresses, commercial establishments, points of interest, rail networks, hiking trails, land utilization, and natural terrain features.

User-Focused Interface

Navigating OpenStreetMap is an intuitive experience. The user-friendly interface empowers individuals to explore and engage with the map effortlessly. Additionally, it permits the extraction of specific data to fulfill unique requirements or seamless integration into other applications.

Figure 3. Key benefits of OpenStreetMap

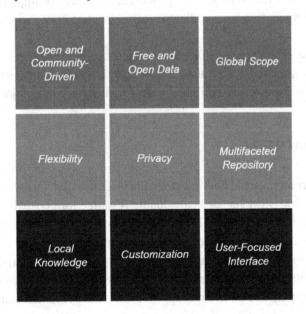

Disadvantages of OpenStreetMap

OpenStreetMap, despite its many advantages, is not without its share of disadvantages:

Quality Control

OSM's reliance on crowd-sourced data means that data quality and accuracy can vary significantly (Haklay, 2010). Ensuring consistent data quality can be challenging, as not all contributors adhere to the same standards or update information regularly.

Limited Points of Interest

OpenStreetMap may lack comprehensive information on points of interest such as hotels, restaurants, and other businesses. This limitation can be frustrating for users who rely on such data for navigation and location-based services.

Incomplete Data

While OpenStreetMap is continually evolving, there may be areas with incomplete or outdated information, especially in less populated regions or developing countries. This can lead to gaps in map coverage.

Complexity for Novice Users

OpenStreetMap's data structure and editing tools can be quite complex, which may deter novice users. It may not be as user-friendly as some commercial mapping platforms, requiring a steeper learning curve.

Reliability of Self-Hosted Data

For users who opt to host their own OpenStreetMap database, maintaining data accuracy, consistency, and access speed can be a significant challenge. It necessitates technical expertise and resources to ensure the reliability of self-hosted data.

Dependency on Volunteers

OSM's data coverage can exhibit geographic disparities due to its reliance on volunteer contributors. Areas with a strong and active OSM community tend to have more detailed and up-to-date maps, while less populous or remote regions may be underrepresented or lack detailed information.

Data Update Lag

OSM updates depend on the willingness and availability of volunteers to contribute new data and edit existing information. As a result, real-time updates may not be as prompt as those provided by commercial map providers, which often have dedicated teams for data collection and maintenance.

Limited 3D Data

OSM's core focus is on 2D mapping, which means that its representation of 3D data, such as building heights, may not be as comprehensive or accurate. While some contributors may add building height information, it may not be consistently available or up-to-date across all regions.

FOCUS OF THE CHAPTER

The focus of this chapter centers on the multifaceted utility of OSM data in enhancing market analysis for businesses. It delineates how OSM serves as a valuable resource for geospatial data analysis, localized marketing, competition insights, supply chain optimization, data-driven decision-making, seamless data integration, market share analysis, consumer behavior insights, and tailored data fusion. Furthermore, the chapter highlights the role of OSM in elevating digital marketing initiatives, providing accessible public data sets, and facilitating environmental impact assessments. It also underscores the ethical considerations essential for responsible data handling and utilization in market analysis, including licensing compliance, privacy protection, data accuracy, transparency, bias mitigation, community engagement, benefit-harm evaluation, data security, and ongoing ethical assessment.

DISCUSSIONS

This section provides an in-depth exploration of the OpenStreetMap for market intelligence and ethical considerations in this context.

OSM for Market Intelligence

Key aspects of leveraging OSM for market intelligence are summarized in Figure 4 and presented as follows:

Geospatial Data Analysis

OSM offers readily accessible geospatial information that can be harnessed for market analysis. It allows for the extraction of data concerning geographical locations, road networks, points of interest, and more, facilitating the examination of market trends and consumer behavior within specific regions. For example, A retail chain can use OSM data to analyze the foot traffic around its stores. By mapping out popular routes and points of interest nearby, the chain can gain insights into customer behavior and can make informed decisions about product placement and promotions.

Localized Marketing Enhancement

The integration of OSM data into local marketing applications and platforms is an effective means to bolster business visibility within particular neighborhoods. This can empower businesses to target their marketing efforts with precision, fostering deeper engagement within local communities (Geoapify, 2023). For example, A small coffee shop can use OSM data to identify nearby events, parks, and transportation hubs. With this information, they can tailor their marketing campaigns and promotions to attract more customers from the local community.

Insights Into Competition

The utilization of OSM data for market share analysis can provide valuable insights into the competitive landscape. This can enable the comparison of a business's presence and distribution with that of competitors across diverse locations. For example, A telecom company can use OSM data to visualize the coverage areas of its network and those of its competitors. This analysis can help them identify areas where they can expand to gain a competitive advantage.

Optimizing Supply Chain and Logistics

For enterprises engaged in shipping and logistics, leveraging OSM data can yield enhanced business intelligence capabilities by optimizing routes, monitoring shipments, and streamlining overall operations.

For example, A courier service can use OSM data to plan the most efficient delivery routes, reducing fuel consumption and delivery times. This optimization can help to improve customer satisfaction and reduce operational costs.

Informed Decision-Making

OSM data can serve as a cornerstone for data-driven decision-making processes across various industries, enabling organizations to make well-informed choices regarding expansion, distribution, and resource allocation. For *example*, A retail chain can use OSM data to identify underserved areas where they can open new stores. They can analyze population density, competitor presence, and accessibility to make strategic expansion decisions.

Seamless Data Integration

OSM data can seamlessly integrate with other sources of business intelligence, including demographic and economic data, to provide a comprehensive perspective on markets and consumer behavior. For *example*, an urban planning department can combine OSM data with demographic statistics to assess transportation needs. This integrated data can inform decisions about public transportation infrastructure improvements.

Analyzing Market Share

A critical component of market intelligence often involves the examination of market share. OSM data can offer a valuable resource for calculating market share by visualizing the distribution of diverse businesses within a given region. This, in turn, can inform strategic decisions related to market expansion or consolidation. For *example*, A fast-food chain can analyze OSM data to understand its market share by mapping the locations of its outlets and those of its competitors. This insight can guide marketing strategies and location planning.

Gaining Consumer Insights

OSM can serve as a valuable resource for a wide spectrum of consumers, including app developers, utilities, governmental bodies, and more. Gaining an understanding of how these various consumer groups harness OSM data can unveil invaluable insights into consumer behavior and preferences. For *example*, A mobile app developer can examine how users access location-based services using OSM data. This analysis can help refine the app's features and user experience based on consumer preferences.

Tailored Data Fusion

Enterprises have the flexibility to merge their proprietary data with OpenStreetMap information, crafting bespoke solutions that cater to their unique market intelligence requisites (Wiki, 2023a). Such amalgamation can encompass a range of data types, including demographic statistics, sales figures, and more. For *example*, an e-commerce company can combine its customer data with OSM data to personalize recommendations and delivery options based on the customer's location, preferences, and past purchases.

Elevating SEO and Digital Marketing Initiatives

OpenStreetMap can also be a potent asset for enhancing digital marketing endeavors. By delving into how users discover businesses on OSM and optimizing their listings accordingly, enterprises can bolster their SEO strategies and drive increased web traffic. For *example,* an online restaurant directory can use OSM data to optimize restaurant listings. This can include adding detailed location information, photos, and customer reviews, improving the restaurants' online visibility and attracting more diners.

Accessible Public Data Sets

OpenStreetMap data is readily available in various formats, free of charge, rendering it easily accessible for businesses seeking to integrate geospatial data into their market intelligence strategies (Christianlauer, 2021). For e*xample*, A small real estate agency can use freely available OSM data to provide detailed neighborhood information on its website. This can enhance the user experience for potential homebuyers.

Environmental Impact Assessment

OSM data can be used to assess the environmental impact of businesses and their activities. By overlaying OSM data with environmental data layers (e.g., pollution levels, and green spaces), organizations can evaluate their ecological footprint and make sustainable business decisions. For example, a manufacturing company can use OSM data to analyze the proximity of its factories to environmentally sensitive areas and residential communities. This analysis can help them implement eco-friendly practices and minimize their impact on the environment, aligning with consumer preferences for sustainability.

Figure 4. OSM for market intelligence

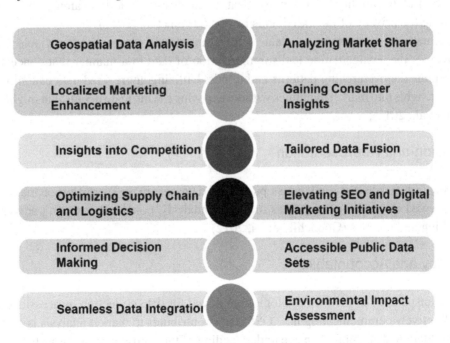

Ethical Considerations

Leveraging OpenStreetMap data for extensive data analytics in the context of market analysis entails several ethical facets that should steer data handling and utilization procedures. These ethical facets are instrumental in ensuring the responsible utilization of data while extracting invaluable insights for market analysis. Below, key ethical considerations in this domain are outlined in Figure 5 and summarized as follows: -

Compliance With Licensing Terms

It is imperative to uphold the licensing terms governing the use of OSM data. Typically, OSM data is made accessible under open licenses like the Open Database License (ODbL). Adhering to these terms, including providing due attribution and adhering to usage constraints, stands as a fundamental aspect of ethical data utilization (OSM, 2021).

Privacy and Anonymization

In the context of privacy, it is imperative to address the potential risks associated with the use of location-based data. This type of data often contains personally identifiable information (PII), which includes details such as an individual's location, daily routines, and preferences. Market analysts must acknowledge the ethical responsibility to ensure that this information is treated with the utmost respect and confidentiality.

Anonymization plays a crucial role in addressing privacy concerns, serving as a fundamental strategy to alleviate potential risks. This method entails altering or eliminating specific identifiers within the data, creating a situation where it becomes difficult or nearly impossible to link information to a particular individual. Through the application of anonymization, analysts can derive valuable insights from data while upholding the privacy of the individuals involved (Pan et al., 2012).

Complementary to anonymization, data aggregation stands out as another viable strategy. This approach involves the amalgamation and summarization of data in a manner that conceals individual details, yet retains the overarching patterns and trends. Utilizing aggregated data can allow analysts to gain valuable insights into market dynamics without exposing the intricate details that might compromise privacy (Pan et al., 2012).

Data Precision and Representation

Ethical responsibility calls for a relentless pursuit of data accuracy. Distorting or manipulating data can lead to skewed or erroneous outcomes in market analysis, potentially exerting adverse effects on decision-making and policies (Goodchild & Li, 2012).

Transparency and Accountability

Maintaining transparency in the methodologies employed for data collection, processing, and analysis is pivotal. Effectively communicating how OSM data contributes to market analysis is essential to empower stakeholders with a comprehensive understanding of the entire process (Floridi & Cowls, 2022).

Instituting clear accountability mechanisms for data management is crucial. This can ensure that individuals responsible for data handling adhere to ethical principles and guidelines (Metcalf & Crawford, 2016) .

Bias Mitigation and Fairness

Vigilance is required to detect biases within OSM data that could potentially sway market analysis outcomes. Mitigating these biases is essential to secure equitable and just results (Diakopoulos, 2016).

Community Engagement

In the context of market analysis using OSM data, active engagement with pertinent stakeholders is indispensable. This includes collaborating with the OSM community and local entities whose data is under examination. Seeking their input, feedback, and cooperation fosters ethical data utilization and minimizes the likelihood of adverse repercussions (Jaljolie et al., 2022).

Benefit-Harm Evaluation

An ethical evaluation of the potential benefits and harms stemming from market analysis is imperative. The objective is to maximize positive outcomes while mitigating any adverse effects on communities or individuals (Floridi & Cowls, 2022).

Figure 5. Ethical consideration for OpenStreetMap

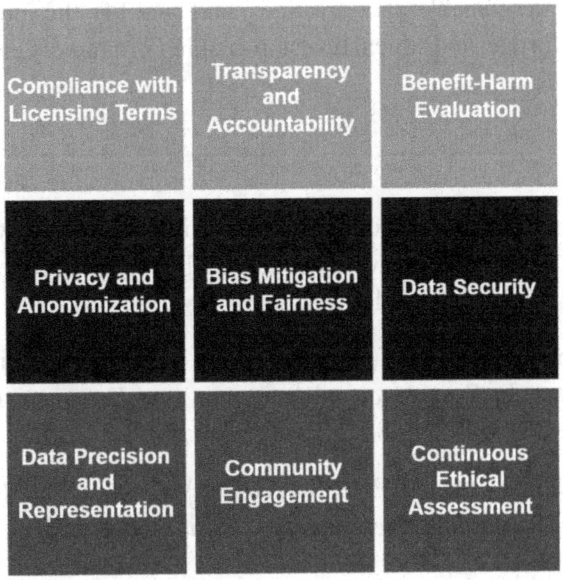

Data Security

Ensuring the security of OSM data and associated market analysis information is fundamental. This involves safeguarding against unauthorized access, data breaches, or misappropriation. Ethical considerations extend to the protection of data from potential security vulnerabilities (Metcalf & Crawford, 2016).

Continuous Ethical Assessment

Continual monitoring and assessment of the ethical implications associated with market analysis using OSM data are essential. This can facilitate the adaptation of practices and policies to address emerging ethical challenges and shifts in the data landscape (Floridi & Cowls, 2022).

CONCLUSION AND FUTURE DIRECTIONS

OpenStreetMap can serve as a valuable resource for market intelligence, offering a multitude of applications that can empower businesses and organizations to enhance their strategies and decision-making processes. By harnessing the geospatial data provided by OSM, businesses can gain insights into market trends, consumer behavior, and competition. They can optimize supply chain operations, make informed expansion decisions, and seamlessly integrate data sources for a comprehensive market perspective. OSM also can support the analysis of market share and provide valuable consumer insights. Its flexibility can allow for tailored data fusion, contributing to customized market intelligence solutions. Furthermore, OSM can help in elevating digital marketing efforts, optimizing SEO strategies, and offering accessible public data sets for businesses seeking geospatial data integration.

The future of market analysis with OpenStreetMap data holds promise for real-time analysis, machine learning-driven predictive insights, sustainability metrics integration, global collaboration for ethical data usage, enhanced data security measures, and the development of user-friendly tools and platforms. These advancements will enable businesses to gain deeper and more timely market insights, align with sustainability goals, ensure responsible data practices, and simplify the integration of OSM data into their strategies, fostering informed and ethical decision-making in a rapidly evolving business landscape.

REFERENCES

Ahmad, M. (2023a). Connecting People and Places: How Citizen Diplomacy and VGI Are Strengthening Disaster Response and Community Development. In Global Perspectives on the Emerging Trends in Public Diplomacy (pp. 195–226). IGI Global.

Ahmad, M. (2023b). Exploring the Role of OpenStreetMap in Mapping Religious Tourism in Pakistan for Sustainable Development. In *Experiences, Advantages, and Economic Dimensions of Pilgrimage Routes*. IGI Global. doi:10.4018/978-1-6684-9923-8.ch002

Ahmad, M. (2023c). Unleashing Business Potential: Harnessing OpenStreetMap for Intelligent Growth and Sustainability. In *Data-Driven Intelligent Business Sustainability*. IGI Global. doi:10.4018/979-8-3693-0049-7.ch013

Ahmad, M., & Ali, A. (2023). Mapping the Future of Sustainable Development Through Cloud-Based Solutions: A Case Study of OpenStreetMap. In Promoting Sustainable Management Through Technological Innovation (pp. 153–176). IGI Global. doi:10.4018/978-1-6684-9979-5.ch011

Ansari, O. B., & Binninger, F. M. (2022). A deep learning approach for estimation of price determinants. *International Journal of Information Management Data Insights*, 2(2), 100101. Advance online publication. doi:10.1016/j.jjimei.2022.100101

Christianlauer. (2021). *Working with OpenStreetMap Data*. https://towardsdatascience.com/working-with-openstreetmap-data-37da18d55822

Diakopoulos, N. (2016). Accountability in algorithmic decision making. *Communications of the ACM*, 59(2), 56–62. Advance online publication. doi:10.1145/2844110

Fleisher, C. S., & Bensoussan, B. E. (2007). Business and competitive analysis. In *Business and Competitive Analysis*. Effective Application of New and Classic Methods.

Floridi, L., & Cowls, J. (2022). A unified framework of five principles for AI in society. In *Machine Learning and the City*. Applications in Architecture and Urban Design. doi:10.1002/9781119815075.ch45

Gebhardt, G. F., Farrelly, F. J., & Conduit, J. (2019). Market intelligence dissemination practices. *Journal of Marketing*, 83(3), 72–90. doi:10.1177/0022242919830958

Geoapify. (2023). *Boosting Business Visibility: OpenStreetMap for Local Marketing*. Geoapify. https://www.geoapify.com/osm-for-local-marketing

Goodchild, M. F. (2007). Citizens as sensors: The world of volunteered geography. In GeoJournal. doi:10.100710708-007-9111-y

Goodchild, M. F., & Li, L. (2012). Assuring the quality of volunteered geographic information. *Spatial Statistics*, 1, 110–120. doi:10.1016/j.spasta.2012.03.002

Grèzes, V. (2015). The definition of competitive intelligence needs through a synthesis model. *Journal of Intelligence Studies in Business*, 5(1). doi:10.37380/jisib.v5i1.111

Haklay, M. (2010). How good is volunteered geographical information? A comparative study of OpenStreetMap and ordnance survey datasets. *Environment and Planning. B, Planning & Design*, 37(4), 682–703. doi:10.1068/b35097

Jaljolie, R., Dror, T., Siriba, D. N., & Dalyot, S. (2022). Evaluating current ethical values of OpenStreetMap using value sensitive design. *Geo-Spatial Information Science*. doi:10.1080/10095020.2022.2087048

Klinkhardt, C., Woerle, T., Briem, L., Heilig, M., Kagerbauer, M., & Vortisch, P. (2021). Using openstreetmap as a data source for attractiveness in travel demand models. In Transportation Research Record (Vol. 2675, Issue 8). doi:10.1177/0361198121997415

Kotler, P., & Keller, K. L. (2021). *Marketing Management*. Pearson Practice Hall.

Köylüoğlu, A., Tosun, P., & Doğan, M. (2021). The Impact of Marketing on the Business Performance of Companies: A Literature Review. *Anemon Muş Alparslan Üniversitesi Sosyal Bilimler Dergisi*, 9(1), 63–74. doi:10.18506/anemon.763875

Mahmoud, M. A., Alomari, Y. M., Badawi, U. A., Ben Salah, A., Tayfour, M. F., Alghamdi, F. A., & Aseri, A. M. (2020). Impacts of marketing automation on business performance. *Journal of Theoretical and Applied Information Technology*, *98*(11).

Mentzer, J. T., & Gundlach, G. (2010). Exploring the relationship between marketing and supply chain management: Introduction to the special issue. *Journal of the Academy of Marketing Science*, *38*(1), 1–4. doi:10.100711747-009-0150-4

Metcalf, J., & Crawford, K. (2016). Where are human subjects in Big Data research? The emerging ethics divide. *Big Data & Society*, *3*(1). doi:10.1177/2053951716650211

Minghini, M., & Frassinelli, F. (2019). OpenStreetMap history for intrinsic quality assessment: Is OSM up-to-date? *Open Geospatial Data. Software and Standards*, *4*(1), 9. doi:10.118640965-019-0067-x

Morgan, R. M., & Hunt, S. D. (1994). The Commitment-Trust Theory of Relationship Marketing. *Journal of Marketing*, *58*(3), 20–38. doi:10.1177/002224299405800302

openstreetmap. (2023a). *What is the history of OSM?* Open Street Map. https://welcome.openstreetmap.org/about-osm-community/history-of-osm/

openstreetmap. (2023b). *Why use OpenStreetMap?* Open Street Map. https://welcome.openstreetmap.org/why-openstreetmap/

OSM. (2021). *OpenStreetMap Copyright and License*. Open Street Map. https://www.openstreetmap.org/copyright

Pan, X., Xu, J., & Meng, X. (2012). Protecting location privacy against location-dependent attacks in mobile services. *IEEE Transactions on Knowledge and Data Engineering*, *24*(8), 1506–1519. doi:10.1109/TKDE.2011.105

Paradza, D., & Daramola, O. (2021). Business intelligence and business value in organisations: A systematic literature review. In Sustainability (Switzerland) (Vol. 13, Issue 20). doi:10.3390u132011382

SarrettaA.NapolitanoM.MinghiniM. (2023). Openstreetmap as an input source for producing governmental datasets: the case of the italian military geographic institute. *The International Archives of the Photogrammetry, Remote Sensing and Spatial Information Sciences, XLVIII-4/W7-2023*, 193–200. ISPRS. doi:10.5194/isprs-archives-XLVIII-4-W7-2023-193-2023

Vidal, J., Carrasco, R. A., Cobo, M. J., & Blasco, M. F. (2023). Data Sources as a Driver for Market-Oriented Tourism Organizations: A Bibliometric Perspective. *Journal of the Knowledge Economy*. doi:10.100713132-023-01334-5

Wichmann, J. R. K., Scholdra, T. P., & Reinartz, W. J. (2023). Propelling International Marketing Research with Geospatial Data. *Journal of International Marketing*, *31*(2), 82–102. doi:10.1177/1069031X221149951

Zhang, L., & Pfoser, D. (2019). Using openstreetmap point-of-interest data to model urban change—A feasibility study. *PLoS One*, *14*(2), e0212606. Advance online publication. doi:10.1371/journal.pone.0212606 PMID:30802251

KEY TERMS AND DEFINITIONS

Community Collaboration: It refers to the joint efforts and partnerships established among individuals, organizations, or communities to achieve common goals.

Consumer Insights: It refers to the understanding gained through the analysis of consumer behavior, preferences, and trends.

Data Fusion: It is the process of integrating and combining information from multiple sources to create a comprehensive and more accurate dataset.

Geospatial Data Analysis: It involves the examination and interpretation of data that is associated with specific geographic locations.

Informed Decision-Making: It is the process of making choices based on a thorough understanding of available information. It involves gathering, analyzing, and interpreting data to assess potential outcomes and risks.

Market Intelligence: It refers to the systematic gathering and analysis of relevant information related to a specific market or industry.

OpenStreetMap (OSM): It is a collaborative and open-source mapping platform that enables users to create, edit, and share geographic data and maps.

Public Data Sets: It is collections of data that are made freely available to the public. These datasets can cover a wide range of topics and may be sourced from government agencies, research institutions, or other organizations.

Quality Control: It is a systematic process implemented to ensure that products or services meet specified standards and fulfill customer expectations.

Chapter 14
Challenges and Solutions of Real–Time Data Integration Techniques by ETL Application

Neepa Biswas
https://orcid.org/0000-0003-2790-1768
Narula Institute of Technology, India

Sudarsan Biswas
RCC Institute of Information Technology, India

Kartick Chandra Mondal
https://orcid.org/0000-0003-3647-5799
Jadavpur University, India

Suchismita Maiti
Narula Institute of Technology, India

ABSTRACT

Business organizations are trying to focus from the traditional extract-transform-load (ETL) system towards real-time implementation of the ETL process. Traditional ETL process upgrades new data to the data warehouse (DW) at predefined time intervals when the DW is in off-line mode. Modern organizations want to capture and respond to business events faster than ever. Accessing fresh data is not possible using traditional ETL. Real-time ETL can reflect fresh data on the warehouse immediately at the occurrence of an event in the operational data store. Therefore, the key tool for business trade lies in real-time enterprise DW enabled with Business Intelligence. This study provides an overview of ETL process and its evolution towards real-time ETL. This chapter will represent the real-time ETL characteristics, its technical challenges, and some popular real-time ETL implementation methods. Finally, some future directions towards real-time ETL technology are explored.

DOI: 10.4018/979-8-3693-0413-6.ch014

INTRODUCTION

Traditional Data warehouse (DW) use to store static data. In DW, strategic analysis is performed on Business data which is integrated from heterogeneous data source. The data is captured, aggregated, cleaned and analyzed for deriving better decisions (Wrembel, 2006; Hong et al., 2009). The analytical decision depends not only on data processing applications, but also on the derived data. The data should be accurate, relevant and timely in nature. The more timely processed data ensure the more better decision making. The decision making process is often delayed in traditional DW due to late propagation of data from the source system to DW in time. Presently, organizations want to access up-to-date data for decision making. So, the concept of real-time ETL technique is introduced (Biswas et al., 2020).

In traditional batch processing ETL, DW refreshment is performed in offline mode in daily, weekly or monthly basis (Vassiliadis, 2009; Biswas et al., 2019). Data is extracted from different types of sources, then it is cleaned and transformed and at last loaded into the DW. These activities are generally performed at night during the warehouse downtime. Any interference is unwanted during the loading and query processing on the DW. These historical data is stored for future analysis purpose.

The way of organizations accessing data is rapidly changing. Nowadays organizations want to access real-time transactional data for taking immediate decision. Currently many industries such as stock exchange, e-commerce, air traffic control, telecommunication etc. have the requirements of correct report based on fresh data in DW as operational decision can be made speedy.

This can't be performed on the status report of yesterday.

Nowadays, the web is considered as important source. In this case, the transactional data that emerge at the source side are not always possible to collect later, if off-line refreshment is performed on the warehouse. Besides, the volume of data for analysis is becoming very high and the response time is shortening. So, the demand is increasing for superior ETL tool. Therefore, the time window is shortening for loading in DW. So the main focus for Business Intelligence (Waas et al., 2013) lies in the DW and the ETL process for supporting continuous data flow (Tho and Tjoa, 2003; Polyzotis et al., 2007) and decreasing downtime.

So, how to define fresh data? Freshness is signifying from minutes to seconds or sub-seconds of data flow delay. The trends of "near real-time" (J¨org and Dessloch, 2009; Chen et al., 2010; Wibowo, 2015) or "real-time" (Cuzzocrea et al., 2014; Patel and Patel, 2022) is going to be the new challenges in technological solutions. Some commercial systems like Informatica PowerCenter, Infosphere Datastage, Oracle Data Integrator, Talend Open Studio, Azure Data Factory etc. are working towards getting fresh data in DW.

In traditional ETL, data warehouse refreshment is done periodically in off-peak time. Due to periodical updation fresh data could not be accessed for analysis purpose. The late arrival of data in warehouse is termed as data latency. Another problem of traditional ETL is off-peak hour loading when all operational and analysis process should be paused. With the introduction of web applications, e-commerce, retail, banking, network traffic monitoring etc. demand running system in 24x7 hours along with latest updated data. To address these issue "near real-time" and further "real-time" mechanism is introduced. Here the main focus is to minimize data latency by identifying the changes immediately in the operational data source and propagate it to warehouse quickly.

Moving towards achieving "real time" implementation, the simple way is to shorten the refreshment cycle. Generally, five to fifteen minutes latency can be categories as "near real time" approach (Vassiliadis and Simitsis, 2008). This solution does not require much changes in the existing operational system.

Table 1. Evolution of ETL process

Category	Mode	Loading frequency	Data flow	Latency
Traditional ETL	Batch	Monthly, weekly, daily	High	Hours
Near real time ETL	Incremental, micro-batch	twice a day, hourly, minutes	Medium	Minutes
Real-time ETL	Incremental, real time	Minutes, seconds, sub-seconds	Low	Minutes, seconds, sub-seconds

Some tools are proposed based on this approach in literature (Vassiliadis et al., 2001; Italiano and Ferreira, 2006; Abrahiem, 2007; J. and Bernardino, 2008). It is a good option for organization dealing with small data warehouse and tolerant of low latency. Workable solution towards near real-time warehouse is introduced in literature (Jain et al., 2012; Ferreira et al., 2013; Suzumura et al., 2010).

The organization of the paper is as follows: In Section 2 describes the technological evolution of real-time ETL. In Section 3, the changing scenario towards real-time ETL is described with an example. Section 4 discusses various challenges during real-time implementation. All the issues for real time ETL implementation are categories according to different stages of ETL. The available solutions are briefly described. At Section 5, various real-time ETL implementation approaches are categories and further discussed based on literature reviews. Section 6 contains briefly discussion on Future Trends in ETL Research. Finally, Section 7 presents the overall summary of the paper and concludes the work.

TECHNOLOGICAL EVOLUTION OF ETL APPLICATION

Formal definition of data warehouse was defined by Bill Inmon in the 1970s. At late 1980s Barry Devlin and Paul Murphy from the IBM researcher laboratory developed the "business data warehouse". At that time, it was used for making report by analysis on stored data. Due to the technological advancement now real-time DW (Mehmood and Anees, 2022) is evolved which can facilitate an organization beyond historical data storing.

The life cycle of data record starts from a business event occurrence. The event record is delivered to central repository of DW. Analytical process is performed on the derived data, which helps for strategic planning and better decision making. To approach real time, the latency between the data acquisition and the corresponding decision making should be minimized. So, the new technological focus is moving from nightly-batch loading of data to real-time data approach (Ali, 2014).

The ETL technology can be classified in three categories. They are: traditional ETL, near real-time ETL and real-time ETL. The classification is done (Farooq and Sarwar, 2010) regarding to technological changes in ETL implementation shown in Table 1. The *ETL mode* is the data loading procedure form the source system which can be either in batch mode or incremental mode. *Loading frequency* indicates the operational interval of the ETL process. *Data flow* is the amount of data. As it is observed that the minimum latency and minimum data flow is the way to implement real-time ETL.

RESEARCH ISSUES AND CHALLENGES

Many organizations have started moving to real-time data aggregation to improve the speed of data flow in warehouse. These techniques involve a lot of challenges (Langseth, 2004; Revathy et al., 2013; Wibowo, 2015). Following are the generic categories of Real-time ETL challenges. The challenges are categories based on different layers of ETL process, namely extraction based problem, transformation based problem and loading based problem. Figure 1 shows the classification of different challenges in implementing real-time ETL. Each of the ETL implementation oriented challenges are briefly discussed here. Interested reader will find various real-time ETL solution approaches in consequtive section.

Extraction Based Problem

Extraction is the first stage of ETL. At first the data is identified and extraction is done. From distributed database, OLTP database, flat files or other file format data can be extracted. The main target of this stage is to convert the heterogeneous data into a single format making useful for transformation stage. Some of the problems that have identified during this phase are presented in Figure 2.

Figure 1. Problems in real-time ETL processing

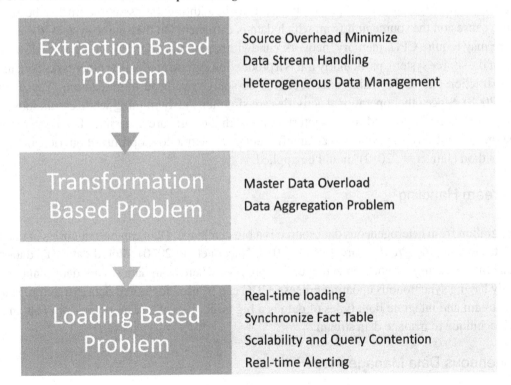

Figure 2. Extraction based problems in ETL process

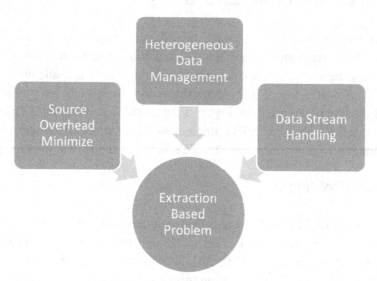

Source Overhead Minimize

"Source overhead" in traditional ETL processing refers to the additional stress and strain that the extraction procedure causes on the source unit from which data is extracted. On the source system, the extraction procedure may require CPU, memory, network bandwidth, and disc I/O. This could slow down the efficiency of the source system, particularly if it is a production system processing other tasks concurrently. During extraction one of the main concern should be source overhead minimization (Vassiliadis and Simitsis, 2008). Since other operational activities are simultaneously running while continuous reading from the source is on the way. Minimum interference with the software is desired. It can slow down the processing. To minimize source overhead an efficient CDC extraction, optimized queries, incremental loading method (Jain et al., 2012) should be applied.

Data Stream Handling

Data integration from heterogeneous data source is a big challenge. Data can be categories in two types, stored data set and *data stream (*Pareek et al., 2018; Naeem et al., 2020*)*. Stored data set's data can be used many times having unsynchronized updating process, where as in data stream data cannot be used repeatedly having synchronous updating process. CDC can be used for stored data extraction. Handling the data stream and integrate both types of data is a big issue. Use of stream processor (Tho and Tjoa, 2003) is technique to manage data stream.

Heterogeneous Data Management

Unstructured or partially structured data formats, like log files or free-form text, may be used by some source systems to store data. It can be difficult to draw out useful information from such data. Using text extraction tools or data parsing techniques can help you extract structured information from semi-structured data or unstructured or. Complex data structures like nested JSON objects or XML files may be present in the source systems. It can be difficult to extract data from these systems, particularly when working with relationships that are hierarchical or multi-level data.

Several issues can arise when integrating data streams from disparate sources in ETL processing. These include a variety of data formats and structures, inconsistencies in data quality, data velocity and volume, data latency and timeliness, schema evolution and versioning, data synchronisation and consistency, security and compliance, error handling and fault tolerance, change data capture (CDC), resource management and scalability, metadata management, distributed processing and parallelization, vendor-specific technology and data. To address these problems, careful architecture design, the selection of appropriate technologies and tools, and the employment of professional data engineers who understand the nuances of working with diverse data sources in ETL procedures are required. It also necessitates continual monitoring, upkeep, and adaptation to changing data source environments.

Transformation Based Problem

In transformation stage extracted data is cleansed and customized according to predefined business rule. Transformation may include cleaning, filtering, joining, splitting, generating surrogate keys, sorting, and transposing row or column, deriving new calculated values, check data quality and applying advanced validation rules. This stage execute the most important operations during the chain processes of ETL. Some of our identified problems is this phase are projected in Figure 3.

Master Data Overhead

Managing master data in the ETL process may bring up special challenges. The term "master data" usually refers to the core data. Client information, product specifications, or personnel records are examples of master data. This information is critical for corporate operations, and any problems with them can have serious consequences. Data can be divided in two types. One is master data accomplished by

Figure 3. Transformation based problems in ETL process

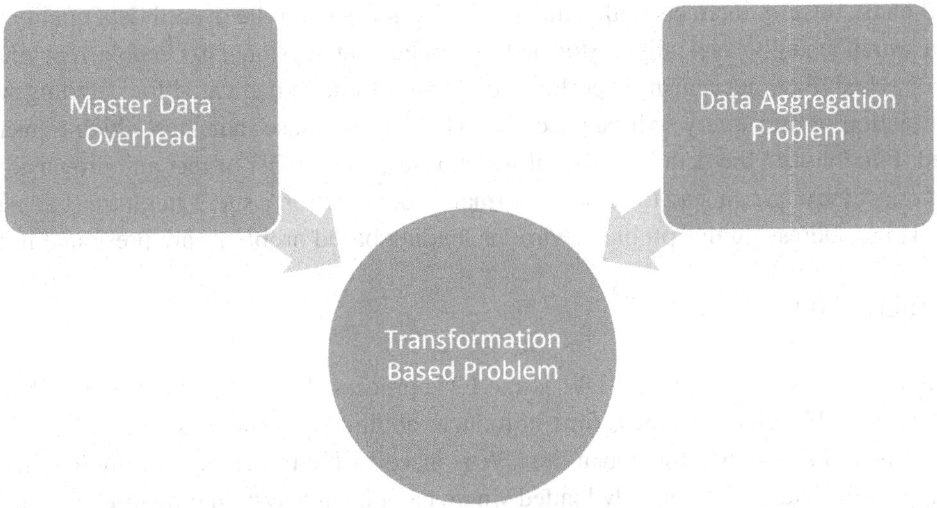

the dimension table doesn't frequently changes. Another is transactional data accomplished by the fact table which is changed frequently. Master data and transactional data are co-related by reference. Master data is needed for transactional data joining process. So fresh master data should always be available in memory. During transformation process in real-time, frequently extraction of same *master data* from *dimension table* can introduce *master data overhead* problem. Some potential solutions to the master data overhead problem are Change Data Capture (CDC), Incremental Loading, Scheduled Extract, Staging Area Optimisation, Cache, and Indexing. Using the aforementioned methods, administrators may reduce the overhead caused by extracting master data from dimension tables during the ETL process, assuring that it remains efficient and does not overburden the source system. Solution mechanism for master data management is addressed in literature (Naeem et al., 2008).

Data Aggregation Problem

The data aggregation problem relates to the difficulty of gathering, aggregating, and processing vast amounts of data from disparate sources into a cohesive format for analysis or data storage. This is an important phase in the data pipeline for organizations seeking valuable insights from their data. The approach used to aggregate data has a considerable impact on the cost, efficiency, and success rate of downstream analytics. In real-time approach minimum amount of data in extracted. Transformation process cannot be applied on this small amount of data in individual refreshment cycle. To address this data aggregation issue a new technique ELT (Extract Load Transform) is introduced where transformation is not performed before each loading. At first loading is done (Waas et al., 2013) then transformation is performed. For applying ELT demanding of an intermediate server for data aggregation is an additional burden.

ELT offers reduced latency, scalability, and flexibility by loading data into storage quickly without transformation, leveraging modern data warehouses and big data platforms for large volumes. On the other hand, ELT may be less efficient than ETL due to the need for complex transformations, which depend on the target storage's processing capabilities.

Loading Based Problem

As the load phase directly interacts with database, it also reflects on the overall data quality. The loading in data warehousing is typically performed by concurrent sessions. To enable real time loading two types of scheduling mechanism is performed. The first one is dedicated for deciding whether an update transaction or user query will be executed. The second phase indicates which transaction will be executed. Finally store the data into central warehouses, usually list of fact and dimension of table. Loading of real-time data can lead to some performance degradation issue. Literature (Langseth, 2004; Zuters, 2011) are addressing this problem. Various loading based problems are presented in Figure 4.

Real-Time Loading

The most important part of building a DW is the ETL process, Even if it run a nightly batch update mode. Processing ETL activities in real-time introduces additional challenges. Generally, the ETL process is performed in DW downtime, when the DW is inaccessible to the user during loading phase. In real-time approach, data is continuously loaded where can't be any system downtime which contradict

Figure 4. Loading based problems in ETL process

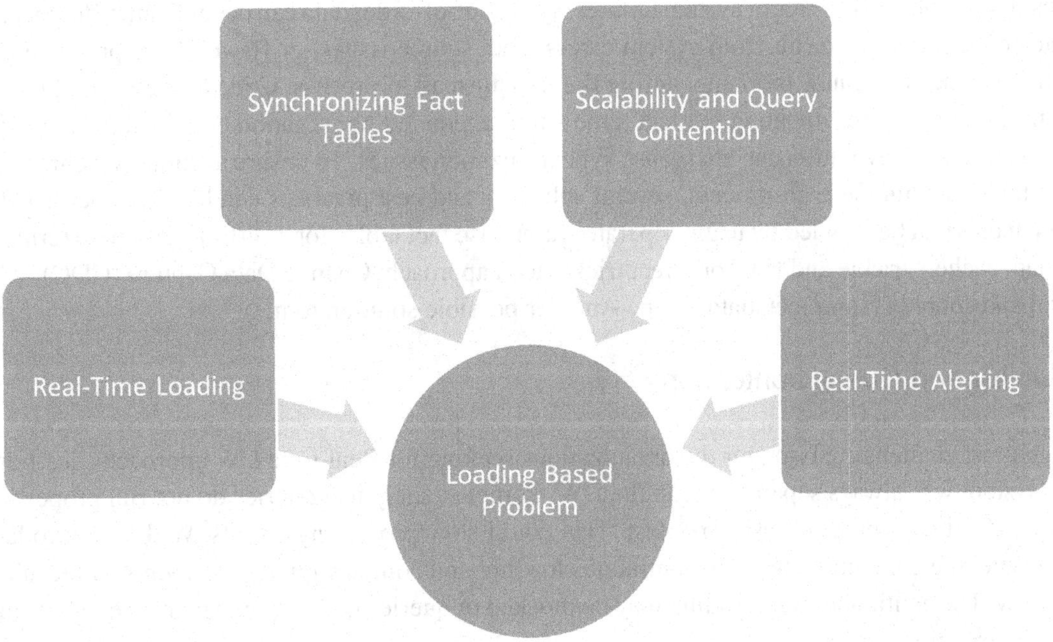

with traditional ETL tools and systems. Real-time loading in an ETL process can significantly impact system performance and concurrent user access. It requires continuous processing of incoming data streams, which can lead to higher CPU, memory, and disk I/O usage compared to batch processing. It also consumes significant network bandwidth, affecting other network-dependent processes. Real-time processing demands low-latency responses, which can lead to data staleness. Persistent processing overhead can affect other applications sharing the same processing resources. Concurrent user access may compete for resources, resulting in slower response times. Locking and blocking issues may occur, potentially causing delays for both processes. Ensuring data consistency and integrity is crucial. Prioritizing real-time loading over user queries is necessary. Mitigation strategies include resource isolation, throttle and prioritization, load balancing and scaling, caching and materialized views, monitoring and alerting, and capacity planning. There are an external real-time data cache or using a direct-trickled feed or a "trickle and flip" approach to overcome this problem.

Synchronizing Fact Tables

Placing real-time data into an existing DW can introduce some inaccuracy in the fact tables. It can lead to synchronization issues between metrics. For example, a warehouse fact table is aggregated at various levels based on a time dimension. There can be a possibility that the aggregated information may be out of synchronization due to real-time data. A month-to-date and week-to-date metrics may result inaccurate when a partial day of data is continuously changes. Fact tables are essential in ETL processes, as they store transactional data about business events like sales and orders. However, synchronization issues can lead to inaccuracies and inconsistencies in reporting and analysis. Common synchronization issues include late arriving data, out-of-order data, duplicates, data integrity violations, data type mismatches, concurrency issues, aggregated values, dimension update issues, and schema evolution. Late arrival data can result from network issues or system failures, while out-of-order data can occur from different orders. Duplicated records can result from system errors, data source issues, or flawed ETL processes. Data type mismatches can cause problems during the transformation process. Concurrency issues can arise from multiple processes updating the fact table simultaneously. Aggregation errors, dimension update issues, and schema evolution can also cause synchronization issues. To ensure accurate synchronization in fact tables within the ETL process, several solutions and best practices can be implemented. These discrepancies can be avoided by using separate warehouse fact tables for real-time data or external real-time data cache. "trickle and flip" or direct trickle feed approach, Change Data Capture (CDC), version control and source system metadata can be Another possible solution to it.

Scalability and Query Contention

It is the most challenging issue for the organizations seeking for Real-time DW approach. The transactional system was always separated from the DW. Complex analytical queries do not run properly with simultaneous user's data accessing request. This could slow processing speeds. With the introduction of real-time, the contention between continuous loading and complex query statements can result poor scalability. The continuous data loading may be blocked or queries may require an unacceptable amount of time to execute.

Simplify and Limiting real-time reporting, upgrading the database by adding more hardware, using a separate and Isolate in a Real-time data cache or applying and managing a "just in time" data merge from External Data Cache or Reverse Just-in-time Data Merge are possible ways to overcome the issue. Concurrent data processing in staging area and OLAP analysis deal with some *OLAP internal inconsistency* issue. Use of data snapshot, RTDC (Real Time Data Cache) (Langseth, 2004) and a *layer-based view* (Lin et al., 2011) are different approaches to overcome this problem.

Real-Time Alerting

Most alerting applications are designed for sending email alert version of report triggered by an event in DW. An email alert is generated after the nightly batch loading in DW. Loading real time data in DW can facilitate the user to be alerted on real-time conditions. Transmission of multiple alerts for a single event is a drawback of this approach. To address the issue, a process to continuously monitor the real-time data and trigger the events and n-Minute Cycle Schedule or Alert Threshold Management are the possible solutions. These solutions still require some upgradations.

REAL-TIME ETL SOLUTION APPROACHES

Typically, the loading process is done at night, downtime of DW. But in real-time approach data is loaded continuously in DW without considering the system downtime. Some of the approaches (Vassiliadis and Simitsis, 2008; Langseth, 2004) for implementing real-time ETL has been categories in three section namely function oriented approaches, data dependent approaches and application based approach. The overall classification is shown in Figure 5. Brief discussion on each categories are presented in the next section.

Figure 5. Classification of real-time ETL approaches

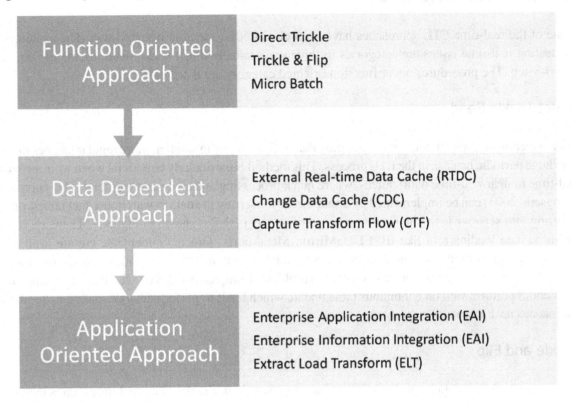

Figure 6. Extraction based problems in ETL process

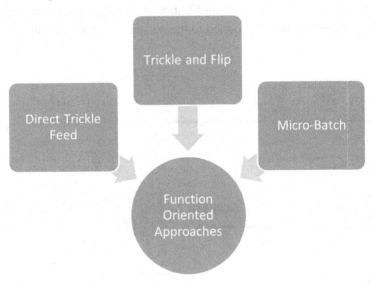

Function Oriented Approaches

Some of the real-time ETL approaches have been classified as function oriented way. The techniques for dealing real-time issues are categories in three ways namely direct trickle feed, trickle & flip and micro-batch. The procedures under function oriented category are listed in Figure 6.

Direct Trickle Feed

Trickle feeding is a way of continuously adding data progressively in smaller, more regular batches rather than huge periodic batches in the ETL process. This method is particularly beneficial when working with real-time or near-real-time data sources, where quick processing and analysis are crucial. This approach (Langseth, 2004) can be implemented by either directly inserting the data in warehouse fact tables, or by inserting into separate location in a real-time partition fact tables as shown in Figure 7. There are some real-time data loading tool like IBM DataMirror, MetaMatrix, Oracle GoldenGate etc are available. They are designed to moving the data from operational system to DW. Continuous queries and update process on same table faces workload mismatch problem. Complex queries by OLTP or other reporting tools could perform well on continuous table update which leads to performance degradation. So, these approaches have a scalability problem.

Trickle and Flip

In this approach, the data is not loaded into the actual warehouse tables. The real time data is continuously stored in staging table having same format as the target table in DW Langseth (2004). Then on a periodic way the trickle process is halted, the staging table is duplicated and the copy is swapped with the fact table, making DW instantly up-to-date. After that the static table become empty and new process starts. Fresh data can be accessed quickly by taking a copy from the staging tables. The process is explained in the Figure 8. With this approach an additional real-time partitions can be applied. Staging table data are duplicated and the copy is flipped to the real-time partition tables.

Figure 7. Direct trickle feed

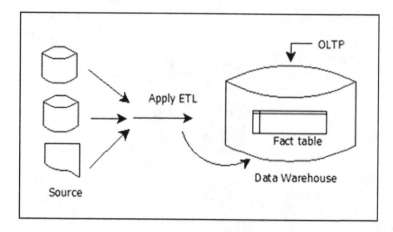

Figure 8. Trickle and flip

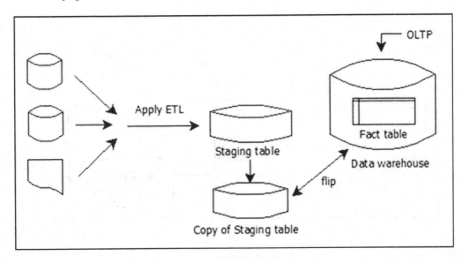

The warehouse is refreshed periodically by the real-time partition. This is not a great idea for the organization dealing with high volume of data. The refreshment cycle to the DW decreases from hours to minutes, still the approach can't meet the real-time criteria. Further modification has been done by implementing "Multi-stage Trickle & Flip" approach (Zuters, 2011). Here more intermediate stages are added between the data flow from the source to DW to overcome conflict between simultaneous loading and query process. From the operational system, small amount of data is continuously copied to 1st staging table. From there the data is continuously moved minutes, hourly and daily cycle wise to next staging area which is partitioned into two parts capable to hold different time domain data with corresponding two real time partitions. Finally data is populated to the warehouse fact table.

Micro-Batch

This approach uses the conventional ETL batches with the use of real time portioning idea (Kimball and Caserta, 2004; Vassiliadis and Simitsis, 2008). The frequency of the batch increases such as hourly basis. Different extraction methods can be used e.g. timestamps, ETL log table, DBMS scrapper, network sniffer etc. After extraction the data is moved into real time partition area

continuously in small regular batches. The data of real time partition is further populated to static data mart once in a day when the system is idle. The real time partition data is vacant after that. The basic operation of this approach is presented in Figure 9. This approach is applicable to those types of DW which is tolerant of hourly latency and for moderate volume of data.

Data Dependent Approaches

Some of the real-time ETL approaches have been classified as data dependent way. The techniques for dealing real-time issues are categories in three ways namely external real-time data catch, change data capture and capture-transform-flow (CTF). Various data dependent approaches under this category are described in this section and presented in figure 10.

Figure 9. Micro-batch ETL

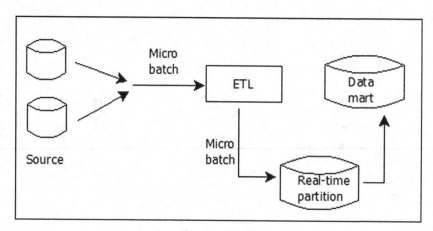

Figure 10. Data dependent approaches in ETL process

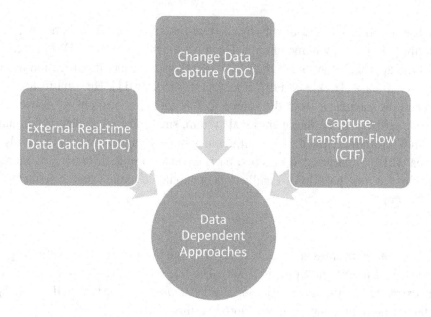

External Real-time Data Catch (RTDC)

External Real-time Data Catch (RTDC) is a technique used in ETL procedures to capture and aggregate real-time data from external sources. When it is important to incorporate continuously changing data into a data warehouse in near real-time, this strategy is used. RTDC is especially useful in situations requiring rapid data updates, such as financial markets, transportation, social media analytics, sensor information monitoring, and other applications that are time-sensitive. In this approach, the real time data is stored in an external real time data cache (RTDC) isolated from the DW (Langseth, 2004). The RTDC can act as another database server for processing real-time data (Revathy et al., 2013). This approach can reduce any additional load avoiding any performance degradation issues and leaving the existing warehouse intact by directing the queries to RTDC which holds real time data. The total process is shown in Figure

Figure 11. Real time data catch (RTDC)

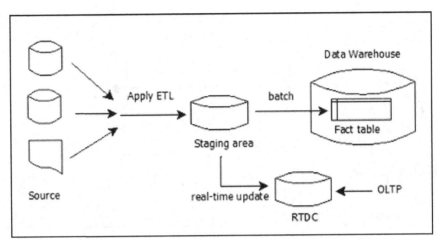

11. This solution provides up-to-the-second data and users don't need to wait for queries execution. Organizations that require large volumes of real-time data and extremely fast query performance might benefit from using this type of in-memory database.

Different configurations can be implemented, either all queries are redirected towards the RTDC or the real-time data is temporarily merged with the warehouse for a particular query execution. Query execution becomes very fast in this approach. It resolves scalability and query contention problem where there is no additional load on DW. The cost of this solution is typically low compared to the trickle feed approaches. Downside is the requirement to create and maintain an additional database. Angara Database Systems, Kx Systems, Blue Coat Systems, InfoCruiser and Oracle TimesTen are some solution providers for supporting real-time data cache.

Change Data Capture (CDC)

Change Data Capture refers to the process of keeping track of any change made to the database. This procedure identifies and extracts only the updated or new data at the source system, and then transmits those changes to the data warehouse. CDC is essential for ensuring data consistency, productivity, and decision-making accuracy throughout the ETL process. It is a new data integration approach, which identify and capture changes occur to data sources and delivery only the changed data to operational system (Attunity, 2009). This approach does not need DW downtime or batch windows of ETL. Some CDC technologies operate in batch mode with a pulling technique. Means, the ETL tool periodically receive a batch for all new changes made up to last receive and execute them. The real time CDC solutions apply a continuous streaming "push" approach for delivering data. The data changed are captured and deliver immediately to the target. The CDC procedure is explained in Figure 12.

It is a cost effective solution. The advantage of CDC is the latency can be cut down to minutes to even seconds which makes the data instantly available eliminating the use of batch windows. Besides, it minimizes the amount of data flow therefore resource requirement is minimized and speed and efficiency is maximized. CDC addresses some business needs like building Operational Data Stores (ODS), Business Activity Monitoring (BAM), Application Integration, Real-time Dashboards, data quality improvement

Figure 12. Change data capture (CDC) process

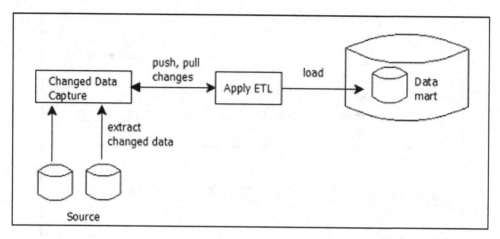

etc. There are several techniques like transactional log, database log scraping & log sniffing, snapshot differential and timestamped index for detecting the changes (Ankorion, 2005;

Bokade et al., 2013). Some research work is going on log-based method is introduced in literature (Shi et al., 2008; Ma and Yang, 2015) for improving the quality of data. There is a web service based approach (Eccles et al., 2010) for modeling of efficient CDC mechanism. A high-performance join on changed data is applied on literature (Tank et al., 2010). There are trigger based approaches for capturing changed data from different data sources mentioned in article (Sukarsa et al., 2012; Valencio et al., 2013).

Capture-Transform-Flow (CTF)

It is a variant of the standard ETL method to simplify the real time data transportation across the heterogeneous database (Kimball and Caserta, 2004; Vassiliadis and Simitsis, 2008). The basic idea is that, transactional data can be moved from the source applying light-weight transformation to the DW staging area. After staging additional complex transformation are applied by micro-batch ETL. Then the data are

Figure 13. Capture-transform-flow

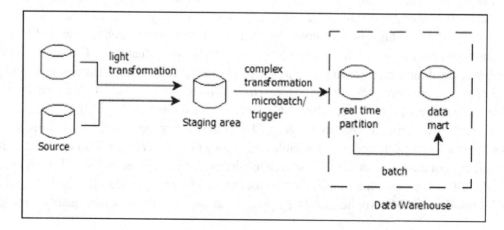

Figure 14. Application based approaches in ETL process

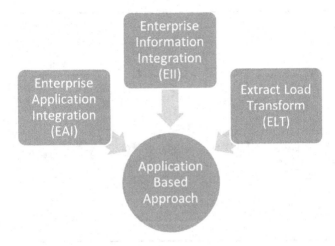

moved to real time partition and from there to static data mart by batch approach. The overall process of Capture-Transform-Flow is shown in Figure 13.

It is a good approach for organizations needs real time report with light integration whose core applications share common period of low activity and allow minimum turbulent data synchronization.

Application Based Approach

Some of the application based techniques have been identified for implementing real-time ETL process. The techniques for dealing real-time issues are categories in three ways namely enterprise application integration, enterprise information integration and extract load transform. The application oriented approaches under this category are described below and presented in figure 14.

Enterprise Application Integration (EAI)

This approach support application integration. This set of technology use to link transactions from different systems using existing applications. The key is to integrating applications rather than integrating the data (Kimball and Caserta, 2004; Vassiliadis and Simitsis, 2008). EAI system builds a set of adapters and a broker which moves business transactions in the form of application independent messages (usually XML) across the integrated network's various systems. Application specific adapters create and execute messages and broker is used to routing those messages between the adapters based on set of rules. Often a message queue is kept between the application and the adapter and between the adapter and broker for providing staging area for asynchronous messages which guaranteed transaction consistency and delivery through the integrated network is shown in Figure 15.

It simplifies advanced process management of organization keeping legacy applications enabling real-time data access and maintaining data integrity as well as enterprise efficiency. EAI is a cost-effective data integration solution for the organization having various applications and data structure without changing them. There can be different levels of application integration.

Figure 15. Enterprise application integration (EAI)

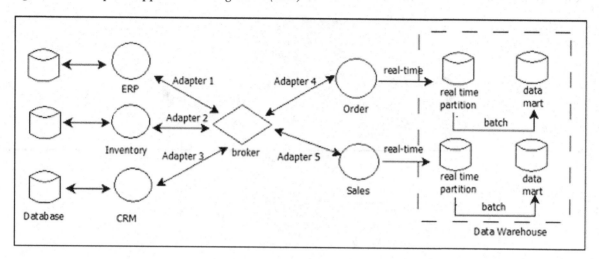

Data-level integration integrates the data stores at the back-end which enable seamless data movement. *Push* or *pull* based integration technique is applied here. Data-level integration is useful for organization does not require any API application.

Data and business process are accessed using *Application-level integration*. It gives the facility to integrate different applications with business logic to maintain the data integrity. It does not have any effect on application interface. This feature is applicable for packaged applications like SAP, Oracle or J.D. Edwards.

Method-level integration It is a complex way of application integration. Here the idea is sharing the methods. Different applications can share a single method or can share each other's methods. Sharing can be archived by hosting on a central server, distributed objects, use of Web services or some other ways.

User interface level integration this method is implemented by integrating existing user interfaces. It is a useful way for mainframe system does not have API and database.

The design of topological architecture can be categories in following ways: *Point-to-Point topology* This approach connects two applications by point-to-point interfaces using a pipe. *Hub-Spoke* The broker (Hub) is kept at central position and connected with different adapters (spokes). Adapters connects different applications converting application data format to hub data format. *Bus* act as a central backbone for communication of messages. Applications send message to the bus through adapters. Each application adapters can convert messages according to required format. Some EAI service provider vendors are available like tibco, IBM WebSphere Message Broker (WMB) and Mule enterprise Service Bus (ESB) for transport of real-time data.

Enterprise Information Integration (EII)

Enterprise Information Integration (EII) is an initiative that merges data from disparate sources within an organisation into a single view, resulting in an extensive and consistent representation of information. EII is concerned with constructing a virtual or distributed view of data across multiple systems without physically transferring or replicating the data. It enables users to query and analyse data in real time, resulting in a unified picture of data from various sources. It is a on demand reporting technique

Figure 16. Enterprise information integration (EII)

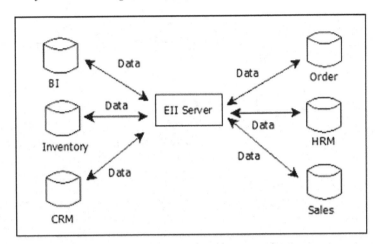

(Kimball and Caserta, 2004; Vassiliadis and Simitsis, 2008). The user can collect the report on demand through a virtual integrated system, which generates a set of queries and deliver the result. EII use data abstraction method which provides a unique interface to view all data of organization. In other words, it provides uniform access to multiple data sources except first load of data to DW. EII offer a virtual real time DW logical view shown in Figure 16. It generates a set of queries on request and applies all necessary transformation to create the resulting data for the user. This approach is useful for zero-latency reporting but applicable to that database contains little or no historical data. EII application offers advantage of relational access upon non-relational sources, allows data exploration prior to the creation of a formal data model and metadata, designed for global access to remote sources. avoiding needless data movement. Challenges of this approaches includes demanding transaction control for Multi-site updates, keys matching across sources, minimal supported transformation, network consume during peak hours, remote result sets have limited number of rows, data types mismatch etc.

Extract Load Transform (ELT)

This is a new approach towards real-time data integration Waas et al. (2013). In real-time scenario continuously small amount of data is extracted. Transformation process cannot be applied on this small amount of data in each refreshment cycle. To overcome this data aggregation problem ELT technique (Singhal and Aggarwal, 2022) can be applied. At first the extracted data is placed in staging area. Here, business constrains and integrity checking can be performed. After that the validated data is loaded directly to the warehouse. After loading, transformation can be applied according to required format in the next stage inside the warehouse. SQL queries are applied for transformation purpose. The overall ELT process is presented in Figure 17. ELT is especially well-suited for situations in where massive amounts of raw data must be processed fast and efficiently. It is commonly utilised in data warehousing, data lakes, and analytical systems where complicated studies on massive amounts of data are performed. The raw data loaded into the target system may require addressing issues related to data quality during the transformation phase. This approach may require significant computational resources depending on the dataset size and the target system's capabilities.

Figure 17. Extract load transform (ELT)

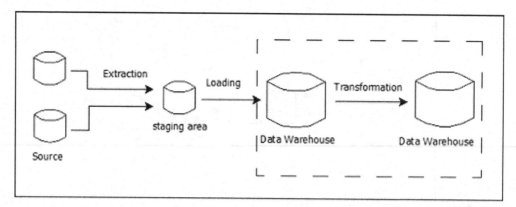

Extensive version ELTA briefly Extract, Load, Transform and Analyse is proposed in literature (Marin-Ortega et al., 2014). Here a stage is added further for analysis of big data from the warehouse by integrating BI technique for better decision making of organization.

FUTURE TRENDS IN ETL RESEARCH

There are many research issues still left open regarding real-time approach. For last few decades new ideas are coming towards data stream processing (Biswas and Mondal, 2021; Naeem et al., 2020) and non-stop query processing issues. Many tech industries have developed their own data stream management system. Still there are some security (Dammak, 2019) and data quality issues like completeness, integrity, validity etc (Gupta and Jolly, 2021; Lebdaoui et al., 2013) need to overcome.

Application of machine learning within the ETL and Data warehousing system can be very beneficial in respect of system automation (Mondal et al., 2020). Inclusion of ML technique for data integration is very demanding now a day. Some efficient real-time workflow scheduling mechanism can overcome the scalability issues have been proposed in literature (Golab et al., 2009; Karagiannis et al., 2013; Song et al., 2010). It is still an open field for researchers for balancing the warehouse update and queries need to explore. Some issues need to consider like setting priority and conflict resolution for updates as well as queries. Future studies might examine cutting-edge methods for data purification, anomaly detection, and real-time data profiling. This can entail using statistical analysis and machine learning methods to quickly identify and fix data quality problems.

The most difficult issue nowadays is integrating streaming data from numerous sources, including sensor networks, IoT devices, and social media feeds (Pareek et al., 2018; Naeem et al., 2020). Real-time data processing is made possible by incorporating Streaming Data Integration with Event-driven Architectures, which respond to events or triggers. Future studies might concentrate on creating effective methods and frameworks for integrating event-driven real-time ETL procedures with high-velocity data sources. This can entail utilising tools like Apache Kafka, Apache Spark, Apache Flink, or other frameworks for stream processing.

Batch processing is still useful for effectively managing Big data (Martins et al., 2016; Mallek et al., 2020) even though real-time ETL is necessary for quick data insights. Future studies might look into hybrid methods that mix batch and real-time processing methods, enabling businesses to carry out both real-time & batch ETL activities within a same framework. Future studies might concentrate on merging real-time ETL with cloud-based services (Oracle, 2015), like serverless computing, auto-scaling capabilities, streaming platforms management etc. to gain greater scalability and cost-efficiency.

CONCLUSION

Today the competitive nature of the business world is established the by use of information technology. There is a high demand to analyze and make decision on fresh and pre-processed data nowadays. So, The enterprises are moving towards the application of the real-time Business Intelligence very quickly. Traditional ETL cannot provide live information. The demand of real-time information in many practical industrial applications incorporated with Business Intelligence features is increasing. By this way business analysis and decision can be made on real-time. In this paper, real-time ETL processing challenges are categories based on three stages of ETL. Corresponding solutions towards each stage of real time ETL is identifies and presented here in a nice way. After that, some popular industry oriented real-time implementation approaches in has been further discussed. Technological constrains and custom solutions for achieving real-time data into warehouse is a profound practical and research domain. Researchers working on this domain can get a brief overview of real-time ETL from this survey. Future research on uncovered area of real-time ETL deserve more attention from the researchers and industry.

REFERENCES

Abrahiem, R. (2007). A new generation of middleware solutions for a near-real time data warehousing architecture. In *IEEE International Conference on Electro/Information Technology*, (pp. 192-197). IEEE. 10.1109/EIT.2007.4374453

Ali, F. S. E. (2014). A survey of real-time data warehouse and ETL. *International Scientific Journal of Management Information Systems*, *9*(3), 03-09.

Ankorion, I. (2005). Change data capture efficient ETL for real-time BI. *Information & Management*, *15*(1), 36.

Attunity. (2009). *Efficient and Real Time Data Integration With Change Data Capture*. An Attunity White Paper. http://download.101com.com/tdwi/ww29/attunity_efficient_and_real-time_di.pdf

Biswas, N., Chattapadhyay, S., Mahapatra, G., Chatterjee, S., & Mondal, K. (2019). A new approach for conceptual extraction-transformation-loading process modeling. [IJACI]. *International Journal of Ambient Computing and Intelligence*, *10*(1), 30–45. doi:10.4018/IJACI.2019010102

Biswas, N., & Mondal, K. C. (2021). Integration of ETL in cloud using spark for streaming data. In *International Conference on Emerging Applications of Information Technology*, (pp. 172-182). Springer.

Biswas, N., Sarkar, A., & Mondal, K. C. (2020). Efficient incremental loading in ETL processing for real-time data integration. *Innovations in Systems and Software Engineering*, *16*(1), 53–61. doi:10.100711334-019-00344-4

Bokade, M. B., Dhande, S. S., & Vyavahare, H. R. (2013). Framework of change data capture and real time data warehouse. In *International Journal of Engineering Research and Technology* (Vol. 2). ESRSA Publications.

Chen, L., Rahayu, W., & Taniar, D. (2010). Towards near real-time data warehousing. In *24th IEEE International Conference on Advanced Information Networking and Applications (AINA)*. IEEE. 10.1109/AINA.2010.54

Cuzzocrea, A., Ferreira, N., & Furtado, P. (2014). Real-time data warehousing: A rewrite/merge approach. In *Data Warehousing and Knowledge Discovery* (pp. 78–88). Springer. doi:10.1007/978-3-319-10160-6_8

Dammak, S., Ghozzi, F., & Gargouri, F. (2019). ETL processes security modeling. [IJISMD]. *International Journal of Information System Modeling and Design*, *10*(1), 60–84. doi:10.4018/IJISMD.2019010104

Eccles, M. J., Evans, D. J., & Beaumont, A. J. (2010). True real-time change data capture with web service database encapsulation. In *Services (SERVICES-1), 2010 6th World Congress on*, pages 128-131. IEEE. 10.1109/SERVICES.2010.59

Farooq, F., & Sarwar, S. M. (2010). Real-time data warehousing for business intelligence. In *Proceedings of the 8th International Conference on Frontiers of Information Technology (FIT'10)*, pages 38:1-38:7. ACM.

Ferreira, N., Martins, P., & Furtado, P. (2013). Near real-time with traditional data warehouse architectures: Factors and how-to. In *Proceedings of the 17th International Database Engineering Applications Symposium (IDEAS'13)*, (pp. 68-75). ACM. 10.1145/2513591.2513650

Golab, L., Johnson, T., & Shkapenyuk, V. (2009). Scheduling updates in a real-time stream warehouse. In *IEEE 25th International Conference on Data Engineering (ICDE'09)*, (pp. 1207-1210). IEEE. 10.1109/ICDE.2009.202

Gupta, N., & Jolly, S. (2021). Enhancing data quality at ETL stage of data warehousing. [IJDWM]. *International Journal of Data Warehousing and Mining*, *17*(1), 74–91. doi:10.4018/IJDWM.2021010105

Hong, Y., Lee, Z., & ... . (2009). Data warehouse performance. In *Encyclopedia of Data Warehousing and Mining* (2nd ed., pp. 580–585). IGI Global.

Italiano, I. C., & Ferreira, J. E. (2006). Synchronization options for data warehouse designs. *Computer*, *39*(3), 53–57. doi:10.1109/MC.2006.104

Jain, T. S. R., & Saluja, S. (2012). Refreshing data warehouse in near real time. *International Journal of Computer Applications*, *46*(18).

Jörg, T., & Dessloch, S. (2009). Near real-time data warehousing using state of-the-art ETL tools. In *Enabling Real-Time Business Intelligence* (pp. 100–117). Springer.

Karagiannis, A., Vassiliadis, P., & Simitsis, A. (2013). Scheduling strategies for efficient ETL execution. *Information Systems*, *38*(6), 927–945. doi:10.1016/j.is.2012.12.001

Kimball, R., & Caserta, J. (2004). *The data warehouse ETL toolkit: Practical techniques for extracting, cleaning, conforming, and delivering data*. John Wiley and Sons.

Langseth, J. (2004). Real-time data warehousing: Challenges and solutions. *DSSResources.com*, 2(08).

Lebdaoui, I., Orhanou, G., & Hajji, S. E. (2013). Data integrity in real-time data warehousing. In *Proceedings of the World Congress on Engineering*, (Vol. 3, pp. 3-5). IEEE.

Lin, Z., Lai, Y., Lin, C., Xie, Y., & Zou, Q. (2011). Maintaining internal consistency of report for real-time OLAP with layer-based view. In *Web Technologies and Applications* (pp. 143–154). Springer. doi:10.1007/978-3-642-20291-9_16

Ma, K., & Yang, B. (2015). Log-based change data capture from schema-free document stores using mapreduce. In *Cloud Technologies and Applications (CloudTech), 2015 International Conference on.* IEEE. 10.1109/CloudTech.2015.7336969

Mallek, H., Ghozzi, F., & Gargouri, F. (2020). Towards extract-transform-load operations in a big data context. [IJSKD]. *International Journal of Sociotechnology and Knowledge Development*, 12(2), 77–95. doi:10.4018/IJSKD.2020040105

Mar'ın-Ortega, P. M., Dmitriyev, V., Abilov, M., & G'omez, J. M. (2014). ELTA: New approach in designing business intelligence solutions in era of big data. *Procedia Technology*, 16, 667–674. doi:10.1016/j.protcy.2014.10.015

Martins, P., Abbasi, M., & Furtado, P. (2016, January). Near-Real-Time Parallel ETL+ Q for Automatic Scalability in Bigdata. In *CS & IT Conference Proceedings* (*Vol. 6*, No. 1). CS & IT Conference Proceedings.

Mehmood E and Anees T. (2022). Distributed real-time ETL architecture for unstructured big data. *Knowledge and Information Systems.* doi:10.1007/s10115-022-01757-7

Mondal, K. C., Biswas, N., & Saha, S. (2020). Role of machine learning in ETL automation. In *Proceedings of the 21st International Conference on Distributed Computing and Networking.* ACM. 10.1145/3369740.3372778

Naeem, M. A., Dobbie, G., & Webber, G. (2008). An event-based near real time data integration architecture. In *12th Enterprise Distributed Object Computing Conference Workshops.* IEEE. 10.1109/EDOCW.2008.14

Naeem, M. A., Mehmood, E., Malik, M. A., & Jamil, N. (2020). Optimizing semi-stream CACHE-JOIN for near-real-time data warehousing. [JDM]. *Journal of Database Management*, 31(1), 20–37. doi:10.4018/JDM.2020010102

Oracle. (2015). *Demystifying data integration for the cloud.* Oracle White paper. Oracle Corporation, Redwood Shores (USA). http://www.audentia-gestion.fr/oracle/data-integration-for-cloud-1870536.pdf

Pareek, A., Khaladkar, B., Sen, R., Onat, B., Nadimpalli, V., & Lakshminarayanan, M. (2018, August). Real-time ETL in Striim. In *Proceedings of the international workshop on real-time business intelligence and analytics* (pp. 1-10). ACM.

Patel, M., & Patel, D. B. (2022). Data Warehouse Modernization Using Document-Oriented ETL Framework for Real Time Analytics. In *Rising Threats in Expert Applications and Solutions* [Singapore: Springer Nature Singapore.]. *Proceedings of FICR-TEAS, 2022,* 33–41.

Polyzotis, N., Skiadopoulos, S., Vassiliadis, P., Simitsis, A., & Frantzell, N. (2007). Supporting streaming updates in an active data warehouse. In *IEEE 23rd International Conference on Data Engineering (ICDE'07)*. IEEE. 10.1109/ICDE.2007.367893

Revathy, S., Saravana, B. B., & Karthikeyan, N. K. (2013). From data warehouse to streaming data warehouse: A survey on the challenges for real time data warehousing and available solutions. *International Journal of Computer Applications*, *975*, 8887.

Shi, J., Bao, Y., Leng, F., & Yu, G. (2008). Study on log-based change data capture and handling mechanism in real-time data warehouse. In *Computer Science and Software Engineering, 2008 International Conference*. IEEE. 10.1109/CSSE.2008.926

Singhal, B., & Aggarwal, A. (2022). ETL, ELT and Reverse ETL: A business case Study. In *2022 Second International Conference on Advanced Technologies in Intelligent Control, Environment, Computing & Communication Engineering (ICATIECE)* (pp. 1-4). IEEE. 10.1109/ICATIECE56365.2022.10046997

Song, J., Bao, Y., & Shi, J. (2010). A triggering and scheduling approach for ETL in a real-time data warehouse. In *Computer and Information Technology (CIT), 2010 IEEE 10th International Conference on*, (pp. 91-98). IEEE. 10.1109/CIT.2010.57

Sukarsa, I. M., Wisswani, N. W., & Darma, I. G. (2012). Change data capture on OLTP staging area for nearly real time data warehouse base on database trigger. *International Journal of Computer Applications*, *52*(11).

Suzumura, T., Yasue, T., & Onodera, T. (2010). Scalable performance of system s for extract-transform-load processing. In *Proceedings of the 3rd Annual Haifa Experimental Systems Conference*. ACM. 10.1145/1815695.1815704

Tank, D. M., Ganatra, A., Kosta, Y. P., & Bhensdadia, C. K. (2010). Speeding ETL processing in data warehouses using high-performance joins for changed data capture (CDC). In *Advances in Recent Technologies in Communication and Computing (ARTCom), 2010 International Conference on*, pages 365-368. IEEE.

Tho, M. N., & Tjoa, A. M. (2003). Zero-latency data warehousing for heterogeneous data sources and continuous data streams. In *5th International Conference on Information Integrationand Web-based Applications Services*, (pp. 55-64). IEEE.

Valencio, C. R., Marioto, M. H., Zafalon, G. F. D., Machado, J., & Momente, J. (2013). Real time delta extraction based on triggers to support data warehousing. In *International Conference on Parallel and Distributed Computing, Applications and Technologies (PDCAT'13)*, (pp. 293-297). IEEE. 10.1109/PDCAT.2013.52

Vassiliadis, P. (2009). A survey of extract - transform - load technology. *International Journal of Data Warehousing and Mining*, *5*(3), 1–27. doi:10.4018/jdwm.2009070101

Vassiliadis, P. and Simitsis, A. (2008). Near real time ETL. *Springer Annals of Information Systems*, *3*(978-0-387-87430-2). New Trends in Data Warehousing and Data Analysis.

Vassiliadis, P., Vagena, Z., Skiadopoulos, S., Karayannidis, N., & Sellis, T. (2001). Arktos: Towards the modeling, design, control and execution of ETL processes. *Information Systems*, *26*(8), 537–561. doi:10.1016/S0306-4379(01)00039-4

Waas, F., Wrembel, R., Freudenreich, T., Thiele, M., Koncilia, C., & Furtado, P. (2013). On-demand ELT architecture for right-time BI: Extending the vision. [IJDWM]. *International Journal of Data Warehousing and Mining*, *9*(2), 21–38. doi:10.4018/jdwm.2013040102

Wibowo, A. (2015). Problems and available solutions on the stage of extract, transform, and loading in near real-time data warehousing (a literature study). In *International Seminar on Intelligent Technology and Its Applications (ISITIA)*.

Wrembel, R. (2006). *Data Warehouses and OLAP: Concepts, Architectures and Solutions: Concepts, Architectures and Solutions*. IGI Global.

Zuters, J. (2011). Near real-time data warehousing with multi-stage trickle and flip. In *Perspectives in Business Informatics Research* (pp. 73–82). Springer. doi:10.1007/978-3-642-24511-4_6

KEY TERMS AND DEFINITIONS

Business Intelligence: It is a branch of data analytics that deals with collecting, analysing, and visualising data. Users can examine this data to learn more about how the company is doing.

Change Data Capture: It is the procedure of locating and collecting changes made to data in a database and then sending those changes instantly to a system or process downstream.

Data Integration: The process of combining data from several sources within an organisation to produce a comprehensive, accurate, and current dataset for BI, data analysis, and other technologies and business processes is known as data integration.

Data Latency: The total amount of time that passes between when data are collected by a source system and when they are made available to the data warehouse is known as data latency.

Data Stream: Data streaming is a process that enables continuous real-time data delivery between a source and a destination.

Data Warehouse: Large volumes of data from many sources are centralised and combined in a data warehouse. With the help of its analytical capabilities, businesses can get more out of their data and make better decisions by gaining useful business insights.

ETL: Extract, transform, and load is a method of integrating data that gathers information from several sources into a single, unified data repository that is then loaded into a data warehouse or other destination system.

Real-Time ETL: As soon as data is acquired, it is processed, transferred, and continuously loaded into a warehouse in real-time and made instantaneously accessible to the various business activities that need it.

Chapter 15
Big Data in Real Time to Detect Anomalies

N. Abinaya
Hindusthan College of Arts and Sciences, India

A. V. Senthil Kumar
ⓘ https://orcid.org/0000-0002-8587-7017
Hindusthan College of Arts and Sciences, India

Ankita Chaturvedi
ⓘ https://orcid.org/0000-0002-0739-5792
IIS University (deemed), India

Ismail Bin Musirin
Universiti Teknologi MARA, Malaysia

Manjunatha Rao
National Assessment and Accreditation Council, India

Gaganpreet Kaur

ⓘ https://orcid.org/0000-0002-3322-1315
Chitkara University Institute of Engineering and Technology, Chitkara University, India

Sarabjeet Kaur
Zakir Husain Delhi College Evening, India

Omar S. Saleh
ⓘ https://orcid.org/0000-0001-8410-0786
Studies, Planning, and Followup Directorate, Iraq

Ravisankar Malladi
ⓘ https://orcid.org/0000-0002-8250-6595
Koneru Lakshmaiah Education Foundation, India

Nitin Arya
India Para Power Lifting, India

ABSTRACT

The proliferation of linked devices and the Internet have made it easier for hackers to infiltrate networks, which can result in cyber attacks, financial loss, healthcare information theft, and cyber war. As a result, network security analytics has drawn a lot of interest from researchers lately, especially in the field of anomaly detection in networks, which is seen to be essential for network security. Current methods are ineffective mostly because of the large amounts of data that linked devices have amassed. It is essential to provide a framework that can manage real-time massive data processing and identify network irregularities. This study makes an effort to solve the problem of real-time anomaly detection. This work has examined both the key features of related machine learning algorithms and the most recent real-time big data processing technologies for anomaly detection. The recognized research problems of massive data processing in real-time for anomaly detection are described at this point.

DOI: 10.4018/979-8-3693-0413-6.ch015

INTRODUCTION

Sensors, connected devices, smart home appliances, smart cities, smartphones, mobile clouds, healthcare applications, multimedia, virtual reality, and autonomous cars are just a few of the emerging technologies that are growing quickly. These technologies also contribute to the massive accumulation of real-time data that is flowing in a network. According to a research, the Internet might see a large community of 50.1 billion linked gadgets by 2020. This anticipated expansion raises serious concerns about network security. The goal of the current study is to give a thorough understanding of the most recent real-time big data technology, applications, and anomaly detection methods. Anomaly detection, machine learning techniques, and real-time big data processing are the three diverse fields that are detailed in this paper's comparative study and relationship. Also, a comprehensive taxonomy built on a comparison of the aforementioned domains is presented. This paper's second goal is to identify and describe the difficulties associated with real-time large data processing for anomaly detection. The most network attacks, with a total of 79,790 security incidents, were reported from the public, information, and financial services industries, and 75% of attacks spread from 0 victims to 1 victim within a given day, (Aburomman et al., 2017) according to a study that examined data from 70 organizations spread across 61 countries. The network infrastructure has also been subject to a variety of cyber attacks. As an illustration, consider phishing, malware, search engine poisoning, bonnets, distributed denial of service attacks, denial of service attacks, spam, and credential comparison. Nowadays, monitoring networking risks has emerged as the main difficulty for most businesses, particularly in well-known industries like government, energy, healthcare, banking, and research facilities. The infrastructure is safeguarded and secured by these firms employing a variety of monitoring methods at great financial expense. Yet, because attackers utilise advanced tactics to access the infrastructure, the current security technologies and log analysis to find attackers operating offline eventually become outdated.

There have been several reports of large-scale, sophisticated cyberattacks against connected devices in 2016. Thousands of Internet-linked gadgets, including cameras, recorders, and other connected devices, were compromised by hackers. Major websites in the United States were attacked by cybercriminals using common home equipment and gadgets. The development of the Internet of Things (IoT) has paved the way for an enormous amount of data generation and flow, creating a barrier for the procedures used to monitor the security of the network infrastructure. (Ahmad, A et al.,2016) According to a recent investigation from Spider Labs, a significant cyber attack on a Singaporean healthcare data centre led to the loss of 1.5 million patient details. Nevertheless, database administrators did not discover and report the data theft for a few days. They discovered unusual activity on one of Sing Health's IT databases, which prompted an alert and the network's closure to prevent a further data breach. Anomaly detection is one of the effective tools used to assure network security since it aids security analysts in seeing potential attacks that might affect the network in the next days or months.

Anomaly detection, in particular, enables early identification of strange or unnecessary patterns in network activity. It continuously analyses crucial network properties and generates an alarm if any anomalies or unusual patterns are found in the network. Network analysts' abilities to scale the enormous number of data have been hampered by the vast volumes of data generated in real time. Thus, it is essential to develop network security analytics performance reports in real-time and close to real-time, as opposed to only using historical monthly and weekly log data. Nevertheless, the current anomaly detection methods fall short of producing sufficient security analytics performance data and are unable to evaluate and detect network threats in real time or close to real time. Also, as a result of the enormous volume, pace, diversity, and reliability of data collected, the present monitoring technologies are no longer able to identify the growing number of new forms of assaults that are discovered in networks every day. In industries like healthcare, manufacturing, telecommunication, banking, education, and transportation, the big data era has created numerous network security challenges and issues that have not yet been resolved. (AhmadS et al., 2017) Of particular concern are network architecture, modelling, data processing and analysis, and anomaly detection. The data must be processed right away in order to identify any possible network risks, but the current standard monitoring technologies are unable to handle huge data, making it difficult to continually monitor network infrastructure and identify anomalous behavior and threats.

Thus, it has become crucial to use a combination of machine learning algorithms linked to big data technologies to overcome the limitations of the existing methodologies in order to analyze real-time large data effectively and find abnormalities. Understanding machine learning will aid in the analysis of

Figure 1. The creation, processing, and anomaly detection steps for large data in real-time

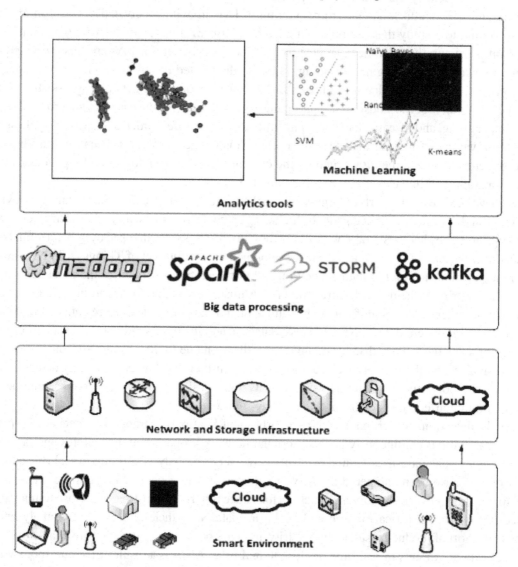

gathered data to identify and monitor the network using algorithms. The large volume of network data may also be processed and streamed in real-time and almost real-time with the aid of different real-time big data technologies.

Figure 1 shows a bottom-up big data processing flow for anomaly detection in real-time, where different smart devices are connected via network technologies. These gadgets produce a large amount of sensor data, which is saved in the cloud and other storage systems. Big data processing tools like Hadoop, (Ahmed et al., 2017) Spark, and Apache Storm are utilized to analyze the stored datasets gathered from sensor devices, and the outcomes are then used for analysis and anomaly detection using machine learning techniques.

SHORTCOMINGS OF EXISTING ANOMALY DETECTION SCHEMES

Sensitivity to Data Quality and Preprocessing

Many anomaly detection schemes are sensitive to data quality and the effectiveness of preprocessing steps. Outliers, missing values, or noisy data can significantly impact the performance of these methods. Ensuring data quality and applying appropriate preprocessing techniques are critical challenges in anomaly detection.(Bradlow, E. T et al., 2017)

Limited Generalizability

Some anomaly detection schemes perform well on specific datasets or within specific domains but struggle to generalize to new, unseen data. (Ahmed et al., 2016) The lack of generalizability hampers the adoption of these methods in real-world scenarios, where data distributions and anomalies may vary. The ability to adapt and generalize to diverse datasets remains an important aspect to address.

Lack of Explainability and Interpretability

As the complexity of anomaly detection models increases, their interpretability often decreases. It becomes challenging to understand the factors contributing to an anomaly detection decision. In domains where interpretability is crucial, such as healthcare or finance, (Bhadani A. K., &JothimaniD. 2016) the lack of explanations can hinder trust and acceptance of the anomaly detection system. The development of more interpretable models and the ability to provide explanations for anomaly detection decisions are important research directions. (Birjali et al., 2017)

Handling Imbalanced Data and Concept Drift

Many real-world datasets exhibit imbalanced distributions, where anomalies are relatively rare compared to normal instances. Anomaly detection schemes need to address the challenge of imbalanced data to prevent biased or inaccurate detections. (CarvalhoJ. V et al., 2018) Additionally, in dynamic environments where data distributions change over time (concept drift), anomaly detection systems should adapt and update their models to maintain accuracy. Developing robust methods that can handle imbalanced data and concept drift is an ongoing challenge in the field. (BirjaliM, et al., 2017)

CRITERIA FOR SELECTING ANOMALY DETECTION APPROACHES FOR REAL-TIME BIG DATA

Real-Time Processing Capability: Anomaly detection approaches should be able to process data in real-time, efficiently handling the high-speed and continuous nature of big data streams.(Casas P, et al., 2016)

Scalability: The selected approach should be scalable to handle large volumes of data in real time without compromising performance. (Chandola V, et al., 2009)

Accuracy: The accuracy of anomaly detection is crucial, and the chosen approach should demonstrate high detection rates while minimizing false positives and false negatives.

Computational Efficiency: Consideration should be given to the computational requirements of the anomaly detection approach, (DBIR, 2015) ensuring that it can process data within the available resources and time constraints.

Flexibility and Adaptability: The chosen approach should be flexible enough to adapt to changing data patterns and accommodate evolving anomalies in real-time big data streams. (Di Mauro, M., & Di Sarno, C2014)

Interpretability: Depending on the application domain, the interpretability of anomaly detection results may be important. (Dromard, J, et al., 2015) The chosen approach should provide explanations or insights into the detected anomalies for effective decision-making.

REVIEW OF LITERATURE

The detection of intrusions in network traffic:

Network security has become a crucial component of all web-based applications, including online transactions, online shopping, (Ellis, B. 2014) and other online companies, as a result of the widespread use of the internet in daily activities. By a variety of internet access methods, internet intrusion results in the loss of data confidentiality. Network intrusions are occasionally referred to as cyberattacks or malicious assaults. Intrusion, (Fan, J et al.,2014) such as variations in data transmission rates, erratic internet use, abrupt changes in access times, etc. Take the following scenario: Using an internet-based method, frequent monitoring of internet usage has been implemented. When network utilization surpasses typical levels when compared to usage patterns from previous data, (Feng, W et al., 2014) the finding is regarded as an incursion. In order to safeguard the network, it has to be found and fixed right away.In this case, it is obvious that detecting abnormalities offers a way to stop network intrusion.(Fernandes G, et al., 2016)

The basic goal of is to find abnormalities in mobile network signalling flow. Have a look at another mobile network instance where the use of anomaly detection techniques is crucial for identifying rapid changes in signal flow. (Fernandes G, et al.,2015) The properties of signal traffic, such as data in terms of TBs, the number of multidimensional data events per second, and the speed of data events per second, are used in this application to identify abnormalities. In the aforementioned research project, (Fernández, et al., 2016) experiments were conducted to find abnormalities using batch processing and real-time analytics.

Computer System Malware Detection

Every type of unwanted activity that seriously harms computer systems is referred to as malware. (GandomiA &HaiderM2015) The computer systems become faulty as a result. For instance, harmful software detected in a computer system causes poor performance, data loss, and resource insecurity. (Gani A et al., 2016) The authors of talk about how anomaly detection may be used to spot patterns in monitored data that differ from normal behaviour. In the aforementioned study, the authors continually tracked VMware stream data performance, including CPU load, memory utilisation, etc., and analyzed the data using an incremental clustering approach to look for anomalies. For real-time anomaly detection, the authors also used Apache Spark and Apache Kafka. (García L et al., 2018)

IoT Outlier Detection

Applications can be fitted with sensors and processors that connect with one another through the internet thanks to the Internet of Things (IoT). In IoT-based applications, outlier identification is still a work in progress. Consider the IoT-based use of communications, where a user may get an unexpected call from attackers. Also, the attackers routinely make fraudulent calls and change their phone numbers. In this case, detecting anomalies assist in spotting fraudulent calls and preventing additional attacks like data loss.Real-time abnormalities in streaming data produced by machines, sensors, the Internet of Things,(HamamotoA, et al., 2017) mobile devices, network data traffic, application logs, etc. are vital, according to. With the help of the Spark environment, the authors tested out the employment of machine learning algorithms like Naive Bayes and Random Forest for the purpose of detecting anomalies in quick datasets. The Random Forest technique was also recommended by the authors as a scalable option since it works better with quick data that expands in size quickly.(Hashem, et al., 2015)

Healthcare Anomalies

The healthcare industry is the most sensitive in terms of real-time anomaly detection since it is essential to lower death rates. To regularly check on the sick patients, a variety of sensors and health monitoring systems are available. Since that healthcare is one of the life-critical industries, real-time analytics are crucial. Take a patient whose heart rate is continually tracked as an example. Let's assume the heart rate being tracked is 120, which is over the usual range. To prevent loss of life, the patient must be treated right away in this circumstance. Thus, it is essential for the healthcare industry to detect irregularities in real time. The study has a strong emphasis on employing machine learning approaches for anomaly identification in healthcare monitoring systems. In this paper, (Hassani, H., & Silva, E. S. 2015) the authors tested supervised machine learning algorithms versus unsupervised machine learning algorithms for anomaly detection. While unsupervised machine learning algorithms like Isolation Forest, Local Outlier Factor, and K-Nearest Neighbor have been employed, supervised machine learning algorithms like Random Forest and Support Vector Machine are used to identify abnormalities.The authors discovered that for anomaly detection, the supervised machine learning approach performs better than the unsupervised technique.

Detection of Credit Card Fraud

In the modern economy, credit cards are essential and are used for numerous consumer and commercial transactions. The possibility of using the credit card fraudulently exists. Credit card fraud is the illicit use of a credit card without the owner's knowledge. Normally, the amount of the transaction, the location of the transaction, and other factors are thoroughly examined in order to identify fraudulent credit card activity. For instance, it is deemed to be fraudulent activity if the amount differs from the typical transaction range. To identify credit card fraud, the authors of offered a number of machine learning methods, including Logistic Regression (LR), Random Forest (RF), Naive Bayes (NB), and Multilayer Perceptron (MLP). Using an experiment with the 2, 84, 807 total transactions and 492 fraudulent transactions from the Kaggle dataset. The Random Forest algorithm, according to the scientists, does a good job of categorizing a transaction as legitimate or fraudulent. It is important to note that our study differs from the studies described above in a number of ways. For example, most investigations of large data processing, anomaly detection, or machine learning approaches have primarily examined these techniques in batch mode rather than in real-time.

On the other hand, our major attention has been on real-time large data processing systems that leverage machine learning to detect anomalies.

i.   The survey of cutting-edge research on real-time large data processing for anomaly detection is one of this paper's primary contributions.
ii. Putting out a taxonomy to group the material that is already out there into groups like big data, anomaly detection, machine learning, modes, data, and applications.
iii. Examining current solutions in light of the suggested taxonomy.
iv. Outlining the difficulties in future research and recommending guidance.

ISSUES IN REAL-TIME ANOMALY DETECTION WITH BIG DATA

Volume and Velocity of Data

The sheer volume and velocity of big data pose significant challenges for real-time anomaly detection. Traditional approaches may not be able to process and analyze data streams in real time, leading to delays in detecting anomalies. Scalable and efficient algorithms are needed to handle the high-speed and continuous flow of data.(Ide, T., Khandelwal, A., &Kalagnanam, 2016)

Data Variety and Complexity

Big data comes in diverse formats, including structured, unstructured, and semi-structured data. This variety adds complexity to anomaly detection as different data types require specific preprocessing and feature extraction techniques. (IqbalR et al., 2016) Handling various data formats in real-time becomes a significant challenge that must be addressed.

Data Quality and Noise

Big data sources often suffer from data quality issues, such as missing values, outliers, or noisy data. These data quality problems can significantly impact the accuracy of anomaly detection. It is crucial to address data quality issues and develop robust techniques that can handle noisy data and outliers without compromising real-time performance.

Scalability and Resource Constraints

Real-time anomaly detection on big data necessitates scalable algorithms and infrastructure to handle large-scale datasets. Resource constraints, such as limited memory, processing power, or bandwidth, can further exacerbate the scalability challenge. Designing efficient algorithms and optimizing resource utilization become essential considerations.

PROBLEMS IN REAL-TIME ANOMALY DETECTION WITH BIG DATA

Latency and Time Sensitivity

Real-time anomaly detection requires detecting anomalies as soon as they occur to minimize the potential impact on critical systems or processes. However, processing and analyzing large volumes of data in real time can introduce latency, resulting in delayed anomaly detection. Reducing latency and achieving timely anomaly detection is a critical problem to address.

False Positives and False Negatives

Balancing the detection of genuine anomalies while minimizing false positives and false negatives is a common challenge in real-time anomaly detection. High false positive rates can lead to alert fatigue and unnecessary interventions, while false negatives can result in critical anomalies being overlooked. Developing techniques to improve the accuracy of anomaly detection and reduce false positives and false negatives is crucial.

Dynamic and Evolving Anomalies

Anomalies in real-world systems are dynamic and constantly evolving. Static anomaly detection models may struggle to adapt to changing patterns and new types of anomalies. Continuous monitoring and updating of anomaly detection models to accommodate dynamic anomalies is a significant problem in real-time big data analytics.

TRENDS IN REAL-TIME ANOMALY DETECTION WITH BIG DATA

Machine Learning and Deep Learning

Machine learning and deep learning techniques are increasingly being applied to real-time anomaly detection on big data. These approaches leverage the ability of models to learn patterns and detect anomalies from large-scale data streams. The utilization of advanced machine learning and deep learning algorithms enables more accurate and automated real-time anomaly detection.

Stream Processing and Complex Event Processing

Stream processing and complex event processing(CEP) technologies are gaining prominence in real-time big data analytics. These techniques allow for the processing and analysis of data streams in real time, enabling faster anomaly detection. Stream processing frameworks, coupled with anomaly detection algorithms, facilitate the timely identification of anomalies within data streams.

Edge Computing and Edge Analytics

The adoption of edge computing and edge analytics in real-time anomaly detection is an emerging trend. Edge devices can process and analyze data locally, reducing the latency associated with sending data to a central server for analysis. By performing anomaly detection at the edge, real-time decision-making becomes faster and more efficient.(Jones,N2016)

Explainable and Interpretable Anomaly Detection

As anomaly detection models become more complex, the need for interpretability and explainability arises. Interpretable anomaly detection techniques provide insights into the reason behind anomaly detections, enabling better understanding and trust in the system. Incorporating explainability into real-time anomaly detection models is an emerging trend in the field.

IMPORTANCE OF IMPLEMENTATION AND EXPERIMENTAL EVALUATION

REALISTIC ASSESSMENT: Implementing and evaluating anomaly detection schemes in real-world scenarios provides a more realistic assessment of their performance. Experimental evaluations allow researchers to observe how the approaches perform in terms of accuracy, efficiency, and scalability when confronted with actual big data streams.(Kakavand M, et al., 2015)

PERFORMANCE COMPARISON: Comparative analysis based on experimental results enables the performance comparison of different anomaly detection schemes. It helps identify the strengths and weaknesses of each approach, enabling researchers and practitioners to make informed decisions when selecting the most suitable scheme for real-time big data anomaly detection.

UNDERSTANDING LIMITATIONS: Implementing and experimenting with different schemes helps to uncover the limitations and shortcomings of each approach. It provides insights into the types of anomalies the methods may struggle to detect, the impact of data distribution and quality, and the computational resources required. Understanding these limitations allows for further research and development to address the identified shortcomings. (Karim A, et al., 2017)

BENCHMARKING: Experimental evaluation of anomaly detection schemes establishes benchmark datasets and evaluation metrics for future studies. By creating standardized benchmarks, researchers can compare the performance of new approaches with existing ones, enabling progress in the field of real-time big data anomaly detection.

EXPERIMENTAL DESIGN AND EVALUATION METRICS

Dataset Selection: Careful consideration should be given to selecting representative datasets that reflect the characteristics of real-time big data. These datasets should include diverse anomalies, varying data distributions, and different levels of noise.

Evaluation Metrics: Defining appropriate evaluation metrics is crucial to assess the performance of anomaly detection schemes. Metrics such as precision, recall, F1-score, and area under the receiver operating characteristic curve (AUC-ROC) are commonly used to evaluate the accuracy and effectiveness of anomaly detection. (Katal A, et al., 2013)

Experimental Setup: The experimental setup should consider the implementation of different anomaly detection schemes using suitable programming languages, frameworks, and tools.

Result Analysis: Analyzing and interpreting the experimental results is crucial for drawing meaningful conclusions. Statistical analysis techniques, such as hypothesis testing and significance analysis, can be employed to determine the statistical significance of the performance differences between different approaches.

MOTIVATION AND EXAMPLES OF USE

The survey of anomalies detection using real-time big data processing has been motivated by the use case scenarios and motivation given in the parts that follow.

According to a 2016 analysis from Cisco, 879 Exabyte more IP traffic would be sent over the Internet in 2020, reaching 2.3 Zettabytes. As a result, the ability of the current security analytics to identify threats in real time is compromised. According to Cisco, non-PC gadgets (smart devices) such tablets, smartphones, smart watches, smart bands, television set-top boxes, smart key chains, smart lamps, smart security cameras, smart Televisions, and smart locks are predicted to account for 71% of all IP traffic in 2020. This causes a massive amount of data to be analyzed in real time at a rapid rate and with more variations, fulfilling the requirements of big data V's. Non-PC gadgets, (Lin W, et al., 2015) on the other hand, present a serious security risk if they are not continuously monitored. Several companies in the US and Europe, including CNN, Twitter, Reddit, The Guardian, and Netflix, were heavily assaulted in October 2016 using smart home devices. Also, as hackers develop new techniques to attack smart devices and protocols, additional dangers are anticipated to materialize in 2021.

By the end of 2018, Gartner estimates that global security spending will have reached an amount of $96 billion. All enterprises will be more aware of the security risk as a result of the outdated and ineffective defenses against assaults offered by current technology. According to forecasts, the U.S. Federal Cybersecurity Market would rise steadily at a compound annual growth rate of 4.4% to $22 billion by

2022. According to another research, the two most important cybersecurity technologies nowadays are deep learning algorithm designs and user and entity behavior analytics (UEBA). Furthermore, during the next five years, this will force the new standards of machine learning solutions to replace Security Information and Event Management (SIEM) of conventional anti-virus. It has also been noted that data stream processing, in which data continually flows into the processing site, has emerged as one of the prospective study fields in next generation applications. Real-time data streams are continuous inflows of data from an external source at predetermined intervals. A few bytes per second to terabytes per second can be used as input data.

The use case scenarios that are provided below and the debate that was just had inspired this article to concentrate on real-time anomaly detection. Current IoT infrastructures include a variety of mobile and connected devices, and their machine-to-machine communication creates enormous amounts of sensor data every second, which are then saved in the cloud. These data have a range of factors, including IP address, data transmission speed, volume, etc. They are heterogeneous in nature. In order to pattern the diverse data provided by these devices for identifying anomalous behavior, it should be tracked and gathered in real-time.

PORTABLE CLOUD: Smartphones include a large number of sensors built into one unit, enabling real-time monitoring, processing, measurement, and device location. Smartphones are able to be used in a broad range of applications because multimedia sensors like the microphone, twin cameras, and fingerprint sensors are included. Due to a lack of resources on the mobile device, all of this sensor data needs to be processed and stored in the cloud. IT services that are accessible at all hours and from any location may be delivered effectively using cloud computing technology for mobile devices.

THE SITUATION INVOLVING AUTONOMOUS VEHICLES: With the help of massive amounts of big data produced by connected devices in vehicles, these driverless cars are redefining the ecology of the automotive sector. Attackers are now focusing on the data of these linked cars in an effort to hack them and take over the entire system, including the ability to instantly deactivate the car. In-vehicle networks (IVN), which include engine control units (ECU), body control modules (BCM), and smartphone integration modules, are now present in the majority of contemporary vehicles. These IVNs offer essential functionalities for the control and safety of vehicles (Symantec Anomaly Detection for Automotive, 2016). To identify abnormalities in the cars, such as rapid increases in speed, detection of radar sensors, camera sensing, excessive fuel consumption, unexpected engine failure, incorrect lane changes, and inaccurate object identification, these modules must be examined in real-time.

In a healthcare setting, real-time anomaly detection enables fast and accurate identification of anomalies by monitoring patient services. This aids decision-making for the hospital and carers, especially as the number of old persons living alone is becoming a social issue for the community and the government. The information may include a number of unusual medical situations, instrument faults, human errors, or be geared towards identifying disease epidemics in a particular region.

These records include a variety of characteristics, including the patient's age, gender, height, blood sugar level, and other information that requires very accurate analysis. Also, an increasing number of IoT device compatibility aids in the collection and analysis of vast amounts of data by the healthcare sector.Moreover, modern medical technology generate a wide range of multimedia data, including high-definition films, images, graphs, and sound files. These multimedia data are full with intricate information that may be used to monitor and diagnose any ailment. Moreover, the need for computational power for multimedia healthcare solutions has prompted the use of cloud services for e-healthcare systems. The integration of multimedia data into electronic health records, on the other hand, presents big data issues, and this data must be watched in real-time to identify any anomalous system behavior.

INSIDER TRADING DETECTION: To catch insider trading early, anomaly detection techniques have been applied to stock markets where data changes in milliseconds. Before the actual information is made public, people make illegal profits by leaking inside knowledge. An impending merger, an acquisition, a terrorist attack, a ruling regarding a certain industry, or any other pertinent information that may have an impact on the stock prices of a particular industry could all be included in the information. By spotting unusual trading activity in the market, insider trading can be identified. To stop people from generating unlawful gains, it needs to be identified in real-time. Attackers start focusing on mobile-connected cars and vehicle-to-vehicle communications networks to get into the control units and body control modules, which offer crucial information about the vehicles, for safety-critical system detection. Moreover, these mobile devices utilize the cloud infrastructure to process, store, and retrieve vital data. Techniques for identifying anomalies in this situation can assist in keeping an eye on the vehicle or alerting it when it has been assaulted or is simply acting strangely.

In contrast, all of the aforementioned use case situations show that employing the current anomaly detection approaches still has its drawbacks and problems. Also, a growing number of brand-new threat kinds are being discovered daily in linked devices. Due to the increased volume, diversity, and velocity of data being collected for analysis, current monitoring technologies are challenged to identify abnormalities.

UNDERSTANDING ANOMALY DETECTION

Definition and Importance: We provide a concise definition of anomalies and emphasize their significance in real-world applications. Readers will understand that anomalies represent abnormal patterns or behaviors that deviate from the norm, and detecting them is crucial for identifying potential threats, frauds, or system malfunctions.

Traditional Approaches vs. Big Data: We compare traditional anomaly detection methods with those tailored for big data. By highlighting the limitations of conventional techniques when applied to big data, readers gain an appreciation for the need to leverage advanced analytics and real-time processing to detect anomalies effectively.

OVERVIEW OF ANAMOLY DETECTION

An important issue that has been studied across a variety of fields and application domains is anomaly detection. Finding patterns in data that deviate from anticipated behaviour is known as anomaly detection. In various application domains, these non-conforming patterns are frequently referred to as anomalies, outliers, discordant observations, exceptions, aberrations, surprises, peculiarities, or contaminants. Anomaly detections are extensively used in a wide range of applications, including cloud computing, healthcare, smart cities, the Internet of Things, and fraud detection. For instance, an unusual computer network traffic pattern may indicate that a compromised machine is disseminating sensitive information to anunauthorised recipient. MAC spoofing, IP spoofing, TCP/UDP fanout, duplicate IP, duplicate MAC, virus identification, bandwidth anomaly detection, and connection rate detection are just a few of the threats that may be found with network monitoring. Anomaly detection also aids in monitoring the patterns of any system, application, or network's typical daily operations. The possibility of high false alarm rates based on unidentified system behaviours is a drawback of the current anomaly detection systems. An anomaly can be classified into three main types. For the purpose of real-time or live anomaly detection, the collective category is often employed.

TYPES OF ANOMALIES

Point anomalies: A point anomaly occurs when a single data instance can be regarded abnormal in relation to the rest of the data.(Liu Q, et al., 2017)

Contextual Anomalies: A contextual anomaly, also known as a conditional anomaly, is when a data instance is abnormal in a certain context. Each instance of data is divided into contextual and behavioral traits.

Collective anomalies: A collective anomaly is a group of connected data instances that are aberrant in relation to the total data set. Although individual data instances in a collective anomaly might not constitute anomalies in and of itself, their existence as a group is abnormal.

For the system to detect anomalies, a number of factors may be taken into account, including timeliness, the rate of changes, scale, conciseness, and event description. The latest application domains, such as image processing, autonomous vehicles, smart homes, flight monitoring, healthcare, network monitoring, sensor networks, fraud detection for safety-critical systems and credit card systems, among others, have been precisely developed for a variety of anomaly detection techniques that we have examined. Many anomaly detection techniques have been developed over time by numerous research institutions and businesses, but it can be difficult to pinpoint the precise difference between normal and abnormal behaviour for various areas due to a number of factors. Additionally, the data has different variations depending on the application domain. In our research, we've examined rigorously a number of anomaly detection methods for keeping track of network traffic patterns. (Liu, X & Nielsen, P. S 2016) To identify any unusual network behaviour, these traffic patterns must be continuously watched. Yet as the number of Internet of Things (IoT) devices and smart linked apps increases, they communicate more data over networks at a faster rate and with more volume and diversity, making it harder for the approaches for detecting abnormalities to identify threats.

*Real-timebigdataprocessing:*Real-time big data processing more crucial than any other processing application, since it is necessary for the continual monitoring of event, messages, activities in network architecture. Hardware and software produce additional quick data for network monitoring. For instance, a log file that contains an in-memory data collection that might change quickly. Fast data is data that dynamically changes over short periods of time, such as seconds or milliseconds. The massive amount of data that enters the pipeline continually can be in any format, including structured, unstructured, and semi-structured. This data provide in-depth details on the messages and events. Streaming data are placed in big data analytics for processing, and big data analytics subsequently assists in the analysis and decision-making for subsequent processes. The use of streaming architecture will provide effective and smooth connection between the network and sensing devices. The following tools, Storm, Splunk, S4, SAP Hana, Spark, can process a large volume of real-time data; their strengths and weaknesses were examined. (Lobato A, et al., 2016)

We are in the big data age, as evidenced by the constant collection, processing, and storing of enormous amounts of data by linked device.We have established a collection of methods and tools that call

Figure 2. List of real-time applications areas

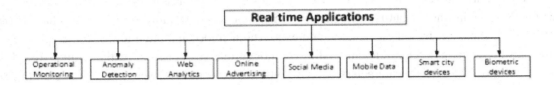

for novel forms of integration in order to extract significant hidden values from big data that is vast, complicated, and varied. Online transactions, emails, music, video, search queries, instant messaging, social networking engagement, health records, photos, click streams, logs, postings, mobile phones and application scientific equipment, and sensors have all produced a variety of different big data structures. Big data is a term used to represent information that is a flood of data, and its effects are being felt in many sectors of society, including business, science, and the arts. The amount of data is anticipated to increase by 50% by 2020, or 40% annually. More than 1 million consumer transactions, or more than 2.5 GB of data, are processed and imported into databases by Walmart alone each hour. As of 2030, when there are anticipated to be 1 trillion sensors, the amount of Internet of Things data may be regarded as little.(MaglarasL.A&JiangJ2014) At that point, IoT data will transform into big data. Several application fields, such as network monitoring and detection, geographic data, vehicle traffic, market prediction, and business forecasting, encounter difficulties as a result of big data features. A lot of companies and organisations worldwide are moving towards real-time reaction, which is seen as a vital choice, as a result of the gathering of vast quantities and diversity of data from various sources in recent years. Fundamentally, it is now essential to make judgements in real time rather than on a weekly or monthly basis due to the accumulation of continually moving data from linked devices and sensors. To get the most value possible from

Moving data requires firms to digest data much more quickly and take prompt response. Improvements in correlation and pattern recognition on a scale of millions of events and continuously churning data streams at microsecond rates are made by real-time event processing. By 2020, there should be a 50% increase in data, or a 40% yearly rise. Each hour, Walmart alone processes and imports more than 1 million consumer transactions, or more than 2.5 GB of data, into databases. By 2030, when there are predicted to be 1 trillion sensors, the volume of IoT data can be viewed as insignificant. IoT data will then change into big data at that moment. Big data characteristics provide challenges in a number of application sectors, including network monitoring and detection, geographic data, automobile traffic, market prediction, and business forecasting (figure 2).

Operational Monitoring: Due to the Internet's strength and reach, operational monitoring is now the most crucial component of streaming data monitoring. Any physical system linked to a network can have its performance monitored through a technique called operational monitoring. Operational monitoring continually records the physical conditions of the systems in data centres, including temperature, fan speed, power supply usage, disc drive utilisation, CPU load, network activity, and storage access time.

Anomaly Detection: The ability to identify abnormalities in real-time data has numerous, useful applications in a variety of fields. In urgent situations, anomaly detection might provide useful information, but trustworthy solutions are still lacking.

In session 2, some of the use cases for programmer that identify abnormalities were covered. Due to their computational flexibility, statistical approaches are commonly utilized in real-time anomaly detection. Sliding thresholds, outlier tests such extreme studentized deviation and k-sigma, change point identification, statistical hypothesis testing, and exponential smoothing are a few of these approaches. Techniques for detecting eccentricity anomalies are more effective than other methods since they don't need the definition of analytic parameters. Web analytics: As commercial websites such as e-commerce and online newspapers grow in popularity, it is necessary to track their activities in real time. This will give businesses insight into how visitors interact with their website and how many people visit a particular product page and how these two factors are related. The majority of web analytics data are cloud-based and accessible via mobile devices. Internet advertising: One of the main sources of real-time data is online advertising. In which administrators monitor a variety of data, including the quantity of sales, the quantity of clicks on any particular adverts, the time of arrival at a website via a contemporary ad exchange, and also that sets bids on the page view. Mobile Data: Cellular data, often known as mobile data, allows smartphone users to access wireless Internet. The origin-to-destination matrix, which makes it easier to identify people's places of origin and current locations on the Internet, may be understood with the use of mobile data. Also, a population group's headcount at a particular site aids in creating a map of the mobility area's density. Wireless communication technology in the smart city can provide real-time monitoring of environmental factors, including temperature, pressure, light, humidity, traffic, and others. A real-time design for the smart city has been adopted, which will guarantee efficient and smooth communication among sensing devices inside the smart city infrastructure. It also takes into account the network's quality of service support, which is essential for real-time applications for smart cities. Biometric devices: In order to make better and more timely judgements, biometric devices are utilized to continuously monitor patients' health data. According to a research, (Mahmood, T & Afzal, U2013) there is a method for inducing human real-time falling behaviour that accelerometer and triaxial gyroscope data may be used to identify. Another study has suggested a method to provide clinicians at a distant place access to information from ICU gadgets in real time. The relevance of real-time processing and its general challenges were highlighted in the aforementioned subsections. Furthermore covered were parameters and the adoption of real-time architecture or strategy for particular application domains. computer learning. The basic goal of machine learning is to provide a system the ability to pick up information from the past or present and use it to anticipate or decide on unknowable future occurrences. Many industries, including banking, autonomous vehicles, manufacturing, retail, marketing, networking, and general science, including chemistry, physics, medical, bioscience, pharmaceutical, insurance, energy, and sustainability, can benefit from machine learning. By preparation and validation utilizing classified datasets, several machine learning methods have been created and deployed to mine relevant information from the data. These algorithms are divided into two main groups: supervised algorithms and unsupervised algorithms. The machine learning algorithm must evaluate a continuous sequence in real-time applications. Real-time streaming of data. The complete dataset is not accessible at runtime as opposed to batch processing. Moreover, real-time applications necessitate making judgements online while processing data in sequential fashion as it is received.

The market's demands to improve energy conservation and raise computing cost will be met by manipulating and altering the current machine learning system. In the near future, machine traffic will increase even further. Machine traffic has already become a crucial component of today's network environment. Network administrators will face a problem in figuring out and monitoring the danger in the network as a result of the projected production of unusual traffic patterns. Current machine learning algorithms are inefficient for numerous learning tasks, computing efficiency, and managing unstructured data, which are necessary to create high accuracy for high-velocity data. They are also incompatible for solving large data categorization challenges. High dimensional data that don't succeed in being modelled have exponentially increased computational complexity.

CUTTING-EDGE BIG DATA PROCESSING TECHNOLOGIES FOR ANOMALY DETECTION BASED ON MACHINE LEARNING

This section's critical analysis of several abnormalities detecting methods. A high performance intrusion detection system with concurrent phases to quickly detect anomalies has been created by merging an ant colony network and a Support Vector Machine. In comparison to other conventional techniques, the SVM plus ant colony optimization algorithm performs better in terms of accuracy rate and running time. To highlight the key differences between the suggested designs, the algorithm's efficiencymust be compared to that of already used methods.

Moreover, a framework built on the pcStream method has been utilized to assess three different types of assaults in order to find malware, data leaks, and device thefts. It is a stream clustering method that is primarily used for maintaining and dynamically identifying temporal contexts. Selecting a parameter might be difficult if you have a lot of training time. The framework establishes network parameter using non-exhaustive grid search across this parameter. Nevertheless, in order for the suggested framework to be compatible with the present method to anomaly detection, it must be proven to be effective.In the meantime, dynamic data stream over anomalies detection is carried out using a reliable random cut forest technique that treats various dimensions separately. It aids in maintaining pairwise distance, which is crucial for computation and anomaly detection. As a consequence, the algorithm's output shows significant promise for combating false alarms. It aids in converting the input map data into a high-dimensional feature space and continuously locating the hyperplane with the greatest margin that most effectively separates training data from the original source. Nevertheless, compared to the bigger datasets that were publicly available, the analyzed datasets were lower in size.

In addition, the Cluster Center and Neighbor Algorithm (CANN) is a model that has been suggested that combines the ability to identify both comparable and dissimilar groups for a given dataset. Also, it improved the effectiveness and efficiency of anomalous detection. It consists of three phases of techniques: the first is a clustering approach to extract the cluster centre, the second is a measure and total of the distance between all the data in the dataset, and the third is cluster centres. Yet, there is a low degree of acceptability for a feature demonstration for improved pattern detecting quality.(Mascaro S, et al., 2014)

Moreover, the industrial Ethernet traffic system models an anomaly detection utilizing structural time series using the expectation maximization approach. Based on a model, the system divides the traffic into four parts that have definite detection implications. The performance of measuring abnormal and low false alarm rate is improved by this approach. Nevertheless, changing the setting is a difficult task.

A model for anomaly detection with high dimensional and large-scale datasets is Hybrid of one-class Support Vector Machine and Deep Belief. This design reduces the computational burden of training and testing the model and provides a high detection rate. Approaching the complexity and scalability issues of one SVM is also beneficial. The design is limited in non-convex loss function even though it can give detection in large dimensions.

The goal of online local adaptive multivariate smoothing is to reduce the high false alarm rate in network intrusion detection systems. To conduct the evaluation, a dataset of HTTP proxy logs is gathered from the networks of several businesses. This method simultaneously detects time and space while improving the genuine anomaly score. The difficulty is in choosing more precise algorithmic parameters without wasting time.

One of the well-known clustering methods that is utilized to identify the abnormal threat in mobile devices is self-organizing maps. The procedure uses three different standards for evaluation: accuracy rate, precision rate, and recall rate. The outcome demonstrates that for KDD Cup99 datasets that are freely available, enhanced SOM can result in greater accuracy rates. The first weight vector takes more time to determine, hence the suggested configuration should be tested with mobile devices.Moreover, increased support vector is well known for spotting anomalies in real-time applications. It delivers higher attack or normal flow categorization accuracy for entering flows. This model used weight assignment for in-the-moment events to boost classification accuracy. Nevertheless, a bottleneck in the suggested methods' parameter selection complexity.

Techniques for Anamolies Detection:

The Nearest Neighbors (NN) algorithm depends on the use of distance measurements. The full sample set is included in NN techniques, together with the data from the set and the desired grouping for each item. For the purpose of categorising the points, the distance between each item in the sampling set must be processed. The k closet passages in the sample set are deemed to be the point in a great distance. Nevertheless, the similarity measure of the NN has a flaw that causes points to be misclassified since it is ineffective at precisely estimating the distance between them, especially when categorising a tiny portion of the features. To determine the closest neighbours at a particular data point, historical data is used. The Nearest Neighbor approach often has applications in classification and prediction, two areas where artificial intelligence technologies are comparable.

As a predictor, the first k-Nearest Neighbour has been used, and this has enabled for testing of its accuracies and scalability. Nevertheless, algorithms have limitations in terms of memory needs and computational complexity for anomaly detection.

For grouping difficulties, Bayesian Networks (BN) have been widely used. Quantitative and qualitative models are divisions of BN. A coordinated non-cyclic network, whose nodes represent the random components in the issue domain and whose edges codify significance links between the factors they interface, speaks to the qualitative component of the system. The model's quantitative component consisted of a configuration of probability distributions on each. Anomalies in vessel tracks can be found using Bayesian networks. By using Bayesian Networks learner to Automatic Identification System data that has been augmented with real-world data, which exhibited different and complementary skills in recognising anomalies, dynamic and static networks are formed.

A decision boundary with the most severe edge between the usual data set and the source was created using Support Vector Machine (SVM). A separating hyperplane in the feature space between two classes is found using the SVM classifier in such a way that the distance between the hyperplane and the open data points of each class is widened. Instead than focusing on optimum classification, the strategy relies on reduced classification threat. Very beneficial when there are many characteristics, m, and few data points, n (m>>n). SVM is a reliable classifier that is used for a variety of classification applications, including network intrusion detection. Extending two-class SVM classifiers to multi-class classifiers is the major goal. This technique is the most successful at categorizing the samples from the NSL-KDD dataset; an intrusion detection system needs a classifier like this.

A decision tree is a structure that resembles a tree and features leaves that signify groups and divisions, which in turn signify the intersections of highlights that cause those classifications. The ID3 and C4.5 algorithms are the best-known methods for naturally creating decision tresses. The two methods use the concept of data entropy to create decision trees from a set of training data. A decision tree also improves the decision boundaries for each cluster by learning about the subgroups that make up the cluster. Decision trees are used to analyse the outcomes from each cluster's decision trees and draw a final conclusion. The normal and abnormal data points in anomaly detection can be grouped using clustering. A collaborative classifier called Random Forest (RF) is utilized to increase accuracy. It entails feature selection and categorization in two steps. Several decision trees will be created using random forest from various data subsets. As only a random fraction of the examples are relevant, each of them captures distinct regularities.

As compared to other conventional classification methods, the Random forest produces minimal classification mistakes, which is one of its main advantages. Four different forms of assaults, including DOS, probe, U2R, and R2L, may be found using the Random forest algorithm. Moreover, RF has been used to the problem of botnet identification because to its high prediction accuracy, capacity for handling a variety of bots, and reliance on data comprised of a very large number and various types of descriptors. (McNeil P, et al., 2016) Nevertheless, the RF requires a significant amount of processing effort when working with huge datasets and complicated estimate techniques.

The fuzzy logic algorithm can make reasonable conclusions in a vague, unclear, and imperfect environment. To find a network abnormality, it employs time interval. Moreover, threshold values are calculated using exponentially weighted moving average approaches, which reflect more recent data with a larger weight. A network segment's traffic can be characterised using a digital signature produced using principal component analysis. By assessing the differences for each variable among all response measurements, it is a statistical technique used to reduce such dimensions multivariate difficulties. Also, without substantially losing information, the answer information can be represented by a smaller fixed number of dimensions. Moreover, it analyses significant information data from logs to identify key activity time periods within the data set and then reduces them so that the new set may accurately describe the consistent behaviour of a network segment.

The ability of ants to determine the quickest route between their nests and food sources is the source of inspiration for Ant Colony Optimization.(Ahmad et al., 2017)Ant Colony Optimization is the process of a population of agents that compete and are globally asynchronous working together to get the best answer. In the context of pattern identification and anomaly detection, ant colonisation optimization and dynamic time wrapping techniques have been applied.

Based on the circumstances of the precedence in learning, Hierarchical Temporal Memory (HTM) has the capacity to forecast the data flow in real-time. Moreover, HTM is frequently used for anomaly detection in distributed real-time systems, primarily because it may produce very accurate results. This method includes a strong framework that aids in improved estimate, categorization, and the online generation of a continuous time-based data sequence. The vehicle controller area network bus uses the HTM to identify anomalous sequences and sends an alarm when these sequences are aberrant.

APPLICATIONS

We have outlined the main use cases for real-time big data processing for anomalous detection in this section. The development of IOT facilitates a variety of applications using sensors that provide significant data that evolves over time. In fact, finding anomalies in such data may assist firms in overcoming a variety of obstacles.Notably, section 2.0 explored the constraints and limitations of various applications, including network intrusion, healthcare, image processing, fraud detection, safety-critical applications, and insider trading detection.

Point anomalies occur when data points in the given dataset are shown upside down or backwards relative to normal points. For instance, point anomaly is the best-known characteristic of user-to-root (U2R) and remote-to-local (R2L) attacks. In actuality, data points aid in identifying unlawful remote and local access credentials. Contextual anomalies identify anomalous effects in the data by identifying associations in datasets and variations in their external behaviour features. For instance, it was discovered that an office building's electricity usage was significantly higher around noon and throughout the workday than it was at night and on the weekends.Collective anomalies are a set of linked data instances that behave differently when compared to the entire dataset. This group of data instances is also known as a collected anomaly. DoS attack, for instanceThese attacks create a variety of connection requests to the web server, but only one of those is reliable since it best matches the overall abnormality.

Anomaly Detection Modes Several modes that are often employed in anomaly detection are covered in this section.Techniques for supervised anomaly detection identify anomalies by creating a set of grouping rules that help forecast future data. Classification-based anomaly detection is an illustration of supervised anomaly detection. The method of semi-supervised anomaly detection models just the typical data. At the testing phase, the other records are classified as outliers. Unsupervised anomaly detection concentrates on data that is label-free and does not require a separate training and testing stage. Clustering-based anomaly detection is a typical illustration. Data the many forms of data utilized in anomaly detection are described in this section. Tabular information seen in relational databases or spreadsheets is known as structured data. Comparing structured data to semi-structured or unstructured data, structured data may be processed for anomaly detection more effectively. Between the categories of structured and unstructured data is semi-structured data. Strict requirements are not met by these data. XML is a type of semi-structured data. Semi-structured data lacks correct formatting and takes longer to spot anomalies than structured data. Unstructured data does not adhere to any set rules or patterns. Social media material, photos, music, IoT sensor data, and video are a few examples of unstructured data. Processing unstructured data for anomaly detection takes a lot of time, memory, and resources. Processing of Huge DataModern technologies use several big data tool types across a range of fields; this section discusses big data tools used for anomaly detection.Spark is a free and open source large data processing technology.

Kafka sends data to Spark, which processes it instantly while utilizing machine learning techniques to look for anomalies. Writing apps for quickly processing massive volumes of data uses the data application programming framework Storm. Similar to Spark, the real-time data processing tool Storm also has advantages and disadvantages. Kafka is mostly used to build real-time data pipelines. The creation of internet streaming apps can also benefit from it. This technique is widely employed in a variety of industries since it can be horizontally gauged, is foolproof, and moves quickly.

Flume is a distributed service used to gather data in real-time, store it temporarily, and send it to a target. A distributed message queuing system is called Amazon Kinesis. Large pipelines and massive data sizes are no problem for it, and Kinesis output may be used with machine learning techniques.

The Hadoop distributed file system, one of the most widely used big data technology frameworks, aids in resolving this scaling issue (HDFS). Large volumes of data have been stored using it across several pieces of commercial hardware. categories of records

We have outlined the various record category types that have been applied to anomaly detection in this section. The incoming and outgoing network traffic of a single device on a network is contained in host-based data. In a single host, the host-based data may be analyzed for anomaly detection utilizing a variety of machine learning methods. All network traffic to and from all devices is included in network-based data. Using various machine learning methods, it may be analyzed for anomaly detection throughout the whole network of linked devices. The use of network-based data facilitates anomaly detection using patterns created by sensor data.

The many types of anomaly detection methodologies, applications, classifications, and modes, as well as data types and big data processing technologies, were all covered in detail in the aforementioned sections.

RESEARCH ISSUES

The most significant research obstacles for real-time big data processing systems for anomaly detection are highlighted in this section. Anomaly detection, real-time large data processing, and machine learning state-of-the-art approaches have been reviewed to determine the research issues, suggestions, and future research objectives. Redundancy: Managing enormous amounts of data created in real-time from several network sensors is essential, especially given the frequent duplication of previously generated data. Although existing big data processing technologies, such as Hadoop and Spark frameworks, have been developed to handle data replication across multiple clusters, these technologies are still insufficient in addressing the challenges related to data redundancy, data quality, inconsistent data, and the cost of maintaining storage. Moreover, these systems lack the schema necessary to reduce redundancy and are unable of storing vast amounts of data. So, it is crucial to create a framework that can manage and minimize duplication concerns in order to meet both existing and future demands. Cost of computing: Some research have concentrated on combining or blending a variety of strategies to improve the effectiveness of anomaly detection, which raises the cost of calculation. Large sample sizes and high dimensionality also lead to problems like high processing costs and algorithmic instability. (Fernandes et al., 2016) Using big data technologies and the cloud will thereby address the problem of computational cost by adding parallel and distributed processing, which aids in the creation of various clusters and minimizes the cost of computing. The cost of high-end chips and processors has decreased due to mass production, therefore using this technology will provide systems more power and enable them to analyze massive amounts of data in real-time at a lower computational cost. The initial consideration in any part of a model's construction is the type of the input data. Data instances such as an object, record, point, vector, pattern, event, case, sample, observation, or entity are examples of input data.

We have elaborated on many record kinds in this section. Each data instance has a different collection of properties, including variables, traits, features, fields, and dimensions. It has binary, category, or continuous properties, (Hashem et al., 2016) among other sorts. Most data instances fall into one of two categories: multivariate or univariate. The variety of input data makes it difficult for anomaly detection algorithms to choose the best algorithm to handle that particular data. Fundamentally, the type of characteristics in that application will determine which anomaly detection approaches are used. By creating a hybrid unsupervised machine learning method, this problem will be solved. Noise and missing values: Network sensors stream a variety of data kinds, including binary, discrete, continuous, audio, video, and picture. Due to the incoming pace of data, these data, which were obtained from multiple deployed sensors over a communication channel, contain noise and missing values. High probability for increasing the false positive alert in anomaly detection can be produced by noise and missing variables. Noise in the input data is caused by a large number of unrelated characteristics, which obscure the real abnormalities. By including an auto noise purification module in the detection framework, these issues will be resolved. By including NA to datasets, the auto cleaning module will also handle the missing value problem. Selection of Parameters: Choosing the right parameters for any machine learning algorithm may be difficult. Consider single, multiple, and hyper parameters before selecting them, especially when working with real-time anomaly detection. Moreover, a collection of parameters that performs well in the early phases of development may not do so in the later stages, and the opposite may be true. One of the main factors affecting how well the algorithms work is their parameters. Moreover, it can significantly speed up or slow down model training. As an alternative, we may develop the parameter-free technique to recognise the node partitions in streaming, directed, bipartite networks and track their development over time to identify events. This problem can be solved by using eccentricity approaches, which reduce the need for parameter selection. Insufficient Architecture: The current design can handle anomaly detection in batch processing and smaller amounts of data, but it cannot handle huge data in real-time. Big data architecture is being developed by organisations to improve performance, but it is fundamentally different from big data when it comes to real-time data. To create a new working environment that meets the demands of both data in motion (rapid) and data at rest, real-time architectural components must integrate analytics and application (big). When big data architecture is not coupled with already-existing corporate data, it is inefficient; similarly, an analysis cannot be finished unless big data correlates it. The architectural problems will be solved by combining various big data technologies with hybrid machine learning methods. Data visualisations: The user must be able to see processed and analyzed data or reports in order to get understanding from them. Nevertheless, choosing the right visualisation techniques for the identification of abnormalities from the numerous linked devices is a hurdle. The design of the anomalous detection visualisation incorporates a variety of visualisation approaches, from basic graphs to 2D and 3D views. When it comes to 2D and 3D output, heat maps, scatter plots, parallel coordinates, and node-link graphs are simple to display. Users must fully comprehend the facts in order to rotate and zoom the displays due to the 3D interaction. This issue may be solved by including the open source visualisation techniques into the framework. In addition, the framework makes it possible for the system to choose the best visualisation style automatically.

Heterogeneity of data: Unstructured data includes virtually all types of data that are created, including interactions on social media, meetings that are recorded, processing of PDF documents, fax transmissions, emails, and more. Structured data is constantly arranged in a highly automated and controllable manner. Although the database integration is strong, unstructured data is utterly unprocessed and disorganised. Dealing with unstructured data is time-consuming and obviously expensive. It is also not possible to convert all of this unstructured data into structured data. Unsupervised hybrid machine learning methods will be used to solve the heterogeneous data problem. the use of real-time big data and hybrid machine learning methods. Technologies will aid in sorting the incoming data into several categories, making it easier to identify the various data kinds and so addressing the heterogeneity issue.

Accuracy: Despite the fact that current technologies are capable of identifying abnormalities, the dependability of the results is still problematic owing to accuracy problems. In some circumstances, increased computing processing and time are necessary to obtain improved precision. This problem will be solved by combining real-time big data technologies with hybrid machine learning algorithms, which develop as an alternative potent meta-learning tool to properly analyse the enormous volume of data created by contemporary apps, while consuming less memory and power. Flume is a distributed service used to gather data in real-time, store it temporarily, and send it to a target. A distributed message queuing system is called Amazon Kinesis. Large pipelines and massive data sizes are no problem for it, and Kinesis output may be used with machine learning techniques. The Hadoop distributed file system, one of the most widely used big data technology frameworks, aids in resolving this scaling issue (HDFS). Large volumes of data have been stored using it across several pieces of commercial hardware.

We have identified upcoming research directions for research communities to develop an adoptable and responsive model for real-time big data processing, which can help to collect data with labelling and convert unstructured data into semi-structured data that will be easier to label in run-time for processing, in addition to the above summarised future research directions on research challenges and recommendations in table 8. The model should also allow for flexible selection of a particular feature and the extraction of parameters for study. It is possible to benchmark various threat kinds and real-time processing using these chosen settings. Similar to this, the suggested model should be more capable and prompt in order to train and retrain the model more effectively. Many of the current efforts do not address model retraining for processing, which will be incredibly helpful in real-time. Modules for offline and online analysis should be included in the model's retraining process.With similarly current incoming real-time data, the future model should include quick, hybrid, and incremental learning algorithms. This will make it easier to choose the appropriate temporal windowing for online analysis. Moreover, tools for multiple level display enhance comprehension of processed and analyzed data. Moreover, by adding cutting-edge visualisation technologies like 3D, 4D, augmented reality, and virtual reality, these methodologies may assist security analytics. Creating a new dataset that combines structured and unstructured data from a variety of contemporary technologies, such as the Internet of Things, 3D printing, smart cities, and other connected gadgets.To address many spread threats throughout the world, developed datasets should be cross-validated with publicly accessible existing datasets.

CONCLUSION AND SOME FINAL THOUGHTS

In this study, we studied machine learning and real-time large data processing with the potential for anomaly detection. We have looked at current research in real-time and anomalous detection from the standpoint of use cases. We were able to determine the difficulties associated with real-time anomaly detection by looking at these use cases. We have outlined the drawbacks and difficulties of the current methods for identifying the abnormal danger in the given area. Also, we had created a taxonomy for our methodology. Additionally, we have discovered that cutting-edge methods provide study difficulties in real-time anomaly detection. This study provided a layer diagram that clarifies the anomaly detection process and may eventually result in the suggestion of a framework for real-time big data processing to find anomalies. The suggested framework will be put into practice using real-time analytics, IOT data sources, gateways, network infrastructure, streaming, clustering/classification algorithms, big data processing technologies, analytics for anomaly identification, and visualisation. Moreover, the study will compare the performance of the proposed framework to existing technologies in terms of accuracy and efficiency in the detection rate using algorithm.

REFERENCES

Aburomman, A. A., & Reaz, M. B. I. (2017). A Novel Weighted Support Vector Machines Multiclass-ClassifierBasedonDifferentialEvolutionforIntrusionDetectionSystems. *Information Sciences*.

Ahmad, A., Paul, A., & Rathore, M. M. (2016). An efficient divide-and-conquer approach for big dataanalyticsinmachine-to-machine communication. *Neurocomputing*, *174*, 439–453. doi:10.1016/j.neucom.2015.04.109

Ahmad, S., Lavin, A., Purdy, S., & Agha, Z. (2017). Unsupervised real-time anomaly detection for streamingdata. *Neurocomputing*, *262*, 134–147. doi:10.1016/j.neucom.2017.04.070

Ahmed, E., Yaqoob, I., Hashem, I. A. T., Khan, I., Ahmed, A. I. A., Imran, M., & Vasilakos, A. V. (2017). The role of big data analytics in Internet of Things. *Computer Networks*, *129*, 459–471. doi:10.1016/j.comnet.2017.06.013

Ahmed, M., Mahmood, A. N., & Hu, J. (2016). A survey of network anomaly detection techniques. *Journal of Network and Computer Applications*, *60*, 19–31. doi:10.1016/j.jnca.2015.11.016

Bhadani, A. K., & Jothimani, D. (2016). *Big Data: Challenges, Opportunities, and Realities. Effective BigDataManagementandOpportunitiesforImplementation*. IGIGlobal.

Birjali, M., Beni-Hssane, A., & Erritali, M. (2017). Analyzing SocialMedia through Big Data usingInfoSphereBigInsightsandApache Flume. *Procedia Computer Science*, *113*, 280–285. doi:10.1016/j.procs.2017.08.299

Bradlow, E. T., Gangwar, M., Kopalle, P., & Voleti, S. (2017). The role of big data and predictive analytics inretailing. *Journal of Retailing*, *93*(1), 79–95. doi:10.1016/j.jretai.2016.12.004

Carvalho, J. V., Rocha, Á., Vasconcelos, J., & Abreu, A. (2018). A health data analytics maturity model for hospital information systems. *International Journal of Information Management*.

Chandola, V., Banerjee, A., & Kumar, V. (2009). Anomaly detection: A survey. *ACM Computing Surveys*, *41*(3), 15. doi:10.1145/1541880.1541882

DBIR. (2015). *2015 Data breach investigations report*. DBIR. http://www.verizonenterprise.com/DBIR/2015/

Di Mauro, M., & Di Sarno, C. (2014). A framework for Internet data real-time processing: A machine-learning approach. *Paper presented at the Security Technology (ICCST), 2014 International Carnahan Conferenceon*. IEEE. 10.1109/CCST.2014.6987044

Dromard, J., Roudière, G., & Owezarski, P. (2015). Unsupervised network anomaly detection in real-timeon big data. *Paper presented at the East European Conference on Advances in Databases andInformationSystems.*

Ellis, B. (2014). *Real-time analytics: Techniques to analyze and visualize streaming data.* John Wiley &Sons.

Erfani, S. M., Rajasegarar, S., Karunasekera, S., & Leckie, C. (2016). High-dimensional and large-scaleanomaly detection using a linear one-class SVM with deep learning. *Pattern Recognition, 58,* 121–134. doi:10.1016/j.patcog.2016.03.028

Fan, J., Han, F., & Liu, H. (2014). Challenges of big data analysis. *National Science Review, 1*(2), 293–314. doi:10.1093/nsr/nwt032 PMID:25419469

Farnaaz, N., & Jabbar, M. (2016). Random ForestModelingforNetworkIntrusionDetectionSystem. *Procedia Computer Science, 89,* 213–217. doi:10.1016/j.procs.2016.06.047

Feng, W., Zhang, Q., Hu, G., & Huang, J. X. (2014). Mining network data for intrusion detection throughcombiningSVMswithantcolonynetworks. *Future Generation Computer Systems, 37,* 127–140. doi:10.1016/j.future.2013.06.027

Fernandes, G., Carvalho, L. F., Rodrigues, J. J., & Proença, M. L. (2016). Network anomaly detection usingIP flows with principal component analysis and ant colony optimization. *Journal of Network and Computer Applications, 64,* 1-11.

Fernandes, G. Jr, Rodrigues, J. J., & Proença, M. L. Jr. (2015). Autonomous profile-based anomaly detectionsystem using principal component analysis and flow analysis. *Applied Soft Computing, 34,* 513–525. doi:10.1016/j.asoc.2015.05.019

Fernández, A., Carmona, C. J., del Jesus, M. J., & Herrera, F. (2016). A view on fuzzy systems for big data:progress and opportunities. *International Journal of Computational Intelligence Systems, 9*(sup1),69-80.

Gandomi, A., & Haider, M. (2015). Beyond the hype: Bigdata concepts, methods, and analytics. *International Journal of Information Management, 35*(2), 137–144.

Gani, A., Siddiqa, A., Shamshirband, S., & Hanum, F. (2016). A survey on indexing techniques for big data:taxonmyandperformance evaluation. *KnowledgeandInformationSystems, 46*(2), 241–284.

García, L., Tomás, J., Parra, L., &Lloret, J. (2018). An m-health application for cerebral stroke detectionandmonitoringusingcloudservices. *International Journal of Information Management.*

Hashem, I. A. T., Chang, V., Anuar, N. B., Adewole, K., Yaqoob, I., Gani, A., & Chiroma, H. (2016). The roleofbigdatainsmartcity. *InternationalJournalofInformationManagement, 36*(5), 748–758.

Hashem, I. A. T., Yaqoob, I., Anuar, N. B., Mokhtar, S., Gani, A., & Khan, S. U. (2015). Theriseof"bigd ata"oncloudcomputing:Reviewandopenresearchissues. *Information Systems, 47,* 98–115. doi:10.1016/j. is.2014.07.006

Hassani, H., & Silva, E. S. (2015). Forecasting with big data: A review. Annals of Data Science, 2(1), 5-19.

Ide, T., Khandelwal, A., & Kalagnanam, J. (2016). Sparse Gaussian Markov Random Field Mixtures forAnomaly Detection. *Paper presented at the Data Mining (ICDM), 2016 IEEE 16th International-Conferenceon*. IEEE.

Introducing WSO2 Data Analytics Server. (2015). Retrieved fromhttps://docs.wso2.com/display/DAS300/Introducing+DAS

Iqbal, R., Doctor, F., More, B., Mahmud, S., & Yousuf, U. (2016). Big data analytics: computational intelligence techniques and application areas. *International Journal of Information Management*.

Jones, N. (2016). *Gartner Identifies the Top 10 Internet of Things*. Gartner. http://www.gartner.com/newsroom/id/3221818

Kakavand, M., Mustapha, N., Mustapha, A., Abdullah, M. T., &Riahi, H. (2015). A survey of anomalydetection using data mining methods for hypertext transfer protocol web services. Journal ofComputerScience,11(1),89.97.

Karim, A., Siddiqa, A., Safdar, Z., Razzaq, M., Gillani, S. A., Tahir, H., & Imran, M. (2017). Big datamanagement in participatory sensing: Issues, trends and future directions. *Future Generation Computer Systems*.

Katal, A., Wazid, M., & Goudar, R. (2013). Big data: Issues, challenges, tools andgood practices. [SixthInternationalConferenceon.]. *PaperpresentedattheContemporaryComputing*, (IC3), 2013.

Lin, W.-C., Ke, S.-W., & Tsai, C.-F. (2015). CANN: An intrusion detection system based on combiningclustercentersandnearestneighbors. *Knowledge-BasedSystems*, 78, 13–21. doi:10.1016/j.knosys.2015.01.009

Liu, Q., Klucik, R., Chen, C., Grant, G., Gallaher, D., Lv, Q., & Shang, L. (2017). *Unsupervised detection of contextual anomaly in remotely sensed data*. Remote Sensing of Environment.

Liu, X., & Nielsen, P. S. (2016). Regression-based Online Anomaly Detection for Smart Grid Data. arXivpreprintarXiv:1606.05781.

Lobato, A., Lopez, M. A., & Duarte, O. (2016). An accurate threat detection system through real-timestream processing. *Grupo de Teleinformática e-Automaçao (GTA), Univeridade Federal do Rio deJaneiro(UFRJ)*,Tech.Rep.GTA-16-08.

Maglaras, L.A., & Jiang, J. (2014). *Intrusion detection and systems using machine learning techniques*. Paper presented at the Science and Information Conference(SAI),2014.

Mahmood, T., & Afzal, U. (2013). Security analytics: Big data analytics for cybersecurity: A review oftrends, techniques and tools. *Paper presented at the Information assurance*. NCIA.

Mascaro, S., Nicholso, A. E., & Korb, K. B. (2014). Anomaly detection in vessel tracks using Bayesiannetworks. *InternationalJournalofApproximateReasoning*, 55(1), 84–98.

McNeil, P., Shetty, S., Guntu, D., & Barve, G. (2016). SCREDENT: Scalable Real-time Anomalies Detectionand Notification of Targeted Malware in Mobile Devices. *Procedia Computer Science*, 83, 1219–1225. doi:10.1016/j.procs.2016.04.254

KEY TERMS AND DEFINITIONS

Anomaly Detection: Generally understood to be the identification of rare items, events or observations which deviate significantly from the majority of the data and do not conform to a well defined notion of normal behaviour.

Cluster Centers: A point to represent central location (usually mean) of the cluster. Cluster centers have been used to represent the points of its cluster.

Contextual Anomalies: If a data instance is anomalous in a specific context (but not otherwise), then it is termed as a contextual anomaly (also referred to as conditional anomaly

Cyberattacks: Attempts to steal, expose, alter, disable, or destroy another's assets through unauthorized access to computer systems.

Mobile Clouds: A new computing paradigm where mobile devices exploit the available cloud computing platform for performing specific tasks and/or accessing data on demand rather than on the individual devices themselves.

Network Traffic: It is the amount of data moving across a computer network at any given time. Network traffic, also called data traffic, is broken down into data packets and sent over a network before being reassembled by the receiving device or computer.

Sensor Data: It is the output of a device that detects and responds to some type of input from the physical environment.

Chapter 16
AI and Big Data Analytics Revolutionizing Industry 5.0:
Unlocking the Power of Smart Manufacturing and Beyond

Shweta Dewangan
https://orcid.org/0000-0002-6539-3357
ICFAI University, India

Sanjeev Kumar
https://orcid.org/0000-0002-7375-7341
Lovely Professional University, India

ABSTRACT

This study intends to investigate the application of artificial intelligence (AI) technologies in Industry 5.0, concentrating on the joint component that promotes interaction and collaboration between humans and machines. The artificial intelligence may improve human capacities, increase productivity, and make it easier to establish new business models. In addition, the study examines the ethical concerns and societal repercussions related to the use of AI in Industry 5.0. The research outlines critical success factors, difficulties, and best practices for effectively collaboratively leveraging AI within the framework of Industry 5.0. The results of this research provide organizations and policymakers with insights and recommendations that can help them use the synergy of AI and Industry 5.0 to generate collaborative innovation and achieve sustainable growth. Human-centricity, socio-environmental sustainability, and resilience are some of the aims that Industry 5.0 has the potential to support.

1. INTRODUCTION

The combination of AI with Industry 5.0 has the potential to completely transform businesses by igniting widespread, cross-organizational creativity and promoting long-term success. Harnessing the potential of AI becomes vital for opening up new prospects and gaining a competitive edge as we reach the era of

DOI: 10.4018/979-8-3693-0413-6.ch016

Figure 1. Industrial revolution and outcomes
(Source: Author compilation)

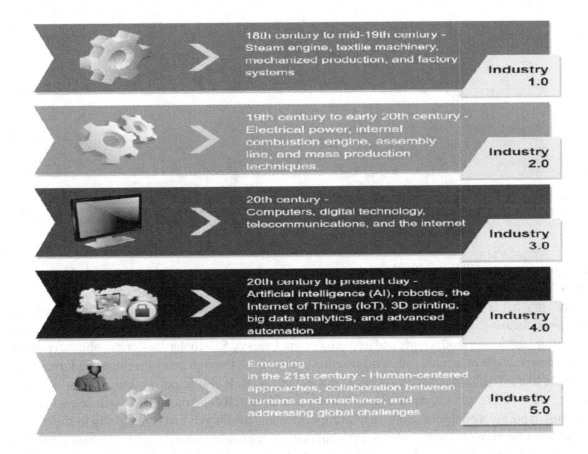

Industry 5.0, which emphasizes the harmonious cohabitation of humans and machines. Human creativity, problem-solving skills, and emotional intelligence are valued in Industry 5.0, marking a significant departure from the entirely automated operations of Industry 4.0. That humans have specific abilities and points of view that machines can't imitate is recognized. Nonetheless, artificial intelligence (AI) technologies have great potential in Industry 5.0 for enhancing human capabilities, automating repetitive jobs, and facilitating data-driven decision-making (Adel, 2022).

In Figure 1 it is mentioned that from industry 0.1 to industry 0.5 major changes seen in the field of technologies. Industry 0.1 started in 18th century that time steam engines, textiles machinery and factory system was used and slowly it change to industry 0.2 which seen up gradation in electric power. More changes seen in industry 3.0 to 5.0 where human develop advance technologies and machine leaning. Many sectors have significantly benefited from AI's ability to learn, reason, and handle large volumes of data. It has boosted production, saved money, and inspired new goods and services by increasing efficiency, precision, and automation. However, AI's actual value comes in its partnership with human workers, whom it may enhance, allowing them to take on greater complexity and driving collaborative innovation (Xian et al., 2023).This article will explore the many facets of AI's incorporation into Industry 5.0, including its design implications, ethical considerations, and societal impact. Case studies

Figure 2. Industry 5.0 and society
(Source: Author compilation)

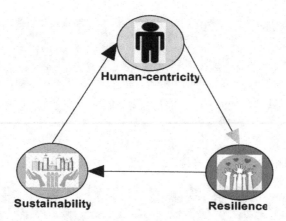

and empirical data will be analyzed to determine what works best when collaborating with AI and what obstacles businesses must overcome (Aheleroff et al., 2022).

Industry 5.0 is a concept that integrates human workers and advanced robotics in manufacturing processes, focusing on sustainable development and societal well-being. It promotes human-robot collaboration, enhancing productivity and job satisfaction. Industry 5.0 emphasizes sustainability, resource management, waste reduction, and environmental conservation through innovative manufacturing technologies like IoT and data analytics (George & George, 2023). It also prioritizes employee well-being, safety, and work-life balance, promoting inclusivity and fairness. By embracing these principles, Industry 5.0 aims to positively impact society, supporting sustainable livelihoods and contributing to community betterment (Tiwari et al., 2022). Industry 5.0 is built upon three fundamental principles: human-centricity, sustainability, and resilience. These principles guide the development and implementation of advanced manufacturing practices in this new era (Ivanov, 2023).

In Figure 2 show the relationship between Human-centricity, sustainability and resilience and it play an important role in industry 5.0. Some more point related to industry 5.0 and society mentioned below:

1. **Human-centricity -**Industry 5.0 prioritizes worker empowerment and well-being. It tries to unite humans and advanced technologies by harnessing their skills and abilities. Human-centric processes, systems, and technology increase human capabilities, promote diversity, and prioritize individual needs and experiences. It facilitates meaningful and gratifying work, directly allowing workers to shape the industry's future (Alves et al., 2023).
2. **Resilience -**Industry 5.0 recognizes the significance of developing resilient and adaptable systems that can withstand disruptions and unforeseen obstacles. Stability requires the design of agile and flexible industrial processes, supply chains, and infrastructure that can effectively respond to varying market conditions, technological developments, and global crises (Aheleroff et al., 2022). Utilizing sophisticated technologies such as artificial intelligence, automation, and data analytics to improve decision-making, optimize operations, and facilitate rapid recovery from disruptions. Industry 5.0 resilience ensures that industries can navigate uncertainty, maintain stability, and continue delivering essential products and services to society (Kaasinen et al., 2022).

3. **Sustainability -**Industry 5.0 acknowledges the urgent need to address environmental issues and transition to a more environmentally friendly and sustainable industrial landscape. Along the entire value chain, from resource extraction and manufacture to distribution and consumption, it encourages adopting sustainable practices and technology (Xu et al., 2021). Sustainability in Industry 5.0 entails reducing waste and pollution, making the best available resources, utilizing renewable energy sources, and implementing circular economy ideas. It aims to balance economic progress, social well-being, and environmental preservation to provide a sustainable future for future generations (ElFar et al., 2021).

2. THE ROLE OF HUMANS IN INDUSTRY

The Vital Roles of Humans in Industry: Training, Explaining, and Sustaining the Responsible Use of Machines. In a constantly changing business, people play three crucial roles in getting the most out of machines. These jobs include teaching people how to use devices, explaining their results, especially in complicated or controversial situations, and sustaining their use responsibly (Nardo et al., 2020).

Firstly, it is up to humans to instruct machines on adequately carrying out various functions. During this phase of training, we will instruct machine learning algorithms, provide data that has been labelled, and impart our expertise. When teaching computers how to traverse complicated situations, the subject experience, contextual awareness, and sophisticated decision-making abilities humans possess are tremendous assets (Deniz, 2020). Humans empower machines to carry out tasks in a precise and time-efficient manner by imparting their knowledge and experience to these machines.

Second, people have the vital job of describing the results of machine-made actions, especially when the results are contradictory or disputed. Machines often make decisions based on complicated formulas, making it hard for people to understand how these machines make their decisions. But people can understand, put these results in perspective, and explain them in a way that is useful to stakeholders and easy for them to understand. This explanation function is essential for building trust, addressing concerns, and making it easier for businesses in various fields to choose based on correct information.

Lastly, it's up to people to make sure tools are used in the right way. As technology improves, ethics and taking care of your responsibilities become more important. People must keep an eye on how technology is used so that it isn't abused, prejudiced, or has unintended effects. People help ensure that technology is used in a safe and fair way and includes everyone by using their best opinion, following social norms, and following rules. They protect responsible behaviour, protect people from possible dangers, and encourage good results for people and society (Maddikunta et al., 2022).

Harnessing AI and Industry 5.0 can lead to significant advancements in the manufacturing and industrial sectors. Industry 5.0 is often considered the next phase of the industrial revolution, building upon Industry 4.0, which focuses on automation and data exchange. Industry 5.0 aims to combine the strengths of both humans and AI to create a more collaborative and efficient working environment (Al Mubarak, 2022). Industry 5.0 promotes a cooperative partnership between humans and AI. Instead of replacing human workers, AI technologies augment their capabilities. AI can handle repetitive and data-intensive tasks, enabling humans to focus on more creative, problem-solving, and strategic aspects of their work. With the help of AI and advanced data analytics, industries can make data-driven decisions faster and more accurately. AI systems can analyze vast amounts of data from various sources to identify patterns, trends, and anomalies, aiding in predictive maintenance, quality control, and supply chain optimization.

By integrating AI technologies, industries can streamline processes, reduce operational inefficiencies, and increase productivity. AI-powered robots and machines can work 24/7 without breaks, leading to continuous production and fewer errors (Rožanec et al., 2022).

AI-powered computer vision systems can be utilized to inspect and ensure product quality during manufacturing. They can detect defects, measure dimensions, and identify imperfections with greater precision and speed than human inspectors. AI can help predict when equipment and machinery will likely fail, enabling companies to perform maintenance before breakdowns occur. It reduces downtime, extends equipment lifespan, and optimizes maintenance costs. AI can optimize the supply chain by analyzing data from suppliers, logistics, and demand patterns. It can predict demand fluctuations, identify potential bottlenecks, and recommend the most efficient routes for shipping and transportation (Huang et al., 2022).AI can assist in producing customized and personalized products at scale. By analyzing customer data, preferences, and behaviour, industries can tailor products to individual needs and offer a more customized experience.Industry 5.0 embraces advanced robotics, harmoniously collaborating with humans. Robots equipped with AI can perform complex tasks, working alongside humans to enhance productivity and safety. However, addressing potential challenges related to AI and Industry 5.0 is essential, such as ethical considerations, data privacy, and ensuring the workforce is adequately trained and unskilled to work effectively with AI systems. Emphasizing responsible AI deployment will be crucial for harnessing the full potential of AI in Industry 5.0 while ensuring a positive impact on society and the workforce (Fazal et al., 2022).

3. HARNESSING AI AND INDUSTRY 5.0 PATHWAY TO COLLABORATIVE INNOVATION

Harnessing AI and Industry 5.0 can pave the way for collaborative innovation, bringing together the strengths of humans and artificial intelligence to drive advancements and transformative changes in various industries.Industry 5.0 emphasizes the collaboration between humans and AI, recognizing that both play crucial roles in innovation. Human workers can leverage AI technologies to augment their capabilities, enhance decision-making, and explore new possibilities (Özdemir &Hekim, 2018). AI can assist in the ideation process by analyzing vast amounts of data, identifying patterns, and proposing novel ideas that human innovators might not have considered. It can lead to the discovery of innovative solutions and concepts. AI can accelerate the prototyping and testing phases of innovation. Through AI simulations and modelling, ideas can be tested virtually, enabling faster iterations and reducing the need for physical prototypes (Özdemir &Hekim, 2018).AI's ability to analyze vast datasets can provide valuable insights into market trends, customer preferences, and emerging opportunities. This data-driven approach can guide innovation efforts in the right direction, increasing the chances of success.

AI can assist researchers and developers in quickly gathering relevant information and knowledge from various sources. This efficiency can lead to faster progress in R&D efforts. AI's ability to process and analyze complex data can help tackle intricate problems that would be challenging for humans alone (Sharma et al., 2020). This collaboration can lead to breakthrough solutions and innovations. Industry 5.0 and AI enable a more agile approach to innovation (Xiao & Yi, 2021). Adapting quickly to changing market conditions and customer demands is critical for staying competitive and relevant. Collaborative innovation with AI should prioritize ethical considerations, ensuring that the technologies developed are inclusive, safe, and beneficial for all stakeholders. AI's ability to learn from data and experiences allows for continuous improvement in the innovation process. This iterative approach enhances the quality of ideas and solutions over time. AI and Industry 5.0, organizations should create a conducive environment that encourages experimentation, risk-taking, and learning. They should invest in upskilling their workforce to effectively collaborate with AI technologies and nurture a culture that values diverse perspectives and teamwork. Furthermore, open partnerships and collaborations with other companies and research institutions can foster knowledge exchange and spark new ideas that lead to transformative innovation (Jaiswal et al., 2022).

4. SCOPE OF AI AND INDUSTRY 5.0 IN FUTURE

The scope of AI and Industry 5.0 in the future, is vast and transformative. These technologies have the potential to revolutionize various industries and significantly impact society.AI can optimize processes, automate repetitive tasks, and improve decision-making, increasing efficiency and productivity across sectors (Verma et al., 2022). With Industry 5.0, human-AI collaboration can enhance productivity and unlock new performance levels. Industry 5.0 will witness the proliferation of advanced robotics that works hand-in-hand with humans. These robots will perform intricate tasks and improve safety and precision in various sectors (Ghobakhloo et al., 2022). AI-enabled predictive maintenance will become more sophisticated, helping companies anticipate equipment failures and reducing downtime and maintenance costs. AI will play a crucial role in healthcare, assisting in diagnosis, drug discovery, personalized medicine, and remote patient monitoring. It can potentially improve healthcare outcomes and make medical services more accessible. AI-powered autonomous vehicles will revolutionize transportation, improving safety, reducing traffic congestion, and increasing the efficiency of logistics and delivery operations. AI and Industry 5.0 can aid in optimizing resource usage, reducing waste, and promoting sustainability across industries, contributing to a greener and more eco-friendly future. AI-driven personalized learning platforms can cater to individual learning needs, making education more effective and accessible.

Additionally, AI can help reskill and upskill the workforce to adapt to the changing job landscape. AI will transform the finance industry by automating processes, detecting fraud, and enabling more accurate risk assessments (Martynov et al., 2019). The widespread adoption of AI and Industry 5.0 will also raise important ethical considerations. Striking a balance between innovation and ensuring AI's responsible and ethical use will be crucial for the future. The future of AI and Industry 5.0 holds immense potential for progress and transformation. However, it's essential to address challenges related to data privacy, ethics, biases, and potential job displacement. Responsible deployment and regulation will ensure that AI and Industry 5.0 contribute positively to society and the economy. As these technologies continue to evolve, they will reshape industries, redefine job roles, and create new opportunities for innovation and growth (Maddikunta et al., 2022)

5. ADVANCED ROBOTICS AND AUTOMATION INDUSTRY 5.0

Advanced robotics and automation play a central role in Industry 5.0, the next phase of the industrial revolution that emphasizes the collaborative integration of humans and machines to drive innovation and productivity.Industry 5.0 promotes the use of collaborative robots, also known as cobots. These robots are designed to work alongside human workers, sharing workspace and tasks. Cobots can assist with repetitive or physically demanding jobs, allowing humans to focus on more complex and creative aspects of their work (Verma et al., 2022). Industry 5.0 robots are highly flexible and adaptable, handling various tasks and quickly switching between them. This agility allows manufacturers to respond rapidly to changing production needs and customization demands (Xian et al., 2023). Industry 5.0 incorporates autonomous mobile robots (AMRs) that can move freely in factories or warehouses. AMRs can transport materials, tools, and finished products, optimizing logistics and reducing human intervention. Advanced robotics in Industry 5.0 is often connected to the Internet of Things (IoT) ecosystem. This connectivity allows robots to gather and exchange real-time data, making data-driven decisions and responding to changing conditions. AI technologies are integrated into robots to enhance their capabilities. AI enables robots to learn from data, optimize their actions, and adapt to new situations autonomously. It empowers robots to become more efficient and perform complex tasks with higher precision.

Advanced robotics equipped with computer vision systems can perform quality control and inspection tasks with high accuracy and speed (Maddikunta et al., 2022). They can identify defects and deviations, ensuring consistent product quality. Industry 5.0 encourages using robots in hazardous environments, such as nuclear facilities, oil rigs, or disaster-stricken areas, where human safety is at risk. Robots can take over dangerous tasks, protecting human workers (Jeong et al., 2014). Augmented Reality assists robot operators in guiding robots during complex tasks. AR overlays visual instructions and information on the physical environment, making it easier for operators to control robots effectively (Vadalà et al., 2020). Robots generate vast amounts of data, which can be analyzed to optimize processes, identify bottlenecks, and continuously improve efficiency (Makhataeva& Varol, 2020).Overall, advanced robotics and automation in Industry 5.0 revolutionize the manufacturing landscape by improving efficiency, safety, and productivity. They enable a collaborative ecosystem where humans and robots work together, leveraging each other's strengths to drive innovation and create a more resilient and agile industrial sector (Lotsaris et al., 2021).

6. TECHNOLOGICAL CHALLENGES FOR INDUSTRY 5.0

Industry 5.0 is the next phase of global industry evolution, building on Industry 4.0's integration of intelligent production systems and advanced information technologies. It focuses on collaboration between humans and machines, customization, and sustainability, with key technological changes expected.

1. **Human-Robot Collaboration:** Unlike the previous industrial revolutions where machines might have replaced human labor, Industry 5.0 emphasizes the synergy between humans and machines. Technologies such as advanced collaborative robots (cobots) will work side by side with humans, learning from them, and vice versa, leading to increased efficiency and productivity.
2. **Enhanced Customization and Personalization:** With the advancements in AI and machine learning, manufacturing systems will be more adaptable and capable of producing highly customized products on demand. This "batch of one" capability will be driven by technologies that can rapidly adjust operational parameters for individual product specifications, catering to the specific needs and preferences of customers.
3. **AI and Big Data Analytics:** AI algorithms will become increasingly sophisticated, able to predict, optimize, and make decisions during the manufacturing process. Big data analytics will allow for

the analysis of vast amounts of data generated by smart sensors embedded within manufacturing equipment, thereby optimizing production quality, precision, and speed.

4. **Digital Twins:** The use of digital twins, or virtual replicas of physical systems, will enable real-time monitoring, simulation, and analysis of manufacturing processes. This technology will help in predicting potential issues before they happen and optimizing the system for better performance.

5. **Sustainable Production:** Industry 5.0 will focus more on sustainable practices, including the efficient use of resources and energy. Innovations in green manufacturing technologies and circular economy principles will aim to reduce waste, lower carbon footprints, and ensure that products are more easily recycled or reused.

6. **Advanced Materials:** Developments in materials science, including the use of nanomaterials and smart materials, will revolutionize product capabilities and manufacturing techniques. These materials will potentially offer unprecedented attributes, such as self-healing or shape-changing abilities.

7. **Edge Computing:** While cloud computing has been a focus of Industry 4.0, Industry 5.0 will see a rise in edge computing, where data processing happens near the source of data generation. This shift will reduce latency, conserve bandwidth, and allow more reliable real-time processing, essential for critical decision-making in manufacturing.

8. **Blockchain for Supply Chain:** The transparency and security provided by blockchain technology will be used for tracking all types of transactions across the supply chain. This ensures product authenticity, facilitates smart contracts, and enhances the traceability of materials.

9. **AR/VR Integration:** Augmented Reality (AR) and Virtual Reality (VR) will be widely adopted for training, maintenance, design, and remote collaboration. These technologies offer immersive experiences and enhance human capabilities, driving efficiency, and accuracy.

10. **5G and Beyond:** The implementation of 5G networks will further facilitate the Internet of Things (IoT) in industrial settings. With higher speeds and lower latency, 5G will support real-time communication for machines and systems, crucial for autonomous operations and remote processes.

7. TECHNOLOGICAL ADVANCEMENTS DEFINING INDUSTRY 5.0

Multiple technological problems are presented by industry 5.0, which is defined by the seamless integration of humans and robots. To the full extent that Industry 5.0 can disrupt industries and spur innovation, it requires interoperability, data management, cybersecurity, AI ethics, a trained workforce, cost and ROI, regulation and compliance, and sustainability. In order for various technologies to communicate effectively, protocols and interfaces must be standardized. It's also crucial to address cybersecurity threats, guarantee ethical AI adoption, and build a competent workforce. Organizations must compare the expenses and returns on investment against the expected returns on investment when considering the importance of training and education for a competent workforce. Sustainable growth depends on navigating the regulatory framework and balancing energy use and environmental effect. Taking on these issues is essential for maximizing the potential of Industry 5.0 in transforming industries and driving innovation.

1. **Interoperability:** Ensuring that diverse technologies can communicate and work together effectively is crucial. Standardizing protocols and interfaces is essential to achieve this.

2. **Data Management:** Handling vast amounts of data generated by IoT devices and AI systems requires robust data management strategies, including storage, processing, and analysis.
3. **Cybersecurity:** With increased connectivity comes heightened cybersecurity risks. Protecting sensitive data and systems from cyber threats is a paramount concern.
4. **AI Ethics:** Ethical considerations surrounding AI, such as bias mitigation and responsible AI deployment, must be addressed to ensure fair and ethical AI-driven decisions.
5. **Skilled Workforce:** Developing a workforce with the necessary skills to operate and maintain Industry 5.0 technologies is a challenge. Training and education are critical.
6. **Cost and ROI:** Implementing Industry 5.0 technologies can be expensive. Organizations must weigh these costs against expected returns on investment.
7. **Regulation and Compliance:** Navigating the regulatory landscape is complex. Adhering to industry-specific regulations while harnessing Industry 5.0 technologies is a challenge.
8. **Sustainability:** Balancing the energy consumption of connected devices and the environmental impact of Industry 5.0 is essential for sustainable growth.

Addressing these technological challenges is crucial for realizing the full potential of Industry 5.0 in transforming industries and driving innovation.

8. FINDINGS

The study explores AI's potential in Industry 5.0, focusing on human-machine interaction and collaboration. It highlights its benefits in improving human capacities, increasing productivity, and establishing new business models. The research also addresses ethical concerns and societal repercussions. The strategy roadmap aims to develop procedures and identify enablers for Industry 5.0 development. AI and Industry 5.0 can revolutionize industries, but ethical considerations, data privacy, and job displacement must be addressed for responsible deployment and regulation.

Industry 5.0 focuses on the collaborative integration of humans and machines, promoting cobots, autonomous mobile robots, and AI technologies. These robots are flexible, adaptable, and can handle repetitive tasks, allowing humans to focus on more creative aspects. They are connected to the IoT ecosystem, enabling real-time data exchange, and can perform quality control and inspection tasks with high accuracy. Augmented Reality assists operators in guiding robots, enhancing efficiency and creating a more resilient and agile industrial sector.

9. CONCLUSION

Industry 5.0, driven by AI and cooperative human-machine interactions, has immense potential across various industries. Cobots, autonomous mobile robots, and AI technologies offer benefits like increased productivity, job enrichment, quality control, real-time data interchange, AR, and resilience. However, ethical concerns like data privacy, job displacement, and regulatory oversight must be addressed. A comprehensive roadmap for Industry 5.0 should balance innovation and social well-being. Organizations and policymakers must adopt human-centric, environmentally responsible, and resilient approaches to harness AI's full potential for societal and industry benefits.

In concluding our exploration of "AI and Big Data Analytics Revolutionizing Industry 5.0: Unlocking the Power of Smart Manufacturing and Beyond," it is evident that the confluence of these advanced technologies marks a paradigm shift not just in manufacturing but in the operational blueprint of various industries globally. Industry 5.0, with its focus on collaboration between humans and smart systems, signifies an era where technology transcends automation of tasks, embedding itself into more strategic roles and augmenting human capabilities.

Artificial Intelligence and Big Data are the twin engines driving this transformation. By harnessing the colossal amounts of data generated in modern industrial processes, companies can gain insights of unprecedented depth and clarity. These insights can fuel AI systems, making them more efficient, self-optimizing, and capable of making complex decisions in real-time, factors that are critical in an era characterized by its fast-changing pace and need for agility and customization.

Moreover, while Industry 4.0 focused on optimizing systems, Industry 5.0 looks beyond, to optimizing the entire value chain. Smart manufacturing becomes not just a way of producing goods, but a comprehensive approach to managing resources, data, and human talent in a way that is efficient, sustainable, and most importantly, in synergy with human ingenuity. In this new industrial landscape, technology does not replace the human workforce; instead, it complements and enhances human skills, leading to new job opportunities, increased productivity, and more innovative products.

However, the path to this bright future is plagued with obstacles. Significant obstacles must be overcome, including data privacy, security, the digital skills divide, and the need for substantial investment in new technologies. Additionally, this transition must be inclusive in order to be sustainable and successful. SMEs must have access to the advantages of AI and Big Data.

Moreover, as this technological evolution continues, ethical considerations should be at the vanguard. The creation and implementation of AI and Big Data must be governed by ethical frameworks that prioritize openness, accountability, and equity. In addition to innovating, the objective should be to do so in a way that respects human rights and promotes the welfare of all stakeholders.

AI and Big Data are ultimately catalysts for a monumental transition in the global industrial landscape. With its emphasis on human-technology symbiosis, Industry 5.0 has the potential to herald in an era of unprecedented productivity, sustainability, and economic expansion. However, this future is contingent on our collective ability to invest prudently in these technologies, upskill the workforce, address ethical implications, and develop robust data security and privacy frameworks. If these challenges are met with innovative and inclusive solutions, then the promise of Industry 5.0 to harmonize human touch and technological prowess will unquestionably revolutionize how we manufacture, work, and ultimately live.

REFERENCES

Adel, A. (2022). Future of industry 5.0 in society: Human-centric solutions, challenges and prospective research areas. *Journal of Cloud Computing (Heidelberg, Germany)*, *11*(1), 1–15. doi:10.118613677-022-00314-5 PMID:36101900

Aheleroff, S., Huang, H., Xu, X., & Zhong, R. Y. (2022). Toward sustainability and resilience with Industry 4.0 and Industry 5.0. *Frontiers in Manufacturing Technology*, *2*, 951643. doi:10.3389/fmtec.2022.951643

Al Mubarak, M. (2022). Sustainably Developing in a Digital World: Harnessing artificial intelligence to meet the imperatives of work-based learning in Industry 5.0. *Development and Learning in Organizations: An International Journal.*

Alves, J., Lima, T. M., & Gaspar, P. D. (2023). Is Industry 5.0 a Human-Centred Approach? A Systematic Review. *Processes (Basel, Switzerland), 11*(1), 193. doi:10.3390/pr11010193

Deniz, N. (2020). The roles of human 4.0 in the industry 4.0 phenomenon. In *Logistics 4.0* (pp. 338–349). CRC Press. doi:10.1201/9780429327636-33

ElFar, O. A., Chang, C.-K., Leong, H. Y., Peter, A. P., Chew, K. W., & Show, P. L. (2021). Prospects of Industry 5.0 in algae: Customization of production and new advanced technology for clean bioenergy generation. *Energy Conversion and Management: X, 10*, 100048.

Fazal, N., Haleem, A., Bahl, S., Javaid, M., & Nandan, D. (2022). Digital management systems in manufacturing using industry 5.0 technologies. In *Advancement in Materials, Manufacturing and Energy Engineering, Vol. II: Select Proceedings of ICAMME 2021* (pp. 221–234). Springer.

George, A. S., & George, A. H. (2023). Revolutionizing Manufacturing: Exploring the Promises and Challenges of Industry 5.0. *Partners Universal International Innovation Journal, 1*(2), 22–38.

Ghobakhloo, M., Iranmanesh, M., Mubarak, M. F., Mubarik, M., Rejeb, A., & Nilashi, M. (2022). Identifying industry 5.0 contributions to sustainable development: A strategy roadmap for delivering sustainability values. *Sustainable Production and Consumption, 33*, 716–737. doi:10.1016/j.spc.2022.08.003

Huang, S., Wang, B., Li, X., Zheng, P., Mourtzis, D., & Wang, L. (2022). Industry 5.0 and Society 5.0—Comparison, complementation and co-evolution. *Journal of Manufacturing Systems, 64*, 424–428. doi:10.1016/j.jmsy.2022.07.010

Ivanov, D. (2023). The Industry 5.0 framework: Viability-based integration of the resilience, sustainability, and human-centricity perspectives. *International Journal of Production Research, 61*(5), 1683–1695. doi:10.1080/00207543.2022.2118892

Jaiswal, A., Arun, C. J., & Varma, A. (2022). Rebooting employees: Upskilling for artificial intelligence in multinational corporations. *International Journal of Human Resource Management, 33*(6), 1179–1208. doi:10.1080/09585192.2021.1891114

Jeong, E., Jang, S., Day, J., & Ha, S. (2014). The impact of eco-friendly practices on green image and customer attitudes: An investigation in a café setting. *International Journal of Hospitality Management, 41*, 10–20. doi:10.1016/j.ijhm.2014.03.002

Kaasinen, E., Anttila, A.-H., Heikkilä, P., Laarni, J., Koskinen, H., & Väätänen, A. (2022). Smooth and resilient human–machine teamwork as an Industry 5.0 design challenge. *Sustainability (Basel), 14*(5), 2773. doi:10.3390u14052773

Lotsaris, K., Fousekis, N., Koukas, S., Aivaliotis, S., Kousi, N., Michalos, G., & Makris, S. (2021). Augmented Reality (AR) based framework for supporting human workers in flexible manufacturing. *Procedia CIRP, 96*, 301–306. doi:10.1016/j.procir.2021.01.091

Maddikunta, P. K. R., Pham, Q.-V., Prabadevi, B., Deepa, N., Dev, K., Gadekallu, T. R., Ruby, R., & Liyanage, M. (2022). Industry 5.0: A survey on enabling technologies and potential applications. *Journal of Industrial Information Integration*, *26*, 100257. doi:10.1016/j.jii.2021.100257

Makhataeva, Z., & Varol, H. (2020). Augmented Reality for Robotics: A Review. *Robotics (Basel, Switzerland)*, *9*(2), 21. doi:10.3390/robotics9020021

Martynov, V. V., Shavaleeva, D. N., & Zaytseva, A. A. (2019). *Information technology is the basis for transformation into a digital society and industry 5.0*. 539–543.

Nardo, M., Forino, D., & Murino, T. (2020). The evolution of man–machine interaction: The role of the humans in Industry 4.0 paradigm. *Production & Manufacturing Research*, *8*(1), 20–34. doi:10.1080/21693277.2020.1737592

Özdemir, V., & Hekim, N. (2018). Birth of Industry 5.0: Making sense of big data with artificial intelligence," the Internet of Things", and next-generation technology policy. *OMICS: A Journal of Integrative Biology*, *22*(1), 65–76. doi:10.1089/omi.2017.0194 PMID:29293405

Rožanec, J. M., Novalija, I., Zajec, P., Kenda, K., Tavakoli Ghinani, H., Suh, S., Veliou, E., Papamartzivanos, D., Giannetsos, T., & Menesidou, S. A. (2022). Human-centric artificial intelligence architecture for industry 5.0 applications. *International Journal of Production Research*, ●●●, 1–26.

Sharma, G. D., Yadav, A., & Chopra, R. (2020). Artificial intelligence and effective governance: A review, critique and research agenda. *Sustainable Futures : An Applied Journal of Technology, Environment and Society*, *2*, 100004. doi:10.1016/j.sftr.2019.100004

Tiwari, S., Bahuguna, P. C., & Walker, J. (2022). Industry 5.0: A macro perspective approach. In Handbook of Research on Innovative Management Using AI in Industry 5.0 (pp. 59–73). IGI Global.

Vadalà, G., Salvatore, S. D., Ambrosio, L., Russo, F., Papalia, R., & Denaro, V. (2020). Robotic Spine Surgery and Augmented Reality Systems: A State of the Art. *Neurospine*, *17*(1), 88–100. doi:10.14245/ns.2040060.030 PMID:32252158

Verma, A., Bhattacharya, P., Madhani, N., Trivedi, C., Bhushan, B., Tanwar, S., Sharma, G., Bokoro, P. N., & Sharma, R. (2022). Blockchain for Industry 5.0: Vision, Opportunities, Key Enablers, and Future Directions. *IEEE Access : Practical Innovations, Open Solutions*, *10*, 69160–69199. doi:10.1109/ACCESS.2022.3186892

Xian, W., Yu, K., Han, F., Fang, L., He, D., & Han, Q.-L. (2023). Advanced Manufacturing in Industry 5.0: A Survey of Key Enabling Technologies and Future Trends. *IEEE Transactions on Industrial Informatics*, 1–15. doi:10.1109/TII.2023.3274224

Xiao, M., & Yi, H. (2021). Building an efficient artificial intelligence model for personalized training in colleges and universities. *Computer Applications in Engineering Education*, *29*(2), 350–358. doi:10.1002/cae.22235

Xu, X., Lu, Y., Vogel-Heuser, B., & Wang, L. (2021). Industry 4.0 and Industry 5.0—Inception, conception and perception. *Journal of Manufacturing Systems*, *61*, 530–535. doi:10.1016/j.jmsy.2021.10.006

KEY TERMS AND DEFINITIONS

AI and Data Analytics: It industries can make data-driven decisions faster and more accurately. AI systems can analyze vast amounts of data from various sources to identify patterns, trends, and anomalies, aiding in predictive maintenance, quality control, and supply chain optimization.

AI and Industry 5.0: These technologies have the potential to revolutionize various industries and significantly impact society.

Augmented Reality: It visual instructions and information on the physical environment, making it easier for operators to control robots effectively.

Automation Industry 5.0: Industry 5.0 robots are highly flexible and adaptable, handling various tasks and quickly switching.

Autonomous Mobile Robots: It can move freely in factories or warehouses. AMRs can transport materials, tools, and finished products, optimizing logistics and reducing human intervention.

Robots Equipped: AI can perform complex tasks, working alongside humans to enhance productivity and safety.

Sustainable Growth: It depends on navigating the regulatory framework and balancing energy use and environmental effect.

Chapter 17
Machine Learning and Sentiment Analysis for Analyzing Customer Feedback:
A Review

Kriti Saroha

iD https://orcid.org/0000-0001-9804-771X

CDAC, Noida, India

Mukesh Sehrawat

IAMR Group of Institutions, India

Vishal Jain

iD https://orcid.org/0000-0003-1126-7424

Sharda University, India

ABSTRACT

The rapid transformation in the business domain enhances the understanding that to achieve competitive advantage, corporates need to understand customer sentiments. The abundance of customer data as customer feedback, product reviews, and posts on social media platforms provides an in-depth insight that can navigate strategic decisions and inflate customer experiences. In this context, the unification of machine learning and sentiment analysis emerges as a potent combination for extracting emotional traces from volumes of unstructured text data. This chapter searches into the sphere of analysis techniques of sentiment analysis for analyzing customer feedback, where the convergence of advanced machine learning techniques with sentiment analysis methods empowers businesses to derive valuable insights from the feedback gathered from various touch points. By decoding sentiments and opinions hidden within textual data, this approach enables organizations to capture a clear view on customer satisfaction, identify their pain points, uncover emerging trends, and tailor offerings accordingly.

DOI: 10.4018/979-8-3693-0413-6.ch017

1. INTRODUCTION

In an age where customers with digital voices are louder and more influential than ever, this association of machine learning and sentiment analysis emerges as a compass for guiding businesses to have a deeper understanding of their clientele. As we navigate through the chapter, we will explore the foundations of sentiment analysis and its significance in the modern business landscape. We will probe into the elaborate working of machine learning algorithms that drive sentiment analysis, unfold their capacity to comprehend the complexities of human expression. Additionally, we will examine various aspects different collaborative approaches with real life applications.

1.1 Understanding Sentiment Analysis

Sentiment analysis, alternatively known as opinion mining, is a natural language processing (NLP) approach that is used to recognize the emotional tone expressed by a customer in a text or other forms of communication. Its objective is to automatically categorize the sentiment of the text, labelling it as positive, negative, or neutral. In some cases, it goes a step further by classifying sentiments into specific categories like "happy", "angry", or "sad". This technique is widely used across various industries for understanding customer opinions, market trends, social media sentiment, and more. Figure 1 explains the sentiment analysis (Tonic, 2018).

Understanding customer sentiment

Figure 1. Sentiment analysis
(Tonic, 2018)

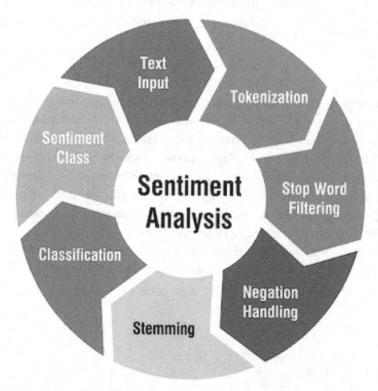

Understanding consumer behaviour is a crucial aspect for businesses in every industry. Customer reviews are on various E-com and social media platforms are a sizable source to know customer sentiments. Various research has been conducted to analyse customer reviews and understand what are the pain points, what factors impact customer satisfaction and recommendation. A study focused on airline passengers' online reviews and found that factors such as seat comfort, staff, food and beverage, entertainment, ground service, and value for money significantly influenced customer satisfaction and recommendation (Ban & Kim, 2019). A different research investigated customer worries about privacy in the retail sector, highlighting factors like retail platforms and the sensitivity of data. These factors were found to influence how privacy concerns affected outcomes in the retail industry (Okazaki et. al., 2020). Additionally, researchers have explored the effect of product reviews, prices, transaction trust, and security on online purchasing decisions among the Islamic millennial generation (Rokhman & Andiani, 2020). Furthermore, the use of machine learning and text analytics has been proposed to classify review sentences as praise or complaint and gain valuable insights from customer reviews (Khedkar & Shinde, 2018). Overall, these studies contribute to the understanding of customer reviews and provide insights for businesses to improve customer satisfaction and make informed decisions (Davis & Tabrizi 2021). Therefore, to enhance profitability, sustainability and achieve competitive advantage businesses seek indebted knowledge of customer sentiment in true sense.

2. APPROACHES OF SENTIMENT ANALYSIS

Sentimental analysis referred as opinion mining which explore, analyse, and organise human feelings (Anand,2021). It involves extracting feelings using NLP technique from various sources such as images and text and aims to determine and categorize the emotional state, attitude, and expression of individuals in different situations (Srinivasan & Subalalitha, 2021). Sentimental analysis is used in various fields, including research, decision support, and market analysis (Sainger, 2021, Bhargava & Rao, 2018). The analysis can be employed across various domains to different types of data, that includes social media posts, reviews, and market trends. The goal of sentimental analysis is to classify and understand the emotions and sentiments behind the text or visual data, providing valuable insights for businesses and researchers. Analyzing customer feedback using big data and machine learning techniques can provide valuable insights into customer preferences, sentiments, and behaviour.

Before moving to the various approaches let us discuss the broad process flow of how sentiment analysis works as also shown in Figure 2 and Figure 3:

1. **Data Collection:** Sentiment analysis starts with a piece of text (input in text, emojis, image form) as input that may be an online review by customer. This text(input) can be a sentence, a paragraph, a review, a tweet, a product description, or any other form of written content.
    - **Feedback Sources:** feedback can be gathered from various sources such as surveys, social media, emails, customer support interactions, and online reviews.
    - **Data Integration:** Data is integrated from different sources into a centralized database or data lake for comprehensive analysis.
2. **Data Preprocessing:** At this stage, the irrelevant information needs to be removed from the text. Before analysis, the text is prepared for analysis as many sentiment analysis algorithms are incapable of analysing emojis, images and other Unicode character. Therefore, it is important to pre-process

the text by eliminating irrelevant elements like punctuation, special characters, and stop words through cleaning and sorting (common words like "and," "the," "is" that don't carry significant meaning).

- ○ **Cleaning and Transformation:** The data is cleansed by removing noise, irrelevant information, and inconsistencies. Convert unstructured data (text) into a structured format for analysis.
- ○ **Sentiment Analysis:** Use Natural Language Processing (NLP) techniques to perform sentiment analysis on textual feedback. This helps in understanding customer emotions and opinions.

3. **Feature Extraction:** The procedure of transforming raw textual data into numerical features is essential. This conversion retains the original information while enhancing the performance compared to applying machine learning algorithms directly to the raw data. Commonly employed techniques of feature extraction are bag-of-words (BoW) representation, TF-IDF (Term Frequency-Inverse Document Frequency), and word embeddings like Word2Vec or GloVe.

- ○ **Keyword Extraction:** Important keywords and phrases are identified within the feedback using techniques like TF-IDF (Term Frequency-Inverse Document Frequency).
- ○ **Topic Modeling:** Implement algorithms like Latent Dirichlet Allocation (LDA) to identify topics within the feedback data.

4. **Machine Learning Models:** At this stage, we train a machine learning model to classify the content as positive, neutral, or negative using the testing dataset. We are free to choose the model architecture, although training a validated, context-aware natural language processing (NLP) model is recommended (like BERT). Machine learning models, such as classification algorithms (e.g., Naive Bayes, Support Vector Machines (SVM), Logistic Regression) or deep learning models (e.g., Recurrent Neural Networks (RNN), Convolutional Neural Networks (CNN)), are trained using labelled data. Labelled data consists of text, emojis, image samples along with their corresponding sentiment labels (positive, negative, neutral).

- ○ **Classification:** Classification models may be built (e.g., Naive Bayes, Support Vector Machines) to categorize feedback into predefined categories (e.g., positive, negative, neutral).
- ○ **Regression:** Regression models can be used to predict customer satisfaction scores based on specific feedback features.
- ○ **Clustering:** May apply clustering algorithms (e.g., K-means) to group similar feedback together. This can help in identifying patterns and common themes.
- ○ **Deep Learning:** Utilize neural networks, especially Recurrent Neural Networks (RNNs) and Long Short-Term Memory (LSTM) networks, for understanding context and generating insights from textual feedback.

5. Big Data Technologies:

- ○ **Distributed Computing:** Leverage big data processing frameworks like Apache Hadoop and Apache Spark to handle large volumes of feedback data efficiently.
- ○ **Real-time Processing:** Implement real-time processing using technologies like Apache Kafka and Apache Storm to analyze feedback as it arrives, enabling immediate responses to customer concerns.

6. **Sentiment Classification:** Once the model is trained, the trained model can classify unseen text, emojis, images or new ones into various sentiment categories. The model attaches a probability

or confidence score for every sentiment class, indicating the chances or probable the text, emoji, image is to be a part of that particular class.

7. **Post-processing:** Post-processing steps may be employed based on the application to improve the results. This could involve thresholding the confidence scores, considering contextual information, or incorporating domain-specific knowledge.

8. **Output:** The output sentiment analysis is the categorize or label the emotions or sentiment express by customer on social media/ e-commerce sites. This label can help businesses, researchers, and individuals to understand that how people feel and express about a specific topic, product, or episode/ incident online.

9. Continuous Improvement:
   - **Feedback Loop:** Integrate the insights derived from customer feedback analysis back into business processes. This continuous feedback loop ensures that customer insights are utilized for product/service improvement and customer satisfaction enhancement.

10. Ethical Considerations:
    - **Data Privacy:** Ensure compliance with data privacy regulations and anonymize customer data to protect privacy.
    - **Bias Detection:** Regularly assess machine learning models for biases to ensure fair and unbiased analysis of customer feedback.

By combining big data technologies with machine learning algorithms, businesses can gain valuable insights from customer feedback, leading to better customer experiences, improved products/services, and increased customer satisfaction.

2.1 Approaches of sentiment analysis: Different approaches are developed in the area of sentiment analysis as shown in Figure 4. Following are the main approaches:

i.   Lexicon based approach
ii.   Rule based approach
iii. Aspects based approach
iv.   Machine learning approach
v.   Hybrid approach
vi.   Other approaches

Let's discuss the approaches of sentiment analysis briefly.

2.1.1 Lexicon Based Approach of Sentiment Analysis

Sentiment analysis using the lexicon-based approach depends on predefined sets of words called sentiment lexicons, which are used to assess the sentiment of a given text. These lexicons contain words or phrases linked to particular sentiment categories like positive or negative. The method computes the complete sentiment score of the text by considering the presence and polarity of words from the lexicon. Here's a brief explanation of how the lexicon-based approach works:

Figure 2. Sentiment Analysis Process
(Pradhan, 2022)

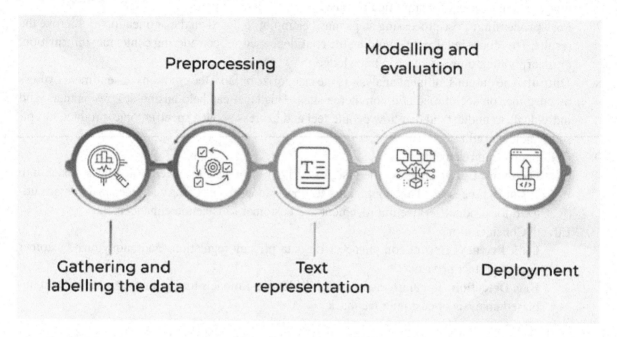

i. **Sentiment Lexicons:** A sentiment lexicon is a collection of words/ phrases that have been manually annotated with sentiment labels. Each word or phrase in the lexicon is assigned a polarity, that indicates whether it's positive, negative, or neutral. Some lexicons also assign strength values to indicate the intensity of sentiment.

Figure 3. General process for sentiment analysis
(Shayaa et al. 2018)

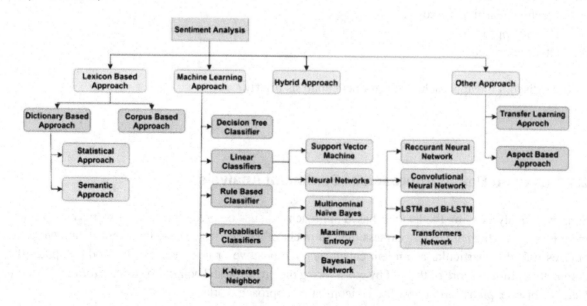

Figure 4. Approaches of sentiment analysis
(Wankhade, Rao & Kulkarni, 2022)

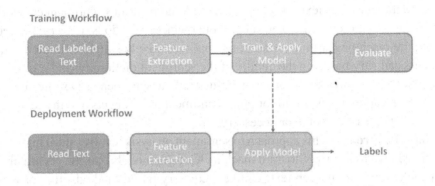

ii. **Text Preprocessing:** It removes punctuation from the input text, converts text to lowercase, and eliminates stop words (common words that don't carry significant sentiment).

iii. **Calculating Sentiment Score:** In the pre-processed text, each word is checked against the lexicon to identify its sentiment polarity. These individual word sentiment scores are combined to compute the total sentiment score for the whole text. This aggregation can involve adding up the polarity scores of words or using more intricate techniques that take into account context and word order.

iv. **Thresholds and Neutral Classification:** Depending on the approach, a threshold may be set to decide if the text is positive, negative, or neutral. For example, if the overall sentiment score is above a certain threshold, the text could be classified as positive; if it's below a different threshold, it could be classified as negative. Text falling in between could be labeled as neutral.

v. **Handling Negation and Intensifiers:** Some lexicon-based approaches take into account negation words (e.g., "not," "no") and intensifiers (e.g., "very," "extremely") that can alter the sentiment of a sentence. For example, "not good" would be treated as negative despite containing the word "good."

vi. **Limitations:** While lexicon-based approaches are simple and easy to implement, they have limitations. They might struggle with sarcasm, idiomatic expressions, and words with multiple meanings. Additionally, they might not capture the nuanced sentiment of complex sentences.

vii. **Domain Adaptation:** One challenge with lexicon-based approaches is that they might not capture sentiment expressions specific to certain domains or contexts. Customizing the lexicon or adapting it to a particular domain can improve accuracy.

Lexicon-based approaches are useful for quick sentiment analysis tasks, especially when you don't have a large labelled dataset for training more complex models. They can provide a basic understanding of sentiment in a text, but for more accurate and nuanced analysis, machine learning models like neural networks (NNs) or ensemble methods are often preferred.

Lexicon based approaches are further bifurcated into Dictionary based and, Corpus based approach.

a. **Dictionary based approach:** This method of sentiment analysis entails using sentiment dictionaries or lexicons, which comprise word lists along with their corresponding sentiment scores or labels. These dictionaries are typically curated based on manual annotation or automated methods.

In this approach, text is analyzed by relating the words in the text to the words in the sentiment dictionary. The sentiment scores or labels of the matched words are then aggregated to find out the overall sentiment of the text. This approach can handle various sentiment categories, including positive, negative, and sometimes neutral or more nuanced emotions. It's a rule-based method that doesn't require machine learning training, making it relatively simple to implement. However, its effectiveness can vary based on the quality of the sentiment dictionary, and it might struggle with sarcasm, idiomatic expressions, and context-dependent sentiments. Despite its limitations, the dictionary-based approach is useful for quick sentiment assessments and in scenarios where more complex models arc not fcasible or necessary.

b. **Corpus based approach:** This approach to sentiment analysis involves utilizing a large collection of text data, known as a corpus, to train machine learning models that can accurately predict sentiment labels for new and unseen text. Unlike dictionary-based methods, the focus is on learning sentiment patterns directly from the data rather than relying on predefined sentiment lexicons. This approach is often used in conjunction with labeled datasets to teach models to recognize contextual cues and linguistic patterns associated with different sentiments.

2.1.2 Machine Learning Approach

In the machine learning method for sentiment analysis, algorithms are trained using labelled data, enabling them to predict sentiment labels for new and unseen text based on what they have learned. This approach leverages the power of computational models to automatically discover patterns and relationships within the text data, ultimately making predictions about the sentiment expressed in the text.

Here's a concise overview of how the machine learning approach to sentiment analysis works. The process is shown in Figure 5.

i. **Data Collection and Labeling:** A dataset is collected where each text sample is paired with its corresponding sentiment label (positive, negative, neutral). This labeled data serves as the training set for the machine learning algorithm.

ii. **Feature Extraction:** Textual information is converted into numerical features that are easily understood by the machine learning algorithms. Commonly used techniques include BoW representation, TF-IDF, and word embeddings.

iii. **Model Selection:** Several machine learning algorithms, like Naive Bayes, Support Vector Machines (SVM), Decision Trees (DT), Random Forests, Gradient Boosting, and Neural Networks (NNs), can be employed for sentiment analysis. The selection of model is based on the factors like dataset size, complexity of the problem, and computational resources.

iv. **Model Training:** The selected algorithm is trained on the labeled dataset. During training, the algorithm learns to associate features extracted from the text with the corresponding sentiment labels.

v. **Hyperparameter Tuning:** Depending on the algorithm, there might be hyperparameters to adjust for optimal performance. These hyperparameters influence how the model learns and generalizes from the training data.

vi. **Model Evaluation:** The trained model is evaluated using separate data that it hasn't seen before (validation or test data). The commonly used evaluation metrics include accuracy, precision, recall, F1-score, and AUC-ROC.

Figure 5. Machine learning based approach
(Surekha & Jayanthi, 2019)

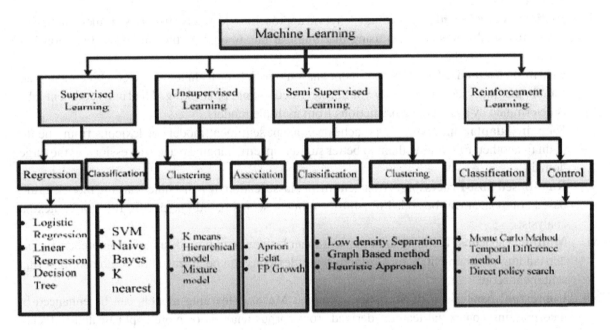

vii. **Predictions:** After the model is trained and assessed, it becomes capable of predicting the sentiment label of new and previously unseen text. The model analyzes the text's features and outputs a sentiment prediction.

viii. **Iterative Improvement:** If the model's performance is not satisfactory, iterations involving hyperparameter tuning, feature engineering, or model selection can be carried out to improve results.

The machine learning approach offers the advantage of adaptability and scalability. It can capture complex relationships between words and sentiment, account for contextual nuances, and perform well across various domains and languages. Nonetheless, this process necessitates a substantial quantity of labelled data for training and considerable computational resources when training more intricate models. It's a commonly and popularly used approach in sentiment analysis due to its capability to handle diverse textual data and provide accurate sentiment predictions.

2.1.3 Hybrid Approach

A hybrid approach to sentiment analysis integrates various techniques or methods in order to improve the accuracy and reliability of sentiment classification. This strategy seeks to utilize the advantages of different approaches while addressing their respective limitations. The objective is to achieve a more nuanced and accurate sentiment analysis result.

Here's a brief overview of how a hybrid approach to sentiment analysis works:

i. **Combining Rule-Based and Machine Learning Methods:** Hybrid approaches might incorporate both rule-based methods (e.g., lexicon-based) and machine learning methods. Rule-based methods can handle specific sentiment expressions, while machine learning models can capture complex context and patterns.

ii. **Dictionary and Machine Learning:** A hybrid approach could involve using a sentiment dictionary to identify seed words and then using machine learning to analyze the context and relationships between these words.

iii. **Ensemble Methods:** Different sentiment analysis models or techniques are combined using ensemble methods, such as majority voting, weighted voting, or stacking. The final sentiment label is determined by aggregating predictions from multiple models.

iv. **Domain Adaptation:** Hybrid approaches can adapt sentiment models or lexicons from one domain to another, fine-tuning them to better suit the specific language and expressions of the target domain.

v. **Rule-Based Post-Processing:** After sentiment classification by a machine learning model, a rule-based component can be added to adjust sentiment scores based on specific rules or contextual analysis.

vi. **Multiple Lexicons:** Utilizing multiple sentiment lexicons can provide a more comprehensive understanding of sentiment. Scores from different lexicons can be averaged or combined for a final sentiment score.

vii. **Contextual Analysis with Statistical Models:** Machine learning models can be enhanced by incorporating contextual features derived from corpus analysis or more sophisticated statistical models.

viii. **Meta-Learning:** Meta-learning techniques can be used to learn how different sentiment analysis methods perform on various types of data and then select the best-performing method for a given input.

ix. The hybrid approach is advantageous because it addresses the limitations of individual methods while benefiting from their strengths. However, implementing a hybrid approach can be more complex and resource-intensive as compared to using a single method. It requires expertise in understanding how to effectively combine different techniques and tailor them to specific analysis goals and domains.

2.1.4 Other Approaches

In addition to the approaches mentioned earlier, there are a few other notable approaches to sentiment analysis:

i. **Aspect-Based Sentiment Analysis (ABSA):** This method concentrates on evaluating sentiments linked to particular aspects or features of a product, service, or topic. It extends beyond general sentiment categorization, offering insights into the distribution of sentiments across various aspects.

ii. **Emotion Analysis:** In contrast to conventional sentiment analysis, emotion analysis strives to recognize and classify distinct emotions conveyed in text, including joy, anger, sadness, fear, and surprise. It offers a more profound insight into the emotional subtleties present in the text.

iii. **Cognitive Sentiment Analysis:** This approach aims to assess the cognitive processes underlying sentiment expressions, including beliefs, intentions, and opinions. It's often used in psychological research and understanding human behavior.

iv. **Biometric Sentiment Analysis:** This unique approach involves using physiological signals like heart rate, facial expressions, and body movements to infer emotional states and sentiments. It's commonly used in human-computer interaction and affective computing.

v. **Network Analysis:** This approach focuses on analyzing sentiment within social networks and understanding how sentiments spread among connected users. It considers the social relationships and influence dynamics in sentiment propagation.

vi. **Temporal Sentiment Analysis:** This approach examines how sentiment changes over time, capturing trends and shifts in public opinion, sentiment during events, and other temporal dynamics.

vii. **Sentiment Summarization:** Rather than classifying sentiment for individual sentences or documents, sentiment summarization aims to create concise summaries that capture the overall sentiment of a longer piece of text.

viii. **Cross-Lingual Sentiment Analysis:** This approach involves analyzing sentiment in text written in multiple languages. It requires models capable of understanding and comparing sentiments across different languages.

ix. **Transfer Learning:** Transfer learning consists of initially training a sentiment analysis model on a broad dataset to establish a foundation, followed by refining it on a narrower, domain-specific dataset. This process enhances the model's performance in the specific domain it is intended for.

x. **Opinion Mining:** Opinion mining is a broader term that encompasses sentiment analysis. It involves extracting opinions, attitudes, and emotions expressed in text, which can include sentiment classification as well as identifying subjective expressions like beliefs and desires.

These various approaches cater to different analytical needs and scenarios, showcasing the versatility and evolving nature of sentiment analysis as a field of study.

3. MACHINE LEARNING ALGORITHMS FOR SENTIMENT ANALYSIS

Machine learning algorithms for sentiment analysis involve training models to recognize patterns and relationships in text data that correlate with different sentiment labels (positive, negative, neutral, etc.).

The process involves several key concepts:

i. **Feature Extraction:** Textual data must be converted into a format that is understood by machine learning algorithms. Commonly used techniques include:
   a. *Bag-of-Words:* It represents text as an assortment of words without considering grammar or word sequence.
   b. *TF-IDF:* It assigns weights to words depending on how often they appear in a document in relation to their occurrence throughout the entire dataset.
   c. *Word Embeddings:* Transforming words into dense vector representations that capture semantic relationships.

ii. **Labelling and Training Data:** A labelled dataset is essential for training the machine learning model. Each text sample in the dataset is paired with its corresponding sentiment label. The dataset is divided into training, validation, and test sets.

iii. **Algorithm Selection:** Various algorithms can be chosen for sentiment analysis, including Naive Bayes, SVM, Logistic Regression, DT, Random Forests, Gradient Boosting, and NNs. The decision relies on factors like the size of the dataset, the complexity of the problem, and the availability of computational resources.

iv. **Model Training:** During training, the algorithm learns to associate the extracted features (words, phrases, etc.) with the corresponding sentiment labels. The aim is to minimize the difference between predicted and actual labels by adjusting internal parameters.

v. **Hyperparameter Tuning:** Many machine learning algorithms have hyperparameters that influence the learning process. Tuning these hyperparameters helps optimize model performance on validation data.

vi. **Model Evaluation:** The trained model is evaluated using separate data that it hasn't seen before (test data). Typical evaluation metrics encompass accuracy, precision, recall, F1-score, and AUC-ROC.

vii. **Predictions:** Once trained, the model can make predictions on new, unseen text data. The model analyzes the features extracted from the text and outputs a predicted sentiment label.

viii. **Overfitting and Generalization:** Models should be monitored for overfitting, where their performance is good on training data but poor on new data. Techniques like regularization and cross-validation help prevent overfitting.

ix. **Ensemble Techniques:** Ensemble methods amalgamate multiple models to enhance overall accuracy and robustness. Examples include Bagging, Boosting, and Stacking.

x. **Transfer Learning:** Models pre-trained on extensive datasets can be adjusted to fine-tune sentiment analysis within a particular domain. This capitalizes on the knowledge acquired from one task to enhance performance in another context.

xi. **Interpretability:** Depending on the algorithm, some models are more interpretable than others. DT and Logistic Regression, for instance, provide insights into how the model makes decisions.

Machine learning algorithms enable sentiment analysis models to capture complex relationships and context in text data, making them adaptable to various domains, languages, and sentiment expressions. However, their performance relies heavily on the quality and diversity of the training data and the algorithm's suitability for the specific task.

3.1 Types of Machine Learning Algorithms

Machine learning algorithms can be categorized into several types based on their characteristics, learning strategies, and applications as shown in Figure 6. Here's a brief explanation of some common types:

i. **Supervised Learning:** In supervised learning, algorithms are trained using labelled data, where each data point includes specific input features and a corresponding known output label. The objective is to establish a relationship between inputs and outputs, enabling predictions or classifications on new, unseen data.

ii. **Unsupervised Learning:** Unsupervised learning entails analyzing data without predefined output labels. Clustering algorithms group similar data points, while dimensionality reduction techniques aim to represent data in a lower-dimensional space.

iii. **Semi-Supervised Learning:** This method merges aspects of both supervised and unsupervised learning, utilizing a limited set of labelled data alongside a larger volume of unlabelled data during the training process.

iv. **Reinforcement Learning:** In reinforcement learning, an agent learns to engage with an environment in order to optimize a reward signal. It learns through trial and error, with the goal of making sequences of decisions that yield the most cumulative reward.

v. **Deep Learning:** Deep learning algorithms use neural networks with multiple layers to learn representations of data. They're especially powerful for tasks such as image and speech recognition, natural language processing, and more.

vi. **Ensemble Methods:** Ensemble methods enhance overall performance by integrating multiple models. Examples include Bagging (Bootstrap Aggregating), Boosting, and Stacking.

vii. **Decision Trees:** These are structured hierarchies that make decisions by following a set of rules derived from data. They are easy to interpret and can manage intricate relationships between different features.

viii. **Support Vector Machines (SVM):** It identifies an optimal hyperplane that effectively separates data into different classes while maximizing the space between them.

ix. **Naive Bayes:** This algorithm, rooted in Bayes' theorem and assuming feature independence, operates probabilistically. It is commonly applied in text classification tasks.

x. **K-Nearest Neighbour (KNN):** It categorizes data points by determining their majority class within the group of their k nearest neighbours in the feature space.

xi. **Principal Component Analysis (PCA):** It is a method for reducing dimensionality that involves mapping data onto a lower-dimensional space, aiming to retain maximum variance in the process.

xii. **Neural Networks:** Neural networks, inspired by the human brain, comprise interconnected nodes (neurons) arranged in layers. Deep neural networks have the capability to grasp intricate patterns and relationships within data.

These examples represent only a subset of machine learning algorithms. Each type possesses unique strengths and limitations, rendering them suitable for specific tasks and data properties. The selection of an algorithm depends on the specific problem, the available data, and the desired results.

3.2 Literature Review of Supervised and Semi-Supervised Machine Learning Methods for Sentiment Analysis of Customer Feedback

Machine learning and sentiment analysis are powerful tools for analyzing customer feedback, providing valuable insights to businesses for improving products, services, and customer experiences. Here's how they can be used in tandem:

Data Collection and Preprocessing: Gather customer feedback from sources like surveys, reviews, social media, and customer support interactions. Pre-process the text data by removing noise, tokenizing, and cleaning the text for analysis. In this chapter we emphases on supervised and semi-supervised machine learning methods. Table 1 presents summary of the literature reviewed.

3.2.1 Challenges

Machine learning algorithms for sentiment analysis face several challenges due to the inherent complexity of human language and the nuances of sentiment expression. Some key challenges include:

Figure 6. Types of machine learning algorithms
(Dutta et. al., 2018)

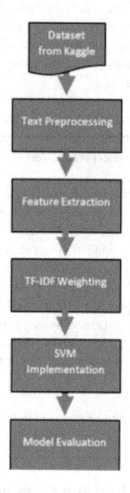

i. **Subjectivity and Context:** Sentiments can be highly subjective and influenced by the context in which words are used. A word may carry different sentiments based on the surrounding words or the overall tone of the text.

ii. **Sarcasm and Irony:** Detecting sarcasm, irony, and other forms of figurative language can pose challenges for algorithms, making accurate interpretation a complex task, as they often involve the opposite sentiment of what's expressed explicitly.

iii. **Ambiguity:** Words with multiple meanings can introduce ambiguity. For instance, "bad" might mean low quality or negative sentiment, depending on the context.

iv. **Negation:** Negation words (e.g., "not," "no") can completely reverse the sentiment of a sentence. Algorithms need to identify and handle negations appropriately.

v. **Domain-Specific Language:** Sentiment expressions can vary greatly across different domains (e.g., medical, legal, informal social media). Algorithms trained on one domain might not perform well in another.

Table 1. Summary of literature review

S. No.	Paper	Insights	Method Used	Findings and Conclusion
1	(Nurcahyawati & Mustaffa, 2023)	In this study, the researchers utilized a technique to assess the classification accuracy of the Vader lexicon annotation method in comparison to manual annotation. The findings indicated that employing Vader in the annotation process yielded higher accuracy values when contrasted with manual annotation.	Vader lexicon annotation process – SVM Algorithm	Customer orientation towards product or service quality is predominantly positive (76% of responses analyzed). Using the Vader lexicon in the annotation process accuracy increased from 86% to 88.57% which results in better accuracy compared to manual annotation.
2	(Uma et. al., 2022)	In this paper, the customer review Sentiment Analysis for polarity classification has been performed using SVM Model and CNN Model on a real-world dataset of web scraped customer reviews, following which the SVM model was deployed to a web application.	SVM Model - CNN Model	SVM achieved 96% accuracy - CNN achieved 94% accuracy
3	(Kumar et.al.,2022)	The author tested various machine learning and swarm intelligence optimization techniques for sentiment analysis on movie review data. The study revealed that the Hybrid Kernel based SVM (HKSVM) achieved impressive results.	Hybrid Kernel based SVM (HKSVM) - Modified Cat Swarm Optimization (MCSO) strategy	The Hybrid Kernel based SVM (HKSVM) proves to be a highly efficient technique for sentiment analysis. The method proposed in the study demonstrated outstanding performance, achieving an accuracy of 96.82%, a sensitivity rate of 97.14%, and impressive scores in specificity, precision, recall, and F-Measure rates.
4	(Zaenal & Astutik, 2023)	In this paper, the authors employ SVM and Radial Basis Function Kernel (RBF) to categorize reviews on the OYO application, aiming to discern user sentiment.	SVM Algorithm Radial basis function kernel	SVM algorithm achieves high accuracy of 78.98%. Whereas accuracy of 80.36% is achieve by using the confusion matrix which means radial basis function kernel produces highest accuracy.
5	(Nur,2023)	In this paper, the authors utilize SVM classifiers to analyze the Twitter dataset, employing various parameters such as accuracy, precision, recall, and F1-score for evaluation.	SVM classifiers - BoW and TF-IDF	SVM with bags of word achieved 88.59% accuracy using Bags of Word (BoW) in comparison with SVM achieved 91.27% accuracy using TF-IDF
6	(Heryadi et.al., 2023)	The researchers utilized the aspect embedding long short-term memory model to forecast aspect sentiment polarization derived from customer feedback on restaurant service. Using aspect text representation as input, they achieved exceptional performance in their predictions.	Aspect Embedding Long Short-Term Memory Model - ReLU, Sigmoid, and Tanh activation functions	Aspect Embedding LSTM model achieves excellent performance. - ReLU activation function achieves higher performance than Sigmoid and Tanh.
7	(Zain, Ramli & Adnan, 2022)	The researcher suggested a machine learning method to examine the application of sentiment analysis in evaluating customer opinions about products, brands, or services.	Machine learning approach for sentiment analysis.	The paper doesn't delve into specific outcomes but rather concentrates on introducing a machine learning method for analyzing customer sentiment from social media feedback. This approach aids businesses in gaining valuable insights and responding effectively to customer sentiments.
8	(Pratama et.al., 2022)	The study demonstrated that Support Vector Machine is proficient at effectively classifying beauty product reviews with high accuracy, making it a viable and practical choice for this task.	SVM method used for classification - Data preprocessing and feature extraction steps performed	SVM demonstrates effective classification of beauty product reviews with an accuracy rate of 80.06%.
9	(Sitepu, Munthe & Harahap, 2022)	The author discusses utilizing the SVM algorithm for performing sentiment analysis on user reviews of Shopee products, achieving a significantly higher accuracy rate in the process.	Preparing the dataset text - Assigning word weights through the TF-IDF method.	In this paper the most positive word: "Good" occurred 4684 times whereas most negative word: 'seller' occurred 68 times. SVM algorithm is applicable for sentiment analysis on Shopee product reviews with 97.3% accuracy. - "Good" is the most representative word for positive opinions, while "Seller" represents the most negative opinions.
10	(Darusman, Arifiyanti & Wati, 2022)	The goal is to create a classification model capable of categorizing tweets as either positive or negative sentiment. This approach aims to be more efficient and effective as compared to the 1-stage feature selection model.	SVM method - Two-stage feature selection	The two-stage feature selection method proves to be more efficient and effective. The model attained an accuracy rate of 64.08% utilizing 841 features. The processing time was 0.033 seconds with a CPU usage of 9.6%.
11	(Maharani et. al., 2023)	In this study, the process involved text preprocessing, data labelling, word weighting, classification, and performance evaluation. Text preprocessing, data labelling, and classification were key steps in the analysis.	Sentiment analysis using Naive Bayes algorithm - Text preprocessing, data labeling, word weighting, classification	- More positive sentiment than negative sentiment - Naive Bayes algorithm accuracy rate of 77.78%
12	(Astuti et. al., 2023)	In this study, the researchers employed sentiment analysis to determine public opinions (both positive and negative) regarding the PLN Mobile Application. They gathered review data from Google Play Store and assessed the dimensions of electricity service quality, including empathy, responsiveness, and reliability.	Sentiment analysis using Naïve Bayes - Analysis based on dimensions of service quality	Naïve Bayes is effective for sentiment analysis. Reliability received the Most negative sentiments with an accuracy of 73%.

Table 1. Continued

S. No.	Paper	Insights	Method Used	Findings and Conclusion
13	(Asthakhuroh, Komarudin & Kholifah, 2023)	The Naive Bayes model used for analyzing customer feedback in sentiment analysis demonstrates excellent performance, as indicated by high accuracy, precision, recall, and AUC values. The provided information does not specify any drawbacks associated with this approach.	Naïve Bayes Classifier method - Sentiment analysis	Sentiment analysis of Pre-Employment Card program on Twitter - Naïve Bayes Classifier method achieved high accuracy, precision, recall, and AUC.
14	(Subramanian et. al., 2023)	This study introduces and tests an ensemble feature selection strategy to address challenges related to feature selections. The results from the experiments demonstrate that the proposed HEVS method surpasses the standard Naive Bayes model in performance.	Filter, wrapper, and hybrid methods for feature selection - Heterogeneous ensemble feature selection method	Heterogeneous ensemble variable selection outperforms Naive Bayes model. - Computational complexity is minimized in the proposed methodology.
15	(Erfina & Lestari, 2023)	In this article, the authors used the K-Fold cross validation and the Naïve Bayes algorithm to determine the polarity of sentiment and the accuracy of the test results.	K-Fold Cross Validation Naïve Bayes algorithm	- Accuracy value of 82% obtained using Naïve Bayes algorithm - Negative sentiment of 82% and positive sentiment of 18%
16	(Patel, Oza & Agrawal, 2023)	In this article, the authors used the BERT algorithm for sentiment analysis in the analysis of the airline reviews dataset and found that BERT outperformed the other machine learning techniques, like Naive Bayes, SVM, and DT.	- Machine Learning algorithms (Naive Bayes, SVM, DT) - Google's BERT algorithm compared with Random Forest	BERT surpassed other machine learning techniques in sentiment analysis. The models underwent evaluation using performance metrics like accuracy, precision, recall, and F1-score.
17	(Ama et. al., 2022)	Companies or UMKM can collect customer feedback by looking at the reviews given by customers. Utilizing the Naïve Bayes algorithm with TF-IDF weighting achieves an accuracy rate of 83%. Additionally, the visualization of the most frequently occurring words reveals that 'good', 'comfortable', and 'use' are prominent terms in positive reviews.	Sentiment analysis - Naïve Bayes algorithm with TF-IDF weighting	- Sentiment analysis achieved 83% accuracy using Naïve Bayes algorithm - Positive reviews mentioned words like 'good', 'comfortable', 'use' while negative reviews mentioned 'material' and 'thin'
18	(Astuti et. al., 2022)	In this paper, the authors used Google Colab and Naïve Bayes approach to predict the sentiment pattern using data from Twitter.	Naïve Bayes algorithm - Machine learning approach	Data from Twitter spanning 14 days between May 16-21, 2022, was gathered, revealing that negative sentiment exceeded positive and neutral sentiment, accounting for 93%. Naïve Bayes is suggested for predicting sentiment patterns, achieving an accuracy of 81% for positive sentiment and 90% for neutral sentiment.
19	(Chan & Im, 2022)	In this study, a stacked CARU network was employed to extract essential information from paragraphs. Additionally, a CNN-based extractor was used to thoroughly analyze entire passages and capture valuable features within their hidden states.	Stacked CARU network for extracting main information - CNN-based extractor with Naïve-Bayes classifier	Empirical investigation on sentiment analysis using proposed models is a combination of classifiers with GloVe embedding on SST-5 and IMDB datasets. Stacked CARU Network improves paragraph-based sentiment analysis. And Naïve-Bayes Classifier connected to CNN-based extractor.
20	(Hossain & Rahman, 2022)	The research applied five supervised machine learning techniques, including DT, KNN classifier, SVM, logistic regression, and random forest classifier to conduct sentiment analysis.	AFINN and VADER sentiment algorithms - DT, KNN classifier, SVM, logistic regression, and random forest classifier	Most of the feedback from customers regarding insurance products was unfavourable or negative - Logistic regression outperforms in high accuracy
21	(Naeem, Logoftu & Muharemi, 2020)	In this study, a machine learning-based text classification solution was developed to categorize customer reviews as positive or negative. This system predicts the overall sentiment of the review text at a document level.	Traditional machine learning with TF-IDF model and deep learning with word2vec approach	Logistic regression achieves highest accuracy, approximately 87% of accuracy.
22	(Hossain et.al., 2022)	In this study, the researchers examined and forecasted customer reviews of halal restaurants using machine learning techniques.	DT, linear SVM, logistic regression, random forest classifier	Majority of customer reviews towards halal restaurants were positive. - Logistic regression outperformed other methods in terms of accuracy.
23	(Tetzlaff et. al., 2019)	The study outlines a practical method for utilizing LASSO regression in online hospitality reviews. This approach resulted in a sentiment dictionary comprising 778 terms, each with specific weights derived from the analysis of 20,000 reviews.	Statistical learning method - LASSO regression	- A sentiment dictionary of 778 terms was created. - The created dictionary accurately predicts online review scores.

Table 1. Continued

S. No.	Paper	Insights	Method Used	Findings and Conclusion
24	(Patrick, Sharief & Mukherjee, 2023)	This paper is on supervised machine learning algorithms, such as linear regression, KNN, SVM, Random Forest, Bagging, and Gradient Boosting, can be used to create sentiment analysis models. The dataset used in this study consisted of feedback from 884 employees, with 802 employees' data being considered reliable. Different lexical resources, including Afinn, VADER, and sentiment from textblob, were used to determine sentiment related to positive leadership dimensions.	The paper utilized supervised machine learning algorithms, that includes linear regression, KNN, SVM, Random Forest, Bagging, and Gradient Boosting, to create a sentiment analysis model. Different lexical resources, such as Afinn, VADER, and sentiment from textblob, were examined for deciding the sentiment related to positive leadership dimension	The dataset used in the study consisted of feedback from 884 employees, with 802 employees' data being considered reliable. The random forest algorithm achieved the highest accuracy of 0.711, while the KNN algorithm achieved an accuracy of 0.515. The paper concludes that sentiment analysis using supervised machine learning algorithms can be efficient in reviewing customer feedback and employee reviews, helping organizations identify customer needs and improve their business profitability. In this study, the random forest algorithm exhibits the highest accuracy.
25	(Komarasamy et. al., 2022)	The study suggests employing the Harmony Random Forest machine learning algorithm and the Gradient Boosting Harmony for sentiment analysis on social media. These methods yield superior results compared to other techniques.	harmony gradient boosting random forest machine learning algorithm, Gradient boosting approach, Harmonic random forest	The harmony gradient boosting random forest method outperforms the gradient boosting approach, that makes ensembles of weak and shallow trees, achieving superior results. The suggested approach utilizes the random forest algorithm, forming ensembles of independent trees, leading to enhanced performance in sentiment classification on social media, with a classification accuracy improvement of 5.68%.
26	(Uma et. al., 2022)	In this article, the customer review Sentiment Analysis for polarity classification has been performed using SVM Model and CNN Model on a real-world dataset of web scraped customer reviews, following which the support vector machine model was deployed to a web application.	The CNN model was also employed for sentiment analysis in customer reviews	The paper focuses on sentiment analysis in customer reviews using SVM and CNN models. Both models outperformed existing models in terms of accuracy and minimal error rate. The SVM model achieved a high accuracy of 96% in polarity classification, while the CNN model achieved an accuracy of 94%. Both models demonstrated much higher accuracy and minimal error rates compared to existing models
27	(Vielma, Verma & Bein, 2023)	The study presents two innovative multi-branch models, namely CNN-GRU and CNN-bidirectional GRU, designed for sentiment analysis using movie reviews sourced from the IMDb dataset.	The paper utilizes the internet movie database (IMDb) dataset, specifically movie reviews, as the input for sentiment analysis. Two novel multi-branch models, CNN-GRU and CNN-bidirectional GRU, are implemented for sentiment analysis. The CNN-bidirectional GRU model combines CNN with bidirectional GRU, which allows the model to consider both past and future context in the text	The research investigates two innovative multi-branch models, namely CNN-GRU and CNN-bidirectional GRU. Both models demonstrate similar accuracy in sentiment analysis. However, the CNN-GRU model achieves this accuracy in a shorter training time compared to the CNN-bidirectional GRU model. This indicates that the CNN-GRU model is a more efficient choice for sentiment analysis tasks, delivering comparable accuracy with a reduced training duration.
28	(Nahumury, Manongga & Iriani, 2022)	The study employs Twitter data to assess the sentiment of the Indonesian public regarding one of the domestic airlines. This analysis utilizes Deep Learning techniques, specifically the RNN with Long Short-Term Memory (LSTM) for training, validation, and prediction.	Deep Learning technique of RNN with Long Short-Term Memory (LSTM)	The study identifies that the negative sentiment towards the airline is higher (56.5%) compared to positive and neutral sentiment. The LSTM model achieves a high accuracy of 98.5% in data training and 92.2% in validation accuracy. The paper suggests that the factors contributing to negative sentiment can be employed as input to improve the airline's business processes.
29	(Zakir & Jinny, 2022)	This paper introduces a technique involving text feature extraction utilizing a CNN and employing logistic regression to evaluate the sentiment polarity of customer reviews. Experimental results demonstrate that this model significantly enhances the performance of sentiment classification.	CNN for text feature extraction - Logistic regression for sentiment polarity analysis	Proposed method improves sentiment classification performance - Uses CNN and Logistic regression
30	(Sumayya et. al., 2022)	In this article, a system is proposed that gives summarised feedback and works on sentiment analysis, which is based on RNN algorithm for keyphrase extraction and sentiment analysis.	Recurrent Neural Network (RNN) algorithm - Key phrase extraction and sentiment analysis	Proposed system provides summarised feedback with key phrases. RNN algorithm used for key phrase extraction and sentiment analysis.
31	(Lin et. al., 2017)	A system is designed where word embeddings represent sentence features within the corpus, and a NN serves as the classifier to accomplish the shared task. Additionally, an ensemble method is employed to obtain the final predictive outcome.	The paper utilizes word embeddings for sentence feature representation. A classifier combining bi-LSTM-CNN is utilized to categorize customer feedback into six tags. An ensemble method is then employed to generate the final prediction.	The paper presents a system that uses word embeddings and a neural network classifier to automatically classify customer feedback into six tags categorization. The proposed method achieved the first rank in terms of micro-averaged F1 and the second rank for accuracy metric among twelve teams in the shared task at IJCNLP
32	(Dhyani, 2017)	In this paper, the authors outline systems developed for the IJCNLP 2017 Shared Task on Customer Feedback Analysis. These systems utilize shallow CNN and Bi-Directional LSTM architectures, with Facebook's FastText serving as the baseline model. Notably, these approaches outperformed all other models specifically in classifying comments and meaningless tags.	Shallow CNN architecture Bi-Directional LSTM architecture	Top 5 systems for Spanish task (Exact-Accuracy and Micro-Average-F1 metrics) - Best performing model for French task (Micro Average F1 by Tags metric). Simple Neural architectures gave competitive performance. - Best performing Model outperformed other models on certain tasks.

Table 1. Continued

S. No.	Paper	Insights	Method Used	Findings and Conclusion
33	(Arifianto et. al., 2020)	This study categorizes user feedback from an Indonesian Internet Service Provider called IndiHome. TF-IDF is considered more suitable for data with extensive or lengthy documents since it assesses the representation based on the entire document. Whereas, Word Embedding is not influenced by the data size.	LSTM combined with Word Embedding - Naive Bayes combined with TF-IDF	LSTM with Word Embedding achieve 87.98% accuracy, as compare to TF-IDF. LSTM is 11.21% higher than Naive Bayes with TF-IDF. Naive Bayes with TF-IDF achieve an accuracy of 76.77%.
34	(Hossen et. al.,2021)	In this study, LSTM and Gated Recurrent Unit (GRU) models were employed to train hotel review data. The accuracy rates for identifying customer opinions were 86% for LSTM and 84% for GRU, respectively.	LSTM and GRUs used for training hotel review Data - Naive Bayes, DT, Random Forest, SVM also tested	- LSTM and GRUs achieve 86% and 84% accuracy in identifying customer opinion. - Naive Bayes, Decision Tree, Random Forest, and SVM achieve lower accuracy rates
35	(Bart, 2019)	The innovative bidirectional backpropagation algorithm transforms a standard feedforward neural network into a straightforward feedback dynamical system. This system minimizes a combined performance measure, ensuring that training in one direction does not interfere with training in the opposite direction.	Bidirectional backpropagation algorithm - Injected noise for convergence and Accuracy improvement	Bidirectional backpropagation converts feedforward Neural Network into feedback dynamical system - Injected noise can speed convergence and improve Accuracy
36	(Chaudhuri & Ghosh, 2016)	HBRNN was created to identify sentiment-specific aspects in review data from the DBS Text Mining Challenge. The study demonstrated the superior performance of HBRNN compared to other methods.	Hierarchical Bidirectional RNN (HBRNN) - Long Short-Term Memory (LSTM) and Bidirectional LSTM (BLSTM)	HBRNN surpasses LSTM and BLSTM models in sentiment analysis, with evaluation metrics including precision, recall, and F1 scores.
37	(Asghar et. al., 2021)	The proposed system, called Senti-eSystem, focuses on creating a sentiment-based electronic system. It combines Fuzzy and Deep Neural Network techniques to measure customer satisfaction, offering assistance to businesses in enhancing the quality of their services and products.	- Senti-e System suggested hybrid fuzzy logic deep neural network which Outperfor previous lexicon-based approaches.	The paper suggests a fuzzy logic approach incorporated into bidirectional Long Short-Term Memory with an attention mechanism. The resulting system, Senti-eSystem, achieves an accuracy of 92.86%, surpassing previous methods based on lexicon-based approaches.
38	(Wu & Li, 2022)	This paper introduces an enhanced algorithm called GBDT-NN, which combines gradient boosting decision trees. The efficiency of this algorithm is confirmed through real customer purchase behaviour data validation.	Improved gradient boosting decision tree algorithm (GBDT-NN) Artificial neural network (ANN	The newly proposed algorithm, GBDT-NN, demonstrated remarkable performance with an accuracy of 96.3% on the test set, showcasing a significant 10.6% enhancement compared to the traditional GBDT algorithm. Additionally, the test AUC of GBDT-NN reached 0.99, indicating a substantial 15.9% improvement over the GBDT algorithm. The approach combines the feature and feature combination screening using GBDT with the subsequent processing of screening outcomes using an ANN.
39	(Al-Qudah et. al., 2020)	In this research, a method for sentiment analysis is introduced. It integrates a neutrality detector model with eXtreme Gradient Boosting and a genetic algorithm, this approach is tailored to precisely forecast and analyze customer feedback about an e-Payment service on an Arabic social network.	Neutrality detector model combined with eXtreme Gradient Boosting - Genetic algorithm for sentiment analysis	This study concentrates on e-government services, particularly the online payment system, eFawateer.com. It investigates the user satisfaction level with these services by using sentiment analysis. By comparing two datasets of client feedback from 2017 and 2019, the research assesses the service's improvement over time. The proposed approach delivers outstanding results in comparison to other methods.
40	(Gumber, Jain & Amutha, 2021)	Gradient Boosting can be used to enhance the accuracy of customer feedback analysis by utilizing a more formalized paradigm to manage overfitting, resulting in superior performance.	ensemble method called Extreme Gradient Boosting - Randomized Search CV for tuning parameters	The model demonstrates a high prediction rate and is straightforward, making it practical for businesses to adopt. Its accuracy and recall, reported at 85.9% and 91.04% respectively, underscore its effectiveness in forecasting customer behaviour.
41	(Bentéjac, Csörgo & Martínez-Muñoz, 2019)	Gradient boosting algorithms such as XGBoost, LightGBM, and CatBoost can be used to enhance the accuracy of customer feedback analysis.	XGBoost, LightGBMCatBoost	In the examined datasets, CatBoost attains the highest generalization accuracy and AUC, albeit with marginal differences. Light GBM proves to be the fastest among the analyzed methods, although it doesn't match the highest accuracy. XGBoost stands as the second-best choice in terms of both accuracy and training speed.
42	(Yurochkin et. al., 2019)	This research introduces a novel challenge that lies at the crossroads of semi-supervised learning and contextual bandits. It draws inspiration from various applications such as clinical trials and ad recommendations. By merging the strengths of both approaches, the study develops a multi-GCN embedded contextual bandit model.	Graph Convolutional Network (GCN) - Linear contextual bandit with semi-supervised missing rewards imputation	The researchers introduce a modified version of the linear contextual bandit with semi-supervised missing rewards imputation. They illustrate how the Graph Convolutional Network (GCN), typically used in semi-supervised learning, can be adapted to this new problem setup. By merging the advantages of both approaches, the authors create a multi-GCN embedded contextual bandit. The effectiveness of these proposed algorithms is substantiated through experiments on various real-world datasets, providing quantitative proof of their efficacy.

Table 1. Continued

S. No.	Paper	Insights	Method Used	Findings and Conclusion
43	(Li et. al., 2021)	This study presents a method for semi-supervised channel state information (CSI) feedback in a massive multiple-input multiple-output (MIMO) system. The approach utilizes CSI data to enhance the practicality of the deep learning-based CSI feedback system.	Semi-supervised learning on CSI feedback 2CsiNet with three classifiers comparisons	The paper proposes a semi-supervised learning approach called S2CsiNet for channel state information (CSI) feedback in a Massive MIMO system, which addresses the challenges of wireless channel environment variation sensing and the lack of pre-labeled CSI data. S2CsiNet improves the feasibility of the DL-based CSI feedback system by incorporating indoor and outdoor environment sensing, resulting in better system performance. The proposed approach reduces the labeled dataset requirement by up to 96.2% through semi-supervised learning, making it more practical in scenarios where labeled data is scarce
44	(Deng, Smith & Quintin, 2020)	This study proposes a strategy that merges a BERT-based multi-classification algorithm using supervised learning with an innovative Probabilistic and Semantic Hybrid Topic Inference Model employing unsupervised learning. The goal is to automate the process of accurately identifying the primary topics or categories, as well as the sub-topics, from textual feedback and support.	semi-supervised learning approach using deep learning and Topic Modeling - BERT-based multi-classification algorithm combined with A Probabilistic and Semantic hybrid Topic Inference (PSHTI) Model	The study introduces a semi-supervised learning method that incorporates deep learning and Topic Modeling. It involves the development of a BERT-based multi-classification algorithm coupled with a Probabilistic and Semantic Hybrid Topic Inference (PSHTI) model.
45	(Dong, Matthew & Biagi, 2021)	In this paper, a semi-supervised multi-task learning paradigm was proposed for text-based intent classification for a customer support service on an E-commerce website, which improved the performance significantly.	Semi-supervised multi-task learning paradigm ALBERT as the backbone encoder	Multi-task learning, adaptive pre-training, and semi-supervised learning improve model performance. Final model shows 20 points increase in average AUC ROC.
46	(Park et. al., 2021)	This study introduced a semi-supervised multi-task learning approach for text-based intent classification in customer support services on an E-commerce website. The implementation of this method led to a significant improvement in performance.	Sentiment propagation using word graph. Customer review analysis for complaint topics	The suggested customer sentiment analysis approach incorporates sentiment propagation and customer review analysis to capture sentiment words beyond conventional vocabulary and non-grammatical language used by customers. It utilizes semi-supervised learning on a word graph generated by a word embedding algorithm to expand sentiment words from a dictionary, encompassing diverse terms. Additionally, the method categorizes reviews into primary complaint topics and establishes an index for customer dissatisfaction by amalgamating "controversy" and "complaint" factors. The "controversy" factor represents the extent of dissatisfaction coverage, while the "complaint" factor signifies the intensity of dissatisfaction.

vi. **Data Imbalance:** Sentiment datasets are often imbalanced, with more instances of one sentiment class than others. This situation can result in models exhibiting biases, performing effectively on the majority class while encountering difficulties with minority classes.

vii. **Lack of Labeled Data:** Collecting high-quality labeled data for sentiment analysis can be time-consuming and expensive. Limited labeled data can affect the performance of machine learning models.

viii. **Noise and Spelling Errors:** Text data often contains noise, including misspellings, typos, and grammatical errors, which can confuse sentiment analysis algorithms.

ix. **Multilingual Sentiment Analysis:** Sentiment analysis across multiple languages presents challenges due to language-specific expressions, cultural nuances, and the need for multilingual models.

x. **Sentiment Evolution:** Sentiments change over time, and models trained on historical data might not generalize well to the present. Temporal sentiment analysis is necessary to capture sentiment shifts.

xi. **Data Preprocessing:** Text preprocessing, including tokenization, stopword removal, and stemming, is crucial for feature extraction. Incorrect preprocessing can lead to distorted results.

xii. **Bias and Fairness:** Sentiment analysis models can inherit biases present in the training data. This can result in unfair predictions and reinforce societal biases.

xiii. **Interpretable Models:** Deep learning models, while powerful, can lack interpretability, making it challenging to understand why they make specific predictions.

Addressing these challenges requires a combination of domain expertise, feature engineering, careful algorithm selection, model validation, data augmentation, and ethical considerations to build accurate and fair sentiment analysis models.

3.3 A Case Study

This section presents a case study as discussed and presented in (Sitepu, Munthe & Harahap, 2022). It employs the SVM algorithm to perform sentiment analysis on customer reviews of Shopee products written in English. The analysis was conducted using secondary data sourced from Kaggle (https://www. kaggle.com/datasets/shymammoth/shopee-reviews), an unstructured document, a dataset containing 1,502,575 records. For this study, a subset of 10,000 records with three attributes, namely- label, text, and Sentiment, were used for analysis. The steps of this process are as shown in the Process stages in Figure 6 (Somantri & Apriliani, 2018, Hafidz & Yanti Liliana 2021).

Dataset & Pre-processing

The text pre-processing was required as the dataset consisted of words/ sentences that were not properly structured. The text pre-processing thus removed unnecessary data or data contained in the text that did

Figure 7. Process framework
(Sitepu, Munthe & Harahap, 2022)

Dataset	Case Folding	Tokenization	Stopwords Removal	Stemming	Lemmatization
"NOTE: DOESN'T INCLUDE THE BLUE SMALL ONE. The delivery was fast, and the quality is real good. Recommended! "	note: doesnt include the blue small one. The delivery was fast, and the quality is real good. recommended!	note doesnt include the blue small one the delivery was fast and the quality is real good recommended	note doesnt include blue small one delivery fast quality real good recommended	note doesnt include blue small one delivery fast quality real good recommend	note doesnt include blue small one delivery fast quality real good recommend
"FAST DELIVERY! Ordered on 3rd Jun, received on the 6th. Can't wait to try it. :) Seller was really helpful and patient when I met with an issue with the courier service."	fast delivery! ordered on 3rd jun, received on the 6th. can'twait to try it. :) seller was really helpful and patient when i met with an issue with the courier service.	fast delivery ordered on 3rd jun received on the 6th cant wait to try it seller was really helpful and patient when i met with an issue with the courier service	fast delivery ordered 3rd jun received 6th cant wait try seller really helpful patient met issue courier service	fast delivery order 3rd jun receive 6th cant wait try seller really helpful patient met issue courier service	fast delivery order rd jun receive th cant wait try seller really helpful patient met issue courier service

not match the required process. The implementation was done using the Python programming language. Case Folding, Tokenization, Stopwords removal, Stemming, and Lemmatization are the different stages for pre-processing text and the results of text processing are presented in the Figure 7.

Feature Extraction

In this step, the text was transformed into a "bag-of-words" representation, serving as a tool for creating features. Different sizes were computed to describe the document, where each item in the list represented the frequency or count of respective entries in the bag-of-words list. The Count Vectorizer class from the Scikit-Learn Python library was utilized during this process. Additionally, the resulting features were saved in a file named feature.pkl, employing the picke module in the Python library.

TF-IDF Weighting

In this phase, the data undergoes transformation into a matrix, and each word was assigned a weight using the Term Frequency-Inverse Document Frequency (TF-IDF) algorithm. This weighting process calculated the TF-IDF values, revealing the similarities between the documents within the dataset.

SVM Implementation

The SVM algorithm was implemented with a linear kernel, and the training data incorporated a parameter C set to 1. The trained model is subsequently employed to classify the data.

Model Evaluation and Result

The model's performance was assessed using error metrics to determine its accuracy. To evaluate the model, the K-fold Cross-Validation (CV) method was employed. In this approach, k=5, meaning the data was divided into 5 training groups for evaluation. Upon examining the dataset, it was observed that the data used was considered good as it contained no duplicates or null values. The findings from the exploratory data analysis in Python are summarized in Table 2.

Figure 8 shows that the dataset consisted of 10,000 records with an average value of 4.76, and a standard deviation of 0.71.

Table 2. Exploratory Data Analysis

Index	Label
count	10000.0
mean	4.7646
std	0.712066

Figure 8. Text pre-processing results

The case folding process transformed the dataset's letters from uppercase to lowercase. Tokenization, performed using the remove_punctuation library in Python, removed all punctuation from strings or user reviews in the dataset. Stopwords removal reduced unimportant words like "the," "was," "and," and "is." The stemming process eliminated word affixes such as prefixes, infixes, suffixes, and confixes, reverting words in the dataset to their basic form; in this test dataset, the "ed" suffix was omitted.

The subsequent step involves applying SVM with TF-IDF weighting on individual words. For this test, a linear kernel is employed with the parameter C set to 1. This process involves training a sentiment model to classify the data. To assess the model's performance, the Cross-Validation (CV) method from the K-fold Python library is utilized. In this specific implementation, 5 data training groups were utilized, denoted by k=5. Following the completion of sentiment analysis, the classification results indicate 5 repetitions. The outcomes indicate a successful classification process with an accuracy rate of 96%. After analyzing the sentiment of Shopee user customer data, a data plot illustrating the results of sentiment analysis classification is generated, as depicted in Figure 9.

Figure 8 illustrates the division of Shopee customer reviews into two categories: "Positive" and "Negative." Among the 10,000 tested user data records, the results reveal 9,719 instances of positive opinions, accounting for 97.19% of the total. Conversely, there are 279 instances of negative opinions, constituting 2.79% of the total.

The subsequent step involves assessing the implemented sentiment model. The evaluation generates precision, recall, f1-score, and accuracy values. Further details are provided in Figure 10 below.

From figure 10, it's evident that the highest scores were achieved in k-folds 0, 1, and 3. In these cases, precision was 1, recall stood at 0.98, f1-score was 0.99, and accuracy was 0.98. When considering the

Figure 9. Customer opinion classification

K-Fold	Precision	Recall	F1-Score	Accuracy
k=0	1.0	0.98	0.99	0.98
k=1	1.0	0.98	0.99	0.98
k=2	1.0	0.97	0.98	0.97
k=3	1.0	0.98	0.99	0.98
k=4	1.0	0.96	0.98	0.96

Figure 10. Evaluation model analysis sentiment SVM

K-Fold	Precision	Recall	F1-Score	Accuracy
k=0	1.0	0.98	0.99	0.98
k=1	1.0	0.98	0.99	0.98
k=2	1.0	0.97	0.98	0.97
k=3	1.0	0.98	0.99	0.98
k=4	1.0	0.96	0.98	0.96

five sentiment analysis models, the average values were calculated. The obtained results show precision = 1, recall = 0.97, f1-score = 0.98, and accuracy = 0.97.

The case study presented that a sentiment analysis model was successfully developed by applying the SVM algorithm to customer reviews of Shopee products in English. The model was tested five times, resulting in average precision, recall, and f1-score values of 1.0, 0.97, and 0.98, respectively. The average accuracy level achieved was 97.3%. Utilizing the Support Vector Machine algorithm with TF-IDF weighting proves to be an effective approach for solving classification problems in sentiment analysis. For future research, a more comprehensive approach could involve comparing multiple classification algorithms and incorporating optimization methods.

3.4 Improving Sentiment Analysis Performance

The performance of sentiment analysis may be improved but is a complex process which may involve a combination of data preprocessing, feature engineering, model selection, and validation techniques. Some of the suggested strategies to enhance sentiment analysis performance are as follows:

i. **Quality Labelled Data:** We need to make sure that the training data is accurately labelled and representative of the sentiment expressions in your target domain. Improving data quality can lead to enhanced model performance.

ii. **Data Augmentation:** Diversity in training data by using techniques like synonym replacement, back-translation, and paraphrasing can help the model generalize better to different expressions.

iii. **Advanced Preprocessing:** Paying more attention to tokenization, stemming, lemmatization, and removing stop words to ensure text features capture meaningful sentiment information.

iv. **Custom Lexicons:** Domain or context specific creation or customization of sentiment lexicons can help the model understand domain-specific expressions and slang.

v. **Feature Engineering:** Experiment with different features, including n-grams, word embeddings, and part-of-speech tags. The right features can improve the model's ability to capture sentiment nuances.

vi. **Handling Negations and Intensifiers:** Design your preprocessing and feature engineering pipelines to appropriately handle negation words and intensifiers that impact sentiment.

vii. **Ensemble Methods:** Combine predictions from multiple models using ensemble techniques like majority voting, weighted voting, or stacking to improve overall performance.

viii. **Hyperparameter Tuning:** Experiment with different hyperparameter settings for the chosen algorithm. Grid search or random search can help you find optimal parameter values.

ix. **Cross-Validation:** Utilize methods such as k-fold cross-validation to assess the performance of the model across various subsets of your dataset, reducing the risk of overfitting.

x. **Regularization:** Implement regularization techniques like L1 and L2 regularization to prevent overfitting and enhance the capability of the model to generalize to new data.

xi. **Transfer Learning:** Fine-tune pre-trained models like BERT or GPT on your sentiment analysis task. These models have already learned rich language representations that can improve performance.

xii. **Bias Mitigation:** Address bias in your data and model predictions by using debiasing techniques and ensuring diversity and fairness in your training data.

xiii. **Temporal Analysis:** Consider incorporating temporal information to account for sentiment shifts over time. Temporal models can capture evolving sentiments more accurately.

xiv. **Regular Model Evaluation:** Continuously evaluate your model's performance on validation and test data. Monitor for degradation in performance and update your model as needed.

xv. **User Feedback Loop:** Incorporate user feedback to identify and rectify instances where the model misclassifies sentiment.

3.5 Real-World Applications

Sentiment analysis using machine learning algorithms for analysing customer feedback has numerous real-world applications across various industries. Here are some examples:

i. **Social Media Monitoring:** Companies are using sentiment analysis to monitor social media platforms for public opinions about their products, services, or brands. This helps them gauge customer satisfaction and determine the areas for improvement.

ii. **Customer Reviews and Feedback:** E-commerce platforms and businesses analyze customer reviews and feedback to understand customer sentiment, gather insights, and make data-driven decisions for product development and developing marketing strategies.

iii. **Financial Markets:** Sentiment analysis is applied to analyze financial news, social media chatter, and market sentiment to predict stock price movements and make informed investment decisions.

iv. **Public Opinion and Politics:** Political campaigns and government bodies use sentiment analysis to gauge public opinions on policies, candidates, and issues, helping them tailor their messaging and strategies.

v. **Healthcare:** Sentiment analysis can be used to monitor patient reviews and feedback about healthcare services, enabling hospitals to improve patient experiences and identify areas for enhancement.

vi. **Brand Reputation Management:** Organizations use sentiment analysis to monitor their online reputation by analyzing mentions across various platforms and addressing negative sentiments promptly.

vii. **Market Research:** Companies use sentiment analysis to gather insights about consumer preferences, trends, and opinions, aiding in product development and marketing strategies.

viii. **Product Launches:** Sentiment analysis helps assess customer reactions to new product launches, allowing companies to make adjustments based on initial feedback.

ix. **Voice of the Customer (VoC) Analysis:** Businesses use sentiment analysis to analyze customer interactions and feedback from call centers, chat logs, and surveys, helping them improve customer service.

x. **Hotel and Restaurant Reviews:** The hospitality industry uses sentiment analysis to monitor online reviews and ratings, helping establishments enhance customer experiences and service quality.

xi. **News and Media Monitoring:** Media organizations use sentiment analysis to understand how news articles and stories are perceived by the public, aiding in journalistic decisions and story coverage.

xii. **Automated Content Moderation:** Sentiment analysis is applied to moderate user-generated content on online platforms, identifying and filtering out inappropriate or offensive content.

xiii. **Online Advertising:** Advertisers use sentiment analysis to tailor their ad campaigns by analyzing user sentiment and targeting content that resonates positively with the audience.

xiv. **Health Monitoring:** Patients' sentiment expressed in their health-related messages, forums, or wearable device data can be analyzed to gain insights into their emotional states and overall well-being.

xv. **Educational Feedback:** Educational institutions analyze student feedback to understand their sentiment towards courses, instructors, and learning experiences, aiming to improve educational quality.

3.6 CONCLUSION

Improving sentiment analysis performance is an iterative process that requires experimentation, fine-tuning, and adaptation to the specific domain and data characteristics. Regularly assessing the model's effectiveness and staying updated with advancements in sentiment analysis techniques can help maintain high-quality results.

REFERENCES

Al-Qudah, D. A., Al-Zoubi, A. M., Castillo-Valdivieso, P. A., & Faris, H. (2020). Sentiment Analysis for e-Payment Service Providers Using Evolutionary eXtreme Gradient Boosting. *IEEE Access : Practical Innovations, Open Solutions, 8*, 189930–189944. doi:10.1109/ACCESS.2020.3032216

Ama, A., Mulya, D., Astuti, Y., & Prasadhya, I. (2022). Analisis Sentimen Customer Feedback Tokopedia Menggunakan Algoritma Naïve Bayes. *Jurnal Sistem Komputer dan Informatika (JSON), 4*(1), 50-50. https://doi: . doi:10.30865/json.v4i1.4783

Anand, D. D. (2021). Implementation and Analysis of Sentimental Analysis on Facial Expression Using HAAR Cascade Methods. [TURCOMAT]. *Turkish Journal of Computer and Mathematics Education, 12*(2), 2787–2793. doi:10.17762/turcomat.v12i2.2308

Arifianto, A., Suyanto, S., Sirwan, A., Desrul, D. R., Prakoso, I. D., Guntara, F. F., Hidayati, D. C., & Murti, R. S. (2020). Developing an LSTM-based Classification Model of IndiHome Customer Feedbacks. *International Conference on Data Science and Its Applications (ICoDSA)*, (pp. 1-5). IEEE. 10.1109/ICoDSA50139.2020.9212863

Asghar, M. Z., Subhan, F., Ahmad, H., Khan, W. Z., Hakak, S., Gadekallu, T. R., & Alazab, M. (2021). Senti-eSystem: A sentiment-based eSystem-using hybridized fuzzy and deep neural network for measuring customer satisfaction. *Software, Practice & Experience, 51*(3), 571–594. doi:10.1002pe.2853

Asthakhuroh, A., Komarudin, R., & Kholifah, D. (2023). Sentiment Analysis with A Case Study of Practice Card on Twitter social media Using Naive Bayes Method. *Jurnal Techno Nusa Mandiri, 20*(1), 8–13. doi:10.33480/techno.v20i1.3709

Astuti, Y., Wahyuni, S. N., Maulina, D., & Sidiq, F. M. (2022). The Data Leakage Sentiment Analysis Using Naive Bayes Algorithm Based on Machine Learning Approach. *5th International Seminar on Research of Information Technology and Intelligent Systems (ISRITI)*, (pp. 215-220). IEEE. 10.1109/ISRITI56927.2022.10052877

Astuti, Y., Yova, R., Faris, S., & Aldiansah, P. (2023). Sentiment Analysis of Electricity Company Service Quality Using Naïve Bayes. [Rekayasa Sistem Dan Teknologi Informasi]. *Jurnal RESTI, 7*(2), 389–396. doi:10.29207/resti.v7i2.4627

Ban, H.-J., & Kim, H.-S. (2019). Understanding Customer Experience and Satisfaction through Airline Passengers' Online Review. *Sustainability (Basel), 11*(15), 4066. doi:10.3390u11154066

Bart, K. (2019). Noise Benefits in Feedback Machine Learning: Bidirectional Backpropagation. In book: *Challenging the Borders of Justice in the Age of Migrations,* (pp. 267-275). IEEE. . doi:10.1007/978-3-030-10892-2_26

Bentéjac, C., Csörgo, A., & Martínez-Muñoz, G. (2019). A comparative analysis of gradient boosting algorithms. *Artificial Intelligence Review, 54*(3), 1937–1967. doi:10.100710462-020-09896-5

Bhargava, M. G., & Rao, D. R. (2018). Sentimental analysis on social media data using R programming. *IACSIT International Journal of Engineering and Technology, 7*(2.31), 80. doi:10.14419/ijet.v7i2.31.13402

Chan, K. H., & Im, S. K. (2022). Sentiment analysis by using Naïve Bayes classifier with stacked CARU. *Electronics Letters, 58*(10), 411–413. doi:10.1049/ell2.12478

Chaudhuri, A., & Ghosh, S. (2016). Sentiment Analysis of Customer Reviews Using Robust Hierarchical Bidirectional Recurrent Neural Network. In book: *Artificial Intelligence Perspectives in Intelligent Systems,* (pp. 249-261). Springer. . doi:10.1007/978-3-319-33625-1_23

Darusman, F. S., Arifiyanti, A. A., & Wati, S. F. A. (2022). A Sentiment Analysis Pedulilindungi Tweet Using Support Vector Machine Method. *Applied Technology and Computing Science Journal, 4*(2), 113–118. doi:10.33086/atcsj.v4i2.2836

Davis, S., & Tabrizi, N. (2021). Customer Review Analysis: A Systematic Review. *IEEE/ACIS 6th International Conference on Big Data, Cloud Computing, and Data Science (BCD).,* (pp. 91-97). IEEE. https://doi: 10.1109/BCD51206.2021.9581965

Deng, X., Smith, R. T., & Quintin, G. (2020). *Semi-Supervised Learning Approach to Discover Enterprise User Insights from Feedback and Support.* arXiv: Learning. https://doi.org//arXiv.2007.09303. doi:10.48550

Dhyani, D. (2017). Exploring Neural Architectures for Multilingual Customer Feedback Analysis. In *Proceedings of the International Joint Conference on Natural Language Processing (IJCNLP),* (pp. 170-173). ACM.

Dong, L., Matthew, C. S., & Biagi, A. (2021). A Semi-supervised Multi-task Learning Approach to Classify Customer Contact Intents. In *Proceedings of the 4th Workshop on e-Commerce and NLP,* (pp. 49–57). Online. Association for Computational Linguistics. 10.18653/v1/2021.ecnlp-1.7

Dutta, N., Umashankar, S., Shankar, V. K., Padmanaban, S., Leonowicz, Z., & Wheeler, P. (2018). Centrifugal Pump Cavitation Detection Using Machine Learning Algorithm Technique. *IEEE International Conference on Environment and Electrical Engineering and IEEE Industrial and Commercial Power Systems Europe.* IEEE. 10.1109/EEEIC.2018.8494594

Erfina, A., & Lestari, R. (2023). Sentiment Analysis of Electric Vehicles using the Naïve Bayes Algorithm. *SISTEMASI, 12*(1), 178–185. doi:10.32520tmsi.v12i1.2417

Gumber, M., Jain, A., & Amutha, A. L. (2021). Predicting Customer Behavior by Analyzing Clickstream Data. *5th International Conference on Computer, Communication and Signal Processing (ICCCSP),* (pp. 1-6). IEEE, 10.1109/ICCCSP52374.2021.9465526

Hafidz, N., & Yanti Liliana, D. (2021). Klasifikasi Sentimen pada Twitter Terhadap WHO Terkait Covid-19 Menggunakan SVM, N-Gram, PSO. [Rekayasa Sistem Dan Teknologi Informasi]. *Jurnal RESTI, 5*(2), 213–219. doi:10.29207/resti.v5i2.2960

Heryadi, Y., Wijanarko, B. D., Fitria Murad, D., Tho, C., & Hashimoto, K. (2023). Aspect-based Sentiment Analysis using Long Short-term Memory Model for Leveraging Restaurant Service Management. *International Conference on Computer Science, Information Technology and Engineering (ICCoSITE),* (pp. 779-783). IEEE. https://doi: 10.1109/ICCoSITE57641.2023.10127708

Hossain, M., Rahman, M. F., Uddin, M. K., & Hossain, M. K. (2023, June 07). S., Rahman, M., Uddin, Md. K., Hossain, Md. (2022). Customer Sentiment Analysis and Prediction of Halal Restaurants Using Machine Learning Approaches. *Journal of Islamic Marketing, 14*(7), 1859–1889. doi:10.1108/JIMA-04-2021-0125

Hossain, M. A., & Rahman, M. F. (2022). Customer Sentiment Analysis and Prediction of Insurance Products' Reviews Using Machine Learning Approaches. *FIIB business review.* https://doi: . doi:10.1177/23197145221115793

Hossen, M. S., Jony, A. H., Tabassum, T., Islam, M., Rahman, M. M., & Khatun, T. (2021). Hotel review analysis for the prediction of business using deep learning approach. *International Conference on Artificial Intelligence and Smart Systems (ICAIS),* (pp. 1489-1494). IEEE. 10.1109/ICAIS50930.2021.9395757

Khedkar, S. A., & Shinde, S. K. (2018). Customer Review Analytics for Business Intelligence. *IEEE International Conference on Computational Intelligence and Computing Research (ICCIC).,* (pp. 1-5). IEEE. https://doi: 10.1109/ICCIC.2018.8782305

Komarasamy, G., Jaganathan, S. C. B., Sridharan, K., Mital, A., & Awal, S. (2022). Harmony Gradient Boosting Random Forest Machine Learning Algorithms for Sentiment Classification. *IEEE 2nd International Symposium on Sustainable Energy, Signal Processing and Cyber Security (iSSSC),* (pp. 1-5). IEEE. https://doi: 10.1109/iSSSC56467.2022.10051210

Kumar, V., Pareek, P., Albuquerque, V. H., Khanna, A., Gupta, D., & Madhumala, R. B. (2022). Multimodal Sentiment Analysis using Kernel Based Support Vector Machine. *Second International Conference on Advanced Technologies in Intelligent Control, Environment, Computing & Communication Engineering (ICATIECE).,* (pp. 1-8). IEEE. https://doi: 10.1109/ICATIECE56365.2022.10046818

Li, H., Zhang, B., Liang, X., Chang, H., Gu, X., & Zhang, L. (2021). *CSI Sensing and Feedback: A Semi-Supervised Learning Approach.* arXiv: Signal Processing. https://doi.org//arXiv.2110.06142. doi:10.48550

Lin, S., Xie, H., Yu, L., & Lai, K. R. (2017). SentiNLP at IJCNLP-2017 Task 4: Customer Feedback Analysis Using a Bi-LSTM-CNN Model. In *Proceedings of the International Joint Conference on Natural Language Processing (IJCNLP),* (pp. 149–154). Asian Federation of Natural Language Processing.

Maharani, P. U., Amalita, N., Amadi, A., & Fitri, F. (2023). Sentiment Analysis of GoRide Services on Twitter social media Using Naive Bayes Algorithm. *UNP Journal of Statistics and Data Science*, *1*(3), 134–139. doi:10.24036/ujsds/vol1-iss3/41

Naeem, S., Logoftu, D., Muharemi, F. (2020). Sentiment Analysis by Using Supervised Machine Learning and Deep Learning Approaches. *Advances in Computational Collective Intelligence*, (pp. 481-491). IEEE. https://doi: . doi:10.1007/978-3-030-63119-2_39

Nahumury, A. J., Manongga, D., Iriani, A. (2022). Analysis Sentiment on Airline Customer Satisfaction Using Recurrent Neural Network. *Journal Eduvest - Journal of Universal Studies, 2*(10), 2119-2129. https://doi: . v2i10.594. doi:10.36418/eduvest

Nur Cahyo, D. D., Farasalsabila, F., Lestari, V. B., Hanafi, Lestari, T., Al Islami, F. R., & Maulana, M. A. (2023). Sentiment Analysis for IMDb Movie Review Using Support Vector Machine (SVM) Method. *Inform: Jurnal Ilmiah Bidang Teknologi Informasi Dan Komunikasi*, *8*(2), 90–95. doi:10.25139/inform. v8i2.5700

Nurcahyawati, V., & Mustaffa, Z. (2023). Vader Lexicon and Support Vector Machine Algorithm to Detect Customer Sentiment Orientation. *Journal of Information Systems Engineering and Business Intelligence.*, *9*(1), 108–118. doi:10.20473/jisebi.9.1.108-118

Okazaki, S., Eisend, M., Plangger, K., Ruyter, K., & Grewal, D. (2020). Understanding the Strategic Consequences of Customer Privacy Concerns: A Meta-Analytic Review. *Journal of Retailing*, *96*(4), 458–473. doi:10.1016/j.jretai.2020.05.007

Park, S., Cho, J., Park, K., & Shin, H. (2021). Customer sentiment analysis with more sensibility. *Engineering Applications of Artificial Intelligence*, *104*, 104356. doi:10.1016/j.engappai.2021.104356

Patel, A., Oza, P., & Agrawal, S. (2023). Sentiment Analysis of Customer Feedback and Reviews for Airline Services using Language Representation Model. *Procedia Computer Science*, *218*, 2459–2467. doi:10.1016/j.procs.2023.01.221

Patrick, H. A., Sharief, P. J. M. H., & Mukherjee, U. (2023). Sentiment Analysis Perspective using Supervised Machine Learning Method. *Fifth International Conference on Electrical, Computer and Communication Technologies (ICECCT)*, (pp. 1-4). IEEE. 10.1109/ICECCT56650.2023.10179807

Pradhan, S. (2022). *A Guide to Sentiment Analysis – Part 2*. Nitor.

Pratama, M. R., Soerawinata, F. A., Zhafari, R. R., Imanda, H. N. (2022). Sentiment Analysis of Beauty Product E-Commerce Using Support Vector Machine Method. *Jurnal RESTI (Rekayasa Sistem dan Teknologi Informasi)*, *6*(2), 269-274. https://doi: . v6i2.3876 doi:10.29207/resti

Rokhman, W., & Andiani, F. (2020). Understanding Muslim Young Consumers on Online Shopping: The role of Customer Review, Price, Trust and Security. *Equilibrium: Journal Ekonomi Syariah*, *8*(2), 297–312. doi:10.21043/equilibrium.v8i2.8655

Sainger, D. G. (2021). Sentiment Analysis - An Assessment of Online Public Opinion: A Conceptual Review. [TURCOMAT]. *Turkish Journal of Computer and Mathematics Education*, *12*(5), 1881–1887. doi:10.17762/turcomat.v12i5.2266

Shayaa, S., Jaafar, N. I., Bahri, S., Sulaiman, A., Seuk Wai, P., Wai Chung, Y., Piprani, A. Z., & Al-Garadi, M. A. (2018). Sentiment Analysis of Big Data: Methods, Applications, and Open Challenges. *IEEE Access : Practical Innovations, Open Solutions, 6*(6), 37807–37827. doi:10.1109/ACCESS.2018.2851311

Sitepu, M.B., Munthe, I.R., & Harahap, S.Z. (2022). Implementation of Support Vector Machine Algorithm for Shopee Customer Sentiment Analysis. *Sinkron: jurnal dan penelitian teknik informatika, 7*(2), 619-627. https://doi: . v7i2.11408 doi:10.33395/sinkron

Somantri, O., & Apriliani, D. (2018). Support Vector Machine Berbasis Feature Selection Untuk Sentiment Analysis Kepuasan Pelanggan Terhadap Pelayanan Warung dan Restoran Kuliner Kota Tegal. [JTIIK]. *Jurnal Teknologi Informasi Dan Ilmu Komputer, 5*(5), 537–548. doi:10.25126/jtiik.201855867

Srinivasan, R., & Subalalitha, C. N. (2021). Sentimental analysis from imbalanced code-mixed data using machine learning approaches. *Distributed and Parallel Databases, 41*, 37–52. doi:10.100710619-021-07331-4 PMID:33776212

Subramanian. R, S., P, G., M, A., M G, D., J, A., & P, D. (2023). Heterogeneous Ensemble Variable Selection to Improve Customer Prediction Using Naive Bayes Model. *International Journal on Recent and Innovation Trends in Computing and Communication, 11*(5s), 64–71. doi:10.17762/ijritcc.v11i5s.6599

Sumayya, K. A., Joseph, R., Saisree, R. K., & Satheesh, T. S. (2022). Sentiment Analysis on Student Feedback Using RNN. *International Journal of Engineering Research in Computer Science and Engineering, 9*(7), 52–57. doi:10.36647/IJERCSE/09.07.Art012

Surekha, L., & Jayanthi, A. (2019). A Movie Review Sentiment Analysis Using Machine Learning Techniques. *International Journal of Recent Scientific Research, 10*(08), 34492–34497. doi:10.24327/ijrsr.2019.1008.3906

Tetzlaff, L., Rulle, K., Szepannek, G., & Gronau, W. (2019). A customer feedback sentiment dictionary: Towards automatic assessment of online reviews. *European Journal of Tourism Research, 23*, 28–39. doi:10.54055/ejtr.v23i.387

Tonic. (2018). A Sentiment Analysis Approach to Predicting Stock Returns. *Medium.*

Uma, R., Sana, H. A., Jawahar, P., & Rishitha, B. V. (2022). Support Vector Machine and Convolutional Neural Network Approach to Customer Review Sentiment Analysis. *1st International Conference on Computational Science and Technology (ICCST).,* (pp. 239-243). IEEE. https://doi: 10.1109/ICCST55948.2022.10040381

Vielma, C., Verma, A., & Bein, D. (2023). Sentiment Analysis with Novel GRU based Deep Learning Networks. *IEEE World AI IoT Congress (AIIoT),* (pp. 0440-0446). IEEE. https://doi: 10.1109/AIIoT58121.2023.10174396

Wankhade, M., Rao, A. C. S., & Kulkarni, C. (2022). A survey on sentiment analysis methods, applications, and challenges. *Artificial Intelligence Review, 55*(7), 5731–5780. doi:10.100710462-022-10144-1

Wu, H., & Li, B. (2022). Customer Purchase Prediction Based on Improved Gradient Boosting Decision Tree Algorithm. *2nd International Conference on Consumer Electronics and Computer Engineering (ICCECE),* (pp. 795-798). IEEE. 10.1109/ICCECE54139.2022.9712779

Yurochkin, M., Upadhyay, S., Bouneffouf, D., Agarwal, M., & Khazaeni, Y. (2019). *Online Semi-Supervised Learning with Bandit Feedback*. arXiv: Learning, arXiv:2010.12574. https://doi.org//arXiv.2010.12574. doi:10.48550

Zaenal, Z., & Astutik, I. R. I. (2023). Sentiment Analysis of OYO App Reviews Using the Support Vector Machine Algorithm. *Procedia of Engineering and Life Science, 3*. doi:10.21070/pels.v3i0.1338

Zain, S., Ramli, N. & Adnan, R. (2022). Customer sentiment analysis through social media feedback: a case study on telecommunication company. *International Journal of Humanities Technology and Civilization, 7*(2), 54-61. https://doi: . v7i2.8739. doi:10.15282/ijhtc

Zakir, H. M., & Jinny, S. V. (2022). Convolutional neural networks method for analysis of e-commerce customer reviews. *AIP Conference Proceedings, 2444*, 030004. doi:10.1063/5.0078372

KEY TERMS AND DEFINITIONS

Big Data: Primarily refers to data sets that are too large or complex to be dealt with by traditional data-processing techniques.

Data Preprocessing: Text preprocessing that includes tokenization, stopword removal, and stemming, and is crucial for feature extraction.

Machine Learning: It is a field of study in artificial intelligence that tries to make machines learn automatically without explicit programming.

Semi-Supervised Learning: This type of machine learning method merges aspects of both supervised and unsupervised learning. It uses a combination of a small amount of labelled data and a large amount of unlabelled data to train models.

Sentiment Analysis: Known as opinion mining, is a natural language processing (NLP) approach used to recognize the emotional tone expressed by an individual in some form of communication.

Supervised Learning: It uses labelled datasets to train algorithms to classify data or predict outcomes accurately.

Unsupervised Learning: In contrast to supervised learning, unsupervised learning algorithms learn patterns exclusively from unlabelled data.

Chapter 18
Case Studies in Big Data Analysis:
A Novel Computer Vision Application to Detect Insurance Fraud

Dwijendra Dwivedi

https://orcid.org/0000-0001-7662-415X

Krakow University of Economics, Poland

Saurabh Batra

Delhi University, India

ABSTRACT

Computer vision technology can be used for instant car damage recognition by analyzing images of damaged vehicles to detect and identify the location and severity of any damages. Technology can accurately classify damage into categories such as small, medium, or high severity. This can help insurance companies and other relevant stakeholders quickly process claims, reduce fraudulent claims, and improve the overall claims process efficiency. The conventional car damage assessment process is time-consuming, labor-intensive, and prone to errors. Computer vision models offer a new solution to detect car insurance fraud by identifying the damage severity and streamlining the claims process. AI can automate the process by analyzing images of damaged cars and generating a breakdown of the damage. The authors propose a unique computer vision process that can help identify small, medium, and high severity of damages and validate investigators' recommendations to detect anomalies in real-time.

1. INTRODUCTION

Insurance fraud is a serious threat that threatens the insurance industry in several ways. It can affect client satisfaction by delaying payouts or conducting lengthy investigations during an already hectic timeframe and reduce profitability through incorrect payouts. An effective method of detecting insurance fraud is

DOI: 10.4018/979-8-3693-0413-6.ch018

through machine learning, which allows insurers to identify suspicious patterns in customer behavior that might indicate fraudulent claims. Deep learning algorithms have the capability of quickly comparing millions of pieces of data in milliseconds. Computer vision technology provides another means of detecting auto insurance fraud, allowing insurers to accurately assess damage. This approach helps prevent fraudulent repair claims with false invoices submitted to collect more from insurers.

Computer vision technology can also be used to inspect damaged cars. By analyzing 360-degree videos, it can analyze images to detect causes of damage such as minor spot damages or isolated injuries and quickly assess repair needs. This system can also be integrated with car rental and repair services to inspect vehicles prior to their repair, detecting the type of damage detected as well as providing a report detailing estimated repair costs. Instead of saving photos or videos locally on systems, this AI solution transmits camera feed directly to a backend platform - eliminating potential customer and middleman agent manipulation of camera feed data Car owners also avoid inflating their claim amounts by misrepresenting past damage in their claim by concealing it entirely, for instance by adding stickers over damaged areas or by covering it with new damage altogether.

AI and data analytics can assist insurers in detecting fraud as it happens and connecting previously disjointed data sets to enhance the process. This provides greater control over fraud prevention while offering customers a seamless customer experience.

Artificial intelligence can also help to prevent fraud. In the past, people have hidden damages on their cars during video inspections to increase the value of their cars. These hidden damages are usually covered with stickers, which make it hard for the tool to detect the true extent of the damage. The latest AI-based solutions offer an automated inspection process that can eliminate manual processes. Using the machine learning model on the image of damaged car, an insurance company can predict the extent of a claim before it is even filed. Machine learning-based workflows analyze the damages, estimating the costs of repair and identifying damaged components.

One of the benefits of this approach is the user-based system, which allows for more personalization in the claims process. It also relies on user behavioral patterns to identify potential problems. our AI-based auto damage inspection approach uses smart accidental damage pattern analysis to separate new or old damages. It can be used by car rental services, car repair services and motor vehicle insurers to streamline the claim process and increase customer satisfaction.

The advent of machine learning in the car insurance industry has transformed the way policies are priced and claimed. These advancements in AI have helped insurers to better price their policies, identify suspicious patterns, and prevent fraud. As more insurers use machine learning for claim processing, they are also improving their customer service. AI can help insurers reduce the number of complaints they receive and make the claims process faster and easier. It can also suggest car insurance add-ons to customers. A machine learning model can analyze a large amount of data to generate a fraud suspicion score. The score is measured by the accuracy of a model's predictions. Compared to rules-based systems, models with higher precision can identify more frauds. Car insurance companies can use these algorithms to develop and implement customized policies to best serve their customers. It can also be used to spot fraudulent claims and flag them for further investigation.

Machine learning is a data-driven, automated approach that helps us identify fraud and reduce human error. With AI, we can process claims quickly and efficiently, reducing our risk of false claims. The auto insurance industry is a huge profit center. It is estimated that fraudulent insurance claims cost US insurers approximately $40 billion[1] each year. By incorporating AI into claims processing, we can reduce the costs of investigating fraudulent claims, and speed up claim settlements. As per insurance information institute auto fraud often includes the resale of storm-damaged vehicles, which are misleadingly repaired and sold, a practice known as "title washing."

To prevent this, standardized state rules for titling vehicles, especially those with flood damage, are essential. Some hurricane-prone states now require "flood vehicle" labels on titles of rebuilt, water-damaged vehicles, with mandatory buyer notification. However, inconsistencies in state laws can lead to some states becoming hotspots

for undisclosed flooded vehicles. The National Insurance Crime Bureau (NICB) combats this by maintaining a database of VINs from flooded vehicles, accessible to both officials and the public via VINCheck®. Additionally, the National Motor Vehicle Title Information System (NMVTIS) collects data on vehicles declared total losses, with nearly complete U.S. vehicle coverage by 2019. Another related issue is the use of counterfeit parts, like airbags, in auto repairs, where dishonest repair shops substitute genuine parts with cheaper counterfeits and claim insurance for the full cost.

The use of computer vision to identify fraud in the auto insurance industry is a relatively new concept. However, recent improvements in computer vision technology have made this method feasible. As a result, insurers can evaluate damage to a vehicle based on video and internal sensors. In addition, they can also perform additional checks on repair quotes. Using this technique, we can detect damage before it's repaired, thereby preventing fraud from occurring.

Machine learning can help insurers detect fraud by identifying patterns and trends in claims. This is especially important in the auto insurance industry where customers often feel cheated when they are overcharged for damages. Using AI to analyze a video is an effective way to detect fraud. Moreover, it provides us with a streamlined and more personalized claim process.

2. LITERATURE STUDY

Jagadevi N Kalshetty et. Al (2022) created a system based on Convolutional Neural Networks (CNN) to analyze damage to automobiles, eliminating the need for physical inspection. Yibo Wang et. Al (2017) used text mining and an LDA- and deep learning-based automobile insurance fraud detection model. Combining LDA with deep learning techniques enables the model to effectively represent automobile insurance fraud behavior. Kalpesh Patil et. Al (2017) studied the problem of car damage classification including some fine-granular categories. They tested various deep learning methods, including training CNNs from scratch, using Convolution Autoencoder-based pre-training with subsequent supervised fine-tuning, and employing transfer learning and found out that transfer learning yielded the most effective results. Jaffrey de Deijn (2018) used CNN in for car damage recognition. Using transfer learning an accuracy of 99% was achieved. This methodology was also used to classify the type, location, and size of the damage, achieving respective accuracies of 75.1%, 68.7%, and 54.2%. Chun Yan et Al. (2020) presents a UBI car insurance rate model using the CNN-HVSVM algorithm, merging CNN's feature extraction with SVM's classification stability and Hull Vector optimization. It effectively correlates driver behavior with insurance rates, offering a fair and practical solution for UBI car insurance rate determination, contributing significantly to the marketization of car insurance rates in China. Kitsuchart Pasupa et al. (2021) compared five deep learning algorithms for car part semantic segmentation, with Mask R-CNN as the baseline. HTC with ResNet-50 emerged as the top performer for instance segmentation on diverse vehicles, achieving 55.2% mean average precision with distinct labels for car sides, and 59.1% with a unified label. GCNet proved most robust in varied weather and lighting, showing less performance degradation on corrupted data. Supavee Tanutammakun (2020) study on car damage classification for car insurance market in Thailand. The damage classification accuracy stands at 74.59%. In terms of repair duration prediction, fuzzy predictions are more accurate when the highest damage percentage is close by, while non-fuzzy predictions are used when the highest damage percentage exceeds 0.5. The Mean Absolute Percentage Error (MAPE) for fuzzy predictions is 27.29%, compared to 24.16% for non-fuzzy predictions. Huosong Xia et. Al (2022) compared different deep learning algorithms for auto fraud risk identification. CNN+LSTM+DNN based model showed the highest accuracy of 89.6% with a precision of 90.7% and recall of 89.6%.

Shao Xiang et. Al (2019) a new net of lightweight convolutional neurons (CNN) with channel mixing operation and multiple size module (L-CSMS) is proposed for the recognition of the severity of plant diseases. Vibhor Kumar Vishnoi (2022) used advanced feature extraction techniques for several crop categories. Sasikala Vallabhajosyula (2021) proposed a technique for automatic detection of plant diseases using deep ensemble neural networks (DENN). DENN's performance surpasses advanced pre-formed models such as ResNet 50 and 101, InceptionV3, DenseNet 121 and 201, MobileNetV3 and NasNet. Sharifah Farhana Syed-Ab-Rahman et. al.(2021) used an in-depth two-stage CNN model for detecting plant diseases and classifying citrus diseases using leaf images. the proposed model delivers 94.37% accuracy in detection and an average precision of 95.8%. Rajeev Kumar Singh et.al(2022) explored AlexNet model for fast and accurate detection of leaf disease in maize plant. Using various iterations such as 25, 50, 75 and 100, the model achieved 99.16% precision. Shantkumari et.al (2021) proposed an adaptive snake segmentation model for segmentation and identification of infected regions. Adaptive snake segmentation model is a two-stage segmentation model, i.e. Common segmentation and absolute segmentation. Namita Sengar et.al (2017) used a threshold based on adaptive intensity for the automated segmentation of powdery mildew disease, making this method invariant for image quality and noise. The proposed method was tested on the complete set of cherry leaf images, which obtained 99% good accuracy. Edson Ampélio Pozza et.al (2022) evaluated computer vision with red- green-blue (RGB) images and machine learning algorithms for detecting seed-based fungi on common beans (Phaseolus vulgaris L.) seeds. The use of spectral indices derived from RGB imagery has extended the training capability of algorithms, demonstrated by the importance of the variables and decision tree used for target prediction by the rf and rpart1SE algorithms. Chandrasen Pandey et.al (2021) proposed an automatic, computer-based method of identifying yellow disease, also known as chlorosis, in a major pulse crop such as Vigna mungo.

Convolutional Neural Networks and its various forms have become a de facto architecture to use for various computer vision related applications by F. Sultana et. al (2018) and Zeiler M.D et. al.(2014) in recent past. The use of Convolutional Neural Networks span across domains and industries. Convolutional Neural Networks have been proven effective in medical imaging by Yamashita et. al. (2018) and Alexander Selvikvåg et. al. (2019). Gupta A. (2021) created a template for leveraging remote sensing, deep learning, and computer vision as a mechanism for future studies in a cost-effective manner. Dwivedi et. Al. (2021) demonstrated a lightweight CNN configuration that results in significantly high validation accuracy.

3. DATA AND METHODOLOGY

In this paper a VGG16 CNN model is used and trained on a custom image dataset. VGG16 is a deep convolution neural network (CNN) model which has achieved state-of-the-art performance on ImageNet Large Scale Visual Recognition Challenge 2014 tasks like object localization and classification. Comprised of 13 convolutional layers and three fully connected layers with 138 million parameters, its simple architecture and rapid training time make it a popular choice for computer vision applications such as recognizing objects in images, text or speech. ImageNet is one of the most used datasets, and deep learning models like ImageNet produce exceptional results across numerous tasks and datasets. They also have an intuitive architecture which makes them simple to learn and use, while their lower number of layers helps avoid overfitting, where too many layers could cause a model's accuracy to decline over time. To address this issue, the VGG16 utilizes gradient clipping to limit weight changes. This technique involves rescaling error derivative during backpropagation to cause less weight adjustments to be implemented into its model's weights. VGG16 offers significant improvements over AlexNet by replacing large kernel-sized filters with a sequence of three 3-by-3 kernel-sized filters, providing improved classification results. It contains 13 convolutional and max-pooling layers as well as an output layer equipped with SoftMax activation and 1000 nodes; its input images consist of 224x224 images cropped from their center location on original images. Dataset is split into training (80%) and validation (20%) datasets. Three datasets' of 1150 cars damaged images were used. Image data augmentation is used to adapt dataset to improve the model performance and reduce the bias. The three models developed are:

1. Car Damage assessment model: To detect car damage if any on the uploaded image.
2. Damage location detection model: To detect the location of damage viz. front, rear or side damage.
3. Severity assessment model: To detect the severity of the damage viz. minor, moderate, or severe.

The decision flow diagram on how these models is used is as follows (Figure 1):

New car image is uploaded as an input data. Damage detected model is executed which detects if the damage is present on the vehicle or not. If no damage is detected a new image can be uploaded to restart the process. Once the damage is detected two more models are executed viz. damage location and damage severity models. Damage location detect the location of the damage front, rear or side. Damage severity detected the severity of the damage minor, moderate or severe. These outputs can be used and checked against the damage reported by the surveyor for car insurance. For example, if the model predicts minor damage and surveyor reports severe damage, the case needs to be explored further for fraud.

4. RESULTS

Three models were developed namely damage detection, damage location and damage severity (Table1). Three different metrics were used to measure the model performance: precision, recall and F1-score. Precision of 91%, 69% and 71% were achieved for the three models respectively with 50 epochs in the model.

Figure 1. The decision flow diagram

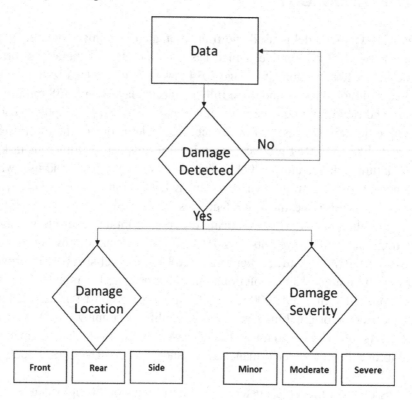

Table 1. Model accuracy

Model	Precision	Recall	F1-Score
Damage detection	0.91	0.90	0.90
Damage location	0.69	0.68	0.68
Damage Severity	0.71	0.70	0.70

5. DISCUSSION AND CONCLUSION

Computer vision helps insurers detect fraud in the claims process by analyzing images and videos of incidents. It can even spot red flags such as fake documents or altered photos; creating alerts when suspicious incidents take place can further aid insurers' fraud fighting efforts. Computer vision technology can also assist insurance businesses by automating inspections of vehicles. Automated solutions use image datasets and deep learning algorithms to detect damages on vehicles automatically and calculate their extent, helping insurance businesses avoid excessive repair claims.

The author verified the accuracy and found that CNN-based model can be used for detecting the damage on the vehicle. This functionality can be extended and used for following applications:

- Detecting insurance fraud if there is a difference between surveyor damage report and model output.

- Reduce the inaccuracy in the reports if any.
- Reduce the time required for surveyor and disbursement.
- Better customer experience.
- As more insurers adopt AI and ML solutions, they will gain access to vast amounts of data that they can then utilize to identify fraudulent activities and customers while increasing business profitability.

6. ADDITIONAL APPLICATIONS

AI can also be utilized to analyze customer sentiment and enhance customer experiences, while helping insurers determine proper policy pricing and detect red flags of fraud. Behavioral analytics are another effective tool that insurers can employ in their fight against fraud. By gathering data from social media and past experiences to assess clients' risks, behavioral analytics can detect red flags such as nervousness or rapid claim submission that may indicate fraud in insurance contracts. Vehicle insurance fraud is an all too prevalent scourge of our industry. It often takes the form of falsifying vehicle details, staging accidents to file claims with insurers, falsifying or exaggerating physical injuries suffered as well as falsifying or falsifying injuries sustained, among many other methods of misconduct. When dealing with stolen vehicles, for instance, models can be trained to recognize suspicious activity like changing vehicle colors and license plate numbers, as well as distinguish between damaged parts and non-destroyed ones - this helps prevent anyone from altering its value for increased insurance policy premiums.

Machine learning can help insurers to identify suspicious behaviors, detect trends in a customer's background check, and recommend insurance add-ons. AI is quickly gaining ground in the insurance industry. More insurers are turning to AI-powered solutions to improve customer service and identify fraud. The internet of things (IoT) has a huge impact on the insurance industry. It provides data and analytics for predictive decision-making. IoT helps insurers to improve efficiency and reduce expenses. But to use the power of the IoT, we need to make sure that our data is analyzed in real time. Using Machine Learning and Artificial Neural Networks, we can do just that. ML makes it possible to create models that predict events, such as how a traffic control system will operate. It can even identify different types of nodes on an IoT network. In addition to providing security, ML can also optimize the way sensors are used. Another important application of ML is in smart cities. City managers can use ML to find and fix problems that are affecting the quality of life. For example, the IoT can provide information on the location of pollution. This information can then be used to reduce emissions. Other applications are smart transportation, smart homes, and smart healthcare. All of these make our lives more efficient and reduces risk.

7. DECLARATION OF CONFLICTING INTERESTS

The authors have not declared any potential conflicts of interest with respect to the research, authorship and/or publication of this article. SAS software has been used for analysis and model building.

REFERENCES

Chikkamath, M., Dwivedi, D., Hirekurubar, R. B., & Thimmappa, R. (2023). Benchmarking of Novel Convolutional Neural Network Models for Automatic Butterfly Identification. In P. K. Shukla, K. P. Singh, A. K. Tripathi, & A. Engelbrecht (Eds.), *Computer Vision and Robotics. Algorithms for Intelligent Systems.* Springer. doi:10.1007/978-981-19-7892-0_27

Deijn, J. D. (2018). Automatic Car Damage Recognition using Convolutional. *Neural Networks.* Advance online publication. doi:10.1016/j.mlwa.2022.100332

Dwivedi, D., & Patil, G. (2022). Lightweight Convolutional Neural Network for Land Use Image Classification. *Journal of Advanced Geospatial Science & Technology*, 2(1), 31–48. https://jagst.utm.my/index.php/jagst/article/view/31

Gupta, A., (2021). Climate Change Monitoring Using Remote Sensing, Deep Learning, And Computer Vision. *Webology, 19*(2). https://www.webology.org/abstract.php?id=1708

Gupta, V., Sengar, N., Dutta, M., Travieso, C., & Alonso, J. (2017). Automated segmentation of powdery mildew disease from cherry leaves using image processing. *Proceedings of the 2017 IEEE International Work Conference on Bioinspired Intelligence (IWOBI),* (pp. 1-4). IEEE. https://doi.org/10.1109/IWOBI.2017.8006454

Kalshetty, J. N., Devaiah, H., Rakshith, K., Koshy, K., & Advait, N. (2022). Analysis of Car Damage for Personal Auto Claim Using CNN. In S. Shakya, V. E. Balas, S. Kamolphiwong, & K. L. Du (Eds.), Sentimental Analysis and Deep Learning (Advances in Intelligent Systems and Computing, Vol. 1408). Springer. doi:10.1007/978-981-16-5157-1_25

Liang, Q., Xiang, S., Hu, Y., Coppola, G., Zhang, D., & Sun, W. (2019). PD2SE-Net: Computer-assisted plant disease diagnosis and severity estimation network. *Computers and Electronics in Agriculture, 157,* 518–529. doi:10.1016/j.compag.2019.01.034

Lundervold, A. S., & Lundervold, A. (2019). An overview of deep learning in medical imaging focusing on MRI. *Zeitschrift für Medizinische Physik, Volume 29*(2), 102-127. doi:10.1016/j.zemedi.2018.11.002

Manjunath, C., Dwivedi, D. N., Thimmappa, R., & Vedamurthy, K. B. (2023). Detection and categorization of diseases in pearl millet leaves using novel convolutional neural network model. In *Future Farming* (Vol. 1, p. 41). Advancing Agriculture with Artificial Intelligence. doi:10.2174/9789815124729123010006

Pandey, C., Baghel, N., Dutta, M. K., Srivastava, A., & Choudhary, N. (2021). Machine learning approach for automatic diagnosis of Chlorosis in Vigna mungo leaves. *Multimedia Tools and Applications, 80*(9), 13407–13427. doi:10.100711042-020-10309-6

Pasupa, K., Kittiworapanya, P., Hongngern, N., & Woraratpanya, K. (2021). Evaluation of deep learning algorithms for semantic segmentation of car parts. *Complex & Intelligent Systems*, 8(5), 1–10. doi:10.100740747-021-00397-8

Patil, K., Kulkarni, M., Sriraman, A., & Karande, S. (2017). Deep Learning Based Car Damage Classification. *Proceedings of the 16th IEEE International Conference on Machine Learning and Applications (ICMLA)*, (pp. 50-54). IEEE. 10.1109/ICMLA.2017.0-179

Pozza, E. A., de Carvalho Alves, M., & Sanches, L. (2022). Using computer vision to identify seed-borne fungi and other targets associated with common bean seeds based on red–green–blue spectral data. *Tropical Plant Pathology*, *47*(1), 168–185. doi:10.100740858-021-00485-7

Shantkumari, M., & Uma, S. (2021). Grape leaf segmentation for disease identification through adaptive Snake algorithm model. *Multimedia Tools and Applications*, *80*(6), 1–19. doi:10.100711042-020-09853-y

Singh, R., Tiwari, A., & Gupta, R. (2022). Deep transfer modeling for classification of Maize Plant Leaf Disease. *Multimedia Tools and Applications*, *81*(5), 6051–6067. Advance online publication. doi:10.100711042-021-11763-6

Sultana, F., Sufian, A., & Dutta, P. (2018). Advancements in Image Classification using Convolutional Neural Network. *2018 Fourth International Conference on Research in Computational Intelligence and Communication Networks (ICRCICN)*, Kolkata, India. 10.1109/ICRCICN.2018.8718718

Syed-Ab-Rahman, S., Hesamian, M. H., & Prasad, M. (2021). Citrus disease detection and classification using end-to-end anchor-based deep learning model. *Applied Intelligence*, *52*(1), 927–938. doi:10.100710489-021-02452-w

Tanutammakun, S. (2020). *Car damage classification for car insurance company by using Colab with convolutional neural networks deep learning method.* https://digital.library.tu.ac.th/tu_dc/frontend/Info/item/dc:181816

Vallabhajosyula, S., Sistla, V., & Kolli, V. K. (2021). Transfer learning-based deep ensemble neural network for plant leaf disease detection. *Journal of Plant Diseases and Protection*, *129*(3), 1–14. doi:10.100741348-021-00465-8

Vishnoi, V., Kumar, K., & Kumar, B. (2022). A comprehensive study of feature extraction techniques for plant leaf disease detection. *Multimedia Tools and Applications*, *80*(1), 367–419. doi:10.100711042-021-11375-0

Wang, Y., & Xu, W. (2017). Leveraging deep learning with LDA-based text analytics to detect automobile insurance fraud. *Decision Support Systems*, *105*, 1–10. doi:10.1016/j.dss.2017.11.001

Xia, H., Zhou, Y., & Zhang, J. (2022). Auto insurance fraud identification based on a CNN-LSTM fusion deep learning model. *International Journal of Ad Hoc and Ubiquitous Computing*, *39*(1/2), 37–47. doi:10.1504/IJAHUC.2022.120943

Yamashita, R., Nishio, M., Do, R. K. G., & Togashi, K. (2018). Convolutional neural networks: An overview and application in radiology. *Insights Into Imaging*, *9*(4), 611–629. doi:10.100713244-018-0639-9 PMID:29934920

Yan, C., Wang, X., Liu, X., Liu, W., & Liu, J. (2020). Research on the UBI Car Insurance Rate Determination Model Based on the CNN-HVSVM Algorithm. *IEEE Access : Practical Innovations, Open Solutions*, *8*(1), 1–1. doi:10.1109/ACCESS.2020.3021062

Zeiler, M. D., & Fergus, R. (2014). Visualizing and Understanding Convolutional Networks. In D. Fleet, T. Pajdla, B. Schiele, & T. Tuytelaars (Eds.), Lecture Notes in Computer Science: Vol. 8689. *Computer Vision – ECCV 2014*. Springer. doi:10.1007/978-3-319-10590-1_53

ENDNOTE

[1] https://www.fbi.gov/stats-services/publications/insurance-fraud#:~:text=Costs%20of%20Fraud,the%20form%20of%20increased%20premiums

Chapter 19
Future Expectations About Big Data Analytics

Santosh Ramkrishna Durugkar
https://orcid.org/0000-0002-5079-2224
Independent Researcher, India

ABSTRACT

There is no future without big data as users, applications are continuously increasing and processed information expected to use in Healthcare, e-Commerce, Aviation, Education, etc. One can say it is just the beginning of big-data-era (BDE) computing. Everyone expects that 'ready to use' data must be available instantly and hence new techniques and algorithms must be developed to store handle and find the required 'relevant' data. However, to predict and find the relevant data many researchers suggested taking care about handling the 'context'. Many people process big datasets with missing contexts, and considering the datasets or attributes as per their convenience. In future it is also expected to focus on data quality because many applications will use this ready to process data as an input. Decision making is possible with recent machine learning applications and selection of data. It involves carefully selecting the data and removing incomplete, invalid, inaccurate data. Therefore, it is suggested to get ready for the future of big data with innovative ways, techniques, and algorithms.

1. INTRODUCTION

In many applications big data can be integrated from a variety of sources and termed *heterogeneous data* (Heterogeneous big data). However, in the future, users '*u*', and devices '*d*' will increase which generates heterogeneous data (text, audio, images, video etc.) that requires handling & retrieving important information. *Future expectation from big-data processing applications requires developing applications based on speedy algorithms representing this heterogeneous data in aggregate form.* However, a centralized coordinator will be necessary if the system involves multiple users, multiple systems etc. In the future, *proper coordination* is the key challenge in handling and processing the big-data. In the future focus should be on developing applications to handle '***contextual data***'. These applications can be termed as *Next-Generation-big-data* (NGBD) processing contextual data. Applications of context

DOI: 10.4018/979-8-3693-0413-6.ch019

data are traffic handling, weather forecasting etc. Therefore processing historical as well as current data requires developing NGBD applications. *We strongly believe these types of systems will serve the next generation of businesses.*

If observing the *trend of digitization*, one can conclude that 'n' users are increasing and the simultaneous increase in the 'n' users added large volume of data in the system. However, this large volume of data is heterogeneous because it is integrated from different sources. Transformation of the data in unique representation is necessary for analysis purposes. Big data analytics helps users fulfilling their daily business needs, identify the customer segment and forecast business strategies. Traditional learning does not support in-depth learning whereas recent machine learning (ML), deep learning (DL) uses supervised & unsupervised learning techniques. Though the datasets are large & consist of 'n' records/ values using classification methods one can classify the features of the datasets. Among those records/ values, one can select a few records as a representative value instead of considering all the records from the given dataset which is known as *sampling*.

To store this large volume of data on a bigger platform 'cloud' service is necessary and one can go for *open source cloud service providers*. Though, this big data resides on the cloud there could be some risks associated with the storage. These risks can be mitigated using the various applications such as *Cassandra service* if there is any issue with the data and safe location can be determined by querying the measurable property such as write/read errors with the disks. A future expectation about big data gives more suggestions like:

- *User must use the data more efficiently & effectively*
- *To process the large volume of data more sophisticated algorithms are required*
- *Along with these parameters there is a more requirement of more intelligent and fast machines.*

In future user's expectations will definitely increase i.e. Algorithm, Machines must process large volume of data and works on *'personalization'*. According to individual users will expect categorizing the big data into different categorizes i.e. user's specific data. This approach will give rise to *predictive analytics*. Another future expectation is migrating the large volume on the cloud. Due to rapid growth of users and data driven applications data size will also increase. Even though users will store the large volume on the cloud, it must incorporate *'data security', 'data integrity' and 'data availability'* i.e. SIA model must be incorporated in big data driven applications. Users will expect processing the large volume of data on the cloud & make it available as and when required. In this case HADOOP, NO-SQL etc. platforms can be very useful. *Transformation of large volume of data on the cloud is possible with the use of AWS, Microsoft Azure, Google Cloud platforms.* As discussed earlier, with the increasing users, application's data size will also increase and requires *skilled persons* to process this big data. These skilled persons will store, process, and analyze the large volume of data. Therefore in future *data analysts, data administrators, data scientist* roles will be high in demand. Many data driven applications and systems works on the *'data'* and it is expected future is 'data driven' which solves many business problems and will definitely help to increase the growth of businesses.

Big data could be the next basic need to enhance the performance and growth of the businesses, retaining the customers and personalizing the user's choices in ecommerce industries etc. Businesses will keep track of their customers using this 'raw data' (big data) to classify their choices, feedbacks etc. Few research studies also suggested working on 'real-time' analysis of this large volume can also transform the business, industries, & living of human beings. Even emphasis can be given on 'You-

Will-Do-It' (YWDI) approach where machine learning based applications will help users to analyze the data at their own. *Main aspect in future expectation is identifying the perfect 'stakeholders' i.e. who will be beneficial after processing of big-data. Few research studies also suggested everything (approach) has two sides i.e. positive and negative.* One can process the large volume within less time which will benefit the businesses, industries and institutes. It could have negative side too because when systems will track all the possible information of users then *providing security to this data would be the major issue.* If the personal information of any user gets compromised then it could lead to serious issue which must be avoided.

2. LITERATURE REVIEW

Future systems will process the heterogeneous data for data driven applications. Data from heterogeneous sources will be processed and presented in the aggregated format (meaningful and easy to access form for the end user). This may require processing the big-data and therefore proposed next generation big-data processing system which deals with the context data. There are many applications and will require many more in future where context data is useful such *as traffic intensity, changing users per applications, weather conditions etc. Therefore these types of systems will serve the next generation business needs.*

In the research paper (Khurana, 2014) author has pointed the change in technological era i.e. use of cloud computing and big data and these two technologies are discussed in this paper. As the term define big data, it deals with the few steps such as, collecting the raw data, processing it, forming and handling the queries (for effective retrieval) etc. These technologies are rapidly changing the face and pace of data driven applications. Cloud computing which refers to the infrastructure, hardware, software where the data will reside. There are public and private cloud service providers and this technology can be divided into the infrastructure as a service, platform as a service, and software as a service. Nowadays, AWS (amazon web services) are changing the face of data driven applications. Along with Amazon there are many cloud service providers such as Google, Microsoft etc. In this paper (Cheng et. al., 2015) authors have focused on integrity and security of the data stores on the cloud. To protect this data one can divide it in multiple parts and store on multiple locations. Securing the big data on cloud authors have proposed a trapdoor function using various data elements to analyze, compare and simulate the responses. In recent era and future applications the data sensitivity will be an important aspect in the cloud computing as big data is being used in many data sensitive applications such as data mining, real time data analysis etc. To store and handle all the queries industries are establishing the data centers – a platform to store and process the data. Authors (Wang et. al., 2017) recognized the big data characteristics such as – volume i.e. large volume of data, variety – data from multiple sources and heterogeneous data, veracity – accuracy of the data or correctness of the data and last velocity – in response to handle the query and returning the relevant results within either the stipulated time or least time than expected. By recognizing these characteristics authors reviewed these technologies i.e. big data and storing this data on clouds. Authors have proposed a framework, known as big data as a service based on the three layers (1) sensing plane (2) cloud plane, (3) application plane. A bicycle sharing system example is illustrated in this paper and the proposed framework gives some suggestions to improve the effectiveness of this system. In the research paper (Wu et. al., 2017) authors have discussed optimization of big data processing by using job sequences and pipelining. A HDM (Hierarchically Distributed Data Matrix) concept is proposed in this paper – hierarchically distributed data matrix. Authors also focused MapReduce framework and Hadoop with advantages and limitations. Authors have suggested that large volume of data is collected from heterogeneous sources. Handling such data became a difficult task. This paper focused on identifying the interesting patterns from this big data which reduces the computational efforts as the data size gets reduced. Authors also suggested using frequent pattern mining could be a useful solution implemented with MapReduce tool. Authors have also surveyed big data analytics & tools involved in this process, quantitative processes involved used to mine required data from large volume.

Important point discussed in this paper, big data processing should be fault tolerant which should be managed by these frameworks. Spark, Flink, Pregel Storm are the few available framework can be used for big data processing. However, when we talk about real world scenario, system must deal with multiple jobs. System deals with the multiple jobs where one can apply pipelining and integration. Feature extraction and classification trainer could be the important modules in this system. Pipelining concept is very useful in handling multiple data streams or multiple components. Only the concern is evolving process where components/data can be re-developed, updated or new components is added. Hence it is not an easy task to manually optimize the performance of each component as this component may have gone through evolving process. One point is clear when system deals with the real time scenario, a chain of operations i.e. pipelining is required. In the paper (Hababeh et. al., 2018) authors have discussed the impacts of the cloud technology in our daily life and keenly pointed the security issues in this regard too. A methodology is proposed in this paper suggests that, one can classify the secure data before using it for analysis or using it in redundancy operations. Hadoop a distributed file system can be used for managing, storing and use of stored data for analysis purpose in decision making operations etc. Important features of any big data projects including redundancy, handling the scalability, executing multiple tasks parallel can be achieved using Hadoop. Authors also mention the use of Map-reduce in scheduling the jobs in distributed file system. Ultimate objective discussed in this paper is securing the big data over the cloud. Authors concern is to secure the data when it is stored on the storage devices, when someone is using it for analysis and when data is in transmission. Along with security paper focuses on access control mechanism (ACL).

This paper (Salloum et. al., 2019) focuses on the data partition as the volume could be so large to handle. Therefore, the authors have suggested, strategies need to be designed to partition the data. This partition could be in terms of consistent data blocks. A model proposed in this paper is based on random sample partition and the blocks generated will be known as RSP blocks. These blocks will act as a representative block of the data set and can be used for predictive modeling. Block-level sampling is proposed in this paper to support data analysis. As discussed earlier, RSP blocks are the representative blocks for the entire data set. Hence, these RSP blocks are quite similar to record-level sampling. During data analysis, samples from these RSP blocks will be selected and the analysis phase completes. This process is executed in parallel to every selected RSP blocks. Integration phase integrate all the outputs by producing the desired result for the entire data. Authors have used data sets up to 1TB, executed the proposed algorithm using RSP blocks and concluded that only a few RSP blocks are required to represent the entire data set. This idea can be termed cluster computing as 'n' RSP blocks are used in parallel and estimation will be done.

This paper (Yang et.al., 2019) focused on the big data acquired in sensing systems. Once the data is received it can be processed but, one important point is **errors encountered** during **sampling and data transfer** from remote systems/devices to the integration unit. To improve the accuracy these errors must be removed, however this task is challenging as data considered is received from sensing devices. Sensing devices senses the environmental data that is not repeatable which needs to be discussed in error removal. This paper emphasizes on accuracy using error recovery in cloud systems. One more important research scope is identified by the author, scalability – if the devices are 'n' and sensed data is large enough then fast error recovery mechanism is necessary. To achieve this speedy recovery, prediction model is proposed by the authors using approximation. To achieve this Euclidean distance metric is used to predict the relevance and error recovery. Authors have given 'n' examples in this paper to illustrate how big data (Terabytes, Exabyte) is generated day by day which became a challenging task to capture, manage and process. It requires strong platform to process the same within a stipulated time. Another important point discussed by the authors is, reliability – with reference to processing the large volume of data within a time requires strong reliability. Meaning is that, algorithms or systems should follow common platform/ standards which help to increase the reliability. To implement this system one has to study data processing and its steps. In data processing error detection and recovery is important to improve the quality of data. Data processing must ensure cleaning of the captured data with lossless strategy.

Authors (Mahmud et.al, 2020) have discussed data partitioning and sampling methods in this paper. We must study shared nothing, shared memory architecture styles used in distributed computing. Partitioning and sampling methods are used in cluster computing to speed up the query processing. In this paper authors have elaborated the working of Hadoop clusters. A sampling method, random sampling partition RSP is also proposed by the authors. Authors also suggested that, to improve the performance and getting better results scaling and speeding up requires strong algorithms. A common strategy that can be used is, divide-and-conquer to form the clusters. MapReduce and Hadoop can be used for implementing the shared nothing architecture. Shared nothing architecture where individual node does not depends on the data and resources. In this paper, authors have discussed an approximate computing which suggests use only selective data instead of using the whole data and producing the approximate results. Authors (Liu & Zhang, 2020) have mentioned the increasing rate of data which brings few challenges and opportunities too. Strong platform i.e. memory, I/O, processing is necessary to process this data. Instead of processing the whole data authors have suggested to use samples. Sampling is nothing but selecting representative data and processing it further. Search engines are dealing with enormous data daily and processes the end user's query within very less time. It is possible just because of the strong platforms and algorithms used to process this large volume of data.

Authors (Sellami et.al, 2020) have proposed a new scalable service approach in this paper. Providing the big-data services through is based on cloud computing and extending to this cloud computing approach authors have proposed a new model based on fuzzy logic in this paper. Big data service is nothing but providing and managing the data. To provide the service various factors needs to be considered such as scalability i.e. large volume of data from 'n' sources, storing this large volume of data, strong algorithm to manage this large volume of data. Software tools such as MapReduce, Spark and Hadoop. Mainly working on the distributed processing systems as the data may reside on the 'n' nodes/ sources and may distributed across the network. Therefore, it become a difficult task to retain the data on these distributed nodes, maintaining the redundancy, updating the results correctly and efficiently, integrating the required data within less time etc. are the important factors affects the quality of service. Authors have also discussed the on-demand services where 'data' is demanded in real time manner. On-demand and big-data service may have few constraints as discussed earlier. However, as the data is large in size/ volume i.e. it may have 'n' datasets and 'm' records. Identifying the correlation between them is important task to reduce the processing time. Providing the data security is another important factor discussed in this paper.

In this paper authors (Zhou & Zhao, 2020) have studied multimedia big data processing. A back-propagation algorithm is trained to handle the errors encountered during processing the big data. Authors have focused on the real time dealing and its complexity due to high dimensionality. Classifying this high dimensional data is somewhat critical task and strong platform i.e. strong system with memory and storage capacity is required. Authors have focused on the multimedia big data processing and integrating the same with reduced errors. Important part in this case is to process the large scale data as objective is to reduce the query computation time. Authors have proposed a radial basis function neural network based on MapReduce cloud computing cluster approach. Important point in this paper is hardware requirements must be strong to deal with large scale data. Authors (Ban et.al, 2015) have focused on the query optimization in distributed databases. Optimizing the query is necessary to speed up the query and increasing the throughput. Authors also emphasized in the communication cost between 'n' devices / nodes. A query mechanism with multi-join technique is proposed in this paper. As the system deals with large volume of data and giving the results to the user within minimum time is necessary, QEP should be ready and executed immediately. This QEP is nothing but optimizing the query (using multi-join condition as stated in the paper) and returning the results to the end users. Authors (Goldin et. al., 2017) have focused on cloud computing infrastructure necessary for big data analysis. Authors have discussed the use of historical data used to train the machine learning based models. Processing the large volume of data is somewhat critical and requires strong hardware platform i.e. memory, processor and other independent devices required if any. Fetching and storing real time data is an important task. Hence, speed up and scale up are important parameters used to decide the performance of the system. In this paper authors (Harerimana et. al. 2018) have discussed big data analytics with respect to healthcare / patient's data. This data is large in size and processing it requires for identifying the better relations. Volume, velocity and variety are the important characteristics of the big data. Healthcare data is sensitive data and required to handle carefully. Dealing with the big data, processing it and deriving the required, accurate and meaningful relations require computational intelligence. This computational intelligence is nothing but strong platform and efficient algorithms. Authors have also noted that existing healthcare infrastructure must be capable enough to handle and process this big data. Integrating data from 'n' sources / devices, processing it and providing the conclusions/decisions in real time is required. MRI scans, ECG, EEG, CT scan, and X- Ray etc. are sources of the data in healthcare industry. Usually, physicians are manually checking these records and giving the medical treatments. Along with these records basic records are also maintained in the hospitals. Hence, large data needs to be stored and processed. At this stage, computational intelligence is applicable.

Use of Apache Hadoop system is discussed in this paper (Thind & Simon, 2019). Cloud systems are the frameworks or you can say the platform where you are doing some operations. Big data is large in size and one can store it on the cloud, manage it and process it whenever required. To manage the large volume of data collected from 'n' sources one can use Hadoop which is open source software. Heterogeneous data i.e. audio, video, text, emails, sensory data etc. collected from 'n' sources and stored on one unique file system. Using Hadoop these datasets are accessible and can be processed as per requirement. In this paper authors have integrated 02 approaches big data and cloud systems. With the cloud system architecture data (big data) stored can be accessible anytime, anywhere.

In this paper authors (Singh, S., & Singh, N. 2012) have explained different trends in big data computing. Daily large volume of data is generated from 'n' sources i.e. businesses, social media, emails, e-commerce etc. Big data computing deals with volume, variety, velocity. Volume is nothing but the size of the data, variety is heterogeneous data and velocity is how your system processes this data i.e. either in batch processing or in real time.

3. FUTURE EXPECTATIONS

3.1 User's Trust

However, user's 'trust' (Cheng et. al., 2015) is necessary to share, process, and analyze the large data associated with them. The main reason is *security breach* where users will feel someone unauthenticated can misuse their 'personal data'. Therefore, in future there would be strong demand in *security applications* to protect the user's data in order to maintain data's integrity, and confidentiality intact and make it available to the concern user as and when required.

E.g. If someone considers a healthcare sector where there is a rapid growth of wearable devices. These devices continuously monitor and gather various parameters of human being. It helps monitoring the critical patients in real time and passes them to the concerned authorities. These devices are playing important role in healthcare sector and in future there use of wearable devices would surely increases. Increase in wearable devices will also increase the data because to store this large volume of data platforms like cloud will play a crucial role. Similar to this there would be increase in data related to aviation sector, automobile sector, real estate etc.

3.2 Sampling

Sampling could be other future expectation about big-data and there are many sampling techniques (Salloum et. al., 2019; Mahmud et.al, 2020; Liu & Zhang, 2020) those can be integrated with the big-data applications. E.g. *Block level sampling* can be used where RSP blocks are the representative blocks for the entire data set. Hence, these RSP blocks are quite similar to *record level sampling. During data analysis samples from these RSP blocks will be selected and analysis phase completes.* Integration phase used in this sampling is integrating all the outputs and representing it in the aggregate form. This idea can be termed as *cluster computing* as '*n*' RSP blocks can be used in parallel.

However, it is suggested that user must target the population, its size and method to be used to apply the sampling. Out of large volume user must focus on few samples and then apply any existing sampling technique to process the selected data. This step can be integrated in the initial stage of data analysis i.e. data selection. It reduces the time complexity of the data analysis methods and algorithms. Other advantage of sampling is, it helps in data profiling which is the primary need of data driven applications.

3.2.1 Segmentation

Processing the large volume of data and creating different discrete groups based on available parameters is known as segmentation. E.g. one can segment the input data based on parameters like gender, geographical location, age etc. Important factor in segmentation is creating the groups by setting the 'threshold' values. One can find such approach is very useful in 'association rule mining', 'sentiment analysis', 'identifying the user's behavior' etc. Segmentation will divide the records/data into different discrete groups.

3.3 Scalability

One more future research area where focus must be given is- scalability. If the data is generated by 'n' users it is expected future systems must be highly scalable. In highly scalable future system handling big-data another expectation would be faster error recovery. In near future data size will increase in proportion to the internet users & numerous applications. "Data storage", "Data cleaning", & "Data freshness" are the important research areas must be focused in order to deal with the Big-data (Hababeh et. al., 2018). In future it is also required to reduce the cost of storage by developing applications focusing on storing & analyzing the data. Even organizations can prefer on-premise storage solution or storing the big-data on the cloud by dividing it into chunks (parts).

3.4 Strong Legislative Framework

In future strong legislative framework/rules must be applied to protect the personal data from hackers. Future systems must be capable enough to handle the large volume of big-data & these systems must prevent unauthorized disclosure, collection and exploitation of user's personal data. Availability of the relevant data on right time from the large volume would be another future expectation about the big-data. It will be more useful in forecasting & predicting in the applications such as weather forecasting etc. To fulfill all the above mentioned expectations intelligent data professionals will be required to collect, process and analyze the big-data. Selection of the right tool to handle big-data would be another expectation of the users. There are many existing tools available to process & analyze the big-data. In future there would be more additional tools those can be developed to handle the big-data. Therefore, a guideline to select the perfect tool is necessary with the help of devising a selection based framework. Motivating the people to change according to future trends of the big-data would be more challenging task. Many people, organizations will resist changing as they may fail to understand the importance of big-data. In future 'transforming' the businesses will is more challenging task & expert data professionals must be in leadership roles of the organizations. Advantage of such systems is it works on the context data as compared to handling large volume of historical data less efforts will be required. (We may use historical data if required to add the relevance in our results)

Next gen big-data processing system we will work on following points:

- *Acquiring the context data*
- *Storing it and integrating it*
- *Processing it*
- *Applying reasoning algorithms*
- *Representing it in abstract meaningful form*
- *Using matching functions f_x to find relevance*
- *Applying database triggers and schema modeling for effective query optimization*

3.5 CIA Model

Other future expectation about big-data is very important i.e. maintaining the data security i.e. confidentiality, integrity and availability. Hence, maintaining its 'consistency' will be a critical task because if system fails to maintain the data consistency then erroneous results will be produced. Future systems

Figure 1. CIA model

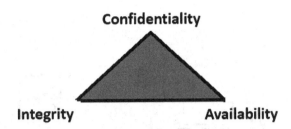

will process this data from low granularity to higher granularity. One more future expectation about the big-data is data protection. A large volume of data will be processed by the future systems & users will expect performance of the system must not be degraded. A framework/model must be designed to tackle the abnormal behavior i.e. unusual activities, attacks etc. Hence, risk assessment would be another expectation about big-data. CIA model can be explained with the help of triangular representation as shown in figure 1.

By including this CIA in the application one can protect only the unique path of the 'cloud' where the data is stored. However there is provision in special application requirement to protect the key data. In this proposed scheme to increase the reliability data or some data parts can be copied and will be stored on different storage parts. Unique data path, including the replicated data path will be protected. Implementing the trapdoor function to strengthen the security authors has implemented the identity based encryption algorithm. Before accessing and sharing the data parts one has to prove its data identity then only access will be granted. Big- data protection is necessary in every application however, while processing the large volume of data performance of the system must not be degraded. After selection of the required attributes ranking of the same can be conducted. A framework / model designed for the proposed system must tackle the abnormal behavior i.e. unusual activities, attacks etc. Hence, risk assessment needs criteria must be defined where one can categorize the risks in terms of low risks, medium risks, negligible risks, high risks etc. Hence, authentication and authorization must be a part of any big data driven application. Additionally, it is also advisable to go for regular 'security audit' and implementation of the 'central administration'. Communication, access and storage must involve a tightened security and all the files could be encrypted using any strong encryption algorithm. It is also suggested to add a 'layer' with your application to track the 'behavior' of the users i.e. implementing 'user behavior analysis'.

3.6 Highly Specialized Predictive Analytical Approach

As discussed in the earlier sections applications of the big-data are more and continuously increasing. In future almost every organization, institute and sector will focus on big data to get the rid of customer retention. Everyone expects customers must remain associated with their businesses which ultimately help in growth of the business. Healthcare, Aviation, Pharmaceuticals, and Education etc. will utilized the big data for 'predictive analytics'. In this 'predictive' approach large volume of data must be processed by the system to get the highly relevant data.

Figure 2. Cloud storage

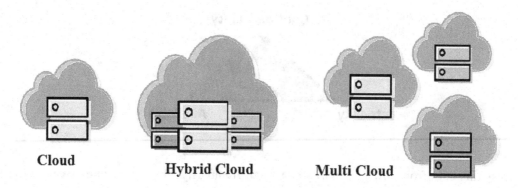

Cloud   Hybrid Cloud   Multi Cloud

3.7 Driving the Autonomous Computing

Many research studies focused on autonomous computing in various sectors like driverless cars, autonomous ships, autonomous machines etc. In future Artificial intelligence and Machine learning will the drive the businesses and will consume large volume of data. Therefore, in future business will expect the maximum uses of big data to be used in autonomous computing.

3.8 Multiple Cloud

Data size will be almost 'double' in future and therefore it will be necessary migrating large volume of data on different clouds. Hence, in future 'multiple clouds' environment will be used to store, process and analyze the big data. Experts from different domains like 'cloud computing', 'heterogeneous computing', 'data analysis' etc. will be high in demand. Figure 2 illustrates the use of single, hybrid and multi cloud architectures.

As the data size will increase, in future many organizations will try to outsource the 'data cleaning' task to third parties. Cloud computing which refers to the infrastructure, hardware, software where the data will reside. There are public and private cloud service providers and this technology can be divided into the infrastructure as a service, platform as a service, and software as a service. Nowadays, AWS amazon web services are changing the face of data driven applications. Along with Amazon there are many cloud service providers such as Google, Microsoft etc.

However, there are many attributes are associated with this technology such as

- *Cost*
- *Ease of use*
- *Elasticity*
- *Performance*
- *Security*
- *Location*
- *Reliability*
- *Flexibility*

Figure 3. Unstructured data

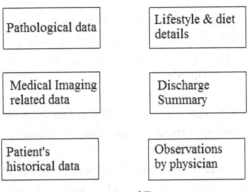

Unstructured Data

3.9 New Tools Understandable by Non-Technical Persons

As discussed in the earlier sections, experts will be high in demand to use big-data driven applications. However, developers must consider the requirements of non-technical persons. It is necessary to know and enlist all the requirements of all the 'stakeholders'. It is expected that in future everyone will use big-data driven applications for 'predictive' and 'prescriptive' analysis. New tools must help all the users in 'decision making' which would help in retaining the customers, improving the business strategies etc.

3.9.1 Predictive modeling

Following are the types of predictive analysis models -

- *Classification model*
- *Outlier's model*
- *Clustering model*
- *Time series analysis*

To develop the model based on predictive analytics user can use any algorithm like K-means algorithm, generalized linear model, Gradient boost model, and Random forest etc. It helps analyzing the historical data in order to identify the different possible future trends and patterns. It enables user better insights to predict the possible future outcomes. User can use any existing methods like time series analysis, logistic regression, neural networks etc. to develop a predictive model. 'Predictive modeling' is very useful in multiple application areas like disaster recovery, town planning, construction (civil works), change management etc.

3.10 Unstructured Data

Large volume of data can be integrated from different sources and requires categorizing it into 'structure', 'unstructured' and 'semi-structured' data. Therefore, new tools must help users handling the large volume and processing the 'unstructured data' (if present). Figure 3 illustrates the example of unstructured data.

This step is necessary to enhance the algorithm's efficiency and effectively producing the desired results. There are many tools available in the market to deal with the structured and unstructured data like, *Power BI, KNIME, Tableau, Apache Hadoop, Rapid Miner, Apache Spark* etc. However, focus should be given on handling the unstructured, structured and semi-structured data. There are tools discussed earlier helps processing these types of data.

E.g. **Sentiment analysis**- it is the key concept in many machine learning applications which identifies the *interest*s of the users. Sentiment analysis driven applications will process this data and identifies different factors affecting the possible growth of business. It is possible with the help of user's feedbacks, comments and ratings. Machine learning algorithms can be applied to process the big data and retrieve different interesting patterns. It helps businesses to improvise their weaker sections by carefully studying the ratings, feedbacks and comments. It is also very important in order to retain the employees by collecting their feedbacks about organization's policies.

3.11 Data's freshness

In future all the big data driven applications will demand 'data freshness' because it will be the basic need of all the businesses. A cloud system based on like 'snowflake' focuses on reducing the latency. This will surely results in higher availability of 'real time' data. Once the real time fresh data is available, it is possible to develop a good *automated decision making systems*. However, user must carefully select the data based on quality and there should be a good data governance policy implemented in the organization. In future to process the real time as well as data from clouds, focus should be on developing applications based on 'no-code' policies. It means any user can easily process the large volume of data using such tools. However, user should have 'proactive approach' to measure the data's freshness. It is up to the user to compare the retrieved fresh data with the existing available data. Though one can say getting the real time fresh data is easier, but there are few challenges in data freshness as listed below-

- *Source of the data changing frequently*
- *Consumption patterns also changes*
- *Dealing with above mentioned issues will take more time*

Hence, organizations must follow guidelines to deal with data freshness. It may involve source analysis, integrating the data from multiple sources, monitoring the data integration, training to the employees etc.

3.12 Key drivers behind the big data analytics

Following are the key drivers behind big data analytics market and must be study, analyzed and implement carefully.

- *Maximum people are adopting IoT enabled devices and technologies.*

- *Digitized records of people.*
- *Reducing cost of electronic devices.*
- *Increasing data driven applications.*
- *Increasing knowledge about recent technologies.*
- *AI (artificial intelligence), ML (machine learning) and automated solutions are available and can be accessed easily.*
- *Easier access of cloud computing services*
- *Affordable solutions to big data*

4. CONCLUSION

With the help of recent technologies like AI (artificial intelligence), and ML (machine learning) new big-data driven applications can be developed. Data can be heterogeneous or homogeneous and divided into structured, unstructured and semi-structured data. Future big data driven applications must process the big data accordingly i.e. by considering all types of data. Future applications must incorporate high level of security protecting the data from unauthorized access.

In future, larger storage space (multiple and hybrid cloud) and skilled persons will be required to process the big data. Every stakeholder will expect '*ready to analyze*' data (processed and cleaned) and therefore can outsource few tasks to third parties. Outsourcing benefits in multiple ways i.e. reduced time to clean and processed the data, and focusing on the selected parameters. There could be a dramatic change in the '*decision making*' applications due to new tools developed to process the big data. '*Big data*' would be the next primary requirement for many businesses, institutes, and organizations. Hence, data experts will be high in demand and more technical as well as non-technical persons must be trained accordingly.

REFERENCES

Ageed, Z. S., Zeebaree, S. R., Sadeeq, M. M., Kak, S. F., Yahia, H. S., Mahmood, M. R., & Ibrahim, I. M. (2021). Comprehensive survey of big data mining approaches in cloud systems. *Qubahan Academic Journal, 1*(2), 29–38. doi:10.48161/qaj.v1n2a46

Ahmed, E. S. A., & Saeed, R. A. (2014). A survey of big data cloud computing security. *International Journal of Computer Science and Software Engineering, 3*(1), 78–85.

Ban, W., Lin, J., Tong, J., & Li, S. (2015, December). Query optimization of distributed database based on parallel genetic algorithm and max-min ant system. In *2015 8th International Symposium on Computational Intelligence and Design (ISCID)* (Vol. 2, pp. 581-585). IEEE. 10.1109/ISCID.2015.199

Cheng, H., Rong, C., Hwang, K., Wang, W., & Li, Y. (2015). Secure big data storage and sharing scheme for cloud tenants. *China Communications, 12*(6), 106–115. doi:10.1109/CC.2015.7122469

Goldin, E., Feldman, D., Georgoulas, G., Castano, M., & Nikolakopoulos, G. (2017, July). Cloud computing for big data analytics in the Process Control Industry. In *2017 25th Mediterranean Conference on Control and Automation (MED)* (pp. 1373-1378). IEEE. 10.1109/MED.2017.7984310

Hababeh, I., Gharaibeh, A., Nofal, S., & Khalil, I. (2018). An integrated methodology for big data classification and security for improving cloud systems data mobility. *IEEE Access : Practical Innovations, Open Solutions, 7,* 9153–9163. doi:10.1109/ACCESS.2018.2890099

Harerimana, G., Jang, B., Kim, J. W., & Park, H. K. (2018). Health big data analytics: A technology survey. *IEEE Access : Practical Innovations, Open Solutions, 6,* 65661–65678. doi:10.1109/ACCESS.2018.2878254

Javadpour, A., Abadi, A. M. H., Rezaei, S., Zomorodian, M., & Rostami, A. S. (2022). Improving load balancing for data-duplication in big data cloud computing networks. *Cluster Computing, 25*(4), 2613–2631. doi:10.100710586-021-03312-5

Khurana, A. (2014). Bringing big data systems to the cloud. *IEEE Cloud Computing, 1*(3), 72–75. doi:10.1109/MCC.2014.47

Liu, Z., & Zhang, A. (2020). Sampling for big data profiling: A survey. *IEEE Access : Practical Innovations, Open Solutions, 8,* 72713–72726. doi:10.1109/ACCESS.2020.2988120

Mahmud, M. S., Huang, J. Z., Salloum, S., Emara, T. Z., & Sadatdiynov, K. (2020). A survey of data partitioning and sampling methods to support big data analysis. *Big Data Mining and Analytics, 3*(2), 85–101. doi:10.26599/BDMA.2019.9020015

Salloum, S., Huang, J. Z., & He, Y. (2019). Random sample partition: A distributed data model for big data analysis. *IEEE Transactions on Industrial Informatics, 15*(11), 5846–5854. doi:10.1109/TII.2019.2912723

Sellami, M., Mezni, H., & Hacid, M. S. (2020). On the use of big data frameworks for big service composition. *Journal of Network and Computer Applications, 166,* 102732. doi:10.1016/j.jnca.2020.102732

Singh, S., & Singh, N. (2012). Big data analytics, 2012 International Conference on Communication. *Information Computing Technology (ICCICT 2012), 4.*

Thind, J. S., & Simon, R. (2019, June). Implementation of Big Data in cloud computing with optimized Apache Hadoop. In *2019 3rd International conference on Electronics, Communication and Aerospace Technology (ICECA)* (pp. 997-1001). IEEE. 10.1109/ICECA.2019.8821854

Wang, X., Yang, L. T., Liu, H., & Deen, M. J. (2017). A big data-as-a-service framework: State-of-the-art and perspectives. *IEEE Transactions on Big Data, 4*(3), 325–340. doi:10.1109/TBDATA.2017.2757942

Wu, D., Zhu, L., Lu, Q., & Sakr, S. (2017). HDM: A composable framework for big data processing. *IEEE Transactions on Big Data, 4*(2), 150–163. doi:10.1109/TBDATA.2017.2690906

Yang, C., Huang, Q., Li, Z., Liu, K., & Hu, F. (2017). Big Data and cloud computing: Innovation opportunities and challenges. *International Journal of Digital Earth, 10*(1), 13–53. doi:10.1080/17538947.2016.1239771

Yang, C., Xu, X., Ramamohanarao, K., & Chen, J. (2019). A scalable multi-data sources based recursive approximation approach for fast error recovery in big sensing data on cloud. *IEEE Transactions on Knowledge and Data Engineering, 32*(5), 841–854. doi:10.1109/TKDE.2019.2895612

Zhou, Z., & Zhao, L. (2020). Cloud computing model for big data processing and performance optimization of multimedia communication. *Computer Communications*, *160*, 326–332. doi:10.1016/j.comcom.2020.06.015

KEY TERMS & DEFINITIONS

Big Data: It refers to large volume of data and has characteristics such as volume, variety and veracity etc.

Classification: It is a supervised method used in machine learning to classify the given input data.

Contextual Data: Data refers to specific events, thing or related to any person.

Heterogeneous Data: Data from various sources and may be in different formats.

Homogeneous Data: Data integrated in same type or format.

Pattern Mining: Knowing the trends during analysis of the data used for future predictions.

Regression: It is a method used in machine learning to predict the relationship between independent and dependent variables.

Compilation of References

Abdul Hussien, T., Rahma, A. M. S., & Abdul Wahab, H. B. (1897). Recommendation Systems For E-commerce Systems An Overview. *Journal of Physics: Conference Series*, *1897*(1), 012024. doi:10.1088/1742-6596/1897/1/012024

Abiodun, O. I., Jantan, A., Omolara, A. E., Dada, K. V., Mohamed, N. A., & Arshad, H. (2018). State-of-the-art in artificial neural network applications: A survey. *Heliyon*, *4*(11), e00938. doi:10.1016/j.heliyon.2018.e00938 PMID:30519653

Abrahiem, R. (2007). A new generation of middleware solutions for a near-real time data warehousing architecture. In *IEEE International Conference on Electro/Information Technology*, (pp. 192-197). IEEE. 10.1109/EIT.2007.4374453

Aburomman, A. A., & Reaz, M. B. I. (2017). A Novel Weighted Support Vector Machines MulticlassClassifierBasedonDifferentialEvolutionforIntrusionDetectionSystems. *Information Sciences*.

Adel, A. (2022). Future of industry 5.0 in society: Human-centric solutions, challenges and prospective research areas. *Journal of Cloud Computing (Heidelberg, Germany)*, *11*(1), 1–15. doi:10.118613677-022-00314-5 PMID:36101900

Adweek. (2023, October 9). How Indeed Is Growing Audience and Revenue With Disney's Data Clean Room. *Adweek*. https://www.adweek.com/programmatic/how-indeed-is-growing-audience-and-revenue-with-disneys-data-clean-room/

Ageed, Z. S., Zeebaree, S. R., Sadeeq, M. M., Kak, S. F., Yahia, H. S., Mahmood, M. R., & Ibrahim, I. M. (2021). Comprehensive survey of big data mining approaches in cloud systems. *Qubahan Academic Journal*, *1*(2), 29–38. doi:10.48161/qaj.v1n2a46

Agrawal, R., & Srikant, R. (2000, June). Privacy-preserving data mining. *SIGMOD Record*, *29*(2), 439–450. doi:10.1145/335191.335438

Aheleroff, S., Huang, H., Xu, X., & Zhong, R. Y. (2022). Toward sustainability and resilience with Industry 4.0 and Industry 5.0. *Frontiers in Manufacturing Technology*, 2, 951643. doi:10.3389/fmtec.2022.951643

Ahmad, M. (2023a). Connecting People and Places: How Citizen Diplomacy and VGI Are Strengthening Disaster Response and Community Development. In Global Perspectives on the Emerging Trends in Public Diplomacy (pp. 195–226). IGI Global.

Ahmad, M., & Ali, A. (2023). Mapping the Future of Sustainable Development Through Cloud-Based Solutions: A Case Study of OpenStreetMap. In Promoting Sustainable Management Through Technological Innovation (pp. 153–176). IGI Global. doi:10.4018/978-1-6684-9979-5.ch011

Ahmad, A., Paul, A., & Rathore, M. M. (2016). An efficient divide-and-conquer approach for big dataanalyticsinmachine-to-machine communication. *Neurocomputing*, *174*, 439–453. doi:10.1016/j.neucom.2015.04.109

Ahmad, M. (2023b). Exploring the Role of OpenStreetMap in Mapping Religious Tourism in Pakistan for Sustainable Development. In *Experiences, Advantages, and Economic Dimensions of Pilgrimage Routes*. IGI Global. doi:10.4018/978-1-6684-9923-8.ch002

Ahmad, M. (2023c). Unleashing Business Potential: Harnessing OpenStreetMap for Intelligent Growth and Sustainability. In *Data-Driven Intelligent Business Sustainability*. IGI Global. doi:10.4018/979-8-3693-0049-7.ch013

Ahmad, S., Lavin, A., Purdy, S., & Agha, Z. (2017). Unsupervised real-time anomaly detection for streaming data. *Neurocomputing*, *262*, 134–147. doi:10.1016/j.neucom.2017.04.070

Ahmad, W., & Quadri, B. S. M. K. (2015). Big Data promises value: Is hardware technology taken onboard? *Industrial Management & Data Systems*, *115*(9).

Ahmed, E. S. A., & Saeed, R. A. (2014). A survey of big data cloud computing security. *International Journal of Computer Science and Software Engineering*, *3*(1), 78–85.

Ahmed, E., Yaqoob, I., Hashem, I. A. T., Khan, I., Ahmed, A. I. A., Imran, M., & Vasilakos, A. V. (2017). The role of big data analytics in Internet of Things. *Computer Networks*, *129*, 459–471. doi:10.1016/j.comnet.2017.06.013

Ahmed, M. A., & Al-Jamimi, H. A. (2013). Machine learning approaches for predicting sofware maintainability: A fuzzy-based transparent model. *IET Software*, *7*(6), 317–326. doi:10.1049/iet-sen.2013.0046

Ahmed, M., Mahmood, A. N., & Hu, J. (2016). A survey of network anomaly detection techniques. *Journal of Network and Computer Applications*, *60*, 19–31. doi:10.1016/j.jnca.2015.11.016

Akter, S., Wamba, S. F., Gunasekaran, A., Dubey, R., & Childe, S. J. (2016). How to improve firm performance using big data analytics capability and business strategy alignment? *International Journal of Production Economics*, *182*, 113–131. doi:10.1016/j.ijpe.2016.08.018

Al Mubarak, M. (2022). Sustainably Developing in a Digital World: Harnessing artificial intelligence to meet the imperatives of work-based learning in Industry 5.0. *Development and Learning in Organizations: An International Journal*.

Al-Abassi, A., Karimipour, H., Pajouh, H., Dehghantanha, A., & Parizi, RM., (2020). Industrial big data analytics: challenges and opportunities. In: Handbook of big data privacy; (pp. 37–61). Springer.

Al-Dulaimi, A. H. (2020). Big data: Definition, characteristics, life cycle, applications, and challenges. *IOP Conference Series. Materials Science and Engineering*, *769*(1), 012007. doi:10.1088/1757-899X/769/1/012007

Alghamdi, T. A., & Javaid, N. (2022). A survey of preprocessing methods used for analysis of big data originated from smart grids. *IEEE Access : Practical Innovations, Open Solutions*, *10*, 29149–29171. doi:10.1109/ACCESS.2022.3157941

Ali, F. S. E. (2014). A survey of real-time data warehouse and ETL. *International Scientific Journal of Management Information Systems*, *9*(3), 03-09.

Alnoukari, M., & Hanano, A. (2017). Integration of business intelligence with corporate strategic management. *Journal of Intelligence Studies in Business*, *7*(2), 5–16. doi:10.37380/jisib.v7i2.235

Al-Qudah, D. A., Al-Zoubi, A. M., Castillo-Valdivieso, P. A., & Faris, H. (2020). Sentiment Analysis for e-Payment Service Providers Using Evolutionary eXtreme Gradient Boosting. *IEEE Access : Practical Innovations, Open Solutions*, *8*, 189930–189944. doi:10.1109/ACCESS.2020.3032216

Alves, J., Lima, T. M., & Gaspar, P. D. (2023). Is Industry 5.0 a Human-Centred Approach? A Systematic Review. *Processes (Basel, Switzerland)*, *11*(1), 193. doi:10.3390/pr11010193

Alzubi, J., Nayyar, A., & Kumar, A. (2018). Machine Learning from Theory to Algorithms: An Overview. *Journal of Physics: Conference Series, 1142*, 012012. doi:10.1088/1742-6596/1142/1/012012

Ama, A., Mulya, D., Astuti, Y., & Prasadhya, I. (2022). Analisis Sentimen Customer Feedback Tokopedia Menggunakan Algoritma Naïve Bayes. *Jurnal Sistem Komputer dan Informatika (JSON), 4*(1), 50-50. https://doi: . doi:10.30865/json.v4i1.4783

Anand, D. D. (2021). Implementation and Analysis of Sentimental Analysis on Facial Expression Using HAAR Cascade Methods. [TURCOMAT]. *Turkish Journal of Computer and Mathematics Education, 12*(2), 2787–2793. doi:10.17762/turcomat.v12i2.2308

Ankorion, I. (2005). Change data capture efficient ETL for real-time BI. *Information & Management, 15*(1), 36.

Ansari, O. B., & Binninger, F. M. (2022). A deep learning approach for estimation of price determinants. *International Journal of Information Management Data Insights, 2*(2), 100101. Advance online publication. doi:10.1016/j.jjimei.2022.100101

Arifianto, A., Suyanto, S., Sirwan, A., Desrul, D. R., Prakoso, I. D., Guntara, F. F., Hidayati, D. C., & Murti, R. S. (2020). Developing an LSTM-based Classification Model of IndiHome Customer Feedbacks. *International Conference on Data Science and Its Applications (ICoDSA),* (pp. 1-5). IEEE. 10.1109/ICoDSA50139.2020.9212863

Asghar, M. Z., Subhan, F., Ahmad, H., Khan, W. Z., Hakak, S., Gadekallu, T. R., & Alazab, M. (2021). Senti-eSystem: A sentiment-based eSystem-using hybridized fuzzy and deep neural network for measuring customer satisfaction. *Software, Practice & Experience, 51*(3), 571–594. doi:10.1002pe.2853

Asthakhuroh, A., Komarudin, R., & Kholifah, D. (2023). Sentiment Analysis with A Case Study of Practice Card on Twitter social media Using Naive Bayes Method. *Jurnal Techno Nusa Mandiri, 20*(1), 8–13. doi:10.33480/techno.v20i1.3709

Astuti, Y., Wahyuni, S. N., Maulina, D., & Sidiq, F. M. (2022). The Data Leakage Sentiment Analysis Using Naive Bayes Algorithm Based on Machine Learning Approach. *5th International Seminar on Research of Information Technology and Intelligent Systems (ISRITI),* (pp. 215-220). IEEE. 10.1109/ISRITI56927.2022.10052877

Astuti, Y., Yova, R., Faris, S., & Aldiansah, P. (2023). Sentiment Analysis of Electricity Company Service Quality Using Naïve Bayes. [Rekayasa Sistem Dan Teknologi Informasi]. *Jurnal RESTI, 7*(2), 389–396. doi:10.29207/resti.v7i2.4627

Attaallah, A., Alsuhabi, H., Shukla, S., Kumar, R., Gupta, B. K., & Khan, R. A. (2022). Analyzing the Big Data Security through a Unified Decision-Making Approach. *Intelligent Automation & Soft Computing, 32*(2), 1071–1088. doi:10.32604/iasc.2022.022569

Attunity. (2009). *Efficient and Real Time Data Integration With Change Data Capture.* An Attunity White Paper. http://download.101com.com/tdwi/ww29/attunity_efficient_and_real-time_di.pdf

Atzori, L., Iera, A., & Morabito, G. (2010). The internet of things: A survey. *Computer Networks, 54*(15), 2787–2805. doi:10.1016/j.comnet.2010.05.010

Ayasdi, (2023). *Resources on how Topological Data Analysis is used to analyze big data.* Avasdi.

International, (2023). Market Intelligence, https://www.b2binternational.com/wp-content/uploads/2013/06/market_intelligence.pdf

Babcock University. (2017). Supervised Machine Learning Algorithms: Classification and Comparison. *International Journal of Computer Trends and Technology, 48*(3), 128–138. doi:10.14445/22312803/IJCTT-V48P126

Bagga, S., & Sharma, A. (2018, August). Big data and its challenges: a review. In *2018 4th International Conference on Computing Sciences (ICCS)* (pp. 183-187). IEEE. 10.1109/ICCS.2018.00037

Bajaj, R. H., & Ramteke, P. P. L. (2014). Big data–the New Era of data. *International Journal of Computer Science and Information Technologies, 5*(2), 1875–1885.

Bakshi, K. (2012). Considerations for Big Data: Architecture and Approaches. In: *Proceedings of the IEEE Aerospace Conference,* (pp. 1–7). IEEE. 10.1109/AERO.2012.6187357

Balazka, D., & Rodighiero, D. (2020). Big Data and the Little Big Bang: An Epistemological (R) evolution". *Frontiers in Big Data, 3,* 31. doi:10.3389/fdata.2020.00031 PMID:33693404

Ban, W., Lin, J., Tong, J., & Li, S. (2015, December). Query optimization of distributed database based on parallel genetic algorithm and max-min ant system. In *2015 8th International Symposium on Computational Intelligence and Design (ISCID)* (Vol. 2, pp. 581-585). IEEE. 10.1109/ISCID.2015.199

Banga, D. &. (2023). Emotion Detection in Speech. *11th International Symposium on Digital Forensics and Security (ISDFS),* (pp. 1-4). Chattanooga, TN, USA.

Banga, D., & Peddireddy, K. (2023). Artificial Intelligence for Customer Complaint Management. *International Journal of Computer Trends and Technology, 71*(3), 1–6. doi:10.14445/22312803/IJCTT-V71I3P101

Ban, H.-J., & Kim, H.-S. (2019). Understanding Customer Experience and Satisfaction through Airline Passengers' Online Review. *Sustainability (Basel), 11*(15), 4066. doi:10.3390u11154066

Bansal, R., Obaid, A. J., Gupta, A., Singh, R., & Pramanik, S. (2021). Impact of Big Data on Digital Transformation in 5G Era. *2nd International Conference on Physics and Applied Sciences (ICPAS 2021).* IOP. 10.1088/1742-6596/1963/1/012170

BarseS.BhagatD.DhawaleK.SolankeY.KurveD. (2023). Cyber-Trolling Detection System. SSRN 4340372.

Bart, K. (2019). Noise Benefits in Feedback Machine Learning: Bidirectional Backpropagation. In book: *Challenging the Borders of Justice in the Age of Migrations,* (pp. 267-275). IEEE. . doi:10.1007/978-3-030-10892-2_26

Beckhard, R. (1972). Organizational issues in the team delivery of comprehensive health care. *The Milbank Memorial Fund Quarterly, 50*(3), 287–316. doi:10.2307/3349351 PMID:5043084

Benatia, M. A., Baudry, D., & Louis, A. (2022). Detecting counterfeit products by means of frequent pattern mining. *Journal of Ambient Intelligence and Humanized Computing, 13*(7), 3683–3692. doi:10.100712652-020-02237-y

Bentéjac, C., Csörgo, A., & Martínez-Muñoz, G. (2019). A comparative analysis of gradient boosting algorithms. *Artificial Intelligence Review, 54*(3), 1937–1967. doi:10.100710462-020-09896-5

Berisha, B., Mëziu, E., & Shabani, I. (2022). Big data analytics in Cloud computing: An overview. *Journal of Cloud Computing (Heidelberg, Germany), 11*(1), 24. doi:10.118613677-022-00301-w PMID:35966392

Bertolucci, J. (2013). Hadoop: From Experiment To Leading Big Data Platform. *Information Week.*

Bhadani, A. K., & Jothimani, D. (2016). *Big Data: Challenges, Opportunities, and Realities. Effective BigDataManagementandOpportunitiesforImplementation.* IGIGlobal.

Bharadiya, J. P. (2023). A Comparative Study of Business Intelligence and Artificial Intelligence with Big Data Analytics. *American Journal of Artificial Intelligence, 7*(1), 24.

Bhargava, M. G., & Rao, D. R. (2018). Sentimental analysis on social media data using R programming. *IACSIT International Journal of Engineering and Technology, 7*(2.31), 80. doi:10.14419/ijet.v7i2.31.13402

Bhattarai, B. P., Paudyal, S., Luo, Y., Mohanpurkar, M., Cheung, K., Tonkoski, R., Hovsapian, R., Myers, K. S., Zhang, R., Zhao, P., Manic, M., Zhang, S., & Zhang, X. (2019). Big data analytics in smart grids: State-of-the-art, challenges, opportunities, and future directions. *IET Smart Grid*, 2(2), 141–154. doi:10.1049/iet-stg.2018.0261

Bhatti, M. (2014). The key performance indicators (KPIs) and their impact on overall organizational performance. *Quality & Quantity*, 48(6), 3127–3143. doi:10.100711135-013-9945-y

Bhave, R., Thakre, B. P., Kamble, V., Gogte, P., & Bhagat, D. (2023). BMSQABSE: Design of a Bioinspired Model to Improve Security & QoS Performance for Blockchain-Powered Attribute-based Searchable Encryption Applications. *International Journal on Recent and Innovation Trends in Computing and Communication*, 2023(11), 527–535. doi:10.17762/ijritcc.v11i5s.7114

Bi, H., Liu, J., & Kato, N. (2021). Deep Learning-based Privacy Preservation and Data Analytics for IoT Enabled Healthcare. IEEE Transactions on Industrial Informatics. IEEE. doi:10.1109/TII.2021.3117285

Big Data's Fourth V . (2023). Spotless Data. https://web.archive.org/web/20180731105912/https:/spotlessdata.com/blog/big-datas-fourth-v

Birjali, M., Beni-Hssane, A., & Erritali, M. (2017). Analyzing SocialMedia through Big Data usingInfoSphereBigInsightsandApache Flume. *Procedia Computer Science*, 113, 280–285. doi:10.1016/j.procs.2017.08.299

Biswas, N., Chattapadhyay, S., Mahapatra, G., Chatterjee, S., & Mondal, K. (2019). A new approach for conceptual extraction-transformation-loading process modeling. [IJACI]. *International Journal of Ambient Computing and Intelligence*, 10(1), 30–45. doi:10.4018/IJACI.2019010102

Biswas, N., & Mondal, K. C. (2021). Integration of ETL in cloud using spark for streaming data. In *International Conference on Emerging Applications of Information Technology*, (pp. 172-182). Springer.

Biswas, N., Sarkar, A., & Mondal, K. C. (2020). Efficient incremental loading in ETL processing for real-time data integration. *Innovations in Systems and Software Engineering*, 16(1), 53–61. doi:10.100711334-019-00344-4

Bizer, C., Boncz, P., Brodie, M. L., & Erling, O. (2012). The meaningful use of big data: Four perspectives — Four challenges. *SIGMOD Record*, 40(4), 56–60. doi:10.1145/2094114.2094129

Boja, C., Pocovnicu, A., & Bătăgan, L. (2012). Distributed Parallel Architecture for Big Data. *Informações Econômicas*, 16(2), 116–127.

Bokade, M. B., Dhande, S. S., & Vyavahare, H. R. (2013). Framework of change data capture and real time data warehouse. In *International Journal of Engineering Research and Technology* (Vol. 2). ESRSA Publications.

Bostock, M. O., Ogievetsky, V., & Heer, J. (2011). D³ Data-Driven Documents. *IEEE Transactions on Visualization and Computer Graphics*, 17(12), 2301–2309. doi:10.1109/TVCG.2011.185 PMID:22034350

Bradlow, E. T., Gangwar, M., Kopalle, P., & Voleti, S. (2017). The role of big data and predictive analytics inretailing. *Journal of Retailing*, 93(1), 79–95. doi:10.1016/j.jretai.2016.12.004

Brown, A. (2018). Operational Efficiency in Big Data Management: A Comparative Study. *International Journal of Information Management*, 36(5), 690–701.

Bucolo, M., Fortuna, L., & Rosa, M. L. (2004). Complex dynamics through fuzzy chains. *IEEE Transactions on Fuzzy Systems*, 12(3), 289–295. doi:10.1109/TFUZZ.2004.825969

Cai-Ming, Z., & Hao-Nan, C. (2020, December). Preprocessing method of structured big data in human resource archives database. In *2020 IEEE International Conference on Industrial Application of Artificial Intelligence (IAAI)* (pp. 379-384). IEEE.

Cao, Z. (2016). *Improving the accuracy and the efficiency of geo-processing through a combinative geo-computation approach* [Doctoral dissertation, UCL University College London].

Carvalho, J. V., Rocha, Á., Vasconcelos, J., & Abreu, A. (2018). A health data analytics maturity model for hospital information systems. *International Journal of Information Management*.

Ceballos, O., Ramírez Restrepo, C. A., Pabón, M. C., Castillo, A. M., & Corcho, O. (2021). SPARQL2Flink: Evaluation of SPARQL Queries on Apache Flink. *Applied Sciences (Basel, Switzerland)*, *11*(15), 7033. doi:10.3390/app11157033

Çelik, O., Hasanbaşoğlu, M., Aktaş, M. S., Kalıpsız, O., & Kanli, A. N. (2019, September). Implementation of data preprocessing techniques on distributed big data platforms. In *2019 4th International Conference on Computer Science and Engineering* (UBMK) (pp. 73-78). IEEE. 10.1109/UBMK.2019.8907230

Cen, L., Ruta, D., & Ng, J. (2015). Big education: Opportunities for Big Data analytics. *2015 IEEE International Conference on Digital Signal Processing (DSP)*, (pp. 502–506). IEEE. 10.1109/ICDSP.2015.7251923

Chandola, V., Banerjee, A., & Kumar, V. (2009). Anomaly detection: A survey. *ACM Computing Surveys*, *41*(3), 15. doi:10.1145/1541880.1541882

Chan, K. H., & Im, S. K. (2022). Sentiment analysis by using Naïve Bayes classifier with stacked CARU. *Electronics Letters*, *58*(10), 411–413. doi:10.1049/ell2.12478

Chaudhuri, A., & Ghosh, S. (2016). Sentiment Analysis of Customer Reviews Using Robust Hierarchical Bidirectional Recurrent Neural Network. In book: *Artificial Intelligence Perspectives in Intelligent Systems*, (pp. 249-261). Springer. . doi:10.1007/978-3-319-33625-1_23

Che, D., Safran, M., & Peng, Z. (2013). From big data to big data mining: challenges, issues, and opportunities. In *Database Systems for Advanced Applications* (pp. 1–15). Springer. doi:10.1007/978-3-642-40270-8_1

Chelladurai, K., & Sujatha, N. (2023). A Survey on Different Algorithms Used in Deep Learning Process. *E3S Web of Conferences*, *387*, 05008.

Chellam, V. V., Veeraiah, V., Khanna, A., Sheikh, T. H., Pramanik, S., & Dhabliya, D. (2023). *A Machine Vision-based Approach for Tuberculosis Identification in Chest X-Rays Images of Patients, ICICC 2023*. Springer.

Chen, C. P., & Zhang, C. Y. (2013). *Data-intensive applications, challenges, techniques and technologies: A survey on big data*. IEEE.

Cheng, H., Rong, C., Hwang, K., Wang, W., & Li, Y. (2015). Secure big data storage and sharing scheme for cloud tenants. *China Communications*, *12*(6), 106–115. doi:10.1109/CC.2015.7122469

Chen, H. C., Chiang, & Storey. (2012). Business intelligence and analytics: From big data to big impact. *Management Information Systems Quarterly*, *36*(4), 1165–1188. doi:10.2307/41703503

Chen, L. e. (2019). Leveraging Big Data for Competitive Advantage: A Case Study in E-commerce. *Journal of Business Analytics*, *2*(1), 45–56.

Chen, L., Rahayu, W., & Taniar, D. (2010). Towards near real-time data warehousing. In *24th IEEE International Conference on Advanced Information Networking and Applications (AINA)*. IEEE. 10.1109/AINA.2010.54

Chen, M., Mao, S., & Liu, Y. (2014). Big data: A survey. *Mobile Networks and Applications, 19*(2), 171–209. doi:10.100711036-013-0489-0

Chen, R. C., Dewi, C., Huang, S. W., & Caraka, R. E. (2020). Selecting critical features for data classification based on machine learning methods. *Journal of Big Data, 7*(1), 52. doi:10.118640537-020-00327-4

Chen, X.-W., & Lin, X. (2014). Big Data Deep Learning: Challenges and Perspectives. *IEEE Access : Practical Innovations, Open Solutions, 2*, 514–525. doi:10.1109/ACCESS.2014.2325029

Chikkamath, M., Dwivedi, D., Hirekurubar, R. B., & Thimmappa, R. (2023). Benchmarking of Novel Convolutional Neural Network Models for Automatic Butterfly Identification. In P. K. Shukla, K. P. Singh, A. K. Tripathi, & A. Engelbrecht (Eds.), *Computer Vision and Robotics. Algorithms for Intelligent Systems.* Springer. doi:10.1007/978-981-19-7892-0_27

Christian Janiescha, C., Dinterb, B., Mikalefc P., & Tona, O. (2022). Business analytics and big data research in information systems. *Journal of business analytics, 5*(1), 1–7. https://doi.org/. doi:10.1080/2573234X.2022.2069426©

Christianlauer. (2021). *Working with OpenStreetMap Data.* https://towardsdatascience.com/working-with-openstreetmap-data-37da18d55822

Chu, V. W., Wong, R. K., Chi, C.-H., Zhou, W., & Ho, I. (2017). The Design of a Cloud-Based Tracker Platform based on system-of-systems service architecture. *Information Systems Frontiers, 19*(6), 1283–1299. doi:10.100710796-017-9768-9

CIGI and Ipsos. (2019). *CIGI-Ipsos Global Survey on Internet Security and Trust.* IPSOS. https://www.ipsos.com/en/2019-cigi-ipsos-global-survey-internet-security-and-trust

Clarke, R. (2016). Big data, big risks. *Information Systems Journal, 26*(1), 77–90.

CNET News. (2011). *Storage area networks need not apply.* CNet News.

Cohen, J., Dolan, B., Dunlap, M., Hellerstein, J. M., & Welton, C. (2009). MAD Skills: New Analysis Practices for Big Data. *Proceedings of the ACM VLDB Endowment.* ACM. 10.14778/1687553.1687576

Cortes, C., & Vapnik, V. N. (1995). Support-vector networks". *Machine Learning, 20*(3), 273–297. doi:10.1007/BF00994018

Cudeck, R. (2000). Exploratory factor analysis. In *Handbook of applied multivariate statistics and mathematical modeling* (pp. 265–296). Elsevier. doi:10.1016/B978-012691360-6/50011-2

Cummings, T. G., & Worley, C. G. (2009). Organization development and change. 8th ed. Mason: Thompson South-Western.

Cuzzocrea, A., Ferreira, N., & Furtado, P. (2014). Real-time data warehousing: A rewrite/merge approach. In *Data Warehousing and Knowledge Discovery* (pp. 78–88). Springer. doi:10.1007/978-3-319-10160-6_8

Cuzzocrea, A., Song, I., & Davis, K. C. (2011). Analytics over Large-Scale Multidimensional Data: The Big Data Revolution! In: *Proceedings of the ACM International Workshop on Data Warehousing and OLAP,* (pp. 101–104). ACM. 10.1145/2064676.2064695

Dammak, S., Ghozzi, F., & Gargouri, F. (2019). ETL processes security modeling. [IJISMD]. *International Journal of Information System Modeling and Design, 10*(1), 60–84. doi:10.4018/IJISMD.2019010104

Darusman, F. S., Arifiyanti, A. A., & Wati, S. F. A. (2022). A Sentiment Analysis Pedulilindungi Tweet Using Support Vector Machine Method. *Applied Technology and Computing Science Journal, 4*(2), 113–118. doi:10.33086/atcsj.v4i2.2836

Davenport, T. H. (2014). How strategists use 'big data' to support internal business decisions, discovery and production. *Strategy and Leadership, 42*(4), 45–50. doi:10.1108/SL-05-2014-0034

Davis, S., & Tabrizi, N. (2021). Customer Review Analysis: A Systematic Review. *IEEE/ACIS 6th International Conference on Big Data, Cloud Computing, and Data Science (BCD).*, (pp. 91-97). IEEE. https://doi: 10.1109/BCD51206.2021.9581965

Davis, K. (2012). *Ethics of Big Data: Balancing risk and innovation.* O'Reilly Media, Inc.

DBIR. (2015). *2015 Data breach investigations report.* DBIR. http://www.verizonenterprise.com/DBIR/2015/

Dean, J., & Ghemawat, S. (2004). *MapReduce: Simplified Data Processing on Large Clusters.* Search Storage.

Decentriq. (2023, October 1). *Case Study: LynxCare* Decentriq. https://www.decentriq.com/request/case-study/lynxcare

Deijn, J. D. (2018). Automatic Car Damage Recognition using Convolutional. *Neural Networks.* Advance online publication. doi:10.1016/j.mlwa.2022.100332

Demchenko, Y., De Laat, C., & Membrey, P. (2014). Defining architecture components of the Big Data Ecosystem. In *Collaboration technologies and systems (CTS) International Conference on,* (pp. 104–112). IEEE. 10.1109/CTS.2014.6867550

Deng, X., Smith, R. T., & Quintin, G. (2020). *Semi-Supervised Learning Approach to Discover Enterprise User Insights from Feedback and Support.* arXiv: Learning. https://doi.org//arXiv.2007.09303. doi:10.48550

Deniz, N. (2020). The roles of human 4.0 in the industry 4.0 phenomenon. In *Logistics 4.0* (pp. 338–349). CRC Press. doi:10.1201/9780429327636-33

Desai, V., & Dinesha, H. A. (2020, November). A hybrid approach to data pre-processing methods. In *2020 IEEE International Conference for Innovation in Technology (INOCON)* (pp. 1-4). IEEE. 10.1109/INOCON50539.2020.9298378

Devi, R., & Judith, D. (2018). Deep Learning Methods for Big Data Analytics. *IJRECE, 6*(4). https://www.researchgate.net/publication/354970200_Deep_Learning_Methods_for_Big_ Data_Analytics #fullTextFileContent.

Dhyani, D. (2017). Exploring Neural Architectures for Multilingual Customer Feedback Analysis. In *Proceedings of the International Joint Conference on Natural Language Processing (IJCNLP),* (pp. 170-173). ACM.

Di Mauro, M., & Di Sarno, C. (2014). A framework for Internet data real-time processing: A machine-learning approach. *Paper presented at the Security Technology (ICCST), 2014 International Carnahan Conferenceon.* IEEE. 10.1109/CCST.2014.6987044

Diakopoulos, N. (2016). Accountability in algorithmic decision making. *Communications of the ACM, 59*(2), 56–62. Advance online publication. doi:10.1145/2844110

DOJ, United States Department of Justice, Office of Privacy and Civil Liberties. (2020). *Overview of the Privacy Act of 1974 (2020 Edition).* US DoJ. https://www.justice.gov/opcl/overview-privacy-act-1974-2020-edition

Dong, L., Matthew, C. S., & Biagi, A. (2021). A Semi-supervised Multi-task Learning Approach to Classify Customer Contact Intents. In *Proceedings of the 4th Workshop on e-Commerce and NLP,* (pp. 49–57). Online. Association for Computational Linguistics. 10.18653/v1/2021.ecnlp-1.7

Dromard, J., Roudière, G., & Owezarski, P. (2015). Unsupervised network anomaly detection in real-timeon big data. *Paper presented at the East European Conference on Advances in Databases andInformationSystems.*

Dutta, N., Umashankar, S., Shankar, V. K., Padmanaban, S., Leonowicz, Z., & Wheeler, P. (2018). Centrifugal Pump Cavitation Detection Using Machine Learning Algorithm Technique. *IEEE International Conference on Environment and Electrical Engineering and IEEE Industrial and Commercial Power Systems Europe.* IEEE. 10.1109/EEEIC.2018.8494594

Dwivedi, D., & Patil, G. (2022). Lightweight Convolutional Neural Network for Land Use Image Classification. *Journal of Advanced Geospatial Science & Technology, 2*(1), 31–48. https://jagst.utm.my/index.php/jagst/article/view/31

Dwivedi, S. K., & Rawat, B. (2015, October). A review paper on data preprocessing: a critical phase in web usage mining process. In *2015 International Conference on Green Computing and Internet of Things (ICGCIoT)* (pp. 506-510). IEEE. 10.1109/ICGCIoT.2015.7380517

Dwork, C. (2006). Differential Privacy. *Automata, languages, and programming*, 1–12. https://doi.org/doi:10.1007/11787006_1

Eccles, M. J., Evans, D. J., & Beaumont, A. J. (2010). True real-time change data capture with web service database encapsulation. In *Services (SERVICES-1), 2010 6th World Congress on*, pages 128-131. IEEE. 10.1109/SERVICES.2010.59

Eckerson, W. W. (2010). *Performance dashboards: Measuring, monitoring, and managing your business*. John Wiley & Sons.

Egan, M. P. (2001). Conclusion: Governance and Market-Building. In *Constructing a European Market* (pp. 260–272). Oxford University Press. doi:10.1093/0199244057.003.0011

El Arass, M. E., Tikito, I., & Souissi, N. (2017). *Data lifecycles analysis: Towards intelligent cycle*. In Fès Proceeding of The second International Conference on Intelligent Systems and Computer Vision, Fès, Morocco. 10.1109/ISACV.2017.8054938

ElFar, O. A., Chang, C.-K., Leong, H. Y., Peter, A. P., Chew, K. W., & Show, P. L. (2021). Prospects of Industry 5.0 in algae: Customization of production and new advanced technology for clean bioenergy generation. *Energy Conversion and Management: X, 10*, 100048.

Ellis, B. (2014). *Real-time analytics: Techniques to analyze and visualize streaming data*. John Wiley &Sons.

EMC. (2012). *Data Science and Big Data Analytics*. EMC Education Services.

Entrepreneur. (2023). Why Both Quantitative and Qualitative Data Are Vital for Results-Driven Businesses. *Entrepreneur.* https://www.entrepreneur.com/science-technology/why-both-quantitative-and-qualitative-data-are-vital-for/361314

Erevelles, S., Fukawa, N., & Swayne, L. (2016). Big Data consumer analytics and the transformation of marketing. *Journal of Business Research, 69*(2), 897–904. doi:10.1016/j.jbusres.2015.07.001

Erfani, S. M., Rajasegarar, S., Karunasekera, S., & Leckie, C. (2016). High-dimensional and large-scale anomaly detection using a linear one-class SVM with deep learning. *Pattern Recognition, 58*, 121–134. doi:10.1016/j.patcog.2016.03.028

Erfina, A., & Lestari, R. (2023). Sentiment Analysis of Electric Vehicles using the Naïve Bayes Algorithm. *SISTEMASI, 12*(1), 178–185. doi:10.32520tmsi.v12i1.2417

Eweek, (2023). Survey: Biggest Databases Approach 30 Terabytes. *Eweek.com.*

Fahad, S. A., & Alam, M. M. A. (2016). modified K-means algorithm for big data clustering. *International Journal of Computer Science and Engineering Technology, 6*(4), 129–132.

Fan, J., Han, F., & Liu, H. (2014). Challenges of big data analysis. *National Science Review, 1*(2), 293–314. doi:10.1093/nsr/nwt032 PMID:25419469

Farnaaz, N., & Jabbar, M. (2016). Random ForestModelingforNetworkIntrusionDetectionSystem. *Procedia Computer Science, 89*, 213–217. doi:10.1016/j.procs.2016.06.047

Farooq, F., & Sarwar, S. M. (2010). Real-time data warehousing for business intelligence. In *Proceedings of the 8th International Conference on Frontiers of Information Technology (FIT'10)*, pages 38:1-38:7. ACM.

Faroukhi, A. Z., El Alaoui, I., Gahi, Y., & Amine, A. (2020). Big data monetization throughout Big Data Value Chain: A comprehensive review. *Journal of Big Data, 7*(1), 3. doi:10.118640537-019-0281-5

Faundeen, J. L. (2014). *The United States Geological Survey science data lifecycle model.* United States Geological Survey.

Fazal, N., Haleem, A., Bahl, S., Javaid, M., & Nandan, D. (2022). Digital management systems in manufacturing using industry 5.0 technologies. In *Advancement in Materials, Manufacturing and Energy Engineering, Vol. II: Select Proceedings of ICAMME 2021* (pp. 221–234). Springer.

Federal Trade Commission. (2019, July 24). *FTC Imposes $5 Billion Penalty, Sweeping New Privacy Restrictions on Facebook.* FTC. https://www.ftc.gov/news-events/news/press-releases/2019/07/ftc-imposes-5-billion-penalty-sweeping-new-privacy-restrictions-facebook

Feng, W., Zhang, Q., Hu, G., & Huang, J. X. (2014). Mining network data for intrusion detection throughcombiningSVMswithantcolonynetworks. *Future Generation Computer Systems, 37*, 127–140. doi:10.1016/j.future.2013.06.027

Fernandes, G., Carvalho, L. F., Rodrigues, J. J., & Proença, M. L. (2016). Network anomaly detection usingIP flows with principal component analysis and ant colony optimization. *Journal of Network and Computer Applications, 64*, 1-11.

Fernandes, G. Jr, Rodrigues, J. J., & Proença, M. L. Jr. (2015). Autonomous profile-based anomaly detectionsystem using principal component analysis and flow analysis. *Applied Soft Computing, 34*, 513–525. doi:10.1016/j.asoc.2015.05.019

Fernández, A., Carmona, C. J., del Jesus, M. J., & Herrera, F. (2016). A view on fuzzy systems for big data:progress and opportunities. *International Journal of Computational Intelligence Systems, 9*(sup1),69-80.

Ferreira, N., Martins, P., & Furtado, P. (2013). Near real-time with traditional data warehouse architectures: Factors and how-to. In *Proceedings of the 17th International Database Engineering Applications Symposium (IDEAS'13),* (pp. 68-75). ACM. 10.1145/2513591.2513650

Few, S. (2006). *Information dashboard design: The effective visual communication of data.* O'Reilly Media.

Few, S. (2009). *Now you see it: Simple visualization techniques for quantitative analysis.* Analytics Press.

Few, S. (2013). *Information dashboard design: Displaying data for at-a-glance monitoring.* O'Reilly Media.

Fleisher, C. S. (2008). Using open source data in developing competitive and marketing intelligence. European Journal of Marketing, 42 (7/8), 853.

Fleisher, C. S., & Bensoussan, B. E. (2007). Business and competitive analysis. In *Business and Competitive Analysis.* Effective Application of New and Classic Methods.

Floridi, L., & Cowls, J. (2022). A unified framework of five principles for AI in society. In *Machine Learning and the City.* Applications in Architecture and Urban Design. doi:10.1002/9781119815075.ch45

Fournier-Viger, P., Gan, W., Wu, Y., Nouioua, M., Song, W., Truong, T., & Duong, H. (2022, April). Pattern mining: Current challenges and opportunities. In *International Conference on Database Systems for Advanced Applications* (pp. 34-49). Cham: Springer International Publishing.

Fox, C. (2018). Data Science for Transport. Springer.

Fuller, C. J. (2023). *What is Tactical Marketing?* Marketing.

Gandomi, A., & Haider, M. (2015). Beyond the hype: Big data concepts, methods, and analytics. *International Journal of Information Management, 35*(2), 137–144. doi:10.1016/j.ijinfomgt.2014.10.007

Gandomi, A., & Haider, M. (2015). Beyond the hype: Bigdata concepts, methods, and analytics. *International Journal of Information Management, 35*(2), 137–144.

Gani, A., Siddiqa, A., Shamshirband, S., & Hanum, F. (2016). A survey on indexing techniques for big data:taxonmyandperformance evaluation. *KnowledgeandInformationSystems, 46*(2), 241–284.

Gao, P., Han, Z., & Wan, F. (2020, October). Big Data Processing and Application Research. In 2020 2nd International Conference on Artificial Intelligence and Advanced Manufacture (AIAM) (pp. 125-128). IEEE.

García, L., Tomás, J., Parra, L., &Lloret, J. (2018). An m-health application for cerebral stroke detectionandmonitoringusingcloudservices. *International Journal of Information Management.*

García, S., Ramírez-Gallego, S., Luengo, J., Benítez, J. M., & Herrera, F. (2016). Big data preprocessing: Methods and prospects. *Big Data Analytics, 1*(1), 9. doi:10.118641044-016-0014-0

Gartner, S. (2020). *65% of the World's population will have personal data covered under modern privacy regulations.* Gartner. https://www.gartner.com/en/newsroom/press-releases/2020-09-14-gartner-says-by-2023--65--of-the-world-s-population-w

Gebhardt, G. F., Farrelly, F. J., & Conduit, J. (2019). Market intelligence dissemination practices. *Journal of Marketing, 83*(3), 72–90. doi:10.1177/0022242919830958

Gegov, A., Arabikhan, F., & Petrov, N. (2014). Linguistic composition based modelling by fuzzy networks with modular rule bases. *Fuzzy Sets and Systems, 269*, 1–29. doi:10.1016/j.fss.2014.06.014

Gegov, A., Sanders, D., & Vatchova, B. (2016). Mamdani fuzzy networks with feedforward rule bases for complex systems modelling. *Journal of Intelligent & Fuzzy Systems, 30*(5), 2623–2637. doi:10.3233/IFS-151911

Gentry, C. (2009). Fully homomorphic encryption using ideal lattices. In *Proceedings of the forty-first annual ACM symposium on Theory of computing (STOC '09).* Association for Computing Machinery, New York, NY, USA. 10.1145/1536414.1536440

Geoapify. (2023). *Boosting Business Visibility: OpenStreetMap for Local Marketing.* Geoapify. https://www.geoapify.com/osm-for-local-marketing

George, A. S., & George, A. H. (2023). Revolutionizing Manufacturing: Exploring the Promises and Challenges of Industry 5.0. *Partners Universal International Innovation Journal, 1*(2), 22–38.

Georgevici, A. I., & Terblanche, M. (2019). Neural networks and deep learning: A brief introduction. *Intensive Care Medicine, 45*(5), 712–714. doi:10.100700134-019-05537-w PMID:30725133

Ghobakhloo, M., Iranmanesh, M., Mubarak, M. F., Mubarik, M., Rejeb, A., & Nilashi, M. (2022). Identifying industry 5.0 contributions to sustainable development: A strategy roadmap for delivering sustainability values. *Sustainable Production and Consumption, 33*, 716–737. doi:10.1016/j.spc.2022.08.003

Ghosh, R., Mohanty, S., Pattnaik, P. K., & Pramanik, S. (2020). Performance Analysis Based on Probablity of False Alarm and Miss Detection in Cognitive Radio Network. *International Journal of Wireless and Mobile Computing, 20*(4), 2020. doi:10.1504/IJWMC.2021.117530

Glanz, K., Rimer, B. K., & Viswanath, K. (Eds.). (2008). *Health behavior and health education: theory, research, and practice.* Wiley.

Golab, L., Johnson, T., & Shkapenyuk, V. (2009). Scheduling updates in a real-time stream warehouse. In *IEEE 25th International Conference on Data Engineering (ICDE'09)*, (pp. 1207-1210). IEEE. 10.1109/ICDE.2009.202

Goldin, E., Feldman, D., Georgoulas, G., Castano, M., & Nikolakopoulos, G. (2017, July). Cloud computing for big data analytics in the Process Control Industry. In *2017 25th Mediterranean Conference on Control and Automation (MED)* (pp. 1373-1378). IEEE. 10.1109/MED.2017.7984310

Goodchild, M. F. (2007). Citizens as sensors: The world of volunteered geography. In GeoJournal. doi:10.100710708-007-9111-y

Goodchild, M. F., & Li, L. (2012). Assuring the quality of volunteered geographic information. *Spatial Statistics*, *1*, 110–120. doi:10.1016/j.spasta.2012.03.002

Goodfellow, I., Bengio, Y., Courville, A., & Bengio, Y. (2016). *Deep learning* (Vol. 1). MIT Press.

Govindarajan, P., & Panneerselvam, S. (2014). Issues and challenges in big. In *Proceedings of the 2nd International Conference on Science* (pp. 265–272). Engineering and Management. http://www.ijaert.org/wp-content/uploads/2014/04/42.pdf

Grèzes, V. (2015). The definition of competitive intelligence needs through a synthesis model. *Journal of Intelligence Studies in Business*, *5*(1). doi:10.37380/jisib.v5i1.111

Gumber, M., Jain, A., & Amutha, A. L. (2021). Predicting Customer Behavior by Analyzing Clickstream Data. *5th International Conference on Computer, Communication and Signal Processing (ICCCSP)*, (pp. 1-6). IEEE, 10.1109/ICCCSP52374.2021.9465526

Gupta, A., (2021). Climate Change Monitoring Using Remote Sensing, Deep Learning, And Computer Vision. *Webology*, *19*(2). https://www.webology.org/abstract.php?id=1708

Gupta, N., & Jolly, S. (2021). Enhancing data quality at ETL stage of data warehousing. [IJDWM]. *International Journal of Data Warehousing and Mining*, *17*(1), 74–91. doi:10.4018/IJDWM.2021010105

Gupta, V., Sengar, N., Dutta, M., Travieso, C., & Alonso, J. (2017). Automated segmentation of powdery mildew disease from cherry leaves using image processing. *Proceedings of the 2017 IEEE International Work Conference on Bioinspired Intelligence (IWOBI)*, (pp. 1-4). IEEE. https://doi.org/10.1109/IWOBI.2017.8006454

Gusmão, A., Horta, N., Lourenço, N., & Martins, R. (2020). Artificial Neural Network Overview. In *Analog IC Placement Generation via Neural Networks from Unlabeled Data* (pp. 7–24). Springer. doi:10.1007/978-3-030-50061-0_2

Hababeh, I., Gharaibeh, A., Nofal, S., & Khalil, I. (2018). An integrated methodology for big data classification and security for improving cloud systems data mobility. *IEEE Access : Practical Innovations, Open Solutions*, *7*, 9153–9163. doi:10.1109/ACCESS.2018.2890099

Hafidz, N., & Yanti Liliana, D. (2021). Klasifikasi Sentimen pada Twitter Terhadap WHO Terkait Covid-19 Menggunakan SVM, N-Gram, PSO. [Rekayasa Sistem Dan Teknologi Informasi]. *Jurnal RESTI*, *5*(2), 213–219. doi:10.29207/resti.v5i2.2960

Haklay, M. (2010). How good is volunteered geographical information? A comparative study of OpenStreetMap and ordnance survey datasets. *Environment and Planning. B, Planning & Design*, *37*(4), 682–703. doi:10.1068/b35097

Hande, T., Dhawas, P., Kakirwar, B., & Gupta, A. (2023, August) Yoga Postures Correction and Estimation using Open CV and VGG 19 Architecture. In *2023 International Journal of Innovative Science and Research Technology*.

Hande, T., Dhawas, P., Kakirwar, B., & Gupta, A. Yoga Postures Correction and Estimation using Open CV and VGG 19 Architecture.

Han, J., Kamber, M., & Pei, J. (2011). *Data mining: concepts and techniques*. Elsevier Science.

Harerimana, G., Jang, B., Kim, J. W., & Park, H. K. (2018). Health big data analytics: A technology survey. *IEEE Access : Practical Innovations, Open Solutions*, 6, 65661–65678. doi:10.1109/ACCESS.2018.2878254

Hariharakrishnan, J., Mohanavalli, S., & Kumar, K. S. (2017, January). Survey of pre-processing techniques for mining big data. In *2017 international conference on computer, communication and signal processing (ICCCSP)* (pp. 1-5). IEEE.

Hashem, I. A. T., Chang, V., Anuar, N. B., Adewole, K., Yaqoob, I., Gani, A., & Chiroma, H. (2016). The roleofbigdatainsmartcity. *InternationalJournalofInformationManagement*, 36(5), 748–758.

Hashem, I. A. T., Yaqoob, I., Anuar, N. B., Mokhtar, S., Gani, A., & Ullah Khan, S. (2015). The rise of "big data" on cloud computing: Review and open research issues. *Information Systems*, 47, 98–115. doi:10.1016/j.is.2014.07.006

Hassani, H., & Silva, E. S. (2015). Forecasting with big data: A review. Annals of Data Science, 2(1), 5-19.

Hassija, V., Chamola, V., Mahapatra, A., Singal, A., Goel, D., Huang, K., Scardapane, S., Spinelli, I., Mahmud, M., & Hussain, A. (2023). Interpreting Black-Box Models: A Review on Explainable Artificial Intelligence. *Cognitive Computation*. doi:10.100712559-023-10179-8

HCLtech, (2023). *Solving Key Business Challenges With a Big Data Lake.* Hcltech.com.

Heang, R. (2017). *Book Review: The use of Market Intelligence in Competitive Analysis.* Digitala Vetenskapliga Arkivet.

Hecht-Nielsen, R. (1992). Theory of the backpropagation neural network. In *Neural networks for per-ception* (pp. 65–93). Academic Press. doi:10.1016/B978-0-12-741252-8.50010-8

Hedin, H., Hirvensalo, I., & Vaarnas, M. (Eds.). (2012). *The Handbook of Market Intelligence.* doi:10.1002/9781119208082

Hemmatian, F., & Sohrabi, M. K. (2019). A survey on classification techniques for opinion mining and sentiment analysis. Artificial intelligence review. doi:10.100710462-017-9599-6

He, P., Zhu, J., He, S., Li, J., & Lyu, M. R. (2017). Towards automated log parsing for large-scale log data analysis. *IEEE Transactions on Dependable and Secure Computing*, 15(6), 931–944. doi:10.1109/TDSC.2017.2762673

Herodotou, H., Lim, H., Luo, G., Borisov, N., Dong, L., Cetin, F. B., & Babu, S. (2011). Starfish: A Self-tuning System for Big Data Analytics. In: *Proceedings of the Conference on Innovative Data Systems Research*, (pp. 261–272).

Heryadi, Y., Wijanarko, B. D., Fitria Murad, D., Tho, C., & Hashimoto, K. (2023). Aspect-based Sentiment Analysis using Long Short-term Memory Model for Leveraging Restaurant Service Management. *International Conference on Computer Science, Information Technology and Engineering (ICCoSITE)*, (pp. 779-783). IEEE. https://doi: 10.1109/ICCoSITE57641.2023.10127708

He, Y., Lee, R., Huai, Y., Shao, Z., Jain, N., Zhang, X., & Xu, Z. (2011). RCFile: A Fast and Spaceefficient Data Placement Structure in MapReduce-based Warehouse Systems. In: *IEEE International Conference on Data Engineering (ICDE)*, (pp. 1199–1208), IEEE. 10.1109/ICDE.2011.5767933

Hilbert, M., & López, P. (2011). The World's Technological Capacity to Store, Communicate, and Compute Information". *Science*, 332(6025), 60–65. doi:10.1126cience.1200970 PMID:21310967

Hong, Y., Lee, Z., & … . (2009). Data warehouse performance. In *Encyclopedia of Data Warehousing and Mining* (2nd ed., pp. 580–585). IGI Global.

Hossain, M. A., & Rahman, M. F. (2022). Customer Sentiment Analysis and Prediction of Insurance Products' Reviews Using Machine Learning Approaches. *FIIB business review*. https://doi: . doi:10.1177/23197145221115793

Hossain, M., Rahman, M. F., Uddin, M. K., & Hossain, M. K. (2023, June 07). S., Rahman, M., Uddin, Md. K., Hossain, Md. (2022). Customer Sentiment Analysis and Prediction of Halal Restaurants Using Machine Learning Approaches. *Journal of Islamic Marketing*, *14*(7), 1859–1889. doi:10.1108/JIMA-04-2021-0125

Hossen, M. S., Jony, A. H., Tabassum, T., Islam, M., Rahman, M. M., & Khatun, T. (2021). Hotel review analysis for the prediction of business using deep learning approach. *International Conference on Artificial Intelligence and Smart Systems (ICAIS)*, (pp. 1489-1494). IEEE. 10.1109/ICAIS50930.2021.9395757

Huang, L., Zhao, Q., Li, Y., Wang, S., Lei, S., & Chou, W. (2017). Reliable and efficient big service selection. *Information Systems Frontiers*, *19*(6), 1273–1282. doi:10.100710796-017-9767-x

Huang, S., Wang, B., Li, X., Zheng, P., Mourtzis, D., & Wang, L. (2022). Industry 5.0 and Society 5.0—Comparison, complementation and co-evolution. *Journal of Manufacturing Systems*, *64*, 424–428. doi:10.1016/j.jmsy.2022.07.010

Hullman, J., & Diakopoulos, N. (2011). Visualization rhetoric: Framing effects in narrative visualization. *IEEE Transactions on Visualization and Computer Graphics*, *17*(12), 2231–2240. doi:10.1109/TVCG.2011.255 PMID:22034342

Hunter, J. D. (2007). Matplotlib: A 2D graphics environment. *Computing in Science & Engineering*, *9*(3), 90–95. doi:10.1109/MCSE.2007.55

IBM Big data & analytics, (2023). *Measuring the Business Value of Big Data Hub*. IBM. www.ibmbigdatahub.com

Ide, T., Khandelwal, A., & Kalagnanam, J. (2016). Sparse Gaussian Markov Random Field Mixtures forAnomaly Detection. *Paper presented at the Data Mining (ICDM), 2016 IEEE 16th InternationalConferenceon*. IEEE.

Ifeyinwa, A. (2019). Review Big Data and Business Analytics: Trends, Platforms, Success Factors and Applications. *Big Data Cogn. Comput.* . doi:10.3390/bdcc3020032

Infosum. (2023, October 9). *Case Study: Retail, Nectar360, and Channel 4 Deliver Up to 122% Sales Uplift for CPGs*. Infosum. https://www.infosum.com/case-studies/ret4il-nectar360-and-channel-4-deliver-up-to-122-sales-uplift-for-cpgs

Interactive Advertising Bureau. (n.d.). *State of Data 2023*. IAB. https://www.iab.com/insights/state-of-data-2023/

International Association of Privacy Professionals. (n.d.). *5 Steps to Prepare for India's Digital Personal Data Protection Act*. IAPP. https://iapp.org/news/a/5-steps-to-prepare-for-indias-digital-personal-data-protection-act/

Introducing WSO2 Data Analytics Server. (2015). Retrieved fromhttps://docs.wso2.com/display/DAS300/Introducing+DAS

Iqbal, R., Doctor, F., More, B., Mahmud, S., & Yousuf, U. (2016). Big data analytics: computational intelligence techniques and application areas. *International Journal of Information Management*.

Ishwarappa & Anuradha, J. (2015). A Brief Introduction on Big Data 5Vs Characteristics and Hadoop Technology. *Procedia Computer Science*, *48*, 319–324.

Italiano, I. C., & Ferreira, J. E. (2006). Synchronization options for data warehouse designs. *Computer*, *39*(3), 53–57. doi:10.1109/MC.2006.104

Ivakhnenko, A. G. & Grigor'evich Lapa, V. (1967). *Cybernetics and forecasting techniques*. American Elsevier Pub. Co.

Ivakhnenko, A. G. (1973). *Cybernetic Predicting Devices*. CCM Information Corporation.

Ivanov, D. (2023). The Industry 5.0 framework: Viability-based integration of the resilience, sustainability, and human-centricity perspectives. *International Journal of Production Research*, *61*(5), 1683–1695. doi:10.1080/00207543.2022.2118892

J¨org, T., & Dessloch, S. (2009). Near real-time data warehousing using state of-the-art ETL tools. In *Enabling Real-Time Business Intelligence* (pp. 100–117). Springer.

Jain, N., & Kumar, R.Department of Electrical Engineering. (2022). A Review on Machine Learning & It's Algorithms. *International Journal of Soft Computing and Engineering*, *12*(5), 1–5. doi:10.35940/ijsce.E3583.1112522

Jain, T. S. R., & Saluja, S. (2012). Refreshing data warehouse in near real time. *International Journal of Computer Applications*, *46*(18).

Jaiswal, A., Arun, C. J., & Varma, A. (2022). Rebooting employees: Upskilling for artificial intelligence in multinational corporations. *International Journal of Human Resource Management*, *33*(6), 1179–1208. doi:10.1080/09585192.2021.1891114

Jaljolie, R., Dror, T., Siriba, D. N., & Dalyot, S. (2022). Evaluating current ethical values of OpenStreetMap using value sensitive design. *Geo-Spatial Information Science*. doi:10.1080/10095020.2022.2087048

Jamil, G. L. (2013). Approaching Market Intelligence Concept through a Case Analysis: Continuous Knowledge for Marketing Strategic Management and its Complementarity to Competitive Intelligence". *Procedia Technology*, *9*, 463–472. doi:10.1016/j.protcy.2013.12.051

Janelle, D. G., & Goodchild, M. F. (2018). Territory, Geographic Information, and the Map. In The Map and the Territory. Springer. doi:10.1007/978-3-319-72478-2_33

Javadpour, A., Abadi, A. M. H., Rezaei, S., Zomorodian, M., & Rostami, A. S. (2022). Improving load balancing for data-duplication in big data cloud computing networks. *Cluster Computing*, *25*(4), 2613–2631. doi:10.100710586-021-03312-5

Jayasingh, R., Kumar, R. J. S., Telagathoti, D. B., Sagayam, K. M., & Pramanik, S. (2022). Speckle noise removal by SORAMA segmentation in Digital Image Processing to facilitate precise robotic surgery. *International Journal of Reliable and Quality E-Healthcare*, *11*(1). 10.4018/IJRQEH.29508

Jeong, E., Jang, S., Day, J., & Ha, S. (2014). The impact of eco-friendly practices on green image and customer attitudes: An investigation in a café setting. *International Journal of Hospitality Management*, *41*, 10–20. doi:10.1016/j.ijhm.2014.03.002

Jha, A. K., Agi, M. A., & Ngai, E. W. (2020). A note on big data analytics capability development in supply chain. *Decision Support Systems*, *38*, 113382. doi:10.1016/j.dss.2020.113382

Jin, D. H., & Kim, H. J. (2018). Integrated Understanding of Big Data, Big Data Analysis, and Business Intelligence: A Case Study of Logistics. *Sustainability (Basel)*, *10*(10), 3778. doi:10.3390u10103778

Jiwat, R. (2016). *The implications of Big Data analytics on Business Intelligence: A qualitative study in China*. ICRTCSE. doi:10.1016/j.procs.2016.05.152

Jones, N. (2016). *Gartner Identifies the Top 10 Internet of Things*. Gartner. http://www.gartner.com/newsroom/id/3221818

Joo, M. G., & Lee, J. S. A. (2005). class of hierarchical fuzzy systems with constraints on the fuzzy rules. *IEEE Transactions on Fuzzy Systems*, *13*(2), 194–203. doi:10.1109/TFUZZ.2004.840096

Kaasinen, E., Anttila, A.-H., Heikkilä, P., Laarni, J., Koskinen, H., & Väätänen, A. (2022). Smooth and resilient human–machine teamwork as an Industry 5.0 design challenge. *Sustainability (Basel)*, *14*(5), 2773. doi:10.3390u14052773

Kaisler, S., Armour, F., Espinosa, J. A., & Money, W. (2013). Big data: Issues and challenges moving forward. In *Proceeding of the 46th Hawaii International Conference on System Sciences*. IEEE. 10.1109/HICSS.2013.645

Kaisler, S., Armour, F., Espinosa, J. A., & Money, W. (2013). Big data: Issues and challenges moving forward. In *System sciences (HICSS), 2013 46th Hawaii international conference on* (pp. 995-1004). IEEE.

Kakavand, M., Mustapha, N., Mustapha, A., Abdullah, M. T., &Riahi, H. (2015). A survey of anomalydetection using data mining methods for hypertext transfer protocol web services. Journal ofComputerScience,11(1),89.97.

Kalshetty, J. N., Devaiah, H., Rakshith, K., Koshy, K., & Advait, N. (2022). Analysis of Car Damage for Personal Auto Claim Using CNN. In S. Shakya, V. E. Balas, S. Kamolphiwong, & K. L. Du (Eds.), Sentimental Analysis and Deep Learning (Advances in Intelligent Systems and Computing, Vol. 1408). Springer. doi:10.1007/978-981-16-5157-1_25

Kamat, P., & Sugandhi, R. (2020). Anomaly Detection for Predictive Maintenance in Industry 4.0- A survey. *E3S Web of Conferences, 170*, 02007.

Karagiannis, A., Vassiliadis, P., & Simitsis, A. (2013). Scheduling strategies for efficient ETL execution. *Information Systems, 38*(6), 927–945. doi:10.1016/j.is.2012.12.001

Karim, A., Siddiqa, A., Safdar, Z., Razzaq, M., Gillani, S. A., Tahir, H., & Imran, M. (2017). Big datamanagement in participatory sensing: Issues, trends and future directions. *Future Generation Computer Systems*.

Kasongo, S. M. (2023). A deep learning technique for intrusion detection system using a Recurrent Neural Networks based framework. *Computer Communications, 199*, 113–125. doi:10.1016/j.comcom.2022.12.010

Katal, A., Wazid, M., & Goudar, R. (2013). Big data: Issues, challenges, tools and good practices. In: *Contemporary Computing (IC3), 2013 Sixth International Conference on*, (pp. 404-409). IEEE.

Katal, A., Wazid, M., & Goudar, R. (2013). Big Data: Issues, challenges, tools and Good practices. *Proceeding of the Sixth International Conference on Contemporary Computing*. IEEE. https://ieeexplore.ieee.org/xpls/abs_all.jsp?arnumber=6612229

Katal, A., Wazid, M., & Goudar, R. (2013). Big data: Issues, challenges, tools andgood practices. [SixthInternationalConferenceon.]. *PaperpresentedattheContemporaryComputing*, (IC3), 2013.

Kaur, G., Goyal, S., & Kaur, H. (2020). Brief Review Of Various Machine Learning Algorithms. SSRN *Electronic Journal*. doi:10.2139/ssrn.3747597

Kelleher, J. D. (2015). *Fundamentals of machine learning for predictive data analytics: Algorithms, worked examples, and case studies*. MIT Press.

Kelley, W. T. (1965). Marketing Intelligence for Top Management". *Journal of Marketing, 29*(4), 19–24. doi:10.1177/002224296502900405

Ketu, S., Kumar Mishra, P., & Agarwal, S. (2020). Performance Analysis of Distributed Computing Frameworks for Big Data Analytics: Hadoop Vs Spark. *Computación y Sistemas, 24*(2). doi:10.13053/cys-24-2-3401

Khan, N., Yaqoob, I., Hashem, I. A., Inayat, Z., Ali, W. K., Alam, M., Shiraz, M., & Gani, A. (2014). Big data: Survey, technologies, opportunities, and challenges. *TheScientificWorldJournal, 712826*, 1–18. doi:10.1155/2014/712826 PMID:25136682

Khedkar, S. A., & Shinde, S. K. (2018). Customer Review Analytics for Business Intelligence. *IEEE International Conference on Computational Intelligence and Computing Research (ICCIC).*, (pp. 1-5). IEEE. https://doi: 10.1109/ICCIC.2018.8782305

Khurana, A. (2014). Bringing big data systems to the cloud. *IEEE Cloud Computing, 1*(3), 72–75. doi:10.1109/MCC.2014.47

Kim, S.-H., Kim, N.-U., & Chung, T.-M. (2013). Attribute relationship evaluation methodology for big data security. *International Conference on IT Convergence and Security (ICITCS)*, (pp. 1–4). IEEE. 10.1109/ICITCS.2013.6717808

Kimball, R., & Caserta, J. (2004). *The data warehouse ETL toolkit: Practical techniques for extracting, cleaning, conforming, and delivering data.* John Wiley and Sons.

Kim, M. K., & Park, J. H. (2017). Identifying and prioritizing critical factors for promoting the implementation and usage of big data in healthcare. *Information Development*, *33*(3), 257–269. doi:10.1177/0266666916652671

Kinsey, S. (2023, February 24). *KPI Dashboards: A comprehensive guide.* Simple KPI. https://www.simplekpi.com/Blog/KPI-Dashboards-a-comprehensive-guide

Kiron, D. P. (2018). *Data-driven: Creating a data culture.* MIT Sloan Management Review Research Report.

Kitchin, R., & McArdle, G. (2016). What makes Big Data, Big Data? Exploring the ontological characteristics of 26 datasets". *Big Data & Society*, *3*(1), 1–10. doi:10.1177/2053951716631130

Klinkhardt, C., Woerle, T., Briem, L., Heilig, M., Kagerbauer, M., & Vortisch, P. (2021). Using openstreetmap as a data source for attractiveness in travel demand models. In Transportation Research Record (Vol. 2675, Issue 8). doi:10.1177/0361198121997415

Kolajo, T., Daramola, O., & Adebiyi, A. (2019). Big data stream analysis: A systematic literature review. *Journal of Big Data*, *6*(1), 47. doi:10.118640537-019-0210-7

Komarasamy, G., Jaganathan, S. C. B., Sridharan, K., Mital, A., & Awal, S. (2022). Harmony Gradient Boosting Random Forest Machine Learning Algorithms for Sentiment Classification. *IEEE 2nd International Symposium on Sustainable Energy, Signal Processing and Cyber Security (iSSSC)*, (pp. 1-5). IEEE. https://doi: 10.1109/iSSSC56467.2022.10051210

Kościelniaka, H., & Puto, A. (2015). BIG DATA in decision making processes of enterprises. *Procedia Computer Science*, *65*, 1052–1058. doi:10.1016/j.procs.2015.09.053

Kotler, P., & Keller, K. L. (2021). *Marketing Management.* Pearson Practice Hall.

Kowalczyk, M., & Buxmann, P. (2014). Big Data and Information Processing in Organizational Decision Processes: A Multiple Case Study. *Business & Information Systems Engineering*, *5*(5), 267–278. doi:10.100712599-014-0341-5

Köylüoğlu, A., Tosun, P., & Doğan, M. (2021). The Impact of Marketing on the Business Performance of Companies: A Literature Review. *Anemon Muş Alparslan Üniversitesi Sosyal Bilimler Dergisi*, *9*(1), 63–74. doi:10.18506/anemon.763875

Krishna, G. S., Supriya, K., & Rao, K. M. (2022, September). Selection of data preprocessing techniques and its emergence towards machine learning algorithms using hpi dataset. In 2022 IEEE Global Conference on Computing, Power and Communication Technologies (GlobConPT) (pp. 1-6). IEEE. 10.1109/GlobConPT57482.2022.9938255

Krishnan, K. (2013). *Data warehousing in the age of big data.* Newnes.

Kukreja, H., N, B., & S, K. (2016). AN INTRODUCTION TO ARTIFICIAL NEURAL NETWORK. *International Journal Of Advance Research And Innovative Ideas In Education*, *1*(5), 27–30.

Kulkarni, A. (2016). A Study on Metadata Management and Quality Evaluation. *Big Data Management*, *4*(7).

Kumar, V. S., & Bagga, T. (2020). Marketing Intelligence: Antecedents and Consequences. Rochester, NY.

Kumar, V., Pareek, P., Albuquerque, V. H., Khanna, A., Gupta, D., & Madhumala, R. B. (2022). Multimodal Sentiment Analysis using Kernel Based Support Vector Machine. *Second International Conference on Advanced Technologies in Intelligent Control, Environment, Computing & Communication Engineering (ICATIECE)., (pp. 1-8). IEEE.* https://doi: 10.1109/ICATIECE56365.2022.10046818

Kwon, D., Kim, H., Kim, J., Suh, S. C., Kim, I., & Kim, K. J. (2019). A survey of deep learning-based network anomaly detection. *Cluster Computing*, *22*(1), 949–961. doi:10.100710586-017-1117-8

Kwon, O., Lee, N., & Shin, B. (2014). Data quality management, data usage experience and acquisition intention of big data analytics. *International Journal of Information Management*, *34*(3), 387–394. doi:10.1016/j.ijinfomgt.2014.02.002

Lackman, C., Saban, K., & Lanasa, J. (2000). The contribution of market intelligence to tactical and strategic business decisions". *Marketing Intelligence & Planning*, *18*(1), 8. doi:10.1108/02634500010308530

Landset, S., Khoshgoftaar, T. M., Richter, A. N., & Hasanin, T. (2015). A survey of open source tools for machine learning with big data in the Hadoop ecosystem. *Journal of Big Data*, *2*(1), 24. doi:10.118640537-015-0032-1

Langseth, J. (2004). Real-time data warehousing: Challenges and solutions. *DSSResources.com*, *2*(08).

Lautenbach, P., Johnston, K., & Adeniran-Ogundipe, T. (2017). Factors influencing bussiness intelligence and analytics usage extent in south african organaisations. *South African Journal of Business Management*, *48*(3), 23–33. doi:10.4102ajbm.v48i3.33

Lebdaoui, I., Orhanou, G., & Hajji, S. E. (2013). Data integrity in real-time data warehousing. In *Proceedings of the World Congress on Engineering*, (Vol. 3, pp. 3-5). IEEE.

LeCun, Y., Boser, B., Denker, J. S., Henderson, D., Howard, R. E., Hubbard, W., & Jackel, L. D. (1989). Backpropagation applied to Handwritten Zip Code recognition. *Neural Computation*, *1*(4), 541–551. doi:10.1162/neco.1989.1.4.541

LeCun, Y., Bottou, L., Bengio, Y., & Haffner, P. (1998). Gradient-based learning applied to document recognition. *Proceedings of the IEEE*, *86*(11), 2278–2324. doi:10.1109/5.726791

Lee, M.-L., Chung, H.-Y., & Yu, F.-M. (2003). Modeling of hierarchical fuzzy systems. *Fuzzy Sets and Systems*, *138*(2), 343–361. doi:10.1016/S0165-0114(02)00517-1

Lee, R., Luo, T., Huai, Y., Wang, F., He, Y., & Zhang, X. (2011). Ysmart: Yet Another SQL-toMapReduce Translator. In: *IEEE International Conference on Distributed Computing Systems (ICDCS), (pp. 25–36). IEEE.*

Leung, C. K. S., & Jiang, F. (2014, December). A data science solution for mining interesting patterns from uncertain big data. In *2014 IEEE Fourth International Conference on Big Data and Cloud Computing* (pp. 235-242). IEEE.

Lewis, P. V. (1985). Defining 'business ethics': Like nailing jello to a wall. *Journal of Business Ethics*, *4*(5), 377–383. doi:10.1007/BF02388590

Liang, Q., Xiang, S., Hu, Y., Coppola, G., Zhang, D., & Sun, W. (2019). PD2SE-Net: Computer-assisted plant disease diagnosis and severity estimation network. *Computers and Electronics in Agriculture*, *157*, 518–529. doi:10.1016/j.compag.2019.01.034

Li, D., Wang, H., Yuan, H., & Li, D. (2016). Software and applications of spatial data mining. *Wiley Interdisciplinary Reviews. Data Mining and Knowledge Discovery*, *6*(3), 84–114. doi:10.1002/widm.1180

Lin, S., Xie, H., Yu, L., & Lai, K. R. (2017). SentiNLP at IJCNLP-2017 Task 4: Customer Feedback Analysis Using a Bi-LSTM-CNN Model. In *Proceedings of the International Joint Conference on Natural Language Processing (IJCNLP), (pp. 149–154). Asian Federation of Natural Language Processing.*

Linardatos, P., Papastefanopoulos, V., & Kotsiantis, S. (2020). Explainable AI: A Review of Machine Learning Interpretability Methods. *Entropy (Basel, Switzerland)*, *23*(1), 18. doi:10.3390/e23010018 PMID:33375658

Lin, L., Liu, T., Hu, J., & Zhang, J. (2014). A privacy-aware cloud service selection method toward data life-cycle. In *Parallel and Distributed Systems (ICPADS) 20th IEEE International Conference on*, (pp. 752–759). IEEE. 10.1109/PADSW.2014.7097878

Lin, W.-C., Ke, S.-W., & Tsai, C.-F. (2015). CANN: An intrusion detection system based on combiningclustercentersandnearestneighbors. *Knowledge-Based Systems*, *78*, 13–21. doi:10.1016/j.knosys.2015.01.009

Lin, Z., Lai, Y., Lin, C., Xie, Y., & Zou, Q. (2011). Maintaining internal consistency of report for real-time OLAP with layer-based view. In *Web Technologies and Applications* (pp. 143–154). Springer. doi:10.1007/978-3-642-20291-9_16

Liu, X., & Nielsen, P. S. (2016). Regression-based Online Anomaly Detection for Smart Grid Data. arXivpreprint-arXiv:1606.05781.

Liu, B. (2020). *Sentiment analysis: mining opinions, sentiments, and emotions*. Cambridge University Press. doi:10.1017/9781108639286

Liu, Q., Klucik, R., Chen, C., Grant, G., Gallaher, D., Lv, Q., & Shang, L. (2017). *Unsupervised detection of contextual anomaly in remotely sensed data*. Remote Sensing of Environment.

Liu, Z., & Zhang, A. (2020). Sampling for big data profiling: A survey. *IEEE Access : Practical Innovations, Open Solutions*, *8*, 72713–72726. doi:10.1109/ACCESS.2020.2988120

Li, W. (2020). Enhancing Big Data Security: A Comprehensive Approach. *Journal of Cybersecurity*, *5*(3), 201–215.

Llave, M. R. (2018). Data lakes in business intelligence: Reporting from the trenches. *Procedia Computer Science*, *138*, 516–524. doi:10.1016/j.procs.2018.10.071

Lobato, A., Lopez, M. A., & Duarte, O. (2016). An accurate threat detection system through real-timestream processing. *Grupo de Teleinformática e-Automaçao (GTA), Univeridade Federal do Rio deJaneiro(UFRJ)*,Tech.Rep.GTA-16-08.

Lotsaris, K., Fousekis, N., Koukas, S., Aivaliotis, S., Kousi, N., Michalos, G., & Makris, S. (2021). Augmented Reality (AR) based framework for supporting human workers in flexible manufacturing. *Procedia CIRP*, *96*, 301–306. doi:10.1016/j.procir.2021.01.091

Lundervold, A. S., & Lundervold, A. (2019). An overview of deep learning in medical imaging focusing on MRI. *Zeitschrift für Medizinische Physik, Volume 29*(2), 102-127. doi:10.1016/j.zemedi.2018.11.002

Ma, K., & Yang, B. (2015). Log-based change data capture from schema-free document stores using mapreduce. In *Cloud Technologies and Applications (CloudTech), 2015 International Conference on*. IEEE. 10.1109/CloudTech.2015.7336969

Maddikunta, P. K. R., Pham, Q.-V., Prabadevi, B., Deepa, N., Dev, K., Gadekallu, T. R., Ruby, R., & Liyanage, M. (2022). Industry 5.0: A survey on enabling technologies and potential applications. *Journal of Industrial Information Integration*, *26*, 100257. doi:10.1016/j.jii.2021.100257

Maglaras, L.A., & Jiang, J. (2014). *Intrusion detection and systems using machine learning techniques*. Paper presented at the Science and Information Conference(SAI),2014.

Mahajan, H. B., Rashid, A. S., Junnarkar, A. A., Uke, N., Deshpande, S. D., Futane, P. R., Alkhayyat, A., & Alhayani, B. (2023). Integration of Healthcare 4.0 and blockchain into secure cloud-based electronic health records systems. *Applied Nanoscience*, *13*(3), 2329–2342. doi:10.100713204-021-02164-0 PMID:35136707

Mahajan, P., Uddin, S., Hajati, F., & Moni, M. A. (2023). Ensemble Learning for Disease Prediction: A Review. *Health Care, 11*(12), 1808. PMID:37372925

Maharani, P. U., Amalita, N., Amadi, A., & Fitri, F. (2023). Sentiment Analysis of GoRide Services on Twitter social media Using Naive Bayes Algorithm. *UNP Journal of Statistics and Data Science, 1*(3), 134–139. doi:10.24036/ujsds/vol1-iss3/41

Mahesh, B. (2019). Machine Learning Algorithms -. *RE:view, 9*(1).

Mahmood, T., & Afzal, U. (2013). Security analytics: Big data analytics for cybersecurity: A review oftrends, techniques and tools. *Paper presented at the Information assurance.* NCIA.

Mahmoud, M. A., Alomari, Y. M., Badawi, U. A., Ben Salah, A., Tayfour, M. F., Alghamdi, F. A., & Aseri, A. M. (2020). Impacts of marketing automation on business performance. *Journal of Theoretical and Applied Information Technology, 98*(11).

Mahmud, M. S., Huang, J. Z., Salloum, S., Emara, T. Z., & Sadatdiynov, K. (2020). A survey of data partitioning and sampling methods to support big data analysis. *Big Data Mining and Analytics, 3*(2), 85–101. doi:10.26599/BDMA.2019.9020015

Makhataeva, Z., & Varol, H. (2020). Augmented Reality for Robotics: A Review. *Robotics (Basel, Switzerland), 9*(2), 21. doi:10.3390/robotics9020021

Makridakis, S. S., Spiliotis, E., & Assimakopoulos, V. (2018). Statistical and Machine Learning forecasting methods. *Concerns and ways forward. PLoS One, 13*(3), e0194889. doi:10.1371/journal.pone.0194889 PMID:29584784

Mallek, H., Ghozzi, F., & Gargouri, F. (2020). Towards extract-transform-load operations in a big data context. [IJSKD]. *International Journal of Sociotechnology and Knowledge Development, 12*(2), 77–95. doi:10.4018/IJSKD.2020040105

Manisha, K. (2017). Recommender System. In *Big Data Environment, 3*(6).

Manjunath, C., Dwivedi, D. N., Thimmappa, R., & Vedamurthy, K. B. (2023). Detection and categorization of diseases in pearl millet leaves using novel convolutional neural network model. In *Future Farming* (Vol. 1, p. 41). Advancing Agriculture with Artificial Intelligence. doi:10.2174/9789815124729123010006

Manyika, J. et al. (2011). *Big data: The next frontier for innovation, competition, and productivity.*

Manyika, J.; Chui, M.; Bughin, J.; Brown, B.; Dobbs, R.; Roxburgh, C.; & Byers, A. H., (2011). *Big Data: The next frontier for innovation, competition, and productivity.* McKinsey Global Institute.

Mar'ın-Ortega, P. M., Dmitriyev, V., Abilov, M., & G'omez, J. M. (2014). ELTA: New approach in designing business intelligence solutions in era of big data. *Procedia Technology, 16*, 667–674. doi:10.1016/j.protcy.2014.10.015

Marchal, S., Jiang, X., State, R., & Engel, T. (2014). A big data architecture for large scale security monitoring. In *Proceeding of the International Congress on Big Data.* IEEE. 10.1109/BigData.Congress.2014.18

Martin, K. E., (2015). Ethical Issues in the Big Data Industry. *MIS Quarterly Executive, 14*(2), 67– 85.

Martins, P., Abbasi, M., & Furtado, P. (2016, January). Near-Real-Time Parallel ETL+ Q for Automatic Scalability in Bigdata. In *CS & IT Conference Proceedings (Vol. 6*, No. 1). CS & IT Conference Proceedings.

Martynov, V. V., Shavaleeva, D. N., & Zaytseva, A. A. (2019). *Information technology is the basis for transformation into a digital society and industry 5.0.* 539–543.

Marx, V. (2013). Biology: The big challenges of big data. *Nature*, *498*(7453), 255–260. doi:10.1038/498255a PMID:23765498

Marynowski, J. E., Santina, A. O., & Andrey, R. P. (2015). Method for Testing the Fault Tolerance of MapReduce Frameworks. *Computer Networks*, *86*, 1–13. doi:10.1016/j.comnet.2015.04.009

Mascaro, S., Nicholso, A. E., & Korb, K. B. (2014). Anomaly detection in vessel tracks using Bayesiannetworks. *InternationalJournalofApproximateReasoning*, *55*(1), 84–98.

Mashey, J.R. (1998). *Big Data ... and the Next Wave of InfraStress. Slides from invited talk.* Usenix.

Mcculloch, W. S., & Pitts, W. (1943). A logical calculus of the ideas immanent in nervous activity. *The Bulletin of Mathematical Biophysics*, *5*(4), 115–133. doi:10.1007/BF02478259

McMahan, B., Moore, E., Ramage, D., Hampson, S. & Arcas, B. (2017). Communication-Efficient Learning of Deep Networks from Decentralized Data. *Proceedings of the 20th International Conference on Artificial Intelligence and Statistics.* MLR Press. https://proceedings.mlr.press/v54/mcmahan17a.html.

McNeil, P., Shetty, S., Guntu, D., & Barve, G. (2016). SCREDENT: Scalable Real-time Anomalies Detectionand Notification of Targeted Malware in Mobile Devices. *Procedia Computer Science*, *83*, 1219–1225. doi:10.1016/j.procs.2016.04.254

Mehmood E and Anees T. (2022). Distributed real-time ETL architecture for unstructured big data. *Knowledge and Information Systems*. doi:10.1007/s10115-022-01757-7

Mentzer, J. T., & Gundlach, G. (2010). Exploring the relationship between marketing and supply chain management: Introduction to the special issue. *Journal of the Academy of Marketing Science*, *38*(1), 1–4. doi:10.100711747-009-0150-4

Metcalf, J., & Crawford, K. (2016). Where are human subjects in Big Data research? The emerging ethics divide. *Big Data & Society*, *3*(1). doi:10.1177/2053951716650211

Mikalef, P., Pappas, I.O., Krogstie, J., & Giannakos, M. (2018). Big data analytics capabilities: a systematic literature review and research agenda. *Inf Syst e-Business Manage.* *6*(3), 547–78.

MIKE 2.0, (2013). *Big Data Solution Offering.* MIKE2.0.

MIKE 2.0, (2018). *Big Data Definition.* MIKE2.0.

Milgram, P. (1994). A taxonomy of mixed reality visual displays. *IEICE Transactions on Information and Systems*, *77*(12), 1321–1329.

Miloslavskaya, N., Senatorov, M., Tolstoy, A., & Zapechnikov, S. (2014). Big data information security maintenance. In *Proceedings of the 7th International Conference on Security of Information and Networks—SIN,* (pp. 89–94). ACM Press. 10.1145/2659651.2659655

Mingers, J., and Walsham, G., (2010). "Towards ethical information systems: The contribution of discourse ethics," (34:4), pp. 833–854.

Minghini, M., & Frassinelli, F. (2019). OpenStreetMap history for intrinsic quality assessment: Is OSM up-to-date? *Open Geospatial Data. Software and Standards*, *4*(1), 9. doi:10.118640965-019-0067-x

Mitchell, T. (1997). *Machine Learning.* McGraw Hill.

Mo, R., Liu, J., Yu, W., Jiang, F., Gu, X., Zhao, X., & Peng, J. (2019, August). A differential privacy-based protecting data preprocessing method for big data mining. In *2019 18th IEEE International Conference On Trust, Security And Privacy In Computing And Communications/13th IEEE International Conference On Big Data Science And Engineering (TrustCom/BigDataSE)* (pp. 693-699). IEEE. 10.1109/TrustCom/BigDataSE.2019.00098

Mohammed Alqahtani, T. (2023). Big Data Analytics with Optimal Deep Learning Model for Medical Image Classification. *Computer Systems Science and Engineering, 44*(2), 1433–1449. doi:10.32604/csse.2023.025594

Monash, C., (2009). eBay's two enormous data warehouses. EBay,

Mondal, K. C., Biswas, N., & Saha, S. (2020). Role of machine learning in ETL automation. In *Proceedings of the 21st International Conference on Distributed Computing and Networking*. ACM. 10.1145/3369740.3372778

Morales-Botello, M. L., Gachet, D., De Buenaga, M., Aparicio, F., Busto, M. J., & Ascanio, J. R. (2021). Chronic patient remote monitoring through the application of big data and internet of things. *Health Informatics Journal, 27*(3), 146045822110309. doi:10.1177/14604582211030956 PMID:34256646

Morgan, R. M., & Hunt, S. D. (1994). The Commitment-Trust Theory of Relationship Marketing. *Journal of Marketing, 58*(3), 20–38. doi:10.1177/002224299405800302

Naeem, S., Logoftu, D., Muharemi, F. (2020). Sentiment Analysis by Using Supervised Machine Learning and Deep Learning Approaches. *Advances in Computational Collective Intelligence*, (pp. 481-491). IEEE. https://doi: . doi:10.1007/978-3-030-63119-2_39

Naeem, M. A., Dobbie, G., & Webber, G. (2008). An event-based near real time data integration architecture. In *12th Enterprise Distributed Object Computing Conference Workshops*. IEEE. 10.1109/EDOCW.2008.14

Naeem, M. A., Mehmood, E., Malik, M. A., & Jamil, N. (2020). Optimizing semi-stream CACHEJOIN for near-real-time data warehousing. [JDM]. *Journal of Database Management, 31*(1), 20–37. doi:10.4018/JDM.2020010102

Nahumury, A. J., Manongga, D., Iriani, A. (2022). Analysis Sentiment on Airline Customer Satisfaction Using Recurrent Neural Network. *Journal Eduvest - Journal of Universal Studies, 2*(10), 2119-2129. https://doi: . v2i10.594. doi:10.36418/eduvest

Najafabadi, M. M., Villanustre, F., Khoshgoftaar, T. M., Seliya, N., Wald, R., & Muharemagc, E. (2016). Deep Learning Techniques in Big Data Analytics. In B. Furht & F. Villanustre, Big Data Technologies and Applications (pp. 133–156). Springer International Publishing. doi:10.1007/978-3-319-44550-2_5

Najafabadi, M., Villanustre, F., Khoshgoftaar, T., Seliva, N., Muharemagic, E., & Wald, R. (2015). Deep learning applications and challenges in big data analytics. *Journal of Big Data, 2*(1), 1. doi:10.118640537-014-0007-7

Narayanan, V. (2014). Using Big-Data Analytics to Manage Data Deluge and Unlock Real-Time Business Insights. *Journal of Equipment Lease Financing., 32*, 1–7.

Nardo, M., Forino, D., & Murino, T. (2020). The evolution of man–machine interaction: The role of the humans in Industry 4.0 paradigm. *Production & Manufacturing Research, 8*(1), 20–34. doi:10.1080/21693277.2020.1737592

Nasteski, V. (2017). An overview of the supervised machine learning methods. *HORIZONS.B, 4*, 51–62.

Nations, U. (2018). *Revision of world urbanization prospects*. United Nations.

Nazari, E., Shahriari, M. H., & Tabesh, H. (2019). BigData Analysis in Healthcare: Apache Hadoop, Apache spark and Apache Flink. *Frontiers in Health Informatics, 8*(1), 14. doi:10.30699/fhi.v8i1.180

Newell, S., & Marabelli, M. (2015). *"Strategic opportunities (and challenges) of algorithmic decision making: A call for action on the long-term societal effects of 'datification,'" The Journal of Strategic Information Systems.* Elsevier B.V.

Nur Cahyo, D. D., Farasalsabila, F., Lestari, V. B., Hanafi, Lestari, T., Al Islami, F. R., & Maulana, M. A. (2023). Sentiment Analysis for IMDb Movie Review Using Support Vector Machine (SVM) Method. *Inform: Jurnal Ilmiah Bidang Teknologi Informasi Dan Komunikasi, 8*(2), 90–95. doi:10.25139/inform.v8i2.5700

Nurcahyawati, V., & Mustaffa, Z. (2023). Vader Lexicon and Support Vector Machine Algorithm to Detect Customer Sentiment Orientation. *Journal of Information Systems Engineering and Business Intelligence., 9*(1), 108–118. doi:10.20473/jisebi.9.1.108-118

O'Shea, K., & Nash, R. (2015). *An Introduction to Convolutional Neural Networks.*

Obaid, H. S., Dheyab, S. A., & Sabry, S. S. (2019, March). The impact of data pre-processing techniques and dimensionality reduction on the accuracy of machine learning. In *2019 9th Annual Information Technology, Electromechanical Engineering and Microelectronics Conference (IEMECON)* (pp. 279-283). IEEE. 10.1109/IEMECONX.2019.8877011

Office of the Attorney General of California. (n.d.). *California Consumer Privacy Act (CCPA).* OAG. https://oag.ca.gov/privacy/ccpa

Okazaki, S., Eisend, M., Plangger, K., Ruyter, K., & Grewal, D. (2020). Understanding the Strategic Consequences of Customer Privacy Concerns: A Meta-Analytic Review. *Journal of Retailing, 96*(4), 458–473. doi:10.1016/j.jretai.2020.05.007

openstreetmap. (2023a). *What is the history of OSM?* Open Street Map. https://welcome.openstreetmap.org/about-osm-community/history-of-osm/

openstreetmap. (2023b). *Why use OpenStreetMap?* Open Street Map. https://welcome.openstreetmap.org/why-openstreetmap/

Oracle. (2015). *Demystifying data integration for the cloud.* Oracle White paper. Oracle Corporation, Redwood Shores (USA). http://www.audentia-gestion.fr/oracle/data-integration-for-cloud-1870536.pdf

OSM. (2021). *OpenStreetMap Copyright and License.* Open Street Map. https://www.openstreetmap.org/copyright

Özdemir, V., & Hekim, N. (2018). Birth of Industry 5.0: Making sense of big data with artificial intelligence," the Internet of Things", and next-generation technology policy. *OMICS: A Journal of Integrative Biology, 22*(1), 65–76. doi:10.1089/omi.2017.0194 PMID:29293405

Pandey, C., Baghel, N., Dutta, M. K., Srivastava, A., & Choudhary, N. (2021). Machine learning approach for automatic diagnosis of Chlorosis in Vigna mungo leaves. *Multimedia Tools and Applications, 80*(9), 13407–13427. doi:10.100711042-020-10309-6

Panigutti, C., Hamon, R., Hupont, I., Fernandez Llorca, D., Fano Yela, D., Junklewitz, H., Scalzo, S., Mazzini, G., Sanchez, I., Soler Garrido, J., & Gomez, E. (2023). The role of explainable AI in the context of the AI Act. *2023 ACM Conference on Fairness, Accountability, and Transparency,* (pp. 1139–1150). ACM. 10.1145/3593013.3594069

Pan, X., Xu, J., & Meng, X. (2012). Protecting location privacy against location-dependent attacks in mobile services. *IEEE Transactions on Knowledge and Data Engineering, 24*(8), 1506–1519. doi:10.1109/TKDE.2011.105

Paradza, D., & Daramola, O. (2021). Business intelligence and business value in organisations: A systematic literature review. In Sustainability (Switzerland) (Vol. 13, Issue 20). doi:10.3390u132011382

Pareek, A., Khaladkar, B., Sen, R., Onat, B., Nadimpalli, V., & Lakshminarayanan, M. (2018, August). Real-time ETL in Striim. In *Proceedings of the international workshop on real-time business intelligence and analytics* (pp. 1-10). ACM.

Park, S., Cho, J., Park, K., & Shin, H. (2021). Customer sentiment analysis with more sensibility. *Engineering Applications of Artificial Intelligence*, *104*, 104356. doi:10.1016/j.engappai.2021.104356

Parmenter, D. (2015). *Key performance indicators: Developing, implementing, and using winning KPIs*. John Wiley & Sons. doi:10.1002/9781119019855

Passlick, J., Lebek, B., & Breitner, M. H. (2017). A Self-Service Supporting Business Intelligence and Big Data Analytics Architecture. In J. M. Leimeister & W. Brenner (Eds.), Proceedings der 13. Interna tionalen Tagung Wirtschaftsinformatik (WI 2017) (pp. 1126–1140). Academic Press.

Pasupa, K., Kittiworapanya, P., Hongngern, N., & Woraratpanya, K. (2021). Evaluation of deep learning algorithms for semantic segmentation of car parts. *Complex & Intelligent Systems*, *8*(5), 1–10. doi:10.100740747-021-00397-8

Patel, A., Oza, P., & Agrawal, S. (2023). Sentiment Analysis of Customer Feedback and Reviews for Airline Services using Language Representation Model. *Procedia Computer Science*, *218*, 2459–2467. doi:10.1016/j.procs.2023.01.221

Patel, M., & Patel, D. B. (2022). Data Warehouse Modernization Using Document-Oriented ETL Framework for Real Time Analytics. In *Rising Threats in Expert Applications and Solutions* [Singapore: Springer Nature Singapore.]. *Proceedings of FICR-TEAS*, *2022*, 33–41.

Patil, K. & Seshadri, R. (2014). Big Data Security and Privacy Issues in Healthcare. *Proceedings - 2014 IEEE International Congress on Big Data, BigData Congress 2014*, (pp. 762–765). IEEE. . https://ieeexplore.ieee.org/document/6906856 doi:10.1109/BigData.Congress.2014.112

Patil, K., Kulkarni, M., Sriraman, A., & Karande, S. (2017). Deep Learning Based Car Damage Classification. *Proceedings of the 16th IEEE International Conference on Machine Learning and Applications (ICMLA)*, (pp. 50-54). IEEE. 10.1109/ICMLA.2017.0-179

Patrick, H. A., Sharief, P. J. M. H., & Mukherjee, U. (2023). Sentiment Analysis Perspective using Supervised Machine Learning Method. *Fifth International Conference on Electrical, Computer and Communication Technologies (ICECCT)*, (pp. 1-4). IEEE. 10.1109/ICECCT56650.2023.10179807

Pedregosa, F., Varoquaux, G., Gramfort, A., Michel, V., Thirion, B., Grisel, O., Blondel, M., Prettenhofer, P., Weiss, R., & Dubourg, V. (2011). Scikit-learn: Machine learning in python. *Journal of Machine Learning Research*, *12*, 2825–2830.

Perer, A., & Liu, S. (2019). Visualization in data science. *IEEE Computer Graphics and Applications*, *39*(5), 18–19. doi:10.1109/MCG.2019.2925493 PMID:31442962

Pichler, M., & Hartig, F. (2023). Machine learning and deep learning—A review for ecologists. *Methods in Ecology and Evolution*, *14*(4), 994–1016. doi:10.1111/2041-210X.14061

Polyzotis, N., Skiadopoulos, S., Vassiliadis, P., Simitsis, A., & Frantzell, N. (2007). Supporting streaming updates in an active data warehouse. In *IEEE 23rd International Conference on Data Engineering (ICDE'07)*. IEEE. 10.1109/ICDE.2007.367893

Popovič, A., Hackney, R., Tassabehji, R., & Castelli, M. (2018). The impact of big data analytics on frms' high value business performance. *Information Systems Frontiers*, *20*(2), 209–222. doi:10.100710796-016-9720-4

Pozza, E. A., de Carvalho Alves, M., & Sanches, L. (2022). Using computer vision to identify seed-borne fungi and other targets associated with common bean seeds based on red–green–blue spectral data. *Tropical Plant Pathology*, *47*(1), 168–185. doi:10.100740858-021-00485-7

Pradha, S., Halgamuge, M. N., & Vinh, N. T. Q. (2019, October). Effective text data preprocessing technique for sentiment analysis in social media data. In *2019 11th international conference on knowledge and systems engineering (KSE)* (pp. 1-8). IEEE. 10.1109/KSE.2019.8919368

Pradhan, S. (2022). *A Guide to Sentiment Analysis – Part 2*. Nitor.

Praful Bharadiya, J. (2023). A Comparative Study of Business Intelligence and Artificial Intelligence with Big Data Analytics. *American Journal of Artificial Intelligence*.

Pramanik, S., & Obaid, A. J., N M, & Bandyopadhyay, S. K. (2023). Applications of Big Data in Clinical Applications. *Al-Kadhum 2nd International Conference on Modern Applications of Information and Communication Technology*. AIP. 10.1063/5.0119414

Pramanik, S., Samanta, D., Ghosh, R., & Bandyopadhyay, S. K. (2021). A New Combinational Technique in Image Steganography. *International Journal of Information Security and Privacy, 15*(3). doi:10.4018/IJISP.2021070104

Pramanik, S., Singh, R. P. and Ghosh, R. (2019). A New Encrypted Method in Image Steganography. *International Journal of Electrical and Computer Engineering, 14*(3), 1412- 1419. DOI: , 2019. doi:10.11591/ijeecs.v13.i3.pp1412-1419

Pramanik, S. (2022). An Effective Secured Privacy-Protecting Data Aggregation Method in IoT. In M. O. Odhiambo, W. Mwashita, & I. G. I. Global (Eds.), *Achieving Full Realization and Mitigating the Challenges of the Internet of Things.*, doi:10.4018/978-1-7998-9312-7.ch008

Pramanik, S. (2023). An Adaptive Image Steganography Approach depending on Integer Wavelet Transform and Genetic Algorithm. *Multimedia Tools and Applications, 2023*(22), 34287–34319. Advance online publication. doi:10.100711042-023-14505-y

Pramanik, S., Galety, M. G., Samanta, D., & Joseph, N. P. (2022). Data Mining Approaches for Decision Support Systems, *3rd International Conference on Emerging Technologies in Data Mining and Information Security*. IOP.

Pratama, M. R., Soerawinata, F. A., Zhafari, R. R., Imanda, H. N. (2022). Sentiment Analysis of Beauty Product E-Commerce Using Support Vector Machine Method. *Jurnal RESTI (Rekayasa Sistem dan Teknologi Informasi), 6*(2), 269-274. https://doi: . v6i2.3876 doi:10.29207/resti

Praveenkumar, S., Veeraiah, V., Pramanik, S., Basha, S. M., Lira Neto, A. V., De Albuquerque, V. H. C., & Gupta, A. (2023). Prediction of Patients' [Springer]. *Incurable Diseases Utilizing Deep Learning Approaches, ICICC, 2023*.

Prestby, J., & Wandersman, A. (1985). A. An empirical exploration of a framework of organizational viability: Maintaining block organizations. *The Journal of Applied Behavioral Science, 21*(3), 287–305. doi:10.1177/002188638502100305

Provost, F., & Fawcett, T. (2013). *Data science for business: what you need to know about data mining and data-analytic thinking*. O'Reilly Media, Inc.

PyTorch. (2023, October 7). *PyTorch Opacus*. GitHub. https://github.com/pytorch/opacus

Qiu, J., Wu, Q., Ding, G., Xu, Y., & Feng, S. (2016). A survey of machine learning for big data processing. *EURASIP Journal on Advances in Signal Processing, 2016*(1), 67. doi:10.118613634-016-0355-x

Rahmaty, M. (2023). Machine learning with big data to solve real-world problems. *Journal of Data Analytics, 2*(1), 9–16. doi:10.59615/jda.2.1.9

Rana, M., & Bhushan, M. (2023). Machine learning and deep learning approach for medical image analysis: Diagnosis to detection. *Multimedia Tools and Applications, 82*(17), 26731–26769. doi:10.100711042-022-14305-w PMID:36588765

Ray, S. (2019, February). A quick review of machine learning algorithms. In *2019 International conference on machine learning, big data, cloud and parallel computing (COMITCon)* (pp. 35-39). IEEE. 10.1109/COMITCon.2019.8862451

Raza, A., Chrysogelos, P., Sioulas, P., Indjic, V., Ailamaki, A., & Anadiotis, A. (2020). GPU-accelerated data management under the test of time. *Conference on Innovative Data Systems Research.*

Redman, T. C. (1998). The impact of poor data quality on the typical enterprise". *Communications of the ACM, 41*(2), 81. doi:10.1145/269012.269025

Reeve, A. (2013). Managing data in motion: Data integration best practice techniques and technologies. Research Gate.

Reinsel, D. (2018, November 27). *The Digitization of the World from Edge to Core.* Seagate Technology. https://www.seagate.com/files/www-content/our-story/trends/files/idc-seagate-dataage-whitepaper.pdf

Resch, B., & Szell, M., (2019). *Human-centric data science for urban studies.*

Reuters. (2019, July 24). *Facebook to pay a record $5 billion U.S. fine over privacy, faces antitrust probe.* Reuters. https://www.reuters.com/article/us-facebook-ftc/facebook-to-pay-record-5-billion-u-s-fine-over-privacy-faces-antitrust-probe-idUSKCN1UJ1L9

Revathy, S., Saravana, B. B., & Karthikeyan, N. K. (2013). From data warehouse to streaming data warehouse: A survey on the challenges for real time data warehousing and available solutions. *International Journal of Computer Applications, 975,* 8887.

Riahi, A., & Riahi, S., (2015). The Big Data Revolution, Issues and Applications. *IJARCSSE, 5*(8).

Ridzuan, F., Wan, Z., & Wan, M. N. (2019). A Review on Data Cleansing Methods for Big Data". *Procedia Computer Science, 161,* 731–738. doi:10.1016/j.procs.2019.11.177

Robbins, H., & Monro, S. (1951). A Stochastic Approximation Method". *Annals of Mathematical Statistics, 22*(3), 400–407. doi:10.1214/aoms/1177729586

Rohini, P., Tripathi, S., Preeti, C. M., Renuka, A., Gonzales, J. L. A., & Gangodkar, D. (2022, April). A study on the adoption of Wireless Communication in Big Data Analytics Using Neural Networks and Deep Learning. In *2022 2nd International Conference on Advance Computing and Innovative Technologies in Engineering (ICACITE)* (pp. 1071-1076). IEEE. 10.1109/ICACITE53722.2022.9823439

Rokhman, W., & Andiani, F. (2020). Understanding Muslim Young Consumers on Online Shopping: The role of Customer Review, Price, Trust and Security. *Equilibrium: Journal Ekonomi Syariah, 8*(2), 297–312. doi:10.21043/equilibrium.v8i2.8655

Rosenblatt, F. (1958). The perceptron: A probabilistic model for information storage and organization in the brain. *Psychological Review, 65*(6), 386–408. doi:10.1037/h0042519 PMID:13602029

Rosenfeld, L. (2006). *Information architecture for the World Wide Web: Designing large-scale web sites.* O'Reilly Media.

Rožanec, J. M., Novalija, I., Zajec, P., Kenda, K., Tavakoli Ghinani, H., Suh, S., Veliou, E., Papamartzivanos, D., Giannetsos, T., & Menesidou, S. A. (2022). Human-centric artificial intelligence architecture for industry 5.0 applications. *International Journal of Production Research,* ●●●, 1–26.

Russell, S. J., & Norvig, P. (2010). *Artificial Intelligence: A Modern Approach* (3rd ed.). Prentice Hall.

Russom, P. (2011). Big Data Analytics. In: TDWI Best Practices Report, (pp. 1–40). TDWI.

Saeed, M. M., Al Aghbari, Z., & Alsharidah, M. (2020). Big data clustering techniques based on Spark: A literature review. *PeerJ. Computer Science*, *6*, e321. doi:10.7717/peerj-cs.321 PMID:33816971

Sagiroglu, S. (2013). Big data: A review. *2013 International Conference on Collaboration Technologies and Systems (CTS)*. IEEE. 10.1109/CTS.2013.6567202

Sahu, M., Dhawale, K., Bhagat, D., Wankkhede, C., & Gajbhiye, D. (2023). Convex Hull Algorithm based Virtual Mouse. *Grenze International Journal of Engineering & Technology (GIJET)*, *9*(2).

Sainger, D. G. (2021). Sentiment Analysis - An Assessment of Online Public Opinion: A Conceptual Review. [TURCO-MAT]. *Turkish Journal of Computer and Mathematics Education*, *12*(5), 1881–1887. doi:10.17762/turcomat.v12i5.2266

Salehinejad, H., Sankar, S., Barfett, J., Colak, E., & Valaee, S. (2018). *Recent Advances in Recurrent Neural Networks*.

Salloum, S., Huang, J. Z., & He, Y. (2019). Random sample partition: A distributed data model for big data analysis. *IEEE Transactions on Industrial Informatics*, *15*(11), 5846–5854. doi:10.1109/TII.2019.2912723

Samanta, D., Dutta, S., Galety, M. G., & Pramanik, S. (2021). A Novel Approach for Web Mining Taxonomy for High-Performance Computing. *The 4th International Conference of Computer Science and Renewable Energies (ICCSRE'2021)*, *2021*. ACL. 10.1051/e3sconf/202129701073

Sarker, I. H. (2019). A machine learning based robust prediction model for real-life mobile phone data. *Internet of Things : Engineering Cyber Physical Human Systems*, *5*, 180–193. doi:10.1016/j.iot.2019.01.007

Sarker, I. H. (2021). Machine learning: Algorithms, real-world applications and research directions. *SN Computer Science*, *2*(3), 1–21. doi:10.100742979-021-00592-x PMID:33778771

Sarker, I. H., Colman, A., & Han, J. (2019). Recencyminer: Mining recencybased personalized behavior from contextual smartphone data. *Journal of Big Data*, *6*(1), 1–21. doi:10.118640537-019-0211-6

Sarker, I. H., Colman, A., Kabir, M. A., & Han, J. (2018). Individualized time series segmentation for mining mobile phone user behavior. *The Computer Journal*, *61*(3), 349–368. doi:10.1093/comjnl/bxx082

Sarker, I. H., Hoque, M. M., Uddin, M. K., & Alsanoosy, T. (2020). Mobile data science and intelligent apps: Concepts, ai-based modeling and research directions. *Mobile Networks and Applications*, 1–19.

Sarker, I. H., & Kayes, A. S. M. (2020). Abc-ruleminer: User behavioral rule based machine learning method for context-aware intelligent services. *Journal of Network and Computer Applications*, *168*, 102762. doi:10.1016/j.jnca.2020.102762

Sarker, I. H., Kayes, A. S. M., Badsha, S., Alqahtani, H., Watters, P., & Ng, A. (2020). Cybersecurity data science: An overview from machine learning perspective. *Journal of Big Data*, *7*(1), 1–29. doi:10.118640537-020-00318-5

SarrettaA.NapolitanoM.MinghiniM. (2023). Openstreetmap as an input source for producing governmental datasets: the case of the italian military geographic institute. *The International Archives of the Photogrammetry, Remote Sensing and Spatial Information Sciences*, *XLVIII-4/W7-2023*, 193–200. ISPRS. doi:10.5194/isprs-archives-XLVIII-4-W7-2023-193-2023

Satyanarayan, A. M. (2016). Vega-Lite: A grammar of interactive graphics. *IEEE Transactions on Visualization and Computer Graphics*, 341–350. PMID:27875150

Sawant, N., & Shah, H. (2013). Big Data Visualization Patterns. In Big Data Application Architecture Q & A, 79-90. Springer. doi:10.1007/978-1-4302-6293-0_7

Schein, E. H. (1985). *Organizational culture and leadership*. Jossey-Bass.

Schläpfer, M., Bettencourt, L. M. A., Grauwin, S., Raschke, M., Claxton, R., Smoreda, Z., West, G. B., & Ratti, C. (2014). The scaling of human interactions with city size. *Journal of the Royal Society, Interface, 11*(98), 20130789. doi:10.1098/rsif.2013.0789 PMID:24990287

Schmidhuber, J. (2022). *Annotated History of Modern AI and Deep Learning.*

Schumann, J., Gupta, P., & Liu, Y. (2010). Application of neural networks in high assurance systems: A survey. In *Applications of Neural Networks in High Assurance Systems* (pp. 1–19). Springer. doi:10.1007/978-3-642-10690-3_1

SCIP. (1991). SCIP Europe established. *Competitive Intelligence Review, 2*(1), 51–52.

Segel, E., & Heer, J. (2010). Narrative visualization: Telling stories with data. *IEEE Transactions on Visualization and Computer Graphics, 16*(6), 1139–1148. doi:10.1109/TVCG.2010.179 PMID:20975152

Sellami, M., Mezni, H., & Hacid, M. S. (2020). On the use of big data frameworks for big service composition. *Journal of Network and Computer Applications, 166*, 102732. doi:10.1016/j.jnca.2020.102732

Shantkumari, M., & Uma, S. (2021). Grape leaf segmentation for disease identification through adaptive Snake algorithm model. *Multimedia Tools and Applications, 80*(6), 1–19. doi:10.100711042-020-09853-y

Sharma, A. (2020). The organization of customer support services". *European Journal of Marketing, 54*(7), 1813–1814. doi:10.1108/EJM-07-2020-974

Sharma, G. D., Yadav, A., & Chopra, R. (2020). Artificial intelligence and effective governance: A review, critique and research agenda. *Sustainable Futures : An Applied Journal of Technology, Environment and Society, 2*, 100004. doi:10.1016/j.sftr.2019.100004

Shayaa, S., Jaafar, N. I., Bahri, S., Sulaiman, A., Seuk Wai, P., Wai Chung, Y., Piprani, A. Z., & Al-Garadi, M. A. (2018). Sentiment Analysis of Big Data: Methods, Applications, and Open Challenges. *IEEE Access : Practical Innovations, Open Solutions, 6*(6), 37807–37827. doi:10.1109/ACCESS.2018.2851311

Shi, J., Bao, Y., Leng, F., & Yu, G. (2008). Study on log-based change data capture and handling mechanism in real-time data warehouse. In *Computer Science and Software Engineering, 2008 International Conference*. IEEE. 10.1109/CSSE.2008.926

Shukla, N., & Fricklas, K. (2018). *Machine learning with TensorFlow*. Manning.

Shukla, S., Kukade, V., & Mujawar, S. (2015). Big Data: Concept, Handling and Challenges: An Overview. *International Journal of Computer Applications, 114*(11), 6–9. doi:10.5120/20020-1537

Shun'ichi, A. (1967). A theory of adaptive pattern classifier. *IEEE Transactions,* (16), 279–307.

Singh, S., & Singh, N. (2012). Big data analytics, 2012 International Conference on Communication. *Information Computing Technology (ICCICT 2012), 4*.

Singhal, B., & Aggarwal, A. (2022). ETL, ELT and Reverse ETL: A business case Study. In *2022 Second International Conference on Advanced Technologies in Intelligent Control, Environment, Computing & Communication Engineering (ICATIECE)* (pp. 1-4). IEEE. 10.1109/ICATIECE56365.2022.10046997

Singh, D., & Srivastava, V. M. (2017, January). Triple band regular decagon shaped metamaterial absorber for X-band applications. In *2017 International Conference on Computer Communication and Informatics (ICCCI)* (pp. 1-4). IEEE.

Singh, R., Tiwari, A., & Gupta, R. (2022). Deep transfer modeling for classification of Maize Plant Leaf Disease. *Multimedia Tools and Applications, 81*(5), 6051–6067. Advance online publication. doi:10.100711042-021-11763-6

Sitepu, M.B., Munthe, I.R., & Harahap, S.Z. (2022). Implementation of Support Vector Machine Algorithm for Shopee Customer Sentiment Analysis. *Sinkron: jurnal dan penelitian teknik informatika, 7*(2), 619-627. https://doi: . v7i2.11408 doi:10.33395/sinkron

Sivarajah, U., Kamal, M. M., Irani, Z., & Weerakkody, V. (2017). Critical analysis of Big Data challenges and analytical methods. *Journal of Business Research, 70*, 263–286. doi:10.1016/j.jbusres.2016.08.001

Ślusarczyk, B., (2018). Industry 4.0: are we ready? Pol J Manag Stud., 17.

Smith, J. (2017). Data Quality in Big Data: A Review. *Journal of Data Analysis14(2)*, 112-125.

Snijders, C.; Matzat, U.; & Reips, U.-D. (2012). "'Big Data': Big gaps of knowledge in the field of Internet". International Journal of Internet Science. **7**: 1–5. Archived on 23 November 2019.

Somantri, O., & Apriliani, D. (2018). Support Vector Machine Berbasis Feature Selection Untuk Sentiment Analysis Kepuasan Pelanggan Terhadap Pelayanan Warung dan Restoran Kuliner Kota Tegal. [JTIIK]. *Jurnal Teknologi Informasi Dan Ilmu Komputer, 5*(5), 537–548. doi:10.25126/jtiik.201855867

Song, J., Bao, Y., & Shi, J. (2010). A triggering and scheduling approach for ETL in a real-time data warehouse. In *Computer and Information Technology (CIT), 2010 IEEE 10th International Conference on*, (pp. 91-98). IEEE. 10.1109/CIT.2010.57

Sowmya, R., & Suneetha, K. R. (2017, January). Data mining with big data. In *2017 11th International Conference on Intelligent Systems and Control (ISCO)* (pp. 246-250). IEEE. 10.1109/ISCO.2017.7855990

Srinivasan, R., & Subalalitha, C. N. (2021). Sentimental analysis from imbalanced code-mixed data using machine learning approaches. *Distributed and Parallel Databases, 41*, 37–52. doi:10.100710619-021-07331-4 PMID:33776212

Steele, J. (2010). *Designing data visualizations*. O'Reilly Media.

Steve, L. (2013). The Origins of 'Big Data': An Etymological Detective Story. *The New York* Times.

Subramanian. R, S., P, G., M, A., M G, D., J, A., & P, D. (2023). Heterogeneous Ensemble Variable Selection to Improve Customer Prediction Using Naive Bayes Model. *International Journal on Recent and Innovation Trends in Computing and Communication, 11*(5s), 64–71. doi:10.17762/ijritcc.v11i5s.6599

Sughasiny, M., & Rajeshwari, J. (2018, August). Application of machine learning techniques, big data analytics in health care sector–a literature survey. In *2018 2nd International Conference on I-SMAC (IoT in Social, Mobile, Analytics and Cloud)(I-SMAC) I-SMAC (IoT in Social, Mobile, Analytics and Cloud)(I-SMAC), 2018 2nd International Conference on* (pp. 741-749). IEEE. 10.1109/I-SMAC.2018.8653654

Sukarsa, I. M., Wisswani, N. W., & Darma, I. G. (2012). Change data capture on OLTP staging area for nearly real time data warehouse base on database trigger. *International Journal of Computer Applications, 52*(11).

Sukhobok, D., Nikolov, N., & Roman, D. (2017, August). Tabular data anomaly patterns. In *2017 International Conference on Big Data Innovations and Applications (Innovate-Data)* (pp. 25-34). IEEE. 10.1109/Innovate-Data.2017.10

Sultana, F., Sufian, A., & Dutta, P. (2018). Advancements in Image Classification using Convolutional Neural Network. *2018 Fourth International Conference on Research in Computational Intelligence and Communication Networks (ICRCICN)*, Kolkata, India. 10.1109/ICRCICN.2018.8718718

Sumayya, K. A., Joseph, R., Saisree, R. K., & Satheesh, T. S. (2022). Sentiment Analysis on Student Feedback Using RNN. *International Journal of Engineering Research in Computer Science and Engineering, 9*(7), 52–57. doi:10.36647/IJERCSE/09.07.Art012

Sun, Z., Zou, H., & Strang, K. (2015). Big Data Analytics as a Service for Business Intelligence. *14th Conference on e-Business, e-Services and e-Society (I3E)*, (pp. 200-211). Springer. 10.1007/978-3-319-25013-7_16

Surekha, L., & Jayanthi, A. (2019). A Movie Review Sentiment Analysis Using Machine Learning Techniques. *International Journal of Recent Scientific Research, 10*(08), 34492–34497. doi:10.24327/ijrsr.2019.1008.3906

Suzumura, T., Yasue, T., & Onodera, T. (2010). Scalable performance of system s for extract-transform-load processing. In *Proceedings of the 3rd Annual Haifa Experimental Systems Conference*. ACM. 10.1145/1815695.1815704

Syed-Ab-Rahman, S., Hesamian, M. H., & Prasad, M. (2021). Citrus disease detection and classification using end-to-end anchor-based deep learning model. *Applied Intelligence, 52*(1), 927–938. doi:10.100710489-021-02452-w

Tank, D. M., Ganatra, A., Kosta, Y. P., & Bhensdadia, C. K. (2010). Speeding ETL processing in data warehouses using high-performance joins for changed data capture (CDC). In *Advances in Recent Technologies in Communication and Computing (ARTCom), 2010 International Conference on*, pages 365-368. IEEE.

Tanutammakun, S. (2020). *Car damage classification for car insurance company by using Colab with convolutional neural networks deep learning method*. https://digital.library.tu.ac.th/tu_dc/frontend/Info/item/dc:181816

Tan, W. T., & Zafar, U. A. (1999). Managing market intelligence: An Asian marketing research perspective". *Marketing Intelligence & Planning, 17*(6), 39.

TensorFlow. (2023, October 7). *TensorFlow Privacy*. GitHub. https://github.com/tensorflow/privacy

Tetzlaff, L., Rulle, K., Szepannek, G., & Gronau, W. (2019). A customer feedback sentiment dictionary: Towards automatic assessment of online reviews. *European Journal of Tourism Research, 23*, 28–39. doi:10.54055/ejtr.v23i.387

Thakur, A. (2021). Fundamentals of Neural Networks. *International Journal for Research in Applied Science and Engineering Technology, 9*(VIII), 407–426. doi:10.22214/ijraset.2021.37362

The Future of Market Intelligence. (2023). More Inclusive, More Proactive, More Personalized. *The Future of Market Intelligence*. https://gis.usc.edu/blog/how-gis-is-taking-advantage-of-big-data/

The Guardian. (2019, March 17). *The Cambridge Analytica scandal changed the world but did not change Facebook*. The Guardian. https://www.theguardian.com/technology/2019/mar/17/the-cambridge-analytica-scandal-changed-the-world-but-it-didnt-change-facebook

Thind, J. S., & Simon, R. (2019, June). Implementation of Big Data in cloud computing with optimized Apache Hadoop. In *2019 3rd International conference on Electronics, Communication and Aerospace Technology (ICECA)* (pp. 997-1001). IEEE. 10.1109/ICECA.2019.8821854

Tho, M. N., & Tjoa, A. M. (2003). Zero-latency data warehousing for heterogeneous data sources and continuous data streams. In *5th International Conference on Information Integrationand Web-based Applications Services*, (pp. 55-64). IEEE.

Tiwari, R. (2023). Ethical And Societal Implications of AI and Machine Learning. *Interantional Journal Of Scientific Research In Engineering And Management, 07*(01).

Tiwari, S., Bahuguna, P. C., & Walker, J. (2022). Industry 5.0: A macro perspective approach. In Handbook of Research on Innovative Management Using AI in Industry 5.0 (pp. 59–73). IGI Global.

Tonic. (2018). A Sentiment Analysis Approach to Predicting Stock Returns. *Medium*.

Truata. (2023, October 9). Case Study: Mastercard Business Intelligence Platform. https://www.truata.com/resources/case-study/case-study-mastercard-business-intelligence-platform/

Tsekouras, G., Sarimveis, H., Kavakli, E., & Bafas, G. A. (2005). hierarchical fuzzy-clustering approach to fuzzy modeling. *Fuzzy Sets and Systems*, *150*(2), 245–266. doi:10.1016/j.fss.2004.04.013

Tyagi, A. K., & G, R. (2019). Machine Learning with Big Data. *SSRN Electronic Journal*.

Tyagi, A. K., & Rekha, G. (2020). Challenges of Applying Deep Learning in Real-World Applications. In R. Kashyap & A. V. S. Kumar (Eds.), (pp. 92–118). Advances in Computer and Electrical Engineering. IGI Global. doi:10.4018/978-1-7998-0182-5.ch004

U.S. Department of Health & Human Services. (n.d.). *Records, Computers and the Rights of Citizens*. US DHH. https://aspe.hhs.gov/reports/records-computers-rights-citizens

Uma, R., Sana, H. A., Jawahar, P., & Rishitha, B. V. (2022). Support Vector Machine and Convolutional Neural Network Approach to Customer Review Sentiment Analysis. *1st International Conference on Computational Science and Technology (ICCST).,* (pp. 239-243). IEEE. https://doi: 10.1109/ICCST55948.2022.10040381

Urbanowicz, R. J., & Moore, J. H. (2009). Learning Classifier Systems: A Complete Introduction, Review, and Roadmap". *Journal of Artificial Evolution and Applications*, *2009*, 1–25. doi:10.1155/2009/736398

Vadalà, G., Salvatore, S. D., Ambrosio, L., Russo, F., Papalia, R., & Denaro, V. (2020). Robotic Spine Surgery and Augmented Reality Systems: A State of the Art. *Neurospine*, *17*(1), 88–100. doi:10.14245/ns.2040060.030 PMID:32252158

Valencio, C. R., Marioto, M. H., Zafalon, G. F. D., Machado, J., & Momente, J. (2013). Real time delta extraction based on triggers to support data warehousing. In *International Conference on Parallel and Distributed Computing, Applications and Technologies (PDCAT'13)*, (pp. 293-297). IEEE. 10.1109/PDCAT.2013.52

Vallabhajosyula, S., Sistla, V., & Kolli, V. K. (2021). Transfer learning-based deep ensemble neural network for plant leaf disease detection. *Journal of Plant Diseases and Protection*, *129*(3), 1–14. doi:10.100741348-021-00465-8

Vassiliadis, P. and Simitsis, A. (2008). Near real time ETL. *Springer Annals of Information Systems*, *3*(978-0-387-87430-2). New Trends in Data Warehousing and Data Analysis.

Vassiliadis, P. (2009). A survey of extract - transform - load technology. *International Journal of Data Warehousing and Mining*, *5*(3), 1–27. doi:10.4018/jdwm.2009070101

Vassiliadis, P., Vagena, Z., Skiadopoulos, S., Karayannidis, N., & Sellis, T. (2001). Arktos: Towards the modeling, design, control and execution of ETL processes. *Information Systems*, *26*(8), 537–561. doi:10.1016/S0306-4379(01)00039-4

Vera-Baquero, A., Palacios, R. C., Stantchev, V., & Molloy, O. (2015). Leveraging big-data for business process analytics. *The Learning Organization*, *22*(4), 215–228. doi:10.1108/TLO-05-2014-0023

Verma, J., & Agrawal, S. (2016). Big data analytics: challenges and applications for text, audio, video, and social media data. International Journal on Soft Computing, Artificial Intelligence and Applications (IJSCAI), 5(1).

Verma, A., Bhattacharya, P., Madhani, N., Trivedi, C., Bhushan, B., Tanwar, S., Sharma, G., Bokoro, P. N., & Sharma, R. (2022). Blockchain for Industry 5.0: Vision, Opportunities, Key Enablers, and Future Directions. *IEEE Access : Practical Innovations, Open Solutions*, *10*, 69160–69199. doi:10.1109/ACCESS.2022.3186892

Vidal, J., Carrasco, R. A., Cobo, M. J., & Blasco, M. F. (2023). Data Sources as a Driver for Market-Oriented Tourism Organizations: A Bibliometric Perspective. *Journal of the Knowledge Economy*. doi:10.100713132-023-01334-5

Vielma, C., Verma, A., & Bein, D. (2023). Sentiment Analysis with Novel GRU based Deep Learning Networks. *IEEE World AI IoT Congress (AIIoT)*, (pp. 0440-0446). IEEE. https://doi: 10.1109/AIIoT58121.2023.10174396

Vishnoi, V., Kumar, K., & Kumar, B. (2022). A comprehensive study of feature extraction techniques for plant leaf disease detection. *Multimedia Tools and Applications*, *80*(1), 367–419. doi:10.100711042-021-11375-0

Vossen, G. (2014). Big data as the new enabler in business and other intelligence. *Vietnam J ComputSci*, *1*(1), 3–14. doi:10.100740595-013-0001-6

Waas, F., Wrembel, R., Freudenreich, T., Thiele, M., Koncilia, C., & Furtado, P. (2013). On-demand ELT architecture for right-time BI: Extending the vision. [IJDWM]. *International Journal of Data Warehousing and Mining*, *9*(2), 21–38. doi:10.4018/jdwm.2013040102

Wamba, S. F., Gunasekaran, A., Akter, S., Ren, S. J., Dubey, R., & Childe, S. J. (2017). Big data analytics and frm performance: Efects of dynamic capabilities. *Journal of Business Research*, *70*, 356–365. doi:10.1016/j.jbusres.2016.08.009

Wang, J., Zhang, W., Shi, Y., Duan, S., & Liu, J., (2018). *Industrial big data analytics: challenges, methodologies, and applications.*

Wang, G., Wang, H., & Long, Z. (2021). Norm approximation of mamdani fuzzy system to a class of integrable functions. *International Journal of Fuzzy Systems*, *23*(3), 833–848. doi:10.100740815-020-01008-3

Wang, H. (2021). Credit Risk Management of Consumer Finance Based on Big Data. *Mobile Information Systems*, *2021*, 1–10. doi:10.1155/2021/7054016

Wang, J., Yang, Y., Wang, T., Sherratt, R. S., & Zhang, J. (2020). Big Data Service Architecture: A Survey. *Journal of Internet Technology*, *21*, 393–405.

Wang, L., & Alexander, C. A. (2015). Big Data Driven Supply Chain Management and Business Administration. *American Journal of Economics and Business Administration*, *7*(2), 60–67. doi:10.3844/ajebasp.2015.60.67

Wang, L.-X., & Mendel, J. M. (1992). Generating fuzzy rules by learning from examples. *IEEE Transactions on Systems, Man, and Cybernetics*, *22*(6), 1414–1427. doi:10.1109/21.199466

Wang, S. (2018). Data cleaning in big data: A survey. *Data Science and Engineering*, *3*(1), 15–30.

Wang, X., Gegov, A., Farzad, A., Chen, Y., & Hu, Q. (2019). Fuzzy network based framework for sofware maintainability prediction. *International Journal of Uncertainty, Fuzziness and Knowledge-based Systems*, *27*(5), 841–862. doi:10.1142/S0218488519500375

Wang, X., Yang, L. T., Liu, H., & Deen, M. J. (2017). A big data-as-a-service framework: State-of-the-art and perspectives. *IEEE Transactions on Big Data*, *4*(3), 325–340. doi:10.1109/TBDATA.2017.2757942

Wang, Y., & Hajli, N. (2017). Exploring the path to big data analytics success in healthcare. *Journal of Business Research*, *70*, 287–299. doi:10.1016/j.jbusres.2016.08.002

Wang, Y., & Xu, W. (2017). Leveraging deep learning with LDA-based text analytics to detect automobile insurance fraud. *Decision Support Systems*, *105*, 1–10. doi:10.1016/j.dss.2017.11.001

Wani, M., & Jabin, S. (2018). *Big Data: Issues*. Challenges, and Techniques in Business Intelligence. doi:10.1007/978-981-10-6620-7_59

Wankhade, M., Rao, A. C. S., & Kulkarni, C. (2022). A survey on sentiment analysis methods, applications, and challenges. *Artificial Intelligence Review*, *55*(7), 5731–5780. doi:10.100710462-022-10144-1

Werbos, P. J. (1974). Beyond Regression: New Tools for Prediction and Analysis in the behavioral sciences. PhD, Harvard University, Cambridge, Massachusetts.

Wibowo, A. (2015). Problems and available solutions on the stage of extract, transform, and loading in near real-time data warehousing (a literature study). In *International Seminar on Intelligent Technology and Its Applications (ISITIA)*.

Wichmann, J. R. K., Scholdra, T. P., & Reinartz, W. J. (2023). Propelling International Marketing Research with Geo-spatial Data. *Journal of International Marketing*, *31*(2), 82–102. doi:10.1177/1069031X221149951

Wiener, M., Saunders, C., & Marabelli, M. (2020). Big-data Business Models: A Critical Literature Review and Multi-perspective Research Framework. *Journal of Information Technology*, *35*(1), 66–91. doi:10.1177/0268396219896811

Witten, I. H. (2016). *Data mining: Practical machine learning tools and techniques*. Morgan Kaufmann.

Witten, I. H., & Frank, E. (2005). *Data mining: practical machine learning tools and techniques*. Morgan Kaufmann.

Wixom, B. H. (2010). The BI-based organization. *MIS Quarterly Executive*, *9*(2), 61–80.

Won, J. Y. (2021). Development and Initial Results of a Brain PET Insert for Simultaneous 7-Tesla PET/MRI Using an FPGA-Only Signal Digitization Method. IEEE Transactions on Medical Imaging. IEEE. . doi:10.1109/TMI.2021.3062066

Wrembel, R. (2006). *Data Warehouses and OLAP: Concepts, Architectures and Solutions: Concepts, Architectures and Solutions*. IGI Global.

Wu, D., Zhu, L., Lu, Q., & Sakr, S. (2017). HDM: A composable framework for big data processing. *IEEE Transactions on Big Data*, *4*(2), 150–163. doi:10.1109/TBDATA.2017.2690906

Wu, H., & Li, B. (2022). Customer Purchase Prediction Based on Improved Gradient Boosting Decision Tree Algorithm. *2nd International Conference on Consumer Electronics and Computer Engineering (ICCECE)*, (pp. 795-798). IEEE. 10.1109/ICCECE54139.2022.9712779

Xia, H., Zhou, Y., & Zhang, J. (2022). Auto insurance fraud identification based on a CNN-LSTM fusion deep learning model. *International Journal of Ad Hoc and Ubiquitous Computing*, *39*(1/2), 37–47. doi:10.1504/IJAHUC.2022.120943

Xian, W., Yu, K., Han, F., Fang, L., He, D., & Han, Q.-L. (2023). Advanced Manufacturing in Industry 5.0: A Survey of Key Enabling Technologies and Future Trends. *IEEE Transactions on Industrial Informatics*, 1–15. doi:10.1109/TII.2023.3274224

Xiao, M., & Yi, H. (2021). Building an efficient artificial intelligence model for personalized training in colleges and universities. *Computer Applications in Engineering Education*, *29*(2), 350–358. doi:10.1002/cae.22235

Xu, X., Lu, Y., Vogel-Heuser, B., & Wang, L. (2021). Industry 4.0 and Industry 5.0—Inception, conception and perception. *Journal of Manufacturing Systems*, *61*, 530–535. doi:10.1016/j.jmsy.2021.10.006

Yaakob, A. M., Gegov, A., & Rahman, S. (2018). Selection of alternatives using fuzzy networks with rule base aggregation. *Fuzzy Sets and Systems*, *341*, 123–144. doi:10.1016/j.fss.2017.05.027

Yamashita, R., Nishio, M., Do, R. K. G., & Togashi, K. (2018). Convolutional neural networks: An overview and application in radiology. *Insights Into Imaging*, *9*(4), 611–629. doi:10.100713244-018-0639-9 PMID:29934920

Yan, C., Wang, X., Liu, X., Liu, W., & Liu, J. (2020). Research on the UBI Car Insurance Rate Determination Model Based on the CNN-HVSVM Algorithm. *IEEE Access : Practical Innovations, Open Solutions*, *8*(1), 1–1. doi:10.1109/ACCESS.2020.3021062

Yang, C., Huang, Q., Li, Z., Liu, K., & Hu, F. (2017). Big Data and cloud computing: Innovation opportunities and challenges. *International Journal of Digital Earth*, *10*(1), 13–53. doi:10.1080/17538947.2016.1239771

Yang, C., Xu, X., Ramamohanarao, K., & Chen, J. (2019). A scalable multi-data sources based recursive approximation approach for fast error recovery in big sensing data on cloud. *IEEE Transactions on Knowledge and Data Engineering, 32*(5), 841–854. doi:10.1109/TKDE.2019.2895612

Yao, A. C. (1982). Protocols for secure computations. *23rd Annual Symposium on Foundations of Computer Science.* IEEE. 10.1109/SFCS.1982.38

Yao, A. C.-C. (1986). How to generate and exchange secrets. *27th Annual Symposium on Foundations of Computer Science.* IEEE. 10.1109/SFCS.1986.25

Yong, A. G., & Pearce, S. (2013). A beginner's guide to factor analysis: Focusing on exploratory factor analysis. *Tutorials in Quantitative Methods for Psychology, 9*(2), 79–94. doi:10.20982/tqmp.09.2.p079

Zaenal, Z., & Astutik, I. R. I. (2023). Sentiment Analysis of OYO App Reviews Using the Support Vector Machine Algorithm. *Procedia of Engineering and Life Science, 3.* doi:10.21070/pels.v3i0.1338

Zaharia, M., Chowdhury, M., Franklin, M. J., Shenker, S., & Stoica, I. (2010). Spark: cluster computing with working sets. In: *Proceedings of the 2nd USENIX conference on Hot topics in cloud computing*, vol. 10

Zain, S., Ramli, N. & Adnan, R. (2022). Customer sentiment analysis through social media feedback: a case study on telecommunication company. *International Journal of Humanities Technology and Civilization, 7*(2), 54-61. https://doi: . v7i2.8739. doi:10.15282/ijhtc

Zakir, H. M., & Jinny, S. V. (2022). Convolutional neural networks method for analysis of e-commerce customer reviews. *AIP Conference Proceedings, 2444*, 030004. doi:10.1063/5.0078372

Zeiler, M. D., & Fergus, R. (2014). Visualizing and Understanding Convolutional Networks. In D. Fleet, T. Pajdla, B. Schiele, & T. Tuytelaars (Eds.), Lecture Notes in Computer Science: Vol. 8689. *Computer Vision – ECCV 2014.* Springer. doi:10.1007/978-3-319-10590-1_53

Zhang, L., & Pfoser, D. (2019). Using openstreetmap point-of-interest data to model urban change—A feasibility study. *PLoS One, 14*(2), e0212606. Advance online publication. doi:10.1371/journal.pone.0212606 PMID:30802251

Zhang, X., Zhou, Y., & Luo, J. (2022). Deep learning for processing and analysis of remote sensing big data: A technical review. *Big Earth Data, 6*(4), 527–560. doi:10.1080/20964471.2021.1964879

Zhao, Z., & Bai, T. (2022). Financial Fraud Detection and Prediction in Listed Companies Using SMOTE and Machine Learning Algorithms. *Entropy (Basel, Switzerland), 24*(8), 1157. doi:10.3390/e24081157 PMID:36010821

Zheng, C., Yu, X., & Jin, Q. (2017). How user relationships affect userperceived value propositions of enterprises on social commerce plat-forms. *Information Systems Frontiers, 19*(6), 1261–1271. doi:10.100710796-017-9766-y

Zheng, P., & Ni, L. M. (2006). Spotlight: The rise of the smart phone. *IEEE Distrib Syst Online., 7*(3), 3. doi:10.1109/ MDSO.2006.22

Zhou, T., Li, B., Wu, C., Tan, Y., Mao, L., & Wu, W. (2019, November). Studies on big data mining techniques in wildfire prevention for power system. In *2019 IEEE 3rd Conference on Energy Internet and Energy System Integration (EI2)* (pp. 866-871). IEEE. 10.1109/EI247390.2019.9061901

Zhou, V., (2019). Machine Learning for Beginners: An Introduction to Neural Networks. *Medium.*

Zhou, L., Pan, S., Wang, J., & Vasilakos, A. V. (2017). Machine learning on big data: Opportunities and challenges. *Neurocomputing, 237*, 350–361. doi:10.1016/j.neucom.2017.01.026

Zhou, Z., & Zhao, L. (2020). Cloud computing model for big data processing and performance optimization of multimedia communication. *Computer Communications*, *160*, 326–332. doi:10.1016/j.comcom.2020.06.015

Zuboff, S., (2015). Big other: surveillance capitalism and the prospects of an information civilization. *Journal of Information Technology, 30*(1). Nature Publishing Group.

Zuters, J. (2011). Near real-time data warehousing with multi-stage trickle and flip. In *Perspectives in Business Informatics Research* (pp. 73–82). Springer. doi:10.1007/978-3-642-24511-4_6

About the Contributors

Munir Ahmad is a Ph.D. in Computer Science. over 24 years of extensive experience in spatial data development, management, processing, visualization, and quality control. He has dedicated expertise in open data, crowdsourced data, volunteered geographic information and spatial data infrastructure. A seasoned professional with extensive knowledge in the field, having served as a trainer for the latest spatial technologies. With a passion for research and over 30 publications in the same field, in 2022, he got PhD degree in Computer Science from Preston University Rawalpindi, Pakistan. He is dedicated to advancing the industry and spreading knowledge through my expertise and experience.

Minakshi Ramteke has completed master technology in computer science & Engineering from RTM Nagpur University. She have 9 years of teaching experience. Her area of interest is Artificial intelligence and machine learning and Big data computing.

Dishant Banga received his Master's Degree in systems Engineering and Engineering Management with specialization in Data Analytics from the University of North Carolina, Charlotte in 2018. His interest includes applications of Machine Learning and Data Science to solve complex business problems. He has participated in various national and international level competitions and secured good rank by developing solutions for complex business problems. Currently, he is working as a Sr. analyst at Bridgetree, LLC. His research interests include developing statistical and machine learning models and applications, artificial intelligence

Saurabh Batra is a data science professional working in analytical consulting with expertise in handling end-to-end data analytics projects across different sectors and markets. He holds an experience of 12+ years and has specialized in the BFSI domain with deep experience in customer analytics. He is a B.tech.(ECE) graduate and holds a degree of Masters in Business Economics from Delhi University. He has delivered data science training and has trained both fresh graduates and lateral experience holders in the past. He has worked on multiple research papers in AI and has presented in some international conferences.

Dhananjay Bhagat, an accomplished educator and technologist, is dedicated to teaching and staying updated on emerging technologies. With a wealth of experience, he has made substantial contributions to education, spanning teaching, research, and innovative projects. He has a 3-year professional background, previously affiliated with Amravati University and currently working at G H Raisoni College of Engineering in Nagpur since February 2022. Driven by a commitment to knowledge sharing, Prof. Bhagat has authored and significantly contributed to diverse books and research papers, including topics like Business Intelligence, Machine Learning, and Natural Language Processing. His papers are published in reputable journals like Scopus, reflecting his dedication to expanding knowledge boundaries. Prof. Dhananjay's skills extend beyond teaching to encompass technical proficiency. He adeptly combines technology and data analysis, showcasing his proficiency in Python, digital marketing, and graphic design tools such as Canva and Fligma, highlighting his versatility.

Neepa Biswas has completed her PhD. from Jadavpur University, M.E. from IIEST, Shibpur. Currently she is working as Assistant Professor, Department of IT, Narula Institute of Technology (JIS Group). Her research Interest is Data Warehousing, ETL processing, Data Mining, IoT, Machine learning, Blockchain.

Ankita Chaturvedi is currently working as an Associate Professor at IIS (deemed to be University), Jaipur and has over 16+ years of teaching experience. She received her Ph.d degree(2011), Master's in Accounting and Business Statistics(2006), and Master's in Economics and Financial Management(2018) from University of Rajasthan, India. She has qualified NET in Commerce in 2015. She is an author or Co-author of more than 46 research papers published in national or international refereed journals, 11 chapters in edited books, 3 books with ISBN number and more than 50 conference contributions. She has received several (22) awards in the field of academics and research. She has supervised around 18 PG dissertations. She is supervising 6 Ph.d Thesis and 6 Ph.d degrees has been awarded under her guidance. She has been convener of various academic events like international conference, training programmes, Research workshop, Board of Studies etc. She has attended various more than 22 FDP's and training programmes.

Pranali Dhawas, Assistant Professor, GHRCE, Nagpur Prof. Pranali Dhawas has completed Bachelor of Engineering and M.tech in Computer Science & Engineering from Rashtrasant Tukdoji Maharaj Nagpur University. She has a valuable teaching experience of more than 3 years. Her expertise and area of research lies in Machine Learning, Artificial Intelligence, Data Mining, Big Data, Cloud Computing, Python,, Computer Network, Data Science, R programming and Pattern Recognition. Prof. Pranali Dhawas has Worked on 3 Book Chapters, 2 copyrights, 1 papers in conference, 3 papers in UGC approved Journals. She has successfully submitted book chapter with title "Implementation of Parallel Computing With Artificial Intelligence in Big Data Analytics" under CRC Publication: (Got Acceptance, Time to get published)

Abhishek M. Dhore is an accomplished educator and technologist with a deep passion for teaching and learning new technologies. With a rich blend of experience and expertise, significant contributions to the field of education, spanning teaching, research, and innovative project endeavors with total experience of 8+ Years which includes previous work at affiliated college at Amravati University and currently working at MIT School of Computing, MIT ADT University Since April 2022. Driven by a commitment to knowledge dissemination, Prof. Abhishek Dhore has authored and contributed to several books and research papers. Notable publications include works on professional ethics, digital electronics, biometric security, and machine learning algorithms also published papers in journals such as Scopus, Springer and web of science. These contributions reflect Prof. Dhore's dedication to advancing the frontiers of knowledge. wears multiple hats, excelling not only in teaching but also in technical skills. As a Power BI Data Analytics Certified Dashboard Developer, Prof. Abhishek blends technology and data analysis seamlessly. Proficiency in Python, digital marketing, and graphic design tools like Canva and Filmora showcases Prof. Abhishek's versatility.

Santosh Durugkar has pursued Ph.D in Software engineering from Amity University Rajasthan Jaipur. He has completed U.G. (B.E.) and P.G. (M.E.) from SPPU, Pune. His area of interests are software engineering, database management, data analysis, information retrieval.

Dwijendra Nath Dwivedi is a professional with 20+ years of subject matter expertise creating right value propositions for analytics and AI. He currently heads the EMEA+AP AI and IoT team at SAS, a worldwide frontrunner in AI technology. He is a post-Graduate in Economics from Indira Gandhi Institute of Development and Research and currently perusing PHD from crackow university of economics Poland. He has presented his research in more than 20 international conference and published several Scopus indexed paper on AI adoption in many areas. As an author he has contributed to more than 8 books and has more than 25 publications in high impact journals. He conducts AI Value seminars and workshops for the executive audience and for power users.

Puneet Gangrade is a technology and privacy analytics leader driving business transformation and data privacy solutions for global companies. He has consistently delivered multi-million dollar business impact through advanced analytics, measurement, machine learning, and cloud platforms. He is experienced with CRM, data strategy, and marketing intelligence in multiple industry verticals as a client growth lead, solutions engineer, and adtech expert. He has an extensive understanding of privacy-safe data collaboration solutions, also known as data clean rooms. He holds a Master's in Marketing Intelligence from Fordham University, New York. He also was awarded the Gold Winner at the 2023 Globee Business Awards for the category 'Technology Marketing Engineer of the Year'. He is also a contributing author of the data analytics and marketing strategy books and has peer-reviewed multiple books. He is a professional member of IEEE and of the invite-only U of Digital Expert Network for AdTech, Digital Advertising, and Martech skills. He has delivered several podcasts, such as the AI in Action podcast (2021) and FunnelReboot podcast (2023), and participated in speaking engagements such as the Ad-World Conference (2022), Data & Analytics Summit at Google (2018), and Data Science Salon (2020).

Ankur Gupta has received the B.Tech and M.Tech in Computer Science and Engineering from Ganga Institute of Technology and Management, Kablana affiliated with Maharshi Dayanand University, Rohtak in 2015 and 2017. He is an Assistant Professor in the Department of Computer Science and Engineering at Vaish College of Engineering, Rohtak, and has been working there since January 2019. He has many publications in various reputed national/ international conferences, journals, and online book chapter contributions (Indexed by SCIE, Scopus, ESCI, ACM, DBLP, etc). He is doing research in the field of cloud computing, data security & machine learning. His research work in M.Tech was based on biometric security in cloud computing.

Vishal Jain is presently working as an Associate Professor at Department of Computer Science and Engineering, School of Engineering and Technology, Sharda University, Greater Noida, U. P. India. Before that, he has worked for several years as an Associate Professor at Bharati Vidyapeeth's Institute of Computer Applications and Management (BVICAM), New Delhi. He has more than 15 years of experience in the academics. He obtained Ph.D (CSE), M.Tech (CSE), MBA (HR), MCA, MCP and CCNA.

He has authored more than 100 research papers in reputed conferences and journals, including Web of Science and Scopus. He has authored and edited more than 45 books with various reputed publishers, including Elsevier, Springer, IET, Apple Academic Press, CRC, Taylor and Francis Group, Scrivener, Wiley, Emerald, NOVA Science, IGI-Global and River Publishers. His research areas include information retrieval, semantic web, ontology engineering, data mining, ad hoc networks, and sensor networks. He received a Young Active Member Award for the year 2012–13 from the Computer Society of India, Best Faculty Award for the year 2017 and Best Researcher Award for the year 2019 from BVICAM, New Delhi.

Kavita Jhajharia was Born in Jhunjhunu, Rajasthan, India, in 1992. She Received her B.Tech. Degree from Rajasthan Technical University, India, in 2013 in Information Technology, and the M.Tech Degree from SRM University, Sonepat, India, in 2016. She has received her PhD from Manipal University Jaipur in 2023. She is Assistant Professor in Manipal University Jaipur since 2016. She is member of ACM. Her Research Professor in Manipal University Jaipur since 2016. She is member of ACM. Her Research interest is VANET, Wireless networking, Machine Learning, Software Engineering and IOT.

Kamlesh Kalbande is working as Assistant Professor at G H Raisoni College of Engineering, Nagpur since June 2012. He is a doctoral student at Department of Electronics & Telecommunication Engineering, G H Raisoni University, Amravati, Maharashtra, India. He has completed graduation and post- graduation in Electronics Engineering. He has been published more than 20 research papers in reputed International Conference & Journals. His research interests includes Machine Learning, Internet of Things, Embedded System and Artificial Intelligence.

Gaganpreet Kaur is currently working as an Associate Professor at Department of Computer Science & Engineering, Chitkara University, Punjab, India. She has obtained Ph.D (CSE),from I.K. Gujral Punjab Technical University, Jalandhar, M.Tech (CSE), from I.K. Gujral Punjab Technical University, Jalandhar and B.Tech (CSE), from Kurukshetra University. She has rich teaching experience of 18+ years. She has published more than 90+ research articles in various peer reviewed, SCI, Scopus Journals, International and National Conferences in the field of computer science. She has published more than 13 Indian patents. She has authored a book on biometrics. She has guided a Ph.D scholar and 38 students have completed M. Tech thesis under her guidance. She has acted as a guest editor for special issue of Special Issue entitled: ■ "Computer-Aided Diagnosis of Pleural Mesothelioma: Recent Trends and Future Research Perspectives" for BioMed Research International. ■ Special Issue entitled "IOT Data Analytics for Financial Economics and Accounting in CMC Press for year 2023. ■ Special Issue entitled " Innovative Tools and Methodologies for Big Data Exploration, Visualization, and Analytics for Neuroscience" for Journal of Integrative Neuroscience, 2023. She has been reviewer and session chair for various conferences. She has delivered expert talk in various colleges and universities. Her research interest includes biometrics, image processing, forensic science, cloud computing, healthcare sector.

Sarabjeet Kaur is presently working in Zakir Husain Delhi College (Eve), Delhi University. She did B.Sc (Hons) and M.Sc (Hons) in Economics from Punjab School of Economics, Guru Nanak Dev University, Amritsar. She did her Phd from Punjab School of Economics, Guru Nanak Dev University, Amritsar. Her area of research is Econometrics and Monetary Economics. She has more than 14years of teaching experience. She has attended various national and international conferences. She has also published articles in national and international journals. She was the co-editor of two edited books.

Ashwini Kukade is an accomplished educator and technologist with a passion for teaching and embracing new technologies along with she is PhD pursuant in Computer Science and Engineering (specialization in Artificial Intelligence and Data Science) She has significant experience in education, including teaching, research, and project ventures. With over 9 years in the field, she has engaged with many institutions under Nagpur University and currently working at G. H. Raisoni College of Engineering, Nagpur which is an excellence hub of technical knowledge. She is a dedicated knowledge disseminator, having authored and contributed to various books and research papers, covering topics such as cloud computing, intelligent mobility, artificial intelligence and machine learning. Her contributions appear in esteemed journals like Scopus, Springer, and Web of Science. Prof. Ashwini Kukade excels in teaching and technical skills. She is a Certified Salesforce Developer, seamlessly integrating technology and data analysis. Her proficiency extends to Python, cloud computing and data science.

A.V.Senthil Kumar is working as a Director & Professor in the Department of Research and PG in Computer Applications, Hindusthan College of Arts and Science, Coimbatore. He has to his credit 19 Book Chapters, 215 papers in International and National Journals, 53 papers in International and National Conferences, and 10 edited books and text books. He is an Editor-in-Chief for various journals. Key Member for India, Machine Intelligence Research Lab (MIR Labs).He is Associate Editor of IEEE Access. He is an Editorial Board Member and Reviewer for various International Journals. He is also a Committee member for various International Conferences. He is a Life member of International Association of Engineers (IAENG), Systems Society of India (SSI), member of The Indian Science Congress Association, member of Internet Society (ISOC), International Association of Computer Science and Information Technology (IACSIT), Indian Association for Research in Computing Science (IARCS), and committee member for various International Conferences

Sanjeev Kumar is an accomplished expert in Food and Beverage. He currently holds the positions of Professor at the Lovely Professional University, Punjab, India. With over a decade of experience in the field, food Service Industry, his research focuses on Alcoholic beverages, Event management and Sustainable Management Practices, Metaverse and Artificial Intelligence. He has published more than 35 research papers, articles and chapters in Scopus Indexed, UGC Approved and peer reviewed Journals and books. Dr. Sanjeev Kumar participated and acted as resource person in various National and International conferences, seminars, research workshops and industry talks and his work has been widely cited.

M. Ravisankar, working as an Associate Professor in Department of Computer Science and Engineering, K.L. deemed to be University, Guntur dist., Andhra Pradesh, India. He has 24 years of teaching experience. Dr. Ravi has received Excellence in Research Award and Best Senior Faculty Award. He has Published 5 Patents and he has published more than 20 articles in Scopus, SCI, WOS and International Journals. His areas of specializations are Data Mining and Artificial Intelligence.

Prathamesh Nimkar is a 3rd year undergraduate student, doing his Bachelor's in Technology (B.Tech.) in Information Technology at Manipal University Jaipur, Rajasthan. His research interests include cloud computing, software engineering, artificial intelligence and machine learning.

Poonam V. Polshetwar is working with CSMSS College of Polytechnic.she is having total 9 years of experience in Teaching (Computer science and Engineering).she had also worked as a Head of the Department in Shreeyash Polytechnic.she has published total 5 international journals.she has completed her ME in CSE in 2018 with 7.43 CGPA grades.she is having Indian Society For Technical Education (ISTE)membership.she has also worked on preparing QR for Hrvesting deep Web interfaces.she thoughts A good teacher is like a candle-it consumes itself to light the way for others.

Tarun Pradhan, a 3rd year undergraduate student, pursuing his bachelor's in technology (B.Tech) in Information technology at Manipal University Jaipur, Rajasthan. His research interests include Artificial Intelligence, Machine learning and Deep Learning. He can be contacted at pradhantarun123@gmail.com

Sabyasachi Pramanik is a professional IEEE member. He obtained a PhD in Computer Science and Engineering from Sri Satya Sai University of Technology and Medical Sciences, Bhopal, India. Presently, he is an Associate Professor, Department of Computer Science and Engineering, Haldia Institute of Technology, India. He has many publications in various reputed international conferences, journals, and book chapters (Indexed by SCIE, Scopus, ESCI, etc). He is doing research in the fields of Artificial Intelligence, Data Privacy, Cybersecurity, Network Security, and Machine Learning. He also serves on the editorial boards of several international journals. He is a reviewer of journal articles from IEEE, Springer, Elsevier, Inderscience, IET and IGI Global. He has reviewed many conference papers, has been a keynote speaker, session chair, and technical program committee member at many international conferences. He has authored a book on Wireless Sensor Network. He has edited 8 books from IGI Global, CRC Press, Springer and Wiley Publications.

Smrity Prasad working as Assistant Professor in the Department of Statistics and Data Science in Christ Deemed to Be University, Bengaluru. Prior to this, she managed Computer Science department in different organization, Bengaluru. Her doctoral work is focused on Image Processing. For her doctoral work, she was associated with Christ University, Bengaluru. Prior to that she completed her MPhil on Requirement Analysis with Object Oriented Development Method. She professes to graduate and master's students on concepts like leveraging Database Technologies, and Information Systems Design and Development. She has a rich experience of 15 years in this profession where she has taught Network Applications, Operation Research and Theory of Computation. She has a lifetime membership of Computer Society of India. Her current research interests include Artificial Intelligence, Machine Learning, IOT and algorithms. Her research papers on Image Processing are published in leading international journals and find place in libraries of universities like Penn State University. Her work in Machine Learning Era in Heart Disease Prediction is well appreciated by academia. She has also edited a book; DELVE-Emerging Trend and Challenges in IT. She has published a book, "New Foundation of Artificial Intelligence". She has presented and published number of papers in national and international journals.

Kashvi Prawal is a Computer Science Student at Penn state University,University Park,Pennsylvania. She is president of Girls Who Code College Loop.She Has done Machine Learning Course From ICT Academy,IIT Kanpur and worked on project Airline Customer Satisfaction Prediction.

Omar S. Saleh earned his B.Sc. in Computer Engineering from the University of Technology-Baghdad in 2006. He received his M.Sc. in Software Engineering from Staffordshire University-APU-Malaysia in

2012. Currently, he has submitted his PhD thesis and is awaiting the final viva. He is presently employed as a lecturer in the Studies, Planning, and Follow-Up Directorate of the Ministry of Higher Education and Scientific Research in Iraq. In his field of expertise, he has authored and co-authored over 30 journal articles, conference publications, and book chapters that delve into the areas of Blockchain, Cloud Computing, Software Architecture, and IoT. Omar is also a reviewer for several indexed journals and has participated in organizing IEEE and other international conferences.

Ramadevi Salunkhe, a renowned researcher and academic, has dedicated her life to pushing the boundaries of knowledge in her field. Born on a bright autumn day on May 02, 1991, in a small town in the Sangli District of Maharashtra,India. After completing her undergraduate studies, pursuing a M.Tech in Computer Science and Engineering at a leading institution Rajarambapu Institute of Technology, Rajaramnagar, Islampur.

Mukesh Sehrawat is presently working with IAMR Group of Institutions, Ghaziabad. He has more than 10 years of industry experience and about 13 years of teaching and research experience. His research interest includes digital marketing, social media marketing and social media influencers.

Index

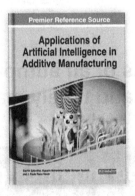

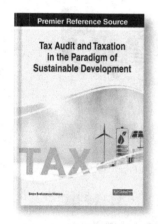   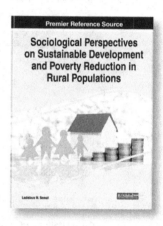

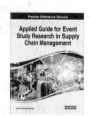
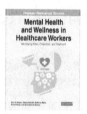

Printed in the United States
by Baker & Taylor Publisher Services